NOTES
ON THE
OLD TESTAMENT
EXPLANATORY AND PRACTICAL

BY

ALBERT BARNES

ENLARGED TYPE EDITION

EDITED BY
ROBERT FREW, D.D.

PSALMS
VOL. I

BAKER BOOK HOUSE
GRAND RAPIDS, MICHIGAN

Library of Congress Catalog Card Number: 55-11630

ISBN: 0-8010-0515-9

First Printing, February 1950
Second Printing, December 1955
Third Printing, September 1958
Fourth Printing, July 1960
Fifth Printing, July 1962
Sixth Printing, February 1965
Seventh Printing, March 1967
Eighth Printing, April 1969
Ninth Printing, October 1970
Tenth Printing, November 1971
Eleventh Printing, July 1973
Twelfth Printing, December 1974
Thirteenth Printing, September 1976
Fourteenth Printing, January 1977
Fifteenth Printing, February 1978
Sixteenth Printing, April 1979
Seventeenth Printing, December 1980
Eighteenth Printing, November 1981

PHOTOLITHOPRINTED BY CUSHING - MALLOY, INC.
ANN ARBOR, MICHIGAN, UNITED STATES OF AMERICA

EDITOR'S PREFACE.

The Psalms have ever been held in the highest appreciation by the Church. We are familiar with the testimonies of Augustine, Luther, and Calvin to the excellence of the Psalms. We know that the piety of the Church has been fed by the Psalms for thousands of years; that they have come singing down through the ages, sustaining the sufferers, and inspiring the heroes of every time. It is a good sign of our times that these precious songs of Zion are attracting more attention amongst us, and that not only on the part of men whose professional duties may be supposed to demand it, but also from men occupying the highest place in literature and politics. The Christian public, not long ago, were surprised and delighted when informed that our great Prime Minister had been whiling away some dreary hours in the House of Commons last session by translating into Greek Toplady's beautiful hymn, "Rock of Ages, cleft for me." We think many will be equally delighted with the following beautiful testimony to the Psalms of David on the part of Mr. Gladstone. He says—"In that book, for well nigh three thousand years, the piety of saints has found its most refined and choicest food, to such a degree, indeed, that the rank and quality of the religious frame may in general be tested, at least negatively, by the height of its relish for them. There is the whole music of the human heart, when touched by the hand of the Maker, in all its tones that whisper or that swell, for every hope and fear, for every joy and pang, for every form of strength and languor, of disquietude and rest. There are developed all the innermost relations of the human soul to God, built upon the platform of a covenant of love and sonship, that had its foundations in the Messiah, while, in this particular and privileged book, it was permitted to anticipate his coming." It is reassuring, in these rationalistic times, to meet in such quarters with so profound a reverence for the Divine Word, and so keen a relish for its beauty, and appreciation of its spiritual power. At the same time, Commentaries on the Psalms and Introductions have greatly multiplied among us of late. For a long time we had almost nothing in our language on this deeply interesting portion of Scripture but the work of Bishop Horne, of the excellence of which, in a purely practical and devotional point of view, it would be impossible to speak too highly; but something was needed that would go deeper down and bring up the precious gems that lay in the hidden depths of the Psalter. We do not forget Bishop Horsley, Professor Bush, and others, or the earlier writers from which Mr. Spurgeon has drawn so largely in his recent work. Yet of really good expositions of the Psalms the number was very small. But now we have Plumer, Perowne, Alexander, M'Michael (on the Pilgrim Psalms), Binnie, Bonar, Spurgeon, and BARNES, with many more on the whole or on detached portions of the book.

The works now named are all of them of high excellence. In Mr. Barnes' three volumes the reader will find the same thorough and painstaking research, the same fulness, the same delightful perspicuity, the same beauty and practical power, that characterized his previous works, and have given them so extended popularity both in this country and in America. Our author sat down to his work on the Psalms with a full conviction of the difficulty of the task, and full knowledge of the peculiar and varied qualifications requisite to enable one to produce a satisfying exposition of this portion of the Word of God. He himself states these qualifications well. Among them he enumerates, after noticing the necessity of Hebrew and other learning, the possession of the imaginative faculty in such strength as will give sympathy with the poetic spirit of the Psalms; and also, and not least, the possession of the devotional element, with deep and long experience of the life of godliness, to enable the expositor to sympathize with the varied feelings and frames of the sanctified heart. The better half of the Psalms must ever remain a sealed book to the unsanctified expositor, however learned or qualified in other respects. Mr. Barnes has risen to a higher level here than many who have trodden in the same path before. Piety and practical experience of Divine things are often prominent, and are never awanting, and rest always on a basis of sound criticism and sober expository judgment. It is this union of the practical and critical element, in just proportion, that constitutes the distinguishing excellence of our author's exposition, and entitles it, we think, to rank among the best, if not to be regarded as indeed the best Commentary on the Psalms, that has yet appeared in our language. The work has also this peculiar feature of interest, that it is the last which, in all probability, the author will issue. His growing weakness of sight, and the infirmities of advancing years, have disposed, if not compelled, him to lay down his pen; and his many labours on the Word of God have found a fitting close in these notes and meditations on a book which furnishes the sweetest music for the soul in the evening of life, and the best preparation for the eternal rest. It is well to cease from the labours of life, and fall asleep with the harp of David making grave sweet melody in one's ears all the way down through the valley of age and the valley of death, to be lost only in the higher melody of angelic harps before the throne.

It remains only to state the peculiarities of this edition. The text has been subjected to careful revision. The reader will not find additional and corrective notes as in the volumes previously edited by us. The reason is twofold. First, the Author's views have been somewhat modified, and his theology has mellowed and ripened with years. Even in those passages where the old peculiarities appear, there is less angularity and more careful and guarded language. We have been particularly struck with the sound and clear views generally expressed on the principles which regulate the interpretation of the Old Testament prophecies, as quoted and appealed to in the New. The principle of accommodation finds little countenance at the hands of our Author. The Messianic Psalms, too, are interpreted in a way that leaves nothing to be desired. The second reason is, that a mere reference to the additional notes, when required, seemed all that was necessary for readers already in possession of the previous volumes of our edition of Barnes.

In the *Appendix*, however, will be found very many and valuable additional notes, in the form of brief extracts, from the best writers and commentators on the Psalms. These extracts have been selected with care, and on the principle of exhibiting the scope of the Psalm, giving special attention to the Messianic Psalms, and of presenting throughout only such things as appeared to us to approach to the character of gems in psalm literature, or at all events to have some special excellence entitling them to be placed under the reader's eye. The works we have mainly used for this purpose are—Hengstenberg, Delitzsch (of which the proof-sheets of the English translation were kindly furnished by Messrs. Clark of Edinburgh), Plumer, Kitto, Thrupp, Perowne, Alexander, Bonar, Calvin, Luther, Horne, Binnie, and Spurgeon. The name of the author in every instance is given along with the extract from his work. The selection is confined within a limited range, and is also in itself limited. The space at our command did not admit of more, and the limitation will perhaps be less regretted if the selection shall be found to be judicious.

Altogether it is believed that these volumes will be found fitting companions for the numerous volumes already issued of Blackie's Edition of the Expository Works of ALBERT BARNES. The Notes on the Psalms, it should be observed, have a close connection with those on Isaiah and Daniel, and form, besides, the necessary complement of the Exposition on the New Testament. The quotations from the Psalms are so abundant in the New Testament, that the author's views on some of the most important passages of Scripture can only be fully obtained by a comparison of the Notes on both places. In a word, the Notes on the Old Testament and on the New are mutually illustrative of one another.

R. F.

PREFACE.

THESE Notes on the Book of Psalms complete my labours in endeavouring to explain and illustrate the sacred Scriptures. At my time of life—with the partial failure of vision with which I have been afflicted for more than twelve years—with the other cares and burdens resting on me—and with the moral certainty that the infirmities of age, if I am spared, must soon come upon me, I could hope to accomplish no more; and I shall attempt no more.

These Notes were commenced more than twelve years ago, and were undertaken in pursuance of a desire long cherished. For this work I had been making preparation for several years previous by the collection of such Commentaries on the Psalms as I could obtain, that might assist me in preparing something on this portion of the Sacred Volume that might at once be useful to others, and might make it my duty and privilege, in this the closing labour of my life, in this department, to contemplate the beauties of this book by a close study—an employment than which none could be more appropriate for one who looks at the end of all his earthly labours as rapidly approaching.

The work has been prosecuted with such leisure as I could command—the whole of it having been written, as all my other Commentaries have been, in the early hours of the morning, uniformly closing my daily task in this respect as the hour of nine was reached. By this arrangement I have secured the time which I have employed in preparing the Notes on the New Testament, on Job, on Isaiah, on Daniel, and now on the Psalms, without entrenching on what I felt might properly be required of me in my pastoral labours; and, at the same time, I have secured to myself personally the inestimable benefit of commencing each day with the contemplation of a portion of the Word of God.

In the long period which has elapsed since these Notes on the Psalms were commenced, I have been frequently compelled to interrupt my studies by the condition of my eyes; and, in more than one instance, the work has been wholly suspended for more than a year at a time, with little hope that it would be resumed again. Some apology, I trust, may be found in these facts for the manifold defects which I have too much reason to suppose will be observed by all who consult these volumes. I have performed my work as well as I could; but I have not accomplished my own cherished hopes in regard to it. It is not what I fondly trusted it might be; it is not what a work on the Psalms should be. Some of the reasons for the failure I have stated at length in the Introduction, § 8.

It is of more interest to me than it can be to the public to say that I cannot close these labours, continued through so many years of my life, without deep emotion. The very fact that *any* work of life is ended, however humble or unimportant it may be in itself, is fitted to suggest solemn reflections to a man's own mind. The nature of the work in which I have thus been engaged is such as to give great additional solemnity to these reflections. He undertakes a work of great responsibility, who engages in the task of endeavouring to explain the Word of God, and who may thus give direction to the views, perhaps, of thousands, on subjects that may affect their destiny for ever.

In looking, now, at a labour of this kind continued for nearly forty years, and entered on with no expectation of the results which have been reached, while I am grateful for the patronage extended to my efforts in this country and abroad, I cannot be insensible to the responsibility of having in that time sent forth to influence my fellow-men more than half a million of volumes of Commentary on the Scriptures in my native land, and perhaps more than this number in England, Scotland, and Ireland; and of having been permitted, to a limited extent at least, thus to speak in the French and Welsh languages, in the languages of India, and in the language spoken by the millions of China.

With such feelings of gratitude, and with, I trust, some proper sense of my responsibility, I now close this part of the labour of my life, and commend these volumes, as I have endeavoured to do those which have gone before them, to the blessing of God.

ALBERT BARNES.

INTRODUCTION.

§ 1. *The title to the Book of Psalms.*—The general title to the Book of Psalms in Hebrew is תְּהִלִּים—*Tehillim*, Psalms, or more fully, סֵפֶר תְּהִלִּים—*Sepher Tehillim*, " Book of Psalms." Sometimes a shorter title is used—תִּלִּים—*Tillim.* Other terms are used as appropriate to particular psalms, as מִזְמוֹרִים—*mizmorim*, or שִׁירִים, *shirim*, songs; or in the singular, מִזְמוֹר, *mizmor*, and שִׁיר, *shir*, a song. These latter titles, however, are not given to the entire collection, but to particular psalms. The former title—*mizmor*—is given to Ps. iii., iv., v., vi., viii., ix., xii., xiii., xv., xix., xx., xxi., xxii., xxiii., and to thirty-nine others, the last being Ps. cxliii., rendered uniformly *a psalm.* The latter title, *shir*, occurs in Ps. xxx., xlv., xlvi., and in twenty-seven other psalms, the last being Ps. cxxxiv., and is uniformly rendered *song*, though it is sometimes connected with the word *mizmor*, psalm, and rendered " A song and psalm," as in Ps. xlviii., lxv., lxvi., lxvii., lxviii., lxxv., lxxxiii., lxxxvii., lxxxviii.; and in Ps. cxxii., cxxiii., cxxiv. it is connected with the word *degrees* : " *A song of degrees.*"

The word *Tehillim* is derived from the verb—הָלַל—*halal*, to praise, as in the word *Hallelujah, Praise Jehovah.* The name is given to the general collection, because praise, more than any one thing else, is the characteristic of the book, and because the collection seems to have been designed to be used in the public praise or worship of God. Probably they were all thus used in Hebrew worship.

The word *Psalms*, as applied to the collection, we have derived from the Greek translation, the word ψαλμὸς, in the plural ψαλμοὶ—*psalmos*, and *psalmoi.* This word is derived from ψάλλω, *psallo*, to touch, to twitch, to pluck—as the hair or beard; and then, to touch or twitch a string, *to twang*, that is, to cause it to vibrate by touching or twitching it with the finger or with a *plectrum* (πλῆκτρον)—an instrument for striking the strings of a lyre, as a quill. Cic. N. D., 2. 59. Hence the word is applied to instruments of music employed in praise, and then to acts of praise in general. The noun—ψαλμός, *psalmos*—*psalm*, means properly *a touching, twang*, as of a bowstring, or of stringed instruments; then a song, as accompanying stringed instruments; and then specifically a psalm or song of praise to God. Thus the verb—ψαλλω, *psallo*—is used in the New Testament as denoting *praise* in the following places:—Rom. xv. 9, "I will confess—and *sing* unto Thy name;" 1 Cor. xiv. 15, "*I will sing* with the spirit, and *I will sing* with the understanding;" Eph. v. 19, "Singing and *making melody* in your heart to the Lord;" James v. 13, "Is any merry? let him *sing psalms*." The verb does not elsewhere occur in the New Testament. The *noun*—ψαλμός, *psalmos*—is used in the New Testament in the following places as denoting psalms in general:—1 Cor. xiv. 26, "Every one of you hath a *psalm*;" Eph. v. 19, "Speaking to yourselves in *psalms*;" Col. iii. 16, "Admonishing one another in *psalms*." In the following places it is applied in the New Testament to the Book of Psalms, considered as a collection of songs of praise;—Luke xx. 42, "David himself saith in the Book of *Psalms*;"—Luke xxiv. 44, "All things must be fulfilled, which were written in the law of Moses, and in the Prophets, and in the *Psalms*, concerning me:" see Notes on that passage;—Acts i. 20, "It is written in the Book of *Psalms*;"—Acts xiii. 33, "It is also written in the second *psalm*." The word does not elsewhere occur in the New Testament.

§ 2. *The authors of the psalms.*—The Psalms thus collected into a book are by no means the production of one poet or one age. They stretch through a long period of Jewish history, certainly from the time of Moses to the time of the return from the captivity of Babylon, and probably later, and they are modified by all the varieties incident to the peculiarities of their respective authors; to individual and national history; to the times in which they were composed. So many of them, however, are the composition of David, that it is customary to speak of them as "The Psalms of David," though it is probable that not much more than half of the psalms in the collection were written by him. Of the one hundred and fifty comprising the collection, according to the enumeration in the Hebrew manuscripts, not quite one half are usually ascribed to him. According to De Wette, seventy-four; to Kennicott, sixty-six; to De Rossi, sixty-seven; to Rosenmüller and Eichhorn, seventy-one; and to Hengstenberg, eighty. It is probable, however, that a portion of the psalms to which no name is prefixed in the title—but how great a portion it is impossible now to determine—is the production of David. Still, so many are known to have been composed by him, and he was so eminent as a poet, as to justify the language which is so frequently employed when they are called familiarly "The Psalms of David."

The following persons are mentioned in the titles as authors of psalms:

(1.) One psalm (xc.) is ascribed to Moses. In regard to the question whether this is to be regarded as a composition of Moses, see Notes on the psalm. No other psalm in the collection is ascribed to him, though not a few specimens of his poetry are preserved in the Pentateuch. Why this was not incorporated with his other writings, or how it was preserved until it obtained a permanent place in the Book of Psalms, cannot now be determined.

(2.) David occupies a prominent position as the author of many of the psalms in the collection, but, as has been remarked above, critics are divided in opinion as to the exact number that should be ascribed to him. In the Hebrew inscriptions of the Psalms, sixty-eight are attributed to him. The difference between this number and that noted above in regard to the opinions of De Wette, Kennicott, De Rossi, Rosenmüller, Eichhorn, Hengstenberg, and others, arises from the variations in the manuscripts in respect to these inscriptions; the different value attached to these inscriptions by various critics; the fact that some psalms, though without a title in the Hebrew, are supposed to be so certainly the production of David as to make it proper to ascribe them to him; and the fact that some of the psalms ascribed to him are supposed by different writers to belong to a later period of the Jewish history than his time, and that consequently the title by which they are attributed to David is an error. There *is* every reason to suppose that some of the psalms now without a title are the composition of David, though it is not known, and cannot now be known, why they are *not* ascribed to him in the titles of the psalms themselves. In consequence of these facts, it is impossible now to determine with exact precision how many of the psalms are to be ascribed to David; though the number is undoubtedly so great that he is to be regarded as the principal author of the collection.

(3.) Twelve of the psalms, Ps. l., lxxiii., lxxiv., lxxv., lxxvi., lxxvii., lxxviii., lxxix., lxxx., lxxxi., lxxxii., lxxxiii., are ascribed to Asaph. These, it will be seen, occupy a place together in the collection, (Ps. lxiii.—lxxxiii.,) with the exception of Ps. l. The reason for this arrangement cannot now be known. De Wette (Einleitung, III. iii.) supposes that, with the exception of Ps. l. and lxxiii., these are improperly ascribed to Asaph, as, in his view, they pertain to later times of the Jewish history, Ps. lxxiv. and lxxix. to the destruction of the temple and the city; Ps. lxxx. to the Exile, etc. Comp. the Notes on the introduction to those psalms.

(4.) Eleven of the psalms, xlii., xliv., xlv., xlvi., xlvii., xlviii., xlix., lxxxiv., lxxxv., lxxxvii., lxxxviii., are ascribed to "the sons of Korah," as the authors, or are "for the sons of Korah." See Notes to the introduction of Ps. xlii. It is not certain whether these were composed *by* "the sons of Korah," or were composed *for* "the sons of Korah;" that is, for the company of musicians to whom the direction of the music in the temple was confided. It is obvious, however, that if the meaning is that they were composed *by* "the sons of Korah," this furnishes no information as to the individual authorship of the psalms. By which *one* of them they were composed, or whether by *more* than one, of course is not indicated by a title so general. De Wette supposes that most of these psalms pertain to the times of the Exile, or to a later period. There is nothing *very* peculiar in the character of these psalms; nothing which in themselves could lead us to conclude that they were composed by those to whom they are ascribed, rather than by David or Asaph.

(5.) Two psalms, lxxxviii., lxxxix., are ascribed to a person called "The Ezrahite." One of these, Ps. lxxxviii., is ascribed to "*Heman* the Ezrahite," and the other, Ps. lxxxix., to *Ethan* the Ezrahite." The former of these is also reckoned among those which pertain to the "sons of Korah." Ethan and Heman were probably, however, different persons, to each of whom the name *Ezrahite* might for some reason be applied. In 1 Kings iv. 31, they are mentioned among others as remarkable for their wisdom: "For he [Solomon] was wiser than all men; than Ethan the Ezrahite, and Heman, and Chalcol, and Darda, the sons of Mahol." In 1 Chron. ii. 6, they are mentioned as "sons of Zerah:" "Zimri, and Ethan, and Heman, and Calcol, and Dara." In 1 Chron. vi. 33, a Heman is mentioned as one of the "sons of the Kohathites:" "Heman, a singer, the son of Joel." So, in 1 Chron. xv. 17, he is mentioned in connexion with Ethan, who is there said to be the son of Kushaiah; and in 1 Chron. xv. 19, he is mentioned as associated with Asaph and Ethan: "So the singers, Heman, Asaph, and Ethan, were appointed to sound with cymbals of brass." In 1 Chron. xxv. 1, Heman is mentioned with Jeduthun, as one of those whose sons "should prophesy with harps, with psalteries, and with cymbals." He is there referred to as associated with Asaph. Comp. 2 Chron. v. 12; xxix. 13, 14; xxxv. 15. Ethan is twice mentioned—1 Kings iv. 31 as above, as a wise man, and 1 Chron. ii. 6, as above. Compare Notes on the introduction to Ps. lxxxviii., lxxxix.

(6.) Two of the psalms, Ps. lxxii. and Ps. cxxvii., are ascribed to Solomon, or are "*for* Solomon." See the Notes on the titles to those psalms. It cannot be positively determined whether those psalms are his composition, or whether they were composed with reference to him or "*for*" him. The latter would seem to be the more probable opinion in regard to Ps. lxxii., so far as can be determined from the contents of the psalm; but still there is nothing which absolutely prevents us from ascribing the two to him as the author.

(7.) Fifteen of the psalms, Ps. cxx.—cxxxiv., are entitled "Songs of Degrees." Of these, four are ascribed to David and one to Solomon. The names of the authors of the others are not mentioned. Comp. the introduction to the Notes on Ps. cxx. They are grouped together because they appear to have been used on certain special occasions, rather than from anything peculiar in the psalms themselves.

(8.) Some of the psalms are ascribed in the Septuagint translation to Jeremiah, to Ezekiel, to Haggai, and to Zechariah. As there is nothing corresponding to this in the Hebrew titles, this must have been, of course, mere conjecture or tradition.

(9.) There remains a pretty large number of the collection the names of whose authors are not mentioned; and, of course, there are now no means of determining the question in regard to the authorship. Such are Ps. i., ii., x., xxxiii., xliii., lxxi., xcii., xciii., xciv., xcv., xcvi., xcvii., xcviii., xcix., c., civ., cv., cvi., cvii., cxi., cxii., cxiii., cxiv., cxv., cxvi., cxvii., cxviii., cxix., cxxxv., cxxxvi., cxxxvii., cxlvi., cxlvii., cxlviii., cxlix., cl. These, it will be seen, are irregularly scattered through the book, though they are, for the most part, near its close.

In regard to the origin and authority of the titles to the several psalms, see § 4.

§ 3. *The formation of the collection and arrangement of the Book of Psalms.*—The Jewish Talmud (Cod. Berachot, 1, 9) ascribes the formation of the Psalter, or the assembling of the Book of Psalms, to David. It is unnecessary to remark that this cannot be a correct opinion, as many of the psalms are indubitably of a later date than the time of David. Most of the Christian fathers, and many critics of modern times, ascribe the collection and arrangement of the book to Ezra, and this is now regarded as the most probable opinion; and if so the collection must have been formed about 450 years before Christ. But though this may be regarded as the correct opinion in regard to the completion of the whole as it now stands, yet there is evidence in the psalms themselves of the existence of smaller collections made before from which the general one was ultimately formed. By whom those smaller collections were made is not now known, nor can it be ascertained what changes may have been made in them when the general collection was formed.

The book is divided in the Hebrew into five minor books or collections, sufficiently marked in their character, and so indicated at the close of each as to make it every way probable that these may have been *published*, so to speak, in the form of different books, or that the later were additions to the first collection or volume. This division is found also in the Septuagint version—a fact which proves that it existed as early as the year 200 before Christ. These portions bear marks of being not *arbitrary* divisions made at the time when the general collection was formed, but distinct and independent collections by different persons. The grouping is not precisely accurate, that is, in the first part, the "Psalms of David" (Ps. i.—xli.), not *all* the psalms of David are included; and there are a few that are not ascribed to him in the title; but still it was so complete at the time, probably, as to make it proper to regard it as a collection of *his* psalms in respect to the purpose for which that collection was made.

The first book embraces the first forty-one psalms, and was, probably, a collection of David's psalms as such, although it does not embrace by any means *all* that he wrote, probably not all that were extant at the time when the collection was made. The *close* of this "book" is indicated by the words "Amen, and Amen," Ps. xli. 13. All the psalms in this collection, except Ps. i., ii., x., and xxxiii., are expressly ascribed to David, and it is every way probable that all were composed by him. In many manuscripts, in the Septuagint, and in the Latin Vulgate, the first psalm is united with the second (as are, also, in other parts of the general collection, Ps. xlii. and Ps. xliii., and Ps. cxvi. and cxvii.). It is probable that this collection was early made, though De Wette has endeavoured to show that it could not have been until after the Exile, as he supposes that Ps. xiv. and xliv. were composed *after* that event. Of this, however, there is no evidence. Of course it is impossible to determine by whom this collection was made. It has been supposed by some that it was as early as the time of Hezekiah, and that it was prepared under his direction, as he is known to have ordered a collection of the proverbs of Solomon to be made and written out (Prov. xxv. 1); and as (2 Chron. xxix. 30) he "commanded the Levites to sing praise unto the Lord with the words of David." (Kitto, *Ency.*)

The second book in the general collection comprises Ps. xlii.—lxxii. This collection is made up of the psalms of "the sons of Korah," Ps. xlii.—xlix.; of one of the psalms of Asaph, Ps. l.; of nineteen psalms of David; of two whose authors are not named; and of one inscribed "to Solomon," or "*for* Solomon," Ps. lxxii. At the end of this collection (Ps. lxxii. 20) the following notice is given: "The prayers of David, the son of Jesse, are ended;" and some have supposed that this was the close of the *entire* psalms preceding it, as one book or collection, Ps. i.—lxxii. Carpzov. Introd. ii. 107. But that this was a different collection, or that there were two collections made by different persons, seems evident from the fact that Ps. liii.

is the same as Ps. xiv., with only slight variations—the variations consisting mainly in the fact that the word *Elohim* is used as the name of God in the latter, in the place of *Jehovah* in the former. It cannot be supposed that a collector would have used the same psalm with such a variation in the same collection. So also Ps. lxx. is but a repetition of Ps. xl. 13—17, with only a similar change.

It may be *suggested* that these two collections may have been subsequently *united,* and may have constituted *one* before the more general collection was made. Thus, the natural *close* of this collection, as of the first collection (Ps. xli. 13), would be with the words "Amen, and Amen," Ps. lxxii. 19. To the *entire* collection—the two combined—these words may have been added (Ps. lxxii. 20), "The prayers of David, the son of Jesse, are ended," meaning that *now* an entire and complete collection of the Psalms of *David* had been made in the *two* combined; or, that *as many had been combined for public worship as were then intended to be used in that service.* This idea would not prevent the supposition that there may have been at that time, in fact, other psalms of David in existence; or that they might have been subsequently introduced into the worship of God in *other* collections.

The third book (Ps. lxxiii.—lxxxix.) consists in part (Ps. lxxiii.—lxxxiii.) of psalms of Asaph, and in part (Ps. lxxxiv.—lxxxix.) of the psalms of the sons of Korah, including one of David (Ps. lxxxvi.). The book contains none of the psalms of David, with the exception of Ps. lxxxvi., and therefore the notice is given at the end of the second book (Ps. lxxii. 20), that "the prayers of David, the son of Jesse, are ended." It was evidently the design of the author of the compilation at the *close* of that book not to admit in the following book *any* of the psalms of David; perhaps it was the intention *not* to collect any more of the psalms of David for the purpose of public worship. Possibly, as De Wette (Einleitung, p. 21) suggests, the author of the collection in the third book put the notice at the end of the second book that David's psalms ended there, it being his intention to make a collection of another kind. *When* this collection was made is unknown. From Ps. lxxxv. it would seem probable that it was made as late as the return from the captivity at Babylon. *That* psalm may have been written by one of the company called "the sons of Korah;" or it may have been composed for their use in the sanctuary. This collection closes, like the two former, with the expressive "Amen, and Amen," Ps. lxxxix. 52.

The fourth collection (Ps. xc.—cvi.) is made up wholly of anonymous psalms, with the exception of Ps. xc., which is ascribed to Moses, and Ps. ci. and ciii., which are ascribed to David. They are psalms which have almost no local references or allusions, which might, for the most part, have been composed in any country or at any period of the world; and which, in their structure and allusions, give no indication of their authors or of the circumstances which led to their composition. Their authorship, except in the three instances above mentioned, cannot now be ascertained; nor is it necessary to determine that question in order fully to understand and appreciate them. They were manifestly designed for public worship, and probably written with the intention of being so used. This book closes (Ps. cvi. 48) with the expression " Amen, Hallelujah."

The fifth and last book (Ps. cvii.—cl.), is miscellaneous in its character, and seems to have been intended to be a collection of *all* the scattered psalms which would be proper for public worship, which had not found a place in the other collections. Part (Psalms cviii., cix., cx., cxxii., cxxiv., cxxxi., cxxxiii., the four last being among the "Songs of Degrees," cxxxviii., cxxxix., cxl., cxli., cxlii., cxliii., cxliv., cxlv.,) are ascribed to David. Part (Psalms cxx.—cxxxiv.) consist of the "Songs of Degrees." The rest (Psalms cvii., cxi., cxii., cxiii., cxiv., cxv., cxvi., cxvii., cxviii., cxix., cxxxv., cxxxvi., cxxxvii., cxlvi., cxlvii., cxlviii., cxlix., cl.) are anonymous. By whom, and when this last collection was made is unknown. It may without improbability, however, be supposed that it was made by the person—Ezra, perhaps—who undertook to collect into one the entire "books" already existing, and who found many psalms that had not been included by the collectors of the previous books, and who, therefore, grouped all these together in a single book, to be added in the general collection to those which had been already classified and arranged.

§ 4. *The titles to the several psalms.*—All the psalms, except thirty-four, have now in the Hebrew titles or superscriptions. Some, however, reckon but twenty-five exceptions, as, according to their view, the phrase, *Hallelujah,* " Praise ye the Lord," occurring at the commencement of several of the psalms, is regarded by them as a title or superscription. The more correct supposition, however, undoubtedly is to regard that phrase as a part of the psalm. To each one of these exceptions the Talmud gives the name of *Orphan Psalms.*

(*a*) The *authorship* of these titles is unknown, and cannot now be ascertained. They are found in the Hebrew; but it is not to be supposed that, so far as the *name* of the author of the psalm is concerned, or so far as they are intended to indicate the author, they were prefixed to the psalm by the authors themselves. The Psalms are not of the nature of epistles or histories, and it cannot be supposed that the author would prefix his name to a mere poem or hymn. The probability, therefore, is, that they were prefixed to the psalms as they came into common use, or by the collectors of the several books, or the collector of the entire book, either as indicating what was the common opinion on the subject of the authorship, and the occasion on which they were composed, or as an inspired record in regard to that authorship and design. The question *by whom* they were prefixed is, however, a point which cannot now be determined. If it were possible to ascertain that, it would do much to determine their authority and worth, but the estimate of their value must now be settled by some other method than this.

(*b*) These titles are of great *antiquity*. The fact that they are found in the Hebrew manuscripts proves this, for there are no Hebrew manuscripts, however ancient, without them. They are found, with some variations, in the Septuagint; and it is thus certain that they existed before that translation was made. This point is also confirmed by the fact that the translators of the Septuagint have, in some instances, copied the Hebrew words in Greek letters, without attempting to translate them; and that, in other instances, the titles which they use are translations of the Hebrew words, and show that they must have been made from a Hebrew original. These facts, however, would not make it necessary to suppose that they had been prefixed by the writers themselves, nor would it be *necessary* to suppose that they were prefixed before the time when the psalms were collected,—either the separate books, or the general collection.

(*c*) The *design* of these titles is either to designate the author of the psalm, or the occasion on which it was composed, or the chief singer to whom it was dedicated, and to whom it seems to have been committed to set it to appropriate music—that is, to arrange the music for a public use of the psalm; or the style of the poetry; or the instrument which was to be used; or the *tune* which was to be sung. Some of the titles simply designate the author, as in many of those ascribed to David; some describe at length the occasion on which they were written, as Ps. xviii., xxx., li., lii., lvi., etc. etc. Some combine several of these things together, the author, the occasion, the style of the poetry, the music to be used, etc., as Ps. lii., liii., liv., lv., lvi. The longest and fullest of these titles is that prefixed to Ps. lx., where we have the dedication to the chief musician, the name of the author, the style of the poetry, the design of the psalm, the instrument of music to be employed, and the historical occasion on which the psalm was composed.

(*d*) It is very difficult at this distance of time to explain the *meaning* of many of these titles, and critics have differed very materially in their conjectures on this subject. The difficulty arises in a considerable degree from our ignorance in regard to the Temple-music, and to the instruments which were employed. The difficulty is the same which would exist two or three thousand years from the present time in explaining a book, now familiar, containing "tunes" of music, and a reference to the instruments of music which are now employed in the public service of God. It might be difficult, if not impossible, so to describe the exact instrument of music used as to be intelligible to a future age; and it would be obviously impossible to explain satisfactorily the *names* of many of the *tunes* which are now in common use—as "Mear," "St. Martin's," "Russia,' "Windham," "Lenox." The difficulty, as has been remarked above, was felt even at the time when the Septuagint version was made, as in several instances the authors of that version have not attempted even to translate the title, but have expressed it in Greek letters answering to the Hebrew. Coverdale, who translated the Bible in 1535, felt the difficulty to be so great that he has omitted nearly all the titles except the names of the authors. In these Notes, as far as an explanation can now be given that is satisfactory or probable, it will be offered in the exposition of the particular psalms.

(*e*) There has been a wide difference of opinion respecting the *authority* of these titles. Not a few modern critics, especially German critics, regard them as of no authority, and argue in respect to the authorship of the psalms, and the time and occasion on which they were composed, as if no such titles were found in the Hebrew. By most of the ancient critics they were considered as genuine, and as having equal authority with the psalms themselves. They were wholly rejected at the close of the fourth century by Theodore of Mopsuestia, one of the ablest and most judicious of the ancient interpreters. Rosenmüller, Hist. Interp. Librorum Sacrorum, P. III., p. 256. Tholuck and Hengstenberg admit their authority. The *objections* to the authority of the title are such as these:—(1.) That the *subscriptions* at the close of the epistles in the New Testament are now regarded as of no historical value, and it is asked why may not the same conclusion be adopted in regard to the titles *prefixed* to the psalms? (2.) That the ancient versions, the Syriac and the Greek especially, exhibit them with great variations, often altering the Hebrew, and sometimes giving a heading where the Hebrew has none. It is asked whether these ancient translators would have taken such liberties if the titles had been considered sacred like the psalms themselves? (*Kitto*).—It is added on this point, that "if ever Ezra settled them, the variations in versions and manuscripts have tended since to make them doubtful." Eichhorn, *Einleitung*, III., p. 490. (3.) It is argued that the titles are at variance with the contents of the psalms. Thus, it is alleged that sometimes the name of the author is incorrectly given, "as when David is named over the psalms referring to the captivity," as in Ps. xiv., xxv., li., lxix. It is also alleged that Ps. cxxxix. cannot be David's, as it is not free from Chaldaisms. It is also said that the occasion on which a psalm was composed is not always correctly specified, as in Ps. xxx.

It is to be observed, however, that these writers sometimes *assume* that a psalm refers to the time of the exile when it would be possible to explain it on the supposition that it was composed at an earlier date; and that it is not always safe to argue from the internal evidence of a psalm against the inscription. A critic affixes his own interpretation to a psalm, and then adopts that as a basis of argument in regard to its origin; whereas often, possibly in all cases, if the inscription were assumed to be correct, it would not be difficult to explain the psalm, by fair rules of interpretation, in accordance with that supposition.

On the whole, it seems to me that these inscriptions are to be regarded as a part of the inspired record, and as having the authority of inspiration. The fact that they are found in the Hebrew,—that they can be traced back to the earliest periods when we have any knowledge of the Hebrew text,—that they have come down to us with that text,—furnishes proof which it seems we cannot now set aside; that they are to be regarded as a part of the text, and that they should not be rejected, except as any other portion of the Hebrew text should be rejected, *i. e.*, only when it can be demonstrated that an error has crept into the text by the fault of transcribers.

§ 5. *The general character of the Book of Psalms.*—The Psalms are mostly lyrical poetry, that is, poetry adapted to the harp or lyre; to be used in connexion with instrumental music; to be *sung*, not *read*. Such poetry was common among the ancients, as it is among the moderns. Anacreon, Alcæus, Stesichorus, Sappho, and Horace were eminent among the ancients as *lyric* poets; and the numerous writers of *songs*, sacred and secular, among the moderns, are to be ranked in the same class. The phrase *lyric poetry* now, however, is frequently applied to that species of poetry which "directly expresses the individual emotions of the poet" (Webster, *Dic.*).

Lyric poetry is, for the most part, an expression of deep *feeling*, and has its foundation *in* feeling or emotion. It is not so much the fruit of the understanding as of the heart; not so much the creation of the imagination as the utterance of deep personal emotion. It embraces in its design and nature all kinds of feeling, and may be joyous, pensive, desponding, triumphant, according to the feelings of the author, or to the occasion; for all these utterances may be *sung*, or may be set to *music*, the varying tones of *music* being adapted to express them all. Hence, in the Psalms, one hundred and fifty in number, and composed by a considerable variety of individuals, and on many different occasions, we have the varied *feelings* of trouble, anguish, fear, hope, joy, trust, thankfulness, devotion to God, penitence for sin, and the exultation of forgiveness,—*the heart moved*, and finding vent for its feelings in words adapted to the melody of the lyre, or the musical tones of the voice. These feelings are expressed in a great variety of modes or forms, and the music was intended, doubtless, to be in accordance with these varied feelings. The Psalms, therefore, comprise compositions of the following classes or orders:—

(1.) Hymns in which the praise of God is the principal and leading object, as (*a*) in general, God is praised as the God of nature and of men, Ps. viii., civ., cxlv.; (*b*) as the God of nature and of the Hebrew people, Ps. xix., xxix., xxxiii., lxv., xciii., cxxxv., cxxxvi., cxlvii.; (*c*) as peculiarly the God of the Hebrew people, Ps. xlvii., lxvi., lxvii., lxxv.; (*d*) as the helper and deliverer of his people, Ps. xlvi., xlviii., lxxv., lxxvi., xviii., xxx., cxxxviii.

(2.) Psalms pertaining to the Hebrew nation; to its history; to the Divine interposition in its behalf; and to its relation to Jehovah. Ps. lxxviii., cv., cvi., cxiv.

(3.) Temple psalms, or songs of Zion. Ps. ii., xv., xxiv., lxxxvii., cxxxii.

(4.) Psalms in relation to trial, calamity, distress, whether of individuals or of the nation. These abound, as Ps. vii., xxii., lv., lvi., cix., xliv., lxxiv., lxxix., lxxx., cxxxvii., lxix., lxxvii., cii., x., xii., xiv., xxxvi., and many others.

(5.) Religious and moral psalms, Ps. xc., cxxxix., xxiii., xci., cxxi., cxxvii., cxxviii., xlii., xliii., ci., cxxxi., i., cxxxiii., cxix.

The *peculiarity* of the Hebrew lyrical poetry as distinguished from the lyrical poetry of other ancient people, and from most of the lyrical poetry in modern times, is its *religion*. It is lyrical poetry on subjects pertaining to religion, or to be employed *in* religion: as expressing religious feeling, and as designed to awaken and foster such feeling. It is intended to raise the heart and the affections towards God; to lift up the thoughts of men from the earth; to inspire confidence in God; to produce consolation as derived from God in times of trouble; to cheer and comfort man in his pilgrimage along a path of sorrow and trouble to a better abode. Much of it can be best characterised by an expression derived from the Bible itself—an expression no less remarkable for its beauty than its truthfulness—as "SONGS IN THE NIGHT" (Job xxxv. 10); songs indicating the joy that may spring up in the soul of man in times of distress and sorrow; songs that show that there *is* joy in the darkness of this world; songs which illustrate the power and the value of religion; songs with which men cheer themselves and each other in their journey towards the grave; songs which even the guilty may pour forth from hearts softened into penitence, and filled with thankfulness in the assurance of pardon.

It is most remarkable that this rich poetry should have sprung up in Palestine, and that it should have been confined to that land. It was not that the land was better adapted to lyric poetry than other lands—for in this respect it could not compare favourably with many other countries, and particularly with Greece. It was not that the events of their history had been such as peculiarly to suggest this kind of composition—for poetry adapted to the lyre or to music abounded elsewhere, and especially in Greece. It was not that the Hebrews had a more poetic imagination than other people—for theirs did not, in this respect, surpass the Greek genius, and whatever there was of poetic imagination in the character of their minds was found with equal richness in Arabia and Persia. Nor was it that their language was peculiarly favourable for this kind of poetry—for in very many respects it was far inferior in this point to the Greek, and had no superiority certainly over the Arabian and Persian.

The fact that their poetry took this turn; the fact that all which they had was religious; the fact that there was literally no poetry in their language that was designed and adapted to the dance, to festive amusements, to Bacchanalian orgies, to scenes of gaiety, frivolity, and vanity; the fact that in *all* the lyric poetry of the Hebrews there is literally nothing in this respect that can be placed by the side of much in the Greek lyric poetry—much in Horace—much in Burns; by the side of the lyric poetry of all lands except Palestine, can be traced only to the idea that the new religion prevailed there, and can be best explained on the supposition that the authors of that poetry were *inspired* to prepare and transmit to future times that which, in all ages, would express the feelings of true devotion, and which might be permanently employed in the praises of God. He will fail to explain the fact that such poetry is found in Palestine alone, and will fail to appreciate its true nature, who does not admit that these "sweet singers" were inspired by the Holy Ghost.

On the general character of Hebrew poetry, see Introduction to the Notes on the Book of Job, sect. v. On "the origin and culture of lyric poetry among the Hebrews," it may be proper to introduce here the following remarks from De Wette's "Commentar ueber die Psalmen," Einleitung, II., pp. 6–12. I copy from the elegant translation of the introduction of De Wette, by Prof. J. Torrey, in the Biblical Repository, Vol. III., pp. 450–456 :—

"If we follow the titles of the Psalms and the common opinion, we must suppose the lyric poetry of the Hebrews, as well as the largest portion of the Psalms themselves, a production of David and his contemporaries. The few specimens of lyric composition which we find before David scarcely enter into consideration, compared with the fertility of his own period. In the earlier history it is but occasionally that the voice of poetry is heard, as in the songs of Moses at the Red Sea, of Deborah, and of Hannah. We are surprised, after so few attempts in lyric poetry, to see so accomplished and fruitful a poet rise up all at once, with several others in his company. So rapid a progress supposes some adequate occasion, some preparatory steps. Now, if we cast our eye over the history of the times immediately preceding the age of David, we are presented with a phenomenon which seems to explain the difficulty. It is Samuel's school of the prophets. Many, as Herder, Eichhorn, Nachtigall, and Rosenmüller, suppose that the composition of psalms was cultivated and brought to perfection in this seminary. Specious as this conjecture appears, it is hardly reconcilable with the facts of the history. It is not intimated that David, before his unction, had any connexion with Samuel. The former tends his father's flock. Indeed Samuel appears to have had no acquaintance with David when he comes to anoint him, 1 Sam. xvi. 6, seq. Yet David is already a skilful minstrel, and famed for his art, ib. ver. 18; he was not, therefore, a disciple of Samuel, at least in minstrelsy. But it is well known that music and song at this period were not separated; we must therefore suppose that David was already a poet, and, as such, known and celebrated. Some time afterwards, it is true, we find David in Samuel's school of the prophets, but it is only on the occasion of his flight from Saul, 1 Sam. xix. 18, seq. It may be possible that Samuel had some acquaintance with David prior to his unction, though no mention is made of it in the account of that transaction, 1 Sam. xvi. But he might have been an object of attention to the prophet without being properly his disciple; or perhaps the youth was his own instructor. Natural capacity, in connexion with frequent practice, might produce the same degree of talent, to say the least, as an artificial system of instruction, like that which we may suppose to have prevailed in the prophetic school. At the same time, it would be an error to imagine that lyric poetry arose amongst the Hebrews all at once, as if it sprung out of the ground. David's contemporaries, the women who celebrated with song and joy his victory over Goliath, practised a species of poetry which, though rude and uncultivated, was truly lyric in its kind; their short poem,

Saul smote his thousands,
But David his ten thousands,

has already the form of the poetic parallelism, and an original and superior mind might easily advance from such a beginning to the highest degree of excellence. We find also, still earlier, in addition to the examples of Moses, Deborah, and Hannah, the practice, particularly among the women, of music and the dance, from which song certainly was not excluded. Jephthah's daughter comes out to meet her father with timbrels and dances, Judges xi. 34. At Shiloh the maidens held a yearly feast with dances, Judges xxi. 21.

It may be questioned whether Samson was not a minstrel, for he is called out to play before the Philistines, Judges xvi. 25, which is commonly understood to refer to the dance, but excludes not the accompaniments of song and instrumental music. But even if he was not, strictly speaking, a musician and singer, yet we meet in him with the first *Mashal* poet, as we have also from the same period the masterly apologue of Jotham. Such facts, though insulated, pre-suppose among a people a considerably high degree of cultivation, or at least of poetical capacity. Indeed, the song of Deborah alone proves that the poetic art was already arrived at a stage of improvement sufficient to account for the origin of the Davidian poetry. Whether a period produces one admirable poem or more is a matter of chance rather than the result of the state of culture. Besides, the times of the Judges and of Samuel constituted the heroic age of the Hebrews, a period peculiarly favourable to the first beginnings and gradual improvement of poetry. 'Such times,' says Eichhorn, 'are poetical under every climate;' but I cannot add with him, 'that poetry, in this case, is like the nation, wild and heroic, breathes only in the warlike trump, and knows no field for practice but that of valour and victory with their attendant train.' The occasions which first called forth the Hebrew poets were, probably enough, connected with war; but when poetry has once sprung into life, she confines herself to no such narrow limits, and draws still other objects within her circle. With feasts of victory, sacrifices, dances, and other rites were united, which might easily have tempered the song to a tone of somewhat softer character. Even warlike songs admit of the gentler emotions, and the song of Deborah is rich in touches of amiable feeling. When it is said they sung to the trumpet, we are certainly not to understand it in the literal sense; the music of the harp, of the flute, and of the timbrel, was the accompaniment even of the songs of war, and these instruments are adapted to the softest tones. We are not then obliged to trace the origin of the sweet and amiable poetry of David's psalms exclusively to Samuel's school of the prophets.

"Unfortunately we know far too little about the prophetic school of Samuel to determine what influence it had on the cultivation of poetry. The passages relating to it are 1 Sam. x. 5 and xix. 19, 20. In the first of these it is undoubtedly implied that the disciples of the prophets had music among them, and their 'prophesying' (הִתְנַבֵּא) has been understood, not without grounds, in the sense of song; for the word נָבִיא sometimes signifies poet, Ex. xv. 20, and נִבָּא, to sing, 1 Chr. xxv. 1, seq. We may suppose, however, that this music was employed simply as a support and accompaniment of the prophetic delivery. The prophets probably delivered their messages, in the earlier times at least, in connexion with music and a vehement action and declamation approaching to a dance. The passage in 2 Kings iii. 15, seq. is remarkable. The prophet Elisha is about to pronounce the answer of the Lord to certain inquiries of Jehoshaphat; but before he does it, he asks for a minstrel; and as the latter strikes the harp, 'the hand of Jehovah comes upon him,' and he utters his reply. The case here, it is true, is different; the prophet does not play and sing himself, but submits to the performance of another; still it shows the constant connexion of music with the prophetic office. Neither is it distinctly asserted in the passages above that the company of the prophets *sung* themselves. The word הִתְנַבֵּא, which is there employed, may not perhaps signify *to sing*, for Saul and Saul's messengers prophecy—הִתְנַבְּאוּ—as soon as they hear the music, without preparation or practice. Their prophesying was perhaps nothing more than a vehement action, dancing, and gesticulation, as we see from the circumstance of Saul's falling down naked. At farthest, they might have joined in the choral song with the company of prophets. Such choral chants were perhaps sung in the school of Samuel, but only for the purposes of devotion and inspiration; and the proper design of this school was to educate youth for the prophetic office, that is, to give counsel from the Lord to a people under a theocratic government. Samuel was a prophet, and history has preserved no remains of any poetical works of his. Is it not most probable that he was aiming to educate his disciples likewise for the prophetic office? Now, it is true that the Hebrews drew no accurate line of distinction between lyric poetry and prophetic eloquence; yet these two always differ, particularly in the mode of delivery; for the lyric poem was probably sung, while the prophetic message was only recited. Supposing, then, Samuel was employed in forming his disciples to be prophetic poets or speakers, what is more natural than to imagine that some of them might feel drawn by genius and inclination to lyric poetry, and succeed in perfecting themselves in this? Yet it lay out of the plan of the prophetic school, and was a thing quite accidental. It is hardly correct, therefore, to consider the prophetic school of Samuel simply as an institution for the cultivation of singing and poetry.

"There were other institutions which may have had an influence still more important and decided than this school of the prophets in promoting the culture of lyric poetry, especially of the religious kind. I refer particularly to those musical schools which, according to the account, 1 Chron. xv. 16, seq., were founded by David in aid of the public worship. Yet I cannot retract the unfavourable opinion I once pronounced* upon these and similar narratives in the Chronicles; I must rather confirm it. Besides the reasons there alleged, which I may not repeat, it seems to me to be a circumstance particularly calculated to excite suspicion, that the psalms and fragments of psalms represented by the Chronicles to have been sung at the dedication of the tabernacle and on similar occasions can hardly have been penned by David, but belong rather to the later and less pure style of the temple poetry. The psalm which is sung, 1 Chron. xvi. 8, seq., is composed of Ps. cv. and xcvi.; but both are productions of a later style. If the Chronicles had presented us on this occasion with a genuine song of David, such as the elegy for which we are indebted to 2 Sam. i., this circumstance would havo contributed not a little to add weight to its authority, but the insertion of these fragments throws suspicion over the whole of the accompanying narrative. The phrase also, quoted 1 Chron xvi. 41, and elsewhere, respecting the Levites who were appointed to give thanks to the

* Beyträge zur Einleit. ins A. T., vol. i., p. 85, sq.

Lord, 'because his mercy endureth for ever,' betrays the later poetry of the temple, an example of which we have in Ps. cxxxvi, where this phrase forms a regular refrain; also Psalms cvi., cvii., and cxviii., in which this phrase occurs appear to belong to a later style of poetry.

"We may imagine that a master like David would not be without companions and assistants in the poetic art; and, in fact, several of David's contemporaries are named in the titles as composers of psalms: but these notices are not always good authority. Solomon, according to the testimony of history, united in himself such richness of lyric invention with the sententious style peculiar to him, that in his time lyric poetry must have attained to a very high degree of perfection. 'Solomon spake three thousand proverbs, and his songs were a thousand and five,' 1 Kings iv. 32. It is singular, however, that with the exception of two which are quite uncertain, no psalms of Solomon are preserved in our present collection; nor do we find any psalm with the author's name belonging to the period after Solomon, not even one which admits of being referred with certainty and of necessity to any particular event in the history of those times; and yet such lyric poems as those of Hezekiah and of Habakkuk clearly evince, that during this period the culture of lyric composition had by no means fallen into neglect. On the contrary, we have many psalms which, according to the results of a sound critical exegesis almost universally acknowledged, must be placed in the times of the captivity, and after the captivity; and these psalms rank, for purity of language, and for sublimity, beauty, and freshness of conception, in the highest class, and are, in no respect, inferior to the poems of David and his contemporaries, *e. g.*, Ps. xlv., lxxiv, lxxix., cvii., and many, if not all, of the Psalms of Degrees. We are here presented, then, with a singular phenomenon. The lyric poetry of the Hebrews, which was cultivated and brought to perfection in the times of David, after producing abundance of fruit, sank into a repose of nearly five hundred years, and then all at once, in the most calamitous period of the state, arose again, survived another golden age, and yielded a second harvest—a phenomenon hardly corresponding with the common course of events. The singularity, however, disappears as soon as we suppose that the collection of Psalms contains several pieces, either anonymous or incorrectly named, which belong to the period extending from David to the captivity. Indeed, it is in the highest degree probable that lyric composition flourished side by side with the prophetic poetry, and that many of the prophets themselves contributed to our present collection, and might reclaim their own productions from David and others. Some of the prophets, too, are actually named by the Septuagint as authors of psalms."

§ 6. *The imprecations in the Psalms.*—Much has been written on the subject of the imprecations in the Psalms, or, as they are called, "The imprecatory psalms;" and perhaps there is no part of the Bible that gives more perplexity and pain to its readers than this; perhaps nothing that constitutes a more plausible objection to the belief that the psalms are the productions of inspired men than the spirit of revenge which they sometimes seem to breathe, and the spirit of cherished malice and implacableness which the writers seem to manifest. There has been probably no explanation offered which has relieved the minds of those who are thus perplexed, or which has furnished a solution wholly satisfactory on the question how this spirit can be reconciled with the precepts of the New Testament and with the requirements of true religion. It is useless to attempt to disguise or to conceal the difficulty, and it may be admitted that most of the explanations which have been suggested leave the difficulty just where it was. Perhaps it is not possible for us to remove all such difficulty, or so to present the subject that questions may not be asked which it would be impossible to answer, and, indeed, what subject is there in mental philosophy, in natural science, in morals, or in theology, on which questions may not be asked which the human powers are not yet competent to answer? In regard to the growth of a blade of grass, questions may be asked which no chemist—no man—*can answer*.

In reference to the imprecations in the Psalms, it will be proper, first, to refer to some specimens of such psalms, that we may know where the difficulty lies; and then to consider in what way, if any, this difficulty may be solved.

The following are among the passages which would be referred to as belonging to that class of psalms. They are not, indeed, *all* that could be selected, but they are *fair* specimens, and there are no others that would involve any difficulty which are not found in these.

Ps. v. 10: "Destroy thou them, O God; let them fall by their own counsels; cast them out in the multitude of their transgressions; for they have rebelled against thee."

Ps. x. 15: "Break thou the arm of the wicked and the evil man: seek out his wickedness till thou find none."

Ps. xviii. 40—42: "Thou hast also given me the necks of mine enemies; that I might destroy them that hate me. They cried, but there was none to save them: even unto the Lord, but he answered them not. Then did I beat them small as the dust before the wind: I did cast them out as the dirt in the streets."

Ps. xxviii. 4: "Give them according to their deeds, and according to the wickedness of their endeavours: give them after the work of their hands; render to them their desert."

Ps. xxxi. 17: "Let me not be ashamed, O Lord; for I have called upon thee: let the wicked be ashamed, and let them be silent in the grave."

Ps. xxxv. 3—8: "Draw out also the spear, and stop the way against them that persecute me: say unto my soul, I am thy salvation. Let them be confounded and put to shame that seek after my soul: let them be turned back and brought to confusion that devise my hurt. Let them be as chaff before the wind: and let the angel of the Lord chase them. Let their way be dark and slippery: and let the angel of the Lord persecute them. For without cause have they hid for me their net in a pit, which without cause they have digged for my soul. Let destruction come upon him at unawares; and let his net that he hath hid catch himself: into that very destruction let him fall."

Ps. xl. 14: "Let them be ashamed and confounded together that seek after my soul to destroy it; let them be driven backward and put to shame that wish me evil."

Ps. lv. 9: "Destroy, O Lord, and divide their tongues: for I have seen violence and strife in the city." 15: "Let death seize upon them, and let them go down quick [*alive, living*] into hell: for wickedness is in their dwellings, and among them."

Ps. lviii. 6—10: "Break their teeth, O God, in their mouth: break out the great teeth of the young lions, O Lord. Let them melt away as waters which run continually: when he bendeth his bow to shoot his arrows, let them be as cut in pieces. As a snail which melteth, let every one of them pass away: like the untimely birth of a woman, that they may not see the sun. Before your pots can feel the thorns, he shall take them away as with a whirlwind, both living, and in his wrath. The righteous shall rejoice when he seeth the vengeance: he shall wash his feet in the blood of the wicked."

Ps. lix. 12—15: "For the sin of their mouth and the words of their lips let them even be taken in their pride: and for cursing and lying which they speak. Consume them in wrath, consume them, that they may not be: and let them know that God ruleth in Jacob unto the ends of the earth. And at evening let them return; and let them make a noise like a dog, and go round about the city. Let them wander up and down for meat, and grudge if they be not satisfied."

Ps. lxviii. 2: "As smoke is driven away, so drive them away: as wax melteth before the fire, so let the wicked perish at the presence of God."

Ps. lxix. 22—25: "Let their table become a snare before them: and that which should have been for their welfare, let it become a trap. Let their eyes be darkened, that they see not; and make their loins continually to shake. Pour out thine indignation upon them, and let thy wrathful anger take hold of them. Let their habitation be desolate; and let none dwell in their tents."

Ps. lxxix. 12: "And render unto our neighbours sevenfold into their bosom their reproach, wherewith they have reproached thee, O Lord."

Ps. lxxxiii. 9—17: "Do unto them as unto the Midianites; as to Sisera, as to Jabin, at the brook of Kison: which perished at Endor: they became as dung for the earth. Make their nobles like Oreb, and like Zeeb; yea, all their princes as Zebah, and as Zalmunna. . . . O my God, make them like a wheel; as the stubble before the wind. As the fire burneth a wood, and as the flame setteth the mountains on fire; so persecute them with thy tempest, and make them afraid with thy storm. Fill their faces with shame; that they may seek thy name, O Lord. Let them be confounded and troubled for ever; yea, let them be put to shame, and perish."

Ps. cix. 6—15: "Set thou a wicked man over him: and let Satan stand at his right hand. When he shall be judged, let him be condemned: and let his prayer become sin. Let his days be few; and let another take his office. Let his children be fatherless, and his wife a widow. Let his children be continually vagabonds, and beg: let them seek their bread also out of their desolate places. Let the extortioner catch all that he hath; and let the strangers spoil his labour. Let there be none to extend mercy unto him: neither let there be any to favour his fatherless children. Let his posterity be cut off; and in the generation following let their name be blotted out. Let the iniquity of his fathers be remembered with the Lord; and let not the sin of his mother be blotted out. Let them be before the Lord continually, that he may cut off the memory of them from the earth."

Ps. cxxxvii. 7—9: "Remember, O Lord, the children of Edom in the day of Jerusalem; who said, Rase it, rase it, even to the foundation thereof. O daughter of Babylon, who art to be destroyed; happy shall he be, that rewardeth thee as thou hast served us. Happy shall he be, that taketh and dasheth thy little ones against the stones."

These are specimens of the class of psalms now under consideration, and though the number might be somewhat increased, yet these examples embrace those which are most difficult to be explained, and involve all the difficulties to be found in this class of the psalms. None could be adduced which *seem* to breathe a more vindictive spirit than these do; none *seem* to be more opposed to the spirit of the New Testament. If, therefore, a solution can be suggested that would be satisfactory in regard to these passages, it would be easy to apply the principles of such a solution to all the similar passages in the Psalms.

The inquiry then occurs in what way, if in any way, the difficulty is to be solved, or what explanations can be suggested.

On this subject the following remarks may be made:—(1.) Whatever difficulty there exists, is created by the Bible itself. The record is one which the sacred writers have themselves made. This fact is proof at least of candour, and of a consciousness on their part that there was *nothing* in this record which was not founded in truth, which did not really occur; that is, that these feelings actually existed in their minds. It cannot be pretended that the writers indulged in feelings which they were unwilling to record; which they were ashamed to make known. In fact, they took all the methods in their power to make them known, and to have the record perpetuated. They not only *recorded* them—put them in a permanent form—but they embodied them in poetry, which was to be employed in the public worship of God; which was to go down to future ages, to direct the devotions of the people of far-distant times. Moreover, if there is any condemnation of this spirit in the Bible—if there was anything wrong in this spirit—we are to remember that the condemnation is found in the very book where these expressions occur —for it is to be assumed here that, so far as the objection lies against these expressions as a part of the Bible—as a part of a pretended revelation—*the Bible is one book;* the Old Testament and the New are parts of the same revelation from God. The Bible, thus in making the record, should be allowed at least to be a book of candour —a book in which there is no attempt to *conceal* what was actually passing in the minds of the writers. There was, it may be presumed some reason for *making* the record which was regarded as not inconsistent with the purpose of a revelation; and it was assumed also that these things would be susceptible of an explanation, which would be consistent with the claim that the Bible was a revelation from God.

(2.) It may be a fair subject of inquiry how much of what is charged as wrong, harsh, and vindictive, may be referred to the spirit of the age in which the Bible was composed, and in which these men lived. This remark is not made on the supposition that the principles of morals and religion change from one age to another; or that they are modified by the circumstances of men; or that the same thing is morally right in one age or country, and morally wrong in another. Truth and holiness, right and wrong, do not change, nor are they dependent on the caprices or the customs of mankind. Still, in order to know exactly what was *meant;* how much words express; what was the precise idea intended to be conveyed by language that was used,—it is necessary for us to place ourselves in the circumstances, and to understand the prevailing customs and habits of the people who used the language. We constantly apply these principles, insensibly it may be, when we read Homer, or when we read the records of knight-errantry, or when we endeavour to understand the poetry of any people in the earlier periods of history. The language which a Covenanter or a Puritan used *may* possibly have expressed no other internal emotion than would be expressed by the milder language which we should use; the rough words which the uneducated and the vulgar use *may* express no different feelings than would be found to exist when the thoughts are conveyed in the smooth tones, and the courtly phrases of those in the higher walks of life. There may be as much bitter feeling beneath silk and satin as beneath a dress made of the skins of wild beasts; in the palace as in the wigwam. It may be possible that those who lived in the earlier ages of the world really *meant* no more by the language which they often used, and which seems to us to be so harsh, so revengeful, and so savage, than we do in the milder tones which we employ, and which we now suppose to be demanded by civilization and Christianity. It is, at least, a supposable case that the people of future times *may* have had conveyed to them as much in the records of *our* literature, and of *our* customs, which they will find it difficult to explain consistently with *their* notions of refinement, civilization, and the spirit of pure religion, as *we* recognise in the language of the Covenanters and the Puritans of Scotland and England, or in the poetic effusions of the days of David. Let us be sure that we understand precisely what they *meant*, and exactly how our own spirit is better than theirs, before we condemn them.

(3.) Part of these passages *may* undoubtedly be regarded as prophetic; expressing what *would be*, rather than indicating any *wish* on the part of the author of the psalms that such things *should* be. In some instances, the passages might have been rendered in the future instead of the imperative mood, with no violation of the laws of the Hebrew language, or the proper principles of interpretation. Several of the passages of this kind which may properly be applied to the Messiah, are undoubtedly of this nature, and those passages are to be interpreted, when the laws of language will admit of such an interpretation, as expressive of what sinners *deserve*, and of what *will* come upon them, and not as indicating any *desire* on the part of the author that it should be so.

It must be admitted, however, that this consideration does by no means remove all the difficulty, nor does it in fact even diminish it. It cannot be affirmed by any one acquainted with the Hebrew language that this solution could be applied to *all* the cases in reference to which the difficulty exists, and there is still an explanation needed to meet the cases which cannot be brought under this rule. In a book claiming to be inspired the objection is, in effect, as great if there is only one such passage as if there are many. The essential difficulty is to explain it consistently with the claim to inspiration at all.

It should be conceded, further, that this explanation is one which cannot be admitted in regard to the most difficult of the passages. No man can show that they are *all* mere predictions of the future; no one can prove that *all* that is implied in these passages is a mere expression of what sin *deserves*, or what *ought* to be inflicted on transgressors. Beyond all question there is, in many cases, an expression of *feeling*—or *desire*—or *wish;* there is language used which implies that there would be gratification—satisfaction—pleasure—if the calamity invoked should come upon the enemies of the writer, or if the punishment should be inflicted on the wicked; there is what is of the nature of *prayer*, that these calamities might come, and that the wicked might be detected, arrested, punished. We cannot on any honest principles interpret these psalms without admitting this; and the objector has a right to ask *how* this feeling can be vindicated; how it can be reconciled with the spirit of Christianity; how it can be shown to be consistent with the belief that the psalms were inspired by the Holy Ghost. This is a fair question to ask, and it is one which a believer in the inspiration of the Bible should be held to answer.

(4.) *Some* of the expressions referred to are a mere record of the feelings of others; of the gratification which *they* would feel in seeing vengeance inflicted on the guilty, even when revenge should be taken in the most barbarous and savage manner. In such a case all that the inspired writer, or the Spirit of inspiration, is responsible for, is *the fairness of the record;* or that he has given an exact statement of the feelings which would be cherished and expressed by those who should inflict the vengeance, or who should experience gratification in seeing it. A man may describe the acts of the American savage, scalping, torturing, murdering by slow degrees women and children, or the acts of cannibals, without being responsible for any of the feelings of the savages in doing this; and the writer of history cannot assuredly be responsible for all or any of the feelings of barbarous delight which a tyrant may have in oppressing his subjects, or for the fury and hatred which leads men to pursue with vengeance their flying victims. The inspired writers who made a record of the cruelty of the sons of Jacob (Gen. xxxiv. 25—29, xlix. 6, 7), or of the act of David in bringing forth the people of Rabbah, and "putting them under saws, and under harrows of iron, and under axes of iron, and making them pass through the brick-kiln" (2 Sam. xii. 31), or the acts of Joab, Ahithophel, Absalom, Nebuchadnezzar, Ahab or Jezebel, cannot be held to be answerable for the feelings which they manifested, or the deeds which they performed, nor is it fair to infer that in making the record they *approved* of what was done. All that the writers can be held to be responsible for is the correctness of the record.

An instance of this kind occurs in Ps. cxxxvii. 8, 9, " O daughter of Babylon, who art to be destroyed; happy shall he be that rewardeth thee as thou hast served us. *Happy shall he be that taketh and dasheth thy little ones against the stones.*" There is nothing to prevent our regarding this as a statement of the actual feelings—the pleasure—the satisfaction—which they would actually *feel* who should wreak vengeance on Babylon. The idea may be, and from anything that appears actually is, that such had been the pride and arrogance of Babylon, such the wrongs which she had done to other people; such her acts of cruelty and oppression,—that they who should overcome, subdue, and destroy her, would have conscious satisfaction and pleasure in bringing deserved punishment on her, even in those forms which men usually regard as savage and barbarous. In this there is nothing which *necessarily* implies that the author of the psalms would approve of it, or that he would have done it himself. If the case is supposed even to indicate the common feelings of the Hebrew people, in view of the destruction of an enemy under which the nation had suffered so much and so long, still it may be a mere record *of* that feeling as a matter of fact, and the Spirit of inspiration is responsible only for a fair account of the feelings which would actually exist.

In one of the methods which have thus been indicated the difficulties in regard to a portion of what are called the *imprecatory psalms* may be removed altogether. These are solutions, however, which cannot be applied to all of them; and if there is any number, however small,—if there is a single one remaining,—to which these solutions cannot be applied, it must be admitted that the actual difficulty still remains; for the Psalms are to be regarded as forming one book; they have, as is fairly implied in the idea that they are inspired, one author—the Holy Spirit; and as it is a principle which must be held by all who regard the Bible as an inspired book, that one text of Scripture fairly interpreted is sufficient to establish the truth of any doctrine, so it must be admitted that a well-founded objection to a single text, fairly interpreted, as really affects the question of inspiration as though there were many passages of that character. Some other solution, therefore, must be found in order to remove the real difficulty in the case.

(5.) A fifth remark, therefore, in regard to the prayers in these passages considered as invocations of vengeance or of punishment on the wicked may be suggested. The real question is, whether under any circumstance such prayers—such imprecations—can be right; and whether, if ever right, the circumstances in the Psalms were such as to make them proper.

To obtain a just view of this, several remarks are to be made.

(*a*) David was a magistrate; a king. He was, by the appointment of God, the civil and military ruler of the nation. His authority was not an usurped authority; nor were his acts those merely of a private man, a man individually wronged. As a king—a magistrate—he was appointed to preserve order; to maintain law; to dispense justice; to detect, arraign, and punish the guilty. As a magistrate, he represented the state; the majesty of the law; the interests of justice. As a magistrate, an act done—an offence committed—a crime in the community, did not respect him as a man—an individual—but as appointed to administer the government and to defend the state. No one can deny that David sustained this relation to the state, and that the duty of maintaining and administering law rested supremely with him. From anything that appears, also, the remark here made is applicable to each of the cases where "imprecations" are found in the Psalms. The question, then, is, whether there is anything in the office and functions of one appointed to make and execute the laws of a land which would render such imprecations justifiable.

(*b*) Punishment is right. It is not wrong that a penalty should be affixed to law; it is not wrong that the penalty of a law should be inflicted; it is not wrong that pain, privation of office, imprisonment, and the loss of life itself, should follow the commission of crime. So all laws determine; so all nations have judged. It is material here to remark that this is *not* an arbitrary thing; that it is not a matter of individual or local feeling. It is laid in our very nature. It is found in all nations. It is acted on among all people. *There is* SOMETHING *in our very nature, account for it as we may, which approves of punishment when properly inflicted; which approves of the appointment of a penalty for crime.* If this is wrong, it is a wrong in our very nature; it is a universal wrong; it is a wrong which has gone into the enactment of all laws—for all law has a penalty. A law without a penalty would be a mockery and a farce. When a man, in accordance with a just sentence of law, is fined, imprisoned, executed, WE APPROVE OF IT. We feel that it is what *ought* to be done, and in this feeling we are conscious of no wrong. We are conscious that we are not to be blamed for approving the sentence which condemns the guilty any more than we are for approving the sentence which acquits the innocent. The foundation of this feeling is laid in the very nature of man, and, therefore, it cannot be evil. No man feels that he is blameworthy when he thus finds himself approving of a just sentence of law; no man feels that this principle of his nature *ought* to be resisted or reversed, so that he would be a better man if he were conscious of the opposite feeling.

(*c*) In accordance with this principle, there are arrangements in every community for detecting and punishing crime. There are laws made which define crime, and designate its just penalty; there are arrangements made for arresting the guilty, and bringing them to trial; there are prisons built in anticipation that there will be men to be punished. There are courts organized for the express purpose of trying offenders; there are penalties affixed by law to different classes of crimes; there are processes prescribed in the law books for arresting, indicting, committing, arraigning, and judging those charged with a violation of law. There is a class of men whose business it is to detect and arrest offenders; there is a class whose business it is to try them; there is a class whose business it is to inflict punishment on them. Hence we have a detective police—men whose calling it is to find out offenders; we have an array of constables, jurymen, and judges; we have sheriffs, keepers of prisons, and executioners. These arrangements are *necessary* in our world. Society could not do without them. No community would be safe without them. No man would feel that his life, his property, his family were secure without them. They enter into the very structure of society as it exists on earth; and if these were abolished, the world would soon be filled with anarchy, bloodshed, and crime.

(*d*) These are lawful, proper, and honourable employments. The business of a detective officer, of a constable, of a sheriff, of a jury-man, of a judge, is as lawful as that of a farmer, a blacksmith, a school-teacher, a physician, a clergyman. No man occupies a more honourable position than the judge of a court, though it be a criminal court; no man is rendering more valuable service to his country than he whose daily business it is to detect offenders, to prosecute for crime, or to administer the laws of a nation. The constable and the judge may go to their work with as conscious a feeling that they are engaged in an honourable work as the farmer or the merchant; and the foreman of a jury who declares that a man arraigned for crime has been found "guilty," and the judge who pronounces the sentence of the law, and the man who executes the sentence, may each one lie down on his bed at night as calmly as the man who during the day has been engaged in sowing seed in his field, or gathering in his harvest, or administering medicine to the sick, or preaching the Gospel. Through all that day the one may be as conscious that he has had no malice towards his fellow-men, no desire of revenge, as the other. In the bosom of each one there may have been only the consciousness of a simple desire to do his duty.

(*e*) It is lawful and proper for such a man to pray;—a detective officer, a constable, a juryman, a judge, a keeper of a prison, *a hang-man*. It is as proper for such a man to pray as any other man. He may pray in his closet and in his family; he may breathe forth a mental prayer when searching for a man charged with an offence, or when bearing a testimony against him, or when sitting in judgment on him, or when inflicting the penalty of the law. He may pray, as other men do, that he may be "diligent in business;" that he may be "fervent in spirit;" that he may "serve the Lord" in that calling. He may pray that he may have grace to be faithful to his trust; firm in his conduct; *successful in what he is appointed to do.* But what is this? It is that the wicked—the guilty—*may* be brought to punishment; that they *may* be punished; that they may receive the due reward for their deeds. It is not malice against an individual; it is not a desire of revenge; it is not the indulgence of any private feeling; it is not conduct inconsistent with the widest benevolence. The officers of justice are engaged in the very work of bringing men to punishment; and why may they not *pray* for success in the work in which they are engaged? Why may not any man who loves the cause of justice, and who desires the security and good order of a community, pray that the wicked may be checked in their career—arrested—confined—punished? Since men lawfully engage in doing the thing, why may they not lawfully pray for the Divine blessing to aid them in doing it?

It is further to be remarked that a magistrate offering such a prayer would have a very different feeling from one who was engaged in an unlawful employment. How can a man engaged in the manufacture and sale of intoxicating drinks *pray?* How can he ask for success in his work? To do this would be to pray that his neighbour, his fellow-men, near or far off, might spend their property for that which would not profit them; might waste their time, ruin their health, cut short their lives, and destroy their souls; that they might be profane, gross, offensive, beastly; that they might be a pest in the community, be led into crime, and find their home in an almshouse, a penitentiary, or an insane asylum; that their families might be beggared, and that a once peaceful home might become a hell; and that the young, the vigorous, the hopeful, the beautiful, the sons of the virtuous and the pious—might go down early to the drunkard's grave; that the hearts of wives, mothers, sisters, and daughters might be crushed and broken, because a husband, a father, a brother, had been made a drunkard. But what fiendish malignity would there be in such a prayer as this! Hence such men do not ask the Divine blessing on their work. But a magistrate may pray, and should pray. He may pray that he may be successful in discharging the duties of his office; in administering justice; in prosecuting for crime; and in pronouncing the sentence of the law. His prayer, in fact, is simply that justice may be done to all; that punishment may be inflicted when it is deserved; and that he may be made an instrument in the hands of God in detecting and punishing crime. At the same time this may be so far from being a vindictive and revengeful spirit, that he himself may be among the most kind and humane men in a community, and when he pronounces the sentence of the law, he may be the only one in the court room that shall weep. Tears may flow fast from his eyes as he pronounces the sentence of the law, while the hardened wretch sentenced to the gallows may be wholly unmoved. It indicated no want of feeling and no malevolent spirit when Washington signed the death-warrant of the accomplished André, for he did it with tears.

In the same way, and with the same spirit, a man may go forth to the defence of his country when invaded, or when one portion of it has risen up in rebellion against a lawful government. A soldier called forth to defend his country may pray; the commander of an army may pray—should pray. But the prayer of such an one may be, and should be, in the line of his duty; for success in that which he has undertaken. It will be a prayer that the enemies of his country may be overcome and subdued. It indicates no malice, no personal feeling, no spirit of revenge, when he prays that the enemies of his country may be scattered as chaff before the wind; or that their counsels may be turned to foolishness; or that he may be successful in subduing them. It is a prayer for the triumph of a righteous cause; and as all his acts *as* a soldier tend to the destruction of the enemies of his country; as he is actually engaged in endeavouring to subdue them; as all his plans contemplate that; as he cannot be successful without that,—if the employment itself is right, it cannot be wrong that he should pray for success in it; that is, that his enemies may be delivered into his hands, and that God would enable him to overcome, to scatter, to subdue them. In this view of the matter there is necessarily no feeling inconsistent with the purest benevolence when the defenders of liberty and law and right apply to themselves the language of Psalm cxlix. :—"Let the high praises of God be in their mouth, and a two-edged sword in their hand; to execute vengeance upon the heathen, and punishments upon the people; to bind their kings with chains, and their nobles with fetters of iron; to execute upon them the judgment written," vers. 6–9.

(*f*) It only remains to be added, as bearing on the point here suggested, that it cannot be *demonstrated* that there is in the psalms that are called "Imprecatory Psalms" any more of malice, or of a spirit of revenge, than there is in the heart of a detective officer, a constable, a sheriff, a juryman, a crown lawyer, a prosecuting attorney, a judge, the keeper of a penitentiary, or an executioner, when he goes to the daily discharge of the duties of his office, and when, in his closet, or in his family, in his morning devotions, he *prays* that he may be faithful and successful in the discharge of his official duties through the day:—for success in any of these duties will be in the line of prayer, and may be in answer to prayer. If the detective officer is successful in ferreting out a burglar or a counterfeiter; if a magistrate is successful in bringing him to justice; if a juryman pronounces an honest verdict finding him guilty; if an attorney is successful in prosecuting the guilty to conviction; if a judge delivers a just sentence; and if the keeper of a prison closes the massive bars and bolts on the guilty,—at night, when they reflect on their work, they may regard their success in the lawful duties of the day as being as real an answer to prayer in the proper business of human life as the waving golden harvest is an answer to the prayers of the pious farmer, or the ship laden with the rich productions of the East, as she glides gallantly into port, should be regarded as an answer to the prayers of the pious merchant;—and until it is *proved* that this may not have been all that was implied in the language of the psalmist, it should not be assumed that the imprecatory psalms breathe a vindictive spirit, or are contrary to the purest and most benevolent feelings of the human heart.

(6.) There is still another solution of the difficulty which has been suggested. It is, substantially, that these expressions *are a mere record of what actually occurred in the mind of the psalmist*, and are preserved to us as an illustration of human nature when partially sanctified. According to this explanation we are not required by any just view of inspiration to vindicate those feelings, or to maintain that such feelings could not occur in the case of an inspired man. One of the main objects of the Psalms is to illustrate religion as it actually exists in the minds of good men in this world; men who are not absolutely perfect, but whose best religious emotions are mingled with many imperfections. According to this view the Spirit of inspiration is no more responsible for these *feelings* on the part of the psalmist than it is for the *acts* of David, Abraham, Jacob, or Peter. The *feelings*—the *acts*—are what they are; the Spirit of inspiration is responsible for a correct record or statement in regard to these acts and feelings:—a record that shall be historically and exactly true. A few remarks may explain this further.

(*a*) It is, then, an admitted fact that David was *not* a perfect man; and the same was undoubtedly true of all the writers of the Psalms. The Bible never claims that they were perfect; it makes a fair record of their faults; it lays down the general principle that none are absolutely free from sin: 1 Kings viii. 46; Eccles. vii. 20; James iii. 2; 1 John i. 8; Job ix. 20. As it is everywhere declared in the Bible that no one is absolutely perfect, and as it is admitted that David, for example, was guilty of wrong *acts*, as in the case of Uriah,—so, for the same reason, it is to be admitted that men, even the best of men, are liable to sin in thoughts and in words as well as in deeds.

(*b*) The proper notion of inspiration does not require us to hold that the men who were inspired were absolutely sinless. There is and must be a manifest and palpable difference between being *inspired*, and being personally *perfect*. Inspiration, in its true nature, secures a truthful record; it does not necessarily secure absolute sanctification. Indeed, inspiration has no necessary connexion with sanctification;—as it is conceivable, certainly, in accordance with the common belief, that Balaam uttered true prophecies respecting the Messiah, yet no one from that fact feels bound to maintain that he was otherwise than a bad man. Livy, Gibbon, Hume, Robertson, were not perfect men, and yet it may be true that they have given a correct account of the events which they profess to record; nor do we argue that because they were faithful historians that therefore, they were perfect men, or that *they* never did or said anything, which, if it were recorded exactly as it occurred, would not be inconsistent with the idea of absolute perfection of character. It is, therefore, a very important principle *that inspiration secures a correct record, not that it implies or secures personal sanctification; and that if it does secure a correct record the limit of responsibility in regard to it is reached.* Assuredly the fact that David in Psalm li. has made a true record in regard to his guiltiness in the case of Uriah, does not prove that he was right or innocent in the fact which is the subject of that record; nor if a record is a record of *feelings* instead of *deeds* does its correctness any more justify or sanction such feelings.

(*c*) It was important and necessary in a revelation from God, in order to meet the wants of the world, that there should be a true representation of religion as it comes in contact with the human heart; as it is in fact illustrated and manifested in the life of *man*, not as it might be in the life of a spotless angel. Assuming, as the Bible does everywhere, that man is depraved; that he has corrupt and evil propensities; that he has passions which by nature are uncontrollable, and that it is the design of religion to teach him how to control and govern them,—what we want is an illustration of religion as it comes in contact with such a heart. If the Bible had described only the feelings and conduct of a *perfect* being, it would be obviously unfit for man, for it would not be adapted to his condition. As man is imperfect and sinful, a representation of religion which would leave the impression that there is no true piety except where there is absolute perfection, would be adapted only to discourage and dishearten, for it would hold up that before his mind which he would feel to be unattainable, and his own consciousness of imperfection would lead him to the painful conclusion that he had no true religion. Hence in the Bible, except in the solitary instance of the Saviour, we have no record of the life of a *perfect* saint. We have a description of piety as it must always be found in the life of man:—as feeble, and struggling, and doubting, and contending with evil passions; as a life of conflict, of mingled light and darkness, good and evil, happiness and sadness, cheerfulness and despondency; as a life where evil often breaks out, where there is a constant effort required to subdue it, and where there is, amidst much that seems to be otherwise, yet truly a constant progress in the soul towards perfection—a perfection not to be obtained in this life, but which is to be consummated in heaven alone. Such a record only is fitted for man; such a record only would properly represent and describe man in his present condition. In another world—in heaven—a true record of man redeemed would be a record of religion without imperfection—as it would now be of the angels. As it is, we have now in the Bible everywhere recorded the lives of imperfect men:—imperfect in their conduct; imperfect in their feelings; imperfect in their words. We have the biographies of Abraham, Isaac, Jacob, of Eli, David, Hezekiah, Moses, Aaron, Josiah, James, John, Peter,—all imperfect but good men; men in whose bosoms there were the strugglings between good and evil principles; in whose lives the evil principle was constantly breaking out, and over whom for the time it seemed to triumph. Hence the painful but honest records which we have of piety in the Bible. In like manner, in order to see and understand what true piety *is* as it is found in connexion with human nature, it might be important that there should be such an illustration of it as we actually find in the Psalms: the *honest* record of what passed through the mind of a good man; of what imperfect man actually feels often, even when it is proper to characterise him as a man of God. Probably there have been few men, very few, even under the influence of the highest forms of piety, who, if they had made an *honest* record of what was passing in their minds at all times—of their wishes, desires, emotions; of their feelings towards their enemies, persecutors, and slanderers—would not have found that the language of the Psalms would *better* express their feelings in this respect than any language which they could find elsewhere;—and is it a forced or an unauthorized thought that even such men as Augustine, Luther, Calvin, Knox, and Edwards, at times when unchristian feelings seemed to have got the ascendancy in their hearts; when they were strongly tempted to give way to passion, or actually gave way to it; when they might have been led to doubt whether men with such feelings *could* have any true religion—may have found consolation in the fact that feelings precisely like theirs sprang up in the hearts of the inspired men who composed the Psalms, and who there made an honest record of what was actually passing in the soul, almost an actual transcript of what they themselves experienced? It need be hardly remarked that if this is a true view of the matter, we are not bound to attempt to vindicate these expressions of passion—any more than we are the conduct of David in the matter of Uriah, or of Peter in denying his Lord.

(*d*) According to this view, the expressions which are used in this record are not presented for our imitation. The mere fact that they are recorded as having occurred in the lives of good men is no evidence that they are right, or are to be followed by us. *All* that occurred in the life of the Redeemer was right, and was recorded that, so far as it might be applicable to us in our circumstances, we might imitate it. If the above remarks are correct, then the record was made for far other purposes than that we should imitate the conduct of those who gave expression to these feelings. Nor should the fact that such feelings actually existed in the minds of good men, or that these "imprecations" are found in their writings, be charged on religion, as if it tended to produce them, any more than the act of adultery and murder on the part of David, or the profaneness of Peter, should be referred to as an illustration of what religion is *adapted* to produce in the hearts and lives of men. Religion is not responsible for these things. The responsibility is in our corrupt nature.

(*e*) If such is a just view of the matter, then all that *inspiration* is responsible for is, the correctness of the *record* in regard to the existence of these feelings:—that is, the authors of the Psalms actually *recorded* what was passing in their own minds. They gave vent to their internal emotions. They state real feelings which they themselves had; feelings which, while human nature remains the same, may spring up in the mind of imperfect man, anywhere, and at any time. They record what other men actually feel; and in making the record, they simply give utterance to what passed through their own hearts. They do not apologize for it; they do not pause to vindicate it; they offer no word in extenuation of it—any more than other sacred writers did when they recorded the *facts* about the errors in the lives of the patriarchs, of David, and of Peter.

In some of these ways it is probable that all the difficulties in regard to the "imprecations" in the Psalms may be met. They who deny the inspiration of the Psalms should be able to show that these are *not* proper explanations of the difficulty; or that they are *not* consistent with any just notions of inspiration.

§ 7. *The practical value of the Book of Psalms.*—It is not a little remarkable that the Psalms, in the estimation of religious persons, hold substantially the same place under the clearer light of the Christian dispensation which they did under the comparatively obscure Hebrew economy, and that with all the additional light which has been imparted under the Christian revelation, the Psalms have not been superseded. The *Christian* looks to the Psalms with an interest as intense as did the ancient Jew; and, as expressive of personal religious experience, as well as for the purpose of a manual for worship, the Psalms are selected by the Christian, from the whole Bible, as they were by the Jew from the books in his possession—the Old Testament. As such, they will retain their value in all times to come, nor will there ever be in our world such an advance in religious light, experience, and knowledge, that they will lose their relative place as connected with the exercises of practical piety. How far this fact is to be regarded as a proof that the authors of the Psalms were inspired; that there was communicated to them a knowledge of the principles and workings of true piety, so in advance of their own age as to be on a level with what will be possessed in the most advanced periods of religious culture; that there must have been an influence on their minds, in composing the Psalms, beyond anything derived from mere poetic genius, is a question which must occur to all reflecting minds. It is a fair question to propose to one who doubts the inspiration of the Psalms, how he will account for this fact, consistently with his idea that the authors of the Psalms were men endowed only as other men of genius are, and with the acknowledged fact that they lived in an age when the views of truth in the world were comparatively obscure. How did it happen that a Hebrew bard, in the matter of deep religious experience and knowledge, placed himself so high as to be a guide to mankind in all coming times, after a new revelation should have been introduced to the world, and after all the attainments which men would have made in the knowledge of religion and of the human heart?

The special value of the Psalms arises (*a*) from the fact that they are adapted to the worship of God; (*b*) from the fact that they are records of deep religious experience.

(*a*) As adapted to the worship of God. For this many of them were originally designed in their very composition; to this the entire book seems to have been intentionally adapted by those who made the collection. It is not necessary to suppose that these sacred songs comprise the whole of the Hebrew lyrical poetry, for as we know that some of the books mentioned in the Old Testament, though inspired, accomplished their purpose and have been lost, so it may have been in regard to a portion of the lyrical poetry of the Hebrews. Many of the words of the Saviour, though all that he spoke was pure truth—truth such as no other man ever spoke—truth such as the Spirit of God imparts—were lost from not having been recorded (John xxi. 25), and in like manner it may have been that truths which were *written* may have accomplished their purpose, and have passed away. But, if there *were* such productions which have not come down to us, we have no reason to doubt that they were of the same general character as those which have survived, and which now constitute the Book of Psalms. Now, it is remarkable that the poetry of the Hebrews is so adapted to public worship above all other poetry, and that the poetic genius of the nation took so exclusively a religious turn. In this respect the Hebrew lyric poetry stands by itself, and is unlike that of every other nation. Among the Greeks there are, indeed, hymns to the gods—hymns designed to be used in the worship of the gods; but this is by no means the general character of their lyric poetry. Among the Persians, the Arabs, the Romans, the Babylonians, there were doubtless such hymns; but this is not the prevailing character of *their* lyric poetry. In the early Scotch, French, Spanish, Italian, and English poetry there *are* such hymns, but this is by no means the exclusive or the predominant character of the early lyric poetry of those nations. Few of all their lyric compositions can be used in the worship of the true God; nor is that which can be thus used always of the most exalted character *as* poetry. The composition of psalms and hymns is a separate poetic art; and though there are specimens, in the hymns in these languages, of the highest kind of lyric excellence, yet it is to be admitted that a large portion of that species of literature would scarcely be regarded as even *respectable*, if it related to other subjects than religion. Of the Hebrews, however, this is their *all*. They have no other poetry whatever. They have none merely amatory or pastoral which will compare with the Bucolics of Virgil, or with much of the poetry of Burns. Their poetry of the religious kind, also, is all of a high order. There is none that can be placed on the same low level with much that is found in the hymn books of most denominations of Christians—very good; very pious; very sentimental; very much adapted, as is supposed, to excite the feelings of devotion—but withal so flat, so weak, so unpoetic, that it would not, in a volume of mere poetry, be admitted to a third or fourth rank, if, indeed, it would find a place at all. It is for him who rejects the idea of *inspiration*, as applied to the Book of Psalms, to account for this fact.

(*b*) The Book of Psalms is a record of deep religious experience. It is this which, in the estimation of religious persons in general, gives it its chief value. It is the guide of young believers; and it becomes more and more the companion, the comforter, and the counsellor, as the believer moves along through the varied scenes of life, and as grey hairs come upon him, and as the infirmities, which pre-intimate the approaching close of all things, press him down. A religious man is rarely, if ever, placed in circumstances where he will not find something in the Psalms appropriate to his circumstances; where he will not find that the Hebrew sacred bard has not gone before him in the depths of religious experience. Hence, in sickness, in bereavement, in persecution, in old age, on the bed of death, the Book of Psalms becomes so invariable and so valuable a companion; and hence, not as a matter of convenience, but as supplying a *want* in the minds of men, and as significant of their value, the Psalms and the New Testament are so often bound together in a single volume. Hence, also, for the aged, for the sick, for those whose powers of vision fail by disease or by years, the Psalms and the New Testament are printed in large type, and bound in convenient forms, that the truths contained in these volumes may be still accessible to the saint ripening for heaven, as the light fails, and as life ebbs away. To the end of the world the Psalms in religious experience will occupy the same place which they now occupy; to the end of the world they will impart comfort to the troubled, and peace to the dying, as they have done in the ages that are past.

§ 8. *The qualifications for preparing a Commentary on the Psalms.*

It is an undoubted fact that there have been more failures in the Commentaries on the Book of Psalms than on any other of the books of the Bible. As yet there has been no Commentary that has met the wants of the Christian world; there are none, whatever anticipations may have been raised, which can be read without feelings of disappointment. For this fact there must be a cause; and that cause is probably to be found in the very peculiar qualifications needed to produce a Commentary on the Psalms:—qualifications which are rarely to be found united in the same person.

A few remarks on the qualifications necessary for preparing such a Commentary may explain the cause of the failures which have occurred; and may, perhaps, also explain the reason why the one now submitted to the public may be found to be an addition to the failures already existing. Every man who prepares a Commentary on the Psalms will probably, at the close of his work, be sensible of a feeling of disappointment in what he had hoped, perhaps what he had expected to do, and will share fully in the feelings of his readers that what is thus submitted to the world is very far from being what a Commentary on this portion of the sacred Scriptures ought to be.

The peculiar qualifications for preparing a Commentary on the Psalms are such as the following:—

(1.) A knowledge of the Hebrew language, particularly as it is affected by the laws of poetry which prevailed among the Hebrews. In all languages there are peculiar rules of poetry; rules by which the sense of the words used is affected, and by which peculiar shades of thought are expressed. In most languages, words have a *poetic* and a *prosaic* sense; and the application of the meaning of a word as used in prose to a passage in poetry might by no means express the idea which was in the mind of the poet. We learn almost insensibly, in reading a language familiar to us, to make this distinction accurately, even when we could not explain it; and we read a psalm, a hymn, a lyric song, without mistaking the meaning. But it is another thing when one undertakes to read a book of poetry in a language different from his native tongue. What is obvious to an Italian, a Frenchman, or a German, in reading poetry in his native language, becomes a matter of difficult acquisition when an Englishman attempts to read the poem. The same thing is true in studying a dead language. It need not be said that there is a peculiar literature in respect to the Greek and Latin poets; and he who can read Herodotus or Livy cannot assume that he has such a full knowledge of the Greek and Latin languages as to qualify him to understand the poetry in those languages. So much depends often on rhythm, on the poetic forms of words, or on the images peculiar to poetry, that a classical education is not complete, nor is the student qualified to apprehend the meaning of the language of a poem, or to appreciate the beauties of its thought and imagery until he has mastered this most difficult part of the rules of language. That the Hebrews, like other people, had such rules and usages, there can be no doubt; for they are to be found in all languages, and there is abundant evidence in the Hebrew poetry itself that they existed among the Jewish people. Yet it may be doubted whether it is possible now so fully to recover the knowledge of those rules and usages as to apply them perfectly in the explanation of the poetic portions of the sacred writings. Much pertaining to the rhythm of the language, much relating to the accents, much connected with the peculiar use of words, it may be impossible now to recover. To show the difficulty of this subject in its bearing on the interpretation of the Psalms, as well as to illustrate the subject of Hebrew poetry, I may refer to the remarks of De Wette, Einleitung, vii. pp. 37—76. An elegant translation of this may be found in the Biblical Repository, vol. iii., pp. 478—514.

(2.) True piety is essential to qualify one to be an interpreter of the Psalms. This is true, in fact, in regard to the interpretation of any portion of the Sacred Volume. As the Bible is a book of religion, employed in describing the nature, the power, and the influence of religion, it is obvious that correct religious feeling, or a practical acquaintance with religion, is necessary in an interpreter. The principle is substantially the same which is required in the interpretation of books on any subject. In a treatise on painting, poetry, sculpture, architecture, there will be things which could not be so well explained as by one who had a practical knowledge of these arts; and in order to the possession of a complete qualification for the interpretation of such a book, an ability to appreciate what is said on those arts must be regarded as indispensable. It is obvious that the mere knowledge of words—of philology—would not be all that would be demanded; nor would any power of explaining local allusions, laws, customs, manners, or geographical or historical references, be all that would be required. Beyond all this, there was in the mind of the writer or author that which he *intended* to express, and which no mere knowledge of language or of customs would be sufficient to explain. To show what the writer *meant* it would be obviously necessary to be able to *understand* him,—to appreciate what he intended to say; to bring out what was *in* his mind; what he thought of—what he felt—what he designed to express. Hence, however valuable a work may be on the Psalms as a philological work, or as illustrating the authorship of a psalm, and the circumstances of the author in its composition, it is plain that we have not reached the main thing unless we have entered into the spirit of the author, and are qualified to understand and appreciate his own feelings in the composition.

(3.) For the reason above stated, there should be in an exposition of the Psalms more than the *mere* possession of piety. *There should be deep religious experience.* There should be an acquaintance with piety in its highest forms of rapture, and in the lowest depths of despondency, darkness, and sorrow. There is no book in the world in which there are such varied expressions of piety, in which there are such diversified forms of religious experience, as in the Book of Psalms. As the Psalms were designed for every age of the world; for persons found in every rank and condition of life; for seasons of joy and of sorrow; for childhood, youth, middle age, old age; for the ignorant and the learned; for times of sickness and of health; for private, social, domestic, and public life; for magistrates and private citizens; for war and peace; for acts of business and acts of charity; for the living and for the dying, and for those that mourn,—so they were designed to form a *manual* that would illustrate religion in all these forms and relations; to be a book in which *any* one, in all the varied conditions of human existence, might be sure that he would find something that would be applicable to himself. If this is so, then it is clear that in order to a good Commentary on the Psalms,—in order that the expositor may be able to enter into the real spirit of the work which he undertakes to explain,—piety of no common order is demanded; a rich and varied religious experience is required that falls to the lot of very few of mankind. Looking simply at *this* qualification of a commentator on the Psalms, we may cease to be surprised that no such Commentary has ever appeared as to leave nothing yet to be desired.

(4.) Poetic taste is an important requisite in a commentator on the Psalms. The Psalms are poetry, and poetry of the most delicate kind. Much of the beauty of the Psalms, and much of their adaptedness to the wants of man, depends on the fact that they *are* poetry. This was a reason why the Spirit of God, in breathing his influence on the men who composed the Psalms, preferred that the sentiments found in them *should be* expressed in poetry rather than in prose, and hence this medium was selected. Among the original endowments of the human mind, that which contemplates *poetry* as among the means of happiness; as adapted to impress truth on the mind; as fitted to arouse the soul to great efforts; as designed to fill the mind with calm, peaceful, pure, patriotic, pious emotions, is one. Possessed by men, indeed (either in the power of producing poetry or of appreciating it) in very different degrees, yet it *is* an endowment of man; and, being such, religion makes use of it to promote its own ends. There are those who will be moved by little besides calm argument, stern logic, severe demonstration; there are those who will be aroused only by the lofty appeals of eloquence; there are those who will be most influenced by the voice of persuasion; there are those who will be awakened from dangerous slumbers only by the denunciations of wrath; there are those in whose minds pure and joyful and holy emotions will be best excited by poetry. It is the province of *song*, as such, to awaken many of the most pure and devoted feelings of piety in the human soul; and the Book of Psalms is the portion of the Sacred Volume by which it is designed and expected that this object will be accomplished as a permanent arrangement.

It is clear, therefore, that he cannot be completely qualified to be a commentator on the Psalms who has not himself such endowments as to appreciate the beauties of poetry; who cannot, in this respect, enter into the feelings of the sacred writer on the one hand, and into the hearts of those who are so made as to be affected by poetry on the other. One of the causes of the *failure* to produce a good Commentary on the Psalms may be traced to this source. A mere philologist; a man who regards nothing as valuable but exact demonstration; a man of prosaic temperament, though he may have piety that is exalted and pure, *may* lack still an important qualification for entering into the true spirit of the Psalms, and for meeting the wants of those who seek for edification and comfort in this portion of the Bible.

(5.) A knowledge of the human heart—of human nature—is an indispensable condition for a good commentator on the Psalms. The Psalms comprise, more than any other book in the Bible, a record of the workings of the heart. Indeed, they pertain mostly *to* the heart. They are not addressed, as the Epistle to the Romans is, to the loftier powers of the understanding, nor do they make such appeals to the imagination as the visions of Isaiah, or the visions of John in Patmos. It is the *heart* which, in the Psalms, is eminently the medium of communication between the Divine Spirit and the soul.

Of all parts of the Bible there is most to illustrate the human heart in the Psalms. All that there is in the heart of man is there in one way or another illustrated, and in an almost endless variety of circumstances. Joy, sorrow, penitence, gratitude, praise, despondency, sadness; love—love to God—love to man;—the feelings experienced in sickness, and on a recovery from sickness;—the anguish, the bitterness of soul, arising from the ingratitude of others; terror at the wrath of God; the dread of death; the peace which religion gives in the prospect of death; the joy of prayer; the light which comes into the soul in answer to earnest supplication; the calmness which springs from devout meditation on the character of God and his law; the light which beams upon the soul after long darkness; the effects of remembered guilt (as in Ps. li.); the feeling of despair when God seems to have forsaken us; the feelings which spring up in the heart on the reception of injuries;—these are a few among the many topics which are found illustrated in the Psalms in the personal experience of the writers, and it is obvious that no one is qualified to comment on these subjects unless he has himself a knowledge of the workings of the human heart. To be able to explain the words used; to state the origin and authorship of the Psalms, and the occasion on which they were composed; to investigate the genuineness and accuracy of the text, and to determine the value of the varied readings; to understand and explain the parallelisms, the rhythm, and the accents employed in the Psalms; to comprehend and appreciate the poetry of the Psalms; or to gather together what Jewish Rabbies and the Christian Fathers have written, or to transplant from Germany what has been produced under Rationalistic views of the Bible, or even what the German mind in its best workings and under the influence of true religion has produced, is *not* all or mainly what is demanded in a Commentary on the Psalms that will meet the wants of those in our own land, or that will illustrate the Psalms in the manner that will be of most value to the great masses of the young, the sick, the bereaved, the tempted, the aged, and the desponding. A man who cannot in this varied manner enter into sympathy with the writers of the Psalms in the workings of the human heart as there illustrated, is not a man who is fully qualified to prepare a Commentary on this book. For some purposes he may, indeed, make a book that will be valuable, but not a book that will be valuable in relation to the real purpose designed to be accomplished by the Psalms—to be a guide and a comfort to believers of every station and condition, in all the varied circumstances of human life, and in all the varied and complicated workings of the human heart.

(6) It may be added that the Book of Psalms, in the main, is so plain, so easy to be understood by the great mass of readers; so expressive of the internal feelings and emotions, as to increase the difficulty in the preparation of a Commentary. The Psalms are so rich; so full of meaning; so adapted to the wants of believers;—they so meet the varied experiences of the people of God, and are so replete with the illustrations of piety; they so touch the deepest fountains of emotion in the soul, that, so far as most of these points are concerned, a *Commentary*, considered as an additional source of light, does not differ materially from a candle considered as affording additional splendour to the sun. What a man finds in the ordinary perusal of the Psalms as a book of devotion, on the subject of deep experimental piety, is so much in advance of what he will usually find in the Commentary, that he turns from the attempt to *explain* them with a feeling of deep disappointment, and comes back to the Book itself as better expressing his emotions, meeting his necessities, and imparting consolation in trial, than anything which the commentator can add. He welcomes the Book of Psalms itself as a comforter and a guide; and in the little volume sold now at so cheap a rate, or appended to his pocket Testament, the common reader of the Bible finds more that is suited to his need than he would in the voluminous commentary of Venema; in all the collections in the Critici Sacri; in the Synopsis of Poole; in the Annotations of Grotius; or in the learned expositions of De Wette—elegant as the work of De Wette is,—or of Tholuck, or Hengstenberg.

When these difficulties in composing a Commentary on the Psalms are considered;—when a man who sits down to write one reflects on the qualifications necessary for the task;—and when under the influence of these thoughts, constantly increasing in magnitude, and pressing upon him more and more as he labours for a dozen years, though at intervals, as I have done, in preparing a Commentary on this portion of Scripture,—whatever ardour of desire or confidence of success he may have had at the commencement of his enterprise, he will cease to wonder, as he progresses in his work, that the efforts of others to prepare a Commentary heretofore have been a failure, and he will not be surprised, should his life be lengthened out to see the result of his own labours, if he finds that the world regards that at which he has toiled so long, and which he hoped might be, in some measure, worthy of the Volume he has undertaken to explain, as but adding another to the long list of unsuccessful attempts to prepare a proper exposition of the Book of Psalms.

THE BOOK OF PSALMS.

PSALM I.

THE first psalm has no title prefixed to it, which is the case, also, with many others, Ps. x., cxvi., cxvii., etc. It is now in vain to attempt to search for the cause of this omission. On the origin and authority of the titles prefixed to the Psalms, see Introduct., § 4. Some have supposed that the reason why no title was affixed to this psalm was that the *general title*, "The Psalms of David," was prefixed to the whole book, and that that was a sufficient indication of the author of this the first in the series. But this is mere conjecture, and this reason would no more make proper the omission of the title to the first psalm than of any other that came under that *general* title. In some manuscripts (2 Codd. de Rossi) this psalm is not numbered; in some others (4 Codd. Kennic., and 3 de Rossi) it is united with the second psalm, and the two are reckoned as one. It is, however, manifestly a distinct composition from the second psalm. It has a unity of its own, as the second has also; and there are almost no two psalms in the whole collection which might not be united with as much propriety as these. It is impossible now to ascertain the authorship of the psalm, though the common opinion is probably the correct one, that it was composed by David. But on what occasion it was written it is now equally impossible to discover. There are no historical allusions in it which would enable us to determine the occasion on which it was written, as there is nothing in it which certainly determines its authorship. The terms employed are of the most general character, and the sentiments are applicable to all times and all lands. It has all the marks of being a general introduction to the *Book* of Psalms, and of having been designed to express in a few sentences the substance of the entire collection, or to state the great principle which would be found to run through the whole of it—*that a righteous life will be attended with prosperity and happiness, and that the life of the wicked will be followed by sorrow and ruin.* This was the great principle of the Jewish Theocracy; and was of sufficient importance to be stated clearly in the commencement of a book that was designed to illustrate so fully the nature and the value of true religion. Comp. Deut. xxvii., xxviii.

The psalm is designed to describe the blessedness or the happiness of the righteous man. This is done "literally and figuratively, positively and negatively, directly and by contrast, with respect both to his character and his condition here and hereafter."—*Professor Alexander*. It is not, however, as Professor Alexander supposes, a "picture of the truly *happy* man;" it is a description of the blessedness of the *righteous* man, in contrast with the condition of the *unrighteous*. The righteous man is indeed prosperous and happy; and it is one design of the psalm to show this. But it is not the *happy* man, as such, that is in the eye of the psalmist; it is the *righteous* man, and the blessedness of *being* righteous.

The psalm is properly made up of two parts—the blessedness of the righteous man, and the unblessedness, *unglück* (*De Wette*), of the wicked or ungodly man.

I. The blessedness of the righteous man, vers. 1—3. This consists also of two minor parts:—

(1.) His character (vers. 1, 2), and this is described also in two forms—negatively and positively.

(*a*) Negatively.—He does *not* walk in the counsel of the ungodly, *nor* stand in the way of sinners, *nor* sit in the seat of the scornful, ver. 1.

(*b*) Positively.—He delights in the law of the Lord, and he has pleasure in meditating continually on his truth, ver. 2.

(2) His prosperity, as the result of being righteous, ver. 3. His condition is compared with that of a tree planted in a well-watered place, whose leaves are always green, and whose fruit never fails; so whatever he does shall prosper.

II. The condition of the unrighteous, or the strong contrast between the un-

PSALM I.

BLESSED *is* the man that walketh not [a] in the counsel of the [1] ungodly, nor standeth in the way

[a] Prov. iv. 14, 15.

[1] Or, *wicked*.

righteous and the righteous, vers. 4—6. Their condition and destiny are expressed in three forms:—

(1) They are like chaff which the wind drives away, ver. 4.

(2) They shall not be acquitted in the judgment, nor have a place among the righteous, ver. 5.

(3) They shall not be approved by God, but shall perish, ver. 6.

1. *Blessed* is *the man.* That is, his condition is a happy or a desirable one. The word here used, אֶשֶׁר, *aishair*, means properly *happiness* or *blessedness.* It is found, however, only in the plural form and in the construct state, and takes the nature and force of an interjection—"O the happiness of the man!" or "O happy man!" Deut. xxxiii. 29: "*Happy* art thou, O Israel!" 1 Kings x. 8: "*Happy* are thy men, *happy* are these thy servants!" Job v. 17: "*Happy* is the man whom God correcteth!" Ps. ii. 12: "*Blessed* are all they that put their trust in him!" See also Ps. xxxii. 1, 2; xxxiii. 12; xxxiv. 8; xl. 4; xli. 1; lxv. 4; lxxxiv. 4, 5, 12, *et al.*, where it is rendered *blessed.* The word is of the most *general* character, and, in itself, would embrace all that is supposed to constitute *real happiness.* The particular kind of blessedness referred to here, as explained in the subsequent part of the psalm, consists in the fact that he avoids the companionship of the wicked; that he has pleasure in the law of the Lord; that he will be prospered in this world; and that he will not perish at last. The word "*man*" here, also, is of the most general character, and is designed to include all men, of all times and of all conditions, who possess the *character* referred to. The term is applicable to the poor as well as to the rich; to the low as well as to the exalted; to the servant as well as to the master; alike to the aged, the middle-aged, and the young. All who have the character here described come under the general description of the *happy man*—the man whose condition is a happy and a desirable one. ¶ *That walketh not.* Whose character is that he does not walk in the manner specified. Professor Alexander renders this, "Who *has not* walked." But it implies more than this; it refers to more than the past. It is the characteristic of the man, always and habitually, that he does not thus walk; it has not only been true in the past, but it is true in the present, and will be true in the future. It is that which distinguishes the man. The word *walk* is often used in the Scriptures to denote a way of life or conduct—since life is represented as a journey, and man as a traveller. Ps. xv. 2: "Who walketh uprightly." Compare 1 Kings ix. 4; Deut. xix. 9; xxviii. 9; Ps. lxxxi. 12, 13; Isa. xxxiii. 15. ¶ *In the counsel.* After the manner, the principles, the plans of this class of men. He does not *take counsel* of them as to the way in which he should live, but from the law of the Lord, ver. 2. This would include such things as these:—he does not follow the *advice* of sinners, 2 Sam. xvi. 20; 1 Kings i. 12; he does not execute the *purposes* or *plans* of sinners, Isa. xix. 3; he does not frame his life according to their views and suggestions. In his plans and purposes of life he is independent of *them*, and looks to some other source for the rules to guide him. ¶ *Of the ungodly.* The wicked. The word here used is general, and would embrace all kinds and degrees of the unrighteous. It is not so specific, and would, in itself, not indicate as definite, or as aggravated depravity, as the terms which follow. The general sentiment here is, that the man referred to is not the companion of wicked men. ¶ *Nor standeth.* This indicates more deliberation; a character more fixed and decided. ¶ *In the way.* The path where they are

of sinners, nor sitteth[b] in the seat of the scornful:

b Jer. xv. 17.

found, or where they usually go. His standing there would be as if he waited for them, or as if he desired to be associated with them. Instead of passing along in his own regular and proper employment, he stations himself in the path where sinners usually go, and lingers and loiters there. Thus he indicates a *desire* to be with them. This is often, in fact, illustrated by men who place themselves, as if they had nothing to do, in the usual situation where the wicked pass along, or where they may be met with at the corners of the streets in a great city. ¶ *Of sinners*, הַטָּאִים, *hattayim*. This word means literally, *those who miss the mark;* then, those who err from the path of duty or rectitude. It is often used to denote any kind or degree of sin. It is more specific than the former word rendered *ungodly*, as denoting those who depart from the path of duty; who fail in regard to the great end of life; who violate positive and known obligations. ¶ *Nor sitteth.* This implies still greater deliberation and determination of character than either of the other words employed. The man here referred to does not casually and accidentally walk along with them, nor put himself in their way by standing where they are ordinarily to be found; but he has become one of them by occupying a seat with them; thus deliberately associating with them. He has an established residence among the wicked; he is permanently one of their number. ¶ *In the seat.* The seat which the scornful usually occupy; the place where such men converse and sit together—as in a ball-room, or in a "club," where wicked men hold their meetings, or where infidels and scoffers are accustomed to assemble. ¶ *Of the scornful*, לֵצִים, *laitzim*. This word properly means those who mock, deride, scoff; those who treat virtue and religion with contempt and scorn. Prov. i. 22; iii. 34; ix. 7, 8; xiii. 1; xv. 12, *et sæpe*. It denotes a higher and more determined grade of wickedness than either of the other words employed, and refers to the consummation of a depraved character, the last stage of wickedness, when God and sacred things are treated with contempt and derision. There is hope of a man as long as he will treat virtue and religion with some degree of respect; there is little or none when he has reached the point in his own character in which virtue and piety are regarded only as fit subjects for ridicule and scorn. We have here, then, a beautiful double gradation or climax, in the nouns and verbs of this verse, indicating successive stages of character. There is, first, casual *walking* with the wicked, or accidentally falling into their company; there is then a more deliberate inclination for their society, indicated by a voluntary putting of oneself in places where they usually congregate, and *standing* to wait for them; and then there is a deliberate and settled purpose of associating with them, or of becoming permanently one of them, by regularly *sitting* among them. So also it is in regard to the *persons* with whom they associate. They are, first, irreligious men in general; then, those who have so far advanced in depravity as to disregard known duty, and to violate known obligations; and then, those who become confirmed in infidelity, and who openly mock at virtue, and scoff at the claims of religion. It is unnecessary to say that, in both these respects, this is an accurate description of what actually occurs in the world. He who casually and accidentally walks with the wicked, listening to their *counsel*, will soon learn to place himself in their way, and to wait for them, desiring their society, and will ultimately be likely to be found identified with open scoffers; and he who indulges in one form of depravity, or

2 But his delight [c] *is* in the law of the LORD; and in his law [d] doth he meditate day and night.

c Job xxiii. 12. d Ps. cxix. 97.

in the neglect of religion in any way, will, unless restrained and converted, be likely to run through every grade of wickedness, until he becomes a confirmed scoffer at all religion. The sentiment in this verse is, that the man who is truly blessed is a man who does none of these things. His associations and preferences are found elsewhere, as is stated in the next verse.

2. *But his delight.* His pleasure; his happiness. Instead of finding his happiness in the society and the occupations of the wicked, he finds it in the truth of God. The law or truth of God is not distasteful to him, but he so delights in it as to desire to become more and more acquainted with it, and to have its truths impressed more and more on his heart. ¶ *In the law of the* LORD. The law of JEHOVAH—the small capitals in the translation indicating here as elsewhere that the original word is JEHOVAH. The word *law* in the Scriptures is used in a considerable variety of significations. The Hebrew word תּוֹרָה, *torah,* properly means *instruction, precept;* and then, an injunction, command, law, in the usual sense of the word. It was applied particularly to the Pentateuch, or law of Moses (comp. Notes on Luke xxiv. 44), as containing the first written and recorded laws of God; and then the word came, in a more general sense, to be applied to all the books of the Old Testament, as being an exposition and application of the law. Here the word undoubtedly refers to the written revelation of the will of God as far as it was then made known. On the same principle, however, the declaration here made would apply to any part of a Divine revelation; and hence the sentiment is, that a truly pious man finds his highest delight in the revealed truths of God. This is often referred to as characteristic of true piety. Comp. Ps. xix. 10; cxix. 97, 99. ¶ *And in his law.* On his law, or his truth. ¶ *He doth meditate.* The word here used, הָגָה, *hagah,* means properly to murmur, to mutter; then, to speak; then, to utter in a low murmuring voice, as is often done by a person in deep meditation; hence, in the usual sense, to meditate on anything; to think of it. So Joshua i. 8: "Thou shalt *meditate* therein [the law] day and night." Ps. lxxvii. 12: "I *meditate* on all thy work." Prov. xv. 28: "The heart of the righteous *meditateth* what to answer." The meaning here is, he thinks of it; he endeavours to understand its meaning; he has pleasure in reflecting on it. It is not a subject which he puts away from him, or in respect to which he is indifferent, but he keeps it before his mind, and has satisfaction in doing it. ¶ *Day and night.* That is, continually—as day and night constitute the whole of time. The meaning is—(*a*) he does this *habitually,* or he intentionally forms the *habit* of meditating on Divine truth, by disciplining his mind in order that he may do it; (*b*) he *takes* time to do it—designedly setting apart suitable portions of each day, that, withdrawn from the cares of life, he may refresh his spirit by contemplating Divine truth, or may become better acquainted with God, and with his duty to him, and may bring to bear upon his own soul more directly the truths pertaining to eternal realities; (*c*) he does this in the intervals of business, the moments of leisure which he may have during the day—having thus an unfailing subject of reflection to which his mind readily reverts, and in which, amid the cares and toils of life, he finds relaxation and comfort; and (*d*) he does it in the wakeful hours of night, when sick and tossed upon his bed, or when, for any other reason, his "eyes are held waking." Ps. lxiii. 5, 6: "My soul shall be

3 And he shall be like a tree
[e] planted by the rivers of water, that bringeth forth his fruit in his season; his leaf also shall

e Jer. xvii. 8.

---

satisfied as with marrow and fatness; and my mouth shall praise thee with joyful lips; when I remember thee upon my bed, and meditate on thee in the night-watches." Ps. cxix. 54: "Thy statutes have been my songs in the house of my pilgrimage." Comp. vers. 23, 48; Ps. cxliii. 5. It is probable that the psalmist had the injunction in his mind which is contained in Josh. i. 8.

3. *And he shall be like a tree.* A description of the happiness or prosperity of the man who thus avoids the way of sinners, and who delights in the law of God, now follows. This is presented in the form of a very beautiful image—a tree planted where its roots would have abundance of water. ¶ *Planted by the rivers of water.* It is not a tree that springs up spontaneously, but one that is set out in a favorable place, and that is cultivated with care. The word "*rivers*" does not here quite express the sense of the original. The Hebrew word (פֶּלֶג *peleg*, from פָּלַג *palag*, to cleave, to split, to divide), properly means *divisions;* and then, channels, canals, trenches, branching-cuts, brooks. The allusion is to the Oriental method of irrigating their lands by making artificial rivulets to convey the water from a larger stream, or from a lake. In this way the water was distributed in all directions. The whole land of Egypt was anciently sluiced in this manner, and it was in this way that its extraordinary fertility was secured. An illustration of the passage may be derived from the account by Maundrell of the method of watering the gardens and orchards in the vicinity of Damascus. "The gardens are thick set with fruit trees of all kinds, kept fresh and verdant by the waters of the Barady.... This river, as soon as it issues out of the cleft of the mountain before mentioned, into the plain, is immediately divided into three streams, of which the middlemost and largest runs directly to Damascus, and is distributed to all the cisterns and fountains of the city. The other two, which I take to be the work of art, are drawn round, the one to the right, and the other to the left, on the borders of the gardens, into which they are let out, as they pass, by little rivulets, and so dispersed over all the vast wood, insomuch that there is not a garden but has a fine, quick stream running through it." Trav., p. 122. A striking allusion to trees cultivated in this manner occurs in Ezek. xxxi. 3, 4: "Behold, the Assyrian was a cedar in Lebanon, with fair branches, and with a shadowing shroud, and of a high stature, and his top was among the thick boughs. The waters made him great, the deep set him up on high, with his rivers running round about his plants, and sent out his little rivers unto all the trees of the field." So Eccles. ii. 4: "I made me pools of water, to water therewith the wood that bringeth forth trees." No particular kind of tree is referred to in the passage before us, but there are abundant illustrations of the passage in the rows of willow, oranges, &c., that stand on the banks of these artificial streams in the East. The image is that of a tree abundantly watered, and that was flourishing. ¶ *That bringeth forth his fruit in his season.* Whose fruit does not fall by the want of nutriment. The idea is that of a tree which, at the proper season of the year, is loaded with fruit. Comp. Ps. xcii. 14. The image is one of great beauty. The fruit is not untimely. It does not ripen and fall too soon, or fall before it is mature; and the crop is abundant. ¶ *His leaf also shall not wither.* By drought and heat. Comp. Notes on Job viii. 16; xv. 32. It is green and flourishing—a striking image of a happy and a prosperous man. ¶ *And whatsoever he doeth shall prosper.* This is a literal statement of what had

not [1] wither; and whatsoever he doeth shall prosper.

4 The ungodly *are* not so: but *are* like the chaff [f] which the wind driveth away.

[1] Or, *fade*.

[f] Matt. iii. 12.

just been put in a figurative or poetic form. It contains a *general* truth, or contains an affirmation as to the natural and proper effect of religion, or of a life of piety, and is similar to that which occurs in 1 Tim. iv. 8: "Godliness is profitable unto all things, having promise of the life that now is, and of that which is to come." This idea of the effect of a life of piety is one that is common in the Scriptures, and is sustained by the regular course of events. If a man desires *permanent* prosperity and happiness, it is to be found only in the ways of virtue and religion. The word "whatsoever" here is to be taken in a *general* sense, and the proper laws of interpretation do not require that we should explain it as *universally* true. It is conceivable that a righteous man—a man profoundly and sincerely fearing God—may sometimes form plans that will not be wise; it is conceivable that he may lose his wealth, or that he may be involved in the calamities that come upon a people in times of commercial distress, in seasons of war, of famine, and pestilence; it is conceivable that he may be made to suffer loss by the fraud and dishonesty of other men; but still as a general and as a most important truth, a life of piety will be followed by prosperity, and will constantly impart happiness. It is this great and important truth which it is the main design of the Book of Psalms to illustrate.

4. *The ungodly* are *not so.* Literally, "Not thus the wicked." For the word *ungodly*, see Notes on ver. 1. The statement that the "wicked are not so," is a general statement applicable alike to their character and destiny, though the mind of the author of the psalm is fixed immediately and particularly on the difference in their *destiny*, without specifying anything particularly respecting their *character*. It is as true, however, that the ungodly do walk in the counsel of the wicked, and stand in the way of sinners, and sit in the seat of the scornful, as it is that the righteous do not; as true that they do *not* delight in the law of the Lord, as it is that the righteous do; as true that the wicked are *not* like a tree planted by the channels of water, as it is that the righteous are. This passage, therefore, may be employed to show what is the character of the ungodly, and in so applying it, what was before *negative* in regard to the righteous, becomes *positive* in regard to the wicked; what was positive, becomes negative. Thus it is true (*a*) that the wicked *do* walk in the counsel of the ungodly; *do* stand in the way of sinners; *do* sit in the seat of the scornful; (*b*) that they do *not* delight in the law of the Lord, or meditate on his word; and (*c*) that they are *not* like a tree planted by the waters, that is green and beautiful and fruitful. Both in character and in destiny the ungodly differ from the righteous. The subsequent part of the verse shows that, while the general truth was in the mind of the writer, the particular thing on which his attention was fixed was, his condition in life—his destiny—as that which could not be compared with a green and fruitful tree, but which suggested quite another image. ¶ *But* are *like the chaff which the wind driveth away.* When the wheat was winnowed. This, in Oriental countries, was commonly performed in the open field, and usually on an eminence, and where there was a strong wind. The operation was performed, as it is now in our country, when a fan or fanning-mill cannot be procured, by throwing up the grain as it is threshed with a shovel, and the wind scatters the chaff, while the grain falls to the ground. See Notes on Matt. iii. 12. The following cut will furnish an

5 Therefore the ungodly shall not stand[g] in the judgment, nor sinners in the congregation of the righteous.

[g] Matt. xxv. 41, 46.

illustration of this as practised in Oriental countries:

AN ANCIENT MODE OF WINNOWING.

This very naturally and appropriately furnished an illustration of the destiny of the wicked. Compared with the righteous, they were like the worthless chaff driven away by the wind. The image is often found in the Scriptures. See Notes on Job xxi. 18; Isa. xvii. 13. Comp. also Ps. xxxv. 5; Isa. xxix. 5; xli. 15; Dan. ii. 35; Hos. xiii. 3. The idea here is, that the wicked are in no respect like the green and fruitful tree referred to in ver. 3. They are not like a tree in *any* respect. They are not even like a decaying tree, a barren tree, a dead tree, for either of these would suggest some idea of stability or permanency. They are like dry and worthless chaff driven off by the wind, as of no value to the farmer—a substance which he is anxious only to separate wholly from his grain, and to get out of his way. The idea thus suggested, therefore, is that of intrinsic worthlessness. It will be, among other things, on this account that the wicked will be driven away—that they are worthless in the universe of God—worthless to all the purposes for which man was made. At the same time, however, there may be an implied contrast between that chaff and the useful grain which it is the object of the farmer to secure.

5. *Therefore.* Because they are thus worthless. ¶ *The ungodly.* See Notes on ver. 1. The wicked in general; the wicked of any kind or degree. ¶ *Shall not stand.* Comp. Notes on ver. 1. The idea is, that they will not be found among those who are acquitted by the Judge, and approved by him. The idea seems to be derived from the act of standing up to be tried, or to receive a sentence. ¶ *In the judgment.* The Chaldee Paraphrase renders this, "in the great day"—understanding it of the day of judgment. The Septuagint and Vulgate render it, "the wicked shall not *rise*—ἀναστήσονται—*resurgent*—in judgment." Most of the Jewish interpreters, following the Chaldee Paraphrase, understand this as referring to the last judgment. *Rosenmüller, in loc.* The truth stated, however, seems to be more *general* than that, though that is probably included. The meaning is, that they would not share the lot of the righteous: in all places, and at all times, where character is determined, and where the Divine estimate of human character is manifested, it would be found that they could not stand the trial, or abide the result, so as to have a place with the righteous. Their true character would in all such cases be shown, and they would be treated like the chaff that is driven away. This would be true alike in those situations of trial in the present life when character is determined, and at the last judgment, when the sentence will be pronounced which will determine the final doom of mankind. ¶ *Nor sinners.* See Notes on ver. 1. ¶ *In the congregation of the righteous.* Be reckoned or regarded as belonging to the righteous. That is, in all the places where the righteous,

6 For the LORD knoweth[h] the way of the righteous: but the way[i] of the ungodly shall perish.

h Job xxiii. 10.

i Prov. xv. 9.

as such, are assembled, they will have no place: where they assemble to worship God; where they meet as his friends; where they unitedly participate in his favour; when, in the last day, they shall be gathered together to receive their reward, and when they shall be assembled together in heaven. The sinner has no place in the congregations of the people of God.

6. *For the Lord knoweth the way of the righteous.* This is given as a *reason* why the wicked would not stand in the judgment with the righteous. The reason is, that the Lord, the great Judge, fully understands the character of those who are his friends, and can discriminate between them and all others, whatever pretences others may make to that character. Only those whom God approves, and loves, as his friends, will be able to stand in the day when the great decision shall be made. No one can impose on him by any mere pretensions to piety; no one can force his way to his favour, or to the rewards of the just, by power; no one can claim this in virtue of rank and station. No one can be admitted to the favour of God, and to the rewards of heaven, whose character is not such that it will bear the scrutiny of the Omniscient eye. Comp. Notes on 2 Tim. ii. 19. Man may be deceived in judging character, but God is not. When it is said that "the Lord knoweth *the way* of the righteous," the word *way* seems to be used to denote the whole of life—the manner of living (Notes, ver. 1), and hence the whole character. Perhaps there is included also the idea that the Lord knows the *result* of their manner of life—the issue to which it leads—and that, therefore, he can properly judge the righteous and assign them to that place in the future world, to wit, heaven, to which their actions tend. ¶ *But the way of the ungodly shall perish.* The way or manner in which the ungodly live shall tend to ruin; their plans, and purposes, and hopes, shall come to nought. Their course, in fact, tends to destruction. None of their plans shall prosper in regard to religion; none of their hopes shall be fulfilled. In this, as in all other respects, they stand in strong contrast with the righteous, alike in this world and the world to come.

PSALM II.

§ 1. *The author.*—This psalm, like the one preceding, is without any title prefixed to it, and, like that, is without anything in the psalm itself to indicate its authorship. Its authorship must be learned, therefore, elsewhere, if it can be ascertained at all. There is, however, every reason to suppose that David was the author; and by those who admit the authority of the New Testament this will not be doubted. The reasons for supposing that its authorship is to be traced to David are the following:—(*a*) It is expressly ascribed to him in Acts iv. 25, 26: "Who by the mouth of thy servant David hast said, Why did the heathen rage, and the people imagine vain things?" etc. There can be no doubt that this psalm is here referred to, and the quotation in this manner proves that this was the common understanding among the Jews. It may be presumed that in a matter of this kind the general tradition would be likely to be correct; and to those who admit the inspiration of the apostles as bearing on points like this, the fact of its being quoted as the production of David is decisive. (*b*) This is the common opinion respecting its origin among Hebrew writers. Kimchi and Aben Ezra expressly ascribe it to David, and they are supposed in this to express the prevailing opinion of the Hebrew people. (*c*) Its place among the Psalms of David may, perhaps, be regarded as a circumstance indicating the same thing. Thus, to the seventy-second psalm there are none which are ascribed expressly to any other author than David (except the fiftieth psalm, which is ascribed to Asaph, or '*for* Asaph,' as it is in the margin), though there are several whose authors are not mentioned; and the common impression has been that this portion of the Book of Psalms was arranged in this manner *because* they were understood by the collector of the Psalms to have been composed by him. (*d*) The character of the composition accords well with this supposition. It is true, indeed, that nothing can be certainly inferred from this consideration respecting its authorship; and that it must be admitted that there are no such peculiarities in the style as to *prove* that David is the author. But the remark now made is, that there is nothing inconsistent with this supposition, and that there is nothing in the sentiment, the style, or the allusions, which might not have flowed from his pen, or which would not be appropriate on the supposition that he was the author. The only objection that could be urged to this would be derived from ver. 6, "I have set my King upon my holy hill of Zion." But this will be considered in another place.

§ 2. *The time when written.*—As we cannot with absolute certainty determine who was the author, it is, of course, not possible to ascertain the exact time when it was composed; nor, if it be admitted that David was the author, can we now ascertain what was the occasion on which it was written. There are no *names* of the kings and people who are represented as conspiring against the Anointed One who is the chief subject of the psalm; and there is no local allusion whatever except in the single phrase the "hill of Zion," in ver. 6. The probability would seem to be that the psalm was not designed to refer to anything which had occurred in the time of the author himself, but, as will be seen in another part of these introductory remarks (§ 4), that the writer intended to refer mainly to the Messiah, who was to come in a distant age, although this may have been *suggested* by something which took place in the time of the writer. The opposition made to David himself by surrounding nations, their attempts to overwhelm the Hebrew people and himself as their king, the fact that God gave him the victory over his foes, and established him as the king of his people, and the prosperity and triumph which he had experienced, may have given rise to the ideas and imagery of the psalm, and may have led him to compose it with reference to the Messiah, between whose treatment and his own there would be so strong a resemblance, that the one might *suggest* the other. If conjecture may be allowed where it is impossible to be certain, it may be supposed that the psalm was composed by David after the termination of the wars in which he had been engaged with surrounding nations, and in which he had struggled for the establishment of his throne and kingdom; and after he had been peacefully and triumphantly established as ruler over the people of God. Then it would be natural to compare his own fortunes with those of the Son of God, the future Messiah, who was to be, in his human nature, his descendant; against whom the rulers of the earth would also "rage," as they had against himself; whom it was the purpose of God to establish on a permanent throne in spite of all opposition, as he had established *him* on *his* throne; and who was to sway a sceptre over the nations of the earth, of which the sceptre that *he* swayed might be regarded as an emblem. Thus understood, it had, in its original composition, no particular reference to David himself, or to Solomon, as Paulus supposed, or to any other of the kings of Israel; but it is to be regarded as having sole reference to the Messiah, in language *suggested* by events which had occurred in the history of David, the author. It is made up of the peaceful and happy reflections of one who had been engaged, in the face of much opposition, in establishing his own throne, now looking forward to the similar scenes of conflict and of triumph through which the Anointed One would pass.

§ 3. *The structure and contents of the psalm.*—The psalm is exceedingly regular in its composition, and has in its structure much of a dramatic character. It naturally falls into four parts, of three verses each.

I. In the first (vers. 1—3) the conduct and purposes of the raging nations are described. They are in the deepest agitation, forming plans against Jehovah and his Anointed One, and uniting their counsels to break their bands asunder, and to cast off their authority, that is, as ver. 6 shows, to prevent the establishment of the Anointed One as King on the holy hill of Zion. The opening of the psalm is bold and abrupt. The psalmist looks out suddenly on the nations, and *sees them* in violent commotion.

II. In the second part (vers. 4—6) the feelings and purposes of God are described. It is implied that he had formed the purpose, by a fixed decree (comp. ver. 7), to establish his Anointed One as king, and he now calmly sits in the heavens and looks with derision on the vain designs of those who are opposed to it. He smiles upon their impotent rage, and goes steadily forward to the accomplishment of his plan. He solemnly declares that he had established his King on his holy hill of Zion, and consequently, that all their efforts must be vain.

III. In the third part (vers. 7—9) the King himself, the Anointed One, speaks, and states the decree which had been formed in reference to himself, and the promise which had been made to him. That decree was, that he should be declared to be the Son of Jehovah himself; the promise was that he should, at his own request, have the nations of the earth for a possession, and rule over them with an absolute sceptre.

IV. In the fourth part (vers. 10—12) the psalmist exhorts the rulers of the nations to yield to the claims of the Anointed One, threatening Divine wrath on those who should reject him, and promising a blessing on those who should put their trust in him.

The psalm is, therefore, regularly constructed, and the main thought is pursued through the whole of it—the exalted claims and ultimate triumph of him who is here called "the Anointed;" the vanity of opposition to his decrees; and the duty and advantage of yielding to his authority. "The several sentences are also very regular in form, exhibiting parallelisms of great uniformity."—*Professor Alexander*. The psalm, in its construction, is one of the most perfect in the book, according to the peculiar ideal of Hebrew poetry.

§ 4. *The question to whom the psalm refers.*—There can be but three opinions as to the question to whom the psalm was designed to refer: (*a*) That in which it is supposed that it refers exclusively to David, or to some other one of the anointed kings of Israel; (*b*) that in which it is supposed that it had this original reference, but has also a secondary reference to the Messiah; and (*c*) that in which it is supposed that it has *exclusive* and *sole* reference to the Messiah.

There are few who maintain the first of these opinions. Even Grotius, in respect to whom it was said, in comparison with Cocceius, that "Cocceius found Christ everywhere, and Grotius nowhere," admits that while, in his view, the psalm had a primary reference to David, and to the Philistines, Moabites, Ammonites, Idumeans, &c., as his enemies, yet, in a more "mystical and abstruse sense, it pertained to the Messiah." The *reasons* why the psalm should not be regarded as referring exclusively to any Hebrew king are conclusive. They are summed up in this one: that the expressions in the psalm are such as cannot be applied exclusively to *any* Hebrew monarch. This will appear in the exposition of this psalm. For like reasons, the psalm cannot be regarded as designed to refer primarily to David, and in a secondary and higher sense to the Messiah. There are no indications in the psalm of any such double sense; and if it cannot be applied exclusively to David, cannot be applied to him at all.

The psalm, I suppose, like Isa. liii., had an original and exclusive reference to the Messiah. This may be shown by the following considerations:—

(1) It is so applied in the New Testament, and is referred to in no other way. Thus, in Acts iv. 24—27, the whole company of the apostles is represented as quoting the first verses of the psalm, and referring them to Christ: "They lifted up their voice to God with one accord, and said, Lord, thou art God . . . who by the mouth of thy servant David hast said, Why did the heathen rage, and the people imagine vain things? The kings of the earth stood up, and the rulers were gathered together against the Lord, and against his Christ. For of a truth against thy holy child Jesus, whom thou hast anointed, both Herod and Pontius Pilate, with the Gentiles, and the people of Israel, were gathered together." If the authority of the apostles, therefore, is to be admitted in the case, there can be no doubt that the psalm was intended to refer to the Messiah. This statement of the apostles may also be adduced as proof that this was, probably, the prevailing mode of interpretation in their age. Again, the psalm is quoted by Paul (Acts xiii. 32, 33) as applicable to Christ, and with reference to the fact that it was a doctrine of the Old Testament that the Messiah was to rise from the dead: "And we declare unto you glad tidings, how that the promise which was made unto the fathers, God hath fulfilled the same unto us their children, in that he hath raised up Jesus again; as it is also written in the second

psalm, Thou art my Son, this day have I begotten thee." And again, in Heb. i. 5, the same passage is quoted by Paul to establish the exalted rank of the Messiah as being above the angels: "For unto which of the angels said he at any time, Thou art my Son, this day have I begotten thee?" These quotations prove that in the estimation of the writers of the New Testament the psalm had an original reference to the Messiah; and the manner in which they make the quotation proves that this was the current belief of the Jews in their day, as they appear to have been under no apprehension that the propriety of the application which they made would be called in question.

(2) But, besides this, there is other evidence that such was the prevailing interpretation among the ancient Hebrews: "In the older Jewish writings, as the Sohar, the Talmud, &c., there is a variety of passages in which the Messianic interpretation is given to the psalm. See the collections by Raym. Martini, Pug. Fid. ed. Carpzov., in several places, and by Schöttgen, de Messia, pp. 227 seq. Even Kimchi and Jarchi confess that it was the prevailing interpretation among their forefathers; and the latter very honestly gives his reasons for departing from it, when he says he prefers to explain it of David, for the refutation of the heretics; that is, in order to destroy the force of the arguments drawn from it by the Christians." (Hengstenberg, Christ., i. 77.)

(3) That it refers to the Messiah is manifest from the psalm itself. This will be apparent from a few subordinate considerations. (*a*) It cannot be applied to David, or to any other earthly king; that is, there are expressions in it which cannot be applied with any degree of propriety to any earthly monarch whatever. This remark is founded particularly on the remarkable use of the word "*Son*" in the psalm, and the promise that "the uttermost parts of the earth" should be placed under the control of him to whom that word is applied. The word *son* is, indeed, of large signification, and is, in a certain sense, applied to the righteous in the plural number, as being the *sons* or the *children* of God by adoption; but it is not so applied in the singular number, and there is a peculiarity in its use here which shows that it was not intended to be applied to an earthly monarch, or to any pious man considered as a child of God. That appellation—*the* Son of God—properly denotes a nearer relation to God than can be applied to a mere mortal of any rank (comp. Notes on John v. 18), and was so understood by the Jews themselves. It is not used in the Old Testament, as applied to an earthly monarch, in the manner in which it is employed here. The remark here made is entirely irrespective of the doctrine which is sometimes supposed to be taught in this passage, of "the eternal generation" of the Son of God, since what is here said is equally true, whether that doctrine is well-founded or not. (*b*) There is an extent of dominion and a perpetuity of empire promised here which could not be applied to David or to any other earthly monarch, but which is entirely applicable to the Messiah (see vers. 8, 10). (*c*) Such, too, is the nature of the promise to those who put their trust in him, and the threatening on those who do not obey him (ver. 12). This is language which will be seen at once to be entirely applicable to the Messiah, but which cannot be so regarded in respect of any earthly monarch. (*d*) There is a strong probability that the psalm is designed to refer to the Messiah, from the fact that they who deny this have not been able to propose any other plausible interpretation, or to show with any degree of probability to whom it *does* refer. There were no Israelitish kings or princes to whom it could be regarded with any show of probability as applicable, unless it were David or Solomon; and yet there are no recorded circumstances in their lives to which it can be regarded as adapted, and there is no substantial agreement among those who maintain that it does refer to either of them. It is maintained by both Rosenmüller and De Wette that it cannot relate to David or Solomon. Some of the modern Jews maintain that it was composed by David respecting himself when the Philistines came up against him (2 Sam. v. 17); but this is manifestly an erroneous opinion, for not only was there nothing in the occurrence there to correspond with the language of the psalm, but there was at that time no particular consecration of the hill of Zion (ver. 6), nor was that mount regarded as holy or sacred until after the tabernacle was erected on it, which was after the Philistine war. The same remark may be made substantially of the supposition that it refers to the rebellion of Absalom, or to *any* of the circumstances in which David was placed.

PSALM II.

WHY [k] do the heathen [1] rage, [l] and the people [2] imagine a vain thing?

k Acts iv. 25, 26. [1] Or, *tumultuously assemble.* *l* Ps. xlvi. 6. [2] *meditate.*

And there is still less reason for supposing that it refers to Solomon, for there is no mention of any rebellion against him; of any general attempt to throw off his yoke; of any solemn consecration of him as king in consequence of, or in spite of such an attempt. (*e*) The psalm *agrees* with the account of the Messiah, or is in its general structure and details applicable to him. This will be shown in the exposition, and indeed is manifest on the face of it. The only plausible objection to this view is, as stated by De Wette, "According to the doctrine of Christianity, the Messiah is no conqueror of nations, bearing an iron sceptre; his kingdom is not of this world." But to this it may be replied, that all that is meant in ver. 9 may be, that he will set up a kingdom over the nations of the earth; that all his enemies will be subdued under him; and that the sceptre which he will sway will be firm and irresistible. See, for the applicability of this to the Messiah, the Notes on ver. 9.

(4) It may be added that the psalm is such as one might *expect* to find in the poetic writings of the Hebrews, with the views which they entertained of the Messiah. The promised Messiah was the object of deepest interest to their minds. All their hopes centered in him. To him they looked forward as the Great Deliverer; and all their anticipations of what the people of God were to be clustered around him. He was to be a Prince, a Conqueror, a Deliverer, a Saviour. To him the eyes of the nation were directed; he was shadowed forth by their pompous religious rites, and their sacred bards sang his advent. That we should find an entire psalm composed with reference to him, designed to set forth his character and the glory of his reign, is no more than what we should expect to find among a people where poetry is cultivated at all, and where these high hopes were cherished in reference to his advent; and especially if to this view of their national poetry, in itself considered, there be added the idea that the sacred bards wrote under the influence of inspiration, nothing is more natural than that we should expect to find a poetic composition having such a sole and exclusive reference. Nothing would have been more *unnatural* than that, with these prevailing views and hopes, and with the fact before us that so much of the Old Testament is sacred poetry, we should have found *no* such production as the second psalm, on the supposition that it had an original and exclusive reference to the Messiah.

1. *Why do the heathen rage.* "Why do nations make a noise?" *Prof. Alexander.* The word *heathen* here—גּוֹיִם *goim*—means properly *nations*, without respect, so far as the *word* is concerned, to the *character* of the nations. It was applied by the Hebrews to the surrounding nations, or to all other people than their own; and as those nations were in fact heathens, or idolators, the word came to have this signification. Neh. v. 8; Jer. xxxi. 10; Ezek. xxiii. 30; xxx. 11; compare אָדָם, Jer. xxxii. 20. The word *Gentile* among the Hebrews (Gr., ἔθνος) expressed the same thing. Matt. iv. 15; vi. 32; x. 5, 18; xii. 21, *et sæpe.* The word rendered *rage*—רָגַשׁ—*ragash*—means to make a noise or tumult, and would be expressive of violent commotion or agitation. It occurs in the Hebrew Scriptures only in this place, though the corresponding Chaldee word—רְגַשׁ—*regash*—is found in Daniel vi. 6, 11, 15—rendered in ver. 6, "assembled together," in the margin "came tumultuously,"—and in ver. 11, 15, rendered *assembled.* The psalmist here sees the nations in violent agitation or commotion, as if under high excitement, engaged in accomplishing some purpose—rushing on to secure something, or to prevent something. The image of a mob, or of a tumultuous unregulated assemblage, would probably convey the idea of the psalmist. The word itself does not enable us to determine how *extensive* this agitation would be, but it is evidently implied that it would be a somewhat *general* movement; a move-

2 The kings of the earth set themselves, and the rulers take

ment in which more than one nation or people would participate. The matter in hand was something that affected the nations generally, and which would produce violent agitation among them. ¶ *And the people.* לְאֻמִּים *Leummim.* A word expressing substantially the same idea, that of *people*, or *nations*, and referring here to the same thing as the word rendered *heathen*—according to the laws of Hebrew parallelism in poetry. It is the *people* here that are seen in violent agitation: the conduct of the *rulers*, as associated with them, is referred to in the next verse. ¶ *Imagine.* Our word *imagine* does not precisely express the idea here. We mean by it, "to form a notion or idea in the mind; to fancy." *Webster.* The Hebrew word — הָגָה—*Hagah*, is the same which, in Ps. i. 2, is rendered *meditate.* See Notes on that verse. It means here that the mind is engaged in deliberating on it; that it plans, devises, or forms a purpose;—in other words, the persons referred to are *thinking* about some purpose which is here called a vain purpose; they are *meditating* some project which excites deep thought, but which cannot be effectual. ¶ *A vain thing.* That is, which will prove to be a vain thing, or a thing which they cannot accomplish. It cannot mean that they were engaged in forming plans which *they* supposed would be vain—for no persons would form such plans; but that they were engaged in designs which the *result* would show to be unsuccessful. The reference here is to the agitation among the nations in respect to the Divine purpose to set up the Messiah as king over the world, and to the opposition which this would create among the nations of the earth. See Notes on ver. 2. An ample fulfilment of this occurred in the opposition to him when he came in the flesh, and in the resistance everywhere made since his death to his reign upon the earth. Nothing has produced more agitation in the world (comp. Acts xvii. 6), and nothing still excites more determined resistance. The truths taught in this verse are (1) that sinners are opposed —even so much as to produce violent agitation of mind, and a fixed and determined purpose—to the plans and decrees of God, especially with respect to the reign of the Messiah; and (2) that their plans to resist this will be vain and ineffectual; wisely as their schemes may seem to be laid, and determined as they themselves are in regard to their execution, yet they *must* find them vain. What is implied here of the particular plans against the Messiah, is true of all the purposes of sinners, when they array themselves against the government of God.

2. *The kings of the earth.* This verse is designed to give a more specific form to the general statement in ver. 1. In the first verse the psalmist sees a general commotion among the nations as engaged in some plan that he sees must be a vain one; here he describes more particularly the cause of the excitement, and gives a nearer view of what is occurring. He now sees kings and rulers engaged in a specific and definite plot against Jehovah and against his Anointed. The word *kings* here is a general term, which would be applicable to all rulers,—as the kingly government was the only one then known, and the nations were under the control of absolute monarchs. A sufficient fulfilment would be found, however, if *any* rulers were engaged in doing what is here described. ¶ *Set themselves.* Or, take their stand. The latter expression would perhaps better convey the sense of the original. It is the idea of taking a stand, or of setting themselves in array, which is denoted by the expression;—they combine; they resolve; they are fixed in their purpose. Comp. Exod. ii. 4; xix. 17; xxxiv. 5. The attitude here is that of firm or determined resistance. ¶ *And the rulers.* A slight addition to the word *kings.* The sense is, that there was a *general* combination

counsel together, against the LORD, and against his [m] anointed,

m Ps. xlv. 7.

saying,

3 [n] Let us break their bands

n Luke xix. 14.

among all classes of rulers to accomplish what is here specified. It was not confined to any one class. ¶ *Take counsel together.* Consult together. Comp. Ps. xxxi. 13, "While they took counsel together against me." The word here used—יָסַד, *yasad*—means properly to found, to lay the foundation of, to establish; then, to be founded (Niph.); to support one's self; to lean upon—as, for example, to lean upon the elbow. Thus used, it is employed with reference to persons reclining or leaning upon a couch or cushion, especially as deliberating together, as the Orientals do in the *divan* or council. Comp. Notes on Ps. lxxxiii. 3. The idea here is that of persons assembled to deliberate on an important matter. ¶ *Against the* LORD. Against *Jehovah*—the small capitals in our common version indicating that the original word is Jehovah. The meaning is, that they were engaged in deliberating *against* Jehovah in respect to the matter here referred to—to wit, his purpose to place the "Anointed One," his King (ver. 6), on the hill of Zion. It is not meant that they were in other respects arrayed against him, though it is true in fact that opposition to God in one respect may imply that there is an aversion to him in *all* respects, and that the same spirit which would lead men to oppose him in any one of his purposes would, if carried out, lead them to oppose him in all things. ¶ *And against his Anointed*—מְשִׁיחוֹ—*his Messiah:* hence our word *Messiah,* or *Christ.* The word means *Anointed,* and the allusion is to the custom of anointing kings and priests with holy oil when setting them apart to office, or consecrating them to their work. Comp. Notes on Matt. i. 1; Dan. ix. 26. The word *Messiah,* or *Anointed,* is therefore of so general a character in its signification that its mere use would not determine to whom it was to be applied—whether to a king, to a priest, or to the Messiah properly so called. The reference is to be determined by something in the connexion. All that the word here necessarily implies is, that there was some one whom Jehovah regarded as his *Anointed one,* whether king or priest, against whom the rulers of the earth had arrayed themselves. The subsequent part of the psalm (vers. 6, 7) enables us to ascertain that the reference here is to one who was *a King,* and that he sustained to Jehovah the relation of *a Son.* The New Testament, and the considerations suggested in the introduction to the psalm (§ 4), enable us to understand that the reference is to the Messiah properly so called—Jesus of Nazareth. This is expressly declared (Acts iv. 25–27) to have had its fulfilment in the purposes of Herod, Pontius Pilate, the Gentiles, and the people of Israel, in rejecting the Saviour and putting him to death. No one can doubt that all that is here stated in the psalm had a complete fulfilment in their combining to reject him and to put him to death; and we are, therefore, to regard the psalm as particularly referring to this transaction. Their conduct was, however, an illustration of the common feelings of rulers and people concerning him, and it was proper to represent the nations in general as in commotion in regard to him.

3. *Let us break their bands asunder.* The bands of Jehovah and of his Anointed. They who are engaged in this combination or conspiracy regard Jehovah and his Anointed as one, and as having one object—to set up a dominion over the world. Hence they take counsel against both; and, with the same purpose and design, endeavour to cast off the authority of each. The word *bands* here refers to the restraints imposed by their authority. The figure is probably taken from fastening a yoke on oxen, or the

asunder, and cast away their cords from us.

4 He that sitteth in the hea-

bands or cords which were used in ploughing—the bands of the yoke being significant of their subjection to the authority or will of another. The same figure is used by the Saviour in Matt. xi. 29: "Take my *yoke* upon you." The idea here is, that it was the purpose of Jehovah and his Anointed to establish a dominion over men, and that it was equally the purpose of the kings and rulers here referred to that it should *not* be done. ¶ *And cast away their cords from us.* The same idea under another form—the cords referring not to that which would bind them as prisoners, but to the ropes or thongs which bound oxen to the plough; and, hence, to that which would bind men to the service of God. The word translated *cords* is a stronger word than that which is rendered *bands.* It means properly what is twisted or interlaced, and refers to the usual manner in which ropes are made. Perhaps, also, in the words "let us cast away" there is the expression of an idea that it could be easily done: that they had only to *will* it, and it would be done. Together, the expressions refer to the purpose among men to cast off the government of God, and especially that part of his administration which refers to his purpose to establish a kingdom under the Messiah. It thus indicates a prevalent state of the human mind as being impatient of the restraints and authority of God, and especially of the dominion of his Son, anointed as King.

The passage (vers. 1—3) proves—(1) that the government of Jehovah, the true God, and the Messiah or Christ, is the same; (2) that opposition to the Messiah, or to Christ, is in fact opposition to the purposes of the true God; (3) that it may be expected that men will oppose that government, and there will be agitation and commotion in endeavouring to throw it off. The passage, considered as referring to the Messiah, had an ample fulfilment (*a*) in the purposes of the high priests, of Herod, and of Pilate, to put him to death, and in the general rejection of him by his own countrymen; (*b*) in the general conduct of mankind—in their impatience of the restraints of the law of God, and especially of that law as promulgated by the Saviour, demanding submission and obedience to him; and (*c*) in the conduct of individual sinners—in the opposition of the human heart to the authority of the Lord Jesus. The passage before us is just as applicable to the world now as it was to the time when the Saviour personally appeared on the earth.

4. *He that sitteth in the heavens.* God, represented as having his home, his seat, his throne in heaven, and thence administering the affairs of the world. This verse commences the second strophe or stanza of the psalm; and this strophe (vers. 4—6) corresponds with the first (vers. 1—3) in its structure. The former describes the feelings and purposes of those who would cast off the government of God; this describes the feelings and purposes of God in the same order, for in each case the psalmist describes what is *done*, and then what is *said:* the nations rage tumultuously (vers. 1, 2), and then say (ver. 3), "Let us break their bands." God sits calmly in the heavens, smiling on their vain attempts (ver. 4), and then solemnly declares (vers. 5, 6) that, in spite of all their opposition, he "has set his King upon his holy hill of Zion." There is much sublimity in this description. While men rage and are tumultuous in opposing his plans, he sits calm and undisturbed in his own heaven. Compare the Notes on the similar place in Isa. xviii. 4. ¶ *Shall laugh.* Will smile at their vain attempts; will not be disturbed or agitated by their efforts; will go calmly on in the execution of his purposes. Comp. as above Isa. xviii. 4. See also Prov. i. 26; Ps. xxxvii. 13; lix. 8. This is,

vens shall laugh: the LORD shall have them in ᵒ derision.

ᵒ Prov. i. 26. [1] Or, *trouble*.

5 Then shall he speak unto them in his wrath, and [1] vex them in his sore displeasure.

of course, to be regarded as spoken after the manner of men, and it means that God will go steadily forward in the accomplishment of his purposes. There is included also the idea that he will look with *contempt* on their vain and futile efforts. ¶ *The* LORD *shall have them in derision.* The same idea is expressed here in a varied form, as is the custom in parallelism in Hebrew poetry. The Hebrew word לָעַג, *laag*, means properly to stammer; then to speak in a barbarous or foreign tongue; then to mock or deride, by imitating the stammering voice of any one. Gesenius, *Lex.* Here it is spoken of God, and, of course, is not to be understood literally, any more than when eyes, and hands, and feet are spoken of as appertaining to him. The meaning is, that there is a result in the case, in the Divine mind, *as if* he mocked or derided the vain attempts of men; that is, he goes calmly forward in the execution of his own purposes, and he looks upon and regards their efforts as vain, as *we* do the efforts of others when we mock or deride them. The *truth* taught in this verse is, that God will carry forward his own plans in spite of all the attempts of men to thwart them. This general truth may be stated in two forms: (1) He sits undisturbed and unmoved in heaven while men rage against him, and while they combine to cast off his authority. (2) He carries forward his own plans in spite of them. This he does (*a*) *directly*, accomplishing his schemes without regard to their attempts; and (*b*) by making their purposes tributary to his own, so making them the instruments in carrying out his own plans. Comp. Acts iv. 28.

5. *Then shall he speak unto them.* That is, this seeming indifference and unconcern will not last for ever. He will not always look calmly on, nor will he suffer them to accomplish their purposes without interposing. When he has shown how he regards their schemes—how impotent they are—how much they are really the objects of derision, considered as an attempt to cast off his authority—he will interpose and declare his own purposes—his determination to establish his king on the hill of Zion. This is implied in the word "*then.*" ¶ *In his wrath.* In anger. His contempt for their plans will be followed by indignation against themselves for forming such plans, and for their efforts to execute them. One of these things is not inconsistent with the other; for the purpose of the rebels may be very weak and futile, and yet their wickedness in forming the plan may be very great. The weakness of the scheme, and the fact that it will be vain, does not change the character of him who has made it; the fact that he is *foolish* does not prove that he is not *wicked.* God will treat the scheme and those who form it as they deserve—the one with contempt, the other with his wrath. The word *wrath* here, it is hardly necessary to say, should be interpreted in the same manner as the word "*laugh*" in ver. 4, not as denoting a feeling precisely like that which exists in the human mind, subject as man is to unreasonable *passion*, but as it is proper to apply it to God—the strong conviction (without passion or personal feeling) of the evil of sin, and the expression of his purpose in a manner adapted to *show* that evil, and to *restrain* others from its commission. It means that he will speak to them *as if* he were angry; or that his treatment of them will be such as men experience from others when they are angry. ¶ *And vex them.* The word here rendered *vex*—בָּהַל, *Bahal*—means in the original or *Kal* form, *to tremble;* and then, in the form here used, the *Piel*, to cause to tremble, to terrify, to strike with consternation. This might be done either by a threat

6 Yet have I [1] set my king [p] upon [2] my holy hill of Zion.

[1] *anointed.* *p* Acts v. 31. [2] *Zion, the hill of my holiness.*

or by some judgment indicative of displeasure or anger. Ps. lxxxiii. 15; Dan. xi. 44; Job xxii. 10. The idea here is that he would alarm them, or make them quake with fear, by what is specified of his purpose; to wit, by his determination to set his King on his holy hill, and by placing the sceptre of the earth in his hands. *Their* designs, therefore, would be frustrated, and if they did not submit to him they must perish (see vers. 9—12). ¶ *In his sore displeasure.* Literally, in his *heat* or *burning*, that is, in his anger; as we speak of one that is *inflamed* with anger, or that *burns* with indignation; or, as we speak of the passions, *kindling into a flame.* The meaning here is, that God would be displeased with their purposes, and that the expression of his design would be adapted to fill them with the deepest alarm. Of course, all such words are to be interpreted in accordance with what we know to be the nature of God, and not in accordance with the same passions in men. God is opposed to sin, and will express his opposition *as if* he felt angry, but it will be in the most calm manner, and not as the result of passion. It will be simply because it *ought* to be so.

6. *Yet have I set my king.* The word *yet* is merely the translation of the conjunction *and.* It is rendered in the Vulgate *but—autem;* and so in the LXX., δὲ. It would be better rendered perhaps by the usual word *and:* "And I have set or constituted my king," &c. This is properly to be regarded as the expression of God himself; as what he *says* in reply to their declared purposes (ver. 3), and as what is referred to in ver. 5. The meaning is, he would speak to them in his anger, and say, "In spite of all your purposes and all your opposition, I have set my king on the hill of Zion." That is, they had *their* plans and God had *his; they* meant to cast off his authority, and to prevent his purpose to set up the Messiah as king; *he* resolved, on the contrary, to carry out his purposes, AND he would do it. The word rendered *set*—נָסַךְ, *nasach*—means, literally, to pour, to pour out, as in making a libation to the Deity, Ex. xxx. 9; Hos. ix. 4; Isa. xxx. 1; then, to pour out oil in anointing a king or priest, and hence to consecrate, to inaugurate, &c. See Josh. xiii. 21; Ps. lxxxiii. 11; Mic. v. 5. The idea here is, that he had solemnly inaugurated or constituted the Messiah as king; that is, that he had formed the purpose to do it, and he therefore speaks *as if* it were already done. The words *my King* refer, of course, to the anointed One, the Messiah, ver. 2. It is not simply *a* king, or *the* king, but "*my* king," meaning that he derived his appointment from God, and that he was placed there to execute *his* purposes. This indicates the very near relation which the anointed One sustains to him who had appointed him, and prepares us for what is said in the subsequent verse, where he is called his *Son.* ¶ *Upon my holy hill of Zion.* Zion was the southern hill in the city of Jerusalem. See Notes on Isa. i. 8. It was the highest of the hills on which the city was built. It was made by David the capital of his kingdom, and was hence called *the city of* David, 2 Chron. v. 2. By the poets and prophets it is often put for Jerusalem itself, Isa. ii. 3; viii. 18; x. 24; xxxiii. 14, *et al.* It did not obtain this distinction until it was taken by David from the Jebusites, 2 Sam. v. 5—9; 1 Chron. xi. 4—8. To that place David removed the ark of the covenant, and there he built an altar to the Lord in the threshing-floor of Araunah the Jebusite, 2 Sam. xxiv. 15—25. Zion became thenceforward the metropolis of the kingdom, and the name was transferred to the entire city. It is to this that the passage here refers; and the meaning is, that in that metropolis or capital God had constituted his Messiah king,

7 I will declare [1] the decree:
the LORD hath said unto me,
Thou [q] *art* my Son; this day have
I begotten thee.

[1] Or, *for a.*

[q] Matt. iii. 17; xvii. 5; Acts xiii. 33.

---

or had appointed him to reign over his people. This cannot refer to David himself, for in no proper sense was he *constituted* or *inaugurated* king in Jerusalem; that is, there was no such ceremony of inauguration as is referred to here. Zion was called the "*holy* hill," or "the hill of my holiness" (Heb.), because it was set apart as the seat of the Theocracy, or the residence of God, from the time that David removed the ark there. That became the place where God reigned, and where his worship was celebrated. This must refer to the Messiah, and to the fact that God had set him apart to reign over his people, and thence over all the earth. The truth taught in this passage is, that God will carry forward his own purposes in spite of all the opposition which men can make, and that it is his deliberate design to make his anointed One—the Messiah—King over all.

7. *I will declare the decree.* We have here another change in the speaker. The Anointed One is himself introduced as declaring the great purpose which was formed in regard to him, and referring to the promise which was made to him, as the foundation of the purpose of Jehovah (ver. 6) to set him on the hill of Zion. The first strophe or stanza (vers. 1–3) is closed with a statement made by the rebels of *their* intention or design; the second (vers. 4–6) with a statement of the purpose of Jehovah; the third is introduced by this declaration of the Messiah himself. The change of the persons speaking gives a dramatic interest to the whole psalm. There can be no doubt that the word "*I*" here refers to the Messiah. The word *decree* — חֹק *hhohk*—means properly something decreed, prescribed, appointed. See Job xxiii. 14. Comp. Gen. xlvii. 26; Exod. xii. 24. Thus it is equivalent to law, statute, ordinance. Here it refers not to a law which he was to obey, but to an ordinance or statute respecting his reign: the solemn purpose of Jehovah in regard to the kingdom which the Messiah was to set up; the *constitution* of his kingdom. This, as the explanation shows, implied two things—(*a*) that he was to be regarded and acknowledged as his *Son,* or to have that rank and dignity (ver. 7); and (*b*) that the heathen and the uttermost parts of the earth were to be given him for a possession, or that his reign was to extend over all the world (ver. 8). The word "*declare*" here means that he would give utterance to, or that he would now himself make a statement in explanation of the reason why Jehovah had determined to establish him as King on his holy hill of Zion. There is great beauty in thus introducing the Messiah himself as making this declaration, presenting it now in the form of a solemn covenant or pledge. The determination of Jehovah (ver. 6) to establish him as King on his holy hill is thus seen not to be arbitrary, but to be in fulfilment of a solemn promise made long before, and is therefore an illustration of his covenant faithfulness and truth. ¶ *The* LORD *hath said unto me.* Jehovah hath said. See vers. 2, 4. He does not intimate *when* it was that he had said this, but the fair interpretation is, that it was *before* the purpose was to be carried into execution to place him as King in Zion; that is, as applicable to the Messiah, before he became incarnate or was manifested to execute his purpose on earth. It is implied, therefore, that it was in some previous state, and that he had come forth in virtue of the pledge that he would be recognised as the Son of God. The passage cannot be understood as referring to Christ without admitting his existence previous to the incarnation, for all that follows is manifestly the result of the exalted rank which God purposed to

give him *as his Son,* or as the result of the promise made to him then. ¶ *Thou* art *my Son.* That is, Jehovah had declared him to be his Son; he had conferred on him the rank and dignity fairly involved in the title THE SON OF GOD. In regard to the general meaning of this, and what is implied in it, see notes on Matt. i. 1; Heb. i. 2, 5; Rom. i. 4; and John v. 18. The phrase "*sons* of God" is elsewhere used frequently to denote the saints, the children of God, or men eminent for rank and power (comp. Gen. vi. 2, 4; Job i. 6; Hos. i. 10; John i. 12; Rom. viii. 14, 19; Phil. ii. 15; 1 John iii. 1); and once to denote angels (Job xxxviii. 7); but the appellation "THE *Son of God*" is not appropriated in the Scriptures to any one but the Messiah. It does not occur before this in the Old Testament, and it occurs but once after this, Dan. iii. 25. See Notes on that passage. This makes its use in the case before us the more remarkable, and justifies the reasoning of the author of the epistle to the Hebrews (i. 5) as to its meaning. The true sense, therefore, according to the Hebrew usage, and according to the proper meaning of the term, is, that he sustained a relation to God which could be compared only with that which a son among men sustains to his father; and that the term, as thus used, fairly implies an equality in nature with God himself. It is such a term as would not be applied to a mere man; it is such as is not applied to the angels (Heb. i. 5); and therefore it must imply a nature superior to either. ¶ *This day.* On the application of this in the New Testament, see Notes on Acts xiii. 33 and Heb. i. 5. The whole passage has been often appealed to in support of the doctrine of the "eternal generation" of Christ, meaning that he was "begotten" from eternity; that is, that his Divine nature was in some sense an emanation from the Father, and that this is from eternity. Whatever may be thought of that doctrine, however, either as to its intelligibility or its truth, there is nothing in the use of the phrase "this day," or in the application of the passage in the New Testament (Acts xiii. 33; Heb. i. 5), to sustain it. The language, indeed, in the connexion in which it is found, does, as remarked above, demonstrate that he had a pre-existence, since it is addressed to him *as the result* of a decree or covenant made with him by Jehovah, and *as the foundation* of the purpose to set him as King on the hill of Zion. The words "this day" would naturally refer to that time when this "decree" was made, or this covenant formed; and as that was before the creation of the world, it must imply that he had an existence then. The time referred to by the meaning of the word is, *that* when it was determined to crown him as the Messiah. This is founded *on* the relation subsisting between him and Jehovah, and implied when in that relation he is called his "Son;" but it determines nothing as to the time *when* this relation commenced. Jehovah, in the passage, is regarded as declaring his purpose to make him King in Zion, and the language is that of a solemn consecration to the kingly office. He is speaking of this as a purpose before he came into the world; it was executed, or carried into effect, by his resurrection from the dead, and by the exaltation consequent on that. Comp. Acts xiii. 33 and Eph. i. 20—22. Considered, then, *as a promise* or *purpose,* this refers to the period before the incarnation; considered as pertaining *to the execution of that purpose,* it refers to the time when he was raised from the dead and exalted over all things as King in Zion. In neither case can the words "this day" be construed as meaning the same as *eternity,* or *from eternity;* and therefore they can determine nothing respecting the doctrine of "eternal generation." ¶ *Have I begotten thee.* That is, in the matter referred to, so that it would be proper to apply to him the phrase "my *Son,*" and to constitute him "King" in Zion. The meaning is, that he had so constituted the relationship of Father and Son *in the case*, that it was proper that the appellation *Son* should be given him, and that he should be regarded and addressed as such. So Prof. Alexander: "The essential meaning of the phrase *I have begotten thee* is simply this, *I am thy Father*." This is, of course, to be understood in accordance with the nature of God, and we are not to bring to the interpretation the ideas which enter into that human relationship. It means that in some proper sense—some sense appropriate to the Deity—such a relation was constituted as would justify this reference to the most tender and important of all human relationships. In what sense that is, is a fair subject of inquiry, but it is not proper to assume that it is in anything like a *literal* sense, or that there can be no *other* sense of the passage than that which is implied in the above-named doctrine; for it *cannot* be literal, and there *are* other ideas that may be conveyed by the phrase than that of "eternal generation." The word rendered "*begotten*" (יָלַד — *Yalad*) determines nothing certainly as to the *mode* in which this relationship was formed. It means properly—(1) to bear, to bring forth as a mother, Gen. iv. 1; (2) to beget, as a father, Gen. iv. 18; and then (3) as applied to God it is used in the sense of creating—or of so creating or forming as that the result would be that a relation would exist which might be compared with that of a father and a son. Deut. xxxii. 18: "Of the Rock that *begat* thee thou art unmindful." Comp. Jer. ii. 27: "Saying to a block [idol], Thou art my father, thou hast *begotten* me." So Paul says, 1 Cor. iv. 15: "In Christ Jesus I have *begotten* you through the Gospel." The full meaning, therefore, of this word would be met if it be supposed that Jehovah had given the Messiah this place and rank in such a sense that it was proper to speak of himself as *the Father* and the Anointed One as *the Son*. And was there not enough in designating him to this high office; in sending him into the world; in raising him from the dead; in placing him at his own right hand—appointing him as King and Lord—to justify this language? Is not this the very thing under consideration? Is it proper, then, in connexion with this passage, to start the question about his eternal generation? Comp. Notes on Rom. i. 4. On this passage Calvin says (*in loc.*), "I know that this passage is explained by many as referring to the eternal generation of Christ, who maintain that in the adverb *to-day* there is, as it were, a perpetual act beyond the limits of time, denoted. But the Apostle Paul is a more faithful and competent interpreter of this prophecy, who in Acts xiii. 33 recalls us to that which I have called a glorious demonstration of Christ. He was said to be begotten, therefore, not that he might be the Son of God, by which he might begin to be such, but that he might be manifested to the world as such. Finally, this begetting ought to be understood not of the mutual relation of the Father and the Son, but it signifies merely that he who was from the beginning hidden in the bosom of the Father, and who was obscurely shadowed forth under the law, from the time when he was manifested with clear intimation of his rank, was acknowledged as the Son of God, as it is said in John i. 14." So Prof. Alexander, though supposing that this is founded on an eternal relation between the Father and the Son, says, "*This day have I begotten thee* may be considered as referring only to the coronation of Messiah, which is an ideal one," vol. i., p. 15. The result of the exposition of this passage may therefore be thus stated: (*a*) The term *Son*, as here used, is a *peculiar* appellation of the Messiah—a term applicable to him in a sense in which it can be given to no other being. (*b*) As here used, and as elsewhere used, it *supposes* his existence before the incarnation. (*c*) Its use here, and the purpose formed, imply that he had an existence *before*

8 Ask of me, and I shall give *thee* the heathen *for* thine inheritance, and the uttermost parts of the earth *for* thy possession.

this purpose was formed, so that he could be personally addressed, and so that a promise could be made to him. (*d*) The term *Son* is not here used in *reference* to that anterior relation, and determines nothing as to the mode of his previous being—whether from eternity essentially in the nature of God; or whether in some mysterious sense begotten; or whether as an emanation of the Deity; or whether created. (*e*) The term, as Calvin suggests, and as maintained by Prof. Alexander, refers here *only* to his being constituted King—to the act of coronation — whenever that occurred. (*f*) This, *in fact*, occurred when he was raised from the dead, and when he was exalted to the right hand of God in heaven (Acts xiii. 33), so that the application of the passage by Paul in the Acts accords with the result to which we are led by the fair interpretation of the passage. (*g*) The passage, therefore, determines nothing, one way or the other, respecting the doctrine of eternal generation, and cannot, therefore, be used in proof of that doctrine.

8. *Ask of me.* That is, of God. This is a part of the "decree" or purpose, as mentioned in ver. 7. That decree embraced not only the design to constitute him as his Son, in the sense that he was to be king in Zion, but also the purpose to give him a dominion embracing "the heathen" and "the uttermost parts of the earth." This wide dominion was to be given him on condition that he would "ask" for it, thus keeping up the idea that Jehovah, as such, is the great source of authority and empire, and that the Messiah, as such, occupies a rank subordinate to him. This relation of the Father and Son is everywhere recognised in the New Testament. As we may be sure that the Messiah *will* ask for this, it follows that the world *will* yet be brought under his sceptre. It may be added that as this wide dominion is promised to the Messiah only on condition that he "asks" for it or prays for it, much more is it true that *we* can hope for this and for no favour from God, unless we seek it by earnest prayer. ¶ *And I shall give* thee. I will give thee. That is, he would ultimately give him this possession. No *time* is specified when it would be done, and the prophecy will be fulfilled if it shall be accomplished in *any* period of the history of the world. ¶ *The heathen.* The *nations* (Notes, ver. 1); that is, the world. In the time of the writer of the psalm, the world would be spoken of as divided into Hebrews and other nations; the people of God and foreigners. The same division is often referred to in the New Testament under the terms Jew and Gentile, as the Greeks divided all the world into Greeks and barbarians. The word would now embrace all the nations which are not under the influence of the true religion. ¶ For *thine inheritance.* Thy heritage; thy portion as my Son. There is an allusion here to the fact that he had constituted him as his Son, and hence it was proper to speak of him as the heir of all things. See Notes on Heb. i. 4. ¶ *And the uttermost parts of the earth.* The farthest regions of the world. This promise would properly embrace all the world as then known, as it is now known, as it shall be hereafter known. ¶ For *thy possession.* That is, as king. This, on the earth, was be to his possession as the Son of Jehovah, constituted as king. It may be remarked here, (*a*) that this can have its fulfilment only in the Lord Jesus Christ. It was not true of David nor of any other Hebrew monarch that he had conceded to him, in fact, any such possession. Their dominions extended, at any time, but little beyond the bounds of Palestine, and embraced a very limited part of the earth—but a small territory, even as compared with many then existing kingdoms. The phrase here used could

9 Thou shalt break them with [r] a rod of iron; thou shalt dash

r Rev. i 27.

never have been applied to the limited and narrow country of Palestine. (*b*) The promise is to be understood as still in full force. It has never been cancelled or recalled, and though its fulfilment has *seemed* to be long delayed, yet as no *time* was specified, its spirit and meaning have not been disregarded. Events have shown that it was not *intended* that it should be speedily accomplished; and events, when no time is specified, should be allowed to be interpreters of the original meaning of the prophecy. (*c*) The promise will yet be fulfilled. It is evidently supposed in the promise that the Messiah *would* ask for this; and it is solemnly affirmed that if he *did*, this wide inheritance would be granted to him. The world, then, is to be regarded as given by covenant to the Son of God, and in due time he will set up his dominion over the earth, and rule over mankind. The period is coming when the actual sceptre swayed over the nations of the earth will be that of the Son of God, and when his right to give laws and to reign will be acknowledged from the rising to the setting sun. This is the only thing in the future that is certainly known to us, and this is enough to make everything in that future bright.

9. *Thou shalt break them with a rod of iron.* That is, evidently, thine enemies; for it cannot be supposed to be meant that he would sway such a sceptre over his own people. The idea is that he would crush and subdue all his foes. He would have absolute power, and the grant which had been made to him would be accompanied with authority sufficient to hold it. That dominion which was to be conceded to him would be not only one of protection to his friends, but also of punishment on his enemies; and the statement here is made prominent because the former part of the psalm had respect to rebels, and the Messiah is here represented as being invested with power sufficient to punish and restrain them. The Vulgate renders this "thou shalt rule;" the Septuagint, "thou shalt feed"—ποιμανεῖς; that is, thou shalt feed them as a shepherd does his flock; thou shalt exercise over them the care and protection of a shepherd. This rendering occurs by a slight change in the *pointing* of the Hebrew word, though the most approved mode of pointing the word is that which is followed in our common translation. De Wette, Hengstenberg, Alexander, Horsley, adopt the common reading. What is said in this verse has been urged as an objection to referring it to the Messiah. The remark of De Wette on this matter has been quoted in the introduction to this psalm, § 4 (3). But it may be observed, while it is everywhere represented that the sceptre of the Messiah over the earth will be a mild sceptre, it is also everywhere stated that he will ultimately crush and overthrow all his foes. Thus in Isa. xi. 4: "He shall smite the earth with the rod of his mouth, and with the breath of his lips shall he slay the wicked." So Ps. cx. 6: "He shall judge among the heathen; he shall fill the places with the dead bodies." So, likewise, Rev. xix. 15: "And out of his mouth goeth a sharp sword, that with it he should smite the nations; and he shall rule them with a rod of iron; and he treadeth the winepress of the fierceness and wrath of Almighty God." So also in Matt. xxv., and elsewhere, it is said that he will come to judgment, and will consign all his foes to appropriate punishment. While it is said that the reign of the Messiah would be a mild reign, and that his kingdom would not be of this world, and while he is represented as the Prince of peace, it is also said that he would be invested with all the authority of a sovereign. While he would have power to protect his friends, he would also have power to humble and

them in pieces like a potter's vessel.

10 Be wise now therefore, O ye kings: be instructed, ye judges of the earth.

crush his foes. The expression *with a rod of iron* refers to the sceptre which he would bear. A sceptre was sometimes made of wood, sometimes of gold, sometimes of ivory, and sometimes of iron. The idea, when the last was the case, was, that the dominion was absolute, and that there was nothing that could resist it. Perhaps the idea of justice or severity would be that which would be most naturally suggested by this. As applicable to the Messiah, it can only mean that his enemies would be crushed and subdued before him. ¶ *Thou shalt dash them in pieces.* The same idea is here expressed in another form, but indicating more particularly the ease with which it would be done. The word rendered "dash them in pieces" means to break in pieces as an earthen vessel, Judges vii. 20; Jer. xxii. 28. It is used to denote the crushing of infants on stones, Ps. cxxxvii. 9. The word *shiver* would well express the idea here—"thou shalt *shiver* them." ¶ *Like a potter's vessel.* A vessel or instrument made by a potter; a vessel made of clay. This is easily broken, and especially with a rod of iron, and the idea here is that he would crush and subdue his enemies as *easily* as this could be done. No image could more happily express the ease with which he would subdue his foes; and this accords with all the representations of the New Testament—that with infinite ease—with a *word*—Christ can subdue his enemies, and consign them to ruin. Comp. Matt. xxv. 41, 46; Luke xix. 27. The sense here is, simply, that the Messiah would be absolute; that he would have power to quell all rebellion against God, and to punish all those that rise up against him; and that on those who are incorrigibly rebellious he would exercise that power, and take effectual means to subdue them. This is merely what is done by all just governments, and is by no means inconsistent with the idea that such a government would be mild and gentle towards those who are obedient. The protection of the righteous makes the punishment of the wicked necessary in all governments, and the one cannot be secured without the other. This verse is applied to the Messiah in the Book of Revelation, ch. ii. 27; xix. 15; comp. xii. 5. See Notes on these passages.

10. *Be wise now, therefore, O ye kings.* This is to be understood as the language of the psalmist. See introduction to the psalm, § 3. It is an exhortation addressed to the rulers and princes whom the psalmist saw engaged in opposition to the purpose of Jehovah (vers. 1—3)—and hence to all rulers and princes—to act the part of wisdom, by not attempting to resist the plans of God, but to submit to him, and secure his friendship. The psalmist cautions them to take warning, in view of what must certainly come upon the enemies of the Messiah; to cease their vain attempts to oppose his reign, and, by a timely submission to him, to ensure his friendship, and to escape the doom that must come upon his foes. The way of wisdom, then, was not to engage in an attempt in which they must certainly be crushed, but to secure at once the friendship of one appointed by God to reign over the earth. ¶ *Be instructed.* In your duty to Jehovah and his Anointed One; that is, in the duty of submitting to this arrangement, and lending your influence to promote it. The word here used, and rendered *be instructed*, means properly to chastise, chasten, correct; and it here means, be admonished, exhorted, or warned. Comp. Prov. ix. 7; Job iv. 3; Ps. xvi. 7. ¶ *Ye judges of the earth.* Ye who administer justice; that is, ye rulers. This was formerly done by kings themselves, as it is now *supposed* to be in monarchical

11 Serve the LORD with fear,
[s] and rejoice with trembling.
12 [t] Kiss the Son, lest he be
angry, and ye perish *from* the
way, when his wrath is kindled

s Heb. xii. 28. t John v. 23.

governments, where the judges act in the name of the king. In Republics, justice is supposed to be administered by the people through those whom *they* have appointed to execute it. The word here is equivalent to rulers, and the call is on those who occupy posts of office and honour not to oppose the purposes of Jehovah, but to bring their influence to the promotion of his designs. At the same time, it cannot be doubted that it is implied that they should seek to be interested personally in his reign.

11. *Serve the* LORD *with fear.* With reverence, and with deep apprehensions of the *consequences* of *not* serving and obeying him. That is, serve him in not opposing, but in promoting his purpose of establishing a kingdom under the Messiah, with the deep apprehension that if you do not do it, he will arise and crush you in his wrath. ¶ *And rejoice.* Prof. Alexander renders this *shout*, and supposes that it refers to the customary recognition of a present sovereign. The word used—גִּיל, *gil*—means properly to move in a circle, to revolve; and then to dance in a circle, to exult, to rejoice. Then, according to Gesenius, it means to tremble, to fear, from the leaping or palpitation of the heart (Job xxxvii. 1; Hos. x. 5; Ps. xxix. 6). Gesenius renders it here "fear with trembling." The common translation, however, better expresses the sense. It means that they should welcome the purposes of Jehovah, and exult in his reign, but that it should be done with a suitable apprehension of his majesty and power, and with the reverence which becomes the public acknowledgment of God. ¶ *With trembling.* With reverence and awe, feeling that he has almighty power, and that the consequences of being found opposed to him must be overwhelming and awful. The *duty* here enjoined on kings and rulers is that of welcoming the purposes of God, and of bringing their influence—derived from the station which they occupy—to bear in promoting the reign of truth upon the earth—a duty binding on kings and princes as well as on other men. The *feelings* with which this is to be done are those which belong to transactions in which the honour and the reign of God are concerned. They are *mingled* feelings, derived from the mercy of God on the one hand, and from his wrath on the other; from the *hope* which his promise and purpose inspires, and from the *apprehension* derived from his warnings and threatenings.

12. *Kiss the Son.* Him whom God hath declared to be his Son (ver. 7), and whom, as such, he has resolved to set as King on his holy hill (ver. 6). The word *kiss* here is used in accordance with Oriental usages, for it was in this way that respect was indicated for one of superior rank. This was the ancient mode of doing homage or allegiance to a king, 1 Sam. x. 1. It was also the mode of rendering homage to an idol, 1 Kings xix. 18; Hos. xiii. 2; Job xxxi. 27. The *mode* of rendering homage to a king by a kiss was sometimes to kiss his hand, or his dress, or his feet, as among the Persians. *De Wette.* The practice of kissing the hand of a monarch is not uncommon in European courts as a token of allegiance. The meaning here is that they should express their allegiance to the Son of God, or recognise him as the authorized King, with suitable expressions of submission and allegiance; that they should receive him as King, and submit to his reign. Applied to others, it means that they should embrace him as their Saviour. ¶ *Lest he be angry.* If you do not acknowledge his claims, and receive him as the Messiah. ¶ *And ye perish* from *the way.* The word *from* in this place is supplied by the translators. It is literally, "And ye perish the way." See Notes on

but a little. Blessed [u] *are* all they that put their trust in him.

u Psa. lxxxiv. 12.

Ps. i. 6. The meaning here seems to be either "lest ye are lost in respect to the way," that is, the way to happiness and salvation; or "lest ye fail to find the way" to life; or "lest ye perish *by* the way," to wit, before you reach your destination, and accomplish the object you have in view. The design seems to be to represent them as pursuing a certain journey or path—as life is often represented (comp. Ps. i. 1)—and as being cut down before they reached the end of their journey. ¶ *When his wrath is kindled.* When his wrath *burns.* Applying to anger or wrath a term which is common now, as when we speak of one whose anger is *heated,* or who is *hot* with wrath. ¶ *But a little.* Prof. Alexander renders this, "For his wrath will *soon* burn." This, it seems to me, is in accordance with the original; the word "little" probably referring to *time,* and not to the intensity of his anger. This accords better also with the connection, for the design is not to state that there will be *degrees* in the manifestation of his anger, but that his anger would not long be delayed. In due time he would execute judgment on his enemies; and whenever his anger began to burn, his enemies must perish. ¶ *Blessed* are *all they that put their trust in him.* Kings, princes, people;—*all,* of every age and every land; the poor, the rich, the bond, the free; white, black, copper-coloured, or mixed; *all* in sickness or health, in prosperity or adversity, in life or in death; *all,* of every condition, and in all conceivable circumstances,—are blessed who put their trust in him. All need him as a Saviour; all will find him to be a Saviour adapted to their wants. All who do this are happy (comp. Notes on Ps. i. 1); all are safe in time and in eternity. This great truth is stated everywhere in the Bible; and to induce the children of men—weak, and guilty, and helpless—to put their trust in the Son of God, is the great design of all the communications which God has made to mankind.

PSALM III.

§ 1. *The author.*—This psalm purports in the *title* to be "A Psalm of David," and is the *first* one to which a title indicating authorship, or the occasion on which a psalm was composed, is prefixed. The title is found in the Chaldee Paraphrase, the Latin Vulgate, the Septuagint, the Syriac, the Arabic, and the Ethiopic versions. It is not, indeed, certain by whom the title was prefixed, but there is no reason to doubt its correctness. The sentiments in the psalm accord with the circumstances in which David was more than once placed, and are such as we may suppose he would *express* in those circumstances.

§ 2. *The occasion on which the psalm was composed.*—The psalm, according to the title, purports to have been written by David, "when he fled from Absalom his son." That is, it was composed at the time when he fled from Absalom—or in view of that event, and as expressive of his feelings on that occasion, though it might have been penned afterwards. Neither of these suppositions has any intrinsic improbability in it; for though at the time when he fled there was, of course, much tumult, agitation, and anxiety, yet there is no improbability in supposing that these thoughts passed through his mind, and that while these events were going forward, during some moments taken for rest, or in the night-watches, he may have given vent to these deep feelings in this poetic form. Kimchi says that it was the opinion of the ancient Rabbins that the psalm was actually composed when David with naked feet, and with his head covered, ascended the Mount of Olives, as he fled from Jerusalem, 2 Sam. xv. 30. It is not necessary, however, to suppose that in these circumstances he would actually give himself to the task of a poetic composition; yet nothing is more probable than that such thoughts passed through his mind, and nothing would be more natural than that he should seize the first moment of peace and calmness—when the agitation of the scene should be in some measure over—to embody these thoughts in verse. Indeed, there is evidence in the psalm itself that it was actually penned on some such occasion. There is (vers. 1, 2) an allusion to the great number of his foes, and to those who had risen up against him, and an expression of his agitation and anxiety in view of that; and there is then a statement that he had, in these circumstances, cried unto the Lord, and that God had heard him out of his holy hill, and that, notwithstanding these alarms, he had been permitted to lie down and sleep, for the Lord had sustained him (vers. 4, 5). In these circumstances—after preservation and peace during what he had apprehended would be a dreadful night—what was more proper, or more natural, than the composition of such a psalm as the one before us?

If the psalm was composed by David, it *was* most probably at the time supposed in the title—the time when he fled from Absalom his son. There is no other period of his life to which it could be regarded as fitted, unless it were the time of Saul, and the persecutions which *he* waged against him. Hitzig indeed supposes that the latter was the occasion on which it was written; but to this it may be replied—(*a*) That there is no direct evidence of this. (*b*) That the title should be regarded as good evidence, unless it can be set aside by some clear proofs. (*c*) That the contents of the psalm are no more applicable to the time of Saul than to the time of Absalom. (*d*) That in the time of the persecutions of Saul, David had not been in such circumstances as are implied in ver. 4, "he heard me *out of his holy hill.*" This, according to the fair construction of the language, must be understood as referring to Mount Zion (comp. Notes, Ps. ii. 6), and implies that David at the time referred to was the established king, and had made that the seat of his authority. This had not occurred in the time of Saul; and there can be no reason for supposing, as Hitzig does, that Mount Horeb is intended.

The flight of David, which is supposed to be referred to here, is described in 2 Sam. xv—xviii. Absalom rebelled against his father; gathered together a great number of the disaffected in the kingdom; and under pretence of performing a vow which he had made, obtained permission to go to Hebron, having given instructions to his followers to meet him, and having made arrangements to be proclaimed king there. So artful had he been, so numerous were his followers, so extensive seemed to be the defection, and so little prepared was David to meet it, that the only prospect of safety seemed to be in flight. With a few attendants David left Jerusalem, and passed over the Mount of Olives, designing to seek a place of refuge. This was to him *the great trial* of his life; for there *is* no greater trial than the ingratitude of a son when he seeks the life of his father. All the circumstances of this case are such that we should suppose that David *would* cry to God in some such language as is found in this psalm.

It is indeed objected by Horsley that there is "nothing in the psalm that had any particular reference to this event," and hence he supposes that the title should be, "Prayer of a Believer for Deliverance from the Atheistical Conspiracy." But there is nothing in the original title that corresponds with this; and there is no need for departing from the common supposition. It is true that there is in the psalm no *express* mention of Absalom; but the same remark may be made of nearly all the psalms. A considerable portion of David's psalms were doubtless composed in view of the circumstances in which the writer was placed, and were designed to be expressive of his own feelings on the occasion, but they were also designed for the Church at large, and were intended to be used in the Church in all times to come, and hence a general form is given to the sentiments, and the local allusion is barely referred to, or omitted altogether. It is, perhaps, also an indication of the nature of true devotion, that it will turn away from, or forget, for the time, the personal and local circumstances of distress, and give utterance to sentiments of piety that will express the feelings of the children of God in all ages and in all circumstances. The psalm thus becomes one of general use; and the language is such as is adapted to the use of the Church in all generations.

It is also objected by De Wette that the psalm is devoid of all the tender feelings which we should suppose the heart of a father would pour out on such an occasion. But to this it may be replied, that this was not the occasion to pour out such feelings. The thoughts are fixed on his own danger; on the number of his enemies; on the suddenness of the peril; on the great ingrati-

PSALM III.

A Psalm of David, when he fled *v* from Absalom his son.

LORD, how are they increased that trouble me? many *are* they that rise up against me.

2 Many *there be* which say of

v 2 Sam. xv., xviii.

tude and crime of those who had risen up against him. It is a time to look to God for help; not a time to express affection for an ungrateful and rebellious son. When this son died—when he was put to death in violation of the commands and entreaties of himself as a king and a father (2 Sam. xviii. 5, 12, 14)—he poured forth *all* his heart in language such as had never been used before, and has never been equalled since, 2 Sam. xviii. 33.

§ 3. *Analysis of the psalm.*—The psalm is naturally and regularly divided into four strophes or parts, each one embracing two verses; and in three of them closed by the word *Selah*, indicating a pause either in the sense, in the melody, or in both. See Notes on ver 2.

I. The first is expressive of the anxiety of the psalmist from the fact that many enemies had risen up against him, vers. 1, 2.

II. The second expresses his confidence in God in the midst of his troubles, vers. 3, 4. He was his shield and his helper, and he heard his prayer out of his holy hill.

III. The third refers to the fact that in his troubles he had, contrary to what there had been reason to apprehend, been permitted to lie down calmly and to sleep, and to arise again in the morning. In view of this, refreshed and invigorated by rest, and having this new proof of the Divine favour and protection, he says that he would not be afraid though ten thousands of people should set themselves against him round about, vers. 5, 6.

IV. In the fourth part, the psalmist calls upon God to arise and save him; for in other times he had smitten his enemies upon their cheek bone, and had broken the teeth of the ungodly, and salvation belonged only unto him, vers. 7, 8.

¶ *A Psalm of David.* Literally, belonging to David; that is, belonging to him as the author. This is marked in the Hebrew as the first verse, and so in the Syriac version, the Latin Vulgate, and the Septuagint, making in the Hebrew, and in each of these versions, nine verses in the psalm instead of eight, as in our translation. This *may* have been prefixed to the psalm by the author himself, for it was not uncommon in ancient times for an author to prefix his name to his own composition, as is commonly done by the apostle Paul in his epistles. It is not absolutely certain, however, that this was done in the Psalms by the authors themselves, but it may have been done by him who collected and arranged the Psalms, indicating the prevalent belief in regard to the authorship, and under the Spirit of inspiration. ¶ *When he fled.* On the occasion of his fleeing. That is, it was composed at that time, or was subsequently composed in remembrance of it. See Introd., § 2. ¶ *From Absalom his son.* See Introd., § 2.

1. LORD, *how are they increased.* How are they multiplied; or, how numerous they are. Perhaps the idea is, that at first they seemed to be comparatively few in number, but had now so multiplied as to endanger his crown and life. This is an appropriate expression on the supposition that it refers to Absalom. At first the number of those who adhered to Absalom was not so great as to excite much alarm; but by the arts of a demagogue, by complaining of the government, by saying that if *he* were made a judge in the land, every man would have justice done him (2 Sam. xv. 4, 5), he won the hearts of the people, and gathered so many under his standard as to make it necessary that the king should flee from Jerusalem to a place of safety. ¶ *That trouble me.* Literally, *my enemies.* The allusion is to those who were now enlisted under Absalom, and who were engaged in endeavouring to overthrow the govern-

my soul, *There* [w] *is* no help for him in God. Selah.

w Psa. lxxi. 11.

ment. ¶ *Many are they that rise up against me.* That is, that have become my enemies.

2. *Many there be which say of my soul.* Or rather, perhaps, of his "*life,*" for so the word here used—נַפְשׁ, *nephesh*—frequently means (Lev. xvii. 11; Deut. xii. 23; Gen. ix. 4; xxxv. 18; 1 Kings xvii. 21). The object of their persecution, as here stated, was not his *soul,* as such, in the sense in which we now understand the word, but his *life;* and they now said that they were secure of that, and that all things indicated that God would not now interfere to save him. They were perfectly sure of their prey. Compare 2 Sam. xvii. 1—4. ¶ There is *no help for him in God.* He is entirely forsaken. He has no power of defending himself, and no hope of escaping from us now, and all the indications are, that God does not intend to interpose and deliver him. Circumstances, in the rebellion of Absalom (2 Sam. xvi. seq.), were such as to seem to justify this taunt. David had been driven away from his throne and his capital. God had not protected him when he had his armed men and his friends around him, and when he was entrenched in a strong city; and now he was a forsaken fugitive, fleeing almost alone, and seeking a place of safety. If God had not defended him on his throne and in his capital; if he had suffered him to be driven away without interposing to save him, much less was there reason to suppose that he would now interpose in his behalf; and hence they exultingly said that there was no hope for his life, even in that God in whom he had trusted. It is no uncommon thing in this world for good men to be in similar circumstances of trial, when they *seem* to be so utterly forsaken by God as well as men, that their foes exultingly say they are entirely abandoned. ¶ *Selah.* סֶלָה. Much has been written on this word, and still its meaning does not appear to be wholly determined. It is rendered in the Targum, or Chaldee Paraphrase, לְעָלְמִין, *lealmin, for ever,* or *to eternity.* In the Latin Vulgate it is omitted, as if it were no part of the text. In the Septuagint it is rendered Διάψαλμα, supposed to refer to some variation or modulation of the voice in singing. Schleusner, *Lex.* The word occurs seventy-one times in the Psalms, and three times in the book of Habakkuk, iii. 3, 9, 13. It is never translated in our version, but in all these places the original word *Selah* is retained. It occurs only in poetry, and is supposed to have had some reference to the singing or cantillation of the poetry, and to be probably a musical term. In general, also, it indicates a pause in the sense, as well as in the musical performance. Gesenius (*Lex.*) supposes that the most probable meaning of this musical term or note is *silence,* or *pause,* and that its use was, in chanting the words of the psalm, to direct the singer *to be silent, to pause a little,* while the instruments played an interlude or harmony. Perhaps this is all that can now be known of the meaning of the word, and this is enough to satisfy every reasonable inquiry. It is probable, if this was the use of the term, that it would commonly correspond with the sense of the passage, and be inserted where the sense made a pause suitable; and this will doubtless be found usually to be the fact. But any one acquainted at all with the character of musical notation will perceive at once that we are not to suppose that this would be invariably or necessarily the fact, for the musical pauses by no means always correspond with pauses in the sense. This word, therefore, can furnish very little assistance in determining the meaning of the passages where it is found. Ewald supposes, differing from this view, that it rather indicates that in the places where it occurs the voice is

3 But thou, O LORD, *art* a shield [1]for me; my glory, and the lifter up of mine head.

4 I cried unto the LORD with

[1] Or, *about*.

to be raised, and that it is synonymous with *up, higher, loud*, or *distinct*, from סַל, *sal*, סָלַל, *salal, to ascend.* Those who are disposed to inquire further respecting its meaning, and the uses of musical pauses in general, may be referred to Ugolin., 'Thesau. Antiq. Sacr.,' tom. xxii.

3. *But thou, O* LORD, art *a shield for me.* Not only in these dangers, but in all dangers. The declaration here has a general form, as if he could trust in him at all times. It shows what his feelings were on the occasion here referred to, when dangers stood thick around him, and what his feelings habitually were in times of peril. The shield was a well-known part of ancient armour, of use, according to the ancient modes of warfare, when swords, and spears, and arrows were employed, but of use only then, since they would constitute no defence against a musket or cannonball. They were usually made of tough and thick hides, fastened to a rim, and so attached to the left arm that they could be readily thrown before the body when attacked, or so that, as they were usually held, the vital parts of the body would be protected. See Notes on Eph. vi. 14—16. From this use of the shield it was natural to speak of God as the *shield*, or the *Protector* of his people—an appellation which is often given to him in the Scriptures (Gen. xv. 1; Deut. xxxiii. 29; 2 Sam. xxii. 3; Ps. xxviii. 7; cxix. 114; cxliv. 2; xxxiii. 20; lxxxiv. 11; Prov. xxx. 5. ¶ *My glory.* My honour, or the source of my honour. That is, he bestows upon me all the honour that I have, and it is my glory that I may put my trust in him. I regard it as an honour to be permitted, in times of danger and trouble, to rely on him—a sentiment in which every true child of God will unite. ¶ *And the lifter up of my head.* The head, in time of trouble and sorrow, is naturally bowed down, as if overpowered with the weight of affliction. See Ps. xxxv. 14: "I bowed down heavily as one that mourneth for his mother;" Ps. xxxviii. 6: "I am bowed down greatly; I go mourning all the day." Comp. Ps. xlii. 5; xliv. 25; lvii. 6; John xix. 30. To lift up the head, therefore, or to raise one up, is to relieve his distresses, or to take away his troubles. Such a helper, David says, he had always found God to be, and he looks to him as one who is able to help him still. That is, he feels that God can so entirely take away his present griefs as to reinstate him in his former happy and honourable condition.

4. *I cried unto the* LORD. That is, in these troubles, as he had always done in affliction. The form of the verb here is *future*—"I will cry" or call unto the Lord; probably, however, designed to state a general habit with him, that when troubles came he always called on the Lord. He speaks now of himself as if in the midst of the trouble; gives utterance to the feeling which he has always had in his sorrows; and says, "I *will* call upon the Lord," thus declaring his purpose to make his appeal confidently to him. Thus, the language is not so much retrospective as it is indicative of the uniform state of his mind in the midst of afflictions. ¶ *With my voice.* Not merely mentally, but he gave utterance to the deep anguish of his soul in words. So the Saviour did in the garden of Gethsemane (Matt. xxvi. 39); and so, perhaps, most persons do in deep affliction. It is natural then to *cry out* for help; and besides the fact that we may hope that *any* prayer then, though mental only, would bring relief by being answered, there is a measure of relief found by the very act of giving *utterance* or *vent* to the deep and, as it were, pent-up feelings of the soul. In calmer times we are satisfied with unuttered aspirations, with gentle

my voice, and he heard me out of his holy hill. Selah.

5 I laid me down and slept; [x]I awaked: for the LORD sustained me.

x Psa. cxxvii. 2.

ejaculations, with sweet mental communion with God; in overwhelming trials we give utterance to our feelings in the earnest *language* of pleading. ¶ *And he heard me.* Or, "then he hears me;" that is, when I call. The psalmist refers to what he had constantly found to be true, that God was a hearer of prayer. ¶ *Out of his holy hill.* Zion. See Notes on Ps. ii. 6. That was the place to which David had removed the ark, and which was regarded, therefore, as the peculiar dwelling-place of the Most High. To him, as dwelling in Zion, prayer was accustomed to be offered, and there he was accustomed to answer prayer. To this fact David here refers as one that had been illustrated in his former days. To that God who *had* thus answered him he felt that he might confidently appeal now. ¶ *Selah.* Indicating another strophe or musical pause. See Notes on ver. 2.

5. *I laid me down and slept.* Notwithstanding these troubles and dangers I had such confidence that God hears prayer, and such calm trust in his protection, that I laid me down gently and slept securely. The psalmist mentions this as a remarkable proof of the Divine protection and favour. He was driven from his capital, his throne, and his home. He was compelled to wander as a poor fugitive, accompanied by only a few friends. He was pursued by enemies, who were numbered by thousands. He was made an exile, and persecuted by his own son; and with this son there were men of age and of experience in war. The forces of his enemies might come upon him at any moment. In these circumstances, persecuted as he was, and under all the anxiety and distress which he felt in view of the ungrateful conduct of his own son, he regarded it as a singular proof of the Divine favour, and as an illustration of the peace which confidence in God gives to those who put their trust in him, that on such a dreadful night he was permitted to lie calmly down and sleep. As such a proof and illustration it may be regarded here:—a proof of the unspeakable value of the Divine favour, and an illustration of the effect of confidence in God in giving calmness and peace of mind in time of trouble. Ps. cxxvii. 2. ¶ *I awaked.* Still safe and secure. He had not been suddenly attacked by his foes, and made to sleep the sleep of death; he had not been crushed by anguish of spirit. That we are "awaked" in the morning after a night's refreshing slumber; that we are raised up again to the enjoyments of life; that we are permitted again to greet our friends and to unite with them in the privileges of devotion, should always be regarded as a new proof of the goodness of God, and should lead to acts of praise. We have no power to awake ourselves; and when we remember how many are taken away from our world each night—how many there are who lie down to sleep to wake no more, we should never rise from a bed of repose without giving our first thoughts in gratitude to our Great Preserver. ¶ *For the* LORD *sustained me.* He kept me from danger; he preserved me from death. And it is as true now as it was then, that God is the supporter of life when men sleep. He guards us; he causes the action of the heart to be continued as it propels the blood through our frame; he secures the gentle heaving of the lungs, both when we slumber and when we wake.

6. *I will not be afraid.* As the result of this new proof of the Divine protection, and in view of all that God has done and has promised, the psalmist now says that he would not be afraid though any number of foes should rise up against him. *Perhaps* this confiding and exulting spirit may be regarded

6 I [y] will not be afraid of ten thousands of people, that have set *themselves* against me round about.

7 Arise, O LORD; save me, O my God; for thou hast smitten all mine enemies *upon* the cheek-

y Psa. xxvii. 1, etc.

in some measure as the *result* of the calm and refreshing slumber which he had enjoyed. The mind as well as the body had been refreshed and invigorated. With the bright light of a new morning he looked with more cheerful views and hopes on the things around him, and felt new strength to meet the dangers to which he was exposed. Who in trouble and sorrow has not felt this? Who has not experienced the influence of the slumbers of a night and of the light of the morning, in giving new vigour and inspiring new hopes, as if the returning day was an emblem of brighter scenes in life, and the passing away of the shades of night a token that all trouble and sorrow would flee away? ¶ *Of ten thousands of people.* Myriads:—Though myriads are arrayed against me. He does not, of course, pretend to any exactness here; but he felt that the number of his enemies was very great. This *was* the case in the rebellion of Absalom. Ahithophel proposed to Absalom to "*choose out* twelve thousand men" with whom he might pursue after David, implying that the number with him was actually much greater than that, (2 Sam. xvii. 1.) ¶ *That have set* themselves *against me.* That have arrayed themselves against me; or that have risen up in rebellion against me. ¶ *Round about.* Intending to hem me in on every side. Of course this was to be apprehended in such a rebellion; yet David says that he could now look with calmness on all this, for he had confidence in God. Comp. Ps. lvi. 3.

7. *Arise, O* LORD. This is a common mode of calling upon God in the Scriptures, as if he had been sitting still, or had been inactive. It is, of course, language taken from human conceptions, for in the intervals of active effort, in labour or in battle, we sit or lie down, and when we engage in toil we arise from our sitting or recumbent posture. So the mind accustoms itself to think of God. The idea is simply that David now calls upon God to interpose in his behalf and to deliver him. ¶ *Save me, O my God.* He was still surrounded by numerous enemies, and he, therefore, calls earnestly upon God to help him. In accordance with a common usage in the Scriptures, and with what is right for all the people of God, he calls him *his* God:—"O *my* God." That is, he was the God whom he recognised as his God in distinction from all idols, and who had manifested himself as his God by the many mercies which he had conferred on him. ¶ *For thou hast smitten all mine enemies.* That is, in former exigencies, or on former occasions. In his conflicts with Saul, with the Philistines, and with the surrounding nations, he had done this; and as the result of all he had established him on the throne, and placed him over the realm. In the remembrance of all this he appeals with the full confidence that what God had done for him before He would do now, and that, notwithstanding he was surrounded with numerous foes, He would again interpose. So we may derive comfort and assurance in present trouble or danger from the recollection of what God has done for us in former times. He who has saved us in former perils can still save us; we may believe that he who did not forsake us in those perils will not leave us now. ¶ Upon *the cheek-bone.* This language seems to be taken from a comparison of his enemies with wild beasts; and the idea is, that God had disarmed them as one would a lion or tiger by breaking out his teeth. The cheek-bone denotes the bone in which the teeth are placed; and to smite that, is to disarm the animal. The

bone; thou hast broken the teeth of the ungodly.

8 Salvation [z] *belongeth* unto the Lord: thy blessing [a] *is* upon thy people. Selah.

z Isa. xliii. 11. a Psa. cxv. 13.

idea here is not that of *insult*, therefore; but the meaning is simply that he had deprived them of the power of doing him wrong. ¶ *Thou hast broken the teeth of the ungodly.* The same idea is here expressed under another form, *as if* the teeth of wild animals were broken out, rendering them harmless. As God had thus disarmed his enemies in times past, the psalmist hoped that he would do the same thing now, and he confidently called on him to do it.

8. *Salvation* belongeth *unto the* LORD. That is, it appertains to God alone to save. The psalmist had no expectation of saving himself; he had no confidence in the unaided prowess of his own arm. If he was to be saved he felt that it was to be only by God, and the praise of this was to be given to Him. The particular reference here is to temporal deliverance, or deliverance from the dangers which surrounded him then; but the declaration is as true of spiritual deliverance—of the salvation of the soul—as it is of deliverance from temporal danger. In both cases it is true that God only saves, and that all the praise is due to him. ¶ *Thy blessing* is *upon thy people.* Or perhaps, rather, "thy blessing be upon thy people," regarding this as a *prayer* rather than an *affirmation.* It is true, indeed, as an affirmation (comp. Ps. ii. 12); but it accords better with the connection here, and is a more appropriate conclusion of the psalm to regard it as a petition, expressing an earnest desire that the blessing of God might ever rest upon his own people. Then the thoughts of the psalmist are turned away from his own perils to the condition of others; from his individual case to that of the Church at large; and he prays that all others may find the same favours from God which he had so richly enjoyed, and which he hoped still to enjoy. It is one of the characteristics of true piety thus to turn from our own condition to that of others, and to desire that what we enjoy may be partaken of by the people of God everywhere.

PSALM IV.

§ 1. *The title of the psalm.*—The title of this psalm is "To the chief Musician on Neginoth. A psalm of David." This phrase in the title, "To the chief Musician," occurs at the beginning of fifty-three psalms, and at the close of the hymn in Hab. iii. 19. It is uniformly rendered "to the chief Musician," and means that the psalm was intended for him, or was to be given to him, probably to regulate the manner of performing it. In no one instance does the title imply that he was the author. The word rendered "Chief Musician," מְנַצֵּחַ—*menatzzaiahh*, is derived from נָצַח—*natzahh*, properly meaning *to shine*, but not used in kal. In the Piel form it means to be conspicuous; to be over anything; to be chief; to be superintendent (2 Chron. ii. 2, 18; xxxiv. 12), and then it means to lead in music. The meaning of the form used here, and in the other places where it occurs as a title to a psalm, is "Chief Musician," or precentor; and the idea is, that the psalm is to be performed under his direction; or that the music is to be directed and adapted by him. In the case before us there is a particular designation of the *instrument* that was to be employed in the music; which occurs also in Ps. vi., liv., lv., lxi., lxvii., lxxvi.; where the same instrument is mentioned as here. In Ps. viii., lxxxi., lxxxiv., another instrument is mentioned; and in Ps. xlv., lx., lxxx., another instrument still. It would seem that the author of the psalm frequently adapted his poem to a particular kind of instrument, but left the further arrangement of the music to the precentor himself. The word *Neginoth*, plural of *Neginah*—נְגִינָה—means properly *stringed instruments.* It occurs in the title of the following psalms, iv., vi., liv., lv., lxvii., lxxvi. It means in these cases that the psalm was designed to be sung with the accompaniment of some stringed instrument, or under the direction of the musician, who presided over the department of stringed instruments. It designates nothing as to the *kind* of stringed instruments which were to be employed.

§ 2. *The author of the psalm.*—This psalm, like the preceding, purports to be a psalm of David, and there is no reason to doubt the correctness of this opinion. Indeed, there is some internal probability that, if the former psalm was composed by him, this was also; for as that appears to be a *morning* psalm (Ps. iii. 5), so this seems to be its counterpart, and to be designed to be an *evening* psalm, vers. 4, 8. The general resemblance in the structure, and the reference in the one to the morning, and in the other to the evening, show that the two were designed, probably, to be a kind of *double* psalm, to be used on the same day, the one in the morning, and the other in the evening. If this is so, and if David was the author of the third psalm, then there is the same reason to suppose that he was the author also of this. It may be added there has been a general concurrence of opinion in the belief that the psalm was written by David.

§ 3. *The occasion on which the psalm was composed.*—There is nothing in the psalm, or in the title, to determine this question, and it is now impossible to settle it with certainty. The Jewish interpreters generally, and most Christian expositors, suppose that it was composed on the same occasion as the preceding, in relation to the rebellion of Absalom. But there is nothing in the psalm itself which will certainly determine this, or which would make it improbable that it might have been composed at some other time in the life of David. It should be said, however, that there is nothing in the psalm which is inconsistent with that supposition, especially as the manifest purpose of the psalm is to make the occasion, whatever it was, one on which to utter great thoughts that would be valuable at all times. There is some internal evidence that this psalm was composed in reference to the same circumstances as the preceding, with this difference, that *that* was when the writer was in the midst of his troubles, and when he thought it a great mercy that he had been permitted to enjoy a night of quiet rest (Ps. iii. 5); *this*, when he had obtained deliverance from those troubles, and now felt that he *could* give himself to calm repose without anxiety and fear, ver. 8.

§ 4. *The contents of the psalm.*—The psalm expresses general confidence in God, and a general sense of security. The writer is conscious, indeed, that he has enemies, and that they would "turn" his "glory into shame" if they could; that they are false men who seek his ruin by detractions (ver. 2), but still he has confidence in God that all will be well. Though he has enemies who are seeking to destroy him, yet his mind is so calm that he feels that he can commit himself confidently to God, and lie down and slumber. The general subject, therefore, of the psalm is the fact that confidence in God will make the mind calm in the midst of troubles, and that reliance on his protecting care will enable us to give ourselves at night to undisturbed repose. The following points occur in the psalm on this general subject.

(*a*) The writer calls on God to hear him, and makes it the ground of his petition that he *had* formerly heard him —that he had enlarged him when he was in distress, ver. 1.

(*b*) He addresses directly his enemies, and gives them counsel as to what *they* ought to do, vers. 2—5. He solemnly appeals to them, and asks them how long they would persevere in attempting to turn his glory into shame, ver. 2; he conjures them to remember that all their efforts must be in vain, since the Lord had set apart him that was godly for himself, and would protect him, ver. 3; he exhorts them to stand in awe, and to fear the consequences of the course which they were pursuing, and exhorts them to take proper time to reflect upon it—to think on it in the night, when alone with God, and when away from the excitements of the day, ver. 4; and he entreats them to become themselves true worshippers of God, and to offer to him the sacrifices of righteousness, ver. 5.

(*c*) He contrasts the sources of his own joy and theirs, vers. 6, 7. They were seeking worldly good, and endeavoured to find their happiness in that alone; he desired more than that, and, as the chief source of his joy, asked that God would lift upon him the light of his countenance. He had experienced this, and he says that God "had put gladness into his heart more than in the time that their corn and wine increased." He had more real happiness in the conscious favour of God than the greatest worldly prosperity without that could afford. Religion will, in time of trouble, give more true happiness than all that the world can bestow.

(*d*) As the result of all, and in view

PSALM IV.

To the [1] chief Musician on Neginoth.
A Psalm of David.

HEAR me when I call, O God of my righteousness: thou hast enlarged me *when I was* in distress; [2] have mercy upon me, and hear my prayer.

2 O ye sons of men, how long

[1] Or, *overseer*, Hab. iii. 19.

[2] Or, *be gracious unto.*

of all these mercies and comforts, he says that he will lie calmly down and sleep. Though he had enemies, his mind is composed and calm; though there may be dangers, he can confide in God; and though he may be less prospered in worldly things than others, he has a joy in religion superior to all that the world can give; and that makes the mind calm as the body is committed to rest in the darkness of the night, ver. 8.

1. *Hear me when I call.* When I pray. The word *hear* in such cases is always used in the sense of "listen to," "hear favourably," or "attend to;" hence in the literal sense it is always true that God *hears* all that is said. The meaning is, "hear and answer me," or grant me what I ask. ¶ *O God of my righteousness.* That is, O my righteous God. This is a common mode of expression in Hebrew. Thus, in Ps. ii. 6, "hill of my holiness," meaning "my holy hill;" Ps. iii. 4, "his hill of holiness," meaning "his holy hill." The psalmist here appeals to God as *his* God—the God in whom he trusted; and as a *righteous* God—a God who would do that which was right, and on whom, therefore, he might rely as one who would protect his own people. The appeal to God as a righteous God implies a conviction in the mind of the psalmist of the justice of his cause; and he asks God merely to do *right* in the case. It is not on the ground of his own claim as a righteous man, but it is that, in this particular case, he was wrongfully persecuted; and he asks God to interpose, and to cause justice to be done. This is always a proper ground of appeal to God. A man may be sensible that in a particular case he has justice on his side, though he has a general conviction that he himself is a sinner; and he may pray to God to cause his enemies to do right, or to lead those whose office it is to decide the case, to do what ought to be done to vindicate his name, or to save him from wrong. ¶ *Thou hast enlarged me* when I was *in distress.* That is, on some former occasion. When he was *pressed* or *confined*, and knew not how to escape, God had interposed and had given him room, so that he felt free. He now implores the same mercy again. He feels that the God who had done it in former troubles could do it again; and he asks him to repeat his mercy. The prayer indicates confidence in the power and the unchangeableness of God, and proves that it is right in our prayers to recall the former instances of the Divine interposition, as an argument, or as a ground of hope that God would again interpose. ¶ *Have mercy upon me.* In my present troubles. That is, Pity me, and have compassion on me, as thou hast done in former times. Who that has felt the assurance that God has heard his prayer in former times, and has delivered him from trouble, will not go to him with the more confident assurance that he will hear him again?

2. *O ye sons of men.* Turning from God to men; from Him in whom he hoped for protection to those who were engaged in persecuting him. We are not, of course, to suppose that they were present with him, but this is an earnest, poetic remonstrance, *as if* they were with him. The reference is doubtless to Absalom and his followers; and he calls them "sons of men," as having human feelings, passions, and purposes, in strong distinction from that righteous God to whom he had just made his solemn appeal. God was holy, true, and just, and he might appeal to Him; they

will ye turn my glory into shame;
how long will ye love vanity, *and*
seek after leasing? Selah.
3 But know that the LORD

were ambitious and wicked, and from them he had nothing to hope. He looked upon God as righteous altogether; he looked upon them as altogether depraved and wicked. God he regarded as his just Protector; them he regarded as seeking only to wrong and crush him. ¶ *How long.* The phrase here used might refer either to *time* or to *extent.* How long in regard to *time,*—or to what *degree* or *extent* will you thus persecute me? The former, however, seems to be the true signification. ¶ Will ye turn *my glory into shame.* My honour, or what becomes my rank and station. If this refers to the rebellion in the time of Absalom, the allusion is to the fact that his enemies were endeavouring to rob him of his sceptre and his crown, and to reduce him to the lowest condition of beggary and want; and he asks with earnestness how long they intended to do him so great injustice and wrong. ¶ *Will ye love vanity.* Comp. Notes on Ps. ii. 1. That is, how long will you act as if you were in love with a vain and impracticable thing; a thing which *must* be hopeless in the end. The idea is, that God had chosen him, and anointed him, and had determined that he should be king (ver. 3), and therefore that their efforts *must be* ultimately unsuccessful. The object at which they were aiming could not be accomplished, and he asks how long they would thus engage in what must, from the nature of the case, be fruitless. ¶ And *seek after leasing.* The word *leasing* is the old English word for *lie.* The idea here is, that they were pursuing a course which would yet prove to be a delusion—the hope of overturning his throne. The same question, in other respects, may be asked now. Men are seeking that which cannot be accomplished, and are acting under the influence of a lie. What else are the promises of permanent happiness in the pursuits of pleasure and ambition? What else are their attempts to overthrow religion and virtue in the world? ¶ *Selah.* See Notes on Ps. iii. 2.

3. *But know.* This is addressed to those whom, in the previous verse, he had called the "sons of men;" that is, his foes. This is designed to show them that their opposition to him must be vain, since God had determined to set him apart for his own service, and would therefore hear his prayer for relief and protection. ¶ *That the* LORD *hath set apart.* That Jehovah had done this; that is, that he had designated him to accomplish a certain work, or that he regarded him as an instrument to perform it. He would, therefore, protect him whom he had thus appointed; and their efforts were really directed against Jehovah himself, and must be vain. ¶ *Him that is godly for himself.* For his own purposes, or to accomplish his own designs. The reference is here undoubtedly to the psalmist himself; that is, to David. The word "godly," as applied to himself, is probably used in contrast with his enemies as being engaged in wicked designs, to wit, in rebellion, and in seeking to dispossess him of his lawful throne. The psalmist felt that his cause was a righteous cause, that he had done nothing to deserve this treatment at their hands; and that he had been originally exalted to the throne because God regarded him as a friend of himself and of his cause; and because he knew that he would promote the interests of that cause. The word here rendered "*godly,*" חָסִיד, *hhasid,* is derived from חֶסֶד, *hesed,* which means desire, ardour, zeal; and then kindness, benignity, love toward God or man. Here the word properly denotes one who has love to God, or one who is truly pious; and it is correctly rendered *godly.* Comp. Ps. xxx. 4, 5; xxxi. 23; xxxvii. 28. The idea is, that as God had appointed him for his own great purposes, the real aim of the rebels was to oppose

hath set apart him that is godly for himself: the LORD will hear when I call unto him.

4 Stand in awe, and sin not;

Jehovah; and the purposes in which they were engaged could not, therefore, be successful. ¶ *The* LORD *will hear when I call unto him.* As I am engaged in his service; as I am appointed to accomplish a certain purpose for him, I may confidently believe that he will hear me, and will deliver me out of their hands. Is not this always the true ground of encouragement to pray—that if God has a purpose to accomplish by us he will hear our prayer, and save us from danger, and deliver us out of the hand of our enemies? And should not this be the main design in our prayers—that God *would* thus spare us that we may accomplish the work which he has given us to do?

4. *Stand in awe.* Still addressed to those who in ver. 2 are called "sons of men;" that is, to his enemies. This is rendered by Prof. Alexander, "Rage and sin not." The Chaldee Paraphrase renders it, "Tremble before him, and sin not." The Latin Vulgate, *Irascimini*—"be angry." The LXX. ὀργίζεσθε καὶ μὴ ἁμαρτάνετε, "Be ye angry, and sin not"—a rendering which Paul seems to have had in his eye in Eph. iv. 26, where the same language is found. It is not necessary, however, to suppose that, in this case, or by so quoting this language, Paul meant to give his sanction to the Septuagint translation of the passage. The truth doubtless is, that he found this language in that version, and that he quoted it, not as a correct translation, but as exactly expressing an idea which he wished to convey,—in the same way as he would have quoted an expression from a Greek classic. It was made to convey an inspired sentiment by his use of it; whether it was a fair translation of the original Hebrew was another question. For the meaning of the sentiment, see Notes on Eph. iv. 26. The original word here—רָגַז, *ragaz*,—means to be moved, disturbed, disquieted, thrown into commotion; and as this may be by anger, fear, or grief, so the word comes to be used with reference to any one of these things.—Gesenius, *Lex.* The connection here would seem to require that it should be understood with reference to *fear*—since we cannot suppose that the writer would counsel them to be moved or agitated by wrath or anger, and since there was no ground for exhorting them to be moved by grief. The true idea is, doubtless, that which is conveyed in our translation—that they were to fear; to stand in awe; to reflect on the course which they were pursuing, and on the consequences of that course, and by so doing to cease from their plans, and to sin no further. God had determined to protect him whom they were engaged in persecuting, and, in prosecuting their plans, they must come into conflict with His power, and be overcome. The counsel, therefore, is just such as may properly be given to all men who are engaged in executing plans of evil. ¶ *And sin not.* That is, by continuing to prosecute these plans. Your course is one of rebellion against Jehovah, since he has determined to protect him whom you are endeavouring to drive from his throne, and any further prosecution of your schemes must be regarded as additional guilt. They had indeed sinned by what they had already done; they would only sin the more unless they abandoned their undertaking. ¶ *Commune with your own heart.* Heb., "Speak with your own heart;" that is, consult your own *heart* on the subject, and be guided by the result of such a deliberation. The language is similar to what we often use when we say, "Consult your better judgment," or "Consult your feelings," or "Take counsel of your own good sense;" as if a man were divided against himself, and his passions, his ambition, or his avarice, were contrary to his own better judgment. The word *heart* here is used in the sense in which we

commune with your own heart upon your bed, and be still. Selah.

5 Offer the sacrifices *b* of righteousness; and put your trust in the LORD.

6 *There be* many that say, Who

b Deut. xxxiii. 19.

---

now use it as denoting the seat of the affections, and especially of right affections; and the meaning is, "Do not take counsel of, or be influenced by, your head, your will, your passions, your evil advisers and counsellors; but consult your own better feelings, your generous emotions, your sense of right, and act accordingly." Men would frequently be much more likely to do right if they would consult their *hearts* as to what should be done than they are in following the counsels which actually influence them. The secret, silent teachings of the *heart*—the heart when unbiassed and uninfluenced by bad counsellors —is often our best and safest guide. ¶ *Upon your bed.* Admirable advice to those who are engaged in plans of wickedness. In the silence of night; in solitary musings on our bed; when withdrawn from the world, and from all the promptings of passion and ambition, and when, if at any time, we cannot but feel that the eye of God is upon us, the mind is most likely to be in a proper state to review its plans, and to inquire whether those plans can be expected to meet the Divine approbation. ¶ *And be still.* When you are thus quiet, reflect on your doings. For a most beautiful description of the effect of night and silence in recalling wicked men from their schemes, see Job xxxiii. 14—17. Comp. Notes on that passage. ¶ *Selah.* This, as explained in the Notes on Ps. iii. 2, marks a musical pause. The pause here would well accord with the sense, and would most happily occur after the allusion to the quiet communion on the bed, and the exhortation to be still.

5. *Offer the sacrifices of righteousness.* Offer righteous sacrifices; that is, sacrifices prompted by right motives, and in accordance with the prescriptions in the law of God. This appears to be addressed also to those who in ver. 2 are called "sons of men;" that is, those who were arrayed against the psalmist. According to the common opinion this psalm was composed by David on occasion of his being driven from his throne and kingdom; and, of course, Zion, the ark, and the tabernacle, were in the hands of his enemies. The exhortation here may be, either that, as his enemies were now in possession of the usual seat of public worship, they would conduct the worship of God by keeping up the regular daily sacrifice; or, more probably, it means that in view of their sins, particularly in this rebellion, and as the result of the calm reflection to which he had exhorted them in ver. 4, they should now manifest their repentance, and their purpose to turn to God, by presenting to him an appropriate sacrifice. They were sinners. They were engaged in an unholy cause. He exhorts them to pause, to reflect, to turn to God, and to bring a sacrifice for their sins, that their guilt might be blotted out. ¶ *And put your trust in the* LORD. That is, turn from your evil ways, and confide in God in all his arrangements, and submit to him. Comp. Ps. ii. 12.

6. There be *many that say.* Some have supposed, as De Wette and others, that the allusion of the psalmist here is to his own followers, and that the reference is to their anxious fears in their misfortunes, as if they were poor and forsaken, and knew not from whence the supply of their wants would come. The more probable interpretation, however, is that the allusion is to the general anxiety of mankind, as contrasted with the feelings and desires of the psalmist himself in reference to the manner in which the desire was to be gratified. That is, the general inquiry among mankind is, Who will show us good?

will show us *any* good? LORD, lift thou up the light of thy countenance upon us.

7 Thou hast put gladness in

Or, where shall we obtain that which seems to us to be good, or which will promote our happiness? ¶ *Who will show us* any *good?* The word "*any*" here is improperly supplied by the translators. The question is more emphatic as it is in the original—"Who will show us *good?*" That is, Where shall happiness be found? In what does it consist? How is it to be obtained? What will contribute to it? This is the *general* question asked by mankind. The *answer* to this question, of course, would be very various, and the psalmist evidently intends to place the answer which *he* would give in strong contrast with that which would be given by the mass of men. Some would place it in wealth; some in honour; some in palaces and pleasure grounds; some in gross sensual pleasure; some in literature; and some in refined social enjoyments. In contrast with all such views of the sources of true happiness, the psalmist says that he regards it as consisting in the favour and friendship of God. To him that was enough; and in this respect his views stood in strong contrast with those of the world around him. The *connection* here seems to be this—the psalmist saw those persons who were arrayed against him intent on their own selfish aims, prosecuting their purposes, regardless of the honour of God and the rights of other men; and he is led to make the reflection that this is the *general* character of mankind. They are seeking for happiness; they are actively employed in prosecuting their own selfish ends and purposes. They live simply to know how they shall be *happy*, and they prosecute any scheme which would seem to promise happiness, regardless of the rights of others and the claims of religion. ¶ LORD, *lift thou up the light of thy countenance upon us.* That is, in contrast with the feelings and plans of others. In the pursuit of what *they* regarded as good they were engaged in purposes of gain, of pleasure, or of ambition; he, on the contrary, asked only the favour of God—the light of the Divine countenance. The phrase, "to lift up the light of the countenance" on one, is of frequent occurrence in the Scriptures, and is expressive of favour and friendship. When we are angry or displeased, the face seems covered with a dark cloud; when pleased, it brightens up and expresses benignity. There is undoubtedly allusion in this expression to the sun as it rises free from clouds and tempests, seeming to smile upon the world. The language here was not improbably derived from the benediction which the High Priest was commanded to pronounce when he blessed the people of Israel (Num. vi. 24—26), "The Lord bless thee, and keep thee; the Lord make his face to shine upon thee, and be gracious unto thee; the Lord lift up his countenance upon thee, and give thee peace." It may be added here, that what the psalmist regarded as the *supreme good*—the favour and friendship of God—is expressive of true piety in all ages and at all times. While the world is busy in seeking happiness in other things—in wealth, pleasure, gaiety, ambition, sensual delights—the child of God feels that true happiness is to be found only in religion, and in the service and friendship of the Creator; and, after all the anxious inquiries which men make, and the various experiments tried in succeeding ages, to find the source of true happiness, all who ever find it will be led to seek it where the psalmist said his happiness was found—in the light of the countenance of God.

7. *Thou hast put gladness in my heart.* Thou hast made me happy, to wit, in the manner specified in ver. 6. Many had sought happiness in other things; he had sought it in the favour of the Lord, and the Lord had given him a degree of happiness which they had never found in the most pros-

my heart, more than in the time *that* their corn and their wine increased.

8 I will [c] both lay me down in peace, and sleep: for thou, LORD, only makest me dwell in safety.

c Psa. iii. 5.

perous worldly condition. This happiness had its seat in the "*heart,*" and not in any external circumstances. All true happiness must have its seat there, for if the heart is sad, of what avail are the most prosperous external circumstances? ¶ *More than in the time.* More than they have had in the time referred to; or, more than I should have in such circumstances. ¶ That *their corn and their wine increased.* When they were most successful and prosperous in worldly things. This shows that when, in ver. 6, he says that many inquired who would show them any *good,* what they aspired after was worldly prosperity, here expressed by an increase of corn and wine. The word rendered *corn* means grain in general; the word rendered *wine* — תִּירוֹשׁ —*térosh*—means properly *must, new wine,* Isa. lxv. 8. The reference here is probably to the joy of harvest, when the fruits of the earth were gathered in, an occasion among the Hebrews, as it is among most people, of joy and rejoicing.

8. *I will both lay me down in peace, and sleep.* The word "*both*" here means *at the same time;* that is, I will alike be in peace, and I will lie down and will sleep; I will have a mind at peace (or, in tranquillity) when I lie down, and will sleep calmly. This is said in view of his confidence in God, and of his belief that God would preserve him. He had put his trust in him; he had sought his happiness in him, and now he felt assured that he had nothing to fear, and, at peace with God, he would lie down and compose himself to rest. This is the counterpart of what is said in Ps. iii. 5. There he says in the morning, that, though surrounded by fear, he *had* been permitted to lie calmly down and sleep; here he says, that, though he *is* surrounded by fear, he has such confidence in God, that he *will* give himself to quiet slumber. His mind was free from anxiety as to the result of the present troubles; he had calm confidence in God; he committed all to him; and thus gave himself to rest. No one can fail to admire the beauty of this; and no one can fail to perceive that entire confidence in God, and an assurance that all things are under his control, are best adapted of all things to give peaceful days and nights. ¶ *For thou,* LORD, *only makest me dwell in safety.* There are two ideas here: (*a*) One a confidence that he would abide in safety; (*b*) the other, that he owed this entirely to the Lord. He had no power to defend himself, and yet he felt assured that he would be safe—for he put his trust entirely in the Lord. The whole language implies unwavering trust or confidence in God, and is thus instructive and useful for all. It teaches us (1) that in the midst of troubles we may put our trust in God; and (2) that religion is adapted to make the mind calm in such circumstances, and to enable its possessor to lie down without anxiety in the slumbers of the night, and to pursue without anxiety the duties of the day.

PSALM V.

§ 1. *Author of the psalm.*—This psalm also purports to be a psalm of David, and there is nothing in it to lead us to doubt that this opinion is correct. It is ascribed to him in all the versions, and by all the ancient Hebrew writers, and the contents are such as we might expect from him.

§ 2. *The occasion on which the psalm was composed.*—This is not specified in the title to the psalm, and there is nothing in the psalm itself that can enable us to determine it with certainty. There can be no improbability in supposing that there were some events in the life of David, or that there were some particular circumstances, which suggested the thoughts in the psalm, but all those local and personal allusions are suppressed, as it does not appear to have been the writer's object to disclose private feelings, but to give utterance to sentiments, though perhaps suggested by private and personal considerations, which might be of permanent use to the church at all times.

There is evidence in the psalm itself that the author at the time of its composition was beset by enemies, and that he was in the midst of peril from the designs of violent men, vers. 6, 8, 9, 10. Who those enemies were, however, he does not specify, for the object was to express sentiments that would be of use to all who might be in similar circumstances, by showing what were the true feelings of piety, and what was the real ground of trust for the people of God at such times; and this object would not have been furthered by any specifications in regard to the foes which surrounded him at the time.

Flaminius (see Rosenmüller) supposes that the psalm was composed in the time of Saul, and in reference to the persecutions which David experienced then; but most interpreters have referred it to the time of Absalom's rebellion. Most of the Jewish writers, according to Kimchi (see De Wette), suppose that it had reference to Doeg and Ahithophel; but, as De Wette remarks, since they lived at different times, it cannot be supposed that the psalm had reference to them both. There is no improbability in supposing that the psalm was composed with reference to the same circumstances as the two preceding,—that important event in the life of David when his own son rose up in rebellion against him, and drove him from his throne. In those prolonged and fearful troubles it is by no means improbable that the royal poet would give utterance to his feelings in more than one poetic effusion, or that some new phase of the trouble would suggest some new reflections, and lead him anew to seek consolation in religion, and to express his confidence in God. The psalm has a sufficient resemblance to the two preceding to accord with this supposition, and it can be read with profit with those scenes in view.

§ 3. *Contents of the psalm.*—The psalm, so far as the sentiment is concerned, may be properly regarded as divided into four parts:—

I. An earnest prayer of the author to God to hear him; to attend to his cry, and to deliver him, vers. 1—3. His prayer in the morning he would direct to him, and with the returning light of day he would look up to him. In his troubles his first act would be each day to call upon God.

II. An expression of unwavering confidence in God as the protector and the friend of the righteous, and the enemy of all wickedness, vers. 4—7. God, he was assured, had no pleasure in wickedness; would not suffer evil to dwell in his presence; would abhor all that was false and deceitful, and he might therefore, in all his troubles, put his trust in him. In view of this fact—this characteristic of the Divine nature—he says that he would enter his holy temple, where prayer was accustomed to be made, with confidence, and worship with profound reverence, ver. 7.

III. Prayer to God, in view of all this, for his guidance and protection in his perplexities, vers. 8—10. He felt himself surrounded by dangers; he was in perplexity as to the true way of safety; his enemies were powerful, numerous, and treacherous, and he beseeches God, therefore, to interpose and to deliver him from them—even by cutting them off. He prays that they might fall by their own counsels, and that, as they had rebelled against God, they might be checked and punished as they deserved.

IV. An exhortation, founded on these views, for all to put their trust in God, vers. 11, 12. What he had found to be true, all others would find to be true; and as he in his troubles had seen reason to put *his* trust in God, and had not been disappointed, so he exhorts all others, in similar circumstances, to do the same.

To the chief musician. See Note on the title to Ps. iv. ¶ *Upon Nehiloth.* The title of Psalm iv. is, "upon Neginoth." As that refers to a musical instrument, so it is probable that this does, and that the idea here is that this psalm was intended particularly for the music-master that had special charge of this instrument, or who presided over those that played on it. Perhaps the idea is that this psalm was specially designed to be accompanied with this instrument. The word here, Nehiloth—נְחִילוֹת, sing. נְחִילָה—is supposed by Gesenius, *Lex.*, to denote a flute, or pipe, as being *perforated*, from חָלַל—*hhalal, to bore.* The word occurs only in this place. Very

PSALM V.

To the chief Musician upon Nehiloth.
A Psalm of David.

1 GIVE ear to my words, O LORD; consider my meditation.

2 Hearken unto the voice of my cry, my King, and my God: for unto thee will I pray.

---

various opinions have been entertained of its meaning. See Hengstenberg, *Com.* The Latin Vulgate and the Septuagint understand it as meaning *inheritance*—the same as נַחֲלָה—*nahhalah*, and as being somehow designed to refer to the people of God *as* a heritage. Lat. Vulg. In finem pro ea, quæ hereditatem consequitur, psalmus David. So the Septuagint—ὑπὲρ τῆς κληρονομούσης. So Luther, Für das Erbe. What was the precise idea affixed to this it is not very easy to determine. Luther explains it, "according to the title, this is the general idea of the psalm, that the author prays for the inheritance or heritage of God, desiring that the people of God may be faithful to him, and may always adhere to him." The true interpretation, however, is evidently to regard this as an instrument of music, and to consider the psalm as adapted to be sung with the instrument of music specified. Why it was adapted particularly to *that* instrument of music cannot now be determined. Horsley renders it "upon the flutes." Comp. Ugolin. Thesau. Ant. Sac.; tom. xxxii. pp. 158—170. ¶ *A Psalm of David.* See introd. to Ps. iii.

1. *Give ear to my words,* O LORD. We naturally incline the ear towards any one when we wish to hear distinctly what he says, and we turn away the ear when we do not. The meaning here is, David prayed that God would be attentive to or would regard his prayer. This form of the petition is, that he would attend to his *words*—to what he was about to *express* as his desire. He intended to express only what he wished to be granted. ¶ *Consider my meditation.* Understand; perceive; for so the word rendered *consider* properly means. He desired that he would regard the real import of what is here called his *meditation;* that is, he wished him not merely to attend to his *words,* but to the secret and unexpressed desires of the soul. The idea seems to be that while his words would be sincere and truthful, yet they could not express *all* his meaning. There were desires of the soul which no language could convey—deep, unuttered "groanings" (comp. Rom. viii. 26, 27), which could not be uttered in language. There is a difference, however, in rendering the word translated *meditation.* Most interpreters regard it as derived from הָגָה, *hagah,* to meditate (see Notes on Ps. i. 2),—and as thus denoting *thought,* or *meditation.* Gesenius and some others regard it as derived from הָגַג, *hagag,* obsolete root,—meaning to set on fire, to kindle; and hence, that it means here *heat,* fervour of the mind; and then, fervent cry, or prayer. See *Rosenmüller* also *in loc.* De Wette concurs with Gesenius, and supposes that it should be rendered *sigh* or complaint. Prof. Alexander renders it *thought.* Horsley renders it "my sighing," but says he is in doubt whether it refers to an "internal desire of the mind," in opposition to *words* in the former part of the verse, or to a "prayer uttered *sotto voce,* like the private prayer usually said by every person before he takes his seat in the church"—the "internal motion of the mind towards God." It is not easy to determine the true meaning, but the probability is that it refers to an internal emotion—a fervent, ardent feeling—perhaps finding partial expression in sighs (Rom. viii. 26), but which does not find expression in words, and which words could not convey. He prayed that God would attend to the *whole* desires of the soul—whether expressed or unexpressed.

2. *Hearken unto the voice of my cry.* My cry for assistance. The word *voice* refers to the utterance of his desires, or to his *expressed* wishes in a time of trouble. ¶ *My King, and my God.* Though he was him-

3 My voice shalt thou hear in the morning, O LORD; in the morning will I direct *my prayer* unto thee, and will look up.

---

self a king, yet he acknowledged his subjection to God as his supreme Ruler, and looked up to Him to protect him in his dangers, and to restore him to his rights. He was, at the same time, his God—his covenant God—to whom he felt that he was permitted to come in the hour of trouble, and whose blessing he was permitted to invoke. ¶ *For unto thee will I pray.* He had no one else to go to in his troubles, and he felt that he *might* approach the living God. It was his fixed purpose—his regular habit—to pray to him, and to seek his favour and friendship, and he felt that he was permitted to do so now.

3. *My voice shalt thou hear in the morning,* O LORD. The voice of prayer. Comp. Notes on Ps. iii. 5. Probably he refers here to a general habit of praying in the morning, though he makes a particular reference to his circumstances at that time. Comp. Ps. lv. 17. The psalmist felt, doubtless, that while it was a general duty and privilege to call upon God with the return of each morning, there was a special reason for it in the circumstances in which he then was. See the introduction to the psalm. He was then surrounded by enemies, and was in danger, and it was only in God that he could hope for protection even for a single day. The propriety of looking to God in the morning by prayer commends itself to any reflecting mind. Who knows what a day may bring forth? Who knows what temptations may await him? Who can protect himself from the dangers which may encompass him? Who can enable us to discharge the duties which are incumbent on us every day? Feeble, helpless, sinful, prone to err, in a world of temptation, and surrounded by dangers alike when we see them and when we do not, there is an obvious fitness in looking to God each morning for his guidance and protection; and the resolution of the psalmist here should be the firm purpose of every man. ¶ *In the morning.* Regularly; each morning. ¶ *Will I direct* my prayer *unto thee.* Marg., as in Heb., *set in order.* The word here used—עָרַךְ, *arach*—means properly to place in a row, to put in order, to arrange, *e.g.*, to place wood upon the altar (Gen. xxii. 9; Lev. i. 7); to arrange the showbread on the table (Ex. xl. 23; Lev. xxiv. 6, 8). There is, not improbably, an allusion to these customs in the use of the word here; and the meaning may be, that his prayer would be a regularly arranged service before God. It would be a kind of morning sacrifice, and it would be arranged and performed with a suitable regard to the nature of the service—the fact that it was rendered to the great God. There would be a devout regard to propriety—a serious and solemn attention to the duties involved in the act as the worship of a holy God. Prayer should not be rash; it should not be performed negligently or with a light spirit; it should engage the profound thought of the soul, and it should be performed with the same serious regard to time and to propriety which was demanded in the solemn and carefully prescribed rites of the ancient temple-service. ¶ *And will look up.* The word here used—צָפָה, *tzaphah*—means, properly, to look about, to view from a distance. In Isa. xxi. 5, it refers to a tower which has a wide prospect. Comp. Cant. vii. 4. The idea here is properly that he would watch, narrowly and carefully (as one does who is stationed on a tower), for some token of Divine favour—for some answer to his prayer—for some Divine interposition—for some intimation of the Divine will. This is, perhaps, equivalent to the Saviour's repeated command to "watch and pray." The notion of looking *up* is not necessarily in the word here used, but it indicates the state of mind where there is deep

4 [d]For thou *art* not a God that
hath pleasure in wickedness;
neither shall evil dwell with thee.
5 The foolish shall not stand [1]
in thy sight: thou hatest all
workers of iniquity.
6 Thou shalt destroy them that

d Hab. i. 13. [1] Or, *before thine eyes.*

and careful solicitude as to the answer to prayer.

4. *For thou art not a God that hath pleasure in wickedness.* The psalmist here refers to a well-known and well-understood characteristic of the Divine Being, that he was holy and pure, and that he could not have any pleasure in furthering the designs of wicked men. This is said with reference to his enemies, who were thus wicked; and the idea is that God would not, and could not, consistently with his nature, further their designs. This is the ground of encouragement which he had to pray—that he was conscious that his own aims were right, and that his cause was just, and that God could not favour the cause of the ungodly. This is still, and always will be, a ground of encouragement in prayer. If we know that our cause is right, we may look to God to favour it; if a cause is wrong, we cannot look to him to interpose to advance it. Good men, therefore, pray; wicked men do not. ¶ *Neither shall evil dwell with thee.* The same idea is here expressed in another form. If God should show favour to the wicked, it would seem as if he admitted them to his habitation, as we do our friends and those in whom we delight. But as God would not do this, the psalmist feels that it was proper for him to call upon Him to deliver him from wicked men.

5. *The foolish.* Referring still to his enemies, as having this character, and urging the fact that they *had* such a character as a reason why God should hear him, and deliver him. The word *foolish* here, הוֹלְלִים *holelim,* is used to denote the wicked, under the common idea in the Scriptures that sin is folly. Comp. Ps. xiv. 1. It is rendered by Professor Alexander, *the proud* or *insolent.* The Chaldee renders it *deriders;* Lat. Vulg. *unjust;* Sept. *transgressors;* Gesenius, *Lex., proud.* So De Wette. The common idea, however, is the correct one, referring to the wicked under the idea that they were *fools,* as all sin is supreme folly. ¶ *Shall not stand in thy sight.* Shall not be allowed to be in thy presence; that is, thou wilt not approve their cause, or favour them. See Notes on Ps. i. 5. ¶ *Thou hatest all workers of iniquity.* All that do wrong. He refers here, also, to a general characteristic of God, but still with an implied and immediate reference to his enemies as sustaining this character, and as a reason why he appealed to God to defend his cause. Nothing is more constantly affirmed in the Scriptures than that God hates all forms of evil.

6. *Thou shalt destroy.* Thou wilt bring to ruin; thou wilt cause to perish; that is, cause to perish as the wicked are caused to perish, by being punished. The idea is that God could not approve their cause; could not favour them; could not give them prosperity, and that they must be overthrown and punished. As in the previous verses, so here, David refers to this as a general characteristic of God, but with an implied reference to his enemies. ¶ *Them that speak leasing.* Lies; the word *leasing* being the old Saxon word to denote falsehood. See Ps. iv. 2. It is not found elsewhere in our common version. The allusion here is to his enemies, and the idea is that they were false and treacherous; a description which will well apply to them on the supposition that this refers to the rebellion of Absalom. See the introduction to the psalm. ¶ *The* Lord *will abhor.* Will hate; will hold in abomination. That is, he will show his abhorrence by punishing such as are here referred to. ¶ *The bloody and deceitful man.* The

speak leasing: the LORD will abhor the [1] bloody and deceitful man.

7 But as for me, I will come *into* thy house in the multitude of thy mercy; *and* in thy fear will I worship toward [2] thy holy temple.

[1] *man of bloods and deceit.*

[2] *the temple of thy holiness.*

man of blood and fraud; the man who sheds blood, and is guilty of treachery and fraud. Marg., *man of bloods and deceit.* The "man of *bloods*,"—"the plural form being commonly used where there is reference to blood-guiltiness or murder."—*Prof. Alexander.* See Gen. iv. 10; Ps. li. 14. The idea seems to be that of shedding *much* blood. The reference here, as before, is to a general characteristic of the Divine mind, with a special reference to the character of David's enemies, as being distinguished for fraud and blood-guiltiness. On the supposition (see introduction) that this refers to the rebellion of Absalom, there can be no difficulty in seeing the propriety of the application. It was on these grounds that the psalmist directed his prayer to God. He was confident that his was a righteous cause; he was as sure that his enemies were engaged in a wicked cause; and he felt, therefore, that *he* might go before God and seek his interposition, with the assurance that all his attributes, as a righteous and holy God, would be enlisted in his favour. God has *no* attribute which can take part with a sinner, or on which a sinner can rely; the righteous can appeal to *every* attribute in the Divine nature as a ground of confidence and hope.

7. *But as for me.* While it is their characteristic that they are wicked, and have no desire to serve God; and while with such characteristics they can have no hope of access to God, and no reason to suppose that he will hear their cry, I am inclined to enter his house, and I feel the assurance that he will listen to my prayer. In character and in feelings he was wholly unlike them. ¶ *I will come* into *thy house.* Indicating his expectation and his hope that he would yet be permitted to enter the courts of the Lord, from which he was now driven away (see the introduction to the psalm), and his purpose thus to acknowledge God. The word *house* here refers to the tabernacle, which was regarded as the house or dwelling place of God. The word was applied to the entire structure, embracing all the courts, as being sacred to God, as the word was subsequently to the whole of the temple. It was the Holy of Holies, however, which was regarded as the peculiar dwelling-place of God, and that none were permitted to enter but the high priest, and he but once in the year. (See Notes on Heb. ix. 1–7.) ¶ *In the multitude of thy mercy.* In thine abundant mercy. He expected to be delivered from his present troubles, and he felt assured that God would permit him again to enter his earthly courts, and to offer his vows and thanksgivings there. ¶ And *in thy fear.* In profound reverence for thee. Fear, or reverence, is often employed to denote devotion or worship. ¶ *Will I worship toward thy holy temple.* The worshippers were not permitted to enter the temple, but worshipped *towards* it; that is, looking towards it, or prostrating themselves towards it as the peculiar dwelling-place of God. If they were in the courts around the temple, they worshipped with their faces towards the place where God was supposed to reside; if they were far away, even in distant lands, they still directed their faces towards Jerusalem and the temple, as the Mohammedans now do towards Mecca. See Notes on Dan. vi. 10. It has been objected, from the use of the word *temple* here, that this psalm could not have been written by David, as the temple was not built until the time of Solomon. But in reply to this it may be observed that the word here used—הֵיכָל, *haikal*—

8 Lead me, O LORD, in thy righteousness because of [1] mine enemies; make thy way straight before my face.

9 For *there is* no [2] faithfulness in [3] their mouth; their inward part *is* [4] very wickedness; their throat *is* an open sepulchre; they flatter with their tongue.

[1] *those which observe me*, Psa. xxvii. 11.

[2] Or, *steadfastness.* [3] *his*, i.e., *in the mouth of any of them.* [4] *wickednesses.*

is a word of large signification, and might be applied to any place of worship. It means, properly, a large and magnificent building, a palace, Prov. xxx. 28; Isa. xxxix. 7; Dan. i. 4; and then, the place where Jehovah was supposed to reside, or the place of his worship; and might be applied to the tabernacle as well as to the temple. In fact, it is *often* applied to the tabernacle that was in use before the building of the temple, 1 Sam. i. 9; iii. 3; 2 Sam. xxii. 7. Comp. Gesenius, *Lex.*

8. *Lead me, O* LORD, *in thy righteousness.* That is, conduct me safely in the manifestation of the principles of justice or righteousness which belong to thy nature. David felt assured that his was a righteous cause, and that he might make his appeal to God on the ground of the justness of that cause. Such a ground of appeal is always proper when we are in danger or in trouble from the injustice of others, for we may always ask of God to interpose, and to cause that which is right to be done. ¶ *Because of mine enemies.* On account of my enemies, or in respect to them; that is, that they may not triumph, but that I may be vindicated and may be delivered from them. ¶ *Make thy way straight before my face.* The way in which thou wouldst have me to walk. That is, mark out or make plain before me the path for me to tread—the path in which thou wilt deliver me. He was in perplexity, and knew not which way to go, and he looks up to God for guidance and direction.

9. *For* there is *no faithfulness in their mouth.* There is nothing in them which can be confided in; nothing in their promises and declarations. They are false and treacherous, and I can, therefore, only appeal to thee. It is easy to see the propriety of this statement, and of those which follow, on the supposition that this refers to the rebellion of Absalom. Absalom had gone to Hebron on a false pretence (2 Sam. xv. 7—10), and every act of his in this whole transaction had been treacherous and false. ¶ *Their inward part.* Not only their external conduct, but their hearts, their principles, their motives. This was fairly to be inferred from their conduct. The object of the psalmist is to show that they were wholly depraved in all that properly constitutes character or that entered into moral conduct. ¶ *Their throat is an open sepulchre.* That is, as the grave is open to receive its victim, so is their throat open to devour or swallow up the peace and happiness of others. The main idea is that they are false, treacherous, not to be confided in, slanderous. This passage, with the following, is employed by the apostle Paul to demonstrate the universal depravity of man. See Notes on Rom. iii. 13. ¶ *They flatter with their tongue.* He had referred to the "inward part," or the *heart*, and to the *throat* as being depraved and evil; he now refers to another member of the body as being equally depraved—the *tongue.* Instead of being employed to utter truth, and to give expression to the real feelings of the heart, it was employed to flatter others, with a view to lead them astray, or to make use of them for base and selfish purposes. The propriety of this representation as applicable to Absalom and his coadjutors no one can fail to see (comp. 2 Sam. xv. 1—6). It is also to an eminent degree the characteristic of the wicked in general. On this, also, see Notes on Rom. iii. 13.

10 [1]Destroy thou them, O God; let them fall [2]by their own counsels; cast them out in the multitude of their transgressions; for they have rebelled against thee.

11 [e] But let all those that put

[1] *Make them guilty.* [2] Or, *from their counsels.*

e Isa. lxv. 13—16.

10. *Destroy thou them, O God.* The word here rendered *destroy* is translated by Prof. Alexander "condemn"—"condemn them; literally, *make them guilty;* that is, recognise and treat them as such." The Hebrew word אָשַׁם, *asham,* means to fail in duty, to transgress, to be guilty; in Hiph., the form used here, according to Gesenius, to "punish; and hence to destroy," (*Lex.*) The idea in the mind of the psalmist seems to have been that he desired, since they were undoubtedly guilty, that God would regard and treat them *as such.* It is not that he wished that God would *make* them guilty; or that, in itself considered, he desired that they should be found to be so, or that, in itself considered, he wished them to be punished or cut off; but it is that, as they *were* guilty, and as they were pursuing a course which tended to overthrow the government of the land, and as they were at war with God and with the best interests of the people, God would interpose and stay their progress,—that he would show himself to be a righteous and just God. There is no evidence of any private malignity in this prayer, or of any spirit of private revenge. It is a prayer which corresponds with all the *efforts,* and consequently with all the *wishes* of every good man, that the violators of law may be arrested and punished. In this, assuredly, there is no wrong. ¶ *Let them fall by their own counsels.* So as to show that they brought this judgment upon themselves. The wish is, that their plans, which were evil, might come to nought, and tend to their own overthrow. That is, the psalmist did not wish to imbrue his hands in their blood, or to be made the agent in their destruction; but he desired that God would himself interpose, so that their own plans might be made the means of quelling the rebellion. If men are so wicked that they must perish, it is desirable that it should be *seen* that they perish by their own guilt and folly. ¶ *Cast them out.* Expel them; drive them away; let them not be successful in taking possession of the throne, and in overturning the government. ¶ *In the multitude of their transgressions.* In the abundance of their sins, or as a consequence of the number and the aggravation of their offences. The design of the psalmist is to fix the attention on the *great number* of their sins as a reason why they should not be successful. Such a prayer is not wrong, for it would not be right to pray that sinners *in* the abundance of their sins, or in consequence of the multitude of their sins, should be successful and prosperous. The fact that they are such sinners is, under a righteous administration, a reason why they should *not* be successful, not why they *should be.* ¶ *For they have rebelled against thee.* This is given as a reason why the psalmist prayed that they should be cut off. It was not that they had wronged *him;* it was because they had rebelled against *God;* and it was right, therefore, to hope and to pray that he would interpose and vindicate his government and law. There is no spirit of private revenge manifested here, and nothing said that would encourage or foster such a spirit. All that is *said* here is but carrying out what every magistrate must *feel* who executes the laws, and is what he endeavours himself to *do;* for it is desirable that the wicked—the violators of the law—the enemies of their country—should be arrested and prosecuted. See General Introduction, § 6.

11. *But let all those that put their trust in thee rejoice.* Comp. Notes on Ps. ii. 12. That is, they have occasion to rejoice in thee and in thy protection.

their trust in thee rejoice; let them ever shout for joy, because thou [1]defendest them: let them also that love thy name be joyful in thee.

12 For thou, LORD, wilt bless the righteous; with favour wilt thou compass him as *with* a shield.

[1] *coverest over*, or, *protectest.*

The wicked have everything to dread, for they must be cut off; but the righteous have every reason to be happy, for they shall partake of the favour of God. This is, at the same time, the earnest expression of a desire that they *might* rejoice, and that the dealings of God with them might be such that they would ever *have occasion* for joy. ¶ *Let them even shout for joy.* Internal joy or happiness is often expressed by shouting, or singing, as the word here used frequently signifies. The meaning is, that they should give every proper expression to their feeling of joy. This may be done by singing, or by grateful ascriptions of praise and gratitude. ¶ *Because thou defendest them.* While the wicked are cut off (ver. 10). The psalmist, in this expression, doubtless had a primary reference to himself, and to those who adhered to him in his righteous cause; but, as is common in the Psalms, he gives to the sentiment a general form, that it might be useful to all who fear and love God. ¶ *Let them also that love thy name.* That love *thee*—the name being often put for the person. This is but another form of designating the righteous, for it is one of their characteristics that they love the name of God. ¶ *Be joyful in thee.* Rejoice in thee—in thine existence, thy perfections, thy government, thy law, thy dealings, thy service;—in all that thou hast revealed of thyself, and in all that thou doest. Comp. Notes on Phil. iii. 1; iv. 4. It is one of the characteristics of the truly pious that they *do* find their happiness in God. They rejoice that there *is* a God, and that he is just such a being as he is; and they take delight in contemplating his perfections, in the evidences of his favour and friendship, in communion with him, in doing his will.

12. *For thou,* LORD, *wilt bless the righteous.* It is one of the characteristics of God that, while he will punish the wicked, he will show favour to the righteous; while he brings deserved punishment upon the one, he will show his favour to the other. ¶ *With favour wilt thou compass him as* with *a shield.* That is, as a shield is thrown round or before one in the day of battle to protect him, so wilt thou throw thy protection around the righteous. For a description of a *shield,* see Notes on Eph. vi. 16. Comp. Notes on Ps. iii. 3. On these accounts, David felt that he might trust in God in the day of trouble and danger; and, on the same account, all who are righteous may put their trust in him now.

PSALM VI.

§ 1. *Title of the psalm.*—This psalm is inscribed "To the chief Musician on Neginoth upon Sheminith." On the meaning of the phrase "Chief Musician on Neginoth," see Notes on the title to Ps. iv. The phrase "upon Sheminith" occurs here for the first time, and modifies the meaning of the title. The word *Sheminith*—שְׁמִינִית—means properly *the eighth,* and corresponds exactly to our word *octave,* the eighth. It means in modern music an interval of seven degrees, or twelve semitones. It contains five full tones, and two semitones. It is supposed by Gesenius (*Lex.*) here to denote "the lowest and gravest notes of the scale, sung by men, the modern *bass* or *basso.*" The word occurs, in the musical use, in 1 Chron. xv. 21, in enumerating various names of musicians, "Mattithiah, and Elipheleh, etc., with harps on the Sheminith to excel;" marg., "or *eighth.*" It is also found in the title to Ps. xii. It does not elsewhere occur in reference to music in the Scriptures. It is probably not possible now to ascertain the precise meaning of the word as applicable to ancient music, and it is not important. The phrase "*upon the octave*" would properly be the true rendering of it; and this was doubtless quite intelligible at the time. It would be difficult to explain many of the musical terms now in use, after the lapse of two or three thousand years. If the term, however, was used, as is supposed by Gesenius, to denote the bass, its meaning is not difficult. It would then mean that the psalm was designed to be sung, accompanied with the instruments designated by *Neginoth*, and with the voices appropriate to this *octave*—the bass voices. The usual bass voice might be supposed to be adapted to the sentiment in the psalm.

§ 2. *The author of the psalm.*—The psalm purports to have been written by David, and there is nothing in the psalm to lead us to doubt the truth of this representation. It may be assumed, therefore, to be his.

§ 3. *The occasion on which the psalm was written.*—In the running title in the English version this psalm is called "David's complaint in his sickness." It is hardly necessary to say that these running titles were prefixed by the translators, and that there is nothing in the Hebrew that corresponds with this. Still, this has been a very prevailing tradition as to the occasion on which this psalm was composed. Bishop Horsley prefixes this title to it:—"A penitential prayer in the character of a sick person," and in the exposition of this psalm supposes that the suppliant is a mystical personage, and that the object is to represent the feelings of a penitent under the image of such a personage, or that "the sick person is the believer's soul labouring under a sense of its infirmities and anxiously expecting the promised redemption; the sickness is the depravity and disorder occasioned by the fall of man." Luther entitles it "A penitential prayer (*Bussgebet*), for the health of the body and the soul." De Wette regards it as the prayer of one oppressed or in trouble, under the image of a sick person; and in this opinion Rosenmüller concurs. Others regard it as a psalm composed in view of sickness, and suppose it was written in consequence of sickness brought upon David in consequence of the rebellion of Absalom. Indeed, there has been a pretty general concurrence among expositors in the sentiment that, as the two previous psalms were composed in view of that rebellion, so this was also. Calvin supposes that it was not composed specifically in view of *sickness*, but of some great calamity that brought David to feel that he was near the borders of the grave, and that was thus the means of bringing the sins of his past life impressively to his remembrance.

In this uncertainty, and this want of positive testimony as to the occasion when the psalm was composed, it is natural to look to the psalm itself, and to inquire whether there are any *internal* indications which will enable us to determine with any degree of probability the circumstances of the writer at the time of its composition. The psalm, then, has the following internal marks as to the occasion on which it was composed:

I. The writer was in the midst of enemies, and in great peril on account of them. "Mine eye is consumed because of grief; it waxeth old because of all mine enemies," ver. 7. "Depart from me, all ye workers of iniquity," ver. 8. "Let all mine enemies be ashamed and sore vexed," ver. 10. We cannot be mistaken, then, in supposing that this was at some period in the life of David, when his numerous enemies pressed hard upon him and endangered his life.

II. He was crushed and broken-hearted on account of these trials; he had not strength of body to bear up under the weight of accumulated woes; he sank under the burden of these troubles and calamities, and was brought near to the grave. There were many and formidable external foes who threatened his life; and there was, on some account, connected with this, deep and crushing *mental* anguish, and the result was actual and dangerous sickness—so that he was led to contemplate the eternal world as near to him. It became a case, therefore, of real sickness caused by peculiar outward troubles. This is manifest from such expressions as the following:—"I am weak; heal me: my bones are vexed" (ver. 2). "In death there is no remembrance of thee; in the grave who shall give thee thanks?" (ver. 5). "I am weary with my groaning; I water my couch with my tears: mine eye is consumed with grief," vers. 6, 7. This is such language as would be used by one who was crushed and broken-hearted with grief, and who, unable to bear up under the weighty load, was laid, as the result of it, on a bed of languishing. It is not uncommon that outward troubles become too great for the feeble human frame to bear, and that, crushed beneath them, the body is laid upon a bed of languish-

PSALM VI.

To the chief Musician on Neginoth upon [1] Sheminith.[f] A Psalm of David.

O LORD, rebuke me not in thine [g] anger, neither chasten me in thy [h] hot displeasure.

[1] Or, *the eighth.*

[f] 1 Chron. xv. 21; Psa. xii., *title.* [g] Jer. x. 24. [h] Psa. ii. 5.

ing, and brought to the borders of the grave, or to the grave itself.

III. The psalmist expresses a feeling which is common in such cases—a deep anxiety on the subject of his own sin, as if these calamities had come upon him on account of his transgressions, and as a punishment for his sins. This is implied in ver. 1:—"O Lord, rebuke me not in thine anger, neither chasten me in thy hot displeasure." He looked upon this as a *rebuke* from God, and construed it as an expression of *hot displeasure.* This is the prompting of natural feeling when one is afflicted, for this inquiry spontaneously arises in the mind, whether the affliction is not on account of some sin which we have committed, and is not to be regarded as proof that God is angry with us. It is an inquiry as proper as it is natural, and David, in the circumstances referred to, seems to have felt its full force.

Taking all these considerations into view, it seems probable that the psalm was composed during the troubles brought upon David in the rebellion of Absalom, and when, crushed by the weight of these sorrows, his strength gave way, and he was laid on a bed of languishing, and brought near to the grave.

§ 4. *The contents of the psalm.*—The psalm contains the following points:—

I. A plea of the author for mercy and compassion in trouble, under the apprehension that God was rebuking and punishing him for his sins, vers. 1, 2. His deep sufferings, described in the following verses, had, as remarked above, led him to inquire whether it was not on account of his sins that he was afflicted, and whether he ought not to regard his sorrow as proof that God was displeased with him for his sins.

II. A description of his sufferings, vers. 2—7. He had been crushed with sorrow, and had become "weak;" his very "bones" were "vexed;" he was drawing near to the grave; he was weary with his groaning; he watered his couch with his tears; his eye was consumed with grief. These sufferings were partly bodily and partly mental; or rather, as suggested above, probably his mental sorrows had been so great as to prostrate his physical frame, and to lay him on a bed of languishing.

III. The assurance that God had heard his prayer, and that he would triumph over all his enemies, and that all his troubles would pass away, vers. 8—10. Hope breaks in suddenly upon his afflicted soul, and, under this exulting feeling, he addresses his enemies, and tells them to depart from him. They could not be successful, for the Lord had heard his prayer. This sudden answer to prayer—this happy turn of thought—often occurs in the Psalms, as if, while the psalmist was pleading, an immediate answer to prayer was granted, and light broke in upon the darkened mind.

1. *O* LORD, *rebuke me not in thine anger.* As if God was rebuking him by the affliction which he was bringing upon him. This is the point on which the attention of the psalmist is now fixed. He had been apparently contemplating his afflictions, and inquiring into their cause, and he was led to the conclusion that it *might* be for his sins, and that his trials were to be interpreted as proof that God was angry with him. He speaks, therefore, of God as visiting him in his *anger*, and in his *hot displeasure*, and pleads with him that he would *not* thus rebuke and chasten him. The word *rebuke* here, like the word rendered *chasten*, properly refers to the reproof of an offender *by words,* but may also be used to denote the reproof which God administers by his providential dealings when he brings judgment upon any one for his sins. This is the meaning here. The psalmist did not apprehend that God would openly *reprove* him for his sins; but he regarded his dealings with him as such a reproof, and he pleads that the tokens of the reproof might be taken away. The whole language is that which indicates a connection between suffering and sin; the feeling

2 Have mercy upon me, O LORD; for I *am* weak: O LORD, heal me; for my bones *i* are vexed.

3 My soul is also sore vexed: but thou, O LORD, how long?

i Psa. li. 8.

which we have when we are afflicted that it must be on account of our sins. ¶ *Neither chasten me.* A word denoting substantially the same thing; used here in the sense of *punishing.* ¶ *In thy hot displeasure.* Literally, *in thy heat.* We speak of anger or wrath as *burning*, or *consuming.* Comp. Gen. xxxix. 19; Num. xi. 33; Deut. xi. 17; Ps. cvi. 40; Job xix. 11; xxxii. 2, 3; Ps. ii. 12.

2. *Have mercy upon me, O* LORD. That is, be gracious to me; or, show me compassion. This language may be used either in view of sin, of suffering, or of danger. It is a cry to God to interpose, and remove some present source of trouble, and may be employed by one who feels that he is a sinner, or by one on a bed of pain, or by one surrounded by enemies, or by one at the point of death, or by one who is looking out with apprehension upon the eternal world. It is commonly, indeed (comp. Ps. li. 1), a cry to God in view of sin, pleading for pardon and salvation; but here it is a cry in view of trouble and danger, outward sorrow and mental anguish, that had overcome the strength of the sufferer and laid him on a bed of languishing. See introduction to the psalm, § 3. ¶ *For I am weak.* The original word here, אֻמְלַל, *umlal*, means properly to languish or droop, as plants do that are blighted, Isa. xxiv. 7, or as fields do in a drought, Isa. xvi. 8, and is here applied to a sick person whose strength is withered and gone. The condition of such an one is beautifully compared with a plant that withers for lack of moisture; and the word is used in this sense here, as referring to the psalmist himself when sick, as the result of his outward and mental sorrows. Such an effect has not been uncommon in the world. There have been numberless cases where sorrow has prostrated the strength—as a plant withers,—and has brought on languishing sickness. ¶ *O* LORD, *heal me.* This is language which would be properly applied to a case of sickness, and therefore it is most natural to interpret it in this sense in this place. Comp. Isa. xix. 22; xxx. 26; Job v. 18; Gen. xx. 17; Ps. lx. 2; 2 Chron. xvi. 12; Deut. xxviii. 27. ¶ *For my bones are vexed.* The word *vexed* we now commonly apply to mental trouble, and especially the lighter sort of mental trouble,—to irritate, to make angry by little provocations, to harass. It is used here, however, as is common in the Scriptures, in reference to torment or to anguish. The bones are the strength and framework of the body, and the psalmist means here to say that the very source of his strength was gone; that that which supported him was prostrated; that his disease and sorrow had penetrated the most firm parts of his body. Language is often used in the Scriptures, also, as if the *bones* actually suffered pain, though it is now known that the bones, as such, are incapable of pain. And in the same manner, also, language is often used, though that use of the word is not found in the Scriptures, as if the *marrow* of the bones were peculiarly sensitive, like a nerve, in accordance with what is the common and popular belief, though it is now known that the marrow of the bones is entirely insensible to suffering. The design of the psalmist here is to say that he was crushed and afflicted in every part of his frame.

3. *My soul is also sore vexed.* The word *soul* here is used in the sense in which it is commonly with us, as denoting the mind. The idea is, that his sorrows were not merely those of the bodily frame. They had a deeper seat than even the bones. His mind, his soul, was full of anguish also, in view of the circumstances which surrounded him, and which had brought

4 Return, O LORD, deliver my soul: oh save me for thy mercies' [k] sake.

k Eph. ii. 7, 8.

5 [l] For in death *there is* no remembrance of thee: in the grave [m] who shall give thee thanks?

l Isa. xxxviii. 18. *m* Psa. lxxxviii. 11.

on these bodily afflictions. ¶ *But thou, O* LORD. This is a broken sentence, as if he had commenced an address to God, but did not complete it. It is as if he had said, "Here I suffer and languish; my sorrows are deep and unmitigated; as for *thee*, O Lord"—as if he were about to say that he had hoped God would interpose; or, that his dealings were mysterious; or, that they seemed strange or severe; but he ends the sentence by no language of complaint or murmuring, but by simply asking "*how long*" these sorrows were to continue. ¶ *How long?* That is, how long wilt thou leave me thus to suffer? How long shall my unmitigated anguish continue? How long will it be ere thou wilt interpose to relieve me? The language implies that in his apprehension it *was* already a long time—as time usually seems long to a sufferer (comp. Job vii. 2—4), and that he was constantly looking out for God to interpose and help him. This is language such as all persons may be inclined to use on beds of pain and languishing. It *seems* indeed long to them now; it will, however, seem short when they look back upon it from the glories of the heavenly world. Comp. 2 Cor. iv. 17, 18.

4. *Return, O* LORD, *deliver my soul.* As if he had departed from him, and had left him to die. The word *soul* in this place is used, as it often is, in the sense of *life*, for in the next verse he speaks of the grave to which he evidently felt he was rapidly descending. ¶ *O save me.* Save my life; save me from going down to the grave. Deliver me from these troubles and dangers. ¶ *For thy mercies' sake.* (*a*) As an act of mere mercy, for he felt that he had no claim, and could not urge it as a matter of right and justice; and (*b*) in order that God's mercy might be manifest, or because he was a merciful Being, and might, therefore, be appealed to on that ground. These are proper grounds, now, on which to make an appeal to God for his interposition in our behalf; and, indeed, these are the *only* grounds on which we can plead with him to save us.

5. *For in death.* In the state of the dead; in the grave. ¶ There is *no remembrance of thee.* They who are dead do not remember thee or think of thee. The *ground* of this appeal is, that it was regarded by the psalmist as a *desirable* thing to remember God and to praise him, and that this could not be done by one who was dead. He prayed, therefore, that God would spare his life, and restore him to health, that he might praise him in the land of the living. A sentiment similar to this occurs in Ps. xxx. 9, "What profit is there in my blood, when I go down to the pit? Shall the dust praise thee? shall it declare thy truth?" So also Ps. lxxxviii. 11, "Shall thy loving-kindness be declared in the grave? or thy faithfulness in destruction?" So also in Isaiah xxxviii. 18, in the language of Hezekiah, "The grave cannot praise thee; death cannot celebrate thee; they that go down into the pit cannot hope for thy truth." See Notes on that passage. A similar sentiment also is found in Job x. 21, 22. See Notes on that passage. In regard to the meaning of this it may be remarked (*a*) that it is to be admitted that there was among the ancient saints much less light on the subject of the future state than there is with us, and that they often, in giving utterance to their feelings, seemed to speak as if all were dark beyond the grave. (*b*) But, though they thus spoke in their sorrow and in their despondency, they also did, on other occasions, express their belief

6 I am weary with my groaning; [1] all the night [n] make I my bed to swim; I water my couch with my tears.
7 Mine eye is consumed be-

[1] Or, *every*. [n] Job vii. 3.

---

in a future state, and their expectation of happiness in a coming world (comp., for example, Ps. xvi. 10, 11; xvii. 15.) (*c*) Does not their language in times of despondency and sickness express the feelings which *we* often have now, even with all the light which we possess, and all the hopes which we cherish? Are there not times in the lives of the pious, even though they have a strong prevailing hope of heaven, when the thoughts are fixed on the grave as a dark, gloomy, repulsive prison, and *so* fixed on it as to lose sight of the world beyond? And in such moments does not *life* seem as precious to us, and as desirable, as it did to David, to Hezekiah, or to Job? ¶ *In the grave.* Heb., בִּשְׁאוֹל, *in Sheol.* For the meaning of the word, see Notes on Isa. v. 14; xiv. 9; Job vii. 9. Its meaning here does not differ materially from the word *grave.* ¶ *Who shall give thee thanks?* Who shall *praise* thee? The idea is that *none* would then praise God. It was the land of *silence.* See Isa. xxxviii. 18, 19. This language implies that David *desired* to praise God, but that he could not hope to do it in the grave.

6. *I am weary with my groaning.* I am exhausted or worn out with it. That is, his sorrows were so deep, and his groaning was so constant, that his strength failed. He became *faint* under the weight of his sorrows. All persons in trouble have experienced this effect—the sense of weariness or exhaustion from sorrow. ¶ *All the night make I my bed to swim.* That is, he wept so much that his bed seemed to be immersed in tears. This is, of course, hyperbolical language, expressing in a strong and emphatic manner the depth of his sorrows. ¶ *I water my couch with my tears.* The word here rendered *water* means to melt, to flow down; then, in Hiph., to cause to flow, to dissolve. The sense here is, that he caused his couch to *flow* or *overflow* with his tears. We would say, he *flooded* his bed with tears. This verse discloses the true source of the trials referred to in the psalm. It was some deep mental anguish—some source of grief—that exhausted his strength, and that laid him on a bed of languishing. No circumstances in the life of David better accord with this than the troubles which existed on account of the ungrateful and rebellious conduct of Absalom, and it is most natural to refer it to this. Many a parent since the time of David has experienced *all*, both mental and bodily, which is here described as a consequence of the ingratitude and evil conduct of his children. The tragedy of "Lear" turns entirely on this.

7. *Mine eye is consumed.* The word here rendered *consumed*—עָשֵׁשׁ, *a-shash*—means properly to fall in, to fall away, and is applied here to the *eye* as pining or wasting away from care, anxiety, and sorrow. Tears were poured forth from the eye, and it seemed to be exhausting itself in this manner. The meaning is, that it had grown *dim*, or that its sight began to fail, like that of an old man, on account of his troubles. Many have understood the word here rendered *eye* as referring to the *countenance;* but it is doubtful whether the word ever has this signification; and at any rate the common signification, referring it to the *eye*, best suits this connection. ¶ *It waxeth old.* It seems to grow old; it experiences the effects commonly produced by age in blunting the power of vision. This is not an uncommon effect of grief and sadness. Even while I am writing this I am called in my pastoral visitations to attend on a young lady lying on a bed of languishing, and probably of death, one of whose symptoms is a quite diminished, and indeed almost

cause of grief; it waxeth old because of all mine enemies.

8 [o] Depart from me, all ye workers of iniquity: for the LORD hath heard [p] the voice of my weeping.

9 The LORD hath heard my supplication; the Lord will receive my prayer.

o Psa. cxix. 115; cxxxix. 19.

p Psa. cxlv. 18.

total loss of vision, as the effect of trouble and disease. ¶ *Because of all mine enemies.* From the trouble which they have brought upon me. The reference here, according to the interpretation proposed of the psalm, is to Absalom and those who were associated with him. Their conduct had been such as to bring upon David this overwhelming tide of sorrows.

8. *Depart from me, all ye workers of iniquity.* Referring, by the "workers of iniquity," to his enemies, as if they now surrounded him, and calling on them *now* to leave him, since God had heard his prayer, and they could not be successful in their purposes. This is an indirect but most emphatic way of saying that God had heard his prayer; and the sentiment in this verse is strongly in contrast with the desponding state of feeling—the deep and dreadful sorrow—indicated in the previous verses. Light broke in suddenly upon him; his prayer had come up before God, and, in some way, he was assured that it would be answered. Already he sees his enemies scattered, and his own cause triumphant; and in this exulting feeling he addresses his foes, and commands them to leave him. This is, therefore, a remarkable and striking proof that prayer may be heard, even while we are speaking to God (comp. Isa. lxv. 24); that the assurance may be conveyed suddenly to the mind that God will hear and answer the prayer which is addressed to him; and also a beautiful illustration of the *effect* of this on a mind overwhelmed with trouble and sorrow, in giving it calmness and peace. ¶ *For the* LORD *hath heard.* That is, my prayer has ascended before him, and I am certain that he regards it favourably, and will answer it. *In what way* he had this assurance he does not inform us. As he was an inspired man, we may suppose that the assurance was given to him directly by the Holy Spirit. *We* are not to expect the *same kind* of assurance that our prayers are heard; we are to look for no revelation to that effect; but there may be *as real* an intimation to the mind that our prayers are heard—as real *evidence*—as in this case. There may be a firm confidence of the mind that God is a hearer of prayer now coming to the soul with the freshness of a new conviction of that truth; and there may be, in trouble and sorrow, a sweet calmness and peace breathed through the soul—an assurance that all will be right and well, *as if* the prayer were heard, and such as there would be if we were assured by direct revelation that it *is* heard. The Spirit of God can produce this in our case as really as he did in the case of David. ¶ *The voice of my weeping.* The voice of prayer that accompanied my weeping, or the voice of the weeping itself—the cry of anguish and distress which was in itself of the nature of prayer.

9. *The* LORD *hath heard my supplication.* Repeating the sentiment in the previous verse, to express his assurance and his joy. Nothing is more natural in such circumstances than to dwell on the joyous thought, and to repeat it to ourselves, that it may make its full impression. ¶ *The* LORD *will receive my prayer.* As he has done it, so he will still do it. This allays all fears of the future, and makes the mind calm. The state of mind here is this:—"The Lord *has* heard my prayer; I am assured that he *will* do it hereafter; I have, therefore, nothing to fear."

10. *Let all mine enemies be ashamed.* Be so brought to see their folly that

10 Let all mine enemies be ashamed and sore vexed: let them return *and* be ashamed suddenly.

they shall be ashamed of their conduct. The wish is that they might be brought to see their own guilt—a wish certainly which it is right to cherish in regard to all evil-doers. ¶ *And sore vexed.* Comp. Notes on Ps. v. 10. The same Hebrew word is used here which occurs in vers. 2, 3, and rendered *vexed.* It is a word which denotes trouble, trembling, consternation; and the meaning here is, that the psalmist prayed that they might be confounded or disconcerted in their plans—a prayer which is certainly proper in regard to all the purposes of the wicked. No one should desire that the purposes of the wicked should prosper; and *not* to desire this is to desire that they may be foiled and overcome in their schemes. This must be the wish of every good man. ¶ *Let them return.* Turn back, or be turned back; that is, let them be repulsed, and compelled to turn back from their present object. ¶ And *be ashamed suddenly.* Heb., "In a moment;" instantaneously. He desired that there might be no delay, but that their discomfiture might be accomplished at once. As it was right to pray that this might occur, so it was right to pray that it might occur without delay, or as speedily as possible. The sooner the plans of sinners are confounded, the better.

PSALM VII.

§ 1. *Author of the psalm.*—This psalm, according to the title, was composed by David; and there is nothing in it that is contrary to this supposition. Indeed, there were many circumstances in the life of David which would suggest the thoughts in this psalm; and the sentiments expressed are such as are frequently found in his other compositions.

§ 2. *Occasion on which the psalm was composed.*—The psalm is said in the title to have been composed as "a song to the Lord, concerning the words (Marg., 'or business,') of Cush the Benjamite." There is no reason to call the correctness of this title in question, but there have been very various opinions as to who this Cush was. It is manifest from the psalm that it was composed in view of some "words" of reviling, or reproach, or slander; something that was done to wound the feelings, or to injure the reputation, or destroy the peace of David.

There have been three opinions in regard to the *Cush* here referred to. (1.) According to the first, *Saul* is the person intended; and it has been supposed that the name *Cush* is given to him as a reproach, and to denote the blackness of his character, as the word *Cush* would denote an Ethiopian, or black man. So it was understood by the author of the Targum or Chaldee Paraphrase, in which it is rendered "an ode which David sang before the Lord on the death of Saul, the son of Kish, of the tribe of Benjamin." But this opinion has no probability. It is not certain that this term *Cush* would, in the time of David, denote one of black complexion; nor is there any probability that it would be used as a term of reproach at all; and as little probability is there that it would be applied by David to Saul if it had been. If the psalm referred to Saul, it is probable, from all that we know of the feelings of David towards the reigning prince, that he would not designate him, in the title of a psalm, in enigmatical and reproachful language. Besides, the injurious treatment of Saul towards David was rather manifested in *deeds* than in *words.* (2.) A second opinion is, that it refers to Shimei, who was of the house of Saul, and who reproached and cursed David as he was flying from Jerusalem on occasion of the rebellion of Absalom, 2 Sam. xvi. 5, seq. It is supposed by those who maintain this opinion that the name was given to him because he was a calumniator and reviler—or, as we would say, a *blackhearted* man. But the same objection exists to this opinion as to that before-mentioned; and besides this, there are several things in the psalm which do not agree with such a supposition. In fact there is no reason for such a supposition, except that Shimei was a calumniator, and that the psalm refers to some such person. (3.) A third opinion is, that it refers to some one of the *name* Cush, of the tribe of Benjamin, who reproached David on some occasion that is now unknown.

This opinion has every degree of probability, and is undoubtedly the correct opinion. David was often reproached and calumniated in his life, and it would seem that, on some occasion now to us unknown, when he was violently reproached in this manner, he gave vent to his feelings in this impassioned ode. No other record was made of the transaction, and the occasion on which it occurred is not known. At the time when it occurred it would be easily understood who was referred to, and the design of the composition was accomplished by the record of the feelings of the author on an occasion that greatly tried his spirit. It is thus of permanent value to the church and the world, for there are few persons that are not on some occasions bitterly reproached, and few who are not disposed to vent their feelings in expressions similar to those in this psalm. One great design of the collection of poems in the Psalms was to show the workings of human nature in a great variety of situations; and hence such a psalm as this has a permanent and general value; and so far as this general use is concerned, it matters little on what occasion, or in reference to what individual, the psalm was composed.

§ 3. *Contents of the psalm.*—The psalm embraces the following points:—

I. A prayer of the psalmist for deliverance from his enemies, and especially from this particular foe that threatened his destruction, vers. 1, 2. This is the general subject of the psalm.

II. He offers this prayer on the ground that he is innocent of the charges that are brought against him;—relying thus on the fact that his was a righteous cause, and appealing to God on this ground, and declaring his willingness to suffer all that his enemy attempted to bring upon him if he was guilty, vers. 3—5.

III. He prays for the interposition of Divine justice on his enemies, on the ground of the general justice of God, and as a part of his general administration over men, vers. 6—9.

IV. In his own hopes, he trusts in the Divine discrimination between innocence and guilt, assured that God would interpose on behalf of the righteous, and that the principles of the Divine administration were opposed to the wicked, vers. 10, 11.

V. He speaks confidently of the ultimate destruction of the ungodly and of the manner in which it would be brought about, vers. 12—16. If they did not turn, they must be certainly destroyed, for God was preparing the instruments of their destruction; and the *means* which he would use would be the very plans of the wicked themselves.

VI. The psalmist says that, as for himself, he would praise the Lord according to his righteousness; that is, would adore and praise him as a righteous God, ver. 17.

The general *subject* of the psalm, therefore, pertains to the feelings which are to be entertained towards revilers and calumniators—towards those who reproach us when we are conscious of innocence of the charges that are alleged against us; and as all good men are liable to be placed in these circumstances, the psalm has a practical and general value.

§ 4. *The title to the psalm.*—The psalm is entitled "*Shiggaion of David.*" The word *Shiggaion*—שִׁגָּיוֹן—occurs only in this place in the singular number, and in Hab. iii. 1 in the plural. "A prayer of Habakkuk upon *Shigionoth.*" It properly means a *song, psalm, hymn* (Gesenius). Prof. Alexander renders it "wandering, error," as if the word were derived from שָׁגָה, *shagah*, to walk, to go astray; and he supposes that it refers to the fact that David was *wandering* or unsettled at the time when the psalm was composed. This reason, however, will not apply to the use of the word in Habakkuk. Solomon Van Til. (Ugolin, Thesau. Sac. Ant., vol. xxxii. pp. 294, 295), supposes that it refers to "a certain inadvertence or oblivion of himself on the part of the author, or powerful seizure of the mind,"—*animi abreptio.* He says that it is commonly supposed to indicate a poem, in which the poet is impelled by his feelings, and drawn along with little regard to the regularity of the numbers or the metre, but in which he pours out his emotions in an erratic or irregular manner from the overflowing of his soul. This seems to me to have been the probable origin of this title, and to have denoted the kind of poetry to which it was applicable. Julius Bartoloccius (Ugolin, xxxii. 484) supposes that it refers to a certain *tone* (the "fifth tone") as peculiarly *sweet* and *soft*, and that this kind of poetry was thus applicable to hymns of joy; and that the term is used here because this psalm is peculiarly sweet and pleasant. There is nothing in

PSALM VII.

Shiggaion *q* of David, which he sang unto the Lord, concerning [1] the words of *r* Cush the Benjamite.

O LORD my God, in thee do I put my trust: save me from all them that persecute me, and deliver me;

2 Lest he tear my soul like a lion, rending *it* in pieces, while *there is* [2] none to deliver.

q Hab. iii. 1. [1] Or, *business.*

r 2 Sam. xvi. [2] *not a deliverer.*

the psalm, however, which would indicate that this is the origin of the title; and the former supposition better meets the case than either this or the opinion of Professor Alexander. I would regard it, therefore, as applicable to a psalm where there was an overflow of feeling or emotion that poured itself out without much regard to regular rhythm, or the laws of metre. It is a psalm of a *wandering* or *irregular metre.* It may not be easy, however, to determine why it is particularly applied to this psalm; it is more easy to see why it should be applied to the hymn in Habakkuk. The Latin Vulgate and the Septuagint render it simply *A psalm.*

1. *O* LORD *my God, in thee do I put my trust.* The psalm opens with an expression of strong confidence in God. The psalmist addresses Jehovah as *his* God, and says that in him he trusts or confides. The word rendered *trust*—חָסָה, *hhasa*—means *to flee;* to flee to a place; to take shelter; and is applied to taking shelter under the shadow or protection of one (Judg. ix. 15; Isa. xxx. 2; Ps. lvii. 1; lxi. 4). The idea here is, that in his troubles he fled to God as a refuge, and felt safe under his protection. ¶ *Save me from all them that persecute me.* That is, protect my life; rescue me from their power. The word *persecute* here refers to those who sought his life, who endeavoured to deprive him of his rights. The *language* would apply to many occasions in the life of David—to the persecutions which he endured by Saul, by Absalom, etc. In this case the language was suggested by the opposition of Cush the Benjamite; and it was this that David had particularly in view. It is probable, however, that, whoever Cush was, he was not alone, but that others were associated with him in his opposition to David; and it was natural also that, in circumstances like these, David should remember his *other* persecutors, and pray that he might be delivered from them all. The prayer, therefore, has a general form, and the desire expressed is that which we all naturally have, that we may be delivered from *all* that troubles us. ¶ *And deliver me.* Rescue me. It would seem from this expression, and from the following verse, that there was more to be apprehended in the case than mere reproachful *words,* and that his life was actually in danger.

2. *Lest he.* Lest *Cush* should do this. See the title, and the introd. to the psalm, § 2. ¶ *Tear my soul like a lion.* Tear or rend my *life*—that is, *me*—like a lion. The word rendered *soul* here—נֶפֶשׁ, *nephesh*—refers, as it properly does elsewhere, to the *life,* and not to the soul, as we use the term, denoting the thinking, immortal part. The simple idea is, that David was apprehensive of his *life,* and, in order to indicate his great peril, he uses language derived from the fierceness of the lion. Such imagery would be well understood in a country where lions abounded, and nothing could more strikingly denote the danger in which David was, or the fierceness of the wrath of the enemy that he dreaded. ¶ *Rending* it *in pieces.* Rending *me* in pieces. Or rather, perhaps, breaking or crushing the bones; for the word used—פָּרַק—*parak* (whence our English word *break*)—means *to break, to crush,* and would apply to the act of the lion crushing or breaking the bones of his victim as he devoured it. ¶ *While* there is *none to deliver.* Denoting the complete destruction which he feared would come upon him. The figure is that of a solitary man seized

3 O LORD my God, if I have done this; if there be iniquity in my hands;
4 If I have rewarded evil unto him that was at peace with me; (yea, I have delivered him that without cause is mine enemy;)

by a powerful lion, with no one at hand to rescue him. So David felt that if God did not interfere, he would fall into the hands of this fierce and wrathful enemy.

3. *O LORD my God.* A solemn appeal to God as to the sincerity and truth of what he was about to say. ¶ *If I have done this.* This thing charged upon me; for it is evident that *Cush,* whoever he was, had accused him of some wrong thing—some wicked action. What that was can only be learned from what follows, and even this is not very specific. So far as appears, however, it would seem to be that he accused David of bringing evil, in some way, upon one who was at peace with him; that is, of wantonly and without provocation doing him wrong, and of so doing wrong that he had the avails of it in his own possession—some spoil, or plunder, or property, that he had taken from him. The charge would seem to be, that he had made a wanton and unprovoked attack on one who had not injured him, and that he had taken, and had still in his possession, something of value that properly belonged to another. Whether the accuser (*Cush*) in this referred to himself or to some other person, does not appear clear from the psalm; but as he was filled with rage, and as the life of David was endangered by him, it would seem most probable that the reference was to himself, and that he felt *he* had been personally wronged. The design of David, in the passage now before us, is to deny this charge altogether. This he does in the most explicit manner, by saying that this was so far from being true, that he had, on the contrary, delivered the life of him that was his enemy, and by adding that, if this were so, he would be willing that the injured man *should* persecute and oppose him, and even trample his life down to the earth. ¶ *If there be iniquity in my hands.* That is, if there is the iniquity referred to; or, in other words, if he had in his possession what had been wrongfully taken from another, to wit, as appears, from this *Cush* who now accused him. The word *iniquity* here denotes an *unjust possession*—a property that had been unjustly taken from another; and, as remarked above, the slanderous charge would seem to have been, that he had taken that property from some one who was at peace with him, and that he retained it contrary to justice. This charge David means peremptorily to deny.

4. *If I have rewarded evil unto him that was at peace with me.* If I have done evil; or if I have requited him that was friendly by some unjust and evil conduct. If I have come upon him wantonly and unprovoked, and have done him wrong. This seems to have been the substance of the accusation; and, as remarked above, it is most probable that the accuser (*Cush*) referred to himself. ¶ *Yea, I have delivered him that without cause is mine enemy.* So far is this from being true, that the very reverse is true. So far from taking advantage of another that was at peace with me, and depriving him of his just rights by fraud or force, it is a fact that I have rescued from impending danger the man that was at war with me, and that was an avowed enemy. It would seem probable that in this he refers to this very Cush, and means to say that there had been some occasion in which he, who was long hostile to him, was wholly in his power, and when he had not only declined to take advantage of him, but had actually interposed to rescue him from danger. An instance of this kind actually occurred in the life of David, in his

5 Let the enemy persecute my soul, and take *it;* yea, let him tread down my life upon the earth, and lay mine honour in the dust. Selah.
6 Arise, O LORD, in thine anger: [s] lift up thyself, because

s Psa. xciv. 1, 2.

treatment of Saul (1 Sam. xxiv. 10, 11); and it is *possible* that David referred to that case, and meant to say that *that* was an indication of his character, and of his manner of treating others. Those who suppose that the whole psalm refers to Saul (see the introduct., § 2), of course regard this as the specific case referred to. There may have been other instances of the same kind in the life of David, and there is no improbability in supposing that on some occasion he had treated this very man, *Cush*, in this way, and that he refers here to that fact.

5. *Let the enemy persecute my soul.* Persecute my *life*, for so the word rendered *soul*, נֶפֶשׁ, *nephesh*, is evidently used here. He was willing, if he had been guilty of the thing charged upon him, that the enemy here referred to should *pursue* or persecute him until he should destroy his life. Compare with this the expression of Paul in Acts xxv. 11. The meaning here is simply that if he were a guilty man, in the manner charged on him, he would be willing to be treated accordingly. He did not wish to screen himself from any just treatment; and if he had been guilty he would not complain even if he were cut off from the land of the living. ¶ *And take* it. Take my life; put me to death. ¶ *Yea, let him tread down my life upon the earth.* The allusion here is to the manner in which the vanquished were often treated in battle, when they were rode over by horses, or trampled by men into the dust. The idea of David is, that if he was guilty he would be willing that his enemy should triumph over him, should subdue him, should treat him with the utmost indignity and scorn. ¶ *And lay mine honour in the dust.* All the tokens or marks of my honour or distinction in life. That is, I am willing to be utterly degraded and humbled, if I have been guilty of this conduct towards him who is my enemy. The idea in all this is, that David did not wish to screen himself from the treatment which he deserved if he had done wrong. His own principles were such that he would have felt that the treatment here referred to would have been right and proper as a recompense for such base conduct; and he would not have had a word to say against it. His desire for the interposition of God, therefore, arose solely from the fact of his feeling that, in these respects, he was entirely innocent, and that the conduct of his enemy was unjust and cruel. ¶ *Selah.* A musical pause, not affecting the sense, but introduced here, perhaps, because the sense of the psalm now demanded a change in the style of the music. See Notes on Ps. iii. 2.

6. *Arise, O* LORD, *in thine anger.* That is, to punish him who thus unjustly persecutes me. See Notes on Psalm iii. 7. ¶ *Lift up thyself.* As if he had been lying in repose and inaction. The idea is derived from a warrior who is called on to go forth and meet an enemy. ¶ *Because of the rage of mine enemies.* Not only of this particular enemy, but of those who were associated with him, and perhaps of all his foes. David felt, on this occasion, that he was surrounded by enemies; and he calls on God to interfere and save him. ¶ *And awake for me.* Or, in my behalf. The word *awake* is a still stronger expression than those which he had before used. It implies that one had been asleep, and insensible to what had occurred, and he addresses God *as if* He had thus been insensible to the dangers which surrounded him. ¶ *To the judgment* that *thou hast commanded.* To execute the judgment which thou

of the rage of mine enemies; and
awake [t] for me *to* the judgment
that thou hast commanded.
7 So shall the congregation of
the people compass thee about:
for their sakes therefore return
thou on high.
8 The LORD shall judge the
people: judge me, O LORD, ac-

t Psa. xliv. 23; lxxiii. 20; Isa. li. 9.

hast appointed or ordered. That is, God had, in his law, commanded that justice should be done, and had proclaimed himself a God of justice—requiring that right should be done on the earth, and declaring himself in all cases the friend of right. David now appeals to him, and calls on him to manifest himself in that character, as executing in this case the justice which he required under the great principles of his administration. He had commanded justice to be done in all cases. He had required that the wicked should be punished. He had ordered magistrates to execute justice. In accordance with these great principles, David now calls on God to manifest *himself* as the friend of justice, and to show, in this case, the same principles, and the same regard to justice which he required in others. It is an earnest petition that he would vindicate his own principles of administration.

7. *So shall the congregation of the people compass thee about.* That is, as the result of thy gracious interposition in defending the righteous, and in bringing just judgment on the wicked. The meaning is, that such an act would inspire confidence in him as a just and holy God, and that, as the result, his people would gather round him to express their gratitude, and to render him praise. In other words, every act of justice on the part of God—all his interpositions to defend his people, and to maintain the principles of righteousness and truth—tend to inspire confidence in him, and to increase the number of his friends. The phrase "the congregation of the people," here, does not necessarily refer to any "congregation," or assembly as such, then existing; but it means that a great congregation—a great multitude—*would* thus encompass him, or that great numbers *would* worship him as the result of his interposition. This the psalmist urges as a motive, or as a reason why God should interpose, that in this way the number of his worshippers would be greatly increased. ¶ *For their sakes.* On their account; or to secure this result in regard to them. ¶ *Return thou on high.* The most probable meaning of this is "ascend thy throne of justice, or thy judgment-seat;" spoken here either as a king ascending his elevated throne (compare Isa. vi. 1), or as ascending to heaven, the place where he dispensed justice. The *language* is *as if* he had come down from his throne—*as if* he had not been engaged in dispensing justice; and David now calls on him to re-ascend the throne, and to execute righteous judgment among men. The effect of this, he says, would be to secure the confidence of his people, and to increase the number of those who would worship him. Of course, this is not to be understood literally, but in a manner appropriate to the Divine majesty. It is language, in this respect, similar to that which is elsewhere used, when the psalmist calls on God *to awake, to arise, to lift up himself.* See ver. 6. Such language is easily understood; and language drawn from the common modes of speaking among men must be used when we speak of God. The whole idea in this passage is that God seemed to delay in the execution of his judgment, and the psalmist entreats him to hasten it.

8. *The* LORD *shall judge the people.* Expressing his confident belief that God *would* interpose, and that his judgment would not much longer be delayed. The proposition is a general one—that God would see that justice would be done to all people; and on

cording *u* to my righteousness, and according to mine integrity *that is* in me.

u Psa. xviii. 20. *v* Rev. ii. 23.

9 Oh let the wickedness of the wicked come to an end; but establish the just: for the righteous God trieth the hearts *v* and reins.

this ground the psalmist pleads that He would now interpose and defend *him* from *his* enemies. ¶ *Judge me, O* LORD. That is, in my present circumstances. Interpose to do justice to my cause, and to vindicate me from these false accusations. ¶ *According to my righteousness.* In this particular case, for to that the proper laws of interpretation require us to confine this. He does not say that he wished his own righteousness to be made the basis of judgment in determining his eternal welfare, or that he depended on his own righteousness for salvation —for that is not the point in question; but he felt that his was, in this case, a righteous cause; that he was not guilty of the charge alleged against him; that he was an injured, wronged, and calumniated man; and he prayed that God would *vindicate* him from these charges, and defend him from those who were unjustly persecuting him. With all our sense of personal unworthiness in the matter of salvation, it is not improper, when we are wronged, to pray that God would interpose and vindicate us in that particular case, according to our innocence of the charges alleged against us. ¶ *And according to mine integrity* that is *in me.* Heb., *my perfection.* That is, his perfection in *this* case; his entire freedom from the charges brought against him; his absolute innocence in respect to the points under consideration. A man may be conscious of *perfect* innocence in respect to a particular matter, and yet have a deep sense of his *general* unworthiness, and of the fact that he is a sinner against God. That I am innocent of a particular act charged on me does not prove that I am guiltless altogether; that I should allege that, and insist on that, and pray to God to vindicate me in that, does not prove that I depend on that for the salvation of my soul, or that I claim absolute perfection before him.

9. *Oh let the wickedness of the wicked come to an end.* Of *all* the wicked; —wickedness not in this particular case only, but wickedness of all forms, and in all lands. The prayer here is a natural one; when a man becomes impressed with a sense of the evil of sin in one form, he wishes that the world may be delivered from it in all forms and altogether. ¶ *But establish the just.* The righteous. This stands in contrast with his desire in regard to the wicked. He prays that the righteous may be confirmed in their integrity, and that their plans may succeed. This prayer is as universal as the former, and is, in fact, a prayer that the world may come under the dominion of the principles of truth and holiness. ¶ *For the righteous God trieth the hearts and reins.* That is, the hearts and reins of all men. He understands the character of all men; he is intimately acquainted with all their thoughts, and purposes, and feelings. To search or try "the heart and the reins" is an expression frequently used in the Bible to denote that God is intimately acquainted with all the thoughts and feelings of men; that is, that he thoroughly understands the character of all men. The word "*heart*" in the Scriptures is often used to denote the seat of the *thoughts;* and the word "*reins*" seems to be used to denote the most secret feelings, purposes, and devices of the soul —as if lodged deep in our nature, or covered in the most hidden and concealed portions of the man. The word *reins,* with us, denotes the kidneys. In the Scriptures the word seems to be used, in a general sense, to denote the inward parts, as the seat of the affections and passions. The Hebrew word כִּלְיָה, *kilyah,* means the same as the word *reins* with us,—the kid-

10 [1] My defence [w] *is* of God, which saveth the upright in heart.

11 [2] God judgeth the righteous,

[1] *buckler* is *upon*. *w* Ps. lxxxix. 18.

[2] Or, *is a righteous judge*.

neys, Exod. xxix. 13, 22; Job xvi. 13; Isa. xxxiv. 6; Deut. xxxii. 14. From some cause, the Hebrews seem to have regarded the *reins* as the seat of the affections and passions, though perhaps only in the sense that they thus spoke of the *inward* parts, and meant to denote the deepest purposes of the soul—as if utterly concealed from the eye. These deep thoughts and feelings, so unknown to other men, are all known intimately to God, and thus the character of every man is clearly understood by him, and he can judge every man aright. The phrase here used—of trying the hearts and reins—is one that is often employed to describe the Omniscience of God. Comp. Jer. xi. 20; xvii. 10; xx. 12; Ps. xxvi. 2; cxxxix. 13; Rev. ii. 23. The particular idea here is, that as God searches the hearts of all men, and understands the secret purposes of the soul, he is able to judge aright, and to determine correctly in regard to their character, or to administer his government on the principles of exact justice. Such is the ground of the prayer in this case, that God, who knew the character of all men, would confirm those who are truly righteous, and would bring the wickedness of the ungodly to an end.

10. *My defence* is *of God.* The meaning here is, that God was his protector, and that in his troubles he confided in him. The original word here, as in Ps. iii. 3; v. 12, is *shield.* See Notes on those verses. ¶ *Which saveth the upright in heart.* Whom he that searches the heart (ver. 9) sees to be upright; or to be sincere, truthful, just. The writer says that it is a characteristic of God that he saves or protects all such; and, conscious of his innocence of the charges against himself, he here appeals to him on that ground, and confides in his protection because he sees that in this respect he was blameless.

11. *God judgeth the righteous.* That is, he pronounces a just judgment on their behalf; he vindicates their character. It is true, in a general sense, that God judges all according to their character; but the particular idea here is, that God will do justice to the righteous; he will interpose to vindicate them, and he will treat them as they ought to be treated when assailed by their enemies, and when reproached and calumniated. The original phrase here is susceptible of two translations; either, *God is a righteous judge*—or, *God is judging,* that is judges, *the righteous.* The sense is not materially varied, whichever translation is adopted. Our common version has probably expressed the true idea; and there the design of the writer is to contrast the manner in which God regards and treats the righteous, with the manner in which he regards and treats the wicked. The one he judges, that is, he does him justice; with the other he is angry every day. ¶ *And God is angry* with the wicked. The phrase *with the wicked* is supplied by our translators, but not improperly, since the writer evidently intends to speak of these in contrast with the righteous. The words *God is angry* must, of course, be understood in a manner in accordance with the Divine nature; and we are not to suppose that precisely the same passions, or the same feelings, are referred to when this language is used of God which is implied when it is used of men. It means that his nature, his laws, his government, his feelings, are all arrayed against the wicked; that he cannot regard the conduct of the wicked with favour; that he will punish them. While his judgment in regard to the righteous must be in their favour, it must just as certainly be *against* the wicked; while he will vindicate the one, he will cut off and

and God is angry *with the wicked* every day.

12 [x] If he turn not, he will whet his sword; he hath bent his bow, and made it ready.

x Matt. iii. 10.

punish the other. Of the truth of this in respect to the Divine character there can be no doubt. Indeed, we could not honour a God—as we could honour no other being—who would deal with the righteous and the wicked alike, or who would have no respect to *character* in the treatment of others, and in his feelings towards them. ¶ *Every day.* Continually; constantly; always. This is designed to qualify the previous expression. It is not excitement. It is not temporary passion, such as we see in men. It is not sudden emotion, soon to be succeeded by a different feeling when the passion passes off. It is the steady and uniform attribute of his unchanging nature to be always opposed to the wicked,—to all forms of sin; and in him, in this respect, there will be no change. The wicked will find him no more favourable to their character and course of life to-morrow than he is to-day; no more beyond the grave, than this side the tomb. What he is to-day he will be to-morrow and every day. Time will make no change in this respect, and the wicked can have no hope on the ground that the feeling of God towards sin and the sinner (as such) will ever be in any way different from what it is at the present moment. This is a fearful truth in regard to the sinner; and both aspects of the truth here stated should make the sinner tremble;—(*a*) that God is angry with him—that all His character, and all the principles of His government and law, are and must be arrayed against him; and (*b*) that in this respect there is to be no change; that if he continues to be wicked, as he is now, he will every day and always—this side the grave and beyond—find all the attributes of God engaged against him, and pledged to punish him. God has no attribute that can take part with sin or the sinner.

12. *If he turn not.* If the wicked person does not repent. In the previous verse the psalmist had said that God is angry with the wicked every day; he here states what must be the consequence to the wicked if they persevere in the course which they are pursuing; that is, if they do not repent. God, he says, cannot be indifferent to the course which they pursue, but he is preparing for them the instruments of punishment, and he will certainly bring destruction upon them. It is implied here that if they *would* repent and turn they would avoid this, and would be saved:—a doctrine which is everywhere stated in the Scriptures. ¶ *He will whet his sword.* He will *sharpen* his sword preparatory to inflicting punishment. That is, *God* will do this. Some, however, have supposed that this refers to the wicked person—the enemy of David—meaning that if he did not turn; if he was not arrested; if he was suffered to go on as he intended, he would whet his sword, and bend his bow, etc.; that is, that he would go on to execute his purposes against the righteous. See Rosenmüller *in loc.* But the most natural construction is to refer it to God, as meaning that if the sinner did not repent, He would inflict on him deserved punishment. The *sword* is an instrument of punishment (comp. Rom. xiii. 4); and to *whet* or *sharpen* it, is merely a phrase denoting that he would prepare to execute punishment. See Deut. xxxii. 41. ¶ *He hath bent his bow.* The bow, like the sword, was used in battle as a means of destroying an enemy. It is here used of God, who is represented as going forth to destroy or punish his foes. The language is derived from the customs of war. Comp. Ex. xv. 3; Isa. lxiii. 1—4. The Hebrew here is, "his bow he has *trodden*," alluding to the ancient mode

13 He hath also prepared for him the instruments of death; he ordaineth his arrows *y* against the persecutors.

y Deut. xxxii. 23; Psa. xlv. 5.

14 Behold, he travaileth with iniquity, and hath conceived mischief, and brought forth falsehood.

15 [1] He made a pit, and digged

[1] *hath digged a pit.*

of bending the large and heavy bows used in war, by *treading* on them in order to bend them. ¶ *And made it ready.* Made it ready to shoot the arrow. That is, He is ready to execute punishment on the wicked; or, all the preparations are made for it.

13. *He hath also prepared for him.* The instruments of punishment are already prepared, and God can use them when he pleases. They are not *to be made ready*, and, therefore, there is no necessity for delay when he shall have occasion to use them. The idea is, that arrangements are made for the destruction of the wicked, and that the destruction must come upon them. The world is full of these arrangements, and it is impossible that the sinner should escape. ¶ *The instruments of death.* The means of putting them to death; that is, of punishing them. The particular means referred to here are *arrows*, as being what God has prepared for the wicked. *Death* here is designed simply to denote punishment, as death would be inflicted by arrows. ¶ *He ordaineth his arrows against the persecutors.* Or rather, as the Hebrew is, "He makes his arrows for burning," that is, "for burning arrows." Horsley renders it, "He putteth his arrows in action against those who are ready for burning." Prof. Alexander, "His arrows to (be) burning he will make." De Wette, "His arrows he makes burning." Lat. Vulgate and Sept., "His arrows he has made for the burning:"—that is, probably for those who are burning with rage; for persecutors. This seems to have been the idea of our translators. The Hebrew word — דָּלַק, *dalak*— —means to burn, to flame; and hence, also, to burn with love, with anxiety, or with zeal or wrath—as persecutors do. But here the word seems properly to be connected with *arrows;* and the sense is, as rendered by Gesenius, "he maketh his arrows *flaming;*" that is, burning—alluding to the ancient custom of shooting ignited darts or arrows into besieged towns or camps, for the purpose of setting them on fire, as well as for the purpose of inflicting greater personal injury. The sense is, that God had prepared the means of certain destruction for the wicked. The reference here is not necessarily to persecutors, but what is said here pertains to all the wicked unless they repent.

14. *Behold, he travaileth with iniquity.* The wicked man does. The allusion here is to the pains and throes of child-birth; and the idea is, that the wicked man labours or struggles, even with great pain, to accomplish his purposes of iniquity. All his efforts, purposes, plans, are for the promotion of evil. ¶ *And hath conceived mischief.* That is, he hath formed a scheme of mischief. The allusion here is common when speaking of forming a plan of evil. ¶ *And brought forth falsehood.* The birth is falsehood; that is, self-deception, or disappointment. It does not mean that falsehood was his aim or purpose, or that he had merely accomplished *a lie;* but the idea is, that after all his efforts and pains, after having formed his scheme, and laboured hard (as if in the pangs of child-birth) to bring it forth, it was abortive. He would be disappointed, and would fail at last. This idea is expressed more distinctly in the following verse, and the design of the whole is to say that any plan or purpose of wickedness must be in the end a failure, since God is a righteous Judge, and will vindicate his own cause.

15. *He made a pit.* The allusion here is undoubtedly to a method of

it, and is [z] fallen into the ditch *which* he made.

16 His mischief shall return upon his own head, and his violent dealing shall come down upon his own pate.

17 I will praise the LORD according to his righteousness; and

z Esth. ix. 25; Ecc. x. 8.

hunting wild beasts which was common in ancient times. It consists in digging a pit-fall, and covering it over with brush and grass so as to deceive the animals, and then enclosing them and driving them into it. See Notes on Isa. xxiv. 17. ¶ *And digged it.* And hollowed it out so as to be large enough to contain his prey, and so deep that he could not escape if he fell into it. The idea is, that the enemy here referred to had laid a secret and artful plan to destroy others. He meant that they should not be aware of his plan until the mischief came suddenly upon them. He was preparing to ruin them, and supposed that he was certain of his prey. ¶ *And is fallen into the ditch* which *he made.* Into the pit-fall which he had constructed for others; as if a man who had made a pit-fall for wild beasts had himself fallen into it, and could not extricate himself. That is, he had been snared in his own devices; his cunning had recoiled on himself, and instead of bringing ruin on others he had only managed to bring it on himself. See this sentiment illustrated in the Notes on Job v. 13. A remarkable instance of the kind may be found in Esther (chap. v.—vii.), in the case of Haman. Indeed, such things are not uncommon in the world, where the cunning and the crafty are involved in the consequences of their own plans, and are taken in meshes from which they cannot free themselves. A straightforward course is easy, and men are safe in it; but it requires more skill than most men are endowed with to manage a crooked and crafty policy safely, or so as to be safe themselves in pursuing such a course. A spider will weave a web for flies with no danger to himself, for he is *made* for that, and acts as if he understood all the intricacies of his own web, and may move safely over it in every direction; but man was made to accomplish his purposes in an open and upright way, not by fraud and deceit; hence, when he undertakes a tortuous and crooked course—a plan of secret and scheming policy—in order to ruin others, it often becomes unmanageable by his own skill, or is suddenly sprung upon himself. No one can overvalue a straightforward course in its influence on our ultimate happiness; no one can overestimate the guilt and danger of a crooked and secret policy in devising plans of evil.

16. *His mischief.* The mischief which he had designed for others. ¶ *Shall return upon his own head.* Shall come upon himself. The blow which he aimed at others shall recoil on himself. This is but stating in another form the sentiment which had been expressed in the two previous verses. The language here used has something of a proverbial cast, and perhaps was common in the time of the writer to express this idea. ¶ *And his violent dealing.* Which he shows to others. The word rendered *violent dealing* means violence, injustice, oppression, wrong. ¶ *Shall come down upon his own pate.* The word here rendered *pate* means properly vertex, top, or crown—as of the head. The idea is that it would come upon himself. He would be treated as he had designed to treat others. The sentiment here expressed is found also in Ps. ix. 15; xxxv. 8; xxxvii. 15. Comp. Eurip. Med. 409, and Lucretius v. 1151.

17. *I will praise the* LORD *according to his righteousness.* That is, particularly as manifested in the treatment of the righteous and the wicked, protecting the one, and bringing deserved punishment upon the other.

will sing praise to the name of the LORD most high.

The purpose of the psalm is to show this. In the course of the psalm the author had declared his full conviction that this was the character of God, and now, in view of this, he says that he will render to him the praise and glory which such a character deserves. He will acknowledge him by public acts of praise as such a God; and will at all times ascribe these attributes to him. ¶ *And will sing praise to the name of the* LORD. To the name of JEHOVAH; that is, to Jehovah himself, the *name* being often used to designate a person, or that by which he is known; and also, in many cases, as in this, being significant, or designating the essential nature of him to whom it is applied. ¶ *Most high.* Exalted above all other beings; exalted above all worlds. The purpose here declared of praising God may refer either to the act which he was then performing in the composition of the psalm, or it may be a purpose in respect to the future, declaring his intention to be to retain in future life the memory of those characteristics of the Divine nature now disclosed to him, and to celebrate them in all time to come. The great truth taught is, that God is to be adored for what he *is*, and that his holy character, manifested alike in the treatment of the righteous and the wicked, lays the foundation for exalted praise.

PSALM VIII.

§ 1. *The author of the psalm.*—This is another psalm purporting to have been written by David, and there is nothing in it that leads us to think otherwise.

§ 2. *The title to the psalm.*—The psalm is addressed "To the chief Musician upon Gittith." In regard to the meaning of the phrase "chief Musician," see Notes on the introduction to Ps. iv. The word *Gittith*—גִּתִּית—occurs but in two other places, also in the titles to the psalms, Ps. lxxxi. 1; lxxxiv. 1. It is supposed to refer to a musical instrument so called, either as being common among the *Gittites* (from גִּתִּי, *Gittites*, or an inhabitant of Gath. See 2 Sam. vi. 10, 11; xv. 18), among whom David for some time resided; or as being derived from גַּת, *Gath*—a wine-press, as denoting an instrument that was used by those accustomed to tread the wine-vat, and intended to accompany the songs of the vintage. The former is the more probable derivation, as it is known that David dwelt for some time among that people, and it is not at all improbable that an instrument of music in use among them should have become common among the Hebrews. Nothing is known, however, as to whether it was a stringed instrument or a wind instrument. Compare, however, Ugolin, Thes. Sac. Ant. xxxii. 487. All that can be ascertained, with any degree of probability about this instrument, is, that as each of the psalms to which this title is prefixed is of a cheerful or joyous nature, it would seem that this instrument was adapted to music of this kind, rather than to that which was pensive or serious. This idea also would agree well with the supposition that it denotes an instrument that was employed by those connected with the vintage. Comp. Isa. xvi. 10.

§ 3. *Occasion on which the psalm was composed.*—Of this nothing is specified in the psalm itself, and it is impossible now to ascertain it. Aben Ezra, and some others, have supposed that it was written when David brought up the ark to the house of Obed-edom the Gittite, as mentioned in 1 Chron. xiii. 12—14. But there is nothing in the psalm adapted to such an occasion. Rüdinger supposes that it was composed in the joy of taking possession of Mount Zion. Others have supposed that it was on occasion of the victory of David over Goliath of Gath; but there is nothing in it adapted to the celebration of such a victory.

If we may judge from the psalm itself, it would seem probable that it was composed by night in the contemplation of the starry heavens—naturally suggesting, in view of the vastness and beauty of the celestial luminaries, the littleness of man. This also filled the mind of the psalmist with wonder that the God who marshals all these hosts should condescend to regard the condition and wants of a being so feeble and frail as man, and should have exalted him as he has done over

PSALM VIII.

To the chief Musician upon *a* Gittith.
A Psalm of David.

O LORD, our Lord, how excellent[b] *is* thy name in all the earth! who hast set thy glory above the heavens.

a Psa. lxxxi. and lxxxiv. *title*.

b Psa. cxlviii. 13.

his works. That it was composed or suggested in the night seems probable, from ver. 3, where the psalmist represents himself as surveying or "considering" the "heavens, the work" of the Divine "fingers," and as making the "moon and the stars" the subject of his contemplation, but not mentioning *the sun*. In such contemplations, when looking on the vastness and grandeur, the beauty and order, of the heavenly hosts, it was not unnatural for the writer to think of his own comparative littleness, and then the comparative littleness of *man* everywhere. No time is more favourable for suggesting such thoughts than the still night, when the stars are shining clearly in the heavens, and when the moon is moving on in the silent majesty of its course. It would seem also, from ver. 2, to be probable that the immediate occasion of this expression of admiration of the name and character of God was some act of condescension on his part in which he had bestowed signal favour on the writer—*as if* he had ordained strength out of the mouth of babes and sucklings—from even the most feeble and helpless. Perhaps it was in view of some favour bestowed on David himself; and his soul is overwhelmed with a sense of the condescension of God in noticing one so weak and feeble and helpless as he was. From the contemplation of this, the thought is naturally turned to the honour which God had everywhere bestowed upon man.

The psalm, though one part of it is applied by the apostle Paul to Christ (Heb. ii. 6, 7), does not appear originally to have had any designed reference to the Messiah, though the apostle shows that its language had a complete fulfilment in him, and in him alone. See Notes on that passage. The psalm is complete in itself, as applicable to man as he was originally created, and according to the purposes of his creation; though it is true that the original design will be carried out and completed only in the dominion which will be granted to the Messiah, who, as a man, has illustrated in the highest manner the original purpose of the creation of the race, and in whom alone the original design will be fully carried out.

§ 4. *Contents of the psalm.*—The psalm embraces the following points:—

I. An admiring recognition of the excellence of the name of God (that is, of God himself);—of that excellence as manifested in all the earth, ver. 1. The excellency referred to, as the subsequent part of the psalm shows, is in his great condescension, and in his conferring such honour on man—a being so feeble as compared with himself, and so unworthy as compared with the glory of the heavens.

II. The immediate occasion of this reflection, or the cause which suggested it, ver. 2. This seems to have been some remarkable manifestation to one who was feeble and helpless, *as if* God had ordained strength out of the mouth of babes and sucklings. It is not improbable, as remarked above, that in this the psalmist refers to himself as having been, though conscious of weakness and helplessness, the means of overcoming the enemies of God, as if God had ordained strength through him, or had endowed him with strength not his own.

III. The psalmist is led into admiration of the condescension of God in bestowing such dignity and honour on man, vers. 3—8. This admiration is founded on two things:—

(1) That the God who had made the heavens, the moon and the stars, should condescend to notice man or creatures so insignificant and unworthy of notice, vers. 3, 4.

(2) The actual honour conferred on man, in the rank which God had given him in the dominion over his works here below; and in the wide extent of that dominion over the beasts of the field, the fowls of the air, and the inhabitants of the seas, vers. 5—8.

IV. The psalm concludes with a repetition of the sentiment in the first verse—the reflection on the excellency of the Divine name and majesty, ver. 9.

1. O LORD. Heb., JEHOVAH. It is an address to God by his chosen and peculiar title, Ex. iii. 14. Compare Notes on Isa. i. 2. ¶ *Our Lord.* The word here used—אֲדֹנָי, *Adonai*—

2 Out of the mouth of [c] babes and sucklings hast thou [1] ordain-

c Matt. xi. 25; xxi. 16; 1 Cor. i. 27.

1 *founded.*

means properly master, lord, ruler, owner, and is such a title as is given to an owner of land or of slaves, to kings, or to rulers, and is applied to God as being the ruler or governor of the universe. The meaning here is, that the psalmist acknowledged JEHOVAH to be the rightful *ruler, king,* or *master* of himself and of all others. He comes before him with the feeling that Jehovah is the universal ruler—the king and proprietor of all things. ¶ *How excellent* is *thy name.* How excellent or exalted art *thou*—the *name* being often used to denote the *person.* The idea is, "How glorious art thou in thy manifested excellence or character." ¶ *In all the earth.* In all parts of the world. That is, the manifestation of his perfect character was not confined to any one country, but was seen in all lands, and among all people. In every place his true character was made known through his works; in every land there were evidences of his wisdom, his greatness, his goodness, his condescension. ¶ *Who hast set thy glory above the heavens.* The word here used, and rendered "*hast set,*" is in the imperative mood—תְּנָה, *tenah—give;* and it should probably have been so rendered here, "which thy glory give thou;" that is, "which glory of thine, or implied in thy name, *give* or *place above the heavens.*" In other words, let it be exalted in the highest degree, and to the highest place, even *above* the heavens on which he was gazing, and which were in themselves so grand, ver. 3. It expresses the wish or prayer of the writer that the name or praise of God, so manifest in the earth, might be exalted in the highest possible degree—be more elevated than the moon and the stars—exalted and adored in all worlds. In His name there was such intrinsic grandeur that he desired that it might be regarded as the highest object in the universe, and might blaze forth above all worlds. On the grammatical construction of this word—תְּנָה—see an article by Prof. Stuart, in the Bibliotheca Sacra, vol. ix. pp. 73—77. Prof. Stuart supposes that the word is not formed from נָתַן, *nathan—to give,* as is the common explanation, but from תָּנָה, *tanah*—to give presents, to distribute gifts, Hos. viii. 9, 10, and that it should be rendered, *Thou who diffusest abroad thy glory over the heavens.*

2. *Out of the mouth.* This passage is quoted by the Saviour in Matt. xxi. 16, to vindicate the conduct of the children in the temple crying, "Hosanna to the Son of David," against the objections of the Pharisees and Scribes, and is perhaps alluded to by him in Matt. xi. 25. It is not affirmed, however, in either place, that it had an original reference to the times of the Messiah, or that it was meant, as used by the psalmist, to denote that *children* would be employed in the praise of God. The language sufficiently expressed the idea which the Saviour meant to convey; and the *principle* or great truth involved in the psalm was applicable to the use which he made of it. The language would, perhaps, most naturally denote that infant children *would* give utterance to the praises of God, as the word *mouth* is used; but still it is not quite certain that the psalmist meant to convey that idea. It is probable, as we shall see, that he meant to say, God had conferred great honour on men—men so humble and weak that they might be compared to infants—by making them the means of overthrowing his enemies, thus showing the greatness of the Divine condescension. ¶ *Babes.* The word here used —עוֹלֵל, *olail*—means properly a boy or child, and is usually connected with the word rendered *sucklings,* Jer. xliv. 7; Lam. ii. 11. It is applied to a boy playing in the streets, Jer. vi. 11; ix. 21; asking for bread,

ed strength, because of thine enemies; that thou mightest still the enemy [d] and the avenger.

d Psa. xliv. 16.

Lam. iv. 4; carried away captive, Lam. i. 5; borne in the arms, Lam. ii. 20; and once to an unborn infant, Job iii. 16. It refers here to a child, or to one who is like a child; and the idea is that those to whom it is applied were naturally unable to accomplish what was done by them, and that God had honoured them, and had shown his own condescension, by making them the instruments of doing what they had done. ¶ *And sucklings.* The word here used—יוֹנֵק, *yonaik*—means a suckling, or a sucking child, a babe, Deut. xxxii. 25. It may be used literally, or employed to denote one who, in respect to strength, may be compared with a babe. The latter is probably the use made of it here. ¶ *Hast thou ordained strength.* The word rendered *ordained*—יָסַד, *yasad* — means to found, to lay the foundation of, as of a building, Ezra iii. 12; Isa. liv. 11. Then it means to establish, appoint, ordain, constitute, etc. The meaning here is, that in what is referred to, there was, as it were, some *basis* or *foundation* for what is called "strength;" *i. e.*, that what is here meant by "strength" rested on *that* as a foundation—to wit, on what was done by babes and sucklings. The word *strength* is rendered by the Septuagint *praise*—*αἶνον*—and this is followed in the quotation in Matt. xxi. 16. The same rendering is adopted in the Latin Vulgate and in the Syriac. The Hebrew word — עֹז, *oz* — properly means *strength, might;* and the idea here would seem to be, that even from babes and sucklings—from those who were in themselves so feeble—God had taken occasion to accomplish a work requiring great *power*—to wit, in "stilling the enemy and the avenger;" that is, he had made those who were so feeble the instruments of accomplishing so great a work. ¶ *Because of thine enemies.* In respect to thine enemies, or in order to accomplish something in regard to them, viz., in "stilling" them, as is immediately specified. The idea is, that there were those who rose up against God, and opposed his government and plans, and that God, in overcoming them, instead of putting forth his own power directly, had condescended to employ those who were weak and feeble like little children. Who these enemies were is not specified, but it is most natural to suppose that the reference is to some of the foes of the author of the psalm, who had been subdued by the prowess of his arm,—by strength imparted to him, though in himself feeble as an infant. ¶ *That thou mightest still.* Mightest cause to *rest*, or to *cease.* The original word—שָׁבַת, *Shabath*—from which our word *Sabbath* is derived, means to rest; to lie by; to sit down; to sit still; and in Hiphil, to *cause* to rest, or to cause to desist; to put an end to, Ezek. xxxiv. 10; Josh. xxii. 25; Psa. xlvi. 9; Prov. xviii. 18. Here it means to bring to an end the purposes of the enemy and the avenger; or, to cause him to *desist* from his designs. ¶ *The enemy.* The enemy of the writer, regarded also as the enemy of God. ¶ *And the avenger.* One who was endeavouring to take revenge, or who was acting as if determined to avenge some imaginary or real wrong. This, too, may refer either to some one who was seeking to revenge himself on the author of the psalm, or who, with the spirit of revenge, stood up against God, and had set himself against him.

In regard to the meaning of this verse, which I apprehend is the *key* to the whole psalm, and which contains the original *germ* of the psalm, or the *thought* which suggested the train of reflection in it, the following remarks may be made:—(*a*) There is no evidence that it was designed to refer originally to infants, or to children of any age, as stating anything which *they* would do in contributing to the praise of God, or as discomfiting sceptics and cavillers by "their instinctive recognition of God's being and glory," as is supposed by Calvin, De Wette, Prof. Alexander, and others. What is said here to be done by "babes and sucklings" has reference to some mighty enemy that had been overcome, not to anything which had been effected by the influence of the recognition of God by little children. It may be doubted, also, whether there *is* any such "instinctive admiration of his works, even by the youngest children," as would be "a strong defence against those who would question the being and glory" of God, as is supposed by Prof. Alexander and others; and, at all events, *that* is not the manifest thought in the passage. (*b*) Nor does it refer merely to *praise* as proceeding from children, as being that by which the effect referred to is accomplished. It is true that this idea is in the translation by the LXX., and true that it is so quoted in Matt. xxi. 16, and true, also, that, *as* quoted by the Saviour, and as originally applied, it was *adapted* to the end which the Saviour had in view—to *silence* the chief priests and Scribes, who objected to the praises and hosannas of the children in the temple; for the psalm, on any interpretation, originally meant that God would accomplish good effects by those who were feeble and weak as children, and this *principle* was applicable to the praises of the children in the temple. But it does not appear that it originally referred to *praise*, either of children or others. It was to some manifested *strength* or *prowess*, by which some enemy, or some one who was seeking revenge, was overcome by the instrumentality of those who might be compared with children on account of their feebleness. From this the psalmist takes occasion to make his reflections on the exalted honour conferred in general on a creature so weak and feeble as man, especially in the wide dominion granted him over the inferior creation. (*c*) This was, not improbably, some enemy of the author of the psalm; but *who* it was is not mentioned. David was often, however, in the course of his life, in such circumstances as are here supposed. Might it not refer to Goliath of Gath—a mighty giant, and a formidable enemy of the people of God, overcome by David, quite a stripling—a child? Would not the language of the psalm agree with that? Was it not true that he was an "enemy" and an "avenger," or one seeking revenge? and was it not true that God had, from one who was a mere child, "ordained strength" to subdue him? (*d*) God had, then, condescended to honour one who was in himself weak and feeble as a child—who had no power of himself to accomplish what had been done. (*e*) This was great condescension on the part of God; and *especially* was it to be so regarded when the eye looked out—as the author of the psalm appears to have done at the time of its composition—on the starry heavens, and contemplated their greatness and grandeur. What astonishing condescension was it that he who marshalled all those hosts should bestow such honour on man! (*f*) It was not, therefore, unnatural to reflect on the greatness of the honour which God had actually bestowed on man, and the dignity to which God had exalted him; and the psalmist is thus, from a particular act of his condescension, led into the beautiful train of reflections on the exalted dominion of man with which the psalm concludes. Thus understood, the psalm has no *original* reference to the Messiah, but still it contains the *principle* on which the apostle reasons in Heb. ii.; for the dignity of *man* is most seen in the Redeemer, and the *actual* conferring of all the dignity and honour referred to in the psalm—the *actual* and *entire* subjugation of the earth to *man*—will be found only in the universal dominion conceded to Him. At the same time, however, there is a foundation for all that the psalmist says in respect to the honour originally conferred on man, and in

3 When I consider thy heavens, the work of thy fingers; the moon and the stars, which thou hast ordained;

4 [e] What is man, that thou art mindful of him? and the son of man, that thou visitest him?

e Psa. cxliv. 3; Heb. ii. 6—9.

his actual dominion over the inferior creation.

3. *When I consider thy heavens.* When I contemplate or look upon. They are called *his* heavens because he made them—because he is the proprietor of them—perhaps because they are his abode. ¶ *The work of thy fingers.* Which thy fingers have made. The fingers are the instruments by which we construct a piece of work—perhaps indicating *skill* rather than *strength;* and hence so used in respect to God, as it is by his *skill* that the heavens have been made. ¶ *The moon and the stars.* Showing, as remarked above, that probably this psalm was composed at night, or that the train of thought was suggested by the contemplation of the starry worlds. It is not improbable that the thoughts occurred to the psalmist when meditating on the signal honour which God had conferred on him, a feeble man (Notes on ver. 2), and when his thoughts were at the same time directed to the goodness of God as the heavens were contemplated in their silent grandeur. ¶ *Which thou hast ordained.* Prepared, fitted up, constituted, appointed. He had fixed them in their appropriate spheres, and they now silently showed forth his glory.

4. *What is man.* What claim has one so weak, and frail, and short-lived, to be remembered by thee? What is there in man that entitles him to so much notice? Why has God conferred on him so signal honour? Why has he placed him over the works of his hands? Why has he made so many arrangements for his comfort? Why has he done so much to save him? He is so insignificant, his life is so much like a vapour, he so soon disappears, he is so sinful and polluted, that the question may well be asked, why such honour has been conferred on him, and why such a dominion over the world has been given him. See these thoughts more fully expanded in the Notes on Heb. ii. 6. ¶ *That thou art mindful of him.* That thou dost *remember* him; that is, think of him, attend to him,—that he does not pass away wholly from thy thoughts. Why should a God who is so vast and glorious, and who has all the starry worlds, so beautiful and grand, to claim his attention—why should he turn his thoughts on *man?* And especially why should he honour him as he *has* done by giving him dominion over the works of his hands? ¶ *And the son of man.* Any descendant of man—any one of the race. What was man, as he was originally made, that such exalted honour should have been conferred on him; and what has any one of his descendants become, in virtue of his native faculties or acquired endowments, that he should be thus honoured? The design is the same as in the former part of the verse, to express the idea that there was nothing in *man,* considered in any respect, that entitled him to this exalted honour. Nothing that man has done since the time when the question was asked by the psalmist has contributed to diminish the force of the inquiry. ¶ *That thou visitest him.* As thou dost; that is, with the attention and care which thou dost bestow upon him; not forgetting him; not leaving him; not passing him by. The word here used —פָּקַד, *pakad*—would properly express a *visitation* for any purpose—for inspection; for mercy; for friendship; for judgment, etc. Here it refers to the *attention* bestowed by God on man in conferring on him such marks of favour and honour as he had done—such attention that he never seemed to forget him, but was constantly coming to him with some new proof of favour. What God has done

5 For thou hast made him a little lower than the angels, and hast crowned him with glory and honour.

6 Thou madest him to have dominion over the works of thy hands: thou [f] hast put all *things* under his feet:

f 1 Cor. xv. 27.

for man since the psalmist wrote this, has done nothing to weaken the force of this inquiry.

5. *For thou hast made him.* Thou hast made man as such; that is, he was such in the original design of his creation, in the rank given him, and in the dominion conceded to him. The *object* here is to show the honour conferred on man, or to show how God has regarded and honoured him; and the thought is, that in his original creation, though so insignificant as compared with the vast worlds over which God presides, he had given him a rank but little inferior to that of the angels. See Notes on Heb. ii. 7. ¶ *A little lower.* The Hebrew word used here—חָסֵר, *hhasar*, means to want, to lack—and then, to be in want, to be diminished. The meaning is, "Thou hast caused him *to want but little;*" that is, he was but little inferior. ¶ *Than the angels.* So this is rendered by the Chaldee Paraphrase: by the Septuagint; by the Latin Vulgate; by the Syriac and Arabic; and by the author of the Epistle to the Hebrews (ch. ii. 7), who has literally quoted the fourth, fifth, and sixth verses from the Septuagint. The Hebrew, however, is—מֵאֱלֹהִים—*than God.* So Gesenius renders it, "Thou hast caused him to want but little of God; that is, thou hast made him but little lower than God." So De Wette, *nur wenig unter Gott.* So Tholuck renders it, *nur um wenig unter Gott.* This is the more *natural* construction, and this would convey an idea conformable to the course of thought in the psalm, though it has been usually supposed that the word here used—אֱלֹהִים, *Elohim* — may be applied to angels, or even men, as in Ps. lxxxii. 1; xcvii. 7; cxxxviii. 1; Ex. xxi. 6; xxii. 8, 9. Gesenius (Thesau. Ling. Heb., p. 95) maintains that the word never has this signification. The authority, however, of the Chaldee, the Septuagint, the Syriac, and the author of the Epistle to the Hebrews, would seem sufficient to show that *that* meaning may be attached to the word here with propriety, and that somehow that idea was naturally suggested in the passage itself. Still, if it were not for these versions, the most natural interpretation would be that which takes the word in its usual sense, as referring to God, and as meaning that, in respect to his dominion over the earth, man had been placed in a condition comparatively but little inferior to God himself; he had made him almost equal to himself. ¶ *And hast crowned him with glory and honour.* With exalted honour. See Notes on Heb. ii. 7.

6. *Thou madest him to have dominion.* Thou didst *cause* him to have, or didst *give* him this dominion. It does not mean that God made or created him for that end, but that he had conceded to him that dominion, thus conferring on him exalted honour. The allusion is to Gen. i. 26, 28. ¶ *Over the works of thy hands.* His works upon the earth, for the dominion extends no further. ¶ *Thou hast put all* things *under his feet.* Hast placed all things in subjection to him. Compare Psa. xlvii. 3; xci. 13; Lam. iii. 34; Rom. xvi. 20; 1 Cor. xv. 25. The language is taken from the act of treading down enemies in battle; from putting the feet on the necks of captives, etc. The idea is that of complete and entire subjection. This dominion was originally given to man at his creation, and it still remains (though not so absolute and entire as this), for nothing is in itself more remarkable than the dominion which *man*, by

7 [1]All sheep and oxen, yea,
and the beasts of the field;
8 The fowl of the air, and the
fish of the sea, *and whatsoever*
passeth through the paths of the
seas.

[1] *Flocks and oxen, all of them.*

---

nature so feeble, exercises over the inferior creation. It is impossible to account for this in any other way than as it is accounted for in the Bible, by the supposition that it was originally conceded to man by his Creator. On the question of the applicability of this to Christ, see Notes on Heb. ii. 6—9.

7. *All sheep and oxen.* Flocks and herds. Gen. i. 26, "over the cattle." Nothing is more manifest than the control which man exercises over flocks and herds—making them subservient to his use, and obedient to his will. ¶ *And the beasts of the field.* Those not included in the general phrase "sheep and oxen." The word rendered *field,* שָׂדֶה, *sadeh*—or the poetic form, as here——שָׂדַי—*Sadai,* means properly a *plain;* a level tract of country; then, a field, or a tilled farm, Gen. xxiii. 17; xlvii. 20, 24; and then the fields, the open country, as opposed to a city, a village, a camp, Gen. xxv. 27; and hence in this place the expression means the beasts that roam at large—wild beasts, Gen. ii. 20; iii. 14. Here the allusion is to the power which man has of subduing the wild beasts; of capturing them, and making them subservient to his purposes; of preventing their increase and their depredations; and of taming them so that they shall obey his will, and become his servants. Nothing is more remarkable than this, and nothing furnishes a better illustration of Scripture than the conformity of this with the declaration (Gen. ix. 2), "And the fear of you, and the dread of you, shall be upon every beast of the earth, and upon every fowl of the air," etc. Comp. Notes on James iii. 7. It is to be remembered that no small number of what are now domestic animals were originally wild, and that they have been subdued and tamed by the power and skill of man. No animal has shown himself superior to this power and skill.

8. *The fowl of the air.* Gen. i. 26, "Over the fowl of the air." Gen. ix. 2, "Upon every fowl of the air." This dominion is the more remarkable because the birds of the air seem to be beyond the reach of man; and yet, equally with the beasts of the field, they are subject to his control. Man captures and destroys them; he prevents their multiplication and their ravages. Numerous as they are, and rapid as is their flight, and strong as many of them are, they have never succeeded in making man subject to them, or in disturbing the purposes of man. See Notes on James iii. 7. ¶ *And the fish of the sea.* Gen. i. 26, "Over the fish of the sea." Gen. ix. 2, "Upon all the fishes of the sea." This must be understood in a general sense, and this is perhaps still more remarkable than the dominion over the beasts of the field and the fowls of the air, for the fishes that swim in the ocean seem to be placed still farther from the control of man. Yet, so far as is necessary for his use and for safety, they are, in fact, put under the control of man, and he makes them minister to his profit. Not a little of that which contributes to the support, the comfort, and the luxury of man, comes from the ocean. From the mighty whale to the shell-fish that furnished the Tyrian dye, or to that which furnishes the beautiful pearl, man has shown his power to make the dwellers in the deep subservient to his will. ¶ And whatsoever *passeth through the paths of the seas.* Everything, in general, that passes through the paths of the sea, as if the ocean was formed with *paths* or *highways* for them to pass over. Some have referred this to man, as passing over the sea and subduing its

9 O LORD, our Lord, how excellent *is* thy name in all the earth!

inhabitants; some, to the *fishes* before spoken of; but the most natural construction is that which is adopted in our received version, as referring to *everything* which moves in the waters. The idea is that man has a wide and universal dominion—a dominion so wide as to excite amazement, wonder, and gratitude, that it has been conceded to one so feeble as he is.

9. *O* LORD, *our Lord, how excellent,* etc. Repeating the sentiment with which the psalm opens, as now fully illustrated, or as its propriety is now seen. The intermediate thoughts are simply an illustration of this; and now we see what occupied the attention of the psalmist when, in ver. 1, he gave utterance to what seems there to be a somewhat abrupt sentiment. We now, at the close of the psalm, see clearly its beauty and truthfulness.

PSALM IX.

§ 1. *Author of the psalm.*—This psalm is ascribed to David, not only in the title, but in all the versions, and there is no reason to doubt the correctness of this. It would not be difficult to show from its contents that the sentiments and style of composition are such as accord with the other compositions of David.

§ 2. *Occasion on which the psalm was composed.*—On this point nothing is intimated expressly in the psalm, unless it be in the title, "To the chief Musician upon Muth-labben." The meaning of this will be considered in another part of the introduction to the psalm (§ 4). It will be seen there that nothing is determined by that title in regard to the origin of the psalm, or the time when it was composed. Neither is there any certain tradition which will determine this, and most that has been written on this point has been mere conjecture, or has arisen out of some interpretation of the enigmatical title "*upon Muth-labben.*" Some have supposed that the word *labben* refers to some foreign king or prince slain by David, and that the psalm was composed on his death. Others, following the Targum, or Chaldee Paraphrase (see § 4), suppose that the person referred to was Goliath of Gath, and that it was composed on his death. Others, as Rüdinger, suppose that it is a psalm of thanksgiving on occasion of the victory over Absalom, and the suppression of his rebellion by his death: a *harsh* and *unnatural* supposition, as if *any* father, in any circumstances, could compose a psalm of praise on occasion of the death of a son. Moeller supposes that it was composed on occasion of a victory over the Philistines by David; Ferrand, who unites this psalm with the following, supposes that the whole refers to the times of the captivity in Babylon, and is a triumphal song of the people over their enemies; and Venema, who also thinks that these two psalms should be united, supposes that Ps. ix. 1-18 refers to David, and to his deliverance from all his enemies, and the remainder to the times of the Maccabees, and the deliverance from the persecutions under Antiochus Epiphanes. Bishop Horsley styles the psalm "Thanksgiving for the extirpation of the Atheistical faction, promised in Psalm x," and supposes that the order should be reversed, and that the whole refers to some great deliverance —either the "overthrow of the Babylonian empire by Cyrus, or the defeat of Haman's plot." The Jewish writers, Jarchi and Aben Ezra, suppose that it was composed on occasion of the defeat and death of some foreign prince. From this variety of views, none of which seem to rest on certain historical grounds, it appears probable that the exact occasion on which the psalm was composed cannot now be ascertained in such a way as to leave no ground for doubt. The only indications of the occasion on which it was written must be found, if at all, in the psalm itself. In the psalm we find the following things, which may, perhaps, be all that is necessary to enable us to understand it.

(*a*) It was composed in view of *enemies* of the writer, or *foes* with whom he had been engaged, ver. 3: "When mine *enemies* are turned back, they shall fall and perish at thy presence." Comp. vers. 6, 13, 19, 20.

(*b*) These were *foreign* enemies, or those who are called *heathen*, that is, belonging to idolatrous nations, ver. 5: "Thou hast rebuked *the heathen.*" Comp. vers. 15, 19.

(*c*) They were *desolating* foes—*invading* foes—those who laid a land waste in their marches, ver. 6: "Thou hast destroyed cities: their memorial is perished with them."

(*d*) The writer had achieved a victory over them, and for this he celebrated the praises of God for his interposition, vers. 1, 2, 10, 11, 15. This victory thus achieved was such as to make him certain of ultimate complete triumph.

(*e*) Yet he was still surrounded by enemies, and he still asks God's merciful interposition in his behalf, ver. 13: "Have mercy upon me, O Lord; consider my trouble which I suffer of them that hate me, thou that liftest me up from the gates of death." Comp. vers. 18—20.

David was not unfrequently in his life in circumstances such as are here supposed, and it is not possible now to determine the *exact* occasion to which the psalm alludes.

§ 3. *The contents of the psalm.*—The psalm embraces two leading subjects—one pertaining to the past and the other to the future, both illustrating the character of God, and both giving occasion to the writer to express his confidence in God. The one relates to deliverance already granted; the other to deliverance still hoped for in his troubles.

I. The first relates to deliverance from trouble, or conquest over foes, already granted, and to the occasion which that furnished for praising God, and for pious reflections on his character.

(1) The psalmist expresses his thanks to God, or pours out the language of praise for mercies that have been received, vers. 1, 2.

(2) The particular reason for this is stated; that God had enabled him to overcome many of his enemies,—the heathen that had risen up against him, who had now been subdued, vers. 3—6.

(3) This gives occasion for pious reflections on the character of God, as one who would endure for ever; as one who had set up his throne to do judgment or right; as one who would be a refuge for the oppressed; as one who might be confided in by all who knew him; as one who would remember the foes of the righteous, and who would not forget the cry of the humble, vers. 7-12. The principal truth taught in this part of the psalm is, that God is a refuge and help for those who are in trouble and danger; that all such may put their trust in Him; and that He will interpose to save them.

II. The second part, constructed in a manner similar to the former, relates to the future, and to what the psalmist *hoped* still from God, in view of the character which He had evinced in his former troubles, vers. 13—20.

(1) The psalmist still needs help, vers. 13, 14. He still has trouble from them that hate him, and he calls upon God still to interpose and lift him up from the gates of death, that he *may* praise him.

(2) He refers to the fact that the heathen, who surrounded him as his foes, had sunk down into the pit which they had made for others; and that their foot was taken in the net which they had hid: referring either to what *had* occurred in the past as the foundation of his present hope, or being so certain that this *would be done* that he could speak of it as if it were now actually accomplished, ver. 15.

(3) This also, as in the former case, gives occasion for pious reflections on the character of God, and on the fact that he would interpose to destroy the wicked, and to protect the righteous, vers. 16—18.

(4) In view of all this, the psalmist calls on God still to interpose—to manifest the same character which He had formerly done, by protecting him, and by overcoming his foes, vers. 19, 20. The principal truth taught in this part of the psalm is, that the wicked will be destroyed; that they, as contradistinguished from the righteous, can hope for no protection from God, but will be cut down and punished.

The condition of the author of the psalm then was, that he *had been* surrounded by foes, and that God had interposed in his behalf, giving him occasion for praise and thanksgiving; that he was still surrounded by formidable enemies, yet he felt assured that God would manifest the same character which He had done formerly, and that he might, therefore, call upon Him to interpose and give him occasion for future praise.

§ 4. *The title of the psalm.*—The psalm is directed to "*the chief Musician upon Muth-labben.*" In regard to the phrase "chief Musician," see Notes on the title to Ps. iv. The phrase, "*upon Muth-labben,*" occurs nowhere else, and very different explanations have been given of its meaning. The Targum, or Chaldee Paraphrase, renders it "To be sung over the man that went out between the camps;" that is, Goliath of Gath; and the author of the Chaldee Paraphrase, evidently supposed it was written on the

PSALM IX.

To the chief Musician upon Muth-labben. A Psalm of David.

I WILL praise *thee*, O LORD, with my whole heart; I will show forth all thy [g] marvellous works.

g Psa. cxxxix. 14.

occasion of his death. The Latin Vulgate renders it, "Pro occultis filii;" and so the Septuagint, ὑπὲρ τῶν κρυφίων τοῦ υἱοῦ—"for the secret things (mysteries) of the Son:" but what idea was attached to those words it is impossible now to determine. The Syriac has this title: "Concerning the Messiah taking his throne and kingdom, and prostrating his foe." Luther renders it, "A Psalm of David concerning a beautiful youth"—von der schönen Jugend. Substantially so also De Wette; Nach der Jungfernweise, den Beniten. Tholuck renders it, "To the chief Musician, after the melody 'Death to the Son' (Tod dem Sohne), a Psalm of David."

After this variety in the explanation of the title, it is certainly not easy to determine the meaning. The most probable opinions may be regarded as two.

(1) That which supposes that it was a melody designed to be sung by females, or with female voices: literally, according to this interpretation, *after the manner of virgins;* that is, with the female voice *treble*, *soprano*, in opposition to the deeper voice of men. Comp. 1 Chron. xv. 20. Forkel, in his History of Musick (Gesch. der Musik, 1, 142), understands it as meaning *virgin measures*, like the German *Jungfrauweis*. Gesenius, who supposes that it refers to the female voice or treble, regards the title—עַל־מוּת—"upon Muth," as being the same as עַל עֲלָמוֹת, in Ps. xlvi., "Upon Alamoth," and supposes that it is derived from עַלְמָה, *almah*—a virgin.

(2) The other opinion is that which supposes that the title is the beginning of some old and well-known melody in common use, and that the idea is, that this psalm was to be sung to that melody. That melody was, as expressed by Tholuck and others, a melody *on the death of a son*, and was set to some hymn that had been composed with reference to such an event. This is founded on the supposition that the national melodies had become in some degree fixed and unchangeable, or that certain melodies or *tunes* originally composed for a particular occasion had become popular, and that the melody would be affixed to new pieces of music. This is common in the East; and, indeed, it is common in all countries. See this idea illustrated in Rosenmüller (Morgenland, No. 800). The meaning, as thus expressed, is, "According to the manner (or, to the air) of the song (or poem) called *Death to the Son.*" Thus understood, it does not refer to the death of Absalom (as some have supposed), since there is nothing in the psalm that would correspond with such a supposition; nor to the death of Goliath, as the Targum supposes; but the composition was to be sung to the well-known air, or tune, entitled "Death to the Son." But when that air was composed, or on what occasion, there is of course no possibility now of ascertaining; and equally impossible is it to recover the *air*, or *tune*. The literal meaning of the title is עַל, *al*, on, or according to—מוּת, *muth*, death—לַבֵּן, *labbain*, to the son.

1. *I will praise* thee, O LORD. That is, in view of the merciful interpositions referred to in the psalm (vers. 3—5), and in view of the attributes of God's character which had been displayed on that occasion (vers. 7—12). ¶ *With my whole heart.* Not with divided affection, or with partial gratitude. He meant that *all* his powers should be employed in this service; that he would give utterance to his feelings of gratitude and adoration in the loftiest and purest manner possible. ¶ *I will show forth.* I will recount or narrate—to wit, in this song of praise. ¶ *All thy marvellous works.* All his works or doings fitted to excite admiration or wonder. The reference here is particularly to what God had done which had given occasion to this psalm, but still the psalmist designs undoubtedly to connect with this the purpose to give a *general* expression of praise in view of *all* that God had done that was fitted to excite such feelings.

2. *I will be glad.* I will rejoice,

2 I will be glad and rejoice in
thee: I will sing praise to thy
name, O thou [h] most high.
3 When mine enemies are
turned back, they shall fall and
perish at thy presence.
4 For thou hast [1] maintained
my right and my cause; thou

h Psa. lxxxiii. 18.

1 *made my judgment.*

and will express my joy. ¶ *And rejoice in thee.* I will exult; I will triumph. That is, he would express his joy *in God*—in knowing that there was such a Being; in all that he had done for him; in all the evidences of his favour and friendship. ¶ *Will sing praise to thy name.* To *thee;* the name often being put for the person. ¶ *O thou Most High.* Thou who art supreme—the God over all. See Notes on Ps. vii. 17.

3. *When mine enemies are turned back.* Who these enemies were, the psalmist does not say. It is clear, however, as was remarked in the introduction, that the psalm was composed (*a*) in view of a victory which *had been* achieved over some formidable enemies; and (*b*) in view of some dangers still impending from a similar source. The literal meaning of the passage here is, "In the turning of my enemies back;" that is, in their retreat, discomfiture, overthrow. So far as the Hebrew form of expression is concerned, this may either refer to what *had been done*, or to what *would be;* and may imply either that they had been turned back, or that the psalmist hoped and believed that they would be; for in either case the fact would show the Divine perfections, and give occasion for gratitude and praise. The *verbs* with which this is connected—"they shall fall and perish"—are indeed in the Hebrew, as in our version, in the future tense; but this does not necessarily determine the question whether the psalmist refers to what *had* occurred or what *would* occur. His attitude is this: he contemplates his enemies as mighty and formidable; he sees the danger which exists when such enemies surround one; he looks at the interposition of God, and he sees that whenever it occurs it would be followed by this consequence, that they would stumble and fall before him. But while this verse does not determine the question whether he refers to what has been, or to what would be, the subsequent verses (4—6) seem to settle it, where he speaks as if this were already done, and as if God had interposed in a remarkable manner in discomfiting his foes. I regard this, therefore, as a reflection on what *had* occurred, and as expressing what was then actually a ground of praise and thanksgiving. ¶ *They shall fall and perish.* A general statement in view of what had occurred, meaning that this would always be the case. ¶ *At thy presence.* Before thee; that is, when thou dost manifest thyself. This was the reason why they would stumble and fall, and is equivalent to saying, that "whenever mine enemies are turned back, the reason why they stumble and fall is *thy presence.* It is the interposition of thy power. It is not to be traced to the prowess of man that they thus turn back, and that they fall and perish; it is to be traced to the fact that *thou art present,*—that thou dost interpose." It is thus an acknowledgment of God as the author of the victory in all cases.

4. *For thou hast maintained my right and my cause.* My righteous cause; that is, when he was unequally attacked. When his enemies came upon him in an unprovoked and cruel manner, God had interposed and had defended his cause. This shows that the psalmist refers to something that had occurred in the past; also that he regarded his cause as right,—for the interposition of God in his behalf had confirmed him in this belief. ¶ *Thou satest in the throne judging right.* As if he had been seated on a bench

satest in the throne [1]judging right.
5 Thou hast rebuked the heathen, thou hast destroyed the wicked, thou hast put out their name [i]for ever and ever.
6 [2]O thou enemy! destructions are come to a perpetual end; and

[1] *in righteousness.*

[i] Prov. x. 7.
[2] Or, *the destructions of the enemy are come to a perpetual end; and* their *cities hast thou destroyed.*

of justice, and had decided on the merits of his cause before he interfered in his behalf. It was not the result of impulse, folly, partiality, or favouritism; it was because he had, as a judge, considered the matter, and had decided that the right was with the author of the psalm, and not with his enemies. As the result of that determination of the case, he had interposed to vindicate him, and to overthrow his adversaries. Compare Ps. viii. 3—8.

5. *Thou hast rebuked the heathen.* Not the heathen in general, or the nations at large, but those who are particularly referred to in this psalm—those who are described as the enemies of the writer and of God. On the word rendered *heathen* here—גּוֹיִם, *goim*—see Notes on Ps. ii. 1. The word *rebuke* here does not mean, as it does usually with us, to chide with words, but it means that he had done this by deeds; that is, by overcoming or vanquishing them. The reference is, undoubtedly, to some of those nations with whom the writer had been at war, and who were the enemies of himself and of God, and to some signal act of the Divine interposition by which they had been overcome, or in which the author of the psalm had gained a victory. De Wette understands this as referring to "barbarians, foreigners, heathen." David, in the course of his life, was often in such circumstances as are here supposed, though to what particular event he refers it would not be possible now to decide. ¶ *Thou hast destroyed the wicked.* The Hebrew here is in the singular number—רָשָׁע—though it may be used collectively, and as synonymous with the word *heathen.* Comp. Isa. xiv. 5; Ps. lxxxiv. 10; cxxv. 3. The Chaldee Paraphrase renders this, "Thou hast destroyed the impious Goliath." The reference is undoubtedly to the enemies meant by the word *heathen,* and the writer speaks of them not only *as* heathen or foreigners, but as characterized by *wickedness,* which was doubtless a correct description of their general character. ¶ *Thou hast put out their name for ever and ever.* As when a nation is conquered, and subdued; when it is made a province of the conquering nation, and loses its own government, and its distinct existence as a people, and its name is no more recorded among the kingdoms of the earth. This is such language as would denote entire subjugation, and it is probably to some such event that the psalmist refers. Nations have often by conquest thus lost their independence and their distinct existence, by becoming incorporated into others. To some such entire subjugation by conquest the psalmist undoubtedly here refers.

6. *O thou enemy!* This verse has been very variously rendered and explained. For an examination of the particular views entertained of it, see particularly Rosenmüller, *in loc.* The reference is doubtless to the enemies mentioned in the previous verses; and the idea is substantially the same—that they were completely overcome and subdued. The phrase, "O thou enemy," is probably to be regarded as the nominative absolute. "The enemy—his destructions or desolations are finished for ever. He will now no more engage in *that* work." The attention of the writer is fixed on them, and on the fact that they will no more engage in the work of desolation. It is not, therefore, properly to be regarded, as it is rendered in the common translation, as

thou hast destroyed cities; [k]their memorial is perished with them.

7 [l]But the LORD shall endure for ever: he hath prepared his throne for judgment:

8 [m]And he shall judge the world

k 2 Kings xix. 25, etc. l Psa. cii. 26. m Rev. xx. 12, 13.

an apostrophe to the enemy, but rather as indicating a state of mind in which the writer is meditating on his foes, and on the fact that they would no more engage in the work in which they had been occupied—of laying cities and towns in ruins. ¶ *Destructions are come to a perpetual end.* That is, *thy* destructions are finished, completed, accomplished. There are to be no more of them. This may either refer to their *acts* causing destruction, or laying waste cities and towns, meaning that they would no more accomplish this work; or to the destruction or ruins which they had caused in laying waste cities —the ruins which marked their career —meaning that the number of such *ruins* was now complete, and that no more would be added, for they themselves were overthrown. The word rendered *destructions* means properly desolations, waste places, ruins, and seem here to refer to the wastes or ruins which the enemy had made; and the true idea is, that such desolations were now complete, or that they would not be suffered to devastate any more cities and fields. Prof. Alexander renders this, "*finished,* completed *are* (*his*) *ruins,* desolations, *for ever; i. e.*, he is ruined or made desolate for ever." ¶ *And thou hast destroyed cities.* That is, in thy desolating career. This, considered as an address to the enemy, would seem to refer to the career of some victor who had carried fire and sword through the land, and whose course had been marked by smoking ruins. This was, however, now at an end, for God had interposed, and had given the author of the psalm a victory over his foe. Prof. Alexander regards this, less properly, as an address to God, meaning that he had destroyed the cities of the enemy. The idea is, rather, that this enemy had been distinguished for spreading desolation and ruin, and that this career was now closed for ever. ¶ *Their memorial is perished with them.* The names of the cities, referring to their utter destruction, and to the character of the warfare which had been waged. It had been utterly barbarous and vicious; the enemy had left nothing to testify even what the city had been, and its name had ceased to be mentioned. See Notes on ver. 5. This seems to be mentioned as a justification of the warfare which the author of the psalm had waged against this enemy, and as showing why God had interposed and had given him the victory.

7. *But the* LORD *shall endure for ever.* Jehovah is eternal—always the same. Though these cities have become desolate, and the enemy has been permitted to triumph, and nations and people have passed away, yet God is ever the same, unaffected by these changes and desolations, and in due time he will always interfere and vindicate his own character, and defend the oppressed and the wronged. ¶ *He hath prepared his throne for judgment.* See ver. 4. He sits as a just judge among the nations, and he will see that right is done. The wicked, though temporarily prosperous, cannot always triumph; and the righteous, though cast down and oppressed, cannot always remain thus, for God, the just Judge, will rise in their defence and for their deliverance. The unchangeableness of God, therefore, is at the same time the ground of confidence for the righteous, and the ground of dread for the wicked. The eternal principles of right will ultimately triumph.

8. *And he shall judge the world in righteousness.* The word here rendered *world* means properly the habitable earth; and then it denotes the inhabitants that dwell upon the earth. The statement here is general,

in righteousness, he shall minister judgment to the people in uprightness.
9 The LORD also will be [1] a refuge for the oppressed, a refuge in times of trouble.
10 And they that know thy name [n] will put their trust in

[1] *an high place.*

n Prov. xviii. 10.

and is suggested by what is referred to in the previous verses. In the particular case on which the psalm turns, God *had* manifested himself as a just Judge. He had overthrown the enemies of himself and of truth; he had interposed in behalf of the righteous: and from this fact the psalmist makes the natural and proper inference that this would be found to be his character in regard to all the world; this indicated what, in all his dealings with men, he would always be found to be; this showed what he would be whenever he in any way pronounced a judgment on mankind. It may be added here that this will be found to be true in the great final judgment; that it will be in accordance with the principles of eternal justice. ¶ *He shall minister judgment.* He will declare or pronounce judgment; he will execute the office of judge. ¶ *To the people.* To all people; to the nations of the earth. This corresponds with what, in the former part of the verse, is called the *world;* and the declaration is, that in his dealings with the dwellers on the earth he will be guided by the strictest principles of justice. ¶ *In uprightness.* In rectitude. He will not be influenced by partiality; he will show no favouritism; he will not be bribed. He will do exact justice to all.

9. *The* LORD *also will be a refuge.* Margin, *an high place.* The margin expresses the more exact sense of the Hebrew word—מִשְׂגָּב, *misgob.* It means properly height, altitude; then a height, rock, crag; and then, as such localities, being inaccessible to an enemy, were sought in times of danger as places of secure retreat, it comes to denote a place of security and refuge, Ps. xviii. 2; xlvi. 7, 11; xlviii. 3; lix. 9, 17; xciv. 22. The declaration here is equivalent to what is so often said, that God is a refuge, a rock, a high tower, a defence; meaning, that those referred to might find safety in him. See Notes on Ps. xviii. 2. ¶ *For the oppressed.* Literally, for those who are *crushed, broken;* hence, the dejected, afflicted, unhappy,—דַּךְ, *dak*—from דָּכַךְ, *dakak*—to beat small; to break in pieces; to crush. The allusion here is to those who are wronged or down-trodden; to the victims of tyranny and injustice. Such may look to God to vindicate them and their cause, and they will not look in vain. Sooner or later he will manifest himself as their protector and their helper. See ver. 12. ¶ *A refuge in times of trouble.* Not only for the oppressed, but for all those who are in trouble. Comp. Ps. xlvi. 1. That is, all such may come to him with the assurance that he will be ready to pity them in their sorrows, and to deliver them. The psalmist had found it so in his own case; and he infers that it would be so in all cases, and that this might be regarded as the general character of God.

10. *And they that know thy name.* All who are acquainted with thee; all those who have been made acquainted with the manifestations of thy goodness, and with the truth respecting thy character. ¶ *Will put their trust in thee.* That is, all who have any just views of God, or who understand his real character, will confide in him. This is as much as to say, that he *has* a character which is worthy of confidence,—since they who know him best most unreservedly rely on him. It is the same as saying that all the revelations of his character in his word and works are such as to make it *proper* to confide in him. The more intimate our knowledge of

thee: for thou, LORD, hast not forsaken them that seek thee.

11 Sing praises to the LORD, which dwelleth in Zion: declare among the people his doings.

12 When he maketh inquisition for blood, he remembereth them: he forgetteth not the cry of the [1] humble.

[1] Or, *afflicted*.

God, the more entirely shall we trust in him; the more we learn of his real character, the more shall we see that he is worthy of universal love. It is much to say of any one that the more he is known the more he will be loved; and in saying this of God, it is but saying that one reason why men do *not* confide in him is that they do not understand his real character. ¶ *For thou,* LORD, *hast not forsaken them that seek thee.* Thou hast never left them when they have come to thee with a confiding heart. David means, doubtless, to refer here particularly to his own case, to derive a conclusion from his particular case in regard to the general character of God. But what is here affirmed is still true, and always has been true, and always will be true, that God does not *forsake* those who put their trust in him. Men forsake *him;* he does not forsake *them.*

11. *Sing praises to the* LORD. As the result of these views of his character, and at the remembrance of his doings. The heart of the psalmist is full of exultation and joy at the remembrance of the Divine interposition, and he naturally breaks out into these strong expressions, calling on others to rejoice also. ¶ *Which dwelleth in Zion.* On the word *Zion,* see Notes on Psalm ii. 6. Comp. Ps. iii. 4; v. 7. As Zion was the place where at this time the tabernacle was set up, and the worship of God was celebrated, it is spoken of as his dwelling-place. ¶ *Declare among the people his doings.* Make general and wide proclamation of what he has done; that is, make him known abroad, in his true character, that others may be brought also to put their trust in him, and to praise him.

12. *When he maketh inquisition for blood.* When he *inquires* after blood; that is, when he comes forth with this view, to wit, for purposes of punishment. There is allusion here to such passages as that in Gen. ix. 5, "And surely your blood of your lives will I require; at the hand of every beast will I require it, and at the hand of man." The idea is, that when blood was shed in murder, God would seek out the murderer; he would require satisfaction of him who had shed the blood; he would punish the offender. The language, *there,* becomes equivalent to that of seeking punishment for murder, and then for sin in general; and the representation *here* is that of God as going forth in the capacity of an executioner of his own laws to inflict punishment on the guilty. ¶ *He remembereth them.* "He remembereth," says Prof. Alexander, "the bloods or murders," since the *word blood,* as in Ps. v. 6, is in the plural—*bloods.* The better interpretation, however, is, that the word "*them*" here refers to the oppressed and the afflicted—for that is the main idea in the passage. See vers. 8, 9. When he goes forth in the earth to execute judgment on the wicked; when he cuts them down in his wrath; when he sweeps them away as with a flood,—the punishment will not be indiscriminate. He will then mark the oppressed, the afflicted, the persecuted, the troubled, and the sad, and will interpose to save them,—delivering them from the storms of wrath. The idea, then, is, that the righteous will not be forgotten; that even in the most fierce and awful of his dispensations he will still regard them, and interpose to save them. ¶ *He forgetteth not the cry of the humble.* Marg., *afflicted.* The margin expresses the true idea. The reference is not to the *humble* in the

13 Have mercy upon me, O LORD; consider my trouble *which I suffer* of them that hate me, thou that liftest me up from the gates of death:

14 That I may show forth all thy praise in the gates of the

common sense of that term, but to the afflicted; the oppressed; to those who are in trouble, ver. 9. He will then remember the cry which in their afflictions they have been long sending up to him.

13. *Have mercy upon me, O* LORD. The cry for mercy implies that though God *had* interposed and granted them surprising deliverances, yet he was still surrounded by enemies, and was still in trouble. See introd. to the psalm, §§ 2, 3. He had been delivered from many troubles, but there were many still pressing upon him, and he now calls on God to interpose further in his behalf, and to grant him entire deliverance from all his sorrows and dangers. The trouble to which he here refers was of the same kind as that adverted to in the former part of the psalm—that arising from the efforts of formidable enemies. ¶ *Consider my trouble.* Do not forget this trouble; bear it in remembrance; look upon its character and its depth, and mercifully interpose to deliver me. ¶ Which I suffer *of them that hate me.* Or, "see my suffering arising from those that hate me; or, which is produced by those who hate me." The design is to fix the attention on the greatness of that suffering as caused by his "haters" or by his enemies,—the foes that were still unsubdued. ¶ *Thou that liftest me up from the gates of death.* Thou on whom I rely to do this; or, who hast done it in times past. The idea is, that he was apparently near to the gates of death, and that the only one who could raise him up was God, and he now invoked His interposition that it might be done. The phrase "gates of death" relates to the prevalent views about the unseen world,—the world where the dead abide. That world was represented as beneath; as a dark and gloomy abode; as enclosed by bars and walls; as entered by gates,—the grave leading to it. See Introd. to Job, § 7 (10), and Notes on Job x. 21, 22. The psalmist felt that he had come near to that dark and gloomy abode, and that God only could rescue him from it; therefore, in the trouble which now threatened his life, he looks to him to interfere and save him.

14. *That I may show forth all thy praise.* That I may praise thee in the land of the living; that I may *finish* the work of praise by rendering to thee all that is due. The idea is, that the dead could not praise God, or that his praise could be uttered only by the living; and he calls on God, therefore, to interpose and save him, that he might yet worship and praise him on the earth. In this sentiment the psalmist utters only what man naturally feels when he looks upon the grave; that it is an end of human plans and pursuits; that it is a land of silence; that the worship of God is not there celebrated. Such language must be regarded as uttered under the impulse of natural feeling, and not as uttered by the deliberate judgment of the mind when calmly contemplating the whole subject. All pious persons have these feelings at times, and it was proper that these feelings should be expressed in the sacred writings, as illustrating human nature even under the influence of religion. The same sentiment occurs in several places, as Ps. cxv. 17, "The dead praise not the Lord, neither any that go down into silence." See Notes on Ps. vi. 5. It is not necessary to say that the sacred writers *had* brighter views at times than these. But who can keep the mind *always* from desponding when it looks at the grave? Who can *always* help feeling that it is a place of darkness and gloom?

daughter of Zion: I will rejoice in thy salvation.

15 The heathen are sunk down in the pit *that* they made: in the net which they hid is their own foot taken.

16 The LORD is known *by* the judgment *which* he executeth:

¶ *In the gates of the daughter of Zion.* As contradistinguished from the "gates of death." Gates in ancient cities were places of concourse, where important transactions were performed; and the "gates" of Jerusalem were regarded as attractive and sacred, because it was *through* them that the people passed on their way to worship God at the tabernacle or in the temple. Hence it is said, Ps. lxxxvii. 2, "The Lord loveth the gates of Zion more than all the dwellings of Jacob." Ps. c. 4, "Enter into his gates with thanksgiving." Comp. Ps. cxviii. 19. The phrase, "daughter of Zion," means Jerusalem. For the reason of this appellation see Notes on Isa. i. 8. The language here used proves that the psalm was composed after Zion or Jerusalem was made the capital of the kingdom and the seat of public worship, and, therefore, that it cannot refer, as is supposed in the Chaldee Paraphrase, to the death of Goliath. ¶ *I will rejoice in thy salvation.* In the salvation which thou wilt bestow on me; here particularly, in delivering him from his dangers. The language, however, is general, and may be employed with reference to salvation of any kind.

15. *The heathen.* Heb., "The nations;" that is, the idolatrous people that were arrayed against him. See Notes on ver. 5. ¶ *Are sunk down.* That is, referring to those who *had* been overcome, as mentioned in ver. 5; or to those who still encompassed him, in respect to whom he was so certain that they *would* be overcome that he could speak of it as a thing already accomplished. According to the former view, it would be an encouragement derived from the past; according to the latter, it would indicate unwavering confidence in God, and the certain assurance of ultimate victory. It is not easy to determine which is the true interpretation. The Hebrew is, "Sunk are the nations in the pit which they have made;" that is, he sees them sinking down to destruction. ¶ *In the pit* that *they made.* In which they designed that others should fall. See Notes on Ps. vii. 15. ¶ *In the net which they hid.* Which they laid for others. The allusion here is to a spring-net made to capture birds or wild beasts. ¶ *Is their own foot taken.* The net here referred to seems to have been particularly a net to take wild beasts by securing one of their feet, like a modern *trap.* The idea is, that they had been brought into the destruction which they had designed for others. See Notes on Ps. vii. 15, 16.

16. *The* LORD *is known* by *the judgment* which *he executeth.* By what he does in his dealings with men, in dispensing rewards and punishments, bestowing blessings upon the righteous, and sending punishments upon the ungodly. That is, his character can be learned from his dealings with mankind; or, by studying the dispensation of his Providence, we may learn what he is. This is always a fair and proper way of estimating *character*, alike in regard to God and man; and it is proper, at all times, to study what God *does,* to learn what he *is.* ¶ *The wicked is snared in the work of his own hands.* The same sentiment which is expressed here occurs in Ps. vii. 16. The idea is that the wicked are the cause of their own destruction; their own devices and designs are the means of their ruin, and they are made their own executioners. It is this to which the writer seems particularly to refer in the former part of the verse, when he says that "the Lord is known by the judgment which he executeth." This great principle is brought out in his dealings with men, that the

the wicked is snared in the work of his own hands. [1] Higgaion. [o] Selah.

17 The wicked shall be turned into hell, *and* all the nations that forget [p] God.

[1] i.e., *meditation.* *o* Psa. xix. 14; xcii. 3.

p Psa. l. 22.

course which wicked men pursue is the cause of their own ruin. The laws of God in a great measure execute themselves, and men bring upon themselves their own destruction. It is the highest perfection of government to make the laws execute themselves. ¶ *Higgaion.* Marg., *Meditation.* This word occurs elsewhere only in the following places, Ps. xix. 14, rendered *meditation;* Ps. xcii. 3, rendered *solemn sound;* Lam. iii. 62, rendered *device.* Its proper meaning is, *murmur; muttering; the utterance of a low sound,* as the low sound of a harp; or the murmuring or muttering of one who talks to himself; and then *meditation.* Comp. Notes on Ps. ii. 1, on the word "*imagine,*"—Marg., *meditate,*—the verb from which this is derived. Gesenius supposes that it is here a musical sound. So it is understood by the LXX.,—ᾠδὴ διαψάλματος. It is not known why it is introduced here. There seems to be nothing in the *sense* which demands it, as there is no particular reason why the reader should pause and meditate *here* rather than in any other place in the psalm. It is doubtless a mere musical pause, though perhaps indicating the *kind* of pause in the music, as some peculiar sound or interlude on the musical instrument that was employed. ¶ *Selah.* Another musical term, see Notes on Ps. iii. 2. This indicates a general pause; the word Higgaion denotes the particular kind of pause.

17. *The wicked.* All the wicked; all who come properly under the denomination of wicked persons. Doubtless the writer had particularly in his eye the enemies with whom he was contending, and in reference to whom the psalm was composed; and he meant to say that *they* would be certainly punished. But what was true in regard to them, was true of all others of similar character, and the statement is therefore made in a universal form—*all* the wicked. ¶ *Shall be turned.* Shall *turn back,* or be turned from their present course. The idea is, that they were now pursuing a certain course, but that they would be turned back from that, or would fail and retreat; and instead of going on to victory, would be defeated, and would sink into hell. The idea is essentially the same as that which is expressed in ver. 3 above:—"When mine enemies are *turned back.*" ¶ *Into hell*—לִשְׁאוֹלָה—*to Sheol,* Hades, *the grave, the world of departed spirits.* This is the usual meaning of this word. See Notes on Luke xvi. 23; Isa. xiv. 9; Job x. 21, 22. Though the word, however, originally denoted the grave, the region of the dead, the world of departed spirits, yet it was also supposed that there was a *distinction* in the condition of the dead; and the word gradually came to denote the abode of the *wicked* portion of the dead, and hence the place of future punishment. So it is undoubtedly used in Luke xvi. 23. It is clear (*a*) that this cannot be understood here as referring to the *grave* in its ordinary sense, for the righteous will be as certainly consigned to the grave, or will as certainly die, as the wicked; (*b*) that it cannot refer to the invisible world, the abodes of the dead, in the ordinary sense of the term—for it is *as* true that the righteous will enter that world as that sinners will. There must be some sense, in which the word is used here, different from that of the grave, or different merely from death as such. This sense can be only one of two—either (1) that the author means that they will be cut off by a sudden and violent death, considered as a calamity or as a punishment; or (2) that he regarded the *Sheol* men-

18 For the needy [q] shall not alway be forgotten: the expecta-

q Isa. xli. 17.

tioned here as a place of punishment. Calvin thinks it is not improbable that the former of these is intended; but it may be observed in regard to this, (*a*) that this is not the language usually employed to denote that idea—the phrase, to be *cut off*, or *cut down*, being that which a writer intending to express that idea, would most naturally use—since the phrase, to be sent to *Sheol*, considered as the grave or the region of the dead, would express nothing peculiar in regard to the wicked; and (*b*) the spirit of the passage seems to demand the idea that the wicked referred to here would be consigned to a place of punishment, that they would be cut off *as* wicked persons, and treated accordingly. This interpretation is strengthened by the other member of the parallelism, where it is said, "and all the nations that forget God;" since it is no more true that the nations "that forget God" will be "turned into the *grave*, or the world of departed spirits," than it is that the nations that serve and obey him will. It seems to me, therefore, that this is one of the passages in which it is clear that the word *Sheol* had connected with it the idea of punishment beyond the grave—of a region where the wicked would be treated according to their deserts, and in a manner different from the treatment of the righteous; that although the general idea of that under-world was that it was a dark and gloomy place, yet that there was *also* the idea that the abode of the wicked there was far more gloomy than that of the righteous; and that it was regarded as a *punishment* to be consigned to that region. It is not necessary to suppose that they had the full idea attached to the word *hell* which we have, any more than that they had the same full and clear idea of *heaven* that we have. Light has come into our world on all these subjects gradually, and there is nothing which requires us to suppose that the earlier sacred writers had the same clear views which the later writers had, or that either of them knew *all* that is to be known. Comp. 1 Pet. i. 10, 11. ¶ And *all the nations that forget God*. All who are strangers to him, or who are ignorant of the true God. See Notes on Rom. ii. 12. From the character and prospective doom of those to whom the psalmist particularly referred in this psalm, he is led to make this *general* remark about all who sustain the same character which they did. Under the administration of the same God those of the same character would share alike, for "there is no respect of persons with him;" and it is the perfection of an impartial government to treat all of the same character in the same manner. If we can, therefore, ascertain how, under his administration, one sinner will be treated in the future world, we can infer how all of the same character will be treated; if we can learn how God will deal with one people, we can infer how he will deal with all. The statement here is, that all the wicked, of whatever nation, will be consigned to punishment in the future world. The phrase here used, "that *forget* God," denotes those who are not disposed or inclined to remember and honour him. The idea seems to be that though they might have known him, they did not choose to retain him in their knowledge, but gave themselves up to a life of idolatry and sin. Comp. Notes on Rom. i. 19—21, 28.

18. *For the needy*. The poor; those who are dependent and helpless. ¶ *Shall not alway be forgotten*. That is, by God. He will interfere and save them by destroying their enemies. He will not suffer the wicked always to persecute and oppress the righteous. In due time he will vindicate his own cause; will deliver the oppressed and down-trodden, and will consign their oppressors to deserved punishment. This is as true now, in regard to all

tion of the poor shall *not* perish for ever.

19 Arise, O LORD; let not man prevail; let the heathen be judged in thy sight.

20 Put them in fear, [r] O LORD; *that* the nations may know themselves *to be but* men. Selah.

r Psa. lxxxiii. 15, 16.

the oppressed and their oppressors, as it was in the time of the psalmist. ¶ *The expectation of the poor.* Of the afflicted and the oppressed. The word *expectation* refers to their hope; their desire; their earnest looking for deliverance. In that state men naturally look for the Divine interposition, and the psalmist says that in that they will not always be disappointed. ¶ *Shall* not *perish for ever.* The word "*not*" is supplied here by our translators, but not improperly. It is thus supplied in the Targum, and in the Syriac, the Vulgate and the Greek. Such forms of construction are not uncommon. Comp. Ps. i. 5; Deut. xxxiii. 6. "The negative is repeated from the preceding member."—*Michaelis.*

19. *Arise, O* LORD. See Notes on Ps. iii. 7. ¶ *Let not man prevail.* Against thee and thy cause. The war waged against the psalmist he regarded as waged against God, and he calls upon him, therefore, to interpose and vindicate his own cause. The word rendered *prevail* is *be strong;* that is, let not man seem to be stronger than thou art, or let him not succeed in his efforts in opposing thy cause. ¶ *Let the heathen be judged in thy sight.* The nations to whom the writer had referred in the psalm, that were arrayed against him and against God. He desired that a just judgment should be passed on them, and that God would vindicate the righteous, and save them from the power of those who oppressed and wronged them.

20. *Put them in fear, O* LORD. From this it is evident that the enemies of the psalmist were bold, daring, confident in their own strength, and in the belief that they would succeed. He prays, therefore, that these bold and daring invaders of the rights of others might be made to stand in awe, and to tremble before the great and terrible majesty of God; that they might thus have just views of themselves, and see how weak and feeble they were as compared with Him. ¶ That *the nations may know.* The nations particularly referred to in this psalm as arrayed against the writer. ¶ *Themselves* to be but *men.* That they may see themselves as they are,—poor, feeble creatures; as nothing when compared with God; that instead of their pride and self-confidence, their belief that they can accomplish any purpose that they choose, they may see that they are not like God, but that they are frail and feeble mortals. The psalmist seems to have supposed that if they understood this, they would be humbled and would desist from their purposes; and he therefore prays that God would interpose and show them precisely what they were. If men understood this, they would not dare to array themselves against their Maker.

PSALM X.

§ 1. *Author and occasion of the psalm.*—This psalm, like Ps. i., ii., and many others, has no title to indicate its authorship; nor is there anything in the psalm itself which can enable us to determine this with any certainty. From the place which it occupies among the acknowledged Psalms of David, it is morally certain that it was regarded by those who arranged the Book of Psalms, as having been composed by him. There is nothing in the psalm to forbid this supposition.

Of course nothing is known as to the occasion on which it was composed. In the Septuagint and the Latin Vulgate, the ninth and tenth Psalms are united, and reckoned as the ninth Psalm; and thenceforward the reckoning proceeds according to this arrangement, the eleventh in the Hebrew being numbered in those versions as the tenth, etc. This arrangement continues to the hundred and thirteenth Psalm inclusive. In those

PSALM X.

WHY standest thou afar off, O LORD? *why* hidest thou *thyself* in times of trouble?

versions, Ps. cxiv. and cxv. of the Hebrew form but one psalm, and the reckoning coincides. But the hundred and sixteenth Psalm in Hebrew is, in those versions, divided into two, and the hundred and forty-seventh Psalm in Hebrew is, in those versions, divided into two, thus completing the number of one hundred and fifty—making the number in the Hebrew, and the Latin Vulgate, and the Septuagint, the same. It is not now known by whom these divisions were made, or on what pretence they were made. There is no known reason for making the divisions of the Psalms that occur in the Septuagint and the Latin Vulgate.

There is no evidence, therefore, that this psalm was composed at the same time, and on the same occasion, as the ninth, and there is nothing in the psalm itself that would necessarily lead to this supposition. It is as independent of that in its structure, as one psalm usually is of another.

So far as appears from the psalm itself, it was composed like the former, and like many others, when the writer was in the midst of trouble; and when, for the time, he seemed to be forsaken by God, ver. 1. The *nature* of that trouble is so far indicated as to show that it arose from the conduct of some formidable enemy, some one who was wicked, some one who was pursuing a secret and underhanded, a clandestine and treacherous course, to destroy the reputation or the life of the author of the psalm. In these circumstances the writer calls upon God to interpose for him. Nothing is indicated, however, by which we can ascertain *who* this enemy was, or on what occasion, in the life of David, the psalm was composed. It is only necessary to add, that there were several occasions in the life of David which corresponded with what is stated in the psalm, and that it is not necessary to understand the particular occasion more clearly in order to see the meaning of the psalm.

§ 2. *Contents of the psalm.*—The psalm is properly divided into two parts.

The first contains an account of the character of the enemy to whom the writer refers, vers. 1-11; the second is an appeal to God to interpose and deliver him from the machinations of this foe, vers. 12-18.

I. The characteristics of the enemy, vers. 1-11. Those characteristics were the following:

(*a*) He was proud, and on that account persecuted the poor, ver. 2.

(*b*) He was a boaster, and especially, it would seem, was one who was disposed to boast of his wealth, ver. 3.

(*c*) He was a practical atheist; one too proud to seek after God, or to acknowledge his dependence on him, ver. 4.

(*d*) His ways were *always* grievous, or adapted to produce evil, and the reason was that he had no just views on moral subjects—that the great principles of truth and right were "far above out of his sight," ver. 5.

(*e*) He was a man who had no apprehensions about the future; one who felt that his course would be one of continued prosperity, and that adversity would never come upon him, ver. 6.

(*f*) He was profane and openly fraudulent, ver. 7

(*g*) He was insidious, artful, and underhanded in his doings; a man who would stoop to any act of duplicity and treachery to accomplish his purposes, vers. 8-10.

(*h*) And he acted as if God had "forgotten," that is, as if God would pass over offences; as though he did not see or regard them, ver. 11.

II. An appeal to God to deliver him from the machinations of this foe, vers. 12-18. This appeal consists of the following parts:

(*a*) A solemn address to God, beseeching him to remember the cry of the humble or the afflicted, ver. 12.

(*b*) Arguments to enforce this appeal, or reasons why God *should* interpose, vers. 13, 14, 15. These arguments are, (1) That he had seen all this; that the effort of the wrong-doer to conceal what he had done was vain; and (2) that the poor and afflicted had committed himself to God with a firm confidence that he would protect those who relied on him.

(*c*) The expression of a solemn and full conviction on the part of the writer of the psalm that God *would* thus interfere, and save those who put their trust in Him, vers. 16-18.

1. *Why standest thou afar off, O* LORD? That is, What is the reason

2 [1]The wicked in *his* pride doth
persecute the poor: [s]let them be
taken in the devices that they
have imagined.
3 For the wicked boasteth of
his [2]heart's desire, and [3]blesseth

[1] *In the pride of the wicked he doth.* [s] Prov. v. 22.
[2] *soul's.* [3] *the covetous blesseth* himself, *he abhorreth the Lord.*

---

why thou doest this? The thought on which this is based is that God might be expected to interpose in a time of trouble, and that his aid might then be looked for. Yet in this case he seemed to be an indifferent spectator of the sorrows and afflictions of the wronged and oppressed. This filled the mind of the writer with surprise, and he could not account for it, especially in view of the character of the person or persons who had wronged the author of the psalm. To *stand afar off* in such circumstances, is an attitude of indifference and unconcern—as when others do not come near us if we are sick, or are bereaved, or are in circumstances of poverty and want. That *man* should do this, would have produced no surprise in the mind of the writer; that *God* should do it was something that filled him with wonder. ¶ Why *hidest thou* thyself? As if God concealed himself, or kept away. He did not manifest himself, but seemed to let the afflicted man suffer alone. ¶ *In times of trouble.* Affliction, sorrow, persecution. The particular trouble referred to here was that which was produced by the machinations of the enemy or enemies whose character is described in the following verses. The question, however, is put in a general form, as if it were strange and unaccountable that God should *ever* fail to interpose in time of trouble. How often has there been occasion to ask this question in our world!

2. *The wicked in his pride.* Marg., *In the pride of the wicked he doth.* The margin is a literal translation of the Hebrew; but the sense is the same. The meaning is, that the fact that the wicked persecuted the poor, in the case referred to, was to be traced to his pride, haughtiness, ambition; that is, in pursuing his own selfish and ambitious purposes, he became utterly regardless of the rights and comforts of others. He esteemed their interest and happiness as unworthy of regard in comparison with his own aims and purposes, and trampled down all their rights in prosecuting his own ends. The term *wicked* here—in the original in the singular number, רָשָׁע, though perhaps used collectively—means properly the *wicked one*, or the *wicked man*, and doubtless refers to some enemy that David had in his eye, and from whom he was at that time suffering wrong. It is not possible now to ascertain with certainty who this was; but as the whole description proceeds in the singular number (vers. 3—11), it is most natural to suppose that this refers to one individual. ¶ *Doth persecute the poor.* יִדְלַק עָנִי. Professor Alexander renders this, "*burns the sufferer.*" Luther, muss der Elende leiden—"must the afflicted suffer." De Wette: ängstigen sich die Elenden. The Latin Vulgate: "When the impious [man] is proud, the poor [man] is burned:" incenditur pauper. So the Septuagint. Gesenius (*Lex.*) supposes it means, *to burn with anguish.* Horsley renders it, "In the exaltation of the impious one the helpless is consumed." But it seems to me that our common version has expressed the true sense. The word rendered *persecuteth* — דָּלַק, *dalak*—means properly to burn, to flame; then to burn with love, with anger; then to burn *after* any one, to persecute. See it explained in the Notes on Ps. vii. 13. According to the most natural application of the word here, it would seem to mean, "In the pride of the wicked, he persecutes the poor or the afflicted;" that is, he burns after him; he is inflamed against him; he hotly pursues

the covetous, *whom* the LORD abhorreth.

him. The word *poor* in this place—עָנִי, *ani*—means the afflicted; the crushed; the downtrodden; those in circumstances of humiliation and poverty. The psalmist doubtless refers to himself as a poor and persecuted man; and the time in his life would seem to be when he was without a protector or friend, probably before he came to the throne. ¶ *Let them be taken in the devices that they have imagined.* The artifice, plan, or scheme, which they have formed. That is, they have formed a scheme to take advantage of, or to destroy others; and the psalmist prays that, as a just retribution, this very calamity may come upon them. No man could have a right to complain if the mischief and wrong which he had devised for others should be brought upon himself; and if it were certain that this in all cases would occur, there could be nothing that would so effectually deter men from wrong-doing. The psalmist, then, simply prays that justice might be done. Compare Notes on Ps. v. 10; vii. 15, 16. The plural form of the verb is used here, but it is not certain that the psalmist had more than one enemy in view, for on expressing his feelings towards that one enemy he may have designed to use language which would be applicable to all in similar circumstances.

3. *For the wicked boasteth of his heart's desire.* Marg., as in Heb., *soul's.* The main idea in this verse seems to be that he is a *boaster*—a man who makes some proclamation about himself as being superior to others, and who, in that proportion, looks with disdain or contempt on others. He vaunts himself, or makes an ostentatious display of something on which he prides himself, as wealth, strength, beauty, talent, prowess, etc. The particular thing here, it would seem, of which he boasted was his natural inclinations; the propensities and passions of his soul; that is, he took pride in himself, in his own passions, desires, lusts, tastes, and made a boastful display of them, as if he regarded them as something honourable, or as something fitted to excite admiration in others. This is not a *very* uncommon characteristic of wicked men; at least it is found in a certain class of wicked men. They pride themselves in *whatever* they have in their character that is peculiar, or that is their own, for the very reason that it is *theirs;* and they become so shameless that they do not hesitate publicly to *boast* of that which should be regarded as a disgrace. A certain class of *young* men are very apt to "boast" of passions and practices which should cover their faces with the burning blush of shame. ¶ *And blesseth the covetous.* Marg., *the covetous blesseth* himself, *he abhorreth the Lord.* Prof. Alexander renders this, "*And winning* (*i.e.,* when he wins) *blesses, despises Jehovah.*" In other words, he hypocritically thanks God for his success, but despises him in his heart. This probably expresses the correct idea. The word rendered *the covetous*—בֹּצֵעַ, *botzaia*—is a participle, from the verb—בָּצַע—*bâtza,* to cut in pieces; then, to plunder, to spoil; and then, to be greedy after gain. Here, the natural construction would seem to be to refer it not to *another,* as one who was covetous, but to *himself,* as greedy, or as succeeding in the object of his desire; as referring to the fact that he *obtained* his heart's desire, and as showing what his feelings were then. He was filled with evil desires, and was so shameless of them that he openly avowed them; and when he obtained the object of his wishes, he did what is here denoted by the word *bless*—as will be explained directly. The idea in the mind of the writer seems to be that he cherished the desire, and made no secret of it, and *obtained* the object of his wishes. The natural explanation

4 The wicked, through the pride of his countenance, will not seek *after God*: [1] God *is* not [t] in all his thoughts.

[1] Or, *all his thoughts* are, There is *no God*, Psa. xiv. 1.

t Eph. ii. 12.

of the *manner* in which he did this is, that it was by plunder, rapine, or spoil, for this would be most literally expressed by the word used. Comp. Prov. i. 19; xv. 27; Jer. vi. 13; viii. 10; Ezek. xxii. 12. It *might* be, however, by unjust gains, or dishonest dealing, 1 Sam. viii. 3; Isa. xxxiii. 15; lvii. 17. The word *bless* here may mean, as in the margin, blesses *himself*; or, as Prof. Alexander supposes, may mean that he blesses *the Lord*, that is, renders hypocritical thanks for his success, and professes to acknowledge that all is the gift of God, while at the same time he expresses contempt for him, and despises him in his heart. If the usual meaning of the word *bless* is to be retained, however, it would seem to be most in accordance with the spirit of the passage that he should *bless himself*, that is, his own talents, skill, power; in other words, that he should attribute all his success to himself. The idea does not seem to be that he was even professedly a religious man, but that he was a proud and vain boaster who attributed all success to himself, and despised God and his claims. It has been supposed by some, however, and with plausibility (De Wette, and others), that the word rendered *bless* here—בֵּרֵךְ, *bairaich*—as in Job i. 5, 11; ii. 9, means, not to *bless*, but to *curse*. See Notes on Job. i. 5. De Wette renders it, Der Räuber lästert schmähend Jehovah. This seems to me to be the true idea—that this braggart or braggadocio did not make any *pretensions* to religion, but was a profane man, and one who despised God and abhorred his cause. ¶ Whom *the* LORD *abhorreth*. Or, more correctly, *despises*, or *abhors the Lord*. That is, he makes shameless boast of his own corrupt and base passions; when he is successful he makes *no* acknowledgment to God, but *curses* him and *despises* or contemns him in his heart. A correct rendering then of the whole would be, "And having obtained, he *curses*—he *despises* Jehovah." Coverdale renders this, "The covetous blesseth himself, and blasphemeth the Lord." We have thus an example of most finished and shameless depravity—but alas! one that was not found in the time of David only.

4. *The wicked, through the pride of his countenance.* In consequence of his pride; or, his pride is the reason of what is here stated. The "pride *of his countenance*" is a phrase that is used because pride shows itself mainly in the countenance, or in a lofty air and manner. The design is to state the influence of pride in producing the effect here specified. ¶ *Will not seek* after God. The phrase "after God," is supplied by our translators. *Something* clearly is to be supplied, and it is plainly something relating to God—either that the wicked man will not seek after God in prayer, or that he will not inquire after the proofs of his existence and attributes; or that he will not seek after his favour, or that he will not endeavour to know the Divine will. All this would be implied in seeking after God; and this is undoubtedly the state of mind that is referred to here. The sinner is unwilling, in any appropriate way, to acknowledge God. ¶ *God is not in all his thoughts.* Marg., "Or, *all his thoughts* are, There is *no God*," Ps. xiv. 1. The literal translation is, "No God [are] all his thoughts." The margin has undoubtedly expressed the meaning better than the translation in the text, since the spirit of the passage is not that the sinner had *no thought* of God, but that he thought *wrong*. The fact that he would not seek God, and that he had said that God had forgotten (ver. 11), shows that he had *some* thoughts of God. The language here

5 His ways are always grievous; thy judgments *are* far above out of his sight: *as for* all his enemies, he puffeth at them.

---

is properly expressive of *belief* or *desire;* either that all his thoughts were that there *is* no God, *i. e.*, that such was the result of all his meditations and reasonings on the subject; or that he wished that it *might* be found to be so. The language will admit of either construction, and in either sense it would express the thoughts of the wicked. Both as a matter of practical belief, and as a matter of desire, the language of the wicked is, "*No God.*" The wicked wish that there were none; he practically believes that there is none. The entire verse, then, expresses the prevailing feelings of a sinner about God:—(*a*) That he *wishes* there were none, and practically *believes* that there is none; and (*b*) that the *reason* or *ground* of these feelings is *pride*. Pride will prevent him from seeking God in the following ways:—(1) It makes him unwilling to recognise his dependence on any being; (2) it makes him unwilling to confess that he is a sinner; (3) it makes him unwilling to pray; (4) it makes him unwilling to seek aid of any one, even God, in the business of life, in the prosecution of his plans, or in sickness and affliction; (5) it makes him unwilling to accede to the terms of reconciliation and salvation proposed by God, unwilling to repent, to believe, to submit to His sovereignty, to acknowledge his indebtedness to mere *grace* for the hope of eternal life. Pride is at the root of all the atheism, theoretical or practical, on the earth; at the root of all the reluctance which there is to seek the favour of God; at the root, therefore, of the misery and wretchedness of the world.

5. *His ways are always grievous.* His paths; his manner of life; his conduct towards God; his dealings with men. The word rendered "*are grievous,*" יָחִילוּ, *yâhhiloo*—has been very variously rendered. The Latin Vulgate renders it, "His ways are defiled." So the Septuagint. Coverdale renders it, "His ways are always filthy." Professor Alexander, "His ways are firm." So De Wette, "Es gelingen seine Wege." Horsley, "His ways are confident." This variety in the interpretation arises from the ambiguity of the original word—חוּל, *hhool.* The meaning of this word, as given by Genesius, is *to turn round, to twist, to whirl;* and hence (1) to dance; (2) to be whirled, or twisted upon anything; (3) to twist oneself with pain, or to be in pain; (4) to bear or bring forth; (5) to tremble, to quake; (6) to be strong or stable, as things twisted are. Hence he translates this passage, "his ways are firm, or stable, *i. e.*, all his affairs prosper." But it seems to me plain that this is not the idea in the mind of the psalmist. He is not dwelling on the *prosperity* of the wicked, or on the result of his conduct, but on his *character*. In the previous verses he had stated some of the traits in his character, and the subsequent verses continue the description; hence it is natural that we should expect to find some peculiar feature of his *character* referred to here, and not that there should be an allusion to the stability of his affairs. It seems to me, therefore, that the exact idea here is, that his ways, or his modes of feeling and conduct were always *perverse* and *forced*, and *hard;* that there was always something tortuous and unnatural about him; that he was not straightforward and honest; that he did not see things as they are, and did not act in a plain and upright manner. ¶ *Thy judgments.* Thy laws; or, the principles of thy government. ¶ Are *far above out of his sight.* They are out of the range of his vision. He does not see them. His thoughts grovel on the earth, and he is never elevated in his views so as to see the great principles of truth. ¶ As for *all his enemies, he puffeth at them.*

6 He hath said in his heart, I shall not be moved; for *I shall* [1] never *be* in adversity.

[1] *unto generation and generation.*

7 His mouth is full of cursing and [2] deceit and fraud; under his tongue *is* mischief and [3] vanity.

[2] *deceits.* [3] Or. *iniquity.*

He treats them with contempt and scorn, as if he had no fear of them, or as if he were entirely confident of his own ability to overcome them. This is an illustration of his pride and self-confidence; for it is the characteristic of the proud and self-confident to boast in this manner. The word rendered "*puffeth*" means to breathe, to blow; and the idea here is, that he acted as though he could sweep them away with a breath.

6. *He hath said in his heart.* The phrase, "he hath said," means that this was his deliberate and settled character. What is here described was no sudden thing. It was not the freak of passion; it was a deliberately formed purpose. The phrase, "in his heart," means that he had purposed this; he had said this to himself in a spirit of self-gratulation and confidence. ¶ *I shall not be moved.* That is, he was confident in his present condition, and he apprehended no changes. He had formed his plans so wisely, that he believed he had nothing to apprehend; he feared neither sickness nor adversity; he dreaded not the power of his enemies; he feared nothing even from the providence of God; he supposed that he had laid the foundation for permanent prosperity. This feeling of self-confidence and of security is sometimes found, to an extent that cannot be justified, in the hearts of even good men (comp. Notes on Job xxix. 18); and it is common among the wicked. See Ps. xlix. 11; Job xxi. 9. ¶ *For* I shall *never* be *in adversity.* Marg., *unto generation and generation.* The margin expresses the correct sense. The idea of the wicked, as expressed here, is that they and their families would continue to be prosperous; that a permanent foundation was laid for honour and success, and for transmitting accumulated wealth and honours down to far distant times. It is a common feeling among wicked men that they can make permanent their titles, and possessions, and rank, and that nothing will occur to reduce them to the humble condition of others. Nothing more clearly shows the pride and atheism of the heart than this; and in nothing are the anticipations and plans of men more signally disappointed. Comp. the case of Shebna; see Notes on Isa. xxii. 15, seq.

7. *His mouth is full of cursing.* Profaneness; blasphemy against God. In the former verse the writer had described the feelings of the *heart;* he now proceeds to specify the open *acts* of the wicked. The meaning is, that the wicked man, as here described, was one who was full of imprecation, swearing, execration;—a *profane* man;—a man who, whatever was his belief about God, would constantly call upon his name, and imprecate his wrath on himself or others. An atheist, strange as it may seem, is as likely to make a frequent use of the name of God, and to call on him, as other men;—just as profane men, who have no belief in the Saviour, swear by Jesus Christ. This passage seems to be referred to by the apostle Paul in Rom. iii. 14, not as a direct quotation, as if the psalmist referred to the point which he was arguing, but as language which expressed the idea that the apostle wished to convey. See Notes on that passage. ¶ *And deceit.* Marg., as in Heb., *deceits.* The meaning is, that he was false and treacherous; and perhaps also that his treachery and fraud were accompanied with the solemn sanction of an oath, or an appeal to God, as is likely to be the case among fraudulent and dishonest men. ¶ *And fraud.* The word here used—תֹּךְ, *toch*—is now commonly supposed to mean rather *oppression* or *violence.* See Gesenius,

8 He sitteth in the lurking-places of the villages; in the secret places doth he murder the innocent: his eyes [1] are privily set against the poor.

9 He lieth in wait [2] secretly, as

[1] *hide themselves.*

[2] *in the secret places.*

Lex. When this is attributed to his *mouth*, it means that what he says—what he requires—what he commands, is unjust, unreasonable, and oppressive. ¶ *Under his tongue.* Perhaps alluding to the serpent, whose poison is concealed at the root of the fang or tooth, and therefore under the tongue. The meaning is, that beneath what the wicked say, though it seems to be harmless, as the tongue of the serpent does, yet there lies mischief and iniquity, as the poison is hidden beneath the serpent's tongue. ¶ Is *mischief.* The word here used means properly labour, toil; then trouble, vexation, sorrow. The meaning here seems to be that there lies under the tongue that which *gives* or *causes* distress; to wit, wrong-doing; injustice to others. ¶ *And vanity.* Marg., *iniquity.* This expresses the idea in the original word. Whatever he *says* is evil, and is fitted to produce trouble and sorrow, as the concealed poison in the mouth of the serpent causes pain and death.

8. *He sitteth in the lurking-places of the villages.* As robbers do, who hide themselves in the vicinity of villages, that they make a sudden descent upon them in the silence of the night, or that they may seize and rob the inhabitants as they go forth in the morning to attend their flocks to the pastures, or to labour in the fields. The word rendered *villages* means properly an enclosure, as a court before a building; and then a village or hamlet, farm-buildings, or farm hamlets, usually erected around an open space; and it is then used to denote the encampment of nomadic tribes, who usually pitch their tents in a circle so as to form an enclosure, Gen. xxv. 16; Isa. xlii. 11. In the neighbourhood of such places,—in the thickets, bushes, or ravines, that might be near such encampments or enclosures,—robbers would naturally secrete themselves, that they might fall upon them suddenly, or that they might seize any one who left the village or encampment for any purpose. So Frazer remarks in his Travels in Chorasan, i. 437: "When the Turkomans design to fall upon a village, they take a position near it in the rear, until in the morning the unsuspecting inhabitants drive out their herds, or leave the villages for some other purpose, and then they suddenly fall upon them." De Wette, *in loc.* ¶ *In the secret places doth he murder the innocent.* From these retreats he suddenly falls upon those who are unsuspicious, and who have done him no wrong. The word *innocent* here does not mean *sinless* in the absolute sense, but it means that they were innocent so far as the robber was concerned. They had done *him* no wrong; they had given him no occasion to make war upon them. ¶ *His eyes are privily set.* Marg., *hide themselves.* The Hebrew word means to hide, to conceal; to lay up in private; to hoard; to keep back; to hold back, etc. Here it means to conceal, to lurk in ambush; and the idea is that his eyes will secretly watch, or keep a look-out for them; that is, that his eyes, or that he himself will be concealed, that he may observe the goings of those whom he intends to make his prey. ¶ *Against the poor.* Or, the wretched, the afflicted, the defenceless. The meaning is, that instead of being a helper of the poor and wretched, he is disposed to take every advantage of them, and deprive them of all their rights and comforts.

9. *He lieth in wait secretly.* Marg., *in the secret places.* See Notes on ver. 8. The object here is merely to illustrate the thought in the previous verse, by an allusion to a lion and a

a lion in his den: he lieth in wait to catch the poor: he doth catch the poor, when he draweth him into his net.

10 [1]He croucheth, *and* humbleth himself, that the poor may fall [2]by his strong ones.

[1] *breaketh himself.* [2] Or, *into his strong parts.*

---

hunter. ¶ *As a lion in his den.* As a lion crouches down in his den, ready to spring upon his prey. That is, the lion is concealed, but is on the look out, and when his prey passes near his den, he suddenly springs upon it and secures it. So it is with the wicked man. He carefully lays his plans. He conceals his purposes. He is himself hidden, or his plans are all hidden. Suddenly he springs upon his victim, who is taken by surprise and has no power of defence or escape. The purpose here is not so much to describe the wicked man *as* a literal robber, as to *compare* the *conduct* of the wicked *with* that of a robber,—one who, like a lion or a hunter, lies concealed until his victim is seen. This will describe the conduct of a large class of men—men who secretly lay plans of seduction, villany, and fraud, and who spring suddenly upon their victims when there is no hope of escape. ¶ *He lieth in wait to catch the poor.* The helpless and defenceless. ¶ *He doth catch the poor, when he draweth him into his net.* As a hunter does the wild beast. Here the same thought is presented under a new image—that of a hunter. He lays his snare, gin, or pit-fall, and when the animal is allured into it, he springs the net suddenly on him, or the animal sinks into the pit, and is secured. See Notes on Ps. vii. 15; ix. 15.

10. *He croucheth.* Marg., *breaketh himself.* Coverdale, "Then smiteth he, then oppresseth he." Prof. Alexander, "And bruised he will sink." Horsley, "And the overpowered man submits." Luther, "He slays, and thrusts down, and presses to the earth the poor with power." This variety of interpretation arises from some ambiguity in regard to the meaning of the original. The word rendered *croucheth*—ודכה, in Chetib or the text,—is in the Keri or margin, ידכה, "and crushed, he sinks down." There is some uncertainty about the form in which the word is used, but it is certain that it does not mean, as in our translation, *he croucheth.* The word דָּכָה, *dachah,* properly means to be broken in pieces, to be crushed; and this idea runs through all the forms in which the word occurs. The true idea, it seems to me, is that this does not refer to the wicked man, but to his victim or victims, represented here by a word in the collective singular; and the meaning is that such a victim, crushed and broken down, sinks under the power of the persecutor and oppressor. "And the crushed one sinks down." ¶ And *humbleth himself.* The word here used—יָשֹׁחַ, *yâshoahh,* — from שׁוּחַ, *shuahh* — means to sink down; to settle down. Here it means to sink down as one does who is overcome or oppressed, or who is smitten to the earth. The idea is, that he is crushed or smitten by the wicked, and sinks to the ground. ¶ *That the poor may fall.* Rather, as in the original, "and the poor fall;" that is, they *do* fall. The idea is, that they do in fact fall by the arm of the persecutor and oppressor who treads them down. ¶ *By his strong ones.* Marg., "Or, *into his strong parts.*" The text here best expresses the sense. The reference is to the strong ones—the followers and abettors of the "wicked" here referred to—his train of followers. The allusion seems to be to this wicked man represented as the head or leader of a band of robbers or outlaws,—strong, athletic men engaged under him in committing robbery on the unprotected. See vers. 8, 9. Under these strong men the poor and the unprotected fall, and are crushed to the earth. The mean-

11 He hath said in his heart, God hath forgotten: [u] he hideth his face; he will never see *it*.
12 Arise, O LORD; O God, lift

[u] Ecc. viii. 11.

ing of the whole verse, therefore, may be thus expressed: "And the crushed one sinks down, and the poor fall under his mighty ones." The word rendered *poor* is in the plural, while the verb *fall* is in the singular; but this construction is not uncommon when the verb precedes. Nordheimer, *Heb. Gram*, § 759, i., *a*. The word rendered *poor* means the wretched or the afflicted, and refers here to those who were unprotected,—the victims of oppression and robbery. The following account of the condition of Palestine at the present time will illustrate the passage here, and show how true the statements of the psalmist are to nature. It occurs in "The Land and the Book," by W. M. Thomson, D.D., Missionary in Syria. He is speaking of the sandy beach, or the sand hills, in the neighbourhood of Mount Carmel, and says, respecting these "sandy downs, with feathery reeds, running far inland, the chosen retreat of wild boars and wild Arabs,"—"The Arab robber lurks like a wolf among these sand heaps, and often springs out suddenly upon the solitary traveller, robs him in a trice, and then plunges again into the wilderness of sand hills and reedy downs, where pursuit is fruitless. Our friends are careful not to allow us to straggle about or lag behind, and yet it seems absurd to fear a surprise here,—Khaifa before, and Acre in the rear, and travellers in sight on both sides. Robberies, however, do often occur, just where we now are. Strange country! and it has always been so." And then quoting the passage before us (vers. 8—10), he adds, "A thousand rascals, the living originals of this picture, are this day crouching and lying in wait all over the country to catch poor helpless travellers. You observe that all these people we meet or pass are armed; nor would they venture to go from Acre to Khaifa without their musket, although the cannon of the castles seem to command every foot of the way." Vol. i., pp. 487, 488.

11. *He hath said in his heart, God hath forgotten.* That is, this is his practical, habitual feeling. He acts as if God had forgotten, or as if God takes no knowledge of what is occurring in the earth. Comp. ver. 6. ¶ *He hideth his face.* God has hidden his face; that is, he does not look on what is occurring. ¶ *He will never see it.* That is, he will never see what is done. It cannot be supposed that any man would deliberately *say* either that the memory of God has failed, or that he will not see what is done upon the earth, but the meaning is, that this is the practical feeling of the wicked man; he acts as if this were so. He is no more restrained in his conduct than he would be if this were his deliberate conviction, or than if he had settled it in his mind that God is regardless of human actions. It is hardly necessary to say that this is a correct description of the conduct of wicked men. If they deliberately believed that God was regardless of human conduct, if they were certain that he would not behold what is done, their conduct would not be different from what it is now. They do not act as if his eye were upon them; they are not restrained by any sense of his presence.

12. *Arise*, O LORD. See Notes on Ps. iii. 7. This commences the second part of the psalm, in which the author calls on God to remember those who were oppressed and wronged by the wicked. By suffering the wicked thus to carry on their plans, God *seemed* to be indifferent to human affairs, and the psalmist, therefore, invokes him to interpose, and to rescue the afflicted from their grasp. ¶ *O God, lift up thine hand.* As one does when he is about to strike, or to exert his power. The prayer is, that God would inter-

up thine hand: forget not the
[1] humble.
13 Wherefore doth the wicked
contemn God? he hath said in
his heart, Thou wilt not require
it.
14 Thou hast seen *it*; for thou
beholdest mischief and spite, to
requite *it* with thy hand: the

[1] Or, *afflicted.*

fere to put down the wicked. ¶ *Forget not the humble.* Marg., *afflicted.* The margin expresses the true sense. The idea is not that God would remember *humble* persons in the sense in which that word is now commonly used, but that he would remember those who were down-trodden, crushed, and afflicted. This is in accordance with the marginal reading in the Hebrew Bibles, which is now usually regarded as the more correct reading.

13. *Wherefore doth the wicked contemn God?* That is, despise him; or treat him with contempt and disregard. On what ground is this done? How is it to be accounted for? What is the proper explanation of so strange a fact? It is to be observed here (*a*) that the psalmist assumes this to be a fact, that the wicked *do* thus contemn or despise God. Of this he had no doubt; of this there can be no doubt now. They act as if this were so; they often speak of him as if this were so. They pay no respect to his commands, to his presence, or to his character; they violate all his laws as if they were not worth regarding; they spurn all his counsels and entreaties; they go forward to meet him as if his wrath were not to be apprehended or dreaded. (*b*) So strange a fact, the psalmist says, ought to be accounted for. There must be some reason why it occurs; and what that reason is, is worth an earnest inquiry. It could not be possible to believe that man—the creature of God, and a creature so weak and feeble—*could* do it, unless the fact were so plain that it could not be denied. It is, then, worth inquiry to learn how so strange a fact can be accounted for; and the solution—the thing which will explain this, and which must be assumed to be true in order to explain it—is stated in the concluding part of the verse. ¶ *He hath said in his heart.* This expression is here repeated for the third time in the psalm. See vers. 6, 11. The idea is, that all this is the work *of the heart,* and indicates the state of the heart. It cannot be regarded as the dictate of the reason or the judgment; but it is to be traced to the wishes, the feelings, the desires, and is to be regarded as indicating the real condition of the human heart. A man habitually desires this; he practically persuades himself that this is so; he acts as if it were so. ¶ *Thou wilt not require it.* Thou wilt not require an account of it; thou wilt not inquire into it. The Hebrew is simply, "Thou wilt not seek;" and the idea is, that God would not make an investigation of the matter. This fact, the psalmist says, would account for the conduct of the wicked. This *is* the actual feeling of wicked men, that they are *not* to give account of their conduct, or that God will not be strict to mark their deeds. Men act *as if* they were not responsible to their Maker, and *as if* it were a settled point that he would never call them to account.

14. *Thou hast seen* it. Thou seest all. Though men act as if their conduct was not observed, yet thou art intimately acquainted with all that they do. The workers of iniquity cannot hide themselves. The idea here is, that although God *seemed* not to notice the conduct of the wicked, and though the wicked acted as if he did not, yet that all this was seen by God, and that he would deal with men according to justice and to truth. ¶ *For thou beholdest mischief.* All that is done on the earth, though perhaps in this case referring particularly to that which gave the psalmist trouble. ¶ *And spite.* The

poor [1] committeth himself unto thee; thou art the helper of the fatherless.

15 [v] Break thou the arm of the wicked and the evil *man*: seek out his wickedness *till* [w] thou find none.

16 The LORD *is* King [x] for ever

[1] *leaveth.* *v* Psa. xxxvii. 17. *w* 2 Kings xxi. 12—15. *x* 1 Tim. vi. 15, 16.

word *spite* with us, though it originally denoted rancour, malice, ill-will, now denotes usually a less deliberate and fixed malice than is indicated by those words, but is used to denote a sudden fit of ill-will excited by temporary vexation. It relates to small subjects, and is accompanied with a desire of petty revenge, and implies that one would be gratified with the disappointment or misfortune of another. The word here, however, in the original, means anger, wrath, malice; and the idea is, that God had seen all the anger of the enemies of the psalmist. ¶ *To requite it with thy hand.* By thine own interposition or agency,—the *hand* being the instrument by which we accomplish anything. The idea is, that the psalmist felt assured that God would not pass this over. Though the wicked acted as if he did not see or regard their conduct, yet the psalmist felt assured that God would not be unmindful of it, but would, in due time, visit them with deserved punishment. ¶ *The poor committeth himself unto thee.* Marg., *leaveth.* The word rendered *poor* is the same as that which occurs in ver. 10. It means here those who are helpless and defenceless; the oppressed and the down-trodden. The word *committeth* or *leaveth* means that he leaves his cause with God; he trusts in his protection and interposition; he gives himself no anxiety as to the result. He knows that God *can* deliver him if he sees that it is best; and he is assured that God *will* do that which it is best should be done. ¶ *Thou art the helper of the fatherless.* That is, this is the general character of God,—the character in which he has revealed himself to man. Comp. Ex. xxii. 22; Deut. x. 18; Isa. i. 17; Ps. lxviii. 5; lxxxii. 3; Jer. xlix. 11; Hos. xiv. 3; Mal. iii. 5; James i. 27. The psalmist here refers to the *general character* of God as that in which all the oppressed, the crushed, the helpless may trust; and he mentions this particular case as one that best illustrated that character.

15. *Break thou the arm of the wicked.* The arm is the instrument by which we effect a purpose, and especially in wielding a sword or a spear, as in battle; and if the arm is broken, we are powerless. The psalmist, therefore, prays that God would render the wicked, in this respect, powerless. ¶ *And the evil* man. Of all the evil, or the wicked. In regard to the prayer here, see Notes on Ps. v. 10. ¶ *Seek out his wickedness* till *thou find none.* Till it is all punished; till there has been a full recompense. This is a wish that no wicked act of his should be forgotten; that exact justice should be rendered. If it is right to punish the wicked at all, it is right to deal with them just as they deserve; if *any* wickedness may properly be punished, all may be; and, whatever may occur, the sinner may be assured that he will not be punished merely for *a part* of his sins. If God punishes the wicked at all, there will be nothing left unpunished.

16. *The* LORD is *King for ever and ever.* That is, he reigns, and he will reign for ever. This is one of the instances which frequently occur in the Psalms, where, though there is a desponding spirit, or an apprehension of danger expressed in the beginning of the poem, it *ends* with the language of exultation and triumph. The psalmist speaks here as if what he had desired was actually accomplished, and as if the enemies that had encompassed him, and all the enemies of the Lord, were actually overthrown, and God now reigned supreme. He was

and ever: the heathen are perished out of his land.
17 LORD, thou hast heard [y] the
desire of the humble: thou wilt
[1] prepare their heart, thou wilt
cause thine ear to hear;
18 [z] To judge the fatherless and

y Isa. lxv. 24. 1 Or, *establish*. z Isa. xi. 4.

so confident that this would be so, that he speaks of it as if it were already done. Comp. Rom. iv. 17; see also Ps. vi. 8, 9; vii. 17; ix. 18. ¶ *The heathen are perished out of his land.* That is, this would so certainly occur that he might speak of it as if it were actually done. The word *heathen* here refers to the enemies of God and of his cause, who are the principal subjects of the psalm. Comp. Ps. ix. 5. The *land*, here, refers to the land of Palestine, or the Holy Land, regarded as a land sacred to God, or in the midst of which he himself dwelt.

17. LORD, *thou hast heard the desire of the humble.* Their desire or their prayer that thou wouldst interpose in their behalf in the time of danger, and rescue them. Comp. Ps. vi. 8, 9. The word *humble* here refers to those who were poor, down-trodden, oppressed; and the original reference is, doubtless, to the psalmist himself, and to his friends. He was so certain that God would interpose, he had such assurance that his prayer would be answered, that his mind was perfectly calm. ¶ *Thou wilt prepare their heart.* Marg., "or, *establish*." The margin seems most accurately to express the meaning of the original word—תָּכִין, *tâchin.* The idea is, that he would settle or confirm their heart; that is, that he would dispel their fears and allay their apprehensions by the assurances of his favour, and by his gracious interposition. They had been full of apprehension and alarm, but the assurances of the Divine favour would establish their hearts and give them peace. ¶ *Thou wilt cause thine ear to hear.* Another form of expressing assurance of the same thing. The idea is, that he would incline his ear, or make it attentive to the cry of his afflicted people.

18. *To judge the fatherless.* That is, to *vindicate* the orphan; to rescue him from the hand of those who would oppress and wrong him. In other words, the psalmist prays that God would manifest himself in his real and proper character as the vindicator of the fatherless (see Notes on ver. 14), or of those who are represented by the fatherless—the feeble and the helpless. ¶ *And the oppressed.* Those who are down-trodden, crushed, and wronged. See Notes on Ps. ix. 9. ¶ *That the man of the earth.* Literally, "the man *from* the earth;" *i. e.*, that man springing from the earth, or created of the dust (Gen. ii. 7)—man frail, short-lived, feeble—should no more set up an unjust authority, trample on the rights of his fellow-worms, or suppose that he is superior to his fellow-creatures. ¶ *May no more oppress.* Marg., *terrify.* The original word means properly to terrify, to make afraid; that is, in this place, to terrify by his harsh and oppressive conduct. It is to be observed here that the original word—אָרַץ, *aratz*—has a very close resemblance in sound to the word rendered *earth*—אֶרֶץ, *eretz*—and that this is commonly supposed to be an instance of the figure of speech called *paronomasia*, when the words have the same sound, but are of different significations. It is not certain, however, that there is in this case any *designed* resemblance, but it is rather to be supposed that it was accidental. In regard to the *prayer* in this verse, it may be proper to observe that there is always occasion to utter it, and will be until the Gospel shall pervade the hearts of all men. One of the most common forms of wickedness in our world is *oppression*—the oppression of the fatherless, of the poor, of the dependent—the oppression of the subjects of government, and the oppression of the slave. One of the most affecting things in regard to this is,

the oppressed, that the man of the earth may no more [1] oppress.

[1] Or, *terrify*.

that it is done by a man made "from the earth,"—a child of dust—a creature composed of clay—of no better mould than others, and soon to return *to* the dust from which he was taken. Yet frail and weak man strives to feel that he is better than those clothed with a skin not coloured like his own, or those born in a more humble condition of life; and, in defiance of all the laws of God, and all the rights of his fellow-men, he crushes and grinds them to the earth. For such sins God will interpose, and he will yet show himself to be the helper of the fatherless and the oppressed. May He hasten the day when oppression and wrong shall cease in the world!

PSALM XI.

§ 1. *Author of the psalm.*—This psalm is ascribed to David, both in the title and in the location which it has among the Psalms. There is nothing in the psalm to make this doubtful, and indeed its structure is so much in accordance with those usually ascribed to David, as to leave no doubt as to its authorship. "The very difficulties of the psalm," says Prof. Alexander, "are proofs of its antiquity, and strong corroborations of the title which ascribes it to David."

§ 2. *Occasion on which it was composed.*—Of this there is no intimation in the title, or in the psalm itself. There is no special reference to any of the incidents of David's life, although some of the thoughts or images were suggested apparently by the recollection of what occurred in the persecutions of Saul or the rebellion of Absalom. Different occasions in the life of David have indeed been referred to as having led to the composition of the psalm. Venema supposes that it was composed when David was in the wilderness of Ziph, and when, betrayed by the inhabitants of the wilderness, and pursued by Saul, his friends began to advise him to seek a place of safety by flight, 1 Sam. xxiii. 14-23. This gave occasion, Venema supposes, for his expressing the sentiment—which is the leading sentiment in the psalm—that when our affairs seem to be hopeless, we are not to be in despair, but are to put our trust still in God. Others have supposed that the psalm was composed when he was in the cave of Adullam (1 Sam. xxii.), and in imminent danger of his life from the persecutions of Saul. A more plausible opinion is that of Amyraldus, who supposes that it was composed when David was in the court of Saul, and when he may have been advised to leave the court—a place of danger—and flee to a place of safety. But it cannot be determined with certainty on which of these occasions the psalm was composed, if it was on either of them. All that is apparent in the psalm itself is, that it was when the author was in danger, and when some of his friends advised him to seek safety by flight, ver. 1. Instead of doing this, David determined to remain where he was, and to put his trust in God, with the belief that he would interpose and deliver him.

§ 3. *Contents of the psalm.*—This psalm may be properly regarded as divided into two parts:

I. The counsel of some timid and fearful friends to the writer, in the circumstances of danger in which he was, to make his escape, and to seek safety by flight, vers. 1-3. They advise him to flee as a bird to the mountain; that is, to flee to a place of security while he could, for he seems to have been surrounded by enemies. The *arguments* by which they enforced this counsel seem to be referred to in vers. 2, 3, and were these: (*a*) that the wicked had made preparations to destroy him, for their bows and arrows were ready, ver. 2; and (*b*) that the condition of affairs was as if the very *foundations* were destroyed; that there was nothing to rest on; and that all his hopes, in his present condition, must be swept away, ver. 3. In these circumstances all his hopes of safety, in their apprehension, was in flight.

II. The views which the author of the psalm entertained on the subject, in reply to this, vers. 4-7. He had unwavering confidence in God; he did not despair; he believed that God would protect him; he believed that the object of God in permitting this was to try the righteous, and that in due time he would come forth and rain snares, fire, and brimstone, upon the ungodly. The state of mind thus

PSALM XI.

To the chief Musician. *A Psalm* of David.

IN the LORD put I my trust: how say ye to my soul, Flee *as* a bird to your mountain?

2 For, lo, the wicked [a] bend *their* bow, they make ready their

a Psa. lxiv. 2—4.

evinced, is that of firmness in trying circumstances; steady confidence in God when things seem to be most adverse; and an assured belief that God will in due time rescue those who put their trust in him. It is the manifestation of firmness against the counsels of the timid; the language of unshaken trust in God when the fearful and unbelieving despair.

For the meaning of the title, see Notes on Ps. v.

1. *In the* LORD *put I my trust.* This, in general, expresses the state of mind of the author—a state of feeling which runs through the entire psalm. It is designed to be an answer to the counsel which others had been giving him to escape, and it implies that he was determined at that time, and always, to put his trust in God. They advised him to flee. In the existing circumstances he felt that that would have implied a want of confidence in God. He determined, therefore, to maintain his present position, and to rely upon the interposition of God in due time. ¶ *How say ye to my soul.* How say ye to *me*—the soul being put for the person himself. *Why* do you say this to me? how can you give me such counsel, as if I were to run away from danger, and to put no trust in God? He seems to have supposed that such an act of flight would have been construed by his enemies, and by the enemies of religion, as evidence that he had no faith or confidence in God. Such circumstances often occur in the world; and when that would be the *fair* and *natural* construction of one's conduct, the path of duty is plain. We are to remain where we are; we are boldly to face the danger, and commit the whole matter to God. ¶ *Flee* as *a bird to your mountain.* This implies that it was supposed there was no longer any *safety* where he then was. The use of the plural number here—"Flee *ye*,"—by a change not uncommon in the Hebrew writings—seems designed to refer to the whole *class* of persons in those circumstances. The mind turns from his own particular case to that of others in the same circumstances; and the language may be designed to imply that this was the *usual* counsel given to such persons; that, on the same principle on which they now advised flight in this particular case, they would also advise flight in all similar cases. That is, they would counsel persons to flee to a place of safety when they were in danger of their life from persecution. This is the common counsel of the world; this would be the ordinary teaching of human prudence. The mountains in Palestine were regarded as places of safety, and were the common refuge of those who were in danger. In their caves and fastnesses, and on their heights, those who were in danger found security, for they could there hide themselves, or could more easily defend themselves, than they could in the plains and in the vallies. Hence they became the place of retreat for robbers and banditti, as well as for the persecuted. The allusion to the *bird* here does not imply that birds sought a refuge in the mountains, and that he was to resemble them in this respect; but the point of the comparison turns on the *rapidity* with which this refuge should be sought: "Fly to the mountains as *swiftly* as a bird flies from danger." Comp. Matt. xxiv. 16; Judges vi. 2; Heb. xi. 38.

2. *For, lo, the wicked bend* their *bow.* These are to be regarded as the words of the persons referred to in the previous verse, who had advised the persecuted psalmist to flee to the mountains. In this verse reasons are suggested for that advice. The reasons are, that the enemy was pre-

arrow upon the string, that they may [1] privily shoot at the upright in heart.

[1] *in darkness.*

3 If the foundations [b] be destroyed, what can the righteous do?

[b] 2 Tim. ii. 19.

paring for an attack, and that at an unexpected moment the attack would be made unless he should effect his escape. Apprised of the danger, he might now make good his escape, and avoid the peril which was impending. The common weapon in war, as in hunting, was the bow and arrow. The process of preparing for the use of the bow consisted in *bending* it, and properly adjusting the arrow. The Hebrew word used here is *tread;* "the wicked *tread upon* the bow;" that is, with a view to bend it. The bow was made of steel, or strong wood, or pieces of ivory framed together, and it often required great strength—beyond the strength of the arm—to bend it so as to adjust the string. Hence the *foot* was placed upon the centre, and the two ends drawn near to each other. ¶ *They make ready their arrow upon the string.* Hebrew, "they *fit* or *fix* the arrow upon the string." That is, they place the end of the arrow in the proper place upon the string of the bow. ¶ *That they may privily shoot at the upright in heart.* Marg., as in the Hebrew, *in darkness.* That is, that they may do it secretly or treacherously. They do not intend to do it in open day, or (as we should say) "in a fair fight;" but they mean to do it when their victim is not aware of their design. The phrase, "the upright in heart," may either denote their own conviction that those whom they designed so to attack were upright in heart—thus knowing that they were innocent; or it may be a statement of the advisers in the case, that those whom they counselled *were* thus upright—a statement on their part that the attack was made on the righteous. The latter is probably the true construction.

3. *If the foundations be destroyed.* These are still to be regarded as the words of the psalmist's advisers; or as an argument why he should make his escape. The word "foundations," here, refers to those things on which society rests, or by which social order is sustained—the great principles of truth and righteousness that uphold society, as the foundations on which an edifice rests uphold the building. The reference is to a destruction of those things in a community, when truth is no longer respected; when justice is no longer practised; when fraud and violence have taken the place of honesty and honour; when error prevails; when a character for integrity and virtue affords no longer any security. This is supposed to be the case in the circumstances referred to in the psalm, when there was no respect paid to truth and justice, and when the righteous, therefore, could find no security. It is under these circumstances the advice is given (ver. 1), that the righteous should seek safety in flight. ¶ *What can the righteous do?* What source of safety or confidence has he? His trust for his own safety, and for the good of society, has always been in the prevalence of just principles, and he has no other resource. Whatever others may do; whatever reliance *they* may place on such things, *he* can have no confidence in fraud, dishonesty, and error—in secret machinations and plans of treachery and deceit. *His* reliance is, and must be, in the prevalence of just principles; in the observance of law; in the diffusion of truth; in plans and deeds which are honourable and pure. When these no longer prevail, the argument is, there is nothing on which he can repose confidence in executing the plans on which his heart is fixed, and his proper course would be to flee (ver. 1). Part of this is true; part not. It *is* true that all the hope of the righteous

4 The LORD *is* in his [c]holy temple, the LORD's throne *is* in heaven: his eyes behold, his eyelids try, the children of men.
5 The LORD trieth the right-

c Hab. ii. 20.

is in the prevalence of principles of truth and justice, and that for the success of the objects nearest to his heart, whether of a private or public nature, he has no other resource or hope; but it is *not* always true, even when injustice, fraud, and error prevail, that he should withdraw from society and seek his safety in flight, and leave the world to its own course. His presence may be the very thing to counteract this; his duty may be to remain and face the evil, and to endeavour to secure a better state of things. So the psalmist understood in his case.

4. *The* LORD is *in his holy temple.* Heb., "Jehovah is in the temple of his holiness." That is, he is in heaven, regarded as his temple or dwelling-place. This is the answer of the psalmist to the suggestions of his advisers that he should flee from danger. The answer is, in substance, that he had nothing to fear; that he had a protector in heaven; and that he might appeal to Him for defence. The idea is, that God, the protector of the righteous, is always in the heavens; that his throne is always accessible; and that to it the persecuted may come, and may *always* be safe. ¶ *The* LORD's *throne* is *in heaven.* God is a king, ruling the universe. As such, the seat of his power or dominion is represented as in heaven, where he administers his government. That throne is fixed, and the affairs of his universe will be administered with justice. The righteous, therefore, may hope in his protection, and need not flee when the wicked assail them. The *idea* here is that of unwavering confidence in God as sitting upon the throne of the universe, and as administering its affairs with justice and truth. Comp. Isa. lxvi. 1, "Heaven is my throne." See Notes on that verse. ¶ *His eyes behold.* He sees everything in all parts of his vast empire, and therefore he knows all the purposes of the wicked, and all the wants of the righteous. The thought here, as one imparting a sense of safety, is, that God *sees* us. He is not ignorant of what our enemies are doing, and he is not ignorant of what we need. If he were, the case would be different. We might then despair of safety, and feel that our enemies could overcome and destroy us. It is much, in the trials of life, to have this assurance—this constant feeling—that God *sees* us. He knows our condition, our wants, our dangers; he knows all that our enemies are doing—all their machinations against us. Knowing all this, we may be assured that he will interpose when it is best that he should interpose, and that he will suffer nothing to come upon us which it is not best that he should permit. When evil befals us, therefore, it does not come because God does not know it, or because he could not prevent it, but because, seeing it all, he judges that it is best that it should thus occur. Comp. Gen. xvi. 13. ¶ *His eyelids try.* That is, they prove, penetrate into, as if by seeing through them. The "eyelids" here are synonymous with the eyes. The form of the language is varied in accordance with a custom common in Hebrew, and there is attributed here to the eyelids what properly belongs to the eyes—the power of seeing. ¶ *The children of men.* All men, good and bad. He knows them all—all their purposes, their designs, their wishes, their dangers. He knows, therefore, what our enemies are doing; he knows what are our perils; and we may safely leave our cause with him. We should not, therefore, listen to the counsel which advises us to flee (ver. 1), but should rather put our trust in him who dwells in the heavens.

5. *The* LORD *trieth the righteous.* That is, he *proves* them, searches them, tests the reality of their piety.

eous: but the wicked, and him that loveth violence, his soul hateth.

6 Upon the wicked he shall rain [1] snares, fire [d] and brimstone, and an [2] horrible tempest: *this shall be* the portion of their cup.

[1] Or, *quick burning coals.* [d] Gen. xix. 24.
[2] Or, *burning.*

His dealings with them are such as to test the genuineness of their religion, and are designed to show their sincerity and the real power of their religious principles. It is not for the purpose of destroying them, or punishing them, that he deals with them as he does, but it is to show the reality of their attachment to him. This language seems here to be used to show the feeling of the persecuted and afflicted author of the psalm. He understood the reason why these calamities were suffered to come upon him,—to wit, as a trial of his faith;—and therefore it was his duty to remain and bear these troubles, and not to attempt to escape from them by flight. He says, therefore, that these troubles in the case of the righteous were in strong contrast with the purpose of the Divine dealings towards the wicked, on whom God would "rain" snares, fire, and brimstone. In their case his judgments were for the purpose of punishing and destroying; in the case of the righteous it was to "try" them, or to test the reality of their religion. ¶ *But the wicked.* The wicked in general. *All* the wicked. ¶ *And him that loveth violence.* Referring particularly here to those who were engaged in persecuting him who was the author of this psalm. They were contemplating acts of violence towards him (ver. 2); he says that all such persons were the objects of the Divine displeasure, and would be appropriately punished. ¶ *His soul hateth;* i. e. *he* hates. God is often spoken of in language appropriate to man; and he is here referred to as having a *soul*,—as he is elsewhere as having eyes, hands, or feet. The meaning is, that all such persons were the objects of the Divine abhorrence, and that the Divine dealings with them were not, as with the righteous, to *try* them, but to *punish* and *destroy* them. Knowing this, the persecuted author of the psalm, instead of fleeing, calmly committed himself and his cause to God.

6. *Upon the wicked.* Upon all the wicked. ¶ *He shall rain.* He shall pour down as in a furious tempest. ¶ *Snares.* It seems rather incongruous to speak of *raining down* "snares," — understanding by the word *snares*, as it is used with us, that which *entangles*, as the snares by which we catch a bird, or by which a wild animal is taken. Comp. Notes on Job xviii. 8—10. The word here used, however, seems to refer to anything by which one is taken in his career or course, or is involved in difficulties; and the meaning is, that God would arrest or seize upon the wicked, as a wild beast is secured by the snares or the toils of the hunter. By their being sent down as in a "rain," is denoted that such means of their arrest and punishment would exist *in abundance*, so that they could not escape. ¶ *Fire and brimstone.* There is probably an allusion here to the destruction of Sodom and Gomorrah, Gen. xix. 24. As those cities were eminent for their wickedness, and were destroyed on account of their guilt, they furnished an illustration of the manner in which God would treat the wicked in all future times. As *they* were destroyed on account of their wickedness, so will all the wicked be destroyed. ¶ *And an horrible tempest.* As a furious blast of wind sweeps away houses and trees, spreading wide desolation, so will the wicked be swept away by the manifestation of the wrath of God. ¶ This shall be *the portion of their cup.* That is, this shall be what they shall *drink.* See Notes on Isa. li. 17. The idea is, that the Lord holds out to them a *cup* for them to drink—a cup containing a deadly mixture. The allusion

7 For the righteous LORD loveth righteousness; his countenance doth behold the upright.

is to the mode of administering punishment by a poisonous draught—not an unfrequent mode of punishment in ancient times. The idea in the whole verse is, that the wicked would be destroyed, and that, therefore, there was nothing ultimately to be apprehended from them. God would protect his own friends, and would destroy all those that sought their hurt. In these circumstances the righteous should confide in him as their protector, and not "flee."

7. *For the righteous* LORD *loveth righteousness.* This would be more correctly rendered, "For Jehovah is righteous; he loves righteousness." The idea is, that God *is* himself righteous, and consequently he loves those who are righteous. He may be confided in, therefore, by the righteous as their friend, and being under his protection they have nothing to fear. ¶ *His countenance doth behold the upright.* The word rendered "countenance" is, in the Hebrew, in the plural number;—literally, "his *faces.*" It is not easy to account for this use of the plural, though it is common in the Scriptures. There *may* be an allusion to the fact that man seems to have two faces—one on the right side, and one on the left, two eyes, two cheeks, two nostrils, etc., as if made up of two persons. Applied to God, it has no other signification than it has when applied to man; nor should we seek to find anything mystical in the fact that the plural form is used. The term here, like the eyelids in ver. 6, is equivalent to *eyes,* since the most remarkable feature of the countenance is the *eyes;* and the idea is, that God *looks upon* the upright; that is, he sees their dangers and their wants; he looks upon them with favour and affection. Being thus constantly under his eye, and being objects of his favourable regard, they can have nothing to fear; or, in other words, they are safe. This, then, is the argument of the righteous man, in reply to the suggestion (ver. 1) that he should "*flee*" from danger. The argument is, that God would be his defender, and that he might safely rely on His protection. The wicked have everything to fear; the righteous, nothing. The one is never safe; the other, always. The one will be delivered out of all his troubles; the end of the other can be only ruin.

PSALM XII.

This psalm purports to be "A Psalm of David," and there is no reason to doubt that it was composed by him. On what occasion it was composed is now unknown, and there is nothing in the psalm itself to enable us to decide. Some have supposed that it was written in view of the persecution of David by Saul; and others, that it was in view of the rebellion of Absalom. There is nothing in the psalm, however, which shows that it has any *special* reference to those persecutions or troubles; nothing which might not have been uttered if those troubles had never occurred. All the expressions in the psalm are of a general character, and seem rather to refer to a prevailing state of iniquity than to any particular manifestation of wickedness as pertaining to the psalmist himself.

The psalm undoubtedly *does* refer to prevailing iniquity, and it is not difficult to determine to what *form* of iniquity it refers. It was a general failure of fidelity among good men; a general withdrawal from active duties of such men as had before been found faithful; a want of that firmness and zeal which it was proper to expect from those who professed to be good men. Particularly it refers to prevailing modes of *speech* among those from whom it was right to expect better things:—a condition in which there was a want of seriousness and sincerity in conversation; in which flattery abounded; in which double meanings in conversation were common; in which promises solemnly made could not be relied on; and in which there was, in consequence, great wrong done to the poor and the unsuspecting—those who, on account of their ignorance and their unsuspicious nature, were greatly injured by putting confidence in such

PSALM XII.

To the chief Musician upon [1] Sheminith. A Psalm of David.

HELP, LORD; for the godly man ceaseth; for the faithful fail from among the children of men.

[1] *the eighth*, Psa. vi., *title*.

promises and assurances. In this state of things the psalmist felt that it was proper to call on God to protect those who were exposed to such wrongs.

The psalm, therefore, is composed of these parts:—

I. A statement of the prevailing condition of things, as a reason why it was proper for God to interpose, vers. 1, 2.

II. The fact that the Lord would interpose in such cases, and would cut off this class of persons, vers. 3-5.

III. The strong contrast between the words of the Lord and the language which was then in prevalent use, ver. 6. The words of the Lord were *pure;* pure as silver tried by the severest tests of fire.

IV. A deep conviction on the part of the psalmist that God *would* be the protector of those who were thus exposed to injury and wrong; particularly he would keep them from the purposes of such a generation for ever, ver. 7.

V. The closing verse, "The wicked walk on every side, when the vilest men are exalted" (ver. 8), seems to be but the carrying out of the idea of the Divine protection in the psalm: "Let the wicked walk about, therefore, on every side when vile men are exalted to power; for God is the protector of his people, and all such men are under his control." Or it may be the statement of a *fact* that wickedness *did* abound, or that men *seemed* to be unrestrained when wicked men were in power, though with the idea that God saw them, and would so check and restrain them that the injured and the wronged would be protected.

The *title* to the psalm—"To the chief Musician upon Sheminith"—is the same as that of the sixth Psalm, except that the words "On Neginoth," used there, are here omitted. See Notes on that psalm.

1. *Help,* LORD. Heb., "Save, JEHOVAH." The idea is that there was no human help, and, therefore, the Divine help is implored. The psalmist saw that those on whom reliance was usually placed for the promotion of the cause of truth and virtue now failed, and hence he invites the Divine interposition. ¶ *For the godly man.* The word here used properly denotes the *merciful* man—חָסִיד, *khasid.* It is a term applied to the righteous, because it is a prominent trait in the character of a pious man that he *is* merciful, kind, benignant. Hence the general character is often denoted by the special characteristic; in the same way as we speak of a pious man as a *good* man, a *just* man, a *righteous* man. The idea suggested by the use of the term here is, that it is *always* a characteristic of a pious man that he is merciful or benignant. Comp. Ps. iv. 3; xxxii. 6, where the same word is rendered *godly;*—Ps. xxx. 4; xxxi. 23; xxxvii. 28; l. 5; lii. 9; lxxix. 2; lxxxv. 8, where it is rendered *saints;*—and Deut. xxxiii. 8; Ps. xvi. 10; lxxxvi. 2; lxxxix. 19, where it is rendered *holy.* ¶ *Ceaseth.* The word here used—גָּמַר, *gamar*—means properly to *bring* to an end; to complete; to perfect. Hence it means to *come* to an end, to cease, to fail. *Gesenius.*—This might occur either by their being cut off by death; or by their ceasing to exert their influence in favour of religion; that is, by a general prevalence of wickedness among those who professed to be the friends of God. The latter seems to be the meaning here, since, in the following verses, the psalmist proceeds to specify the manner in which they "*fail;*" not by death, but by speaking vanity, falsehood, and flattery. That is, their conduct was such that their influence *failed*, or was *lost* to the community. No reliance could be placed on them, and, therefore, the psalmist so earnestly calls on God for his interposition. The idea is, that when men professing religion become conformed to the world,—when they live like other men,—when they cease

2 They speak vanity every one with his neighbour: *with* flattering lips, *and* with [1] a double heart, do they speak.

[1] *an heart and an heart.*

3 The LORD shall cut off all flattering lips, *and* the tongue that speaketh [2] proud [e] things;

[2] *great.*
e 1 Sam. ii. 3; Dan. vii. 8, 25.

to exert an influence in favour of piety,—when they fall into habits of sin, it is a time to call on God with special earnestness for his aid. Often such conduct on the part of the professed friends of religion makes such an appeal to God more proper than even the death of good men does, for, in the latter case, their influence is simply *withdrawn;* in the former, not only is this influence which they *might* exert lost to the church, but there is a positive bad influence to be counteracted. The fall of a professor of religion into sin is a greater loss to the church than his death would be. ¶ *For the faithful.* Those who profess *faith;* those who are bound by their vows *to be* faithful to God and to his cause. The word is equivalent to *the believing,* and is properly expressive of trust or faith in God. ¶ *Fail from among the children of men.* Fail, as above noted, by their misconduct; by being false to the trust committed to them.

2. *They speak vanity.* This is a statement of the *manner* in which the "godly" and the "faithful" fail, as stated in ver. 1. One of the ways was that there was a disregard of truth; that no confidence could be placed on the statements of those who professed to be pious; that they dealt falsely with their neighbours. The word *vanity* here is equivalent to *falsehood.* What they spoke was a vain and empty thing, instead of being the truth. It had no *reality,* and could not be depended on. ¶ *Every one with his neighbour.* In his statements and promises. No reliance could be placed on his word. ¶ With *flattering lips.* Heb., "Lips of *smoothness.*" The verb from which the word here used is derived—חָלַק, *hhalak*—means properly to divide, to distribute; then, to make things equal or smooth; then, to make smooth or to shape, as an artisan does, as with a plane; and then, *to make things smooth with the tongue,* that is, *to flatter.* See Ps. v. 9; Prov. v. 3; xxvi. 28; xxviii. 23; xxix. 5. The meaning is, that no confidence could be placed in the statements made. There was no certainty that they were founded on truth; none that they were not intended to deceive. Flattery is the ascribing of qualities to another which he is known not to possess,—usually with some sinister or base design. ¶ And *with a double heart.* Marg., as in Heb., *a heart and a heart;* that is, as it were, with two hearts, one that gives utterance to the words, and the other that retains a different sentiment. Thus, in Deut. xxv. 13, the phrase in Hebrew, *a stone and a stone* means, as it is translated, "divers weights"—one stone or weight to buy with, and another to sell with. So the flatterer. He has one heart to give utterance to the words which he uses towards his neighbour, and another that conceals his real purpose or design. No confidence, therefore, could be placed in such persons. Comp. Notes on Job xxxii. 22.

3. *The* LORD *shall cut off.* This might be rendered, "May the Lord cut off," implying a wish on the part of the psalmist that it might occur. But probably the common rendering is the correct one. It is the statement of a solemn truth, designed for warning, that all such persons would be punished. ¶ *All flattering lips.* The meaning is, that he will cut off all *persons* who use flattery; that is, he will cut them off from the favours which he will show to his own people, or will punish them. The word here used is the common one to denote disowning or excommunicating, and

4 Who have said, With our tongue will we prevail; our lips *are* [1] our own: who *is* lord over us?

5 For the oppression of the poor, for the sighing of the needy, now will I arise, saith the LORD;

[1] *with us.*

derives its meaning from the act of separating offenders from a community. See Gen. xvii. 14; Lev. xvii. 10; xviii. 29; xx. 3, 6; *et sæpe.* ¶ And *the tongue that speaketh proud things.* That boasts, or is self-confident. For an example of this, see Isa. xxviii. 15; and compare the Notes on that passage. It was this disposition to falsehood, flattery, and boasting, which constituted the fact stated in ver. 1, that "godly" and "faithful" men—men on whom reliance might be placed, whose word might be trusted, and whose promised aid in the cause of truth might be depended on—had seemed to "fail" among men. That is, no such men could be found.

4. *Who have said.* Who habitually say. This does not mean that they had formally and openly said this—for none would be likely to do so—but that they had practically and really said this by their conduct. They acted as if it were the real principle on which they framed their lives, that they might use their tongues as they pleased. ¶ *With our tongue.* Literally, "as to," or "in respect to our tongue;" that is, by our tongue. It was by the tongue that they expected to accomplish their purposes. It was not by direct power, or by violence, but by the power of speech. ¶ *Will we prevail.* Literally, "We will do mightily;" that is, they would accomplish their purposes. They relied on the power of speech—on their ability in influencing others; in deceiving others; in persuading others to fall in with their plans. ¶ *Our lips* are *our own.* That is, we may use them as we please; no one has a right to control us in the use of what properly belongs to ourselves. It cannot be meant that they intended to assert this openly as a right, for there are perhaps none who will not admit in words that they are responsible for what they *say,* as well as for what they *do.* But their conduct was such that this was the fair interpretation to be placed on what they said. They *would* speak this if they openly professed and avowed what was their real opinion. ¶ *Who* is *lord over us?* That is, who has a right to control us in the case? There are many who practically avow this as a principle of conduct, and who seem to feel that they are not responsible for their *words,* however much they may admit their responsibility for their *actions.* There is usually a greater degree of recklessness among men in regard to their speech than in regard to their *conduct;* and many a man who would shrink from doing another wrong by an act of dishonesty in business, may be utterly reckless as to doing him wrong by an unkind remark.

5. *For the oppression of the poor.* That is, on account of the wrong done to the poor in the manner specified above—by the abuse of the power of speech. On account of the slanders uttered against them, or the frauds perpetrated on them by the abuse of this power. The reference is to the wrongs done when no confidence could be placed in men's words; when they uttered words of "vanity" and "flattery" (ver. 2); when promises were made only to be broken, and obligations assumed never to be fulfilled. In such a state of things the *poor* were the most likely to suffer. In performing service for others—in daily labour on a farm or in a mechanical employment—they would depend for support on the promises made by their employers; and when their pay was withheld, they and their families must suffer. Comp. James v. 4. Rich men, having other resources, would not thus suffer; but the poor must always suffer when there is in the

I will set *him* in safety *from him that* [1] puffeth at him.
6 The words of the LORD *are* [f] pure words; *as* silver tried in a furnace of earth, purified seven times.

[1] Or, *would ensnare him.*

f Psa. cxix. 140.

community a disregard of the obligation of promises. In like manner, the poor would be most likely to "be taken in" by the acts of unprincipled men, and to be deceived in their small dealings with them. Other classes of the community would be on their guard; but the poor, unacquainted with the arts of cunning men, are always liable—though on a small scale, yet of importance to them—to be wronged by the false statements and promises of those against whom they can have no redress. ¶ *For the sighing of the needy*, etc. The word *needy* here is synonymous with *poor*. It refers to those in humble circumstances, who were peculiarly liable to be wronged by deceitful statements and promises. ¶ *I will set* him *in safety*. I will make him safe. I will save him from the evils which they thought to bring upon him. The general idea is, that God is the vindicator of the poor and the oppressed. ¶ From him that *puffeth at him*. Professor Alexander renders this, "I will place in safety him that shall pant for it." Gesenius renders it, "Whom they puffed at; *i. e.*, the oppressed." The language in the original is difficult. It may mean either "he pants for it," or "he puffs at him;" and the meaning can only be determined by the connexion. That would rather seem to be what is indicated in our common version; to wit, that the persons referred to as oppressing the poor and needy, *puffed at* them; that is, they looked upon them with contempt, and felt that with a puff of their breath they could blow them away. They regarded them as insignificant and worthless. By this construction, also, the connexion with the main statement will be best preserved—that the injury referred to in the psalm was done by *words*, by the breath of the mouth—thus indicating that by a *word* or a *breath* they could destroy them.

6. *The words of the* LORD. In contrast with the words of the persons referred to in vers. 2—4. Their words were vanity, flattery, and falsehood; and no reliance could be placed on them. In contrast with these words, the words of the Lord were pure. They *were* to be relied on. All his sayings were true and faithful. The design is to bring *his* words into contrast with the sayings of such men, and to show how much more safety there is in relying on his promises than on the promises made by such men. Man failed, but God would not. Reliance could not be placed on the words of even the professedly "godly" and "faithful" (ver. 1), but entire confidence might be placed in the words of Jehovah. All his words were true, pure, faithful, so that even when his own professed friends failed, and no confidence could be placed in them, yet there was still reason for unwavering confidence in God himself. ¶ Are *pure words*. That is, they are without any mixture of falsehood—for this idea is implied in the comparison which the psalmist makes when he says that they are like silver purified in the furnace, that is, from which all the dross has been removed. ¶ As *silver tried in a furnace of earth*. The word here rendered *furnace* properly means a *workshop*. Perhaps it corresponds nearly with our word *laboratory*, as the term is now used by chemists. It evidently refers to some place where the metal was tried and purified. The words rendered "of earth" literally mean "*on* the earth," or "*in* the earth." The language does not mean that the "furnace" was *made* of earth, as would seem to be implied in our version, but that the "furnace" or laboratory was erected *on* the

7 Thou shalt keep them, O LORD, thou shalt preserve [1] them from this generation for ever.

8 The wicked walk on every side, when the vilest [2] men are exalted.

[1] *him*, i.e., *every one of them.*

[2] *of the sons of men.*

earth, or *in* the earth. It may refer to something like a crucible placed on the ground, around which a fire of intense heat could be made. It is probable that some such structure would be made near the mines where ore was obtained, and that the ore would be thus purified from dross before it was removed. ¶ *Purified seven times.* By passing it seven times—that is, very often—through the fire. The word *seven* in the Scriptures denotes a complete or perfect number, and is often used to denote *frequency.* The idea here would seem to be that the process was repeated until the silver became entirely pure. The sense is, that the words of the Lord are *perfectly pure.* There is no admixture of falsehood in his statements; there is no deception in his promises; there is no flattery in what he says. This was the ground of confidence on the part of the psalmist—that while men (even those who professed to be good men) so failed that no reliance could be placed on their statements, the most perfect trust could be reposed on all the statements of God.

7. *Thou shalt keep them.* That is, the persons referred to in ver. 5—the poor and the needy who were suffering from the wrongs inflicted on them. The idea is, that God would guard and defend them. They were safe in his hands. Comp. Ps. xxxvii. 3—7. ¶ *From this generation.* This generation, or this race of detractors, flatterers, and oppressors. The idea is, that that entire generation was eminently wicked, and that none but God could deliver the poor and the needy from their designs. ¶ *For ever.* That is, *constantly*, or as long as they would need the Divine protection. God would not interpose and save them from the *present* trouble, and then leave them to the designs of their enemies, but he would *always* interpose as often as there was any need of his help. That is, they were now, and would be at all times, entirely safe. They had nothing to fear, for God was their refuge and their help.

8. *The wicked walk on every side.* Everywhere. They have full license, or seem to be wholly unrestrained. ¶ *When the vilest men are exalted.* Marg., "The vilest of the sons of men are exalted." This expression has been very variously translated. Bishop Horsley renders it, "When the scorn of the sons of men is exalted." De Wette, "They exalt themselves; terror to the sons of men." Luther, "Where such wicked people rule among the sons of men." Hengstenberg, "Like exaltation is disgrace to the sons of men." Prof. Alexander seems inclined to favour this last view. According to this interpretation, the meaning is, that "although the wicked are now in the ascendant, and the righteous are treated with contempt, this disgrace is really an exaltation, because only......in man's judgment, not in God's, who will abundantly indemnify his people for the dishonour put upon them." The word rendered in our version "the vilest"—זֻלּוּת, *zullooth*—means, according to Gesenius, *trembling, terror.* It occurs nowhere else in the Scriptures. The *verb* from which it is derived—זָלַל, *zalal*—means to shake, to tremble; then (as one shakes out, or casts away worthless things) to be vile, abject, despised, worthless. Perhaps, however, the common version expresses the idea more accurately than any of these proposed amendments. I would offer the following as a fair translation of the passage: "The wicked walk on every side; [it is] as the lifting up, or the exaltation of vileness among the sons of

PSALM XIII.

To the [1] chief Musician. A Psalm of David.

HOW long wilt thou forget me, O LORD? for ever? how long wilt thou hide [g] thy face from me?

[1] Or, *overseer*. [g] Psa. lxxxviii. 14.

men." That is, the state of things is as if the vilest were exalted, or were honoured. It seems to be the very exaltation of wickedness or depravity in the world. A state of things exists in which, from the prevalence of iniquity, the wicked seem to go unrestrained; in which no regard is paid to truth; in which falsehood and flattery abound; and it is *as if* honour were done to the worst forms of sin, and the most abandoned seem to be the most exalted. This appears to be the reason in the mind of the psalmist why the Divine interposition is necessary; with this idea the psalm commences, and with this it appropriately closes. There was a state of wide-spread depravity and successful iniquity, as if all honour were conferred on wicked and abandoned men, while the virtuous were oppressed and degraded. The psalm expresses *confidence* in God—confidence in his faithful word and promises; but the psalmist sees a state of things wherein it was eminently desirable that God should interpose, for the righteous seemed to have failed out of the earth, and the wicked seemed to be wholly in the ascendancy.

PSALM XIII.

This psalm consists properly of three parts:—

I. A complaint as of one who was forsaken by God; who was persecuted, and who saw no means of deliverance; who took counsel with his own heart how he might be delivered, but who found no way in which it could be done, vers. 1, 2.

II. An earnest prayer to God that He would interpose; that He would attend to the cry of the sufferer; that He would enlighten his mind; that his enemy might not be allowed to prevail against him, and rejoice over his fall, vers. 2, 3.

III. A cheerful confidence in God that he would grant this favour, and interpose in his behalf, vers. 5, 6.

This is entitled, "A Psalm of David," and there is no reason to suppose that he was not the author. Yet there are in it no indications of the time when it was written or of the circumstances under which it was composed. It would *seem* to have been in a time of persecution, and it would be most natural to refer its composition to the persecutions which David experienced from Saul. Most of the Rabbinical writers understand it as referring to the whole Hebrew people, and as expressing their sentiments and feelings in times of persecution in general. Kimchi understands it as referring to the present exile and trials of the Jewish people. *De Wette.*—The psalm, though undoubtedly composed with reference to the peculiar circumstances and trials of the author, contains sentiments applicable at all times to believers, and may be regarded as exemplifying the way in which pious feeling expresses itself in times of persecution and trial. Individuals are not unfrequently in circumstances in which the language of this psalm exactly expresses the feelings of their hearts; and the psalm is of great and permanent value, therefore, in the church, as illustrating the fact that good men may sometimes *feel* desolate and forsaken, as if even God had left them; the fact that they will, in such circumstances, cry earnestly to God for his interposition; and the fact that they will have, and will manifest, as the result of such an appeal to God, a cheerful confidence in his protecting care.

The title—"To the chief Musician" (marg., *overseer*)—is the same as that prefixed to the fourth Psalm, with the omission of the words "*On Neginoth.*" See the Notes on that title.

1. *How long wilt thou forget me, O* LORD? Literally, *until when.* The psalmist breaks out into this cry *in the midst* of his troubles. He had apparently borne them as long as he could. It seemed as if they would never come to an end. We may presume that he had been patient and unmurmuring; that he had borne his trials long with the hope and belief that they would soon terminate; that he had waited patiently for deliver-

2 How long shall I take counsel in my soul, *having* sorrow in my heart daily? how long shall mine enemy be exalted over me?

ance, uttering no words of complaint; but *now* he begins to despair. He feels that his troubles will never end. He sees no prospect of deliverance; no signs or tokens that God would interpose; and he breaks out, therefore, in this language of tender complaint, as if he was utterly forsaken, and would be for ever. The mind, even of a good man, is not unfrequently in this condition. He is borne down with troubles. He has no disposition to murmur or complain. He bears all patiently and long. He hopes for relief. He looks for it. But relief does not come; and it seems now that his troubles never *will* terminate. The darkness deepens; his mind is overwhelmed; he goes to God, and asks—not with complaining or murmuring, but with feelings bordering on despair—whether these troubles never will cease; whether he may never hope for deliverance. ¶ *For ever?* He had been forgotten so long, and there appeared to be so little prospect of deliverance, that it seemed as if God never would return and visit him with mercy. The expression denotes a state of mind on the verge of despair. ¶ *How long.* Referring to a second aspect or phase of his troubles. The first was, that he seemed to be *forgotten.* The second referred to here is, that God seemed to hide his face from him, and he asked how long *this* was to continue. ¶ *Wilt thou hide thy face from me.* Favour—friendship—is shown by turning the face benignantly towards one; by smiling upon him;—in Scriptural language, by "lifting up the light of the countenance" upon one. See Notes on Psalm iv. 6. Aversion, hatred, displeasure, are shown by turning away the countenance. God seemed to the psalmist thus to show marks of displeasure towards him, and he earnestly asks *how long* this was to continue.

2. *How long.* This refers to the third aspect of the case, or the third phase of the trouble, *i.e.*, that he was perplexed and embarrassed, having a deep and heavy sorrow in his heart, and he asks how long *this* was to continue. ¶ *Shall I take counsel in my soul.* This refers to the methods which he endeavoured to devise to escape from trouble. He was perplexed, persecuted, and apparently forsaken; and being thus apparently forsaken, he was constrained to attempt to devise some plan for his own deliverance, without interposition or help from on high. He was under a necessity of relying on himself; and he asks *how long* this was to continue, or when he might hope that God would interpose to aid him by *his* counsels, and thus to deliver him. ¶ Having *sorrow in my heart daily.* Every day; constantly. That is, there was no intermission to his troubles. The sorrow in his heart seems to have been not merely that which was caused by troubles from without, but also that which sprang from the painful necessity of attempting to form plans for his own relief,—plans which seemed to be in vain. ¶ *How long shall mine enemy be exalted over me?* This is the fourth form or phase of his trouble, and he asks how long *this* was to continue. This clause suggests perhaps the exact form of the trial. It was that which arose from the designs of an enemy who persecuted and oppressed the psalmist, and who had done it so effectually that he seemed to have triumphed over him, or to have him completely in his power. All the other forms of the trial—the fact that he seemed to be forgotten; that God had apparently averted his face; that he was left to form plans of deliverance which seemed to be vain, were connected with the fact here adverted to, that an *enemy* had persecuted him, and had been suffered to gain a triumph over him. Who this enemy was we do not know.

3 Consider *and* hear me, O LORD my God; lighten mine eyes, lest I sleep [h] the *sleep of* death;

4 Lest mine enemy say, I have prevailed against him; *and* those that trouble me rejoice when I am moved.

5 But I have trusted in thy

h Jer. li. 39.

3. *Consider* and *hear me.* Literally, "Look, hear me." God had seemed to avert his face as if he would not even look upon him (ver. 1); and the psalmist now prays that he *would* look upon him—that he would regard his wants—that he would attend to his cry. So we pray to one who turns away from us as if he were not disposed to hear, and as if he cared nothing about us. ¶ *Lighten mine eyes.* The allusion here is, probably, to his exhaustion, arising from trouble and despair, as if he were about to die. The sight grows dim as death approaches; and he seemed to feel that death was near. He says that unless God should interpose, the darkness would deepen, and he must die. The prayer, therefore, that God would "enlighten his eyes," was a prayer that he would interpose and save him from that death which he felt was rapidly approaching. ¶ *Lest I sleep the* sleep of *death.* Literally, "Lest I sleep the death;" that is, *in* death, or, as in the common version, the sleep of death. The idea is, that death, whose approach was indicated by the dimness of vision, was fast stealing over him as a sleep, and that unless his clearness of vision were restored, it would soon end in the total darkness—the deep and profound sleep—of death. Death is often compared to sleep. See Notes on 1 Cor. xi. 30; John xi. 11, 13; 1 Thess. iv. 14; Daniel xii. 2. The resemblance between the two is so obvious as to have been remarked in all ages, and the comparison is found in the writings of all nations. It is only, however, in connexion with Christianity that the idea has been fully carried out by the doctrine of the resurrection; for as we lie down at night with the hope of awaking to the pursuits and enjoyments of a new day, so the Christian lies down in death with the hope of awaking in the morning of the resurrection to the pursuits and enjoyments of a new and eternal day. Everywhere else death is to the mind a long and unbroken sleep. Comp. Jer. li. 39, 57.

4. *Lest mine enemy say, I have prevailed against him.* I have overpowered him; I have conquered him. That is, to triumph over him as having obtained a complete victory. ¶ *And those that trouble me.* Heb., *My adversaries.* The reference here is the same as in the former member of the verse. It is to the enemies that seemed almost to have triumphed over him already, and under whose power he was ready to sink. ¶ *Rejoice.* Exult; triumph. ¶ *When I am moved.* Moved from my steadfastness or firmness; when I am overcome. Hitherto he had been able to hold out against them; now he began to despair, and to fear that they would accomplish their object by overcoming and subduing him. His ground of apprehension and of appeal was, that by his being vanquished the cause in which he was engaged would suffer, and that the enemies of religion would triumph.

5. *But I have trusted in thy mercy.* In thy favour; thy friendship; thy promises. His original confidence had been in God only, and not in himself. That confidence he still maintained; and now, as the result of that, he begins to exult in the confidence that he would be safe. The idea is, "I have trusted in the mercy of God; I still trust, and I will trust for ever." ¶ *My heart shall rejoice in thy salvation.* The word *salvation* here does not refer to salvation in the future world, but to deliverance from his present troubles, or to God's interposition in putting him into a condition

mercy; my heart shall rejoice in thy salvation.

6 I will sing unto the LORD, because he hath dealt bountifully with me.

of safety. The idea is, that he had entire confidence that God *would* interpose, and that there would yet be cause to rejoice in that salvation as actually accomplished. He now calls on his heart to rejoice in the assurance that it would be his. So with us. There will not only be rejoicing in salvation when actually accomplished, but there may, and should be, in the firm conviction that it will be ours.

6. *I will sing unto the* LORD, *because he hath dealt bountifully with me.* The word which is here rendered *dealt bountifully*—גָּמַל, *gamal*—means properly to *deal* with any one; to *treat* any one well or ill; and then, to requite, or recompense. When used absolutely, as it is here, it is commonly employed in a good sense, meaning to deal favourably, or kindly, towards any one; to treat any one with favour. It means here that God had shown him kindness or favour, and had thus laid the foundation for gratitude and praise. The psalm closes, therefore, with expressions of joy, thankfulness, triumph. Though it begins with depression and sadness, it ends with joy. This is often observable in the Psalms. In the commencement it often occurs that the mind is overwhelmed with sorrow, and there is earnest pleading with God. Light, under the influence of prayer, breaks in gradually upon the soul. The clouds disperse; the darkness disappears. New views of the goodness and mercy of God are imparted; an assurance of his favour is brought to the soul; confidence in his mercy springs up in the heart; and the psalm that began with sorrowful complaining ends with the language of praise and of joy. So, too, it is in our own experience. Afflicted, depressed, and sad, we go to God. Everything seems dark. We have no peace—no clear and cheerful views—no joy. As we wait upon God, new views of his character, his mercy, his love, break upon the mind. The clouds open. Light beams upon us. Our souls take hold of the promises of God, and we, who went to his throne sad and desponding, rise from our devotions filled with praise and joy, submissive to the trials which made us so sad, and rejoicing in the belief that all things will work together for our good.

PSALM XIV.

This purports to be one of David's psalms, and there is no reason to doubt the correctness of the superscription. Yet we are entirely ignorant of the time and the circumstances of its composition. There is nothing in the psalm that throws any light on this point, and conjecture would be vain. It would seem to have been composed under the influence of an affecting conviction of the depth and extent of human depravity, and in view of prevalent impiety and neglect of God; but such a state of things was not confined to any one period of the life of David, as it is not to any one country or period of the world. Unhappily there has been no country and no age in which, in view of existing facts, such a psalm as this might not have been composed; or in which the entire proof on which the psalmist relies to support his melancholy conclusions, might not have been found.

The psalm embraces the following points:—

I. A statement of prevalent depravity, particularly in denying the existence of God, or in expressing the wish that there were no God, ver. 1.

II. The evidence of this, vers. 2-4. This is found in two things:—(*a*) first, in the representation that the Lord looked down from heaven for the very purpose of ascertaining whether there were any that "understood and sought after God," and that the result of this investigation was that *all* had gone aside, and had become defiled with sin, vers. 2, 3. (*b*) The second proof is a prevailing disposition on the part of the wicked to judge severely of the conduct of God's people; to magnify their errors and

PSALM XIV.

To the chief Musician. *A Psalm* of David.

THE fool hath said in his heart, *There is* no God. They are corrupt; they have done abominable works; *there is* none that doeth good.

faults; to make use of their imperfections to sustain themselves in their own course of life—represented by their "eating up the sins of God's people as they eat bread," ver. 4. There was an utter want of kindness and charity in regard to the imperfections of others; and a desire to find the people of God so offending that they could, by *their* imperfections and faults, sustain and vindicate their own conduct in neglecting religion. The idea is that, in their apprehension, the religion of such persons was not desirable,—that the God whom they professed to serve could *not* be God.

III. Yet, the psalmist says, they were not wholly calm and satisfied with the conclusion which they were endeavouring to reach, that there was no God. Notwithstanding their expressed wish or desire (ver. 1), that there was, or that there might be no God, their minds were not at ease in that conclusion or desire.

They were, says the psalmist, "in great fear," for there *was* evidence which they could not deny or resist that God was "in the generation of the righteous," or that there was a God such as the righteous served, ver. 5. This evidence was found in the manifestation of his favour towards them; in his interposition in their behalf, in the proof which could not be resisted or denied that he was their friend. These facts produced "fear" or apprehension in the minds of the wicked, notwithstanding all their efforts to be calm.

IV. The psalmist says that their course was designed to bring shame upon the counsel or purposes of the "poor" (that is, the people of God, who were mainly among the poor, or the humble and oppressed classes of the community)—because *they* regarded God as their refuge, ver. 6. As God was their *only* refuge, as they had no human hope or reliance, as *all* their hope would fail if their hope in God failed, so the attempt to show that there was no God was adapted and designed to overwhelm them with shame and confusion—still more to aggravate their sufferings by taking away their only hope, and leaving them to despair. Their religion was their only consolation, and the purpose of those who wished that there were no God was to take even this last comfort away.

V. The psalm closes, in view of these thoughts, with an earnest prayer that God would interpose to deliver his poor and oppressed people, and with the statement that *when* this should occur, his people would rejoice, ver. 7. Instead of their low and oppressed condition—a condition wherein their enemies triumphed over them, and endeavoured still further to aggravate their sorrows by taking away even their faith in God—they would rejoice in him, and in the full proof of his existence and of his favour towards them.

The psalm, therefore, is designed to describe a condition of things in which wickedness abounds, and when it takes this form—an attempt to show that there is no God; that is, when there is a prevalence of *atheism*, and when the design of this is to aggravate the sufferings and the trials of the professed friends of God by unsettling their faith in the Divine existence.

The title is the same as in Ps. xi. and xii. Comp. Notes on the title to Ps. iv.

1. *The fool.* The word *fool* is often used in the Scriptures to denote a wicked man—as sin is the essence of folly. Comp. Job ii. 10; Ps. lxxiv. 18; Gen. xxxiv. 7; Deut. xxii. 21. The Hebrew word is rendered *vile person* in Isaiah xxxii. 5, 6. Elsewhere it is rendered *fool, foolish,* and *foolish man.* It is designed to convey the idea that wickedness or impiety is essential folly, or to use a term in describing the wicked which will, perhaps, more than any other, make the mind averse to the sin—for there is many a man who would see more in the word *fool* to be hated than in the word *wicked;* who would rather be called a *sinner* than a *fool.* ¶ *Hath said.* That is, has *thought,* for the reference is to what is passing in his mind. ¶ *In his heart.* See Notes on Ps. x. 11. He may not have said this to others; he may not have taken the position openly before

2 The LORD looked down from heaven upon the children of men, to see if there were any that did understand, *and* seek God.

the world that there is no God, but such a thought has passed through his mind, and he has cherished it; and such a thought, either as a matter of belief or of desire, is at the foundation of his conduct. He *acts* as if such were his belief or his wish. ¶ There is *no God.* The words "there is" are not in the original. The literal rendering would be either "no God," "nothing of God," or "God is not." The idea is that, in his apprehension, there is no such thing as God, or no such being as God. The more correct idea in the passage is, that this was the *belief* of him who is here called a "fool;" and it is doubtful whether the language would convey the idea of *desire*—or of a *wish* that this might be so; but still there can be no doubt that such *is* the wish or desire of the wicked, and that they listen eagerly to any suggestions or arguments which, in their apprehension, would go to demonstrate that there is no such being as God. The *exact* state of mind, however, indicated by the *language* here, undoubtedly is that such was the opinion or the belief of him who is here called a fool. If this is the true interpretation, then the passage would prove that there have been men who were atheists. The passage would prove, also, in its connexion, that such a belief was closely linked, either as a cause or a consequent, with a corrupt life; for this statement immediately follows in regard to the character of those who are represented as saying that there is no God. As a matter of fact, the belief that there is no God is commonly founded on the desire to lead a wicked life; or, the opinion that there is no God is embraced by those who in fact lead such a life, with a desire to sustain themselves in their depravity, and to avoid the fear of future retribution. A man who wishes to lead an upright life, *desires* to find evidence that there is a God, and to such a man nothing would be more dark and distressing than anything which would compel him to doubt the fact of God's existence. It is only a wicked man who finds pleasure in an argument to prove that there is no God, and the wish that there were no God springs up only in a bad heart. ¶ *They are corrupt.* That is, they have done corruptly; or, their conduct is corrupt. ¶ *They have done abominable works.* They have done that which is to be abominated or abhorred; that which is to be detested, and which is fitted to fill the mind with horror. ¶ There is *none that doeth good.* Depravity is universal. All have fallen into sin; all fail to do good. None are found who are disposed to worship their Maker, and to keep his laws. This was originally spoken, undoubtedly, with reference to the age in which the psalmist lived; but it is applied by the apostle Paul, Rom. iii. 10 (see Notes on that passage), as an argument for the universal depravity of mankind.

2. *The* LORD *looked down from heaven.* The original word here—שָׁקַף, *shakaph*—conveys the idea of *bending forward*, and hence of an intense and anxious looking, as we bend forward when we wish to examine anything with attention, or when we look out for one who is expected to come. The idea is that God looked intently, or so as to secure a close examination, upon the children of men, for the express purpose of ascertaining whether there were any that were good. He looked at all men; he examined all their pretensions to goodness, and he saw none who could be regarded as exempt from the charge of depravity. Nothing could more clearly prove the doctrine of universal depravity than to say that an Omniscient God made *an express examination* on this very point, that he looked over all the world, and that in the multitudes which passed under the notice of his eye not *one* could be

3 They are all gone aside, they are *all* together become [1] filthy; *there is* none that doeth good, no, not one.

[1] *stinking.*

found who could be pronounced righteous. If God could not find such an one, assuredly man cannot. ¶ *Upon the children of men.* Upon mankind; upon the human race. They are called "children," or *sons* (Hebrew), because they are all the descendants of the man that God created—of Adam. Indeed the original word here is *Adam*—אָדָם. And it may be questionable whether, since this became in fact a proper name, designating the first man, it would not have been proper to retain the idea in the translation — "the sons of Adam;" that is, all his descendants. The phrase occurs frequently to denote the human race, Deut. xxxii. 8; Ps. xi. 4; xxi. 10; xxxi. 19; xxxvi. 7; lvii. 4; *et sæpe.* ¶ *To see if there were any that did understand.* If there were one acting wisely—to wit, in seeking God. "Acting wisely" here stands in contrast with the folly referred to in the first verse. Religion is always represented in the Scriptures as true wisdom. ¶ And *seek God.* The knowledge of him; his favour and friendship. Wisdom is shown by a *desire* to become acquainted with the being and perfections of God, as well as in the actual possession of that knowledge; and in no way can the true character of man be better determined than by the actual interest which is felt in becoming acquainted with the character of him who made and who governs the universe. It is one of the clearest proofs of human depravity that there *is* no prevailing desire among men thus to ascertain the character of God.

3. *They are all gone aside.* This verse states the result of the Divine investigation referred to in the previous verse. The result, as seen by God himself, was, that *all* were seen to have gone aside, and to have become filthy. The word rendered "gone aside" means properly to go off, to turn aside or away, to depart; as, for example, to turn out of the right way or path, Ex. xxxii. 8. Then it means to turn away from God; to fall away from his worship; to apostatize, 1 Sam. xii. 20; 2 Kings xviii. 6; 2 Chron. xxv. 27. This is the idea here—that they had all apostatized from the living God. The word "all" in the circumstances makes the statement as universal as it can be made; and no term could be used more clearly affirming the doctrine of universal depravity. ¶ *They are* all *together become filthy.* The word "*all*" here is supplied by the translators. It was not necessary, however, to introduce it in order that the idea of universal depravity might be expressed, for that is implied in the word rendered *together*, יַחְדָּו, *yahhdâv.* That word properly conveys the idea that the same character or conduct pervaded all, or that the same thing might be expressed of all those referred to. They were *united* in this thing—that they had become defiled or filthy. The word is used with reference to *persons*, as meaning that they are all *in one place*, Gen. xiii. 6; xxii. 6; or to *events*, as meaning that they occurred *at one time*, Ps. iv. 8. They were all as one. Comp. 1 Chron. x. 6. The idea is that, in respect to the statement made, they were alike. What would describe one would describe all. The word rendered "become filthy" is, in the margin, rendered *stinking.* In Arabic the word means to become *sharp*, or *sour* as milk; and hence the idea of becoming corrupt in a moral sense. Gesenius, *Lex.* The word is found only here, and in the parallel Ps. liii. 3, and in Job xv. 16, in each of which places it is rendered *filthy.* It relates here to character, and means that their character was morally corrupt or de-

4 Have all the workers of iniquity no knowledge? who eat up my people *as* they eat bread, and call not upon the LORD.

---

filed. The term is often used in that sense now. ¶ There is *none that doeth good, no, not one.* Nothing could more clearly express the idea of universal depravity than this expression. It is not merely that no one could be found who did good, but the expression is repeated to give emphasis to the statement. This entire passage is quoted in Rom. iii. 10—12, in proof of the doctrine of universal depravity. See Notes on that passage.

4. *Have all the workers of iniquity no knowledge?* Literally, "Do they not know, all the workers of iniquity, eating my people, they eat bread; Jehovah they call not." The several statements in this verse in confirmation of the fact of their depravity are —(*a*) that they have no knowledge of God; (*b*) that they find pleasure in the errors and imperfections of the people of God—sustaining themselves in their own wickedness by the fact that the professed friends of God are inconsistent in their lives; and (*c*) that they do not call on the name of the Lord, or that they offer no worship to him. The whole verse might have been, and should have been put in the form of a question. The first statement implied in the question is, that they have *no knowledge.* This can be regarded as a proof of guilt only (1) as they have opportunities of obtaining knowledge; (2) as they neglect to improve those opportunities, and remain in voluntary ignorance; and (3) as they do this from a design to practise wickedness. See this argument stated at length by the apostle Paul in Rom. i. 19—28. Comp. Notes on that passage. *This* proof of human depravity is everywhere manifested still in the world, —in the fact that men have the opportunities of gaining the knowledge of God if they chose to do it; in the fact that they voluntarily neglect those opportunities; and in the fact that the reason of this is that they love iniquity. ¶ *Who eat up my people* as *they eat bread.* They sustain themselves in their own course of life by the imperfections of the people of God. That is, they make use of their inconsistencies to confirm themselves in the belief that there is no God. They argue that a religion which produces no better fruits than what is seen in the lives of its professed friends can be of no value, or cannot be genuine; that if a professed belief in God produces no happier results than are found in their lives, it could be of no advantage to worship God; that they are themselves as good as those are who profess to be religious, and that, therefore, there can be no evidence from the lives of the professed friends of God that religion is either true or of any value. No inconsiderable part of the evidence in favour of religion, it is intended, shall be derived from the lives of its friends; and when that evidence is not furnished, of course no small part of the proof of its reality and value is lost. Hence so much importance is attached everywhere in the Bible to the necessity of a consistent life on the part of the professed friends of religion. Comp. Isa. xliii. 10. The words "my people" here are properly to be regarded as the words of the psalmist, identifying himself with the people of God, and speaking of them thus as *his own people.* Thus one speaks of his own family or his own friends. Comp. Ruth i. 16. Or this may be spoken by David, considered as the head or ruler of the nation, and he may thus speak of the people of God as his people. The connexion does not allow of the construction which would refer the words to God. ¶ *And call not upon the* LORD. They do not worship Jehovah. They give this evidence of wickedness that they do not pray; that they do not invoke

5 [1] There were they in great fear: [i] for God *is* in the generation of the righteous.

6 Ye have shamed the counsel

[1] *they feared a fear.*

i Psa. liii. 5.

the blessing of their Maker; that they do not publicly acknowledge him as God. It is remarkable that this is placed as the last or the crowning thing in the evidence of their depravity; and if rightly considered, it is so. To one who should look at things as they are; to one who sees all the claims and obligations which rest upon mankind; to one who appreciates his own guilt, his dependance, and his exposure to death and woe; to one who understands aright why man was made,—there can be no more striking proof of human depravity than in the fact that a man in no way acknowledges his Maker,—that he renders him no homage,—that he never supplicates his favour,—never deprecates his wrath,—that, amidst the trials, the temptations, the perils of life, he endeavours to make his way through the world *as if there were no God.* The highest crime that Gabriel could commit would be to renounce all allegiance to his Maker, and henceforward to live *as if* there were no God. All other iniquities that he might commit would spring out of *that,* and would be secondary to *that.* The great sin of man consists in renouncing God, and attempting to live as if there were no Supreme Being to whom he owes allegiance. All other sins spring out of that, and are subordinate to it.

5. *There were they in great fear.* Marg., as in Heb., *they feared a fear.* The idea is, that they were in great terror or consternation. They were not *calm* in their belief that there was no God. They endeavoured to be. They wished to satisfy themselves that there was no God, and that they had nothing to dread. But they could not do this. In spite of all their efforts, there was such proof of his existence, and of his being the friend of the righteous, and consequently the enemy of such as they themselves were, as to fill their minds with alarm. Men cannot, by an effort of will, get rid of the evidence that there is a God. In the face of all their attempts to convince themselves of this, the demonstration of his existence will press upon them, and will often fill their minds with terror. ¶ *For God* is *in the generation of the righteous.* The word *generation* here, as applied to the righteous, seems to refer to them as a *race,* or as a *class* of men. Comp. Ps. xxiv. 6; lxxiii. 15; cxii. 2. It commonly in the Scriptures refers to a certain age or duration, as it is used by us, reckoning an age or generation as about thirty or forty years (comp. Job xlii. 16); but in the use of the term before us the idea of an *age* is dropped, and the righteous are spoken of merely as a *class* or *race* of persons. The idea here is, that there were such manifest proofs that God was among the righteous, and that he was their friend, that the wicked could not resist the force of that evidence, however much they might desire it, and however much they might wish to arrive at the conclusion that there was no God. The evidence that he *was* among the righteous would, of course, alarm them, because the very fact that he was the friend of the righteous demonstrated that he must be the enemy of the wicked, and, of course, that they were exposed to his wrath.

6. *Ye have shamed.* The address here is made directly to the wicked themselves, to show them the baseness of their own conduct, and, perhaps, in connexion with the previous verse, to show them what occasion they had for fear. The idea in the verse seems to be, that as God was the protector of the "poor" who had come to him for "refuge," and as they had "shamed the counsel of the poor" who had done this, they had real occasion for alarm. The phrase

of the poor; because the LORD *is*
his refuge.
7 [1] Oh that the salvation of
Israel *were come* [k] out of Zion!
When the LORD bringeth back
the captivity of his people, Jacob

[1] *who will give.*

k Rom. xi. 26.

"ye have shamed" seems to mean that they had *despised* it, or had treated it with derision, that is, they had laughed at, or had mocked the purpose of the poor in putting their trust in Jehovah. ¶ *The counsel.* The purpose, the plan, the act—of the poor; that is, in putting their trust in the Lord. They had derided this as vain and foolish, since they maintained that there was no God (ver. 1). They therefore regarded such an act as mere illusion. ¶ *The poor.* The righteous, considered *as* poor, or as afflicted. The word here rendered *poor*—עָנִי, *ani* — means more properly, afflicted, distressed, needy. It is often rendered *afflicted,* Job xxxiv. 28; Ps. xviii. 27; xxii. 24; xxv. 16; lxxxii. 3; *et al.* In Ps. ix. 12 and x. 12 it is rendered *humble.* The common rendering, however, is "poor," but it refers properly to the righteous, with the idea that they are afflicted, needy, and in humble circumstances. This is the idea here. The wicked had derided those who, in circumstances of poverty, depression, want, trial, had no other resource, and who had sought their comfort in God. These reproaches tended to take away their last consolation, and to cover them with confusion; it was proper, therefore, that they who had done this should be overwhelmed with fear. If there is anything which deserves punishment it is the act which would take away from the world the last hope of the wretched—*that there is a God.* ¶ *Because the* LORD *is his refuge.* He has made the Lord his refuge. In his poverty, affliction, and trouble, he has come to God, and put his trust in him. *This* source of comfort, the doctrine of the wicked—that there "was no God"—tended to destroy. Atheism cuts off every hope of man, and leaves the wretched to despair. It would put out the last light that gleams on the earth, and cover the world with total and eternal night.

7. *Oh that the salvation of Israel.* Marg., *Who will give,* etc. The Hebrew literally is, "Who will give out of Zion salvation to Israel?" The word *Israel* refers primarily to the Hebrew people, and then it is used generally to denote the people of God. The wish here expressed is in view of the facts referred to in the previous verses —the general prevalence of iniquity and of practical atheism, and the sufferings of the people of God on that account. This state of things suggests the earnest desire that from all such evils the people of God might be delivered. The expression in the original, as in the margin, "*Who will give,*" is a common expression in Hebrew, and means the same as in our translation, "*Oh that.*" It is expressive of an earnest desire, as if the thing were in the hand of another, that he would impart that blessing or favour. ¶ *Out of Zion.* On the word *Zion,* see Notes on Isa. i. 8. It is referred to here, as it is often, as the seat or dwelling-place of God; the place from whence he issued his commands, and from whence he put forth his power. Thus in Ps. iii. 4, "He heard me out of his holy hill." Ps. xx. 2, "The Lord . . . . strengthen thee out of Zion." Ps. cxxviii. 5, "The Lord shall bless thee out of Zion." Here the phrase expresses a wish that God, who had his dwelling in Zion, would put forth his power in granting complete deliverance to his people. ¶ *When the* LORD *bringeth back.* Literally "In Jehovah's bringing back the captivity of his people." That is, the particular salvation which the psalmist prayed for was that Jehovah would return the captivity of his people, or restore them from captivity. ¶ *The captivity of*

shall rejoice, *and* Israel shall be glad.

his people. This is *language* taken from a captivity in a foreign land. It is not necessary, however, to suppose that any such literal captivity is here referred to, nor would it be necessary to infer from this that the psalm was written in the Babylonian captivity, or in any other particular exile of the Hebrew people. The truth was, that the Hebrews were often in this state (see the Book of Judges, *passim*), and this language came to be the common method of expressing any condition of oppression and trouble, or of a low state of religion in the land. Comp. Job xlii. 10. ¶ *Jacob shall rejoice.* Another name for the Hebrew people, as descended from Jacob, Isa. ii. 3; xli. 21; x. 21; xiv. 1; Amos vii. 2; *et sæpe.* Professor Alexander renders this, "Let Jacob exult; let Israel joy." The idea seems to be, that such a restoration would give great joy to the people of God, and the language expresses a desire that this might soon occur—perhaps expressing the idea also that in the certainty of such an ultimate restoration, such a complete salvation, the people of God might *now* rejoice. Thus, too, it will not only be true that the redeemed will be happy in heaven, but they may exult even now in the prospect, the certainty, that they *will* obtain complete salvation.

PSALM XV.

This psalm refers to a single subject, but that the most important which can come before the human mind. It is the question, Who is truly religious? who will enter heaven? who will be saved? The psalm contains a statement of what real religion is; one of the most explicit and formal of the statements which we have in the Old Testament on that subject. The form in which the matter is presented is that of a *question* in the first verse, and of the *answer* to that question in the other verses of the psalm.

I. The question, ver. 1. The question is, Who shall be permitted to reside with God in his tabernacle? who shall be entitled to the privilege of dwelling on his holy hill (that is, Zion, regarded as the dwelling-place of God, and the emblem of heaven)? In other words, Who has such a character as to be entitled to hope for the favour and friendship of God?

II. The answer, vers. 2-5. The answer embraces the following particulars:—

(1) The man who is upright, just, honest, truthful, ver. 2.

(2) The man who treats his neighbour properly; who does not slander or reproach him; who does not readily listen to calumnious reports in regard to him, ver. 3.

(3) The man who regards the righteous and the wicked as they should be regarded; who looks with proper disapprobation on all who are "vile" in their character, and with true respect on all who fear the Lord, ver. 4.

(4) The man who is faithful to an engagement, though it proves to be against his own interest, ver. 4.

(5) The man who does not take advantage of the necessities of others, who does not put out his money "to usury," and who, if a magistrate, does not take a bribe to induce him to condemn the innocent, ver. 5.

These are characteristics of true religion everywhere, and it is as true now as it was when this psalm was composed that it is only those who possess this character who have a right to regard themselves as the friends of God, or who have a well-founded hope of dwelling with him in heaven.

The psalm purports, in the title, to be "A Psalm of David." It is not known on what occasion it was written, nor is it material to know this in order to understand the psalm. It has been supposed by some that it was composed on the occasion when the ark was carried up from the house of Obed-edom (2 Sam. vi. 12, seq.), but there is nothing in the psalm itself which should lead us to refer it to that occasion, or to any other special occasion. It seems rather—like Ps. i.—to be adapted to all times and all places. It contains a general illustration of the nature of true religion, and there has been no state of things in the world in which such a psalm might not be appropriately composed; there is none in which it may not be appropriately read and pondered.

PSALM XV.

A Psalm of David.

LORD, who shall [1] abide in thy tabernacle? who shall dwell in thy holy hill?

2 He that walketh uprightly, and worketh righteousness, and speaketh the truth in his heart.

3 *He that* backbiteth not with

[1] *sojourn.*

---

1. LORD, *who shall abide in thy tabernacle?* Marg., *sojourn.* The Hebrew word means properly to *sojourn;* that is, to abide in a place *as* a sojourner or stranger; not permanently, but only for a while. The idea in this place is taken from the word *tabernacle* or *tent,* with which one naturally associates the thought of sojourning, rather than that of a permanent abode. Comp. Heb. xi. 9. It should not be inferred, however, that it is meant here that the residence with God would be *temporary.* The idea of permanency is fully expressed in the other member of the sentence, and the language here is only such as was customary in speaking of the righteous—language derived from the fact that in early times men dwelt in tents rather than in permanent habitations. ¶ *Who shall dwell in thy holy hill?* Zion, regarded as the dwelling-place of God, and the type of heaven—the eternal abode of the Most High. See Notes on Ps. ii. 6. The question is equivalent to asking, Who is qualified to dwell with God? who may properly be regarded as his friend? who has a title to his favour? who is truly pious? By us the same question would be put in another form, though implying the same thing: Who is qualified to become a member of the church; who has evidence of true conversion and real piety? who is he who is prepared for heaven?

2. *He that walketh uprightly.* Heb., "walking perfectly;" that is, one who walks or lives *perfectly.* The word "*walk*" in the Scriptures is often used to denote the manner of life;—life being represented as a journey. See Notes on Ps. i. 1. The word here rendered "uprightly," or, in the Hebrew, *perfectly,* means that which is complete in all its parts; where no part is wanting or is defective. See the word explained in the Notes on Job i. 1. The word is not used in the sense in which it is often employed now, as denoting absolute freedom from sin, but as meaning that the character was *complete* in all its parts; or that the person referred to was upright alike in regard to God and to man. See the sentiment here expressed explained in the Notes on Isa. xxxiii. 15. ¶ *And worketh righteousness.* Does right. That is, he does what is proper to be done in relation to God and to man. Compare Micah vi. 8. The doctrine is everywhere laid down in the Scriptures that no man can be a friend of God who does not do habitually what is *right.* See 1 John iii. 6—10. ¶ *And speaketh the truth in his heart.* He uses language that is sincere, and that is in accordance with his real belief. This is opposed to all mere outward professions, and all hypocritical pretences. His religion has its seat in the heart, and is not the religion of forms; his acts are the expressions of upright intentions and purposes, and are not performed for selfish and hypocritical ends. This is everywhere the nature of true religion.

3. He that *backbiteth not with his tongue.* The word *backbite* means to censure; slander; reproach; speak evil of. The Hebrew word—רָגַל, *ragal*—a verb formed from the word *foot,* means properly *to foot it,* and then *to go about.* Then it means to go about as a tale-bearer or slanderer; to circulate reports unfavourable to others. It is not improperly rendered here *backbite;* and the idea is, that it is essential to true piety that one should *not* be a slanderer, or should *not* circulate evil reports in regard to others. On the use of the *tongue,* see Notes on James iii. 2—11.

his tongue, nor doeth evil to his neighbour, nor [1] taketh up a reproach against his neighbour.

[1] Or, *receiveth*, or, *endureth*.

4 In whose eyes a vile person is contemned; but he honoureth them that fear the LORD. *He that* sweareth to *his own* hurt, and changeth not.

¶ *Nor doeth evil to his neighbour.* That does his neighbour no harm. This refers to injury in any way, whether by word or deed. The idea is, that the man who will be admitted to dwell on the holy hill of Zion, the man who is truly religious, is one who does no injury to any one; who always does that which is right to others. The word *neighbour* usually refers to one who resides near us; and then it denotes all persons who are near to us in the sense that we have business relations with them;—all persons with whom we have anything to do. It is used in this sense here as referring to our dealings with other persons. ¶ *Nor taketh up a reproach.* Marg., or *receiveth*, or, *endureth.* The idea is that of *taking up*, or receiving as true, or readily giving credit to it. He is slow to believe evil of another. He does not grasp at it greedily as if he had pleasure in it. He does not himself originate such a reproach, nor does he readily and cheerfully credit it when it is stated by others. If he is constrained to believe it, it is only because the evidence becomes so strong that he cannot resist it, and his believing it is contrary to all the desires of his heart. This is true religion everywhere; but this is contrary to the conduct of no small part of the world. There are large classes of persons to whom nothing is more acceptable than reproachful accusations of others, and who embrace no reports more readily than they do those which impute bad conduct or bad motives to them. Often there is nothing more marked in true conversion than the change which is produced in this respect. He who delighted in gossip and in slanderous reports of others; who found pleasure in the alleged failings and errors of his neighbours; who gladly lent a listening ear to the first intimations of this kind, and who cheerfully contributed his influence in giving circulation to such things, augmenting such reports as they passed through his hands,—now sincerely rejoices on hearing everybody well spoken of, and does all that can be done consistently with truth to check such reports, and to secure to every man a good name.

4. *In whose eyes a vile person is contemned.* That is, who does not show respect to a man of base or bad character on account of his wealth, his position, or his rank in life. He estimates character as it is in itself, and not as derived from rank, relationship, or station. While, as stated in the previous verse, he is not disposed to take up a false or evil report against another, he is at the same time disposed to do justice to all, and does not honour those who do not deserve to be honoured, or apologise for base conduct because it is committed by one of exalted station or rank. Loving virtue and piety for their own sake, he hates all that is opposite; and where conduct *deserves* reprobation, no matter where found, he does not hesitate to avow his conviction in regard to it. The sentiment here is substantially the same as in Psalm i. 1. See Notes on that verse. ¶ *But he honoureth them that fear the* LORD. No matter in what rank or condition of life they may be found. Where there is true piety he honours it. He is willing to be known as one that honours it, and is willing to bear all the reproach that may be connected with such a deeply cherished respect, and with such an avowal. Comp. Psalm i. 1. ¶ He that *sweareth to* his own *hurt, and changeth not.* Who has made a promise, or entered into a contract,

5 *He that* putteth not out his money to usury, [l] nor taketh reward against the innocent. He

l Ezek. xviii. 8, 17; xxii. 12.

that is likely to turn out contrary to his expectations, to his own disadvantage; but who still adheres to his engagement. If the thing itself is wrong; if he has made a promise, or pledged himself to do a wicked thing, he cannot be under obligation to execute it; he should at once abandon it (comp. Notes on Matt. xiv. 9); but he is not at liberty to violate an agreement simply because it will be a loss to him, or because he ascertains that it will not be, as he supposed, to his advantage. The principles here laid down will extend to all contracts or agreements, pecuniary or otherwise, and should be a general principle regulating all our transactions with our fellow-men. The only limitation in the rule is that above stated, when the promise or the contract would involve that which is morally wrong.

5. He that *putteth not out his money to usury.* The word *usury* formerly denoted legal interest, or a premium for the *use* of money. In this sense the word is no longer used in our language, but it always now denotes *unlawful* interest; "a premium or compensation paid, or stipulated to be paid, for the use of money borrowed or retained, beyond the rate of interest established by law." *Webster.*—The Hebrew word used here—נֶשֶׁךְ, *neshech*—means *interest,* that is, a premium or compensation for the use of money in any manner, or to any extent. The reference is to the law of the Hebrews, which forbade such a loaning of money to the poor, and especially to poor Israelites, Ex. xxii. 25; Lev. xxv. 35, 36, 37. Although this was forbidden in respect to the Israelites, yet the lending of money on interest, or "usury" in a lawful sense, was allowed towards "strangers," or towards the people of other nations. See Deut. xxiii. 19, 20. The ground of the distinction was, that the Hebrews were regarded as a nation of brethren; that, as such, they should be willing to accommodate and aid each other; that they should not do anything that could be regarded as unbrotherly. In respect to other people it was allowed, not because it was proper to take advantage of their wants, and to oppress them, but because this peculiar reason did not exist in regard to them. That might be improper *in a family,* among brothers and sisters, which would be entirely proper towards those who did not sustain this peculiar relation; and we may conceive of cases—such cases in fact often occur—when it would be unkind in the highest degree to exact interest of a brother, or an intimate friend, while it is perfectly proper to receive the ordinary allowance for the use of money in our business transactions (that is, the ordinary rate of interest) of those who do not sustain to us this peculiar relation. The fact that it was allowed to the Hebrews to take interest of the people of other nations, shows that there was nothing morally wrong in the thing itself; and, in fact, there can be no reason why a man, to whom it is an accommodation, should not *pay* for the use of money as well as for the use of any other property. The thing forbidden here, therefore, is not the taking of interest in any case, but the taking of interest in such a way as would be oppressive and hard,—as of a Hebrew demanding it from his poor and needy brother; and, by consequence, it would forbid the exacting of unusual and unlawful rates of interest, or taking advantage of the necessities of others—by evading the provisions of law, and making their circumstances an occasion of extortion. In one word, the thing forbidden is a harsh, grasping, griping disposition; a disposition to take advantage of the embarrassments of others to increase our own gains.

that doeth these *things* shall never [m] be moved.

m 2 Pet. i. 10.

Kindness, and an accommodating spirit in business transactions, are as much demanded now by the principles of religion as they were when this psalm was written, or as they were under the law which forbade the taking of interest from a poor and needy brother. ¶ *Nor taketh reward against the innocent.* Who does not take a bribe; that is, does not accept a pecuniary consideration, or any other consideration, to induce him to decide a cause against justice. He is not, in any way, to allow any such considerations to influence him, or to sway his judgment. The taking of bribes is often expressly forbidden in the Scriptures. See Ex. xxiii. 8; Deut. xvi. 19; xxvii. 25; Prov. xvii. 23. ¶ *He that doeth these* things *shall never be moved.* That is, in answer to the question in ver. 1, he shall be permitted to "abide in the tabernacle" of God, and to "dwell in his holy hill." He shall have a solid foundation of hope; he is a friend of God, and shall enjoy his favour for ever. In other words, these things constitute true religion; and he who has such a character will obtain eternal life. His foundation is sure; he will be safe in all the storms of life, and safe when the cold waves of death beat around him. Comp. Matt. vii. 24, 25.

PSALM XVI.

This psalm expresses a confident expectation of eternal life and happiness, founded on the evidence of true attachment to God. It expresses the deep conviction that one who loves God will not be left in the grave, and will not be suffered to see permanent "corruption," or to perish in the grave, for ever.

The contents of the psalm are the following:—

(1) An earnest prayer of the author for preservation on the ground that he had put his trust in God, ver. 1.

(2) A statement of his attachment to God, vers. 2, 3, founded partly on his consciousness of such attachment (ver. 2), and partly on the fact that he truly loved the friends of God, ver. 3.

(3) A statement of the fact that he had no sympathy with those who rejected the true God; that he did not, and would not, participate in their worship. The Lord was his portion, and his inheritance, vers. 4, 5.

(4) Thankfulness that the lines had fallen unto him in such pleasant places; that he had had his birth and lot where the true God was adored, and not in a land of idolaters, vers. 6, 7.

(5) A confident expectation, on the ground of his attachment to God, that he would be happy for ever; that he would not be left to perish in the grave; that he would obtain eternal life at the right hand of God, vers. 8-11. This expectation implies the following particulars:—

(*a*) That he would never be moved; that is, that he would not be disappointed and cast off, ver. 8.

(*b*) That, though he was to die, his flesh would rest in hope, ver. 9.

(*c*) That he would not be left in the regions of the dead, nor suffered to lie for ever in the grave, ver. 10.

(*d*) That God would show him the path of life, and give him a place at his right hand, ver. 11.

Nothing can be determined with certainty in regard to the *occasion* on which the psalm was composed. It is such a psalm as might be composed at any time in view of solemn reflections on life, death, the grave, and the world beyond; on the question whether the grave is the end of man, or whether there will be a future. It is made up of happy reflections on the lot and the hopes of the pious; expressing the belief that, although they were to die, there was a brighter world beyond—although they were to be laid in the grave, they would not always remain there; that they would be released from the tomb, and be raised up to the right hand of God. It expresses more clearly than can be found almost anywhere else in the Old Testament a belief in the doctrine of the resurrection—an assurance that those who love God, and keep his commandments, will not always remain in the grave.

The psalm is appealed to by Peter (Acts ii. 25-31), and by Paul (Acts

PSALM XVI.

[1] Michtam of David.

PRESERVE me, O God: for in thee do I put my trust.

2 *O my soul*, thou hast said unto the LORD, Thou *art* my Lord: [n] my goodness *extendeth* not to thee;

[1] Or, *A golden* Psalm, Psa. lvi.—lx.

n Job xxxv. 7, 8.

xiii. 35-37), as referring to the resurrection of Christ, and is adduced by them in such a manner as to show they regarded it as proving that He would be raised from the dead. It is not necessary to suppose, in order to a correct understanding of the psalm, that it had an *exclusive* reference to the Messiah, but only that it referred to him in the highest sense, or that it had its complete fulfilment in him. Comp. Introduction to Isaiah, § 7, iii. It undoubtedly expressed the feelings of David in reference to himself—his own hopes in view of death;—while it is true that he was directed to use language in describing his own feelings and hopes which could have a *complete* fulfilment only in the Messiah. In a more full and complete sense, it was true that *he* would not be left in the grave, and that *he* would not be allowed "to see corruption." It was actually true in the sense in which David used the term as applicable to himself that he would not be "left" *permanently* and *ultimately* in the grave, under the dominion of corruption; it was *literally* true of the Messiah, as Peter and Paul argued, that he did not "*see* corruption;" that he was raised from the grave without undergoing that change in the tomb through which all others must pass. As David used the language (as applicable to himself), the hope suggested in the psalm will be fulfilled in the future resurrection of the righteous; as the words are to be *literally* understood, they could be fulfilled only in Christ, who rose from the dead *without* seeing corruption. The argument of Peter and Paul is, that this prophetic language was found in the Old Testament, and that it could have a *complete* fulfilment only in the resurrection of Christ. David, though he would rise as he anticipated, did, *in fact*, return to corruption. Of the Messiah it was literally true that his body did *not* undergo any change in the grave. The reference to the Messiah is, that it had its highest and most complete fulfilment in him. Comp. Notes on Acts ii. 25-31.

The *title* of the psalm is, "Michtam of David." The word *Michtam* occurs only in the following places, in all of which it is used as the title of a psalm: Ps. xvi., lvi., lvii,, lviii., lix., lx. Gesenius supposes that it means a *writing*, especially a poem, psalm, or song; and that its sense is the same as the title to the psalm of Hezekiah (Isaiah xxxviii. 9), where the word used is rendered *writing*. According to Gesenius the word here used—מִכְתָּם, *Michtam*—is the same as the word employed in Isaiah—מִכְתָּב, *Michtab*—the last letter ב, *b*, having been gradually changed to ם, *m*. Others, unaptly, Gesenius says, have derived the word from כֶּתֶם; *Chethem*, *gold*, meaning a *golden* psalm; that is, precious, or pre-eminent. De Wette renders it, *Schrift*, writing. It is, perhaps, impossible now to determine why some of the psalms of David should have been merely termed *writings*, while others are mentioned under more specific titles.

1. *Preserve me, O God.* Keep me; guard me; save me. This language implies that there was imminent danger of some kind—perhaps, as the subsequent part of the psalm would seem to indicate, danger of death. See vers. 8—10. The idea here is, that God was able to preserve him from the impending danger, and that he might hope he would do it. ¶ *For in thee do I put my trust.* That is, my hope is in thee. He had no other reliance than God; but he *had* confidence in him—he felt assured that there *was* safety there.

2. O my soul, *thou hast said unto the* LORD. The words "O my soul" are not in the original. A literal rendering of the passage would be, "Thou hast said unto the Lord," etc., leaving something to be supplied. De Wette renders it, "To Jehovah I call; thou art my Lord." Luther, "I have said to the Lord." The Latin Vulgate, "Thou, my soul, hast said to

3 *But* to the saints that *are* in the earth, and *to* the excellent, [o] in whom *is* all my delight.

o Mal. iii. 17.

the Lord." The LXX., "I have said unto the Lord." Bishop Horsley, "I have said unto Jehovah." The speaker evidently is the psalmist; he is describing his feelings towards the Lord, and the idea is equivalent to the expression "*I* have said unto the Lord." Some word must necessarily be understood, and our translators have probably expressed the true sense by inserting the words, "O my soul." The state of mind indicated is that in which one is carefully looking at himself, his own perils, his own ground of hope, and when he finds in himself a ground of just confidence that he has put his trust in God, and in God alone. We have such a form of appeal in Ps. xlii. 5, 11; xliii. 5, "Why art thou cast down, O my soul?" ¶ *Thou* art *my Lord.* Thou hast a right to rule over me; or, I acknowledge thee as my Lord, my sovereign. The word here is not *Jehovah,* but *Adonai*—a word of more general signification than *Jehovah.* The sense is, I have acknowledged Jehovah to be my Lord and my God. I receive him and rest upon him as such. ¶ *My goodness* extendeth *not to thee.* This passage has been very variously rendered. Professor Alexander translates it, "My good (is) not besides thee (or, beyond thee);" meaning, as he supposes, "My happiness is not beside thee, independent of, or separable from thee." So De Wette, "There is no success (or good fortune) to me out of thee." Others render it, "My goodness is not such as to entitle me to thy regard." And others, "My happiness is not obligatory or incumbent on thee; thou art not bound to provide for it." The Latin Vulgate renders it, "My good is not given unless by thee." Bishop Horsley, "Thou art my good—not besides thee." I think the meaning is, "My good is nowhere except in thee; I have no source of good of any kind—happiness, hope, life, safety, salvation—but in thee. My good is not without thee." This accords with the idea in the other member of the sentence, where he acknowledges Jehovah as his Lord; in other words, he found in Jehovah all that is implied in the idea of an object of worship—all that is properly expressed by the notion of a *God.* He renounced all other gods, and found his happiness—his all—in Jehovah.

3. But *to the saints that* are *in the earth.* This verse also has been very variously rendered. Our translators seem to have understood it, in connexion with the previous verse, as meaning that his "goodness," or piety, was not of so pure and elevated a character that it could in any way extend to God so as to benefit him, but that it *might* be of service to the saints on earth, and that so, by benefiting them, he might show his attachment to God himself. But if the interpretation of the previous verse above proposed be the correct one, then this interpretation cannot be admitted here. This verse is probably to be regarded as a further statement of the evidence of the attachment of the psalmist to God. In the previous verse, according to the interpretation proposed, he states that his happiness—his all—was centered in God. He had no hope of anything except in him; none beyond him; none besides him. In this verse he states, as a further proof of his attachment to him, that he regarded with deep affection the saints of God; that he found his happiness, not in the society of the wicked, but in the friendship of the excellent of the earth. The verse may be thus rendered:—"As to the saints in the earth (or in respect to the saints in the earth), and to the excellent, all my delight is in them." In the former verse he had stated that, as to God, or in respect to God, he had no source of blessing, no hope, no joy, beyond him, or independent of him; in this verse he says that in respect to the saints—the excellent of the earth—

4 Their sorrows shall be multiplied *that* [1] hasten *after* another *god:* their drink-offerings of

[1] Or, *give gifts to another.*

all his delight was in them. Thus he was conscious of true attachment to God and to his people. Thus he had what must ever be essentially the evidence of true piety—a feeling that God is all in all, and real love for those who are his; a feeling that there is nothing *beyond* God, or *without* God, that can meet the wants of the soul, and a sincere affection for all who are his friends on earth. De Wette has well expressed the sense of the passage, "The holy, who are in the land, and the noble,—I have all my pleasure in them." ¶ *In the earth.* In the land; or, perhaps, more generally, *on earth.* God was in heaven, and all his hopes *there* were in *him.* In respect to those who dwelt on the earth, his delight was with the saints alone. ¶ *And to the excellent.* The word here used means properly *large, great,* mighty; then it is applied to *nobles, princes, chiefs;* and then to those who excel in moral qualities, in piety, and virtue. This is the idea here, and thus it corresponds with the word *saints* in the former member of the verse. The idea is that he found his pleasure, not in the rich and the great, not in princes and nobles, but in those who were distinguished for virtue and piety. In heaven he had none but God; on earth he found his happiness only in those who were the friends of God. ¶ *In whom is all my delight.* I find all my happiness in their society and friendship. The true state of my heart is indicated by my love for them. Everywhere, and at all times, love for those who love God, and a disposition to find our happiness in their friendship, will be a characteristic of true piety.

4. *Their sorrows shall be multiplied.* The word here rendered *sorrows*—עַצְּבוֹת, *atztzeboth*—may mean either *idols* or *sorrows.* Comp. Isa. xlviii. 5; Ps. cxxxix. 24; Job ix. 28; Ps. cxlvii. 3. Some propose to render it, "Their idols are multiplied;" that is, many are the gods which others worship, while I worship one God only. So Gesenius understands it. So also the Chaldee Paraphrase renders it. But the common construction is probably the correct one, meaning that sorrow, pain, anguish, must always attend the worship of any other gods than the true God; and that therefore the psalmist would not be found among their number, or be united with them in their devotions. ¶ That *hasten* after *another* god. Prof. Alexander renders this, "Another they have purchased." Bishop Horsley, "Who betroth themselves to another." The LXX., "After these things they are in haste." The Latin Vulgate, "Afterwards they make haste." The Hebrew word—מָהַר, *mahar*—properly means to hasten; to be quick, prompt, apt. It is twice used (Ex. xxii. 16) in the sense of *buying* or *endowing;* that is, procuring a wife by a price paid to her parents; but the common meaning of the word is to hasten, and this is clearly the sense here. The idea is that the persons referred to show a *readiness* or *willingness* to forsake the true God, and to render service to other gods. Their conduct shows that they do not hesitate to do this when it is proposed to them; that they embrace the first opportunity to do it. Men hesitate and delay when it is proposed to them to serve the true God; they readily embrace an opposite course,—following the world and sin. ¶ *Their drink-offerings of blood.* It was usual to pour out a drink-offering of wine or water in the worship of idol gods, and even of the true God. Thus Jacob (Gen. xxxv. 14) is said to have set up a pillar in Padan-aram, and to have "poured a drink-offering thereon." Comp. Ex. xxix. 40, 41; xxx. 9; Lev. xxiii. 13; Numb. xv. 5. The phrase "drink-offerings *of blood*" would seem to imply that the blood of the animals slain

blood will I not offer, nor take
up their names *p* into my lips.
5 The LORD *is* the portion *q* of
[1] mine inheritance and of my
cup: thou maintainest my lot.

p Hos. ii. 17. *q* Lam. iii. 24. [1] *my part.*

in sacrifice was often mingled with the wine or water that was thus poured out in the services of the heathen gods. So Jarchi, Aben Ezra, and Michaelis suppose. It would seem, also, that the worshippers themselves *drank* this mingled cup. They did this when they bound themselves by a solemn oath to perform any dangerous service. *De Wette.*—The eating, and consequently the drinking of blood, was solemnly forbidden to the Israelites (comp. Gen. ix. 4; Lev. iii. 17; vii. 26; xvii. 10); and the idea here is, that the psalmist had solemnly resolved that he would not partake of the abominations of the heathen, or be united with them in any way in their worship. ¶ *Nor take up their names into my lips.* As objects of worship. That is, I will not in any way acknowledge them as gods, or render to them the homage which is due to God. The very mention of the name of any other god than the true God was solemnly forbidden by the law of Moses (Ex. xxiii. 13), "And make no mention of the name of other gods, neither let it be heard out of your mouth." So the apostle Paul says (Eph. v. 3), "But fornication, and all uncleanness, or covetousness, let it not once be *named* among you, as becometh saints." The idea in these places seems to be, that the mere *mention* of these things would tend to produce dangerous familiarity with them, and by such familiarity take off something of the repugnance and horror with which they should be regarded. They were, in other words, to be utterly avoided; they were never to be thought of or named; they were to be treated as though they were not. No one can safely so familiarize himself with vice as to render it a frequent subject of conversation. Pollution will flow into the heart from words which describe pollution, even when there is no intention that the use of such words should produce contamination. No one can be familiar with stories or songs of a polluted nature, and still retain a heart of purity. "The very passage of a polluted thought through the mind leaves pollution behind it." How much more is the mind polluted when the thought is dwelt upon, and when utterance is given to it in language!

5. *The* LORD is *the portion of mine inheritance.* In contradistinction from idols. The margin here is, *of my part.* The word properly means *lot, portion, part;* and is applicable to the portion of booty or plunder that fell to any one; or to the portion of land that belonged to any one in the division of an estate, 2 Kings ix. 10, 36, 37. The meaning here is, that Jehovah was the being whom the psalmist worshipped as God, and that he sought no possession or comfort which did not proceed from him. ¶ *And my cup.* The allusion here is to what we drink; and hence the term is used in the sense of *lot* or *portion.* See Notes on Isa. li. 17. Comp. Notes on Ps. xi. 6. The idea here is this:—"The cup that I drink—that cheers, refreshes, and sustains me—is the Lord. I find comfort, refreshment, happiness, in him alone; not in the intoxicating bowl; not in sensual joys; but in God—in his being, perfections, friendship." ¶ *Thou maintainest my lot.* Thou dost defend my portion, or that which is allotted to me. The reference is to what he specifies in the following verse as his inheritance, and he says that that which was so valuable to him was sustained or preserved by God. He was the portion of his soul; he was the source of all his joy; he maintained or preserved all that was dear to his heart.

6 The lines are fallen unto me in pleasant *places*; yea, I have a goodly heritage.

7 I will bless the LORD, who hath given me counsel; my reins also instruct me in the night-seasons.

8 [r] I have set the LORD always before me: because *he* [s] *is* at my right hand, I shall not be moved.

r Acts ii. 25, etc.

s Psa. lxxiii. 23—26.

6. *The lines.* The word here used refers to the *lines* employed in measuring and dividing land, Amos vii. 17; 2 Sam. viii. 2. Hence the word comes to denote a portion of land that is *measured out* (or that is *surveyed off*) to any one,—his possession or property; and hence the word refers to the condition in life. The meaning here is, that in running out such a survey, *his* inheritance had been fixed in a pleasant and desirable part of the land. ¶ *Are fallen unto me.* Referring to the appropriation of the different parts of the land by lot. The idea is, that the land was surveyed into distinct portions, and then that the part which fell to any one was determined by lot. This was actually the case in distributing the land of Canaan, Numb. xxvi. 55; xxxiii. 54; xxxvi. 2; Josh. xv.—xix. ¶ *In pleasant* places. In a pleasant or desirable part of the land. ¶ *Yea, I have a goodly heritage.* A good, a desirable inheritance. The meaning is, that he regarded it as a desirable heritage that he lived where the true God was known; where he enjoyed his favour and friendship.

7. *I will bless the* LORD, *who hath given me counsel.* Probably the reference here is to the fact that the Lord had counselled him to choose him as his portion, or had inclined him to his service. There is nothing for which a heart rightly affected is more disposed to praise God than for the fact that by his grace it has been inclined to serve him; and the time when the heart was given away to God is recalled ever onwards as the happiest period of life. ¶ *My reins,* etc. See Notes on Ps. vii. 9. The *reins* are here put for the mind, the soul. They were regarded as the seat of the affections, Jer. xi. 20; Job xix. 27. The meaning here is, that in the wakeful hours of night, when meditating on the Divine character and goodness, he found instruction in regard to God. Comp. Ps. xvii. 3. Everything then is favourable for reflection. The natural calmness and composure of the mind; the stillness of night; the starry heavens; the consciousness that we are alone with God, and that no human eye is upon us,—all these things are favourable to profound religious meditation. They who are kept wakeful by night *need* not find this an unprofitable portion of their lives. Some of the most instructive hours of life are those which are spent when the eyes refuse to close themselves in slumber, and when the universal stillness invites to contemplation on Divine things.

8. *I have set the* LORD *always before me.* By night as well as by day; in my private meditations as well as in my public professions. I have regarded myself always as in the presence of God; I have endeavoured always to feel that his eye was upon me. This, too, is one of the certain characteristics of piety, that we always feel that we are in the presence of God, and that we always act as if his eye were upon us. Comp. Notes on Acts ii. 25. ¶ *Because* he is *at my right hand.* The right hand was regarded as the post of honour and dignity, but it is also mentioned as a position of defence or protection. To have one at our right hand is to have one near us who can defend us. Thus, in Ps. cix. 31, "He shall stand at the right hand of the poor, to save him," etc. So Psalm cx. 5, "The Lord at thy right hand shall strike through kings in the day of his wrath." Ps. cxxi. 5, "The Lord is

9 Therefore my heart is glad, and my glory rejoiceth: my flesh also shall [1] rest in hope.

[1] *dwell confidently.*

thy Keeper; the Lord is thy shade upon thy right hand." The idea is, that as we use the right hand in our own defence, we seem to have an additional and a needed helper when one is at our right hand. The sense here is, that the psalmist felt that God, as his Protector, was always near him; always ready to interpose for his defence. We have a somewhat similar expression when we say of any one that he is "*at hand;*" that is, he is near us. ¶ *I shall not be moved.* I shall be safe; I shall not be disturbed by fear; I shall be protected from my enemies. See Ps. x. 6; xv. 5. Comp. Ps. xlvi. 5. The language here is that of one who has confidence in God in time of great calamities, and who feels that he is safe under the Divine favour and protection.

8. *Therefore my heart is glad.* In view of this fact, that my confidence is in God alone, and my belief that he is my Protector and Friend. See Notes on Acts ii. 26. ¶ *And my glory rejoiceth.* The LXX. translate this, "my tongue," and this translation is followed by Peter in his quotation of the passage in Acts ii. 26. See Notes on that passage. The meaning here is, that whatever there was in him that was honourable, dignified, or glorious,—all the faculties of his soul, as well as his heart,—had occasion to rejoice in God. His whole nature—his undying soul—his exalted powers as he was made by God—all—all, found cause of exultation in the favour and friendship of God. The heart—the understanding—the imagination—the whole immortal soul, found occasion for joy in God. ¶ *My flesh also.* My body. Or, it may mean, his whole person, he himself, though the direct allusion is to the body considered as lying in the grave, ver. 10. The language is such as one would use of *himself* when he reflected on his own death, and it is equivalent to saying, "I myself, when I am dead, shall rest in hope; my soul will not be left to abide in the gloomy place of the dead; nor will my body remain permanently in the grave under the power of corruption. In reference to my soul and my body—my whole nature—I shall descend to the grave in the hope of a future life." ¶ *Shall rest.* Marg., *dwell confidently.* The Hebrew is literally "shall dwell in confidence" or hope. The word here rendered "shall rest" means properly to let oneself down; to lie down, Num. ix. 17; Ex. xxiv. 16; then, to lay oneself down, to lie down, as, for example, a lion lying down, Deut. xxxiii. 20; or a people in tents, Num. xxiv. 2; and hence, to rest, to take rest, Judges v. 17; and then to abide, to dwell. — *Gesenius, Lex.* Perhaps the sense here is that of *lying down,* considered as lying in the grave, and the expression is equivalent to saying, "When I die I shall lie down in the grave in hope or confidence, not in despair. I shall expect to rise and live again." ¶ *In hope.* The word here used means *trust, confidence, security.* It is the opposite of despair. As used here, it would refer to a state of mind in which there was an expectation of living again, as distinguished from that state of mind in which it was felt that the grave was the end of man. What is particularly to be remarked here is, that this trust or confidence extended to the "flesh" as well as to the "soul;" and the language is such as would be naturally used by one who believed in the resurrection of the body. Language of this kind occurs elsewhere in the Old Testament, showing that the doctrine of the resurrection of the body was one to which the sacred writers were not strangers, and that although the doctrine was not as explicitly and formally stated in the Old Testament as in the New, yet that it was a doctrine which had been at some time communicated to man. See Notes on Isa. xxvi. 19; Dan. xii. 2. As applicable

10 For thou wilt not leave [t] my soul in hell: neither wilt thou

t Acts iii. 15.

to David, the language here used is expressive of his belief that *he* would rise again, or would not perish in the grave when his body died; as applicable to the Messiah, as applied by Peter (Acts ii. 26), it means that when *he* should die it would be with the hope and expectation of being raised again without seeing corruption. The language is such as to be applicable to both cases; and, in regard to the interpretation of the *language*, it makes no difference whether it was supposed that the resurrection would occur before the body should moulder back to dust, or whether it would occur at a much more remote period, and long *after* it had gone to decay. In either case it would be true that it was laid in the grave "*in hope*."

10. *For thou wilt not leave.* The language here used implies, of course, that what is here called the soul would be *in* the abode to which the name hell is given, but *how long* it would be there is not intimated. The thought simply is, that it would not be *left* there; it would not be suffered to *remain* there. Whether it would be restored to life again in a few days, or after a longer period, is not implied in the term used. It would be fulfilled, though, as in the case of the Lord Jesus, the resurrection should occur in three days; or though, as in the case of David, it would occur only after many ages; or though, as Abraham believed of Isaac if he was offered as a sacrifice (Heb. xi. 19), he should be restored to life at once. In other words, there is no allusion in this language to *time*. It is only to the *fact* that there would be a restoration to life. ¶ *My soul.* De Wette renders this, *my life.* The Hebrew word—נֶפֶשׁ, *nephesh*—which occurs very frequently in the Scriptures, means properly *breath;* then, the vital spirit, life; then, the rational soul, the mind; then, an animal, or animated thing—that which *lives;* then, oneself. Which of these senses is the true one here must be determined from the connexion, and the meaning could probably be determined by a man's asking himself what *he* would think of if he used similar language of himself—"I am about to die; my flesh will go down to the grave, and will rest in hope,—the hope of a resurrection; my breath—my soul—will depart, and I shall be dead; but that life, that soul, will not be extinct: it will not be *left* in the grave, the abode of the dead; it will live again, live on for ever." It seems to me, therefore, that the language here would embrace the immortal part—that which is distinct from the body; and that the word here employed may be properly understood of the soul as we understand that word. The psalmist probably understood by it that part of his nature which was *not* mortal or decaying; that which properly constituted his *life.* ¶ *In hell*—לִשְׁאוֹל, *to Sheol.* See Notes on Ps. vi. 5; Isa. v. 14. This word does not necessarily mean *hell* in the sense in which that term is now commonly employed, as denoting the abode of the wicked in the future world, or the place of punishment; but it means the region or abode of the dead, to which the grave was regarded as the door or entrance—the under-world. The idea is, that the soul would not be suffered to remain in that under-world—that dull, gloomy abode (comp. Notes on Job x. 21, 22), but would rise again to light and life. This language, however, gives no sanction to the words used in the creed, "he descended into *hell*," nor to the opinion that Christ went down personally to "preach to the spirits in prison"—the souls that are lost (comp. Notes on 1 Peter iii. 19); but it is language derived from the prevailing opinion that the soul, through the grave, descended to the

suffer thine Holy One to see corruption.

under-world—to the abodes where the dead were supposed still to reside. See Notes on Isa. xiv. 9. As a matter of fact, the soul of the Saviour at his death entered into "paradise." See Notes on Luke xxiii. 43. ¶ *Neither wilt thou suffer.* Literally, "thou wilt not *give;*" that is, he would not give him over to corruption, or would not suffer him to return to corruption. ¶ *Thine Holy One.* See Notes on Acts ii. 27. The reading here in the text is in the plural form, "thy holy *ones;*" the marginal reading in the Hebrew, or the Keri, is in the singular, "thine Holy *One.*" The singular form is followed by the Chaldee Paraphrase, the Latin Vulgate, the Septuagint, the Arabic, and in the New Testament, Acts ii. 27. The Masorites have also pointed the text as if it were in the singular. Many manuscripts and earlier editions of the Bible, and all the ancient versions, read it in the same manner. It is probable, therefore, that this is the true reading. The Hebrew word rendered *holy one*—חָסִיד, *hhâsid*—means properly kind, benevolent, liberal, good, merciful, gracious, pious. *Gesenius, Lex.*—It would be applicable to *any* persons who are pious or religious, but it is here restricted to the one whom the psalmist had in his eye—if the psalm referred to himself, then to himself; if to the Messiah, then to him. The term is several times given to the Saviour as being especially adapted to him. See Mark i. 24; Luke iv. 34; Acts iii. 14; comp. Luke i. 35. It is applied to him as being eminently holy, or as being one whom God regarded as peculiarly his own. As the passage here is expressly applied to him in the Acts of the Apostles (ch. ii. 27), there can be no doubt that it was intended by the Spirit of inspiration to designate him in this place, whatever reference it may have had primarily to David himself. ¶ *To see.* That is, to experience; to be acquainted with. The word is used often to denote perceiving, learning, or understanding anything by experience. Thus, "*to see life,*" Eccl. ix. 9; "*to see death,*" Ps. lxxxix. 48; "*to see sleep,*" Eccl. viii. 16; "*to see famine,*" Jer. v. 12; "*to see good,*" Ps. xxxiv. 12; "*to see affliction,*" Lam. iii. 1; "*to see evil,*" Prov. xxvii. 12. Here it means that he would not *experience* corruption; or would not return to corruption. ¶ *Corruption*—שַׁחַת, *shahhath.* This word is frequently used in the Scriptures. It is translated *ditch* in Job ix. 31; Ps. vii. 15; *corruption* (as here), in Job xvii. 14; Ps. xlix. 9; Jonah ii. 6; *pit,* in Job xxxiii. 18, 24, 28, 30; Ps. ix. 15; xxx. 9; xxxv. 7; Prov. xxvi. 27; Isa. xxxviii. 17; li. 14; Ezek. xix. 4; xxviii. 8; *grave,* in Job xxxiii. 22; and *destruction,* in Ps. lv. 23. The common idea, therefore, according to our translators, is the grave, or a pit. The *derivation* seems not to be certain. Gesenius supposes that it is derived from שׁוּחַ, *shuahh—to sink or settle down;* hence, a pit or the grave. Others derive it from שָׁחַת, *shahhath,* not used in Kal, to destroy. The verb is used in various forms frequently; meaning to destroy, to ruin, to lay waste. It is translated here by the Latin Vulgate, *corruptionem;* by the Septuagint, *διαφθοράν,* corruption; by the Arabic in the same way. The same word which is employed by the LXX. is employed also in quoting the passage in the New Testament, where the argument of Peter (Acts ii. 27), and of Paul (Acts xiii. 35, 36, 37), is founded on the supposition that such is the sense of the word here; that it does not mean merely *the pit,* or *the grave;* that the idea in the psalm is *not* that the person referred to would not go down to the grave, or would not *die,* but that he would not moulder back to dust in the grave, or that the *change* would not occur to him in the grave which does to those who lie long in the tomb. Peter and

Paul both regard this as a distinct prophecy that the Messiah would be raised from the grave *without* returning to corruption, and they argue from the fact that David *did* return to corruption in the grave like other men, that the passage could not have referred mainly to himself, but that it had a proper fulfilment, and its highest fulfilment, in the resurrection of the Lord Jesus Christ. This interpretation the believer in the inspiration of Peter and Paul is bound to defend, and in reference to this it may be remarked, (1) that it cannot be demonstrated that this is *not* the meaning of the word. The word may be as *fairly* derived from the verb *to corrupt*, as from the verb to *sink down*, and, indeed, *more* naturally and *more* obviously. The grammatical form would rather suggest this derivation than the other. (2) It *is* a fair construction of the original word. It is such a construction as may be put upon it without any *forced* application, or any design to defend a theory or an opinion. In other words, it is not a mere *catch*, or a grasp at a *possible* meaning of the word, but it is a rendering which, on every principle of grammatical construction, may be regarded as a *fair* interpretation. Whatever may have been the exact idea in the mind of David, whether he understood this as referring only to himself, and to the belief that he would not *always* remain in the grave, and under the power of corruption; or whether he understood it as referring primarily to himself, and ultimately and mainly to the Messiah; or whether he understood it as referring solely to the Messiah; or whether he did not at all understand the language which the Holy Spirit led him to employ (comp. Notes on 1 Pet. i. 11, 12), it is equally true that the sense which the apostles put on the words, in their application of the passage to the Messiah, is a suitable one. (3) The ancient versions, as has been seen above, confirm this. Without an exception they give the sense of *corruption*—the very sense which has been given to the word by Peter and Paul. The authors of these versions had no theory to defend, and it may be presumed that they had a just knowledge of the true meaning of the Hebrew word. (4) It may be added that this interpretation accords with the connexion in which the word occurs. Though it may be admitted that the connexion would not *necessarily* lead to this view, yet this interpretation is in entire harmony with the statements in the previous verses, and in the following verse. Thus, in the previous verse, the psalmist had said that "his flesh would rest in hope,"—a sentiment which *accords* with either the idea that he would at some future period be raised from the grave, and would not perish for ever, though the period of the resurrection might be remote; or with the idea of being raised up so soon that the body would not return to corruption, *i. e.*, before the change consequent on death would take place. The sentiment in the following verse also agrees with this view. That sentiment is, that there is a path to life; that in the presence of God there is fulness of joy; that at his right hand there are pleasures for evermore—a sentiment, in this connexion, founded on the belief of the resurrection from the dead, and equally true whether the dead should be raised immediately or at some remote period. I infer, therefore, that the apostles Peter and Paul made a legitimate use of this passage; that the argument which they urged was derived from a proper interpretation of the language; that the fair construction of the psalm, and the fact that David *had* returned to corruption, fully justified them in the application which they made of the passage; and that, therefore, it was the design of the Holy Spirit to convey the idea that *the Messiah* would be raised from the dead without undergoing the change which others undergo in the grave; and that it was thus *predicted* in the Old Testament, that he *would be* raised from

11 Thou wilt show me the path [u] of life: in thy presence *is* fulness of joy; [v] at thy right hand [w] *there are* pleasures [x] for evermore.

u Matt. vii. 14. *v* Matt. xxv. 33. *w* Jude 24. *x* Psa. xxxvi. 8.

the dead in the manner in which he was.

11. *Thou wilt show me the path of life.* In this connexion this means that though he was to die,—to descend to the regions of the dead, and to lie down in the dark grave,—yet there *was* a path again to the living world, and that that path would be pointed out to him by God. In other words, he would not be suffered to remain among the dead, or to wander away for ever with those who were in the under world, but he would be brought back to the *living* world. This is language which, in this connexion, could be founded only on a belief of the resurrection of the dead. The word "life" here does not necessarily refer to heaven—to eternal life—though the connexion shows that this is the ultimate idea. It is life in contradistinction from the condition of the dead. The highest form of life is that which is found in heaven, at the right hand of God; and the connexion shows it was that on which the eye of the psalmist was fixed. ¶ *In thy presence.* Literally, "with thy face." Before thy face; or, as the sense is correctly expressed in our version, *in thy presence.* The reference is to God's presence in heaven, or where he is supposed to dwell. This is shown by the additional statement that the joy mentioned was to be found at his "right hand"—an expression which properly refers to heaven. It is not merely a return to earth which is anticipated; it is an exaltation to heaven. ¶ Is *fulness of joy.* Not partial joy; not imperfect joy; not joy intermingled with pain and sorrow; not joy which, though in itself real, does not satisfy the desires of the soul, as is the case with much of the happiness which we experience in this life,—but joy, full, satisfying, unalloyed, unclouded, unmingled with anything that would diminish its fulness or its brightness; joy that will not be diminished, as all earthly joys must be, by the feeling that it must soon come to an end. ¶ *At thy right hand.* The right hand is the place of honour (Notes, ver. 8). Comp. Mark xvi. 19; Heb. i. 3; Acts vii. 56; and it here refers to the place which the saints will occupy in heaven. This language could have been used only by one who believed in the doctrine of the resurrection and of the future state. As applicable to the author of the psalm, it implies that he had a firm belief in the resurrection of the dead, and a confident hope of happiness hereafter; as applicable to the Messiah, it denotes that he would be raised up to exalted honour in heaven; as applicable to believers now, it expresses their firm and assured faith that eternal happiness and exalted honour await them in the future world. ¶ There are *pleasures for evermore.* Happiness that will be eternal. It is not enjoyment such as we have on earth, which we feel is soon to terminate; it is joy which can have no end. Here, in respect to any felicity which we enjoy, we cannot but feel that it is soon to cease. No matter how secure the sources of our joy may seem to be, we know that happiness here cannot last long, for life cannot long continue; and even though life should be lengthened out for many years, we have no certainty that our happiness will be commensurate even with our existence on earth. The dearest friend that we have may soon leave us to return no more; health, the source of so many comforts, and essential to the enjoyment of any comfort here, may soon fail; property, however firmly it may be secured, may "take to itself wings and fly away." Soon, at any rate, if these things do not leave us, we shall leave them; and in respect to happiness from them, we shall be as though

PSALM XVII.

A Prayer of David.

HEAR [1] the right, O LORD, attend unto my cry; give ear unto my prayer, *that goeth* [2] not out of feigned lips.

[1] *justice.*
[2] *without lips of deceit.*

they had not been. Not so will it be at the right hand of God. Happiness there, whatever may be its nature, will be eternal. Losses, disappointment, bereavement, sickness, can never occur there; nor can the anticipation of death, though at the most distant period, and after countless millions of ages, ever mar our joys. How different in all these things will heaven be from earth! How desirable to leave the earth, and to enter on those eternal joys!

PSALM XVII.

This psalm is entitled "A Prayer of David." By whom the title was prefixed to it, is not known; but there can be no doubt of its appropriateness. It *is*, throughout, *a prayer*—fervent, earnest, believing. It was evidently uttered in the view of danger—danger arising from the number and the designs of his enemies; but on what particular occasion it was composed cannot now be determined. There were many occasions, however, in the life of David for the utterance of such a prayer, and there can be no doubt that in the dangers which so frequently beset him, he often poured out such warm and earnest appeals to God for help. *Who* the enemies referred to were cannot now be ascertained. All that is known of them is that they were "deadly" or bitter foes, that they were prosperous in the world, and that they were proud (vers. 9, 10); that they were fierce and greedy, like a lion hunting its prey (ver. 12); that they were men whose families were in affluence, and men who lived for this world alone, ver. 14.

The points which constitute the prayer in the psalm are the following:—

1. The prayer itself, as an earnest appeal or supplication to God to do what was equal and right, vers. 1, 2.

2. A reference of the author of the psalm to himself, and to his own life and character, as not deserving the treatment which he was receiving from others, vers. 3, 4.

3. An earnest petition on this ground for the Divine interposition, vers. 5-9.

4. A description of the character of his enemies, and a prayer on the ground of that character, that God would interpose for him, vers. 10-14.

5. The expression of a confident hope of deliverance from *all* enemies; a looking forward to a world where he would be rescued from *all* troubles, and where, in the presence of God, and entering on a new life, he would awake in the likeness of God and be satisfied, ver. 15. The psalm terminates, as the anticipations of all good men do amid the troubles of this life, in the hope of that world where there will be no trouble, and where they will be permitted to dwell for ever with God.

1. *Hear the right.* Marg., as in Hebrew, *justice.* The prayer is, that God would regard that which was *right* in the case, or that he would vindicate the psalmist from that which was wrong. It is the expression of his confident assurance even in the presence of God that his cause was right, and that he was asking only that which it would be consistent for a *just* God to do. We can offer an acceptable prayer only when we are sure that it would be right for God to answer it, or that it would be consistent with perfect and eternal justice to grant our requests. It is to be observed here, however, that the ground of the petition of the psalmist is not that *he* was righteous, that is, he did not base his petition on the ground of his own merits, but that his *cause* was righteous; that he was unjustly oppressed and persecuted by his enemies. We cannot ask God to interpose in our behalf because we have a claim to his favour on the ground of our own merit; we may ask him to interpose because wrong is done, and his glory will be promoted in securing that which is just and right. ¶ *Attend unto my cry.* The word here used—רִנָּה, *rinnah*—means either a shout of joy, Ps. xxx. 5; xlii. 4; xlvii. 1; or a mournful cry,

2 Let my sentence come forth from thy presence; let thine eyes behold the things that are equal.

3 Thou hast proved *y* mine heart; thou hast visited *me* in the

y Psa. cxxxix. 23.

outcry, wailing, Ps. lxi. 1; *et sæpe.* It is expressive, in either case, of deep feeling which vents itself in an audible manner. Here it denotes the earnest *utterance* of prayer. ¶ *Give ear unto my prayer.* See Notes on Ps. v. 1. ¶ That goeth *not out of feigned lips.* Marg., as in Heb., *without lips of deceit.* That is, that is sincere, or that proceeds from the heart. The utterance of the lips does not misrepresent the feelings of the heart. True prayer is that in which the lips *do* represent the real feelings of the soul. In hypocritical prayer the one is no proper representation of the other. It is evident that the prayer here was not mere *mental* prayer, or a *mere* desire of the heart. It was *uttered* prayer, or *oral* prayer; and, though private, it was in the form of uttered words. The feeling was so great that it was expressed in an audible cry to God. Deep emotion usually finds vent in such audible and fervent expressions. Compare the Saviour's earnest prayer in the garden of Gethsemane, Luke xxii. 41, seq.

2. *Let my sentence.* Heb., *my judgment.* The allusion is to a judgment or sentence as coming from God in regard to the matter referred to in the psalm, to wit, the injuries which he had received from his enemies. He felt that they had done him injustice and wrong; he felt assured that a sentence or judgment from God in the case would be in his favour. So Job often felt that if he could bring his case d rectly before God, God would decide in his favour. Comp. Job xxiii. 1—6. ¶ *Come forth from thy presence.* From before thee. That is, he asks God to pronounce a sentence in his case. ¶ *Let thine eyes behold.* He asked God to examine the case with his own eyes, or attentively to consider it, and to see where justice was. ¶ *The things that are equal.* The things that are just and right. He felt assured that his own cause was right, and he prays here that justice in the case may be done. He felt that, if that were done, he would be delivered from his enemies. As between ourselves and our fellow-men, it is right to pray to God that he would see that exact justice should be done, for we may be able to feel certain that justice is on our side, and that we are injured by them; but as between ourselves and God, we can never offer that prayer, for if justice were done to us we could not but be condemned. Before him our plea must be for mercy, not justice.

3. *Thou hast proved mine heart.* In this verse he refers to his own character and life in the matter under consideration, or the consciousness of his own innocence in respect to his fellow-men who are persecuting and opposing him. He appeals to the Great Searcher of hearts in proof that, in this respect, he was innocent; and he refers to different forms of trial on the part of God to show that after the most thorough search he would find, and did find, that in these respects he was an innocent man, and that his enemies had no occasion to treat him as they had done. It is still to be borne in mind here that the trial which the psalmist asks at the hand of God was not to prove that he was innocent towards *Him,* or that he had a claim to His favour on account of his own personal holiness, but it was that he was innocent of any wrong towards those who were persecuting him, or, in other words, that after the most searching trial, even by his Maker, it would be found that he had given *them* no cause for treating him thus. The word here rendered "proved" means *to try, to prove, to examine,*—especially metals, to test their genuineness. See Notes on Ps. vii. 9, 10;

night; thou hast tried me, *and* shalt find nothing: I am purposed *that* my mouth [z] shall not transgress.

4 Concerning the works of men, by the [a] word of thy lips I

z Psa. xxxix. 1, 2; Prov. xiii. 3.

a Prov. ii. 10—15.

Job xii. 11. The psalmist here says that God had tried or searched *his heart.* He knew all his motives. He had examined all his desires and his thoughts. The psalmist felt assured that, after the most thorough trial, even *God* would not find anything in his heart that would justify the conduct of his enemies towards him. ¶ *Thou hast visited* me. That is, for the purpose of inspecting my character, or of examining me. The English word *visit,* like the Hebrew, is often used to denote a visitation for the purpose of inspection and examination. The idea is, that God had come to him for the very purpose of *examining* his character. ¶ *In the night.* In solitude. In darkness. When I was alone. In the time when the thoughts are less under restraint than they are when surrounded by others. In a time when it can be seen what we really *are;* when we do not put on appearances to deceive others. ¶ *Thou hast tried me.* The word here used—צָרַף, *tzaraph*—means properly *to melt, to smelt,* sc., metals, or separating the pure metal from the dross. The meaning is, that God, in examining into his character, had subjected him to a trial as searching as that employed in purifying metals by casting them into the fire. ¶ And *shalt find nothing.* Thou wilt find nothing that could give occasion for the conduct of my enemies. The future tense is here used to denote that, even if the investigation were continued, God would find nothing in his heart or in his conduct that would warrant their treatment of him. He had the most full and settled determination *not* to do wrong to them in any respect whatever. Nothing *had* been found in him that would justify their treatment of him; he was determined so to live, and he felt assured that he would so live, that nothing of the kind *would* be found in him in time to come. ¶ *I am purposed.* I am fully resolved. ¶ *My mouth shall not transgress.* Transgress the law of God, or go beyond what is right. That is, I will utter nothing which is wrong, or which can give occasion for their harsh and unkind treatment. Much as he had been provoked and injured, he was determined not to retaliate, or to give occasion for their treating him in the manner in which they were now doing. Prof. Alexander renders this "My mouth shall not exceed my thought;" but the common version gives a better idea, and is sanctioned by the Hebrew. Comp. Gesenius, *Lex.*

4. *Concerning the works of men.* In respect to the works or doings of men. The reference is here probably to the ordinary or common doings of mankind, or to what generally characterises the conduct of men. As their conduct is so commonly, and so characteristically wicked, wickedness may be spoken of as their "work," and it is to this doubtless that the psalmist refers. In respect to the sinful courses or "paths" to which men are so prone, he says that he had kept himself from them. This is in accordance with what he says in the previous verse, that he had given no occasion by his conduct for the treatment which he had received at the hands of his enemies. ¶ *By the word of thy lips.* Not by his own strength; not by any power which he himself had, but by the commands and promises of God,—by what had proceeded from *his* mouth. The reference is doubtless to *all* that God had spoken:—to the law which prescribed his duty, and to the promises which God had given to enable him to walk in the path of uprightness. He had relied on the word of God as inculcating duty; he had submitted to it

have kept *me from* the paths of the destroyer.
5 Hold up my goings in thy paths, *that* my footsteps [1] slip not.

[1] *be not moved.*

6 I have called upon thee, for thou wilt hear me, O God: incline thine ear unto me, *and hear* my speech.

as authority; he had found encouragement in it in endeavouring to do right. ¶ *I have kept* me. I have preserved myself. I have so guarded my conduct that I have not fallen into the sins which are so common among men. ¶ *The paths of the destroyer.* The paths which the "destroyer" treads; the course of life which such men lead. The idea is, not that he had been able to save himself from violence at their hands, but that he had been enabled to avoid their mode of life. The word rendered *destroyer* is from a verb which means *to break, to rend, to scatter*, and would properly refer to acts of violence and lawlessness. He had kept himself from the modes of life of the violent and the lawless; that is, he had been enabled to lead a peaceful and quiet life. He had given no occasion to his enemies to treat him as a violent, a lawless, a wicked man.

5. *Hold up my goings in thy paths.* He had been enabled before this to keep himself from the ways of the violent by the word of God (ver. 4); he felt his dependence on God still to enable him, in the circumstances in which he was placed, and under the provocations to which he was exposed, to live a life of peace, and to keep himself from doing wrong. He, therefore, calls on God, and asks him to sustain him, and to keep him still in the right path. The verb here used is in the infinitive form, but used instead of the imperative. *De Wette.*—Prof. Alexander renders this less correctly, "My steps have laid hold of thy paths;" for he supposes that a prayer here "would be out of place." But prayer can never be *more* appropriate than when a man realises that he owes the fact of his having been hitherto enabled to lead an upright life only to the "word" of God, and when provoked and injured by others he feels that he might be in danger of doing wrong. In such circumstances nothing can be more proper than to call upon God to keep us from sin. ¶ That *my footsteps slip not.* Marg., as in Heb., *be not moved.* The idea is, "that I may be firm; that I may not yield to passion; that, provoked and wronged by others, I may not be allowed to depart from the course of life which I have been hitherto enabled to pursue." No prayer could be more appropriate. When we feel and know that we have been wronged by others; when our lives have given no cause for such treatment as we receive at their hands; when they are still pursuing us, and injuring us in our reputation, our property, or our peace; when all the bad passions of our nature are liable to be aroused, prompting us to seek revenge, and to return evil for evil, then nothing can be more proper than for us to lift our hearts to God, entreating that *he* will keep us, and save us from falling into sin; that he will enable us to restrain our passions, and to subdue our resentments.

6. *I have called upon thee, for thou wilt hear me, O God.* The meaning of this is, "I have called on thee heretofore, and will do it still, because I am certain that thou wilt hear me." That is, he was encouraged to call upon God by the conviction that he would hear his prayer, and would grant his request. In other words, he came to God in faith; in the full belief of his readiness to answer prayer, and to bestow needed blessings. Comp. John xi. 42; Heb. xi. 6. ¶ *Incline thine ear unto me.* See Notes on ver. 1. ¶ *My speech.* My prayer. The reference here, as in ver. 1, is to prayer *uttered* before God, and not mere mental prayer.

7 Show thy marvellous loving-kindness, O thou that savest [1] by thy right hand them which put their trust *in thee* from those that rise up *against them*.

8 Keep me as the apple of the

[1] Or, *them which trust* in thee *from those that rise up against thy right hand.*

---

7. *Show thy marvellous loving-kindness.* The literal translation of the original here would be, "*distinguish thy favours.*" The Hebrew word used means properly *to separate; to distinguish;* then, *to make distinguished* or *great*. The prayer is, that God would *separate* his mercies on this occasion from his ordinary mercies by the manifestation of greater powers, or by showing him special favour. The ordinary or common mercies which he was receiving at the hand of God would not meet the present case. His dangers were much greater than ordinary, his wants were more pressing than usual; and he asked for an interposition of mercy corresponding with his circumstances and condition. Such a prayer it is obviously proper to present before God; that is, it is right to ask him to suit his mercies to our peculiar necessities; and when special dangers surround us, when we are assailed with peculiarly strong temptations, when we have unusually arduous duties to perform, when we are pressed down with peculiarly severe trials, it is right and proper to ask God to bestow favours upon us which will correspond with our peculiar circumstances. His ability and his willingness to aid us are not measured by our ordinary requirements, but are equal to any of the necessities which can ever occur in our lives. ¶ *O thou that savest by thy right hand.* Marg., "*that savest those that trust* in thee *from those that rise up against thy right hand.*" The Hebrew will admit of either construction, though that in the text is the more correct. It is, literally, "Saving those trusting, from those that rise up, with thy right hand. The idea is, that it was a characteristic of God, or that it was what he usually did, to save by his own power those that trusted him from those who rose up against them. That is, God might be appealed to to do this now, on the ground that he was *accustomed* to do it; and that, so to speak, he would be acting "in character" in doing it. In other words, we may ask God to do what he is accustomed to do; we may go to him in reference to his well-known attributes and character, and ask him to act in a manner which will be but the regular and proper manifestation of his nature. We could not ask him to do what was contrary to his nature; we cannot ask him to act in a way which would be *out of character*. What he has done for men always, we may ask him to do for us; what is entirely consistent with his perfections, we may ask him to do in our own case. ¶ *By thy right hand.* By thy power. The right hand is that by which we execute our purposes, or put forth our power; and the psalmist asks God to put forth his power in defending him. See Isa. xli. 10; Job xl. 14; Ps. lxxxix. 13. ¶ *From those that rise up* against them. From their enemies.

8. *Keep me as the apple of the eye.* Preserve me; guard me; defend me, as one defends that which is to him most precious and valuable. In the original there is a remarkable strength of expression, and at the same time a remarkable confusion of gender in the language. The literal translation would be, "Keep me as the little man—the daughter of the eye." The word *apple* applied to the eye means the *pupil*, the little aperture in the middle of the eye, through which the rays of light pass to form an image on the retina (*Johnson, Webster*); though *why* it is called the *apple* of the eye the lexicographers fail to tell us. The Hebrew word—אִישׁוֹן, *Ishon*—means properly, *a little man*, and is given to the apple or pupil of the eye, "in which, as in a mirror, a person sees

eye, hide me under the shadow
of thy wings,
9 From the wicked that [1] oppress me, *from* my [2] deadly enemies *who* compass me about.

10 They are inclosed in their own fat: with their mouth they speak proudly.
11 They have now compassed us in our steps; they have set

[1] *waste.*

[2] *enemies against the soul.*

his own image reflected in miniature." This comparison is found in several languages. The word occurs in the Old Testament only in Deut. xxxii. 10; Ps. xvii. 8; Prov. vii. 2; where it is rendered *apple;* in Prov. vii. 9, where it is rendered *black;* and in Prov. xx. 20, where it is rendered *obscure.* The other expression in the Hebrew—"*the daughter* of the eye"—is derived from a usage of the Hebrew word *daughter,* as denoting that which is dependent on, or connected with (*Gesenius, Lex.*), as the expression "daughters of a city" denotes the small towns or villages lying around a city, and dependent on its jurisdiction, Num. xxi. 25, 32; xxxii. 42; Josh. xvii. 11. So the expression *daughters of song,* Eccl. xii. 4. The idea here is, that the little image is the *child* of the eye; that it has its birth or origin there. The prayer of the psalmist here is, that God would guard him, as one guards his sight—an object so dear and valuable to him. ¶ *Hide me under the shadow of thy wings.* Another image denoting substantially the same thing. This is taken from the care evinced by fowls in protecting their young, by gathering them under their wings. Comp. Matt. xxiii. 37. Both of the comparisons here used are found in Deut. xxxii. 10—12; and it is probable that the psalmist had that passage in his eye—"He instructed him, he kept him as the apple of his eye; as an eagle stirreth up her nest, fluttereth over her young, spreadeth abroad her wings, taketh them, beareth them on her wings; so the Lord alone did lead him." Comp. also Ps. xxxvi. 7; lvii. 1; lxi. 4; lxiii. 7; xci. 1, 4.

9. *From the wicked that oppress me.* Marg., *That waste me.* The margin expresses the sense of the Hebrew. The idea is that of being wasted, desolated, destroyed, as a city or country is by the ravages of war. The psalmist compares himself in his troubles with such a city or country. The *effect* of the persecutions which he had endured had been like cities and lands thus laid waste by fire and sword. ¶ From *my deadly enemies.* Marg., *My enemies against the soul.* The literal idea is, "enemies against my life." The common translation expresses the idea accurately. The sense is, that his enemies sought his life. ¶ Who *compass me about.* Who surround me on every side, as enemies do who besiege a city.

10. *They are inclosed in their own fat.* The meaning here is, that they were prosperous, and that they were consequently self-confident and proud, and were regardless of others. The phrase occurs several times as descriptive of the wicked in a state of prosperity, and as, therefore, insensible to the rights, the wants, and the sufferings of others. Comp. Deut. xxxii. 15, "But Jeshurun waxed fat and kicked: thou art waxed fat, thou art grown thick, thou art covered with fatness; then he forsook God which made him," etc. Job xv. 27, "Because he covereth his face with his fatness, and maketh collops of fat on his flanks." Ps. lxxiii. 7, "Their eyes stand out with fatness." Ps. cxix. 70, "Their heart is as fat as grease." ¶ *With their mouth they speak proudly.* Haughtily; in an arrogant tone; as a consequence of their prosperity.

11. *They have now compassed us.* Myself, and those who are associated with me. It would seem from this that the psalmist was not alone. It is to be observed, however, that there is a difference of reading in the Hebrew

their eyes bowing down to the earth;

12 [1] Like as a lion *that* is greedy of his prey, and as it were a young lion [2] lurking in secret places.

13 Arise, O LORD, [3] disappoint him, cast him down: deliver my

[1] *The likeness of him* (that is, *of every one of them*) is *as a lion* that *desireth to ravin.*

[2] *sitting.* [3] *prevent his face.*

text. The Masoretic reading is *us*; the Hebrew text is *me*, though in the other expression the plural is used—"*our* steps." There is no impropriety in supposing that the psalmist refers to his followers, associates, or friends, meaning that the wrong was done not to him alone, but to others connected with him. The meaning of *compassed* is, that they *surrounded* him on every side. Wherever he went, they were there. ¶ *In our steps.* Wherever we go. ¶ *They have set their eyes.* As those do who are intent on any thing; as the lion does that is seeking its prey (ver. 12). They looked keenly and directly at the object. They did not allow their eyes to wander. They were not indifferent to the object of their pursuit. ¶ *Bowing down to the earth.* That is, as the translators evidently understood this, having their *eyes* bowed down to the ground, or looking steadily to the ground. The image, according to Bishop Horsley, is borrowed from a hunter taking aim at an animal upon the ground. A more literal translation, however, would be, "They have fixed their eyes to lay me prostrate upon the ground." The Hebrew word—נָטָה, *natah*—means properly *to stretch out, to extend;* then, *to incline, to bow, to depress;* and hence the idea of *prostrating;* thus, to make the shoulder bend downwards, Gen. xlix. 15; to bring down the mind to an object, Ps. cxix. 112; to bow the heavens, Psa. xviii. 9. Hence the idea of prostrating an enemy; and the sense here clearly is, that they had fixed their eyes intently on the psalmist, with a purpose to prostrate him to the ground, or completely to overwhelm him.

12. *Like as a lion.* Marg., *The likeness of him* (that is, *of every one of them*) is *as a lion* that *desireth to ravin.* The meaning is plain. They were like a lion intent on securing his prey. They watched the object narrowly; they were ready to spring upon it. ¶ That *is greedy of his prey.* "He is craving to tear." *Professor Alexander.*—The Hebrew word rendered "*is greedy,*" means *to pine, to long after, to desire greatly.* The Hebrew word rendered "of his prey," is a verb, meaning *to pluck, to tear, to rend in pieces.* The reference is to the lion that desires to seize his victim, and to rend it in pieces to devour it. ¶ *And, as it were, a young lion,* Hebrew, "And like a young lion." ¶ *Lurking in secret places.* Marg., as in Heb., *sitting.* The allusion is to the lion crouching, or lying in wait for a favourable opportunity to pounce upon his prey. See Notes on Ps. x. 8–10. There is no special emphasis to be affixed to the fact that the "*lion*" is alluded to in one member of this verse, and the "*young lion*" in the other. It is in accordance with the custom of parallelism in Hebrew poetry where the same idea, with some little variation, is expressed in both members of the sentence. See Introduction to Job, § 5.

13. *Arise, O* LORD. See Notes on Ps. iii. 7. ¶ *Disappoint him.* Marg., *prevent his face.* The marginal reading expresses the sense of the Hebrew. The word used in the original means *to anticipate, to go before, to prevent;* and the prayer here is that God would come *before* his enemies; that is, that he would cast himself in their way *before* they should reach him. The enemy is represented as marching upon him with his face intently fixed, seeking his destruction; and he prays that God would interpose, or that He would come to his aid *before* his

soul from the wicked, [1] *which is*
thy [c] sword:
14 From men [2] *which are* thy

[1] Or, *by thy*. c Isa. x. 5.

hand, O Lord, from men of the
world, *which have* their portion in
this [d] life, and whose belly thou

[2] by *thine*. d Luke xvi. 25.

enemy should come up to him. ¶ *Cast him down.* That is, as it is in the Hebrew, make him bend or bow, as one who is conquered bows before a conqueror. ¶ *Deliver my soul from the wicked.* Save my life; save me from the designs of the wicked. ¶ Which is *thy sword.* The Chaldee Paraphrase renders this, "Deliver my soul from the wicked man, who deserves to be slain with thy sword." The Latin Vulgate, "Deliver my soul from the wicked man; thy spear from the enemies of thy hand." So the LXX., "Deliver my soul from the wicked; thy sword from the enemies of thy hand." The Syriac, "Deliver my soul from the wicked, and from the sword." De Wette renders it, "Deliver my soul from the wicked by thy sword." Prof. Alexander, "Save my soul from the wicked (with) thy sword." So Luther, "With thy sword." The Hebrew will undoubtedly admit of this latter construction, as in a similar passage in ver. 10 of this psalm; and this construction is found in the margin: "By thy sword." The sentiment that the wicked *are* the "sword" of God, or the instruments, though unconsciously to themselves, of accomplishing his purposes, or that he makes them the executioners of his will, is undoubtedly favoured by such passages as Isa. x. 5—7 (see Notes on those verses), and should be properly recognised. But such a construction is not necessary in the place before us, and it does not well agree with the connexion, for it is not easy to see why the psalmist should make the fact that the wicked were instruments in the hand of God in accomplishing his purposes a *reason* why He should interpose and deliver him from them. It seems to me, therefore, that the construction of De Wette and others, "Save me from the wicked *by* thy sword," is the true one. The psalmist asked that God would interfere by his own hand, and save him from danger. The same construction, if it be the correct one, is required in the following verse.

14. *From men* which are *thy hand.* Marg., *From men* by *thy hand.* Here the rendering in the common version would be still more harsh than in the previous verse, since it is at least unusual to call men "the hand" of God, in the sense that they are his instruments in accomplishing his purposes. The more obvious construction is to regard it as a prayer that God would deliver him by his own hand from *men*—from men that rose up against him. Comp. 2 Sam. xxiv. 14. ¶ *From men of the world.* A better construction of this would be "from men; from the world." The psalmist prays first that he may be delivered from men by the hand of God. He then *repeats* the prayer, "from men, I say," and then adds, "from the world." He desires to be rescued entirely from such worldly plans, devices, purposes;—from men among whom nothing but worldly principles prevail. ¶ Which have *their portion in* this *life.* Their portion—their lot—is among *the living;* that is, they have nothing to look forward to—to hope for in the world to come. They are, therefore, governed wholly by worldly principles. They have no fear of God; they have no regard to the rights of others further than will be in accordance with their own worldly interest. Men whose portion is wholly in this life will make everything subordinate to their worldly interests. ¶ *And whose belly thou fillest with thy hid* treasure. The meaning of this portion of the verse is that, in respect to the object for which they lived, they were successful. They lived only for the world, and they obtained what the

fillest with thy hid *treasure:* [1] they are full of children, and leave the rest of their *substance* to their babes.

15 As for me, I will behold thy [e] face in righteousness: I

[1] Or, *their children are full.*

[e] 1 John iii. 2.

world had to bestow. They *had* prosperity in their purposes in life. The word "*hid*" here — *hid treasure* —means that which is hoarded, secreted, carefully guarded; and the word commonly refers to the practice of secreting from public view valuable treasures, as silver and gold. It is possible, however, that the reference here is to the fact that God has hidden these objects in the depths of the earth, and that it is necessary to *search* for them carefully if men would obtain them. Comp. Job xxviii. 1—11. The phrase "whose belly thou hast filled" means that their appetite or cravings in this respect were satisfied. They had what they wanted. ¶ *They are full of children.* Marg., *their children are full.* The margin probably expresses the sense of the Hebrew better than the text. The literal rendering would be, "satisfied are their sons;" that is, they have enough to satisfy the wants of their children. The expression "they are full of children" is harsh and unnatural, and is not demanded by the original, or by the main thought in the passage. The obvious signification is, that they have enough for themselves and for their children. ¶ *And leave the rest of their* substance *to their babes.* That is, what remains after their own wants are supplied, they leave to their babes. They not only have enough for the supply of their own wants and the wants of their children during their own lives, but they also leave an inheritance to their children after they are dead. The word rendered *babes* properly means little children, though it seems here to be used as denoting children in general. The meaning is, that they are able to provide for their children after they themselves are dead. Compare the description of worldly prosperity in Job xxi. 7—11.

15. *As for me.* In strong contrast with the aims, the desires, and the condition of worldly men. *They* seek their portion in this life, and are satisfied; *I* cherish no such desires, and have no such prosperity. I look to another world as my home, and shall be satisfied only in the everlasting favour and friendship of God. ¶ *I will behold thy face.* I shall see thee. Comp. Matt. v. 8; 1 Cor. xiii. 12; 1 John iii. 2. This refers naturally, as the closing part of the verse more fully shows, to the future world, and is such language as would be employed by those who believe in a future state, and by no others. This is the highest object before the mind of a truly religious man. The bliss of heaven consists mainly, in his apprehension, in the privilege of seeing God his Saviour; and the hope of being permitted to do this is of infinitely more value to him than would be all the wealth of this world. ¶ *In righteousness.* Being myself righteous; being delivered from the power, the pollution, the dominion of sin. It is this which makes heaven so desirable; without this, in the apprehension of a truly good man, no place would be heaven. ¶ *I shall be satisfied.* While *they* are satisfied with this world, I shall be satisfied only when I awake in the likeness of my God. Nothing can meet the wants of my nature; nothing can satisfy the aspirings of my soul, until that occurs. ¶ *When I awake.* This is language which would be employed only by one who believed in the resurrection of the dead, and who was accustomed to speak of death as a *sleep*—a calm repose in the hope of awaking to a new life. Comp. Notes on Ps. xvi. 9-11. Some have understood this as meaning "when I awake to-morrow;" and they thence infer that this was an evening song (comp. Ps. iv. 8); others have supposed that it had a more general sense,—mean-

shall be satisfied, when I awake, with thy likeness.

ing "*whenever* I awake;" that is, while men of the world rejoice in their worldly possessions, and while this is the first thought which they have on awaking in the morning, *my* joy when I awake is in God;—in the evidence of his favour and friendship;—in the consciousness that I resemble him. I am surprised to find that Professor Alexander favours this view. Even De Wette admits that it refers to the resurrection of the dead, and that the psalm can be interpreted only on the supposition that it has this reference, and hence he argues that it could not have been composed by David, but that it must have been written in the time of the Exile, when that doctrine had obtained currency among the Hebrews. The interpretation above suggested seems to me to be altogether too low a view to be taken of the sense of the passage. It does not meet the state of mind described in the psalm. It does not correspond with the deep anxieties which the psalmist expressed as springing from the troubles which surrounded him. He sought repose from those troubles; he looked for consolation when surrounded by bitter and unrelenting enemies. He was oppressed and crushed with these many sorrows. Now it would do little to meet that state of mind, and to impart to him the consolation which he needed, to reflect that he could lie down in the night and awake in the morning with the consciousness that he enjoyed the friendship of God, for he had that already; and besides this, so far as this source of consolation was concerned, he would awake to a renewal of the same troubles to-morrow which he had met on the previous day. He needed some higher, some more enduring and efficient consolation; something which would meet *all* the circumstances of the case; some source of peace, composure, and rest, which was beyond all this; something which would have an existence where there was *no* trouble or anxiety;—and this could be found only in a future world. The obvious interpretation of the passage, therefore, so far as its sense can be determined from the connexion, is to refer it to the awaking in the morning of the resurrection; and there is nothing in the language itself, or in the known sentiments of the psalmist, to forbid this interpretation. The word rendered *awake*—קוּץ, *kootz*—used only in Hiphil, means *to awake;*—to awake from sleep, Ps. iii. 5; cxxxix. 18; or from death, 2 Kings iv. 31; Jer. li. 39; Isa. xxvi. 19; Job xiv. 12; Dan. xii. 2. ¶ *With thy likeness.* Or, *in* thy likeness; that is, resembling thee. The resemblance doubtless is in the moral character, for the highest hope of a good man is that he may be, and will be, like God. Comp. Notes on 1 John iii. 2. I regard this passage, therefore, as one of the incidental proofs scattered through the Old Testament which show that the sacred writers under that dispensation believed in the doctrine of the resurrection of the dead; that their language was often based on the knowledge and the belief of that doctrine, even when they did not expressly affirm it; and that in times of trouble, and under the consciousness of sin, they sought their highest consolation, as the people of God do now, from the hope and the expectation that the righteous dead will rise again, and that in a world free from trouble, from sin, and from death, they would live for ever in the presence of God, and find their supreme happiness in being made wholly like him.

PSALM XVIII.

This psalm is found, with some unimportant variations, in 2 Samuel xxii. In that history, as in the inscription of the psalm here, it is said to have been composed by David on the occasion when the Lord "delivered him from the hand of all his enemies, and from the hand of Saul." There can, therefore, be no doubt that David was the author, nor can there be any as to the occasion on which it was composed. It is a song of victory, and is beyond doubt the most sublime ode that was ever composed on such an occasion. David, long pursued and harassed by foes who sought his life, at length felt that a complete triumph was obtained, and that he and his kingdom were safe, and he pours forth the utterances of a grateful heart for God's merciful and mighty interposition, in language of the highest sublimity, and with the utmost grandeur of poetic imagery. Nowhere else, even in the sacred Scriptures, are there to be found images more beautiful, or expressions more sublime, than those which occur in this psalm.

From the place which this psalm occupies in the history of the life of David (2 Sam. xxii.), it is probable that it was composed in the latter years of his life, though it occupies this early place in the Book of Psalms. We have no reason to believe that the principle adopted in the arrangement of the Psalms was to place them in chronological order; and we cannot determine why in that arrangement this psalm has the place which has been assigned to it; but we cannot well be mistaken in supposing that it was composed at a somewhat advanced period of the life of David, and that it was in fact among the last of his compositions. Thus in the Book of Samuel, it is placed (ch. xxii.) immediately preceding a chapter (xxiii.) which professes (ver. 1) to record "the last words of David." And thus in the title it is said to have been composed when "the Lord had delivered him out of the hand of *all* his enemies," an event which occurred only at a comparatively late period of his life. The circumstance which is mentioned in the title—"and out of the hand of Saul"—does not necessarily conflict with this view, or make it necessary for us to suppose that it was composed immediately after his deliverance from the hand of Saul. To David, recording and recounting the great events of his life, that deliverance would occur as one of the most momentous and worthy of a grateful remembrance, for it was a deliverance which was the foundation of all his subsequent successes, and in which the Divine interposition had been most remarkable. At any time of his life it would be proper to refer to this as demanding special acknowledgment. Saul had been among the most formidable of all his enemies. The most distressing and harassing events of his life had occurred in the time of his conflicts with him. God's interpositions in his behalf had occurred in the most remarkable manner, in delivering him from the dangers of that period of his history. It was natural and proper, therefore, in a general song of praise, composed in view of *all* God's interpositions in his behalf, that he should refer particularly to those dangers and deliverances. This opinion, that the psalm was composed when David was aged, which seems so obvious, is the opinion of Jarchi and Kimchi, of Rosenmüller and De Wette. The strong imagery, therefore, in the psalm, describing mighty convulsions of nature (vers. 6–16), is to be understood, not as a literal description, but as narrating God's gracious interposition in the time of danger, *as if* the Lord had spoken to him out of the temple; *as if* the earth had trembled; *as if* its foundations had been shaken; *as if* a smoke had gone out of his nostrils; *as if* he had bowed the heavens and come down; *as if* he had thundered in the heavens, and had sent out hailstones and coals of fire, etc.

From the fact that there are variations, though not of an essential character, in the two copies of the psalm, it would seem not improbable that it had been revised by David himself, or by some other person, after it was first composed, and that one copy was used by the author of the Book of Samuel, and the other by the collector and arranger of the Book of Psalms. These variations are not important, and by no means change the essential character of the psalm. It is not very easy to see *why* they *were* made, if they were made designedly, or to account for them if they were not so made. They are such as the following: The introduction, or the title of it, is adapted, in the psalm before us, to the purposes for which it was designed, when it was admitted into the collection. "To the chief Musician, a Psalm of David, the servant of the Lord, who spake unto the Lord the words," etc. The first verse of Ps. xviii., "I will love thee, O Lord, my strength," is not found in the psalm as it is in the Book of Samuel. The second verse of the psalm is, "The Lord is my rock, and my fortress, and my deliverer; my God, my strength, in whom I will trust; my buckler, and the horn of my salvation, and my high tower." In Samuel, the corresponding passage is, "The Lord is my rock, and my fortress, and my deliverer; the God of my rock, in him will I trust; he is my shield, and the horn of my salvation, my high tower, and my refuge, my saviour; thou savest me from violence." In ver. 4, the reading is, "The sorrows of death compassed me" etc.; in Samuel, "The waves of death compassed me." Similar variations, affecting the words, without materially affecting the sense, occur in vers. 2, 3, 4, 6, 7, 8, 11, 12, 13, 14, 15, 16, 19, 20, 21, 23, 24, 25, 26, 27, 28, 29, 30, 32, 33, 34, 35, 36, 37, 38, 39, 40, 41, 42, 43, 44, 45, 47, 48, 49, 50, and 51, of the psalm.* See these passages arranged in Rosenmüller's Scholia, vol. i., pp. 451–458. In no instance is the sense very materially affected, though the variations are so numerous.

It is impossible now to account for these variations. Hammond, Kennicott, and others, suppose that they occurred from the errors of transcribers. But to this opinion Schultens opposes unanswerable objections. He refers particularly (*a*) to the multitude and variety of the changes; (*b*) to the condition or state of the codices; (*c*) to the nature of the variations, or to the fact that changes are made in words, and not merely in letters of similar forms which might be mistaken for each other. See his arguments in Rosenmüller, Schol., vol. i., pp. 441–443. It seems most probable, therefore, that these changes were made by design, and that it was done either by David, who revised the original composition, and issued two forms of the poem, one of which was inserted in the history in Samuel, and the other in the collection of the Psalms; or that the changes were made by the collector of the Psalms, when they were arranged for public worship. The former supposition is a possible one; though, as the psalm was composed near the close of the life of David, it would seem not to be very probable. The most natural supposition, therefore, is, that the changes were made by the collector of the Psalms, whoever he might be, or by the person who presided over this part of public worship in the temple, and that the changes were made for some reason which we cannot now understand, as better adapting the psalm to musical purposes. Doederlein supposes that the recension was made by some later poet, for the purpose of "polishing" the language; of giving it a more finished poetic form; and of adapting it better to public use; and he regards both forms as "genuine, elegant, sublime; the one more ancient, the other more polished and refined." It seems most probable that the changes were made with a view to some rhythmical or musical effect, or for the purpose of adapting the psalm to the music of the temple service. Such changes would depend on causes which could be now little understood, as we are not sufficiently acquainted with the music employed in public worship by the Hebrews, nor are we now competent to understand the effect which, in this respect, would be produced by a slight change of phraseology. Variations of a similar nature now exist in psalms and hymns which could not be well explained or understood by one who was not familiar with our language and with our music, and which, after as long an interval as that between the time when the Psalms were arranged for musical purposes and the present time, would be wholly unintelligible.

The psalm embraces the following subjects:—

I. A general acknowledgment of God, and thanks to him, as the Deliverer in the time of troubles, and as worthy to be praised, vers. 1–3.

II. A brief description of the troubles and dangers from which the psalmist had been rescued, vers. 4, 5.

III. A description, conceived in the highest forms of poetic language, of the Divine interposition in times of danger, vers. 6–19.

IV. A statement of the psalmist that this interposition was of such a nature as to vindicate his own character, or to show that his cause was a righteous cause; that he was right, and that his enemies had been in the wrong; that God approved his course, and disapproved the course of his enemies: or, in other words, that these interpositions were such as to prove that God was just, and would deal with men according to their character, vers. 20–30.

V. A recapitulation of what God had done for him, in enabling him to subdue his enemies, and a statement of the effect which he supposed would be produced on others by the report of what God had done in his behalf, vers. 31–45.

VI. A general expression of thanksgiving to God as the author of all these

* *i.e.*, after the notation in the Hebrew Psalter, which accords with the numbering of the verses *in Samuel*.

PSALM XVIII.

To the chief Musician. *A Psalm* of David, the servant *f* of the LORD, who spake unto the LORD the words *g* of this song in the day *that* the LORD delivered him from the hand of all his enemies, and from the hand of Saul: And he said,

I WILL love *h* thee, O LORD, my strength.

f Psa. xxxvi., *title*. *g* 2 Sam. xxii. *h* 1 John iv. 19.

---

blessings, and as worthy of universal confidence and praise, vers. 46–50.

THE TITLE. ¶ *To the chief Musician.* See Notes to the title of Psalm iv. ¶ A Psalm *of David*. The words "A Psalm" are not here in the original, and may convey a slightly erroneous impression, as if the psalm had been composed for the express purpose of being used publicly in the worship of God. In the corresponding place in 2 Sam. xxii., it is described as a "Song" of David:—"And David spake unto the Lord the words of this *song*." It was originally an expression of his private gratitude for God's distinguishing mercies, and was afterwards, as we have seen, probably adapted to purposes of public worship by some one of a later age. ¶ *The servant of the* LORD. This expression also is wanting in 2 Sam. xxii. It is undoubtedly an addition by a later hand, as indicating the general character which David had acquired, or as denoting the national estimate in regard to his character. The same expression occurs in the title to Ps. xxxvi. The Chaldee Paraphrase translates this title: "To be sung over the wonderful things which abundantly happened to the servant of the Lord, to David, who sang," etc. The use of the phrase here—"the servant of the Lord"—by him who made the collection of the Psalms, would seem to imply that he regarded the psalm as having a sufficiently public character to make it proper to introduce it into a collection designed for general worship. In other words, David was not, in the view of the author of the collection, a private man, but was eminently a public servant of Jehovah; and a song of grateful remembrance of God's mercies to him was entitled to be regarded as expressing the appropriate feelings of God's people in similar circumstances in all times. ¶ *Who spake unto the* LORD. Composed it as giving utterance to his feelings towards the Lord. ¶ *The words of this song in the day* that *the* LORD *delivered him*. When the Lord *had* delivered him; when he felt that he was completely rescued from *all* his foes. This does not mean that the psalm was composed on a particular day when God had by some one signal act rescued him from impending danger, but it refers to a calm period of his life, when he could review the past, and see that God had rescued him from *all* the enemies that had ever threatened his peace. This would probably, as has been suggested above, occur near the close of his life. ¶ *From the hand of all his enemies*. Out of the hand, or the power. There is here a *general* view of the mercy of God in rescuing him from *all* his foes. ¶ *And from the hand of Saul*. Saul had been one of his most formidable enemies, and the wars with him had been among the most eventful periods of the life of David. In a general review of his life, near its close, he would naturally recur to the dangers of that period, and to God's gracious interpositions in his behalf, and it would seem to him that what God had done for him in those times deserved a special record. The original word here—כַּף, *kaph*—is not the same as in the corresponding place in 2 Sam. xxii.—יָד, *yad*—though the idea is substantially the same. The word here used means properly the *palm* or *hollow* of the hand; the word used in Samuel means the hand itself. Why the change was made we have not the means of ascertaining. ¶ *And he said*. So 2 Sam. xxii. 2. What follows is what he said.

1. *I will love thee, O* LORD. This verse is not found in the song in 2 Sam. xxii. It appears to have been added after the first composition of the psalm, either by David as expressive of his ardent love for the Lord in view of his merciful interpositions in his behalf, and on the most careful and most mature review of those mercies, or by the collector of the Psalms when they were adapted to purposes of public worship, as a proper commencement of the psalm—expressive of the feeling which the general tenor of the psalm was fitted to inspire. It is impossible now to determine by

2 The LORD *is* my rock, and my fortress, and my deliverer; my God, my [1] strength, in whom I will trust; my buckler, and the horn of my salvation, *and* my high tower.

[1] *rock.*

whom it was added; but no one can doubt that it is a proper commencement of a psalm that is designed to recount so many mercies. It is the feeling which all should have when they recall the goodness of God to them in their past lives. ¶ *My strength.* The source of my strength, or from whom all my strength is derived. So Ps. xxvii. 1, "The Lord is the strength of my life." Ps. xxviii. 8, "He is the saving strength of his anointed." Comp. Ps. xxix. 11; xlvi. 1; lxxiii. 26; lxxxi. 1; cxl. 7.

2. *The* LORD is *my rock.* The idea in this expression, and in the subsequent parts of the description, is that he owed his safety entirely to God. He had been unto him *as* a rock, a tower, a buckler, etc.—that is, he had derived from God the protection which a rock, a tower, a citadel, a buckler furnished to those who depended on them, or which they were designed to secure. The word "rock" here has reference to the fact that in times of danger a lofty rock would be sought as a place of safety, or that men would fly to it to escape from their enemies. Such rocks abound in Palestine; and by the fact that they are elevated and difficult of access, or by the fact that those who fled to them could find shelter behind their projecting crags, or by the fact that they could find security in their deep and dark caverns, they became places of refuge in times of danger; and protection was often found there when it could not be found in the plains below. Comp. Judges vi. 2; Ps. xxvii. 5; lxi. 2. Also, Jos. Ant., b. xiv., ch. xv. ¶ *And my fortress.* He has been to me *as* a fortress. The word *fortress* means a place of defence, a place so strengthened that an enemy could not approach it, or where one would be safe. Such fortresses were often constructed on the rocks or on hills, where those who fled thither would be doubly safe. Comp. Job xxxix. 28. See also Notes on Isa. xxxiii. 16. ¶ *And my deliverer.* Delivering or rescuing me from my enemies. ¶ *My God.* Who hast been to me a God; that is, in whom I have found all that is implied in the idea of *God*—a Protector, Helper, Friend, Father, Saviour. The notion or idea of a *God* is different from all other ideas, and David had found, as the Christian now does, all that is implied in that idea, in Jehovah, the living God. ¶ *My strength.* Marg., *My rock.* So the Hebrew, although the Hebrew word is different from that which is used in the former part of the verse. Both words denote that God was a refuge or protection, as a rock or crag is to one in danger (comp. Deut. xxxii. 37), though the exact difference between the words may not be obvious. ¶ *In whom I will trust.* That is, I have found him to be such a refuge that I *could* trust in him, and in view of the past I *will* confide in him always. ¶ *My buckler.* The word here used is the same which occurs in Ps. iii. 3, where it is translated *shield.* See Notes on that verse. ¶ *And the horn of my salvation.* The *horn* is to animals the means of their defence. Their strength lies in the horn. Hence the word is used here, as elsewhere, to represent that to which we owe our protection and defence in danger; and the idea here is, that God was to the psalmist what the horn is to animals, the means of his defence. Comp. Ps. xxii. 21; lxxv. 4, 5, 10; xcii. 10; cxxxii. 17; cxlviii. 14. ¶ And *my high tower.* He is to me what a high tower is to one who is in danger. Comp. Prov. xviii. 10, "The name of the Lord is a strong tower: the righteous runneth into it, and is safe." The word here used occurs in Ps. ix. 9, where it is rendered "refuge." (Marg., *A high place.*) See Notes on that verse.

3 I will call upon the LORD *who is worthy* [i] to be praised: so [k] shall I be saved from mine enemies.

4 The sorrows of death compassed me, and the floods of [1] ungodly men made me afraid.

i Rev. v. 11—13. *k* Psa. l. 15. [1] *Belial.*

Such towers were erected on mountains, on rocks, or on the walls of a city, and were regarded as safe places mainly because they were inaccessible. So the old castles in Europe,—as that at Heidelberg, and generally those along the Rhine,—were built on lofty places, and in such positions as not to be easily accessible.

3. *I will call upon the* LORD. The idea here is, that he would constantly call upon the Lord. In all times of trouble and danger he would go to him, and invoke his aid. The experience of the past had been such as to lead him to put confidence in him in all time to come. He had learned to flee to him in danger, and he had never put his trust in him in vain. The idea is, that a proper view of God's dealings with us in the past should lead us to feel that we may put confidence in him in the future. ¶ Who is worthy *to be praised.* More literally, " Him who is to be praised I will call upon, Jehovah." The prominent—the leading thought is, that God is a being every way worthy of praise. ¶ *So shall I be saved from my enemies.* Ever onward, and at all times. He had had such ample experience of his protection that he could confide in him as one who would deliver him from all his foes.

4. *The sorrows of death compassed me.* Surrounded me. That is, he was in imminent danger of death, or in the midst of such pangs and sorrows as are supposed commonly to attend on death. He refers probably to some period in his past life—perhaps in the persecutions of Saul—when he was so beset with troubles and difficulties that it seemed to him that he must die. The word rendered *sorrows*—חֶבֶל, *hhebel*—means, according to Gesenius, *a cord, a rope,* and hence *a snare, gin, noose;* and the idea here is, according to Gesenius, that he was taken as it were in the snares of death, or in the bands of death. So Ps. cxvi. 3. Our translators, however, and it seems to me more correctly, regarded the word as derived from the same noun differently pointed—חֵבֶל, *hhaibel*—meaning *writhings, pangs, pains,* as in Isa. lxvi. 7; Jer. xiii. 21; xxii. 23; Hos. xiii. 13; Job xxxix. 3. So the Chaldee Paraphrase, " Pangs as of a woman in childbirth came around me." So the Vulgate, *dolores.* So the LXX., ὠδῖνες. The corresponding place in 2 Sam. xxii. is, " The *waves* of death." The word which is used there—מִשְׁבָּר, *mishbar* — means properly waves which break upon the shore—*breakers.* See Ps. xlii. 7; lxxxviii. 7; Jonah ii. 3. Why the change was made in the psalm it is not possible to determine. Either word denotes a condition of great danger and alarm, as if death was inevitable. ¶ *And the floods of ungodly men.* Marg., as in Heb., *Belial.* The word *Belial* means properly *without use* or *profit;* and then worthless, abandoned, wicked. It is applied to wicked men as being *worthless* to society, and to all the proper ends of life. Though the term here undoubtedly refers to *wicked* men, yet it refers to them as being worthless or abandoned—low, vulgar, useless to mankind. The word rendered *floods*—נַחַל, *nahhal*—means in the singular, properly, a stream, brook, rivulet; and then, a torrent, as formed by rain and snow-water in the mountains, Job vi. 15. The word here used refers to such men as if they were poured forth in streams and torrents—in such multitudes that the psalmist was likely to be overwhelmed by them, as one would be by floods of water. ¶ *Made me afraid.* Made me apprehensive of losing my life. To what particular period of his life he here refers it is impossible now to determine.

5 The [1] sorrows of hell compassed me about: the snares of death prevented me.

6 In my distress I called upon the LORD, and cried unto my God: he heard my voice out of his temple, and my cry came before [l] him, *even* into his ears.

7 Then the earth shook and trembled; the foundations also

[1] Or, *cords*.

l 2 Chron. xxx. 27.

5. *The sorrows of hell.* Marg., *cords.* The word here used is the same which occurs in the previous verse, and which is there rendered *sorrows.* It is correctly translated here, as in that verse, *sorrows,* though the parallelism would seem to favour the interpretation in the margin,—*cords.* If it means *sorrows,* the idea is, that such sufferings encompassed him, or seized upon him, as we associate in idea with the descent to the under-world, or the going down to the dead. If it means *cords,* or *bands,* then the idea is, that he was seized with pain as if with cords thrown around him, and that were dragging him down to the abodes of the dead. Luther, De Wette, Prof. Alexander, Hengstenberg, and others render the word, in each of these places, *bands.* On the word here rendered *hell,* שְׁאוֹל, *Sheol,* see Notes on Isa. xiv. 9. It means here *the under-world, the regions of the dead.* It is a description of one who was overcome with the dread of death. ¶ *The snares of death.* The word *snares* refers to the gins, toils, nets, which are used in taking wild beasts, by suddenly throwing cords around them, and binding them fast. The idea here is, that *Death* had thus thrown around him its toils or snares, and had bound him fast. ¶ *Prevented me.* The word here used in Hebrew, as our word *prevent* did originally, means to *anticipate, to go before.* The idea here is that those snares had, as it were, suddenly rushed upon him, or seized him. They came before him in his goings, and bound him fast.

6. *In my distress.* This refers, most probably, not to any particular case, but rather indicates his general habit of mind, that when he was in deep distress and danger he had uniformly called upon the Lord, and had found him ready to help. ¶ *I called upon the* LORD. I prayed. That is, he invoked God to help him in his trouble. He relied not on his own strength; he looked not for human aid; he looked to God alone. ¶ *And cried unto my God.* The word used here denotes an earnest cry for help. Comp. Job xxxv. 9; xxxvi. 13. ¶ *He heard my voice out of his temple.* That is, he, being in his temple, heard my voice. The word rendered *temple* (comp. Notes on Ps. v. 7) cannot refer here to the temple at Jerusalem, for that was built after the death of David, but it refers either to *heaven,* considered as the temple, or dwelling-place of God, or to the *tabernacle,* considered as his abode on earth. The sense is not materially varied, whichever interpretation is adopted. Comp. Ps. xi. 4. ¶ *And my cry came before him.* He heard my cry. It was not intercepted on the way, but came up to him. ¶ Even *into his ears.* Indicating that he certainly heard it. Comp. Gen. xxiii. 10; xliv. 18; l. 4; Ex. x. 2: Ps. xxxiv. 15.

7. *Then the earth shook and trembled.* The description which follows here is one of the most sublime that is to be found in any language. It is taken from the fury of the storm and tempest, when all the elements are in commotion; when God seems to go forth in the greatness of his majesty and the terror of his power, to prostrate everything before him. We are not to regard this as descriptive of anything which literally occurred, but rather as expressive of the fact of the Divine interposition, *as if* he thus came forth in the greatness of his power. There is no improbability indeed in supposing that in some of the dangerous periods of

of the hills moved and were
shaken, because he was wroth.
8 There went up a smoke [1] out
of his nostrils, and fire out of his
mouth devoured: coals were
kindled by it.
9 He bowed [m] the heavens also,
and came down: and darkness
was under his feet.

[1] *by.* [m] Psa. cxliv. 5, etc.

David's life, when surrounded by enemies, or even when in the midst of a battle, a furious tempest *may* have occurred that seemed to be a special Divine interposition in his behalf, but we have no distinct record of such an event, and it is not necessary to suppose that such an event occurred in order to a correct understanding of the passage. All that is needful is to regard this as a representation of the mighty interposition of God; to suppose that his intervention was as direct, as manifest, and as sublime, *as if* he had *thus* interposed. There are frequent references in the Scriptures to such storms and tempests as illustrative of the majesty, the power, and the glory of God, and of the manner in which he interposes on behalf of his people. See Ps. cxliv. 5–7; xlvi. 6–8; xxix.; Job xxxvii. 21–24; xxxviii. 1; Nahum i. 3; and particularly Habakkuk iii. 3–16. The description in Habakkuk strongly resembles the passage before us, and both were drawn doubtless from an actual observation of the fury of a tempest. ¶ *The foundations also of the hills moved.* The mountains seemed to rock on their foundations. In the corresponding place in 2 Sam. xxii. 8 the expression is, "The foundations *of heaven* moved and shook;" that is, that on which the heavens seem to rest was agitated. Many suppose that the expression refers to the mountains as if they bore up the heavens; but De Wette more properly supposes that the reference is to the heavens as a building or an edifice resting on foundations. Why the change was made in revising the psalm from the "foundations of *the heavens*" to the "foundations of *the hills*," it is impossible now to determine. ¶ *Because he was wroth.* Literally, "Because it was inflamed (or enkindled) to him;" that is, because he was angry. Anger is often compared to a raging flame, because it seems to consume everything before it. Hence we speak of it as *heated*, as *burning*. So we say of one that he is *inflamed by passion*. The expression here is sublime in the highest degree. God seemed to be angry, and hence he came forth in this awful manner, and the very earth trembled before him.

8. *There went up a smoke out of his nostrils.* Marg., *by his*; that is, as it is understood in the margin, the smoke seemed to be produced *by* his nostrils, or to be caused by his breathing. The comparison, according to Rosenmüller and De Wette, is derived from wild beasts when excited with anger, and when their rage is indicated by their violent breathing. Comp. Ps. lxxiv. 1; Deut. xxix. 20; Isa. lxv. 5. ¶ *And fire out of his mouth devoured.* That is, the clouds seemed to be poured forth from his nostrils, and the lightning from his mouth. So in Habakkuk iii. 5: "Before him went the pestilence, and burning coals went forth at his feet." ¶ *Coals were kindled by it.* Everything seemed to glow and burn. The lightning, that appeared to flash from his mouth, set everything on fire. The heavens and the earth were in a blaze.

9. *He bowed the heavens also.* He seemed to bend down the heavens,—to bring them nearer to the earth. "He inclines the canopy of the heavens, as it were, towards the earth; wraps himself in the darkness of night, and shoots forth his arrows; hurls abroad his lightnings, and wings them with speed." Herder, Spirit of Hebrew Poetry (Marsh), ii. 157. The allusion is still to the tempest, when the clouds run low; when they

10 And he rode upon a cherub, and did fly; yea, he did fly upon the wings of the wind.

11 He made darkness his secret place: his pavilion [n] round about

[n] Psa. xxvii. 5.

seem to sweep along the ground; when it appears as if the heavens were brought nearer to the earth—as if, to use a common expression, "the heavens and earth were coming together." ¶ *And came down.* God himself seemed to descend in the fury of the storm. ¶ *And darkness was under his feet.* A dark cloud; or, the darkness caused by thick clouds. Comp. Nahum i. 3, "The Lord hath his way in the whirlwind and in the storm, and the clouds are the dust of his feet." Deut. iv. 11, "the mountain burned . . . with thick darkness." v. 22, "These words the Lord spake out of the thick darkness." Ps. xcvii. 2, "Clouds and darkness are round about him." The idea here is that of awful majesty and power, as we are nowhere more forcibly impressed with the idea of majesty and power than in the fury of a storm.

10. *And he rode upon a cherub.* Comp. Notes on Isa. xiv. 13; xxxvii. 16. The cherub in the theology of the Hebrews was a figurative representation of power and majesty, under the image of a being of a high and celestial nature, "whose form is represented as composed from the figures of a man, ox, lion, and eagle," Ezek. i., x. Cherubs are first mentioned as guarding the gates of Paradise, Gen. iii. 24; then as bearing the throne of God upon their wings through the clouds, Ezek. i., x.; and also as statues or images made of wood and overlaid with gold, over the cover of the ark, in the inner sanctuary of the tabernacle, and of the temple, Ex. xxv. 18, *seq.*; 1 Kings vi. 23–28. Between the two cherubim in the temple, the Shechinah, or visible symbol of the presence of God, rested; and hence God is represented as "dwelling between the cherubim," Ex. xxv. 22; Num. vii. 89; Ps. lxxx. 1; xcix. 1. The cherubim are not to be regarded as real existences, or as an order of angels like the seraphim (Isa. vi. 2, 3), but as an imaginary representation of majesty, as emblematic of the power and glory of God. Here God is represented as "riding on a cherub;" that is, as coming forth on the clouds regarded as a cherub (comp. Ezek. i.), as if, seated on his throne, he was borne along in majesty and power amidst the storm and tempest. ¶ *And did fly.* He seemed to move rapidly on the flying clouds. ¶ *Yea, he did fly upon the wings of the wind.* Rapidly as the clouds driven along by the wind. The "*wings* of the wind" are designed to represent the *rapidity* with which the wind sweeps along. Rapid motion is represented by the flight of birds; hence the term wings is applied to winds to denote the rapidity of their movement. The whole figure here is designed to represent the majesty with which God seemed to be borne along on the tempest. Herder renders it, "He flew on the wings of the storm."

11. *He made darkness his secret place.* Herder has beautifully rendered this verse,

> "Now he wrapped himself in darkness;
> Clouds on clouds enclosed him round."

The word rendered *secret place*—סֵתֶר, *saither*—means properly *a hiding;* then something hidden, private, secret. Hence it means a covering, a veil. Comp. Job xxii. 14; xxiv. 15. In Ps. lxxxi. 7 it is applied to thunder: "I answered thee in the *secret place* of thunder;" that is, in the secret place or retreat,—the deep, dark cloud, whence the thunder seems to come. Here the meaning seems to be, that God was encompassed with darkness. He had, as it were, wrapped himself in night, and made his abode in the gloom of the storm. ¶ *His pavilion.* His *tent*, for so the word means. Comp. Ps. xxvii. 5; xxxi. 20. His abode was in the midst of clouds and waters, or watery clouds.

him *were* dark waters *and* thick clouds [o] of the skies.

12 At the brightness *that was* before him his thick clouds passed, hail-*stones* and coals of fire.

13 The LORD also thundered [p] in the heavens, and the Highest gave his voice; hail-*stones* and coals of fire.

14 Yea, he sent out his arrows, and scattered them; and he shot

o Psa. xcvii. 2.

p 1 Sam. vii. 10.

¶ *Round about him.* Perhaps a more literal translation would be, "the things round about him—his tent (shelter, or cover)—were the darkness of waters, the clouds of the skies." The idea is, that he seemed to be encompassed with watery clouds. ¶ *Dark waters.* Heb., *darkness of waters.* The allusion is to clouds filled with water; charged with rain. ¶ *Thick clouds of the skies.* The word rendered *skies* in this place—שְׁחָקִים, *shehhâkim*—means, in the singular, *dust,* as being fine; then a cloud, as a cloud of dust; then, in the plural, it is used to denote *clouds,* Job xxxviii. 37; and hence it is used to denote the region of the clouds; the firmament; the sky; Job xxxvii. 18. Perhaps a not inaccurate rendering here would be, "clouds of clouds;" that is, clouds rolled in with clouds; clouds of one kind rapidly succeeding those of another kind—inrolling and piled on each other. There are four different kinds of clouds; and though we cannot suppose that the distinction was accurately marked in the time of the psalmist, yet to the slightest observation there *is* a distinction in the clouds, and it is possible that by the use of two terms here, both denoting clouds—one thick and dense, and the other clouds as resembling dust—the psalmist meant to intimate that clouds *of all kinds* rolled over the firmament, and that these constituted the "pavilion" of God.

12. *At the brightness* that was *before him.* From the flash—the play of the lightnings that seemed to go before him. ¶ *His thick clouds passed.* Or, vanished. They seemed to pass away. The light, the flash, the blaze, penetrated those clouds, and seemed to dispel, or to scatter them. The whole heavens were in a blaze, as if there were no clouds, or as if the clouds were all driven away. The reference here is to the appearance when the vivid flashes of lightning seem to penetrate and dispel the clouds, and the heavens seem to be lighted up with a universal flame. ¶ *Hail*-stones. That is, hail-stones followed, or fell. ¶ *And coals of fire.* There *seemed* to be coals of fire rolling along the ground, or falling from the sky. In the corresponding place in 2 Sam. xxii. 13 the expression is, "Through the brightness before him were coals of fire kindled." That is, fires were kindled by the lightning. The expression in the psalm is more terse and compact, but the reason of the change cannot be assigned.

13. *The* LORD *also thundered in the heavens.* Thunder is often in the Scriptures described as the voice of God. See the magnificent description in Ps. xxix.; comp. Job xl. 9, "Canst thou thunder with a voice like him?" So 1 Sam. vii. 10; xii. 18; Ps. lxxvii. 18; Job xxxvii. 4. ¶ *And the Highest gave his voice.* God, the most exalted Being in the universe, uttered his voice in the thunder; or, the thunder was his voice. ¶ *Hail*-stones, *and coals of fire.* Accompanying the thunder. The *repetition* seems to be because these were such striking and constant accompaniments of the storm.

14. *Yea, he sent out his arrows.* The word *arrows* here probably refers to the lightnings mentioned in the other clause of the verse. Those lightnings scattered around, and accomplishing such destruction, seemed to be arrows sent forth from the hand of God. ¶ *And scattered them.* Herder refers this to the lightnings; De Wette, to the enemies of the

out lightnings, and discomfited them.

15 Then [q] the channels of waters were seen, and the foundations of the world were discovered at thy rebuke, O LORD, at the blast of the breath of thy nostrils.

16 He sent from above, he took me, he drew me out of [1] many waters.

17 He delivered me from my strong enemy, and from them which hated me: for they were too strong for me.

q Psa. cvi. 9.

1 Or, *great*.

psalmist. The latter seems to be the more correct interpretation, though the enemies of the psalmist are not here particularly specified. They seem, however, to have been in his eye throughout the psalm, for it was the victory achieved over them by the Divine interposition that he was celebrating throughout the poem. ¶ *And he shot out lightnings.* As arrows; or, as from a bow. ¶ *And discomfited them.* Literally to impel, to drive; then, to put in commotion or consternation. The allusion is to an army whose order is *disturbed*, or which is thrown into confusion, and which is, therefore, easily conquered. The idea is that David achieved a victory over all his enemies, *as if* God had scattered them by a storm and tempest.

15. *Then the channels of waters were seen.* In 2 Sam. xxii. 16 this is, "And the channels of the sea appeared." The idea is that, by the driving of the storm and tempest, the waters were driven on heaps, leaving the bottom bare. In the place before us the word used, "waters"—מַיִם, *mayim*—would denote waters of any kind—seas, lakes, rivers; in the corresponding place in 2 Samuel, the word used—יָם, *Yâm*—denotes, properly, the sea or the ocean. The word rendered *channels* means a pipe or tube; then a channel, or bed of a brook or stream, Isa. viii. 7; Ezek. xxxii. 6; and then the bottom of the sea or of a river. The allusion is to the effect of a violent wind, driving the waters on heaps, and seeming to leave the bed or channel bare. ¶ *The foundations of the world were discovered.* Were laid open; were manifested or revealed. Men seemed to be able to look down into the depths, and to see the very foundations on which the earth rests. The world is often represented as resting on a foundation, Ps. cii. 25; Isa. xlviii. 13; Zech. xii. 1; Prov. viii. 29; see Notes on Job xxxviii. 4. ¶ *At thy rebuke.* At the expression of his anger or displeasure; as if God, in the fury of the tempest, was expressing his indignation and wrath. ¶ *At the blast of the breath of thy nostrils.* At the breathing forth of anger, as it were, from his nostrils. See Notes on ver. 8.

16. *He sent from above.* He interposed to save me. All these manifestations of the Divine interposition were from above, or from heaven; all came from God. ¶ *He took me.* He took hold on me; he rescued me. ¶ *He drew me out of many waters.* Marg., *great waters*. Waters are often expressive of calamity and trouble, Ps. xlvi. 3; lxix. 1; lxxiii. 10; cxxiv. 4, 5. The meaning here is, that God had rescued him out of the many troubles and dangers that encompassed him, as if he had fallen into the sea and was in danger of perishing.

17. *He delivered me from my strong enemy.* The enemy that had more power than I had, and that was likely to overcome me. It is probable that the allusion here in the mind of the psalmist would be particularly to Saul. ¶ *And from them which hated me.* From all who hated and persecuted me, in the time of Saul, and ever onward during my life. ¶ *For they were too strong for me.* I had no power to resist them, and when I was about to sink under their opposition and malice, God interposed and rescued me. David, valiant and bold

18 They prevented me in the day of my calamity: but [r] the LORD was my stay.
19 He brought me forth also into a large place: he delivered me, because he delighted in me.
20 The LORD rewarded [s] me according to my righteousness; according to the cleanness of my hands hath he recompensed me.
21 For I have kept the ways of the LORD, and have not wickedly departed from my God.
22 For all his judgments *were* before me, and I did not put away his statutes from me.

r 1 Sam. xxx. 6; Psa. iii. 1—5.

s 1 Sam. xxiv. 17, 20.

as he was as a warrior, was not ashamed, in the review of his life, to admit that he owed his preservation not to his own courage and skill in war, but to God; that his enemies were superior to himself in power; and that if God had not interposed he would have been crushed and destroyed. No man dishonours himself by acknowledging that he owes his success in the world to the Divine interposition.

18. *They prevented me.* They anticipated me, or went before me. See Notes on ver. 5. The idea here is that his enemies came before him, or intercepted his way. They were in his path, ready to destroy him. ¶ *In the day of my calamity.* In the day to which I now look back as the time of my peculiar trial. ¶ *But the* LORD *was my stay.* My support, or prop. That is, the Lord upheld me, and kept me from falling.

19. *He brought me forth also into a large place.* Instead of being hemmed in by enemies, and straitened in my troubles, so that I seemed to have no room to move, he brought me into a place where I had ample room, and where I could act freely. Comp. Notes on Ps. iv. 1. ¶ *He delivered me.* He rescued me from my enemies and my troubles. ¶ *Because he delighted in me.* He saw that my cause was just, and he had favour towards me.

20. *The* LORD *rewarded me according to my righteousness.* That is, he saw that I did not deserve the treatment which I received from my enemies, and therefore he interposed to save me. Comp. Notes on Ps. xvii. 3. ¶ *According to the cleanness of my hands.* So far as my fellow-men are concerned. I have done *them* no wrong. ¶ *Hath he recompensed me.* By rescuing me from the power of my enemies. It is not inconsistent with proper views of piety—with true humility before God—to feel and to say, that so far as our fellow-men are concerned, we have not deserved ill-treatment at their hands; and, when we are delivered from their power, it is not improper to say and to feel that the interposition in the case has been according to justice and to truth.

21. *For I have kept the ways of the* LORD. I have obeyed his laws. I have not so violated the laws which God has given to regulate my conduct with my fellow-men as to deserve to be treated by them as a guilty man. ¶ *And have not wickedly departed from my God.* "I have not been a sinner from my God;"—an apostate; an open violator of his law. The treatment which I have received, though it would be justly rendered to an open violator of law, is not that which I have merited from the hand of man.

22. *For all his judgments.* All his statutes, ordinances, laws. The word *judgment* is commonly used in this sense in the Scriptures, as referring to that which God has *judged* or determined to be right. ¶ Were *before me.* That is, I acted in view of them, or as having them to guide me. They were constantly before my eyes, and I regulated my conduct in accordance with their requirements. ¶ *And I did not put away his statutes from me.* I did not reject them as the guide of my conduct.

23 I was also upright [1] before
him, and I kept myself from mine
[t] iniquity.
24 Therefore hath the LORD
recompensed me according to
my righteousness, according to
the cleanness of my hands [2] in
his eyesight.
25 With the merciful thou wilt
show thyself merciful; with an

[1] *with.* [t] Psa. xxxvii. 27.

[2] *before his eyes.*

23. *I was also upright before him.* Marg., *with.* The meaning is that he was upright in his sight. The word rendered *upright* is the same which in Job i. 1 is rendered *perfect.* See Notes on that passage. ¶ *And I kept myself from mine iniquity.* From the iniquity to which I was *prone* or *inclined.* This is an acknowledgment that he *was* prone to sin, or that if he had acted out his natural character he would have indulged in sin—perhaps such sins as had been charged upon him. But he here says that, with this natural proneness to sin, he had restrained himself, and had *not* been deserving of the treatment which he had received. This is one of those incidental remarks which often occur in the Scriptures which recognise the doctrine of depravity, or the fact that the heart, even when most restrained, is by nature inclined to sin. If this psalm was composed in the latter part of the life of David (see the introd.), then this must mean either (*a*) that in the review of his life he felt it had been his general and habitual aim to check his natural inclination to sin; or (*b*) that at the particular periods referred to in the psalm, when God had so wonderfully interposed in his behalf, he felt that this had been his aim, and that he might now regard that as a reason why God had interposed in his behalf. It is, however, painfully certain that at some periods of his life—as in the matter of Uriah—he *did* give indulgence to some of the most corrupt inclinations of the human heart, and that, in acting out these corrupt propensities, he was guilty of crimes which have for ever dimmed the lustre of his name and stained his memory. These painful facts, however, are not inconsistent with the statement that in his general character he *did* restrain these corrupt propensities, and *did* "keep himself from his iniquity." So, in the review of our own lives, if we are truly the friends of God, while we may be painfully conscious that we have often given indulgence to the corrupt propensities of our natures,—over which, if we are truly the children of God, we shall have repented,—we may still find evidence that, as the great and habitual rule of life, we *have* restrained those passions, and *have* "kept ourselves" from the particular forms of sin to which our hearts were prone.

22. *Therefore hath the* LORD *recompensed me.* By delivering me from my enemies. The Divine interpositions in his behalf had been of the nature of a *reward* or *recompense.* ¶ *According to my righteousness.* As if I were righteous; or, his acts of intervention have been such as are appropriate to a righteous life. The psalmist does not say that it was *on account* of his righteousness as if he had *merited* the favour of God, but that the interpositions in his behalf had been such as to show that God regarded him as righteous. ¶ *According to the cleanness of my hands.* See Notes on ver. 20. ¶ *In his eyesight.* Marg., as in Heb., *before his eyes.* The idea is that God *saw* that he was upright.

25. *With the merciful.* From the particular statement respecting the Divine dealings with himself the psalmist now passes to a general statement (suggested by what God had done for him) in regard to the general principles of the Divine administration. That general statement is, that *God deals with men according to their character;* or, that he will adapt his providential dealings to the conduct of men. They will find him to be such towards them as they have

upright man thou wilt show thyself upright;
26 With the pure thou wilt show thyself pure; and with the froward [u] thou wilt [1] show thyself froward.
27 For thou wilt save the

u Prov. iii. 34. 1 Or, *wrestle.*

shown themselves to be towards him. The word *merciful* refers to one who is disposed to show kindness or compassion to those who are guilty, or to those who injure or wrong us. ¶ *Thou wilt show thyself merciful.* Thou wilt evince towards him the same character which he shows to others. It is in accordance with this that the Saviour teaches us to pray, "And forgive us our debts, as we forgive our debtors," Matt. vi. 12. And in accordance also with this he said, "For if ye forgive men their trespasses, your heavenly Father will also forgive you: but if ye forgive not men their trespasses, neither will your Father forgive your trespasses," Matt. vi. 14, 15. ¶ *With an upright man.* Literally, a perfect man. See Job i. 1, where the same word is used in the original, and rendered *perfect.* The idea is that of a man who is *consistent,* or whose character is complete in all its parts. See Notes on Job i. 1. ¶ *Thou wilt show thyself upright.* Thou wilt deal with him according to his character. As he is faithful and just, so will he find that he has to do with a God who is faithful and just.

26. *With the pure.* Those who are pure in their thoughts, their motives, their conduct. ¶ *Thou wilt show thyself pure.* They will find that they have to deal with a God who is himself pure; who loves purity, and who will accompany it with appropriate rewards wherever it is found. ¶ *And with the froward.* The word here used—עִקֵּשׁ, *ikkaish*—means properly *perverse;* a man of a perverse and wicked mind. It is derived from a verb—עָקַשׁ, *akash*—which means, *to turn the wrong way, to wrest, to pervert.* It would be applicable to a man who perverts or wrests the words of others from their true meaning; who prevaricates or is deceitful in his own conduct; who is not straightforward in his dealings; who takes advantage of circumstances to impose on others, and to promote his own ends; who is sour, harsh, crabbed, unaccommodating, unyielding, unkind. It is rendered *perverse* in Deut. xxxii. 5; Prov. viii. 8; xix. 1; xxviii. 6; *froward* here, and in 2 Sam. xxii. 27; Ps. ci. 4; Prov. xi. 20; xvii. 20; xxii. 5; and *crooked* in Prov. ii. 15. The word does not occur elsewhere in the Old Testament. ¶ *Thou wilt show thyself froward.* Marg., *wrestle.* In the corresponding place in 2 Sam. xxii. 27 it is rendered, "Thou wilt show thyself unsavory;" though the same word is used in the original. In the margin in that place, as here, the word is *wrestle.* The original word in each place—פָּתַל, *pathal*—means *to twist, to twine, to spin;* and then, to be twisted; to be crooked, crafty, deceitful. In the form of the word which occurs here (Hithpa), it means, *to show oneself crooked, crafty, perverse.* (Gesenius, *Lex.*) It cannot mean here that God would assume such a character, or that he would *be* crooked, crafty, perverse in his dealings with men; for no one can suppose that the psalmist meant to ascribe such a character to God; but the meaning plainly is, that God would deal with the man referred to according to his real character: instead of finding that God would deal with them *as if* they were pure, and righteous, and merciful, such men would find that he deals with them *as they are,*—as perverse, crooked, wicked.

27. *For thou wilt save the afflicted people.* From the particular tokens of Divine favour towards himself in affliction and trouble, the psalmist now draws the general inference that this was the character of God, and that others in affliction might hope for his interposition as he had done.

afflicted people; but wilt bring
down high [v] looks.
28 For thou wilt light my
[1] candle; [w] the LORD my God
will enlighten my darkness.

v Prov. vi. 16, 17. [1] Or, *lamp*, Job xxix. 3.

29 For by thee I have [2] run
through a troop; and by my God
have I leaped over a wall.
30 *As for* God, his way *is* perfect: the word of the LORD is

w Prov. xx. 27. [2] *broken*.

¶ *But wilt bring down high looks.* Another general inference probably derived from the dealings of God with the proud and haughty foes of the psalmist. As God had humbled them, so he infers that he would deal with others in the same way. "High looks" are indicative of pride and haughtiness. Comp. Ps. ci. 5; Prov. vi. 17; xxi. 4; Isa. ii. 11 (Notes); x. 12; Dan. vii. 20.

28. *For thou wilt light my candle.* Marg., *lamp.* The word *lamp* best expresses the idea. In the Scriptures *light* is an image of prosperity, success, happiness, holiness, as darkness is the image of the opposite. See Notes on Job xxix. 2, 3; comp. also Job xviii. 6; xxi. 17; Prov. xx. 27; xxiv. 20; Ps. cxix. 105; cxxxii. 17; Isa. lxii. 1. The meaning here is, that the psalmist felt assured that God would give him prosperity, *as if* his lamp were kept constantly burning in his dwelling. ¶ *The* LORD *my God will enlighten my darkness.* Will shed light on my path, which would otherwise be dark:—will impart light to my understanding; will put peace and joy in my heart; will crown me with his favour. Comp. Notes on Ps. iv. 6.

29. *For by thee I have run through a troop.* Marg., *broken.* The word *troop* here refers to bands of soldiers, or hosts of enemies. The word rendered *run through* means properly to *run;* and then, as here, to run or rush upon in a hostile sense; to rush with violence upon one. The idea here is that he had been enabled to rush with violence upon his armed opposers; that is, to overcome them, and to secure a victory. The allusion is to the wars in which he had been engaged. Comp. cxv. 1. ¶ *And by my God.* By the help derived from God. ¶ *Have I leaped over a wall.* Have I been delivered, as if I had leaped over a wall when I was besieged; or, I have been able to scale the walls of an enemy, and to secure a victory. The probability is that the latter is the true idea, and that he refers to his successful attacks on the fortified towns of his enemies. The general idea is, that all his victories were to be traced to God.

30. As for *God.* The declaration in this verse is suggested by the facts narrated in the previous verses. The contemplation of those facts leads the thoughts of the author of the psalm up to the Great Source of all these blessings, and to these general reflections on his character. "As for God," that is, in respect to that Great Being, who has delivered *me*, his ways are all perfect; his word is tried; he is a shield to all those who trust in him. ¶ *His way is perfect.* That is, his doings are perfect; his methods of administration are perfect; his government is perfect. There is nothing wanting, nothing defective, nothing redundant, in what he does. On the word *perfect*, see Notes on Job i. 1. ¶ *The word of the* LORD *is tried.* Marg., *refined.* The idea is, that his word had been tested as silver or any other metal is in the fire. The psalmist had confided in him, and had found him faithful to all his promises. Compare Notes on Ps. xii. 6. In a larger sense, using the phrase the "word of the Lord" as denoting the revelation which God has made to mankind in the volume of revealed truth, it has been abundantly tested or tried, and it still stands. It has been tested by the friends of God, and has been found to be all that it promised to be for support and consolation in trial; it has been tested by the changes which have occurred in

[1] tried; [x] he *is* a buckler [y] to all those that trust in him.

31 For who *is* God save the LORD? or who *is* a rock save our God.

32 *It is* God [z] that girdeth me with strength, and maketh my way perfect.

33 He maketh my feet like hinds' *feet*, and setteth me upon my high places.

[1] *refined.* *x* Psa. xii. 6. *y* Prov. xxx. 5. *z* 2 Cor. iii. 5.

the progress of human affairs, and has been found fitted to meet all those changes; it has been tested by the advances which have been made in science, in literature, in civilization, and in the arts, and it has shown itself to be fitted to every stage of advance in society; it has been tested by the efforts which men have made to destroy it, and has survived all those efforts. It is settled that it will survive all the revolutions of kingdoms and all the changes of dynasties; that it will be able to meet all the attacks which shall be made upon it by its enemies; and that it will be an unfailing source of light and comfort to all future ages. If persecution could crush it, it would have been crushed long ago; if ridicule could drive it from the world, it would have been driven away long ago; if argument, as urged by powerful intellect, and by learning, combined with intense hatred, could destroy it, it would have been destroyed long ago; and if it is not fitted to impart consolation to the afflicted, to wipe away the tears of mourners, and to uphold the soul in death, that would have been demonstrated long ago. In all these methods it has been "tried," and as the result of all, it has been proved as the only certain fact, in regard to a *book* as connected with the future—that the Bible will go down accredited as a revelation from God to the end of the world. ¶ *He is a buckler.* Or, a *shield*, for so the original word means. See Notes on Ps. iii. 3.

31. *For who* is *God save the* LORD? Who is God except Jehovah? The idea is, that no other being has evinced the power, the wisdom, and the goodness which properly belong to the true God; or, that the things which are implied in the true nature of *God* are found in no other being. ¶ *Or who* is *a rock save our God?* See ver. 2. There is no one who can furnish such safety or defence; no one under whose protection we can be secure in danger. Comp. Deut. xxxii. 31.

32. It is *God that girdeth me with strength.* Who gives me strength. The word *girdeth* contains an allusion to the mode of dress among the orientals, the long flowing robe, which was *girded up* when they ran or laboured, that it might not impede them; and, probably, with the additional idea that girding the loins contributed to strength. It is a common custom now for men who run a race, or leap, or engage in a strife of pugilism, to gird or bind up their loins. See Notes on Job xl. 7; and on Matt. v. 38—41. ¶ *And maketh my way perfect.* Gives me complete success in my undertakings; or, enables me so to carry them out that none of them fail.

33. *He maketh my feet like hinds'* feet. So Habakkuk iii. 19, "He will make my feet like hinds' feet, and he will make me to walk upon mine high places." The *hind* is the female deer, remarkable for fleetness or swiftness. The meaning here is, that God had made him alert or active, enabling him to pursue a flying enemy, or to escape from a swift-running foe. ¶ *And setteth me upon my high places.* Places of safety or refuge. The idea is, that God had given him security, or had rendered him safe from danger. Comp. Deut. xxxii. 13. Swiftness of foot, or ability to escape from, or to pursue an enemy, was regarded as of great value in ancient warfare. Achilles, according to the descriptions of

34 He teacheth my hands to war, so that a bow of steel is broken by mine arms.

35 Thou hast also given me the shield of thy salvation: and thy right hand hath holden me up, and thy [1] gentleness hath made me great.

36 Thou hast enlarged my steps under me, that my [2] feet did not [a] slip.

37 I have pursued mine enemies, and overtaken them: neither did I turn again till they were consumed.

[1] Or, *with thy meekness thou hast multiplied me.* [2] *ancles.* *a* Prov. iv. 12.

Homer, was remarkable for it. Comp. 2 Sam. ii. 18; 1 Chron. xii. 8.

34. *He teacheth my hands to war.* Comp. Ps. cxliv. 1. The skill which David had in the use of the bow, the sword, or the spear,—all of which depends on the hands,—he ascribes entirely to God. ¶ *So that a bow of steel is broken by mine arms.* This is mentioned as an instance of extraordinary strength, as if he were able to *break* a bow made of metal. The original word rendered *steel* means properly *brass.* Wood was doubtless first used in constructing the bow, but metals came afterwards to be employed, and brass would naturally be used before the manufacture of steel was discovered. Rosenmüller *in loc.*

35. *Thou hast also given me the shield of thy salvation.* Thou hast saved me as with a shield; thou hast thrown thy shield before me in times of danger. See Notes on Ps. v. 12. ¶ *And thy right hand hath holden me up.* Thou hast sustained me when in danger of falling, as if thou hadst upheld me with thine own hand. ¶ *And thy gentleness hath made me great.* Marg., "or, *with thy meekness thou hast multiplied me.*" The word here rendered *gentleness*, evidently means here *favour, goodness, kindness.* It commonly means *humility, modesty,* as applied to men; as applied to God, it means *mildness, clemency, favour.* The idea is, that God had dealt with him in gentleness, kindness, clemency, and that to this fact alone he owed all his prosperity and success in life. It was not by any claim which he had on God; it was by no worth of his own; it was by no native strength or valour that he had been thus exalted, but it was wholly because God had dealt *kindly* with him, or had showed him *favour.* So all our success in life is to be traced to the *favour*—the *kindness*—of God.

36. *Thou hast enlarged my steps under me.* The idea here is, "Thou hast made room for my feet, so that I have been enabled to walk without hindrance or obstruction. So in Psalm xxxi. 8, "Thou hast set my feet in a large room." The idea is, that he was before straitened, compressed, hindered in his goings, but that now all obstacles had been taken out of the way, and he could walk freely. ¶ *That my feet did not slip.* Marg., *mine ancles.* The Hebrew word here rendered in the text *feet,* and in the margin *ancles,* means properly *a joint; small joint;* especially the *ancle.* The reference here is to the *ancle,* the joint that is so useful in walking, and that is so liable to be sprained or dislocated. The meaning is that he had been enabled to walk firmly; that he did not *limp.* Before, he had been like one whose ancles are weak or sprained; now he was able to tread firmly. The Divine favour given to him was *as if* God had given strength to a lame man to walk firmly.

37. *I have pursued mine enemies, and overtaken them.* He had not only routed them, but had had strength to pursue them; he had not only pursued them, but he had been enabled to come up to them. The idea is that of complete success and absolute triumph. ¶ *Neither did I turn again.* I was not driven back, nor was I weary and exhausted, and compelled to give over the pursuit. ¶ *Till they were consumed.* Till they were all either slain or made captive, so that

38 I have wounded them, that
they were not able to rise: [b] they
are fallen under my feet.
39 For thou hast girded me
with strength unto the battle:
thou hast [1] subdued under me
those that rose up against me.
40 Thou hast also given me
the necks of mine enemies, that
I might destroy them that hate
me.
41 They cried, but *there was*
none to save *them*: *even* unto the

b 2 Sam. v. 20. [1] *caused to bow.*

the hostile forces vanished. None of my enemies were left.

38. *I have wounded them*, etc. I have so weakened them—so entirely prostrated them—that they were not able to rally again. This does not refer so much to wounds inflicted on *individuals* in the hostile ranks as to the *entire* host or army. It was so weakened that it could not again be put in battle array. The idea is that of successful pursuit and conquest. ¶ *They are fallen under my feet.* I have completely trodden them down—a common mode of denoting entire victory, Ps. cxix. 118; Isa. xxv. 10; Lam. i. 15; Dan. viii. 13; Luke xxi. 24.

39. *For thou hast girded me with strength unto the battle.* See Notes on ver. 32. Comp. Job xii. 18; Prov. xxxi. 17. ¶ *Thou hast subdued under me.* Marg., as in Heb., *caused to bow.* That is, God had caused them to submit to him; he had enabled him to overcome them;—still acknowledging that all this was from God, and that the praise was due to Him, and not to the power of his own arm.

40. *Thou hast also given me the necks of mine enemies.* Their necks to tread upon, as the result of victory; or their necks to be subject to me, as the neck of the ox is to his owner. The phrase is sometimes used in this latter sense to denote subjection (comp. Jer. xxvii. 12); but it is more commonly, when applied to war, used in the former sense, as denoting complete triumph or conquest. It was not uncommon to trample on the necks of those who were overcome in battle. See Josh. x. 24; Ezek. xxi. 2; Gen. xlix. 8. The word used here—עֹרֶף, *oreph*—means properly *neck, nape*, the back of the neck; and hence, *to give the neck* means sometimes to turn the back, as in flight; and the phrase would admit of that meaning here. So Gesenius (*Lex.*) understands it. So also De Wette: "Thou turnest my enemies to flight." It seems to me, however, that the more probable interpretation is that of complete subjection,—as when the conqueror places his foot on the necks of his foes. This is confirmed by the next member of the sentence, where the psalmist speaks of the complete *destruction* of those who hated him. ¶ *That I might destroy them that hate me.* That have pursued and persecuted me in this manner. The idea is that of utterly overcoming them; of putting an end to their power, and to their ability to injure him.

41. *They cried.* They cried out for help, for mercy, for life. In modern language, "they begged for quarter." They acknowledged that they were vanquished, and entreated that their lives might be spared. ¶ *But* there was *none to save* them. To preserve their lives. No help appeared from their own countrymen; they found no mercy in me or my followers; and God did not interpose to deliver them. ¶ Even *unto the* LORD. As a last resort. Men appeal to everything else for help before they will appeal to God; often when they come to him it is by constraint, and not willingly; if the danger should leave them, they would cease to call upon him. Hence, as there is no real sincerity in their calling upon God—no real regard for his honour or his commands—their cries are not heard, and they perish. The course of things with a sinner, however, is often such that, despairing of salva-

LORD, but [c] he answered them
not.
42 Then did I beat them small
as the dust before the wind; I
did cast them out as the dirt in
the streets.
43 Thou hast delivered me
from the strivings of the people;
and thou hast made me the head

c Jer. xi. 11.

tion in any other way, and seeing that this is the only true way, he comes with a heart broken, contrite, penitent, and then God never turns away from the cry. No sinner, though *as* a last resort, who comes to God in *real* sincerity, will ever be rejected. ¶ *But he answered them not.* He did not put forth his power to save them from my sword; to keep them alive when they were thus vanquished. Had they cried unto him *to save their souls,* he would undoubtedly have done it; but their cry was for life—for the Divine help to save them from the sword of the conqueror. There might have been many reasons why God should not interpose to save them from the regular consequences of valour when they had been in the wrong and had begun the war; but there would have been no reason why he should not interpose if they had called upon him to save them from their sins. There may be many reasons why God should not save sinners from the *temporal* judgments due to their sins—the intemperate from the diseases, the poverty, and the wretchedness consequent on that vice,—or the licentious from the woes and sorrows caused by such a course of life; but there is no reason, in any case, why God should not save from the eternal consequences of sin, if the sinner cries sincerely and earnestly for mercy.

42. *Then did I beat them small as the dust before the wind.* As the fine dust is driven by the wind, so they fled before me. There could be no more striking illustration of a discomfited army flying before a conqueror. De Wette says correctly that the idea is, "I beat them small, and scattered them as dust before the wind." ¶ *I did cast them out as the dirt in the streets.* In the corresponding place in 2 Sam. xxii. 43, this is, "I did stamp them as the mire of the street, and did spread them abroad." The idea in the place before us is, that he *poured them out,* for so the Hebrew word means, as the dirt or mire in the streets. As that is trodden on, or trampled down, so they, instead of being marshalled for battle, were wholly disorganized, scattered, and left to be trodden down, as the most worthless object is. A similar image occurs in Isa. x. 6, where God is speaking of Sennacherib: "I will send him against an hypocritical nation......to tread them down like the mire of the streets."

43. *Thou hast delivered me from the strivings of the people.* From the *contentions* of the people; or, from the efforts which they have made to overcome and subdue me. The allusion is to the efforts made by the people, under the guidance of their leaders. It is not "strivings" *among* his own followers, but the efforts, the strivings, the contentions of his enemies, who endeavoured to obtain the mastery over him, and to subdue him. ¶ *Thou hast made me the head of the heathen.* The head of the *nations;* that is, the nations round about. In other words, he had, by the Divine aid, brought them into subjection to him, or so subdued them that they became tributary to him. The word "*heathen*" with us expresses an idea which is not necessarily connected with the original word. That word is simply *nations*—גּוֹיִם, *goim.* It is true that those nations *were* heathens in the present sense of the term, but that idea is not necessarily connected with the *word.* The meaning is, that surrounding *nations* had been made subject to him; or that he had been made to rule over them. David, in fact, thus brought the surrounding

of the heathen: a [d] people *whom* I have not known shall serve me.

44 [1] As soon as they hear of me, they shall obey me: the [2] strangers shall [3] submit themselves unto me.

d Isa. lv. 5.
[1] *At the hearing of the ear.*
[2] *sons of the stranger.*
[3] *lie,* or, *yield feigned obedience.*

people under subjection to him, and made them tributary. In 2 Sam. viii. he is said to have subdued Philistia, and Moab, and Syria, and Edom, in all of which countries he put "garrisons," and all of which he made tributary to himself. ¶ *A people whom I have not known shall serve me.* People that I had not before heard of. This is the language of confident faith that his kingdom would be still further extended, so as to embrace nations before unknown to him. His past victories, and the fact that his kingdom had been so established and was already so extended, justified the expectation that it would be still further enlarged; that the fame of his conquests would reach other nations, and that they would willingly yield themselves to him. After the victories which he had achieved, as celebrated in this psalm, that might be expected to follow as a matter of course. It is the triumphant exultation of a conqueror, and it seems to have been his expectation, not that his successors would extend the empire, but that other nations would become voluntarily subject to him.

44. *As soon as they hear of me, they shall obey me.* Marg., as in Heb., *At the hearing of the ear.* That is, their submission will be prompt and immediate. The fame of my victories will be such as to render resistance hopeless; my fame, as at the head of a mighty empire, will be such as to lead them to desire my friendship and protection. ¶ *The strangers.* Marg., as in Hebrew, *The sons of the stranger.* The word refers to *foreigners,* to those of other nations. His name and deeds would inspire such respect, or create such a dread of his power, that they would be glad to seek his friendship, and would readily submit to his dominion. ¶ *Shall submit themselves unto me.* Marg., *yield feigned obedience.* The Hebrew word here used—כָּחַשׁ, *chahash*—means properly *to lie, to speak lies;* then, to deceive, or disappoint; then, to feign, to flatter, to play the hypocrite. It is manifestly used in this sense here, as referring to those who, awed by the terror of his name and power, would come and profess subjection to him as a conqueror. Yet the use of the word here implies that he was aware that, in many cases, this would be only a *feigned* submission, or that the homage would be hypocritical; homage inspired by terror, not by love. Undoubtedly much of the professed subjection of conquered nations is of this kind, and it would be well if all conquerors understood this as David did. He accepted, indeed, the acquiescence and the submission, but he understood the cause; and this knowledge would only tend to make his throne more secure, as it would save him from putting confidence or trust where there was no certainty that it would be well placed. Towards David as a sovereign there was much real loyalty, but there was also much professed allegiance that was false and hollow; allegiance which would endure only while his power lasted, and which would only wait for an opportunity to throw off the yoke. In respect to God, also, there are not a few who "*feignedly* submit" to him, or who yield feigned obedience. They, too, are awed by his power. They know that he is able to destroy. They see the tokens of his greatness and majesty, and they come and profess submission to him—a submission founded on terror, not on love; a submission which would cease at once could they be assured of safety if

45 The strangers shall fade away, and be afraid out of their close places.
46 The LORD liveth: and blessed *be* my rock; and let the God of my salvation be exalted.
47 *It is* God that [1] avengeth

[1] *giveth avengements for me.*

they should renounce their allegiance to him. And as David was not ignorant of the fact that not a little of the professed submission to him was false and feigned,—so, in a much higher sense—in a much more accurate manner—God is aware of the fact that many who profess to be subject to him are subject in profession only; that if they could do it with safety, they would throw off the very appearance of loyalty, and carry out in reality what exists in their hearts. It must have been sad for David to reflect how greatly the number of his professed subjects might have been diminished, if none had been retained but those who truly loved his reign, and respected him as a sovereign; it is sad to reflect how greatly the number of the professed friends of God would be diminished, if all those should withdraw who have yielded only feigned obedience to him! Yet the Church would be the better and the stronger for it.

45. *The strangers shall fade away.* Heb., "The sons of the stranger." That is, foreigners. The word rendered *fade away*—נָבֵל, *nabal*—means properly to wilt, wither, fall away, as applicable to flowers, leaves, or plants, Ps. i. 3; xxxvii. 2; Isa. i. 30; xxviii. 1. Here it means that those foreign nations would diminish in numbers and in power, until they should wholly disappear. The idea is, that all his foes would vanish, and that he and his kingdom would be left in peace. ¶ *And be afraid out of their close places.* The word rendered *be afraid* means *to tremble*—as those do who are in fear. The word rendered *close places* means places that are shut up or enclosed, as fortified cities or fortresses. The reference is to their places of retreat, towns, castles, fortresses. The meaning is, that they would find such places to be no security, and would *tremble out of them;* that is, they would flee out of them in consternation and alarm. The general thought is that of ultimate complete security for himself and his kingdom, or entire deliverance from all his enemies.

46. *The* LORD *liveth.* Jehovah—the name here used—is often described as the *living God* in contradistinction to idols, who are represented as without life, Deut. v. 26; Josh iii. 10; 2 Kings xix. 4; Ps. xlii. 2; Matt. xvi. 16; 1 Thess. i. 9. Comp. Ps. cxv. 5; cxxxv. 16. It is probably in allusion to this idea that the phrase "The Lord *liveth*" is used here. It is a joyful exclamation in view of all that God had done; of all the deliverances which he had wrought for the author of the psalm. In the remembrance of all this the psalmist says that God had shown himself to be the *living*, that is, the *true* God. These interpositions furnished abundant demonstration that Jehovah *existed,* and that he was worthy of adoration and praise *as* the true God. So, in view of mercy and salvation, the heart of the redeemed exultingly exclaims, "The Lord lives,—there *is* a living God." ¶ *And blessed* be *my Rock.* God, who has shown himself to be a refuge and a protector. See Notes on ver. 2. ¶ *And let the God of my salvation be exalted.* The God who has saved me from my enemies. Let him be *exalted,* be praised, be honoured, be adored. Let his name be exalted above all idol gods; above all the creatures that he has made. The wish is, that His name might be made *prominent;* that all creatures might praise and honour Him.

47. It is *God that avengeth me.* Marg., *giveth avengements for me.* The marginal reading is a literal translation of the Hebrew. The meaning is, that God had punished

me, and [1] subdueth the people under me.

48 He delivereth me from mine enemies; yea, thou liftest me up above those that rise up against me: thou hast delivered me from the [2] violent man.

49 Therefore will I [3] give thanks unto thee, O LORD, among the heathen, and sing praises unto thy name.

[1] *destroyeth.*

[2] *man of violence.* [3] Or, *confess.*

---

the enemies of the author of the psalm for all the wrongs which they had done to him. Comp. Rom. xii. 19. ¶ *And subdueth the people under me.* Marg., *destroyeth.* The idea is that he had *subdued* the nations so that they became obedient to him. The primary notion of the word used here—from דָּבַר, *dabar*—is to set in a row; to range in order; to connect; to lead; to guide;—then, to reduce to order; to subdue. This God had done in respect to the nations. Instead of being rebellious and tumultuous, God had reduced them to obedience, and had thus set him over a kingdom where all were subject to order and to law.

48. *He delivereth me from mine enemies.* From all my foes. ¶ *Yea, thou liftest me up above those that rise up against me.* So that I triumph over them. Instead of being subdued by them, and trampled under their feet, I am exalted, and they are humbled. ¶ *Thou hast delivered me from the violent man.* Marg., as in Heb., *man of violence;* the man characterised by injustice and wrong; the man who endeavoured to overcome and subdue me by force and arms. There is probably a special allusion here by the psalmist to Saul as his great enemy, but perhaps he had also in his eye others of the same kind, and the meaning may be that he had been delivered from *all* of that class of men.

49. *Therefore will I give thanks unto thee.* Marg., *confess.* The Hebrew word—יָדָה, *yadah*—in the form used here, means properly *to profess, to confess, to acknowledge;* then especially to acknowledge or recognise blessings and favours; in other words, to give thanks, to praise. The idea here is that he would make a public *acknowledgment* of those blessings which he had received; or that he would cause the remembrance of them to be celebrated among the nations. ¶ *Among the heathen.* Among the *nations.* See Notes on ver. 43. The meaning here is, that he would cause these blessings to be remembered by making a record of them in this song of praise; a song that would be used not only in his own age and in his own country, but also among other nations, and in other times. He would do all in his power to make the knowledge of these favours, and these proofs of the existence of the true God, known abroad and transmitted to other times. The apostle Paul uses this language (Rom. xv. 9) as expressing properly the fact that the knowledge of God was to be communicated to the "*Gentiles:*" "As it is written, For this cause will I confess to thee among the *Gentiles.*" The word "heathen" or *nations,* in the passage before us, corresponds precisely with the meaning of the word *Gentiles;* and Paul has used the language of the psalm legitimately and properly as showing that it was a doctrine of the Old Testament that the truths of religion were not to be confined to the Jews, but were to be made known to other nations. ¶ *And sing praises unto thy name.* Unto thee;—the *name* often being used to denote the person. The meaning is, that he would cause the praises of God to be celebrated among foreign or heathen nations, as the result of what God had done for him. Far, probably, very far beyond what David anticipated when he penned this psalm, this has been done. The psalm itself has been chanted by mil-

50 Great deliverance giveth he to his king; and showeth mercy to his anointed, to David, and to his seed for [f] evermore.

f Rom. xi. 29.

lions who were not in existence, and in lands of which the psalmist had no knowledge; and, connected as it has been with the other psalms in Christian worship, it has contributed in an eminent degree to extend the praises of God far in the earth, and to transmit the knowledge of him to generations as they succeeded one another. What David anticipated is, moreover, as yet only in the progress of fulfilment. Millions not yet born will make use of the psalm, as millions have done before, as the medium of praise to God; and down to the most distant times this sacred song, in connexion with the others in the Book of Psalms, will contribute to make God known in the earth, and to secure for him the praises of mankind.

50. *Great deliverance giveth he to his king.* To David, as king. The word in the original, which is rendered "deliverance," means properly *salvation,* and is here in the plural number. It refers not to *one* act of Divine interposition, but to the *many* acts (referred to in the psalm) in which God had interposed to save him from danger and from death. The phrase "to *his* king" refers to the fact that God had appointed him to reign, and to administer the government for *him.* He did not reign on his own account, but he reigned for God, and with a view to do his will. ¶ *And showeth mercy to his anointed.* To him who had been set apart to the kingly office by a solemn act of anointing. Comp. 1 Sam. xvi. 13; 2 Sam. ii. 4–7; v. 3, 17; xii. 7; comp. 2 Kings ix. 3, 6, 12. It is in allusion to this custom that the Messiah is called the *Anointed,* or the *Christ.* See Notes on Matt. i. 1. ¶ *To David, and to his seed.* To his descendants, or posterity. There is an undoubted reference here to the promises made to David in regard to his successors on the throne. See 2 Sam. vii. 12–16, 25, 26, and Ps. lxxxix. 19–37. ¶ *For evermore.* This expresses the confident expectation of David that the government would remain in his family to the latest times. This expectation was founded on such promises as that in 2 Sam. vii. 12, 13: "I will set up thy seed after thee, which shall proceed out of thy bowels, and I will establish his kingdom; he shall build an house for my name, and I will establish the throne of his kingdom for ever." Also 2 Sam. vii. 16: "And thine house and thy kingdom shall be established for ever before thee; thy throne shall be established for ever." See also Ps. lxxxix. 36: "His seed shall endure for ever, and his throne as the sun before me." The perpetuity of this kingdom is found, in fact, in the reign of the Messiah, a descendant of David, in whose eternal reign these promises will receive an ample fulfilment. See Isa. ix. 7. Comp. Luke i. 32, 33. The temporal reign passed wholly away in the process of time from the descendants of David; the spiritual reign is perpetual in the Messiah. How far *David* understood this it is not important to inquire, and it would be impossible to determine. It is sufficient for the proper understanding of the place to remember (*a*) that there will have been a strict fulfilment of the promise, according to the full import of the language, in the Messiah, the Son of David; and (*b*) that, however this may have been understood by David who recorded the promise, the real author of the promise was the Holy Spirit, and that the real meaning of the promise, as thus recorded, was that it should be fulfilled as it has been. In this, as in all other cases, the inquiry to be made in interpreting the language is not how the sacred penman understood it, but what was meant by the real author, the Spirit of God,—and whe-

ther the prediction, according to that meaning, has been fulfilled. When a man employs an amanuensis, the inquiry in regard to what is written is not how the amanuensis understood it, but how he who dictated what was written intended it should be understood. Applying this principle, the prediction here and elsewhere, in regard to the perpetuity of the reign of David and his posterity, has been, and is, fulfilled in the most ample manner. "Great David's greater Son" SHALL REIGN FOR EVER AND EVER.

PSALM XIX.

This very beautiful psalm is designed to illustrate the superiority of revealed truth above the light of nature in showing the character and perfections of God. In doing this, there is no attempt in the psalm, as there should be none on our part in explaining it, to *undervalue* or *disparage* the truths about God revealed by nature. All that could now be said in regard to the works of creation, as illustrating the Divine perfections, is really admitted by the psalmist (vers. 1-6); and yet this is placed in strong contrast with the revelations disclosed in the "law of the Lord," that is, in his revealed word (vers. 7-11). The revelations of nature, and the higher revelation by inspiration, belong to the same system of religion, and are alike designed to illustrate the being, the perfections, and the government of God. The friend of religion should claim the one as well as the other; the defence of the Bible as a revelation from God should not lead us to disparage or undervalue the disclosures respecting God as made by nature. He who asserts that a revelation is necessary to mankind, and who maintains that the light of nature is not sufficient for the wants of man, should nevertheless concede all that can be known from the works of God about the Creator; should rejoice in all that truth; and should be willing that all should be learned that can be learned about God from his works. When all this is admitted, and all this learned, there will be still an ample field for the higher disclosures which revelation claims to make.

Nor did the psalmist apprehend that the revelations about God which are made in his works would be in *conflict* with those which are made in his word. He evidently felt, in looking at these works of creation, that he was learning truths which would in no manner contradict the higher truths communicated by revelation; that the investigation of the one might be pursued to any extent without showing that the other was needless, or bringing the truth of the other into peril.

This psalm consists properly of three parts: I. The revelation of God in his works, vers. 1—6. II. The higher and more glorious revelation of himself in his law, vers. 7—10. III. The bearing of these truths on the present character and conduct of the author, and consequently their adaptedness to produce the same effect on others, vers. 11—14;—(*a*) in *warning* men of the nature of sin, and thus keeping them from transgression, ver. 11; (*b*) in making them aware of the extent and depth of sin, and especially of secret faults, ver. 12; (*c*) in leading them to pray earnestly that they may be cleansed from secret faults, and be kept back or restrained from presumptuous sins, vers. 12, 13; (*d*) in leading them to pray earnestly that their words and thoughts may be made acceptable to God, ver. 14.

The psalm is said in the title to be "A Psalm of David;" and there is nothing in the psalm itself to create a doubt in regard to the correctness of this statement. It is impossible, however, to determine when, or in what circumstances, it was composed; for there are no internal marks which will fix it at any particular period of the life of the author. There is no allusion either to persecution or to triumph;—to private, domestic, or public life,—or to any of the known circumstances of the history of David. If a conjecture may be allowed, it would seem not improbable that it was composed in those calm periods of his history when he led a shepherd-life; when he had abundant time to contemplate the movements of the heavenly bodies by day and by night, and to meditate on them in contrast with the higher truths which God had made known in his law.

Rosenmüller conjectured at one time that the psalm was originally *two*, and that the two were afterwards united into one. De Wette also looked favourably on this supposition. Rosenmüller, however, subsequently saw occasion to retract

PSALM XIX.

To the chief Musician. A Psalm of David.

THE heavens [g] declare the glory
of God: and the firmament
showeth his handywork.
2 Day unto day uttereth

g Rom. i. 19, 20.

this, and to adopt the opinion that it was originally one composition. This is undoubtedly the correct idea, as appears not only from the fact that there is no evidence that these were *two* psalms, and from the general character and construction of the psalm, but from the fact that the conclusion (vers. 12—14) seems to be based on the contemplation of *all* the truth which God in any way makes known to the soul. On the supposition that the psalm is *one*, this is a proper termination of the whole composition. On the other supposition, no small part of the beauty of the psalm would be lost.

In respect to the meaning of the title, "To the chief Musician," see the introduction to Ps. iv.

1. *The heavens declare the glory of God.* They announce, proclaim, make known his glory. The word *heavens* here refers to the material heavens as they appear to the eye—the region of the sun, moon, and stars. The Hebrew word is used in the Scriptures uniformly in the plural number, though in our common translation the singular number is often used. Gen. i. 1, 8, 9, 14, 17, 20; vi. 17; vii. 11, 19, 23; *et sæpe.* The plural, however, is often retained, but without any special reason why it should be retained in one place rather than in another. Gen. ii. 1, 4; Deut. x. 14; Ezra ix. 6; Ps. ii. 4; viii. 1, 3; xviii. 13. The original idea may have been that there was one heaven above another—one in which the sun was placed, another in which the moon was placed, then the planets, the fixed stars, etc. Above all was supposed to be the place where God dwells. The word *glory* here means that which *constitutes* the glory or honour of God—his wisdom, power, skill, faithfulness, benevolence, as seen in the starry worlds above us, the silent, but solemn movements by day and by night. The idea is, that these convey to the mind a true impression of the greatness and majesty of God. The reference here is to these heavens as they appear to the naked eye, and as they are observed by all men. It may be added that the impression is far more solemn and grand when we take into the estimate the disclosures of the modern astronomy, and when we look at the heavens, not merely by the naked eye, but through the revelations of the telescope. ¶ *And the firmament.* See Notes on Daniel xii. 3. The word rendered *firmament*—רָקִיעַ, *râkia,* means properly an *expanse,*—that which is *spread out*—and is applied to the heavens as they appear to be spread out or expanded above us. The word occurs elsewhere in the following places, and is always rendered *firmament* in our common version, Gen. i. 6, 7 (twice), 8, 14, 15, 17, 20; Ps. cl. 1; Ezek. i. 22, 23, 25, 26; x. 1; Dan. xii. 3. The word *firmament*—that which is *firm* or fixed—is taken from the word used by the translators of the Septuagint, *στερέωμα,* from the idea that the heavens above us are a *solid concave.* In the Scriptures the stars are represented as placed in that expanse, so that if it should be rolled together as a tent is rolled up, they would fall down to the earth. See Notes on Isa. xxxiv. 4. The reference in the passage before us is to the heavens as they appear to be spread out over our heads, and in which the stars are fixed. ¶ *Showeth his handywork.* The heavens make known the work of his hands. The idea is that God had made those heavens by his own hands, and that the firmament, thus adorned with sun, and moon, and stars, showed the wisdom and skill with which it was done. Comp. Ps. viii. 3.

2. *Day unto day.* One day to another; or, each successive day. The day that is passing away proclaims the lesson which it had to

speech, and night unto night showeth knowledge.

3 *There is* no speech nor language, [1] *where* their voice is not heard.

[1] *without their voice heard,* or, *without* these *their voice is heard.*

convey from the movements of the heavens, about God; and thus the knowledge of God is accumulating as the time moves on. Each day has its own lesson in regard to the wisdom, the power, and the goodness of God, and that lesson is conveyed from one day to another. There is a perpetual testimony thus given to the wisdom and power of the Great Creator. ¶ *Uttereth speech.* The word here rendered *uttereth* means properly *to pour forth; to pour forth copiously as a fountain.* Comp. Prov. xviii. 4; i. 23; xv. 2, 28. Hence the word means to utter; to declare. The word *speech* means properly *a word;* and then, a lesson; or that which speech conveys. The idea is, that the successive days thus impart instruction, or convey lessons about God. The *day* does this by the returning light, and by the steady and sublime movement of the sun in the heavens, and by all the disclosures which are made by the light of the sun in his journeyings. ¶ *And night unto night showeth knowledge.* Knowledge respecting God. Each successive night does this. It is done by the stars in their courses; in their order; their numbers; their ranks; their changes of position; their rising and their setting. There are as many lessons conveyed to man about the greatness and majesty of God by the silent movements of each night as there are by the light of the successive days—just as there may be as many lessons conveyed to the soul about God in the dark night of affliction and adversity, as there are when the sun of prosperity shines upon us.

3. There is *no speech nor language* where *their voice is not heard.* Marg., *Without* these *their voice is heard.* Heb., *Without their voice heard.* The idea in the margin, which is adopted by Professor Alexander, is, that when the heavens give expression to the majesty and glory of God, it is not by *words,*—by the use of language such as is employed among men. That is, there is a silent but real testimony to the power and glory of their great Author. The same idea is adopted substantially by De Wette. So Rosenmüller renders it, "There is no speech to them, and no words, neither is their voice heard." High as these authorities are, yet it seems to me that the idea conveyed by our common version is probably the correct one. This is the idea in the Septuagint and Latin Vulgate. According to this interpretation the meaning is, "There is no nation, there are no men, whatever may be their language, to whom the heavens do not speak, declaring the greatness and glory of God. The language which they speak is universal; and however various the languages spoken by men, however impossible it may be for them to understand each other, yet all can understand the language of the heavens, proclaiming the perfections of the Great Creator. *That* is a universal language which does not need to be expressed in the forms of human speech, but which conveys great truths alike to all mankind." That the passage cannot mean that there is *no* speech, that there are *no* words, or that there is *no* language in the lessons conveyed by the heavens, seems to me to be clear from the fact that alike in the previous verse (ver. 2), and in the following verse (ver. 4), the psalmist says that they *do* use speech or language, "Day unto day uttereth *speech;*" "their *words* unto the end of the world." The phrase "*their* voice" refers to the heavens (ver. 1). They utter a clear and distinct voice to mankind; that is, they convey to men true and just notions of the greatness of the Creator. The meaning, then, it seems to me, is that the same great lessons about God are

4 Their [1] line is gone out through all the earth, and their words to the end of the world.

[1] Or, *rule*, or, *direction*.

In them hath he set a tabernacle for the sun,

5 Which *is* as a bridegroom coming out of his chamber, *and*

conveyed by the heavens, in their glory and their revolutions, to all nations; that these lessons are conveyed to them day by day, and night by night; that however great may be the diversities of speech among men, these convey lessons in a universal language understood by all mankind; and that thus God is making himself constantly known to all the dwellers on the earth. All men can understand the language of the heavens, though they may not be able to understand the language of each other. Of the truth of this no one can doubt; and its beauty is equal to its truth.

4. *Their line.* That is, of the heavens. The word here used—קַו, *kav*—means properly a cord, or line; (*a*), a measuring line, Ezek. xlvii. 3; Job xxxviii. 5; Isa. xliv. 13; and then (*b*) a cord or string as of a lyre or other instrument of music; and hence *a sound.* So it is rendered here by the LXX., *φθόγγος*. By Symmachus, *ἦχος*. By the Vulgate, *sonus.* De Wette renders it *Klang*, sound. Prof. Alexander dogmatically says that this is "entirely at variance with the Hebrew usage." That this sense, however, is demanded in the passage seems to be plain, not only from the sense given to it by the ancient versions, but by the parallelism, where the term "*words*" corresponds to it:—

"Their *line* is gone out through all the earth;
Their *words* to the end of the world."

Besides, what could be the sense of saying that their *line*, in the sense of a *measuring line*, or *cord*, had gone through all the earth? The plain meaning is, that sounds conveying instruction, and here connected with the idea of sweet or musical sounds, had gone out from the heavens to all parts of the world, conveying the knowledge of God. There is no allusion to the notion of the "music of the spheres," for this conception was not known to the Hebrews; but the idea is that of sweet or musical sounds, not harsh or grating, as proceeding from the movements of the heavens, and conveying these lessons to man. ¶ *And their words.* The lessons or truths which they convey. ¶ *To the end of the world.* To the uttermost parts of the earth. The language here is derived from the idea that the earth was a plane, and had limits. But even with our correct knowledge of the figure of the earth, we use similar language when we speak of the "uttermost parts of the earth." ¶ *In them.* That is, in the heavens, ver. 1. The meaning is, that the sun has his abode or dwelling-place, as it were, in the heavens. The *sun* is particularly mentioned, doubtless, as being the most prominent object among the heavenly bodies, as illustrating in an eminent manner the glory of God. The sense of the whole passage is, that the heavens in general proclaim the glory of God, and that this is shown in a particular and special manner by the light, the splendour, and the journeyings of the sun. ¶ *Hath he set a tabernacle for the sun.* A *tent;* that is, a dwelling-place. He has made a dwelling-place there for the sun. Comp. Habak. iii. 11, "The sun and moon stood still in their habitation."

5. *Which* is *as a bridegroom coming out of his chamber.* That is, when he rises in the morning. He rises from the darkness of the night, and comes forth as the bridegroom comes out of the chamber where he has slept. The allusion is to the bright, and joyful, and cheerful aspect of the rising sun. The image of the bridegroom is employed because we associate with a bridegroom the idea of hilarity, cheerfulness, joy. The essential image is that the sun seems to rise from a

rejoiceth as a strong man to run a race.

6 His going forth *is* from the end of the heaven, and his circuit unto the ends of it: and there is nothing hid from the heat thereof.

7 The [1] law of the LORD *is*

[1] *doctrine.*

night of repose, as man does in the morning, and that after such a night of repose he goes forth with cheerfulness and alacrity to the employments of the day. The figure is an obvious but a very beautiful one, though there is a transition from the image employed in the previous verse, where the sun is represented as dwelling in a tent or tabernacle fitted up for it in the heavens. In the next member of the sentence the figure is again changed, by his being represented as a man prepared to run a race. ¶ And *rejoiceth as a strong man to run a race.* As a man who is vigorous and powerful, when he enters on a race. He is girded for it; he summons all his strength; he seems to exult in the idea of putting his strength to the test, and starting off on his career. Comp. Notes on 1 Cor. ix. 24–27. The same comparison which is employed here occurs in the Zendavesta, ii. 106. *De Wette.*—The idea is that the sun seems to have a long journey before him, and puts forth all his vigour, exulting in the opportunity of manifesting that vigour, and confident of triumphing in the race.

6. *His going forth.* The psalmist now *describes* that race which he has to run, as borne over the entire circuit of the heavens, from one end of it to another,—sweeping the whole space across the firmament. ¶ Is *from the end of the heaven.* From one end of the heaven; that is, from the East, where he starts. ¶ *And his circuit.* The word here used—תְּקוּפָה, *tekoophah*—means properly *a coming about*, or *a return*, as of the seasons, or of the year. It is found only in Ex. xxxiv. 22, "At the year's *end;*" 1 Sam. i. 20, "When the time was *come about*" (Marg., *in revolution of days*); 2 Chron. xxiv. 23, "At the end of the year" (Marg., *in the revolution of the year*). The word here does not refer to the fact that the sun comes round to the starting-point on the following day, but to the sweep or circuit which he makes in the heavens from one end of it to the other,—travelling over the entire heavens. ¶ *Unto the ends of it.* That is, to the other side of the heavens. The plural term is here used perhaps from the idea of *completeness*, or to denote that there was nothing beyond. The complete journey was made. ¶ *And there is nothing hid from the heat thereof.* The rays of the sun penetrate everywhere. Nothing escapes it. It is not a mere march for show and splendour; it is not an idle and useless journey in the heavens; but all things,—vegetables, birds, beasts, men,—all that lives,—feel the effect of his vital warmth, and are animated by his quickening influence. Thus the sun in his goings illustrates the glory of God. The psalmist was fully alive to the splendour, the glory, and the value of this daily march over the heavens, and shows that while, as in the remainder of the psalm, he dwells on the law of the Lord as having another sphere, and in its place more fully illustrating the Divine glory, he is not by any means insensible to the grandeur and beauty of the *works* of God as showing forth the Divine perfections.

7. *The law of the* LORD. Marg., *doctrine.* The word here used—תּוֹרָה, *torah*—is that which is commonly employed in the Old Testament with reference to the law of God, and is usually rendered *law.* The word properly means *instruction, precept,* from a verb signifying *to teach.* It is then used with reference to instruction or teaching in regard to conduct, and is thus applied to all that God has communicated to guide mankind. It does not here, nor does

it commonly, refer exclusively to the *commands* of God, but it includes all that God has revealed to teach and guide us. It refers here to *revealed truth* as contradistinguished from the truth made known by the works of creation. Comp. Notes on Ps. i. 2. There are *six* epithets used in these verses (7–9) to describe the revealed truth of God, all referring to the same truths, but with reference to some distinct view of the truths themselves, or of their effect on the soul: to wit, *law*, *testimony*, *statutes*, *commandment*, *fear*, and *judgments*. Of the revealed truth of God, thus characterized by distinct epithets, a particular statement is first made in each case in regard to the truth itself as viewed in that special aspect, and then the effects of that revealed truth on the soul are described corresponding with that truth as so viewed. Thus, of the "*law* of the Lord" it is said (*a*) that it is *perfect*, (*b*) that it *converts* the soul;—of the "*testimony* of the Lord," (*a*) that it is *sure*, (*b*) that it makes the simple *wise*;—of the "*statutes* of the Lord," (*a*) that they are *right*, (*b*) that they *rejoice* the heart;—of the "*commandment* of the Lord," (*a*) that it is *pure*, (*b*) that it *enlightens* the eyes;—of the "*fear* of the Lord," (*a*) that it is *clean*, (*b*) that it *endures for ever*;—of the "*judgments* of the Lord," (*a*) that they are *true* and *righteous*, (*b*) that they are more to be desired than gold, and that they are sweeter than honey and the honey-comb; that men are warned by them, and that in keeping them there is great reward. ¶ Is *perfect*. On the meaning of the word here used, see Notes on Job i. 1. The meaning is that it lacks nothing in order to its completeness; nothing in order that it might be what it should be. It is complete as a revelation of Divine truth; it is complete as a rule of conduct. As explained above, this refers not only to the *law* of God as the word is commonly employed now, but to the *whole* of Divine truth as revealed. It is absolutely true; it is adapted with consummate wisdom to the wants of man; it is an unerring guide of conduct. There is nothing there which would lead men into error or sin; there is nothing essential for man to know which may not be found there. ¶ *Converting the soul.* The *particular* illustration of the perfection of the law is seen in the fact that it "*converts* the soul;" that is, that it *turns* it from the ways of sin to holiness. The glory of the *works* of God—the heavens, the firmament, the sun, as described in the previous verses—is, that they convey the *knowledge* of God around the world, and that the world is filled with light and life under the genial warmth of the sun; the glory of the *law*, or the revealed truth of God, is, that it bears directly on the *soul* of man, turning him from the error of his ways. and leading him to pursue a life of holiness. It is not said of the "law" of God that it does this by its own power, nor can there be any design here to exclude the doctrine of the Divine agency on the soul; but the statement is, that when the "law" of God *is* applied to the heart, or when the truth of God *is* made to bear on that heart, the legitimate effect is seen in turning the sinner from the error of his ways. This effect of truth is seen everywhere, where it is brought into contact with the heart of man. By placing this *first*, also, the psalmist may perhaps have intended to intimate that this is the *primary design* of the revelation which God has given to mankind; that while great and important effects are produced by the *knowledge* which goes forth from the works of God, converting power goes forth only from the "law" of God, or from revealed truth. It is observable that none of the effects here (vers. 7–12) ascribed to the revealed truth of God, under the various forms in which it is contemplated, are ascribed to the knowledge which goes forth from the contemplation of his works, vers. 1–6. It is not *scientific truth* which converts men, but *revealed truth.* ¶ *The testimony of* perfect, [1] converting the soul: the testimony of the LORD *is* sure, making wise the simple.

[1] *restoring.*

8 The statutes of the LORD *are* right, rejoicing the heart: the commandment of the LORD *is* pure, enlightening the eyes.

the LORD. The word here used—עֵדוּת, *aidooth*—means properly *that which is borne witness to*, and is applied to revealed truth as that which *God bears witness to*. In reference to the truth of what is stated *he* is the witness or the voucher; it is that which *he* declares to be true. Hence the term is applicable to *all* that is revealed as being that which he affirms to be true, and the word may be applied to historical truths; or to precepts or laws; or to statements respecting himself, respecting man, respecting the way of salvation, respecting the fallen world. On all these subjects he has borne witness in his word, pledging his veracity as to the correctness of the statements which are thus made. The word, therefore, refers to the whole of what is revealed in his word, considered as that to the truth of which *he bears witness*. The word is often used in this sense: Ps. lxxxi. 5; cxix. 14, 31, 36, 88, 99, 111, 129, 144, 157; Jer. xliv. 23. It is often also applied to the two tables of the law laid up in the ark, which is hence called "the ark of the *testimony*:" Ex. xvi. 34; xxv. 16, 21, 22; xxvi. 33; xxx. 26, *et sæpe*. ¶ Is *sure*. Established, firm. That "testimony," or that revealed truth, is not unsettled, vacillating, uncertain. It is so certain that it may be relied on; so well established, that it cannot be shaken. ¶ *Making wise the simple*. The word rendered *simple*—פְּתִי, *pethi*—means *simplicity*, *folly*, Prov. i. 22; and then, simple in the sense of being *open to persuasion*, *easily seduced*: Prov. vii. 7; xxii. 3; xxvii. 12; Ps. cxvi. 6. Then it means *credulous*, Prov. xiv. 15; and *inexperienced*, Ps. xix. 7. Gesenius, *Lex.* The meaning here is evidently *inexperienced* in the sense of being ignorant or untaught. It refers to those who need spiritual guidance and direction, and is applicable to men as they are by nature, as untaught, or needing instruction, but with the idea that their minds are susceptible to impressions, or are open to conviction. Those who are naturally destitute of wisdom, it makes wise. The statement is, that that testimony, or revealed truth, makes them wise in the knowledge of God, or imparts to them real instruction.

8. *The statutes of the* LORD. The word here rendered *statutes* properly means *mandates, precepts*—rules given to any one to guide him, Ps. ciii. 18; cxi. 7. It refers to the laws of God considered as *appointed*, or as the result of Divine *authority*. The *verb* from which this word is derived (Hiphil) means to set over, to give the oversight, to appoint. Hence the idea of laws, or statutes, as the result of such an appointment, or such an authority. ¶ Are *right*. Are equal, just, proper. They are such as are founded in wisdom and equity; not such as are the mere result of arbitrary appointment. The idea is that they are not merely *appointed*, or made binding by *authority*, but that they are in themselves equitable and just. ¶ *Rejoicing the heart*. Making the heart glad by the fact that they *are* equitable and just,—and glad as the result of obedience. It is always a source of true happiness when we can feel that we are under just and equal laws;—laws in themselves right, and laws administered *in* righteousness and truth. ¶ *The commandment of the* LORD. An appellation of the law of God from the idea of *setting up*, *appointing*, *constituting*; hence, of *charging*, or *commanding*. The idea here is not so much that the thing is right in itself as that it is *appointed* or *ordered* by God; that it is what he requires. The term is one that is often applied to the laws

9 The fear of the LORD *is* clean, enduring for ever: the judgments of the LORD *are* [1] true *and* righteous altogether,

[1] *truth.*

of God, Deut. vi. 1; vii. 11; Lev. iv. 13; Gen. xxvi. 5; Ex. xv. 26; xvi. 28; Ps. lxxviii. 7; lxxxix. 31; cxix. 6, 10, 19, 21, 32, 35, 47, 48, 60, 66, 73, 86, 96, 98, 115, 127, 131, 143, 151, 166, 172, 176. ¶ Is *pure.* Free from all stain; from all imperfection; from any corrupt tendency. ¶ *Enlightening the eyes.* That is, giving us light and knowledge. The *eyes* are mentioned, as it is by them that we see where to go. The reference here is undoubtedly to the mind or soul as being enlightened by the truth of God. We are made by these commandments to *see* what is right and proper; to understand what we should do.

9. *The fear of the* LORD. The word rendered *fear* in this place—יִרְאָה, *yireah*—means properly *fear, terror*, Jonah i. 10; then, reverence, or holy fear, Ps. ii. 11; v. 7; and hence, reverence towards God, piety, religion,—in which sense it is often used. Comp. Prov. i. 7; Job xxviii. 28; Isa. xi. 2. Hence, by metonymy, it means the *precepts* of piety or religion. It is used evidently in this sense here, as referring to revelation, or to revealed truth, in the sense that it promotes proper *reverence* for God, or secures a proper regard for his name and worship. ¶ Is *clean.* The word here used— טָהוֹר, *tâhor*—means properly clear, pure, in a physical sense, as opposed to filthy, soiled; then, in a ceremonial sense, as opposed to that which is profane or common (Lev. xiii. 17), and then, in a moral sense, as a clean heart, etc., Ps. xii. 6; li. 10. It is also applied to pure gold, Ex. xxv. 11. The sense here is, that there is nothing in it that tends to corrupt the morals, or defile the soul. Everything connected with it is of a pure or holy tendency, adapted to cleanse the soul and to make it holy. ¶ *Enduring for ever.* Standing to all eternity. Not temporary; not decaying; not destined to pass away. It stands firm now, and it will stand firm for ever. That is, the law of God, considered as adapted to make the heart holy and pure, is eternal. What it is now it will always be. What its teaching is now it will continue to be for ever. ¶ *The judgments of the* LORD. The word here rendered *judgments* refers also to the revealed truth of God, with the idea that that has been *judged* or *determined* by him to be right and to be best. It is the result of the Divine adjudication as to what is true, and what is best for man. The word is often used in this sense. Comp. Exod. xxi. 1; Lev. xviii. 5; xxvi. 43; comp. Ps. ix. 7, 16; x. 5. ¶ Are *true.* Marg., *truth.* So the Hebrew. That is, they accord entirely with the *truth*, or are a correct representation of the reality of things. They are not arbitrary, but are in accordance with what is right. This supposes that there is such a thing as *truth* in itself, and the Divine law conforms to that;—not that God determines a thing by mere will, and that it is, therefore, right. God is infinitely perfect, and what he does will be always right, for that is in accordance with his nature; but still his judgments are right, not because he *makes* that to be right which is determined by his will, but because his will is always in accordance with what *is* right. ¶ And *righteous altogether.* That is, they are, without exception, just; or, they are altogether or wholly righteous. There is no one of them which is not just and proper. All that God determines, whether in giving or in executing his laws,—all in his requirements, and all in the administration of his government,—is always and wholly righteous. It is precisely what it *should be* in the case, and is, therefore, worthy of universal confidence.

10 More to be desired *are they* than gold, yea, than much fine gold; sweeter also than honey and [1] the honeycomb.

11 Moreover by them is thy servant warned: *and* in keeping of them *there is* great reward.

[1] *the dropping of honeycombs.*

10. *More to be desired* are they *than gold.* That is, his law; or, as in the preceding verse, his judgments. They are more *valuable* than gold; they are of such a nature that the soul should more desire to be in possession of them than to be in possession of gold, and should value them more. The psalmist here and in the following verses describes his estimate of the worth of revealed truth as he perceived it. In the previous verses he had shown its value in the abstract; he here speaks of his own feelings in regard to it, and shows that *he* esteems it more than he did the objects most prized and valued among men. ¶ *Yea, than much fine gold.* The word here used—פָּז, *poz*—means properly that which is purified or pure, and thus becomes an epithet of gold, particularly of gold that is purified. It is rendered *fine gold* here, as in Ps. cxix. 127; Prov. viii. 19; Cant. v. 11, 15; Isa. xiii. 12; Lam. iv. 2; and *pure gold* in Ps. xxi. 3. The word does not occur elsewhere. Gold is an article of principal value among men; and the object here is to show that to a pious mind the revealed truth of God is esteemed to be the most valuable of all things—a treasure above all which men can accumulate, and all which men can prize. Every truly pious heart will respond to the sentiment expressed here. ¶ *Sweeter also than honey.* Honey, the sweetest of all substances, and regarded as an article of luxury, or as most grateful to the taste. It entered largely into the food of the inhabitants of Palestine, as it does now in Switzerland and in some parts of Africa. The idea is that the truth of God, as revealed, is more grateful to the heart, or affords more pleasure to the soul, than that which is esteemed as the highest luxury to the palate. The meaning is, that it is loved; it is pleasant; it is agreeable; it is not regarded merely as *necessary*, and admitted to the soul because it is needful, as medicine is, but it is received into the soul because it is delighted in, or is more agreeable and pleasant than the most luscious article of food is to the taste. To this, also, the heart of every one who "has tasted the good word of God" will respond. ¶ *And the honeycomb.* Marg., *dropping of honeycombs.* So the Hebrew. The allusion is to honey that drops from the combs, and therefore the most pure honey. That which is *pressed* from the combs will have almost inevitably a mixture of bee-bread and of the combs themselves. That which naturally *flows* from the comb will be pure.

11. *Moreover by them is thy servant warned.* The word here used—זָהַר, *zahar*—means, properly, to be bright, to shine; then, to cause to shine, to make light; and then, to admonish, to instruct, to warn. The essential idea here is, to *throw light on a subject*, so as to show it clearly; that is, to make the duty plain, and the consequences plain. Comp. Lev. xv. 31; Ezek. iii. 18; xxxiii. 7. The word is rendered *admonished* in Eccl. iv. 13; xii. 12; *warn*, and *warned*, in Ps. xix. 11; 2 Kings vi. 10; 2 Chron. xix. 10; Ezek. iii. 17–21; xxxiii. 3–9; *teach*, in Exod. xviii. 20; and *shine*, in Dan. xii. 3. It does not elsewhere occur. ¶ And *in keeping of them* there is *great reward.* Either as the result of keeping them, or in the act of keeping them. In the former sense it would mean that a careful observance of the laws of God will be *followed* by rewards hereafter; in the other sense, that the *act* of keeping them will be attended with so much peace and happiness as to constitute of itself an ample reward. In both these senses is the assertion

12 Who can understand *his* errors? cleanse thou me from secret *faults*.

here made a correct one. Both will be found to be true. It is not easy to determine which is the true sense. Perhaps the language implies both. The phrase "thy servant" refers to the author of the psalm, and shows that in this part of the psalm, in speaking of the "sweetness" of the law of God, and of its value as perceived by the soul, and of the effect of keeping that law, he is referring to his own experience.

12. *Who can understand* his *errors?* The word rendered *errors* is derived from a verb which means to wander, to go astray; then, to do wrong, to transgress. It refers here to wanderings, or departures from the law of God, and the question seems to have been asked in view of the purity, the strictness, and the extent of the law of God. In view of a law so pure, so holy, so strict in its demands, and so extended in its requirements,—asserting jurisdiction over the thoughts, the words, and the whole life,—who can recall the number of times that he has departed from such a law? A sentiment somewhat similar is found in Ps. cxix. 96, "I have seen an end of all perfection; thy commandment is exceeding broad." The language is such as every man who has any just sense of the nature and the requirements of the law, and a just view of his own life, must use in reference to himself. The reason why any man is elated with a conviction of his own goodness is that he has no just sense of the requirements of the law of God; and the more any one studies that law, the more will he be convinced of the extent of his own depravity. Hence the importance of preaching the law, that sinners may be brought to conviction of sin; hence the importance of presenting it constantly before the mind of even the believer, that he may be kept from pride, and may walk humbly before God. And who *is* there that can understand his own errors? Who can number up the sins of a life? Who can make an estimate of the number of impure and unholy thoughts which, in the course of many years, have flitted through, or found a lodgment in the mind? Who can number up the words which have been spoken and should not have been spoken? Who can recall the forgotten sins and follies of a life—the sins of childhood, of youth, of riper years? There is but one Being in the universe that can do this. To him all this is known. Nothing has escaped his observation; nothing has faded from his memory. Nothing can prevent his making a full disclosure of this if he shall choose to do so. It is in his power at any moment to overwhelm the soul with the recollection of all this guilt; it is in his power to cover us with confusion and shame at the revelation of the judgment-day. Our only hope—our only security—that he will not do this, is in his mercy; and that he may not do it, we should without delay seek his mercy, and pray that our sins may be so blotted out that they shall *not* be disclosed to us and to assembled worlds when we appear before him. ¶ *Cleanse thou me from secret* faults. The word here rendered *secret* means that which is hidden, covered, concealed. The reference is to those errors and faults which had been hidden from the eye of him who had committed them, as well as from the eye of the world. The sense is, that the law of God is *so* spiritual, and *so* pure, and *so* extended in its claims, that the author of the psalm felt that it must embrace many things which had been hidden even from his own view,—errors and faults lying deep in the soul, and which had never been developed or expressed. From these, as well as from those sins which had been manifest to himself and to the world, he prayed that he might be cleansed. These are the things that pollute the soul; from these the soul

13 Keep back thy servant also from presumptuous *sins;* let them not have dominion [g] over me: then shall I be upright, and I shall be innocent from [1] the great transgression.

14 Let the words of my mouth,

g Rom. vi. 12—14. [1] Or, *much.*

must be cleansed, or it can never find permanent peace. A man who does *not* desire to be cleansed from all these "secret faults" cannot be a child of God; he who is a child of God will pray without ceasing that from these pollutions of the soul he may be made pure.

13. *Keep back thy servant also.* Restrain thy servant; or, do not suffer him to commit those sins. ¶ *From presumptuous* sins. The word here used is manifestly designed to stand in some respects in contrast with the *secret faults* mentioned in the previous verse. The word—זֵד, *zaid*—means properly that which is *boiling, swelling, inflated;* then *proud, arrogant;* with the accessory notion of shameless wickedness or impiety. Gesenius, *Lex.* The word is rendered *proud* in Ps. lxxxvi. 14; cxix. 21, 51, 69, 78, 85, 122; Prov. xxi. 24; Isa. xiii. 11; Jer. xliii. 2; Mal. iii. 15; iv. 1. It does not occur elsewhere. The prevailing thought is that of *pride,* and the reference is particularly to sins which proceed from self-confidence; from reliance on one's own strength. The word does not mean *open* sins, or *flagrant* sins, so much as those which spring from self-reliance or pride. The prayer is substantially that he might have a proper distrust of himself, and might not be left by an improper reliance on his own power to the commission of sin. This also is said in view of the extent and spirituality of the law of God—expressing the earnest desire of the author of the psalm that he might not be left to violate a law so pure and holy. ¶ *Let them not have dominion over me.* Let them not *reign* over me; that is, let them not get the mastery or the ascendancy over me. Let me not become the slave of sin; so subject to it that it shall domineer over me. Sin often secures that kind of triumph or mastery over the mind, making a slave of him who yields to it. The pious man alone is a true freeman. He is emancipated from the dominion of sin, and walks in true liberty: see John viii. 32, 36; Gal. v. 1. ¶ *Then shall I be upright.* Heb., *I shall be perfect.* On the meaning of the word here used, see Notes on ver. 7. It means here that he would be truly a servant of God; or, that he would have this evidence that he was a friend of God, that he was kept from the indulgence of secret faults, and from open transgressions—that is, his piety would have completeness of parts; or, it would be shown to be true and genuine. It cannot be demonstrated from the use of the word that he supposed that he would be absolutely perfect or free from all sin. See Notes on Job i. 1. ¶ *And I shall be innocent.* This does not mean that he would be absolutely innocent, or free from all sin; but it means here, as it is explained in the following phrase, that he would be innocent of the great transgression, or would be free from that. ¶ *From the great transgression.* Marg., as in Hebrew, *much.* It does not refer to any one specific offence, but it means that he would be free from the transgression which would exist if he were *not* cleansed from secret faults, and if he were *not* kept back from presumptuous sins. He would be saved from the great guilt which would ensue if he should give unchecked indulgence to secret faults, and if he should be allowed to commit the open sins which were the result of pride and over-weening self-confidence.

14. *Let the words of my mouth.* The words that I speak; *all* the words that I speak. ¶ *And the meditation of my heart.* The thoughts of my heart. ¶ *Be acceptable in thy*

and the meditation of my heart, be acceptable in thy sight, O LORD, my [1] strength and my redeemer.

[1] *rock.*

sight. Be such as thou wilt approve; or, be such as will be *pleasing* to thee; such as will give thee delight or satisfaction; such as will be agreeable to thee. Comp. Prov. xiv. 35; Isa. lvi. 7; lx. 7; Jer. vi. 20; Exod. xxviii. 38; Lev. xxii. 20, 21; xix. 5. This supposes (*a*) that God has such control over our thoughts and words, that he can cause us to order them aright; (*b*) that it is proper to pray to him to exert such an influence on our minds that our words and thoughts may be right and pure; (*c*) that it is one of the sincere desires and wishes of true piety that the thoughts and words *may be* acceptable or pleasing to God. The great purpose of the truly pious is, not to please themselves, or to please their fellow-men, (comp. Gal. i. 10), but to please God. The great object is to secure acceptance with him; to have such thoughts, and to utter such words, that He can look upon them with approbation. ¶ *O* LORD *my strength.* Marg., as in Hebrew, *rock.* Comp. Notes on Ps. xviii. 2. ¶ *And my redeemer.* On the word here used, see Notes on Job xix. 25; comp. Isa. xli. 14; xliii. 14; xliv. 6, 24; xlvii. 4; lxiii. 16. The two things which the psalmist here refers to in regard to God, as the appellations dear to his heart, are (*a*) that God is his *Rock*, or *strength;* that is, that he was his defence and refuge; and (*b*) that he had *rescued* or *redeemed* him from sin; or that he looked to him as alone able to redeem him from sin and death. It is not necessary to inquire here how far the psalmist was acquainted with the plan of salvation as it would be ultimately disclosed through the great Redeemer of mankind; it is sufficient to know that he had an *idea* of redemption, and that he looked to God *as* his Redeemer, and believed that he could rescue him from sin. The psalm, therefore, which begins with a contemplation of God *in his works,* appropriately closes with a contemplation of God *in redemption;* or brings before us the great thought that it is not by the knowledge of God as we can gain it from his works of creation that we are to be saved, but that the most endearing character in which he can be manifested to us is in the work of redemption, and that wherever we *begin* in our contemplation of God, it becomes us to *end* in the contemplation of his character as our Redeemer.

PSALM XX.

This psalm purports to be "A Psalm of David," nor is there any reason to doubt that he wrote it. Of the precise occasion on which it was composed nothing can be known with certainty, for there is no historical statement on the point, and there is nothing in the psalm to indicate it. It would seem, however, from the psalm, that it was composed on some occasion when the king was about going to war, and that it was designed to be used by the people of the nation, and by the king and his hosts mustered for war, as expressing mutually their wishes in regard to the result, and their confidence in each other and in God. Or if it was not designed to be *used* by the people actually, it was intended to be a poetic expression of the real feelings of the king and the people in regard to the enterprise in which he was embarked.

According to this idea, and as seems to me to be manifest on the face of the psalm, it is composed of alternate parts *as if* to be used by the people, and by the king and his followers, in alternate responses, closing with a chorus to be used by all. If it was intended to be employed in public service, it was doubtless to be sung by alternate choirs, representing the people and the king.

The whole may be divided into three strophes or parts:—

I. The first strophe, vers. 1–5.

(*a*) THE PEOPLE, vers. 1–5. They pray that the Lord would defend the king in the day of trouble; that the name of the God of Jacob would defend him; that he would send him help from the sanctuary, and strengthen

PSALM XX.

To the chief Musician. A Psalm of David.

THE LORD hear thee in the day of trouble; the name of the God of Jacob [1] defend thee.

[1] *set thee on an high place.*

him out of Zion; that he would remember his offerings and accept his burnt sacrifice; that he would grant him according to his own heart, and fulfil all his counsel.

(*b*) THE KING, ver. 5, part first. He says, as expressive of the feeling with which the expedition was undertaken, "We will rejoice in thy salvation, and in the name of our God we will set up our banners."

II. The second strophe, ver. 5 (latter part), and ver. 6.

(*a*) THE PEOPLE, ver. 5, latter clause; expressing a desire for his success and triumph, "The Lord fulfil all thy petitions."

(*b*) THE KING, ver. 6; expressing confidence of success from the observed zeal and co-operation of the people:—"Now know I that the Lord saveth his anointed; he will hear him from his holy heaven with the saving strength of his right hand."

III. GENERAL CHORUS OF ALL, vers. 7–9. This is the language of exultation and triumph in God; of joyful trust in him. "Some," is the language of this chorus, "trust in chariots and some in horses, but we will remember the name of the Lord our God," ver. 7. Then they see their enemies fallen and subdued, while their armies stand upright and firm, ver. 8. Then they call, in joyful exultation and triumph, on God as *the great King over all*, and supplicate his mercy and favour, ver. 9.

This is, therefore, a *patriotic* and *loyal* psalm, full of confidence in the king as he starts on his expedition, full of desire for his success, and full of confidence in God; expressing union of heart between the sovereign and the people, and the union of all their hearts in the great God.

On the meaning of the phrase in the title, "To the chief Musician," see Notes on the title to Ps. iv.

1. *The* LORD *hear thee in the day of trouble.* According to the view expressed in the introduction to the psalm, this is the language of the people praying for their king, or expressing the hope that he would be delivered from trouble, and would be successful in what he had undertaken, in the prosecution of a war apparently of defence. The word "trouble" here used would seem to imply that he was beset with difficulties and dangers; perhaps, that he was surrounded by foes. It seems that he was going forth to war to deliver his country from trouble, having offered sacrifices and prayers (ver. 3) for the purpose of securing the Divine favour on the expedition. The *point* or the *moment* of the psalm is when those sacrifices had been offered, and when he was about to embark on his enterprise. At that moment the people lift up the voice of sympathy and of encouragement, and pray that those sacrifices might be accepted, and that he might find the deliverance which he had desired. ¶ *The name of the God of Jacob.* The word *name* is often put in the Scriptures for the person himself; and hence this is equivalent to saying, "May the God of Jacob defend thee." See Ps. v. 11; ix. 10; xliv. 5; liv. 1; Exod. xxiii. 21. Jacob was the one of the patriarchs from whom, after his other name, the Hebrew people derived their name *Israel*, and the word seems here to be used with reference to the *people* rather than to the ancestor. Comp. Isa. xliv. 2. The God of Jacob, or the God of Israel, would be synonymous terms, and either would denote that he was the Protector of the nation. As such he is invoked here; and the prayer is, that the Great Protector of the Hebrew people would now defend the king in the dangers which beset him, and in the enterprise which he had undertaken. ¶ *Defend thee.* Marg., as in Hebrew, *set thee on a high place.* The word means the same as *defend* him, for the idea is that of being set on a high place, a tower, a mountain, a lofty rock, where his enemies could not reach or assail him.

2 Send [1] thee help from the sanctuary, [2] and strengthen thee out of Zion.

[1] *thy help.* [2] *support.*

3 Remember all thy offerings, and [3] accept thy burnt sacrifice. Selah.

[3] *turn to ashes,* or, *make fat.*

2. *Send thee help.* Marg., *thy help.* So the Hebrew. The idea is, such help as he needed; such as would make him safe. ¶ *From the sanctuary.* From the *tabernacle,* or the holy place where God was worshipped, and where he was supposed to reside, Ex. xxviii. 43; xxix. 30; xxxv. 19; xxxix. 1. This was his seat; his throne; where he abode among the people. Here, too, it would seem that he had been worshipped, and his aid implored, in view of this expedition; here the royal psalmist had sought to secure the Divine favour by the presentation of appropriate sacrifices and offerings (ver. 3). The prayer here is, that God would accept those offerings, and hear those supplications, and would now send the desired help from the sanctuary where he resided; that is, that he would grant his protection and aid. ¶ *And strengthen thee.* Marg., as in Hebrew, *support thee.* The idea is, that he would grant his upholding hand in the day of peril. ¶ *Out of Zion.* The place where God was worshipped; the place where the tabernacle was reared. See Notes on Ps. ii. 6.

3. *Remember all thy offerings.* On the meaning of the word here used, see Notes on Isa. i. 13, where it is rendered *oblations.* The word occurs often in the Scriptures, and is sometimes rendered *offering,* and sometimes *oblation.* The word means an offering of any kind or anything that is presented to God, except a bloody sacrifice,—anything offered as an expression of thankfulness, or with a view to obtain his favour. It is distinguished from bloody sacrifices, which are expressed by the word in the following clause. The word here employed occurs in the Psalms only in the following places: xx. 3; xl. 6; xcvi. 8; where it is rendered *offering* and *offerings;*—xlv. 12, rendered *gift;*—lxxii. 10, rendered *presents;*—and cxli. 2, rendered *sacrifice.* The use of the word in this place proves that such offerings had been made to God by him who was about to go forth to the war; and the prayer of the people here is that God would *remember* all those offerings; that is, that he would grant the blessing which he who had offered them had sought to obtain. ¶ *And accept.* Marg., *turn to ashes,* or *make fat.* The Hebrew word—דָּשֵׁן, *dashain*—means properly to make fat, or marrowy, Prov. xv. 30; to pronounce or regard as fat; to be fat or *satiated,* or *abundantly satisfied,* Prov. xiii. 4. It conveys also the notion of reducing to ashes; perhaps from the fact that the victim which had been fattened for sacrifice was reduced to ashes; or, as Gesenius supposes (*Lex,* see דָּשֵׁן), because "ashes were used by the ancients for *fattening,* i. e., manuring the soil." The prayer here seems to be that God would "pronounce the burnt-offering *fat;*" that is, that he would regard it favourably, or would accept it. This proves, also, that a sacrifice *had* been made with a view to propitiate the Divine favour in regard to the expedition which had been undertaken; that is, a solemn act of devotion, according to the manner of worship which then obtained, had been performed with a view to secure the Divine favour and protection. The example is one which suggests the propriety of always entering upon any enterprise by solemn acts of worship, or by supplicating the Divine blessing; that is, by acknowledging our dependence on God, and asking his guidance and his protecting care. ¶ *Thy burnt sacrifice.* The word here used denotes *bloody offerings;* see Notes on Isa. i. 11. These offerings were designed especially for the

4 Grant thee according to thine heart, and fulfil all thy counsel.
5 We will rejoice in thy salvation, and in the name of our God we will set up *our* banners: the LORD fulfil all thy petitions.
6 Now know I that the LORD saveth his anointed: he will hear him from [1] his holy heaven [2] with the saving strength of his right hand.

[1] *heaven of his holiness.*

[2] *by the strength of the salvation of.*

expiation of sin, and for thus securing the Divine favour. They were an acknowledgment of guilt, and they were offered with a view to secure the pardon of sin, and, in connexion with that, the favour of God. In similar circumstances *we* approach God, not by an offering which *we* make, whether bloody or bloodless, but through the one great sacrifice made by the Redeemer on the cross for the sins of the world.

4. *Grant thee according to thine own heart.* According to thy wishes; according to the desires of thy heart. ¶ *And fulfil all thy counsel.* All that thou hast designed or undertaken in the matter; that is, may he enable thee to execute thy purpose.

5. *We will rejoice in thy salvation.* According to the idea of the psalm suggested in the introduction, this is a response of the king and those associated with him in going forth to battle. It expresses the joy which they would have in the expected deliverance from danger, and their conviction that through his strength they would be able to obtain it. The word *salvation* here means *deliverance;* to wit, from the anticipated danger. The phrase implies that *God* would interpose to save them; it expresses alike their confidence in that, and the fact that such a deliverance would fill their hearts with joy and rejoicing. ¶ *And in the name of our God.* This indicates a sense of dependence on God, and also that the enterprise undertaken was in order to promote his honour and glory. It was not in their own strength, nor was it to promote the purposes of conquest and the ends of ambition; it was that God might be honoured, and it was with confidence of success derived from his anticipated aid. ¶ *We will set up* our *banners.* We will erect our standards; or, as we should say, *we will unfurl our flag.* All people, when they go to war, have standards or banners, whether flags or some other ensigns, around which they rally; which they follow; under which they fight; and which they feel bound to defend. Each nation has its own standard; but it is difficult to determine what precisely was the form of the standards used among the ancient Hebrews. Military standards, however, were early used (comp. Numb. i. 52; ii. 2, 3, 10, 18, 25; x. 14, 25), and indeed were necessary whenever armies were mustered for war. For the forms of ancient standards, see the article in Kitto's Cyclopædia of Bib. Lit., art. *Standards.* ¶ *The* LORD *fulfil all thy petitions.* The prayers offered in connexion with the sacrifice referred to in ver. 3 (comp. ver. 4). This, according to the view suggested in the introduction, is the response of the people, expressing their desire that the king might be successful in what he had undertaken, and that the prayers which had been offered for success might be answered.

6. *Now know I that the* LORD *saveth his anointed.* Saveth, or will save, the king, who had been *anointed,* or consecrated by anointing to that office. Comp. Notes on Ps. ii. 2. This, according to the view given in the introduction, is the response of *the king.* It expresses his confident assurance of success from the interest which the people had expressed in the enterprise, as referred to in the previous verses, and from the earnestness of their prayers in his behalf and in behalf of the enterprise. They had

7 Some *trust* in chariots, and some in horses: but we will remember the name of the LORD our God.

8 They are brought down and fallen; but we are risen, and stand upright.

manifested such zeal in the cause, and they had offered so earnest petitions, that he could not doubt that God would smile favourably on the undertaking, and would grant success. ¶ *He will hear him from his holy heaven.* Marg., *from the heaven of his holiness.* So the Hebrew. Comp. 1 Chron. xxi. 26; 2 Chron. vii. 14; Neh. ix. 27, 28; Ps. xiv. 2; cii. 19. Heaven is represented as the dwelling-place of God, and it is there that he hears and answers our prayers. The meaning of the word *hear* in this passage is, that he will *favourably hear*, or regard; that is, that he will *answer* the petition, or grant the request. ¶ *With the saving strength.* That is, he will interpose with that saving strength. Literally, "*with the strengths of salvation.*" The answer to the prayer will be manifest in the strength or power put forth by him to save. ¶ *Of his right hand.* The right hand is the instrument by which mainly we execute our purposes; and by constant use it becomes in fact more fully developed, and is stronger than the left hand. Hence it is used to denote *strength.* See Ex. xv. 6; Judges v. 26; Notes on Ps. xvii. 7; xviii. 35.

7. *Some* trust *in chariots.* This (see introd. to the psalm) seems to be a *general chorus* of the king and the people, expressing the fullest confidence in God, and showing the true ground of their reliance. The general meaning is, that their entire trust was in God. This is put in strong contrast with others, who relied, some on their chariots, and some on their horses, while *they* relied alone on God. They who trusted in horses and in chariots would be overcome; they who trusted in God alone would triumph. The word rendered chariots—רֶכֶב, *raichaib*—means properly *riding*, and then a vehicle for riding, a wagon, a chariot. Here it refers to the war-chariot, or the vehicle for carrying armed men into battle. These furnished great advantages in war, by the speed with which they could be driven against an enemy, and by the facilities in fighting from them. They were usually very simple. They consisted of "a light pole suspended between and on the withers of a pair of horses, the after end resting on a light axletree, with two low wheels. Upon the axle stood a light frame, open behind, and floored for the warrior and his charioteer, who both stood within. On the sides of the frame hung the war-bow, in its case; a large quiver with arrows and darts had commonly a particular sheath. In Persia, the chariots, elevated upon wheels of considerable diameter, had four horses abreast; and in early ages, there were occasionally hooks or scythes attached to the axles."—Kitto, *Cyclo.* In early ages these constituted a main reliance in determining the result of a battle. ¶ *And some in horses.* Some in cavalry, commonly a very material reliance in war. The use of horses in war was early known in the world, for we find mention of them in the earliest periods of history. ¶ *But we will remember the name of the* LORD *our God.* That is, we will remember God—the name, as before remarked, often being used to denote the person. The meaning is, We will not forget that our reliance is not on armies, but on God, the living God. Whatever instrumentality we may employ, we will remember always that our hope is in God, and that he only can give success to our arms.

8. *They are brought down and fallen.* That is, those who trust in chariots and horses. The reference here is undoubtedly to the enemies against whom the king was about to wage war, and the language here is indicative of his certain conviction

9 Save, Lord: let the King hear us when we call.

that they would be vanquished. So certain was he now of this that he could speak of it as if it were already done. "They *are* brought down." He sees them in anticipation prostrate and subdued; he goes forth to war with the certainty on his mind that this would occur. The word rendered *brought down*—כָּרַע, *châra*—means *to bend, to bow* (as the knees); and then it refers to one who bows down before an enemy, that is, one who is subdued, Isa. x. 4; lxv. 12; Ps. lxxii. 9; lxxviii. 31. ¶ *But we are risen, and stand upright.* That is, he sees this in anticipation. He is certain of success and triumph. Depressed though we may now be, yet we are certain of victory.

9. *Save,* Lord. "Jehovah, save." This is still an earnest prayer. Confident as they are of success and triumph, yet they do not forget their dependence on God; they do not forget that victory must come from his hand. There was, indeed, exultation, but it was exultation in the belief that God would grant success—an exultation connected with, and springing from prayer. Prayer is not inconsistent with the most confident anticipation of success in any undertaking; and confidence of success can only spring from prayer. ¶ *Let the King.* That is, let *God,* spoken of here as the Great King. The connexion and the parallelism demand this interpretation, for to God only is this prayer addressed. He is here invoked as the supreme monarch. A king going forth to war implores the protection of a greater king than himself—the King of all nations; and who, therefore, had the disposal of the whole result of the conflict in which he was about to engage. ¶ *Hear us when we call.* As we now call on him; as we shall call on him in the day of battle. Thus the close of the psalm corresponds with the beginning. In the beginning (vers. 1–4) there is an earnest *desire* that God would hear the suppliant in the day of trouble; in the close there is an earnest *prayer* to him from all the people that he *would* thus hear. The desire of the blessing goes forth in the form of prayer, for God only can grant the objects of our desire. The whole psalm, therefore, is an expression of a strong confidence in God; of a sense of the most complete dependence on him; and of that assurance of success which often comes into the soul, in an important and difficult undertaking, when we have committed the whole cause to God. The psalm, too, is a model for us to imitate when we embark in any great and arduous enterprise. The desire for success should be accompanied with earnest prayer and supplication on our part; and when our friends express the desire that we may be successful, there should have been on our part such acts of devotion—such manifest reliance on God—such religious trust—that they can simply pray for our success to be in accordance with our own prayer. Never should we look for success unless our undertaking has been preceded by prayer; and when our best preparations have been made, our hope of success is not primarily and mainly in them, but only in God.

PSALM XXI.

This psalm likewise purports to be "A Psalm of David," and there is no cause to doubt the correctness of the superscription which ascribes it to him. There is, however, no certain intimation at what time of his life, or on what occasion, it was composed, and it is impossible to determine these points.

The most probable supposition in regard to its composition seems to me to be, that it is a song of thanksgiving for the victory secured in answer to the prayer of himself and the people in the previous psalm. Nothing can be argued, indeed, on this point, from the mere fact that it stands in close connexion with the previous psalm; but there are, it seems to me, internal marks that this was its design, and that it is the expression of a heart overflowing with gratitude, and,

PSALM XXI.

To the chief Musician. A Psalm of David.

THE king shall joy in thy strength, O LORD; and in thy salvation how greatly shall he rejoice!

2 Thou hast given him his heart's desire, and hast not withholden the request of his lips. Selah.

3 For thou preventest him with the blessings of goodness: thou settest a crown of pure gold on his head.

---

therefore, recalling not merely the immediate blessings of a recent victory, but also the other blessings with which God had crowned his life, vers. 3, 4.

Thus understood in regard to its origin, the psalm may be regarded as divided into the following parts:—

I. Thanksgiving for success, or for granting the object which had been so earnestly sought, vers. 1-7. In this thanksgiving the psalmist says that God had not only granted what had been asked (vers. 1-3), but that he had greatly *exceeded* this:—he had granted far more than had been the literal request. He had added blessings which had not been specifically sought; he had made those blessings permanent and eternal, vers. 4-7.

II. The general truth that *all* the foes of God would thus be overcome, and that the cause of truth would be finally triumphant, vers. 8-12. This was *suggested* by the victory which had been achieved. As God had granted *that* victory,—as he had so easily subdued the enemies of himself and of his people, —as he had gone so far beyond the expectations and the hopes of those who had gone forth to the conflict, the idea is naturally suggested that it would be thus with *all* his foes, and that there would be ultimately a complete victory over them.

III. The expression of an earnest *desire* that God might be thus exalted, and might thus achieve a complete and final victory, ver. 13.

For the meaning of the phrase, "To the chief Musician," in the title to the psalm, see Notes on Ps. iv.

1. *The king shall joy in thy strength.* King David, who had achieved the victory which he had desired and prayed for, Ps. xx. This is in the third person, but the reference is doubtless to David himself, and is to be understood as his own language. If it be understood, however, as the language of *the people,* it is still an ascription of praise to God for his favour to their king. It seems better, however, to regard it as the language of David himself. The word "*strength*" here implies that all the success referred to was to be traced to God. It was not by the prowess of a human arm; it was not by the valour or skill of the king himself; it was by the power of God alone. ¶ *And in thy salvation.* In the salvation or deliverance from foes which thou hast granted, and in all that thou doest to save. The language would embrace *all* that God does to save his people. ¶ *How greatly shall he rejoice!* Not only does he rejoice now, but he ever will rejoice. It will be to him a constant joy. Salvation, now to us a source of comfort, will always be such; and when we once have evidence that God has interposed to save us, it is accompanied with the confident anticipation that this will continue to be the source of our highest joy for ever.

2. *Thou hast given him his heart's desire.* See Notes on Ps. xx. 4. This had been the prayer of the people that God would "grant him according to his own heart, and fulfil all his counsel," and this desire had now been granted. All that had been wished; all that had been prayed for by himself or by the people, had been granted. ¶ *And hast not withholden.* Hast not denied or refused. ¶ *The request of his lips.* The request, or the desire which his lips had uttered. The meaning is, that his petitions had been fully granted. ¶ *Selah.* See Notes on Ps. iii. 2.

3. *For thou preventest him.* Thou goest before him; thou dost anticipate him. See Ps. xvii. 13, margin. Our word *prevent* is now most commonly used in the sense of *hinder, stop,* or

4 He asked life of thee, *and* thou gavest *it* him, *even* length of days for ever and ever.

intercept. This is not the original meaning of the English word; and the word is never used in this sense in the Bible. The English word, when our translation was made, meant to *go before,* to *anticipate,* and this is the uniform meaning of it in our English version, as it is the meaning of the original. See Notes on Job iii. 12. Comp. Ps. lix. 10; lxxix. 8; lxxxviii. 13; xcv. 2; cxix. 147, 148; Amos ix. 10; Notes on 1 Thess. iv. 15. The meaning here is, that God had *anticipated* him, or his desires. He had gone before him. He had designed the blessing even before it was asked. ¶ *With the blessings of goodness.* Blessings *indicating* goodness on his part; blessings adapted to promote the "good" or the welfare of him on whom they were bestowed. Perhaps the meaning here is, not only that they *were* good, but they *seemed* to be good; they were not "blessings in disguise," or blessings as the result of previous calamity and trial, but blessings where there was no trial—no shadow—no appearance of disappointment. ¶ *Thou settest a crown of pure gold on his head.* This does not refer to the time of his coronation, or the period when he was crowned a king, but it refers to the victory which he had achieved, and by which he had been made truly a king. He was crowned with triumph; he was shown to be a king; the victory was like making him a king, or setting a crown of pure gold upon his head. He was now a conqueror, and was indeed a king.

4. *He asked life of thee.* An expression similar to this occurs in Ps. lxi. 5, 6, "For thou, O God, hast heard my vows; . . . Thou wilt prolong the king's life, and his years to many generations." The expression in both cases implies that there had been a prayer for *life,* as if life were in danger. The expression itself would be applicable to a time of sickness, or to danger of any kind, and here it is used doubtless in reference to the exposure of life in going into battle, or in going forth to war. In this apprehended peril he prayed that God would defend him. He earnestly sought protection as he went forth to the perils of war. ¶ And *thou gavest* it *him.* Thou didst hear and answer his prayer. He was saved from danger. ¶ Even *length of days for ever and ever.* Thou didst grant him more than he asked. He sought life for himself; thou hast not only granted that, but hast granted to him the assurance that he should live in his posterity to all generations. The idea is, that there would be an indefinite continuation of his race. His posterity would occupy his throne, and there would be no end to his reign thus prolonged. Beyond all his petitions and his hopes, God had given the assurance that his reign would be permanent and enduring. We cannot suppose that he understood this as if it were a promise made to him personally, that *he* would live and would occupy the throne for ever; but the natural interpretation is that which would refer it to his posterity, and to the perpetuity of the reign of his family or descendants. A similar promise occurs elsewhere: 2 Sam. vii. 13, 16; comp. Notes on Ps. xviii. 50. It is by no means an uncommon thing that God gives us more than we asked in our prayers. The offering of prayer is not only the means of securing the blessing which we asked, but also often of securing much more important blessings which we did not ask. If the expression were allowable it might be said that the prayer *suggested* to the Divine mind the conferring of all needed blessings, or it indicates such a state of mind on the part of him who prays that God *takes occasion* to confer blessings which were not asked;—as a request made by a child to a parent for a specific favour is followed not only by granting *that* favour, but by

5 His glory *is* great in thy salvation: honour and majesty hast thou laid upon him.

6 For thou hast [1] made him most blessed for ever: thou hast [2] made him exceeding glad[a] with thy countenance.

[1] *set him* to be *blessings*, Gen. xii. 2.

[2] *gladded him with joy.*
[a] Ps. iv. 6, 7; xvi. 11.

bestowing others of which the child did not think. The state of mind on the part of the child was such as to *dispose* the parent to grant much larger blessings.

5. *His glory is great in thy salvation.* Not in himself; not in anything that he has done, but in what thou hast done. The fact that thou hast saved him, and the manner in which it has been done, has put upon him great honour. He felt indeed that his condition as king, and as to the prospects before him, was one of great "glory" or honour; but he felt at the same time that it was not in *himself*, or for anything that *he* had done: it was only in the "*salvation*" which *God* had conferred upon him. Every child of God, in like manner, has great "glory" conferred upon him, and his "glory" will be great for ever; but it is not in himself, or in virtue of anything that he has done. It is "great" in the "salvation" of God, (*a*) in the *fact* that God has interposed to save him; and (*b*) in the *manner* in which it has been done. The highest honour that can be put upon man is in the fact that God will *save* him. ¶ *Honour and majesty hast thou laid upon him.* (*a*) In making him a king; (*b*) in the victories and triumphs which thou hast now given him, placing on his head, as it were, a brighter crown; (*c*) in the promised perpetuity of his reign. So we may say of the ransomed sinner—the child of God—now. Honour and majesty have been laid on him, (*a*) in the fact that God has redeemed him; (*b*) in the manner in which this has been accomplished; (*c*) in his adoption into the family of God; (*d*) in the rank and dignity which he occupies as a child of God; (*e*) in the hope of immortal blessedness beyond the grave.

6. *For thou hast made him most blessed for ever.* Marg., as in Heb., *set him* to be *blessings.* The expression in our translation, as it is now commonly understood, would mean that God had made him *happy* or *prosperous.* This does not seem to be the sense of the original. The idea is, that he had made him a blessing to mankind or to the world; or, that he had made him to be a source of blessing to others. Blessings would descend through him; and though in the consciousness of this fact he would be *happy*, and in that sense be "blessed," yet the idea is rather that blessings would be imparted or scattered through him. Blessings would abound to others through his own reign; blessings through the reigns of those who should succeed him in the throne; blessings would be imparted to men as far as the import of the promise extended, that is, for ever, ver. 4. The word "for ever" here undoubtedly, as it was used by the Spirit of inspiration, was designed to refer to the eternal blessings which would descend on mankind through the Messiah, the illustrious descendant of David. How far David himself understood this, is not a material inquiry. He was undoubtedly directed by the Spirit of inspiration to use such language as would fairly and properly express this. It is right, therefore, for *us* so to regard it, and so to interpret and apply it. ¶ *Thou hast made him exceeding glad.* Marg., as in Heb., *gladded him with joy.* The Hebrew phrase means, as it is expressed in our translation, that he had been made very glad, or very happy. The favours of God to him, alike in his protection and in the promises which had been made in reference to the future, were such as to make him happy in the highest de-

7 For [b] the king trusteth in the LORD, and, through the mercy of the Most High, he shall not be moved.

b 1 Sam. xxx. 6; Ps. xxvi. 1.

8 Thine hand shall find [c] out all thine enemies: thy right hand shall find out those that hate thee.

c Amos ix. 2, 3.

gree. ¶ *With thy countenance.* With thy favour. By lifting the light of thy countenance upon him; or, as we should express it, by *smiling* upon him. See Notes on Ps. iv. 6.

7. *For the king.* David, the author of the psalm. ¶ *Trusteth in the* LORD. All these blessings have resulted from his confiding in God, and looking to him for his favour and protection. ¶ *And through the mercy of the Most High.* The favour of Him who is exalted above all;—the most exalted Being in the universe. The word *mercy* here is equivalent to *favour.* He had already experienced God's favour; he looked for a continuance of it; and through that favour he was confident that he would never be shaken in his purposes, and that he would never be disappointed. ¶ *He shall not be moved.* He shall be firmly established. That is, his throne would be firm; he himself would live a life of integrity, purity, and prosperity; and the promises which had been so graciously made to him, and which extended so far into the future, would all be acomplished. The truth taught here is, that however firm or prosperous our way seems to be, the continuance of our prosperity, and the completion of our hopes and our designs, depend wholly on the "mercy" or the favour of the Most High. Confiding in that, we may feel assured that whatever changes and reverses we may experience in our temporal matters, our ultimate welfare will be secure. Nothing can shake a hope of heaven that is founded on his gracious promises as made through a Saviour.

8. *Thine hand shall find out.* That is, Thou wilt find out,—the hand being that by which we execute our purposes. This verse commences a new division of the psalm (see the introd.),—in which the psalmist looks forward to the complete and final triumph of God over *all* his enemies. He looks to this in connexion with what God had done for him. He infers that he who had enabled him to achieve such signal conquests over his own foes and the foes of God would not withdraw his interposition until he had secured a complete victory for the cause of truth and holiness. In connexion with the promise made to him respecting his permanent reign and the reign of his successors on the throne (ver. 4), he infers that God would ultimately subdue the enemies of truth, and would set up his kingdom over all. ¶ *All thine enemies.* However they may attempt to conceal themselves,—however they may evade the efforts to subdue them,—yet they shall *all* be found out and overcome. As this was intended by the Spirit of inspiration, it undoubtedly refers to the final triumph of truth on the earth, or to the fact that the kingdom of God will be set up over all the world. All that are properly ranked among the enemies of God,—all that are in any way opposed to him and to his reign,—will be found out and conquered. All the worshippers of idols,—all the enemies of truth,—all the rejecters of revelation, — all the workers of iniquity,—all that are infidels or scoffers,—shall be found out and subdued. Either by being made to yield to the claims of truth, and thus becoming the friends of God,—or by being cut off and punished for their sins,—they will be all so overcome that God shall reign over all the earth. An important truth is further taught here, to wit, that no enemy of God can escape him. There is no place to which he can flee where God will not find him. "There is

9 Thou shalt make them as a fiery [d] oven in the time of thine anger: the LORD shall swallow them up in his wrath, and the fire [e] shall devour them.

10 Their [f] fruit shalt thou destroy from the earth, and their seed from among the children of men.

d Mal. iv. 1. e Isa. xxvi. 11. f Ps. xxxvii. 28.

no darkness, nor shadow of death, where the workers of iniquity may hide themselves," Job xxxiv. 22. ¶ *Thy right hand.* See Notes on Ps. xvii. 7. ¶ *Those that hate thee.* All thine enemies.

9. *Thou shalt make them as a fiery oven in the time of thine anger.* Thou shalt consume or destroy them, as if they were burned in a heated oven. Or, they shall burn, *as if* they *were* a flaming oven; that is, they would be wholly consumed. The word rendered *oven*—תַּנּוּר, *tannoor*—means either an *oven* or a *furnace.* It is rendered *furnace* and *furnaces* in Gen. xv. 17; Neh. iii. 11; xii. 38; Isa. xxxi. 9; and, as here, *oven* or *ovens*, in Exod. viii. 3; Lev. ii. 4; vii. 9; xi. 35; xxvi. 26; Lam. v. 10; Hos. vii. 4, 6, 7; Mal. iv. 1. It does not occur elsewhere. The oven among the Hebrews was in the form of a large *pot*, and was heated from within by placing the wood inside of it. Of course, while being heated, it had the appearance of a furnace. The meaning here is that the wicked would be consumed or destroyed *as if* they were such a burning oven; as if they were set on fire, and burned up. ¶ *The* LORD *shall swallow them up in his wrath.* The same idea of the utter destruction of the wicked is here presented under another form—that they would be destroyed as if the earth should open and swallow them up. Perhaps the allusion in the language is to the case of Korah, Dathan, and Abiram, Num. xvi. 32; comp. Ps. cvi. 17. ¶ *And the fire shall devour them.* The same idea under another form. The wrath of God would utterly destroy them. That wrath is often represented under the image of *fire.* See Deut. iv. 24; xxxii. 22; Ps. xviii. 8; Matt. xiii. 42; xviii. 8; xxv. 41; Mark ix. 44; 2 Thess. i. 8. Fire is the emblem by which the future punishment of the wicked is most frequently denoted.

10. *Their fruit.* Their offspring; their children; their posterity; for so the parallelism demands. The *fruit* is that which the tree produces; and hence the word comes to be applied to children as the production of the parent. See this use of the word in Gen. xxx. 2; Exod. xxi. 22; Deut. xxviii. 4, 11, 18; Ps. cxxvii. 3; Hos. ix. 16; Micah vi. 7. ¶ *Shalt thou destroy from the earth.* Thou shalt utterly destroy them. This is in accordance with the statement so often made in the Scriptures, and with what so often occurs in fact, that the consequences of the sins of parents pass over to their posterity, and that they suffer in consequence of those sins. Comp. Exod. xx. 5; xxxiv. 7; Lev. xx. 5; xxvi. 39; comp. Notes on Romans v. 12–19. ¶ *And their seed.* Their posterity. ¶ *From among the children of men.* From among men, or the human family. That is, they would be entirely cut off from the earth. The truth taught here is, that the wicked will ultimately be destroyed, and that God will obtain a complete triumph over them, or that the kingdom of righteousness shall be at length completely established. A time will come when truth and justice shall be triumphant, when all the wicked shall be removed out of the way; when all that oppose God and his cause shall be destroyed, and when God shall show, by thus removing and punishing the wicked, that he is the Friend of all that is true, and good, and right. The *idea* of the psalmist probably was that this would yet occur on the earth; the *language* is

11 For they intended evil against thee; they imagined a mischievous device *which* [g] they are not able *to perform:*
12 Therefore shalt thou [1] make them turn their [2] back, *when* thou shalt make ready *thine arrows* upon thy strings against the face of them.

g Ps. ii. 1—4. [1] Or, *set them as a butt.* [2] *shoulder.*

such, also, as may be applied to that ultimate state, in the future world, when all the wicked shall be destroyed, and the righteous shall be no more troubled with them.

11. *For they intended evil against thee.* Literally, "They stretched out evil." The idea seems to be derived from *stretching out* or laying snares, nets, or gins, for the purpose of taking wild beasts. That is, they formed a plan or purpose to bring evil upon God and his cause: as the hunter or fowler forms a purpose or plan to take wild beasts or fowls. It is not merely a purpose in the head, as our word "intended" would seem to imply; it supposes that arrangements had been entered into, or that a scheme had been formed to injure the cause of God,—that is, through the person referred to in the psalm. The purposes of wicked men against religion are usually much more than a mere *intention.* The intention is accompanied with a scheme or plan in their own mind by which the act may be accomplished. The evil here referred to was that of resisting or overpowering him who was engaged in the cause of God, or whom God had appointed to administer his laws. ¶ *They imagined a mischievous device.* They thought, or they purposed. The word rendered "mischievous device"—מְזִמָּה, *mezimmah* —means properly *counsel, purpose;* then *prudence, sagacity;* then, in a bad sense, *machination, device, trick.* Gesenius, *Lex.* Prov. xii. 2; xiv. 17; xxiv. 8. ¶ Which *they are not able* to perform. Literally, "they could not;" that is, they had not the power to accomplish it, or to carry out their purpose. Their purpose was plain; their guilt was therefore clear; but they were prevented from executing their design. Many such designs are kept from being carried into execution for the want of power. If all the devices and the desires of the wicked were accomplished, righteousness would soon cease in the earth, religion and virtue would come to an end, and even God would cease to occupy the throne.

12. *Therefore shalt thou make them turn their back.* Marg., *Thou shalt set them as a butt.* The word *back* also is rendered in the margin *shoulder.* The word translated *therefore* means in this place *for,* and the rendering "*therefore*" obscures the sense. The statement in this verse in connexion with the previous verse, is, that they would not be able to "perform" or carry out their well-laid schemes, *for* or *because* God would make them turn the back; that is, he had vanquished them. They were going forward in the execution of their purposes, but God would interpose and turn them back, or compel them to *retreat.* The word rendered *back* in this place — שְׁכֶם, *shechem* — means properly *shoulder,* or, more strictly, the *shoulder-blades,* — that is, the part where these approach each other behind; and then the upper part of the back. It is not, therefore, incorrectly rendered by the phrase "thou shalt make them turn *the back.*" The expression is equivalent to saying that they would be defeated or foiled in their plans and purposes. ¶ When *thou shalt make ready* thine arrows *upon thy strings.* Comp. Notes on Ps. xi. 2. That is, when God should go forth against them, armed as a warrior. ¶ *Against the face of them.* Against them; or, in their very front. He would meet them as they seemed to be marching on to certain conquest, and would discomfit them. It would not be by a side-blow, or by skilful

13 Be thou exalted, LORD, in thine own [h] strength: *so* will we sing and praise thy power.

h Job ix. 19.

manœuvre, or by turning their flank and attacking them in the rear. Truth meets error boldly, face to face, and is not afraid of a fair fight. In every such conflict error will ultimately yield; and whenever the wicked come openly into conflict with God, they must be compelled to turn and flee.

13. *Be thou exalted,* LORD, *in thine own strength.* This is the concluding part of the psalm (see the introd.), expressing a desire that God *might* be exalted over all his foes; or that his own strength might be so manifestly put forth that he would be exalted as he ought to be. This is the ultimate and chief desire of all holy created beings, that God might be exalted in the estimation of the universe above all other beings,—or that he might so triumph over all his enemies as to reign supreme. ¶ So *will we sing and praise thy power.* That is, as the result of thy being thus exalted to proper honour, we will unite in celebrating thy glory and thy power. Comp. Rev. vii. 10—12; xii. 10; xix. 1—3. This will be the result of all the triumphs which God will achieve in the world, that the holy beings of all worlds will gather around his throne and "sing and praise his power." The *thought* in the psalm is that God will ultimately triumph over all his foes, and that this triumph will be followed by universal rejoicing and praise. Come that blessed day!

PSALM XXII.

I. *The author of the psalm.*—This psalm is said to have been composed by David:—"A Psalm of David;" comp. Notes on the title of Psalm iii. It cannot be absolutely demonstrated that these titles to the psalms are all of them correct, as it cannot be supposed that they were affixed to them by the authors of the psalms themselves; and it is not absolutely known by whom they were prefixed. Of course there is no certain evidence that they were attached to the psalms by an inspired writer. Still they are to be presumed to be correct unless there is some clear evidence to the contrary. In this case there seems to be none. There is nothing in the psalm itself that is inconsistent with the supposition, and there are no historical evidences in the case which would make it necessary for us to set the title aside. The affixing of this title to the psalm undoubtedly implies that it was the prevailing opinion, at the time when the collection of Psalms was made, that this was a psalm of David. Rosenmüller indeed doubts this; but he assigns no historical reasons for the doubt. Hitzig supposes that the author was Jeremiah, on the ground, as he says, that it is "in the broad and flowing style" of Jeremiah, but this is mere conjecture.

It is not necessary, however, to suppose that David, though he was the author of the psalm, refers to himself. If it be admitted that he was inspired, or even if *this* should be doubted, it would still be an open question to whom the psalm refers,—whether to himself as an individual;—whether to an *imaginary* sufferer, designing to illustrate the feelings of piety in a time of sorrow;—whether to the people of God, considered collectively;—or whether to the Messiah. The mere fact of the *authorship* of the psalm determines none of these questions.

It is not known, and it cannot now be determined, on what occasion the psalm was written. It is expressive of the feelings of a pious sufferer,—of one who appears to be forsaken by God and by man. Perhaps there may have been occasions in the life of David to which the expressions in the psalm may have been applicable; but if so, it is impossible now to determine on which *one* of these trials of his life the psalm was composed. There is no one period in which, from the historical records of his life, we could be able to make out all the circumstances which are mentioned in the psalm. There are, however, expressions in it which in their intensity, as expressing wretchedness and woe, seem to go beyond anything that occurred in his experience, and which lead naturally to the question whether he did not refer to some other than himself.

II. *The contents of the psalm.*—Various divisions of the psalm have been proposed, but there are no *marked* and *prominent* divisions in the psalm itself. Hengstenberg, and after him Prof. Alexander, divide it into three parts, or strophes, (1) vers. 1–10; (2) vers. 12–21; (3) vers. 22–31. According to this, each strophe, as Hengstenberg remarks, would consist of ten verses,—with an intermediate verse between the 10th and the 12th (ver. 11) connecting the first and second parts. Professor Alexander supposes that ver. 21 is a connecting link also between the second and third parts.

This division, however, seems fanciful and arbitrary; and it will present a more simple and clear view of the psalm to regard it as embracing two main things:—I. The condition of the sufferer; and II. His consolations or supports in his trials.

I. The condition of the sufferer. This consists of two parts:—(1) His sufferings as derived from God, or as they spring from God; (2) as they are derived from men, or as they spring from the treatment which he receives from men.

(1.) As they are derived from God, vers. 1, 2.

(*a*) He is forsaken of God, ver. 1.

(*b*) He cries to him day and night (or continually), and receives no answer, ver. 2.

His prayer seems not to be heard, and he is left to suffer apparently unpitied and alone.

(2) His sufferings as derived from men, as produced by the treatment which he received from men.

Here there are *five* specifications; *five* sources of his affliction and sorrow.

First. He was despised, reproached, derided by them in the midst of his other sufferings, vers. 6, 7, 8;—especially his piety, or confidence in God was ridiculed, for it now seemed as if God had abandoned him.

Second. His enemies were fierce and ravenous as strong bulls of Bashan, or as a ravening and roaring lion, vers. 12, 13.

Third. His sufferings were intense, so that his whole frame was relaxed and prostrated and crushed; he seemed to be poured out like water, and all his bones were out of joint; his heart was melted like wax; his strength was dried up like a potsherd; his tongue clave to his jaws, and he was brought into the dust of death, vers. 14, 15.

Fourth. His enemies pierced his hands and his feet, ver. 16.

Fifth. They stripped him of his raiment, and parted his garments among themselves, ver. 18.

II. His consolations or supports in his trials. These are scattered through the psalm, and consist of the following things:—

(1) His unshaken confidence in God as holy, ver. 3.

(2) His faith in God as the hearer of prayer, and especially on the ground that he *had* heard prayer in times past, vers. 4, 5.

(3) The fact that he had been himself early devoted to God, and cast upon him as his Protector from very childhood, and trained up for him, vers. 9, 10, 11.

(4) The anticipated effect or result of what he was then suffering, or the things to be accomplished *by* his sufferings, vers. 19–31. There are mainly *two* things implied here as to the anticipated result of his sufferings:—

(*a*) The establishment of a great principle that would *encourage* the friends of God, or those whom the sufferer calls his "brethren," vers. 22–26.

(*b*) The world would be converted as the result of his sufferings, and the kingdom of God would be set up everywhere among men, vers. 27–31.

These views of the psalm are apparent on its face, or are such as are suggested by the analysis without reference to the inquiry who was the author, or to whom it refers. The analysis of the psalm, however, necessarily leads—

III. To the inquiry *to whom the psalm refers*:—

(1.) It refers to a sufferer, and it is designed to describe his condition and his feelings, when apparently forsaken by God and man. At the same time, he is a *pious* sufferer, or one who has real trust in God, though God *appears* to have forsaken him.

(2.) There seems to be no reason to suppose that the psalm refers to David himself, or that he means to describe his own feelings and condition. He was indeed a sufferer; and he often refers to his own sufferings in the Psalms. It is true, also, that there are expressions in this psalm which would be applicable to him, or which might refer to his condition. But there are none which can be regarded as *exclusively* applicable to him, and there are some which could *not* be applied to him. Of the latter class are the expressions, "They pierced my hands and my feet," ver. 16; "They part my garments among them, and cast lots upon my vesture," ver. 18. We know of no circumstances in the life of David to which these expressions would be applicable; we have no reason to suppose that there were any in which what is here said would have been literally true of him. On the other hand, this language cannot with propriety be regarded as *figurative*, for we cannot conceive of any circumstances which would be described by such figures of speech. The whole cast of the psalm, moreover, is different from those in which David refers to his own sufferings.

(3.) The psalm refers to a case not then actually before the psalmist, but to some case that might or would occur, as an individual or as a representative case. So far as the mere *language* of the psalm is concerned, this might have been a case purely imaginary, and the design might have been to describe a pious sufferer who seemed to be forsaken both by God and man, or to illustrate the nature of true submission to God *in* such trials. In other words, it might have been a *supposed* case intended to show the nature of real religion under the severest forms of suffering; and, as a poet, the author of the psalm may have pictured to himself such an instance in order to show what the feelings of true piety would suggest in such circumstances, or what would be the effect of true religion then. It is true that this interpretation would not be quite obvious and natural, for we usually find such descriptions connected with real cases; but I am merely saying that *so far as the language of the psalm is concerned*, if we had no other way to ascertain its meaning, this interpretation would be allowable,—and if we could not attach the psalm properly to any real person, this explanation would be admissible. But in this case such an interpretation is unnecessary, for there *is* a real person to whom the language is applicable, and one to whom we may properly suppose an inspired writer would refer in the language which is here used.

(4.) The psalm refers, therefore, I apprehend, originally and exclusively, to the Messiah. The proof of this is to be found in such circumstances as the following:—

(*a*) Portions of it are expressly applied to him in the New Testament. The cry in ver. 1, "My God, my God, why hast thou forsaken me?" is the very one used by the Redeemer when on the cross, Matt. xxvii. 46. The language (ver. 8), "He trusted in the Lord that he would deliver him; let him deliver him, seeing he delighted in him," is the taunt which his enemies used as they passed by the cross, Matt. xxvii. 43. The language (ver. 18), "They part my garments among them, and cast lots upon my vesture," is more than once expressly applied to him; and, in one instance, with the unequivocal statement that it was done "that the Scripture might be fulfilled," John xix. 24. Comp. Luke xxiii. 34.

(*b*) We have evidence derived from the early Jewish interpreters. The modern Jews, indeed, affirm that it has no reference to the Messiah, for they reject the idea of a suffering Messiah altogether. Some of them suppose that it refers to David, and endeavour to find a fulfilment of it in his persecutions and trials. Others, as Kimchi and Jarchi, suppose that the psalm is applicable to the suffering Jewish people, and apply it to them in their trials and dispersions, as if *they* were forsaken of God. Some have supposed that it refers to the condition of the Jews in Babylon. But this was not the prevailing interpretation among the ancient Jewish interpreters. See Jo. H. Michaelis, Com. in Ps., p. 138; and Schöttgen de Messiâ, p. 232, *seq.* It is true that the opinion of the ancient Jews does not *demonstrate* that the psalm refers to the Messiah; but the fact that they *held* that opinion is an important circumstance in showing what is its fair and obvious interpretation, for there was everything to induce *them* to reject this explanation. In general, the Jews who lived in the times referred to here were opposed to the idea of a suffering Messiah; and the fact that they admitted the applicability of the psalm to the Messiah must have embarrassed them not a little in their early controversies with Christians; for the early Christians with one voice maintained that it referred to the Messiah, and that it was fulfilled in Jesus of Nazareth. The correspondence between the psalm and his sufferings was one of the arguments on which they relied in proving that he was the Christ; and if the Jews admitted that the psalm had reference to the Messiah, they would find it hard to meet the force of this argument. Their admission, therefore, under these circumstances, that it referred to the Messiah, could have arisen only from the fair and obvious interpretation of the psalm which it was not easy to set aside.

(*c*) The internal character of the psalm shows that it refers to the Messiah. This will appear more conclusively in the course of the exposition, in the entire correspondence as will be seen there between the psalm and the sufferings of the Redeemer. It will be found that many of the expressions in the psalm are as applicable to him as they would be if they were *history* instead of *prophecy;* if they had been penned *after*, instead of having been penned *before* his sufferings occurred. It is sufficient here to refer to the expressions in vers. 1, 7, 8, 16, 18, and to the Notes on those passages.

(*d*) There is no improbability in supposing that David here refers to the Messiah. It cannot be denied that there *is*, in the Old Testament, from some cause, a frequent reference to a personage who was expected to appear in future time, and who was called *the Messiah.* And it cannot be denied that he is often represented as a sufferer, and that his humiliation and sufferings are often described. *Somehow*, beyond all question, the Jewish writers had formed the conception of such a personage, and they exhaust the powers of their native tongue in their description of his person and his work. He was, in fact, their "*hero;*"—he to whom they always looked, and on whom their descriptions usually terminated, wherever they began. Comp. Notes on Isa. liii. and Dan. ix. Now, if it be admitted that the Jewish writers were *inspired*, and that this view of the Messiah had been furnished by the Spirit of inspiration, nothing is more natural than to expect to find such descriptions of the Messiah as occur in this psalm; and if it should be said that they were *not* inspired, and that this anticipation was wholly a poetic fiction,—a matter of national vanity,—a mere favourite *idea* of the nation,—nothing would even then be more natural than that there should be a frequent reference to this imaginary person in their writings; and nothing would be more probable than that we should find frequent reference to him in the writings of one who was so deeply imbued with the national spirit, and who occupied so high a position among the poets of the nation, as David. Inspired or uninspired, then, there is the strongest probability that there would be in their poetic writings such allusions to the Messiah as we have in this psalm.

An examination of the objections to the interpretation which refers the psalm to the Messiah, may be found in Hengstenberg's Christology, vol. i, pp. 145-147.

The *title* of the psalm is, "To the chief Musician upon Aijeleth Shahar." On the meaning of the expression *chief Musician*, see Notes on the title to Psalm iv. The expression *Aijeleth Shahar* is rendered in the margin, *the hind of the morning*. The word *Aijeleth*—אַיֶּלֶת—means a *hind*, and is used as a term of endearment towards a female, Prov. v. 19. It is found in Gen. xlix. 21, "Naphtali is a *hind* let loose." Also in 2 Sam. xxii. 34; Job xxxix. 1; Ps. xviii. 33; Cant. ii. 7; iii. 5; Hab. iii. 19;—in each of which places it is rendered in the singular *hind*, and in the plural *hinds.* The word *Shahar* — שַׁחַר—means *the aurora, the dawn, the morning.* "The phrase 'hind of the dawn' probably stands for the morning sun scattering his first rays upon the earth, as the Arabian poets call the rising sun *the gazelle*, comparing his rays with the horns of that animal." *Gesenius, Lex.*—The image is one of gladness, *as if* the rays of the sun leaped and bounded over the hills with joyousness as the hart or hind does. But why such a title is given to this psalm can be only a matter of conjecture. It would seem most probable that these words were the beginning of some other psalm or hymn that was sung to a set piece of music, and that the design was, as indicated by this title, that this psalm was to be sung to the same tune. A tune might not improbably be known then, as it is in fact sometimes now, by the first or opening words of the piece which was commonly sung in that measure. Thus we have hymns so constantly sung to certain tunes that the mention of the first line would be a sufficient suggestion of the strain of music in which it was to be sung. It would be, for example, sufficient to say that it was to be sung to the same tune as "From Greenland's icy mountains;" or, "All hail the power of Jesus' name;" or, "I would not live alway." Other views of the meaning of the phrase may be seen in Rosenmüller, *Com. in loc.* Rosenmüller himself adopts the views here expressed, and sustains his opinion by the authority of Bochart.

PSALM XXII.

To the chief Musician upon [1] Aijeleth Shahar. A Psalm of David.

1 MY *i* God, my God, why hast thou forsaken me? *why art thou so* far from [2] helping me, *and from* the words of my *k* roaring?

[1] Or, *the hind of the morning.*

i Matt. xxvii. 46; Luke xxiv. 44.
[2] *my salvation.* *k* Heb. v. 7.

1. *My God, my God.* These are the very words uttered by the Saviour when on the cross (Matt. xxvii. 46); and he evidently used them as best adapted of all the words that could have been chosen to express the extremity of his sorrow. The fact that he employed them may be referred to as *some* evidence that the psalm was designed to refer to him; though it must be admitted that this circumstance is no conclusive proof of such a design, since he might have used words having originally another reference, as best fitted to express his own sufferings. The language is abrupt, and is uttered without any previous intimation of what would produce or cause it. It comes from the midst of suffering—from one enduring intense agony—as if a new form of sorrow suddenly came upon him which he was unable to endure. That new form of suffering was the feeling that now he was forsaken by the last friend of the wretched,—God himself. We may suppose that he had patiently borne all the other forms of trial, but the moment the thought strikes him that he is forsaken of God, he cries out in the bitterness of his soul, under the pressure of anguish which is no longer to be borne. All other forms of suffering he could bear. All others he had borne. But this crushes him; overpowers him; is beyond all that the soul can sustain,—for the soul may bear all else but this. It is to be observed, however, that the sufferer himself still has confidence in God. He addresses him as *his* God, though he seems to have forsaken him:—"*My* God; MY God." ¶ *Why hast thou forsaken me?* Why hast thou abandoned me, or left me to myself, to suffer unaided and alone? As applicable to the Saviour, this refers to those dreadful moments on the cross when, forsaken by men, he seemed also to be forsaken of God himself. God did not interpose to rescue him, but left him to bear those dreadful agonies alone. He bore the burden of the world's atonement by himself. He was overwhelmed with grief, and crushed with pain; for the sins of the world, as well as the agonies of the cross, had come upon him. But there was evidently more than this;—*what* more we are unable fully to understand! There was a higher sense in which he was forsaken of God; for no mere physical sufferings, no pains of dying even on the cross, would have extorted this cry. If he had enjoyed the light of his Father's countenance; if these had been merely physical sufferings; if there was nothing else than what is apparent to our view in the record of those sufferings, we cannot suppose that this cry would have been heard even on the cross. There is evidently some sense in which it was true that the dying Saviour was given up to darkness—to mental trouble, to despair, *as if* He who is the last hope of the suffering and the dying—the Father of mercies—had withdrawn from him; *as if* he were personally a sinner; *as if* he were himself guilty or blameworthy on account of the sins for which he was making an expiation. In some sense he experienced what the sinner will himself experience when, for his own sins, he will be at last forsaken of God, and abandoned to despair. Every word in this wonderful exclamation may be supposed to be emphatic. "*Why.*" What is the cause? How is it to be accounted for? What end is to be answered by it? "*Hast thou.*" Thou, my Father; thou, the comforter of those in trouble; thou, to whom the suffering and the dying may look when all else fails. "*Forsaken.*" Left me to suffer alone;

2 O my God, I cry in the daytime, but thou hearest not: and in the night-season, and [1] am not silent.

[1] there is *no silence to me.*

3 But thou *art* holy, *O thou* that inhabitest the praises [l] of Israel.

l Ps. lxv. 1.

withdrawn the light of thy countenance—the comfort of thy presence—the joy of thy manifested favour. "*Me.*" Thy well-beloved Son; me, whom thou hast sent into the world to accomplish thine own work in redeeming man; me, against whom no sin can be charged, whose life has been perfectly pure and holy;—why, now, in the extremity of these sufferings, hast thou forsaken *me,* and added to the agony of the cross the deeper agony of being abandoned by the God whom I love, the Father who loved me before the foundation of the world, John xvii. 24. There is a reason why God should forsake the wicked; but why should he forsake his own pure and holy Son in the agonies of death? ¶ Why art thou so *far from helping me?* Marg., *from my salvation.* So the Hebrew. The idea is that of one who stood *so far off* that he could not hear the cry, or that he could not reach out the hand to deliver. Comp. Ps. x. 1. ¶ And from *the words of my roaring.* The word here used properly denotes the roaring of a lion, Job iv. 10; Isa. v. 29; Zech. xi. 3; and then the outcry or the groaning of a person in great pain, Job iii. 24; Ps. xxxii. 3. It refers here to a loud cry for help or deliverance, and is descriptive of the intense suffering of the Redeemer on the cross. Comp. Matt. xxvii. 50; Luke xxiii. 46.

2. *O my God, I cry in the daytime.* This, in connexion with what is said at the close of the verse, "and in the night-season," means that his cry was incessant or constant. See Notes on Ps. i. 2. The whole expression denotes that his prayer or cry was continuous, but that it was not heard. As applicable to the Redeemer it refers not merely to the moment when he uttered the cry as stated in ver. 1, but to the continuous sufferings which he endured as if forsaken by God and men. His life in general was of that description. The whole series of sorrows and trials through which he passed was *as if* he were forsaken by God; *as if* he uttered a long continuous cry, day and night, and was not heard. ¶ *But thou hearest not.* Thou dost not *answer* me. It is *as if* my prayers were not heard. God *hears* every cry; but the answer to a prayer is sometimes withheld or delayed, as if he did not hear the voice of the suppliant. Comp. Notes on Dan. x. 12, 13. So it was with the Redeemer. He was permitted to suffer without being rescued by Divine power, *as if* his prayers had not been heard. God *seemed* to disregard his supplications. ¶ *And in the night-season.* As explained above, this means *constantly.* It was literally true, however, that the Redeemer's most intense and earnest prayer was uttered in the night-season, in the garden of Gethsemane. ¶ *And am not silent.* Marg., there is *no silence to me.* Heb., "There is not silence to me." The idea is, that he prayed or cried incessantly. He was never silent. All this denotes intense and continuous supplication, supplication that came from the deepest anguish of the soul, but which was unheard and unanswered. If Christ experienced this, who may not?

3. *But thou* art *holy.* Thou art righteous and blameless. This indicates that the sufferer had still unwavering confidence in God. Though his prayer seemed not to be heard, and though he was not delivered, he was not disposed to blame God. He believed that God was righteous, though he received no answer; he doubted not that there was some sufficient reason why he was not answered. This is applicable, not only to the Redeemer, in whom it

4 Our fathers trusted in thee: they trusted, and thou didst deliver them.

5 They cried unto thee, and were delivered: they trusted in thee, and were not confounded.

was most fully illustrated, but also to the people of God everywhere. It expresses a state of mind such as all true believers in God have—confidence in him, whatever may be their trials; confidence in him, though the answer to their prayers may be long delayed; confidence in him, though their prayers should seem to be *un*answered. Comp. Notes on Job xiii. 15. ¶ O thou *that inhabitest the praises of Israel.* That dwellest where praise is celebrated; that seemest to dwell in the midst of praises. The language here refers to the praises offered in the tabernacle or temple. God was supposed to dwell there, and he was surrounded by those who praised him. The sufferer looks upon him as worshipped by the multitude of his people; and the feeling of his heart is, that though he was himself a sufferer—a great and apparently unpitied sufferer—though he, by his afflictions, was not permitted to unite in those lofty praises, yet he could own that God was worthy of all those songs, and that it was proper that they should be addressed to him.

4. *Our fathers trusted in thee.* This is a plea of the sufferer as drawn from the character which God had manifested in former times. The argument is, that he had interposed in those times when his people in trouble had called upon him; and he now pleads with God that he would manifest himself to *him* in the same way. The argument derives additional force also from the idea that he who now pleads was descended from them, or was of the same nation and people, and that he might call them his ancestors. As applicable to the Redeemer, the argument is that he was *descended* from those holy and suffering men who had trusted in God, and in whose behalf God had so often interposed. He identifies himself with that people; he regards himself as one of their number; and he makes mention of God's merciful interposition in their behalf, and of the fact that he had not forsaken *them* in their troubles, as a reason why he should now interpose in his behalf and save him. As applicable to others, it is an argument which the people of God may always use in their trials—that God has thus interposed in behalf of his people of former times who trusted in him, and who called upon him. God is always the same. We may strengthen our faith in our trials by the assurance that he never changes; and, in pleading with him, we may urge it as an argument that he *has* often interposed when the tried and the afflicted of his people have called upon him. ¶ *They trusted, and thou didst deliver them.* They confided in thee; they called on thee; thou didst not spurn their prayer; thou didst not forsake *them.*

5. *They cried unto thee.* They offered earnest prayer and supplication. ¶ *And were delivered.* From dangers and trials. ¶ *They trusted in thee, and were not confounded.* Were not disappointed. Literally, "they were not *ashamed.*" That is, they had not the confusion which those have who are disappointed. The idea in the word is, that when men put their trust in anything and are disappointed, they are conscious of a species of *shame* as if they had been foolish in relying on that which proved to be insufficient to help them; as if they had manifested a want of wisdom in not being more cautious, or in supposing that they could derive help from that which has proved to be fallacious. So in Jer. xiv. 3, "Their nobles have sent their little ones to the waters; they came to the pits, and found no water; they returned with their vessels empty; *they were ashamed and confounded,* and covered their heads." That is, they

6 But I *am* a worm, [l] and no
man; a reproach of men, and
despised [m] of the people.
7 All [n] they that see me laugh

l Isa. xli. 14. *m* Isa. liii. 3.
n Mark xv. 29, etc.

me to scorn: they [1] shoot out the
lip, they shake [o] the head, *saying*,
8 He [2] trusted on the LORD
that he would deliver him: let

[1] *open.* *o* Ps. cix. 25.
[2] *rolled* himself.

felt as if they had acted *foolishly* or *unwisely* in expecting to find water there. Comp. Notes on Job vi. 20. In the expression here, "they trusted in thee, and were not confounded," it is meant that men who confide in God are never disappointed, or never have occasion for shame as if herein *they* had acted foolishly. They are never left to feel that they had put their trust where no help was to be found; that they had confided in one who had deceived them, or that they had reason to be ashamed of their act as an act of foolishness.

6. *But I am a worm, and no man.* In contrast with the fathers who trusted in thee. They prayed, and were heard; they confided in God, and were treated as men. I am left and forsaken, as if I were not worth regarding; as if I were a grovelling worm beneath the notice of the great God. In other words, I am treated as if I were the most insignificant, the most despicable, of all objects,—alike unworthy the attention of God or man. By the one my prayers are unheard; by the other I am cast out and despised. Comp. Job xxv. 6. As applicable to the Redeemer, this means that he was forsaken alike by God and men, as if he had no claims to the treatment due to *a man.* ¶ *A reproach of men.* Reproached by men. Comp. Isa. liii. 3, and the Notes on that verse. ¶ *Despised of the people.* That is, of the people who witnessed his sufferings. It is not necessary to say how completely this had a fulfilment in the sufferings of the Saviour.

7. *All they that see me laugh me to scorn.* They deride or mock me. On the word used here—לָעַג, *laag*—see Notes on Ps. ii. 4. The meaning here is to mock, to deride, to treat with scorn. The idea of *laughing* is not properly in the word, nor would that necessarily occur in the treatment here referred to. How completely this was fulfilled in the case of the Saviour, it is not necessary to say. Comp. Matt. xxvii. 39, "And they that passed by, reviled him." There is no evidence that this literally occurred in the life of David. ¶ *They shoot out the lip.* Marg., *open.* The Hebrew word—פָּטַר, *patar*—means properly *to split, to burst open;* then, as in this place, it means to open wide the mouth; to stretch the mouth in derision and scorn. See Ps. xxxv. 21, "They opened their mouth wide against me." Job xvi. 10, "They have gaped upon me with their mouth." ¶ *They shake the head.* In contempt and derision. See Matt. xxvii. 39, "Wagging their heads."

8. *He trusted on the* LORD *that he would deliver him.* Marg., *He rolled* himself *on the* LORD. The margin expresses the true sense of the Hebrew word. The idea is that of being under the pressure of a heavy burden, and of *rolling* it off, or casting it on another. Hence the word is often used in the sense of committing to another; entrusting anything to another; confiding in another. Ps. xxxvii. 5, "Commit thy way unto the Lord;" Marg., as in Heb., "*Roll* thy way upon the Lord." Prov. xvi. 3, "*Commit thy works unto the Lord,*" Marg., as in Heb., "*Roll.*" The language here is the taunting language of his enemies, and the meaning is that he had professed to commit himself to the Lord as if he were his friend; he had expressed confidence in God, and he believed that his cause was safe in His hand. This, too, was actually fulfilled in the case of the Saviour. Matt. xxvii. 43: "He trusted in God; let him deliver him

him deliver *p* him, [1] seeing he delighted in him.

9 But thou *art* he that took me out of the womb; thou [2] didst make me hope *when I was* upon my mother's breasts.

[1] Or, *if he delight in him.*
p Ps. xci. 14.

[2] Or, *keptest me in safety.*

now, if he will have him." It is one of the most remarkable instances of blindness and infatuation that has ever occurred in the world, that the Jews should have used this language in taunting the dying Redeemer, without even suspecting that they were fulfilling the prophecies, and demonstrating at the very time when they were reviling him that he was the true Messiah. ¶ *Let him deliver him.* Let him come and save him. Since he professes to belong to God; since he claims that God loves him and regards him as his friend, let him come now and rescue one so dear to him. He is hopelessly abandoned by men. If God chooses to have one so abject, so despised, so forsaken, so helpless, let him come now and take him as his own. *We* will not rescue him; we will do nothing to save him, for we do not need him. If God wants him, let him come and save him. What blasphemy! What an exhibition of the dreadful depravity of the human heart was manifested in the crucifixion of the Redeemer! ¶ *Seeing he delighted in him.* Marg., *if he delight in him.* The correct rendering is, "for he delighted in him." That is, it was claimed by the sufferer that God delighted in him. If this is so, say they, let him come and rescue one so dear to himself. Let him show his friendship for this vagrant, this impostor, this despised and worthless man!

9. *But thou* art *he that took me out of the womb.* I owe my life to thee. This is urged by the sufferer as a reason why God should now interpose and protect him. God had brought him into the world, guarding him in the perils of the earliest moments of his being, and he now pleads that in the day of trouble God will interpose and save him. There is nothing improper in applying this to the Messiah. He was a man, with all the innocent propensities and feelings of a man; and no one can say but that when on the cross,—and perhaps with peculiar fitness we may say when he saw his mother standing near him (John xix. 25),—these thoughts may have passed through his mind. In the remembrance of the care bestowed on his early years, he may now have looked with an eye of earnest pleading to God, that, if it were possible, he might deliver him. ¶ *Thou didst make me hope.* Marg., *Keptest me in safety.* The phrase in the Hebrew means, Thou didst cause me to trust or to hope. It may mean here either that he was made to cherish a hope of the Divine favour *in very early life,* as it were when an infant at the breast; or it may mean that he had *cause* then to hope, or to trust in God. The former, it seems to me, is probably the meaning; and the idea is, that from his earliest years he had been led to trust in God; and he now pleads this fact as a reason why he should interpose to save him. Applied to the Redeemer as a man, it means that in his earliest childhood he had trusted in God. His first breathings were those of piety. His first aspirations were for the Divine favour. His first love was the love of God. This he now calls to remembrance; this he now urges as a reason why God should *not* withdraw the light of his countenance, and leave him to suffer alone. No one can prove that these thoughts did *not* pass through the mind of the Redeemer when he was enduring the agonies of desertion on the cross; no one can show that they would have been improper. ¶ *Upon my mother's breast.* In my earliest infancy. This does not mean that he literally cherished hope *then,* but that he had done it in the earliest period of his life, as the first act of his conscious being.

10 I was cast upon thee from the womb; thou [q] *art* my God from my mother's belly.

11 Be not far from me, for trouble *is* near; for *there is* [1] none to help.

12 Many bulls have compassed me: strong *bulls* of Bashan have beset me round.

13 They [2] gaped upon me *with* their mouths, *as* a ravening and a roaring lion.

q Isa. xlvi. 3; xlix. 1.
1 *not a helper.*
2 *opened their mouths against me.*

10. *I was cast upon thee from the womb.* Upon thy protection and care. This, too, is an argument for the Divine interposition. He had been, as it were, thrown early in life upon the protecting care of God. In some peculiar sense he had been more unprotected and defenceless than is common at that period of life, and he owed his preservation then entirely to God. This, too, *may* have passed through the mind of the Redeemer on the cross. In those sad and desolate moments he may have recalled the scenes of his early life—the events which had occurred in regard to him in his early years; the poverty of his mother, the manger, the persecution by Herod, the flight into Egypt, the return, the safety which he then enjoyed from persecution in a distant part of the land of Palestine, in the obscure and unknown village of Nazareth. This too may have occurred to his mind as a reason why God should interpose and deliver him from the dreadful darkness which had come over him now. ¶ *Thou* art *my God from my mother's belly.* Thou hast been my God from my very childhood. He had loved God as such; he had obeyed him as such; he had trusted him as such; and he now pleads this as a reason why God should interpose for him.

11. *Be not far from me.* Do not withdraw from me; do not leave or forsake me. ¶ *For trouble is near.* Near, in the sense that deep sorrow has come upon me; near, in the sense that I am approaching a dreadful death. ¶ *For* there is *none to help.* Marg., as in Heb., *not a helper.* There were those who *would* have helped, but they could not; there were those who *could* have helped, but they would not. His friends that stood around the cross were unable to aid him; his foes were unwilling to do it; and he was left to suffer unhelped.

12. *Many bulls have compassed me.* Men with the fierceness and fury of bulls. Comp. Isa. li. 20; Ps. lxviii. 30. ¶ *Strong* bulls *of Bashan.* The country of Bashan embraced the territory which was on the east of the Jordan, north of Gilead, which was given to the half tribe of Manasseh: comp. Gen. xiv. 5 with Joshua xii. 4–6. It was distinguished as pasture land for its richness. Its trees and its breed of cattle are frequently referred to in the Scriptures. Thus in Deut. xxxii. 14, "rams of the breed of Bashan" are mentioned; in Isa. ii. 13, Zech. xi. 2, "oaks of Bashan" are mentioned in connexion with the cedars of Lebanon; in Amos iv. 1, "the kine of Bashan" are mentioned. The bulls of Bashan are here alluded to as remarkable for their size, their strength, and their fierceness; and are designed to represent men that were fierce, savage, and violent. As applied to the Redeemer, the allusion is to the fierce and cruel men that persecuted him and sought his life. No one can doubt that the allusion is applicable to his persecutors and murderers; and no one can show that the thought indicated by this phrase also may not have passed through the mind of the Redeemer when on the cross.

13. *They gaped upon me* with *their mouths.* Marg., as in Heb., *opened their mouths against me.* That is, they opened their mouths wide as if they would devour me, as a lion does when he seizes upon his prey. In ver. 7 they are represented as "opening" the mouth for another purpose—that of derision or scorn; here they

14 I am poured out like water,
and all my bones are [1] out of
joint: my heart is like wax; it
is melted in the midst of my
bowels.
15 My strength is dried up
like a potsherd; and my tongue
cleaveth to my jaws; and thou
hast brought me into the dust of
death.
16 For dogs [r] have compassed
me; the assembly of the wicked

1 Or, *sundered*.

r Rev. xxii. 15.

---

are described as if they were fierce and wild beasts ready to fall upon their prey. ¶ As *a ravening and roaring lion.* The word *ravening* means *voraciously devouring,* and the allusion in the Hebrew word is to the lion as he *tears* his prey—טֹרֶף, *toreph*—rending it in pieces to devour it. All this is designed to denote the greediness with which the enemies of the Redeemer sought his life.

14. *I am poured out like water.* The sufferer now turns from his enemies, and describes the effect of all these outward persecutions and trials on himself. The meaning in this expression is, that all his strength was gone. It is remarkable that we have a similar expression, which is not easily accounted for, when we say of ourselves that "we are as weak as water." An expression similar to this occurs in Joshua vii. 5: "The hearts of the people melted, and became as water." Comp. Lam. ii. 19; Ps. lviii. 7. ¶ *My bones are out of joint.* Marg., *sundered.* The Hebrew word—פָּרַד, *parad*—means *to break off, to break in pieces, to separate by breaking;* and then, *to be separated,* or *divided.* It is not necessary to suppose here that his bones were *literally* dislocated or "put out of joint," any more than it is necessary to suppose that he was literally "poured out like water," or that his heart was literally "melted like wax" within him. The meaning is that he was utterly prostrated and powerless; he was *as if* his bones had been dislocated, and he was unable to use his limbs. ¶ *My heart is like wax.* The idea here also is that of debility. His strength seemed all to be gone. His heart was no longer firm; his vigour was exhausted. ¶ *It is melted in the midst of my bowels.* Or, within me. The word *bowels* in the Scriptures is not restricted in its signification as it is with us. It embraces the upper parts of the viscera as well as the lower, and consequently would include that part in which the heart is situated. See Notes on Isa. xvi. 11. The meaning here is that his heart was no longer firm and strong. As applied to the Redeemer, this would refer to the prostration of his strength in his last struggle; and no one can prove that *these* thoughts did not pass through his mind when on the cross.

15. *My strength is dried up like a potsherd.* A *potsherd* is a fragment of a broken pot, or a piece of earthenware. See Notes on Isa. xlv. 9; Job ii. 8. The meaning here is, that his strength was not vigorous like a green tree that was growing, and that was full of sap, but it was like a brittle piece of earthenware, so dry and fragile that it could be easily crumbled to pieces. ¶ *And my tongue cleaveth to my jaws.* See Notes on Job xxix. 10. The meaning here is, that his mouth was dry, and he could not speak. His tongue adhered to the roof of his mouth so that he could not use it,—another description of the effects of intense thirst. Comp. John xix. 28. ¶ *And thou hast brought me into the dust of death.* Or, as we should say, *to dust—to the grave*—to the dust where death reigns. See Notes on Dan. xii. 2. The meaning is, that he was near death; or, was just ready to die. Who can show that the Redeemer when on the cross may not in his own meditations have gone over these very expressions in the psalm as applicable to himself?

16. *For dogs have compassed me.* Men who resemble dogs;—harsh,

have inclosed me: they [s] pierced my hands and my feet.

s John xix. 23; xx. 25—27.

snarling, fierce, ferocious. See Notes on Phil. iii. 2; Rev. xxii. 15. No one can doubt that this is applicable to the Redeemer. ¶ *The assembly of the wicked have inclosed me.* That is, they have surrounded me; they have come around me on all sides so that I might not escape. So they surrounded the Redeemer in the garden of Gethsemane when they arrested him and bound him; so they surrounded him when on his trial before the Sanhedrim and before Pilate; and so they surrounded him on the cross. ¶ *They pierced my hands and my feet.* This passage is attended with more difficulty than perhaps any other part of the psalm. It is remarkable that it is nowhere quoted or referred to in the New Testament as applicable to the Saviour; and it is no less remarkable that there is no express statement in the actual history of the crucifixion that either the hands or the feet of the Saviour were pierced, or that he was *nailed* to the cross at all. This was not *necessarily* implied in the idea of crucifixion, for the hands and the feet were sometimes merely *bound* to the cross by cords, and the sufferer was allowed to linger on the cross thus suspended until he died from mere exhaustion. There can be no doubt, however, that the common mode of crucifixion was to nail the hands to the transverse beam of the cross, and the feet to the upright part of it. See the description of the crucifixion in the Notes on Matt. xxvii. 31, 32. Thus Tertullian, speaking of the sufferings of Christ, and applying this passage to his death, says that "this was the peculiar or proper—*propria*—severity of the cross."—Adv. Marcionem, iii. 19, ed. Würtz, I. p. 403. See Hengstenberg's Christology, 1,139. The great difficulty in this passage is in the word rendered in our version, *they pierced*—כָּאֲרִי, *kaari.* It occurs only in one other place, Isa. xxxviii. 13, where it means *as a lion.* This would undoubtedly be the most natural interpretation of the *word* here, unless there were good reasons for setting it aside; and not a few have endeavoured to show that this *is* the true rendering. According to this interpretation, the passage would mean, "As lions, they [that is, my enemies] surround (gape upon) my hands and my feet; that is, they threaten to tear my limbs to pieces." *Gesenius, Lex.* This interpretation is also that of Aben Ezra, Ewald, Paulus, and others. But, whatever may be the true explanation, there are very serious objections to this one. (*a*) It is difficult to make sense of the passage if this is adopted. The preceding word, rendered in our version "inclosed," can mean only *surrounded* or *encompassed,* and it is difficult to see how it could be said that a lion could "surround" or "encompass" *the hands and the feet.* At all events, such an interpretation would be harsh and unusual. (*b*) According to this interpretation the word "*me*"—"inclosed *me*"—would be superfluous; since the idea would be, "they enclose or surround *my hands and my feet.*" (*c*) All the ancient interpreters have taken the word here to be a verb, and in all the ancient versions it is rendered as if it were a verb. Even in the *Masora parva* (Jewish) it is said that the word here is to be taken in a different sense from what it has in Isa. xxxviii. 13, where it plainly means a lion. Gesenius admits that all the ancient interpreters have taken this as a verb, and says that it is "certainly possible" that it may be so. He says that it may be regarded as a participle formed in the Chaldee manner (from כּוּר, *kur*), and in the plural number for כָּאֲרִים, *kaarim,* and says that in this way it would be properly rendered, *piercing my hands and my feet;* that is, as he says, "my enemies, who are understood in the dogs." From such high authority, and from the uniform mode of interpreting the word among the ancients, it may be regarded as morally certain that the word is a *verb*, and that it is not to be rendered, as in Isa. xxxviii. 13, "*as a lion.*" The material question is, What does the verb mean? The verb—כּוּר, *kur*—properly means *to dig, to bore through, to pierce.* Thus used, according to Gesenius, it would mean *piercing;* and if the word used here is a verb, he supposes that it would refer to the enemies of David as wounding him, or piercing him, "with darts and weapons." He maintains that it is applicable to David literally, and he sees no reason to refer it to the Messiah. But, if so, it is natural to ask why *the hands* and *the feet* are mentioned. Certainly it is not usual for darts and spears thrown by an enemy to injure the hands or the feet particularly; nor is it customary to refer to the hands or the feet when describing the effects produced by the use of those weapons. If the reference were to the enemies of David as wounding him with darts and spears, it would be much more natural to refer to the *body* in general, without specifying any of the particular members of the body. De Wette renders it *fesseln*—"they *bind* my hands and my feet." He remarks, however, in a note, that according to the ancient versions, and the Codices of Kennicott and De Rossi, it means *durchbohren*—bore through. Aquila, Symmachus, and Jerome in five codices, says he, render it *bind.* The Septuagint renders it ὤρυξαν—they *pierced.* The Latin Vulgate the same, *foderunt.* See the Syriac. For these reasons it seems to me that the common rendering is the true one, and that the meaning is, that, in some proper sense, the enemies here referred to "pierced or bored through" the hands and the feet of the sufferer. Evidently this could *not* be literally applied to David, for there is not the least authority for supposing that this ever happened to him; nor, as has been shown, was such a thing probable. A casual dart, or the stroke of a spear, *might* indeed strike the hand or the foot; but it would be unusual and remarkable if they should strike those members of the body and leave the other parts uninjured, so as to make this a matter for special notice; and even *if* they did strike those parts, it would be every way unlikely that they would *pierce them,* or *bore* them *through.* Such an event would be so improbable that we may assume that it did *not* occur, unless there was the most decisive evidence of the fact. Nor is there the least probability that the enemies of David would pierce his hands and feet deliberately and of design. I say nothing in regard to the fact that they never had him in their possession so that they *could* do it; it is sufficient to say that this was not a mode of punishing one who was taken captive in war. Conquerors slew their captives; they made them pass under yokes; they put them under saws and harrows of iron (comp. 2 Sam. xii. 31; 1 Chron. xx. 3); but there is not the slightest evidence that they ever tortured captives in war by piercing the hands and the feet. But, as has been remarked above, there is every reason to believe that this was the ordinary mode of crucifixion. I conclude, therefore, that this must have had original reference to the Messiah. It is no objection to the interpretation that this passage is not expressly referred to as having been fulfilled in the Redeemer; for there are undoubtedly many passages in the prophets which refer to the Messiah, which are not formally applied to him in the New Testament. To make it certain that the prophecy referred to him, and was fulfilled in him, it is not necessary that we should find on record an actual application of the passage to him. All that is necessary in the case is, that it should *be* a prophecy; that it should have been spoken before the event; and that to him it should be fairly applicable.

17 I [t] may tell all my bones: they look *and* stare upon me.

t Isa. lii. 14.

18 They part my garments among them, and cast lots upon my vesture.

17. *I may tell all my bones.* That is, I may count them. They are so prominent, so bare, that I can see them and count their number. The idea here is that of emaciation from continued suffering or from some other cause. As applied to the Redeemer, it would denote the effect of long protracted suffering and anxiety on his frame, as rendering it crushed, weakened, emaciated. Comp. Notes on Isa. lii. 14; liii. 2, 3. No one can prove that an effect such as is here referred to may not have been produced by the sufferings of the Redeemer. ¶ *They look* and *stare upon me.* That is, either my bones,—or, my enemies that stand around me. The most obvious construction would refer it to the former,—to his bones,—*as if* they stood out prominently and stared him in the face. Rosenmüller understands it in the latter sense, as meaning that his enemies gazed with wonder on such an object. Perhaps this, on the whole, furnishes the best interpretation, as there is something unnatural in speaking of a man's own bones staring or gazing upon him, and as the image of his enemies standing and looking with wonder on one so wretched, so crushed, so broken, is a very striking one. This, too, will better agree with the statement in Isa. lii. 14, "Many were astonished at thee;" and Isa. liii. 2, 3, "He hath no form nor comeliness, and when we shall see him, there is no beauty that we should desire him;"—"we hid, as it were, our faces from him; he was despised, and we esteemed him not." It accords also better with the statement in the following verse; "*they*," that is, the same persons referred to, "part my garments among them."

18. *They part my garments among them.* They divide; they apportion. This refers merely to the *fact* that they made such a division or distribution of his garments; the *manner* in which it was done, is specified in the other part of the verse. The word *garments* is a general term, and would be applicable to any part of the raiment. ¶ *And cast lots upon my vesture.* That is, upon the part here represented by the word *vesture*, they *cast lots.* There was a general division of his garments by agreement, or in some other mode not involving the use of the *lot;* on some particular portion, here indicated by the word *vesture*, the lot was cast to determine whose it should be. The word thus rendered *vesture*—לְבוּשׁ, *lebush*—does not necessarily denote any particular article of raiment, as distinguished from what is meant by the word rendered *garments.* Both are general terms denoting clothing, raiment, vestment; and either of the terms might be applied to any article of apparel. The original words used here would not *necessarily* designate one article of raiment as disposed of without the lot and another specified portion by the lot. But although it could not be argued beforehand from the mere use of the language that such would be the case, yet if that should occur, it would be natural and not improper to apply the language in that sense, and as therein completely fulfilled. As a matter of fact this was literally fulfilled in the crucifixion of the Saviour. By remarkable circumstances which no human sagacity could have foreseen or anticipated, there occurred a general division of a portion of his raiment, without an appeal to the lot, among the soldiers who were engaged in crucifying him, and a specific disposal of *one* article of his raiment by the lot, Matt. xxvii. 35; Luke xxiii. 34; John xix. 23, 24. It never occurred in the life of David, as far as we know, or have reason to believe, that his enemies stripped him, and divided his garments among themselves; and the description here, therefore, could be

19 But be not thou far from me, O LORD: O my strength, haste thee to help me.

20 Deliver my soul from the sword; my [1] darling from the [2] power of the dog.

21 Save me from the lion's

[1] *only one.* [2] *hand.*

applicable only to some one else. It was completely fulfilled in the Saviour; and this verse, therefore, furnishes the fullest proof that the psalm refers to him. At the same time it should be observed that these circumstances are such that an impostor could not have secured the correspondence of the events with the prediction. The events referred to were not under the control of him whose garments were thus divided. They depended wholly on others; and by no art or plan could an impostor have so arranged matters that all these things should have appeared to be fulfilled in himself.

19. *But be not thou far from me, O* LORD. O JEHOVAH. Others—all others—have forsaken me, and left me to perish. Now, in the day of my desertion and my peril, be thou near to me. See ver. 11. This is the burden of the prayer in the whole psalm, that God would not leave him, but sustain and deliver him. Comp. ver. 1. ¶ *O my strength.* Source of my strength; thou on whom I rely for support and deliverance. ¶ *Haste thee to help me.* Help me speedily. Come to support me; come to deliver me from these dreadful sorrows. This is not necessarily a prayer to be rescued from *death,* but it would be applicable to deliverance from those deep mental sorrows that had come upon him—from this abandonment to unutterable woes.

20. *Deliver my soul from the sword.* The word *soul* here means *life,* and denotes a living person. It is equivalent to "deliver *me.*" The *sword* is used to denote an instrument of death, or anything that pierces like a sword. Comp. 2 Sam. xi. 24, 25. As applied to the Saviour here, it may mean those extreme mental sufferings that were like the piercing of a sword. ¶ *My darling.* Marg., *my only one.* Prof. Alexander, *my lonely one.* De Wette, *my life.* The Hebrew word—יָחִיד, *yahhid*—means *one alone, only,* as of an only child;—then one alone, as forsaken, solitary, wretched, Ps. xxv. 16; lxviii. 6;—then it means one only, *the* only one, in the sense of *most dear, darling.* Here, according to Gesenius (*Lex.*), it is used poetically for *life,* as being something most dear, or as denoting all that we have, and, therefore, most precious. Comp. Job ii. 4. This is the most probable interpretation here, as it would thus correspond with the expression in the first part of the verse, "deliver my *soul.*" ¶ *From the power of the dog.* Marg., as in Heb., *from the hand.* The enemy is represented, as in ver. 16, as a *dog* (see Notes on that verse); and then that enemy is spoken of as inflicting death by his hand. There is a little incongruity in speaking of a *dog* as having hands, but the image before the mind is that of the enemy with the *character* of a dog, and thus there is no impropriety in using in reference to him the language which is commonly applied to a man.

21. *Save me from the lion's mouth.* His enemies represented as fierce and ravening lions, comp. ver. 13. ¶ *For thou hast heard me.* The word *heard* in this place is equivalent to *saved*—or saved in answer to prayer. The fact of *hearing* the prayer, and *answering* it, is regarded as so identical, or the one as so certainly following from the other, that they may be spoken of as the same thing. ¶ *From the horns of the unicorns.* The idea here is, that he cried to God when exposed to what is here called "the horns of the unicorns." That is, when surrounded by enemies as fierce and violent as wild beasts,—as if he were among "unicorns" seeking his life,—he had called upon God, and God had heard him. This would refer to some

[u] mouth: for thou hast heard me from the horns of the [v] unicorns.

22 I [w] will declare thy name unto my brethren: in the midst of the congregation will I praise thee.

23 Ye [x] that fear the LORD, praise him: all ye the seed of

u 2 Tim. iv. 17. v Isa. xxxiv. 7. w Ps. xl. 9; Heb. ii. 11, 12.

x Ps. cxv. 11, 13.

former period of his life, when surrounded by dangers, or exposed to the attacks of wicked men, and when he had called upon God, and had been heard. There were not a few occasions alike in the life of David and in the life of the Saviour, to which this would be applicable. The fact that he *had* thus been delivered from danger, is now urged as an argument why God was to be regarded as able to deliver him again, and why the prayer might be offered that he would do it; comp. vers. 9–11. To see the force of this it is not necessary to be able to determine with accuracy what is meant here by the word rendered *unicorn,* or whether the psalmist referred to the animal now denoted by that term. The existence of such an animal was long regarded as fabulous; but though it has been proved that there *is* such an animal, it is not *necessary* to suppose that the psalmist referred to it. Gesenius renders the word—רְאֵם, *reem*—*buffalo* (*Lex.*). So also De Wette. See Notes on Job xxxix. 9, 10, where the meaning of the word is fully considered. The word occurs elsewhere only in Numb. xxiii. 22; xxiv. 8; Deut. xxxiii. 17; Ps. xxix. 6; xcii. 10; Isa. xxxiv. 7, in all which places it is rendered *unicorn,* or *unicorns.*

22. *I will declare thy name.* I will make thee known; that is, thine existence; thy perfections; thy law; thy method of salvation. As the result or effect of the interposition which he desired, and for which he prayed, he says that he would diffuse a knowledge of God. This is an expression of true piety, and is a statement of what in a pure mind will always be consequent on a gracious Divine interposition,—a purpose to make the character of the benefactor known. Comp. Ps. li. 12, 13; xviii. 48, 49. As applicable to the Redeemer, it means that he would make the name of God known to men, or that *through him* that name would be made known. ¶ *Unto my brethren.* Comp. John xx. 17; Rom. viii. 29. The word *brethren* would embrace literally brothers; kinsfolk; countrymen; then, those of the same opinion, profession, or religion; then, in a still larger sense, the human race as descended from a common parent. As having reference to the Redeemer, it would embrace here not only those who were his immediate followers and whom he called brethren,—not only those of his own nation,—but the human family in general, towards whom he consented to sustain this relation. Comp. Notes on Heb. ii. 10—12, where this passage is quoted and expressly applied to our Saviour. ¶ *In the midst of the congregation.* Among the people assembled to worship there. See Notes on Heb. ii. 12. This is the place where praise is commonly celebrated, and he says that *there* he would make known the goodness of God. Comp. Isa. xxxviii. 19, 20. It is not necessary to show that this was *literally* done by the Redeemer. It is enough to observe that this is the usual language of piety, and that the effect of his work has been to cause the praises of God to be celebrated in tens of thousands of the congregations of his saints.

23. *Ye that fear the* LORD. A phrase denoting those who are pious. ¶ *Praise him.* This is language which may be supposed to be addressed by the speaker in the great congregation. In the previous verse he had said that he *would* praise God "in the midst of the congregation;" he here speaks *as if* he *were* in that congregation, and addressing them. He, therefore, calls on them to praise

Jacob, glorify him; and fear
him, all ye the seed of Israel.
24 For he hath not despised
nor abhorred the affliction of the
afflicted, neither hath he hid his
face from him; but when he
[y] cried unto him, he heard.
25 My praise *shall be* of thee in
the great congregation: [z] I [a] will
pay my vows before them that
fear him.
26 The meek [b] shall eat and be
satisfied: they shall praise the

y Heb. v. 7. *z* Ps. lxvi. 13—16. *a* Ps. cxvi. 14; Eccles. v. 4, 5. *b* Matt. v. 5.

and honour God. ¶ *All ye the seed of Jacob, glorify him.* The descendants of Jacob; that is, all who are true worshippers of God. ¶ *And fear him.* Honour him, worship him. See Notes on Ps. v. 7. ¶ *All ye the seed of Israel.* Another name for Jacob (Gen. xxxii. 28), and designed to denote also all who are true worshippers of Jehovah.

24. *For he hath not despised nor abhorred the affliction of the afflicted.* This expresses the belief that his prayer had been heard. The fact that he had been thus heard is here assigned to be the ground or reason for the exhortation in the previous verse, addressed to all the pious. The Lord had heard *his* prayer, and this was a reason why others should also confide in the Lord, and feel assured that he would likewise hear their prayers. ¶ *Neither hath he hid his face from him.* That is, *permanently, constantly, finally, completely.* He has not wholly abandoned me, but though he seemed to forsake me, it was for a time only; and his friendship has not been ultimately and for ever withdrawn. It was indeed the foundation of all the petitions in this psalm that the Lord *had* hid his face from the sufferer (ver. 1); but, from this verse, it seems that it was only for a time. That which he passed through was a temporary darkness, succeeded by the clear manifestations of the Divine favour. The Lord heard his prayer; the Lord showed that he had not utterly forsaken him. ¶ *But when he cried unto him, he heard.* Showing that now he had the evidence and the assurance that his prayer *had* been heard. As applicable to the Redeemer on the cross, this means that though the darkness seemed to continue till death, yet it was not an utter forsaking. His prayer was heard; his work was accepted; the great object for which he came into the world would be accomplished; he himself would rise triumphantly from his sufferings; and the cause which he came to establish, and for which he died, would finally prevail in the world. Comp. Heb. v. 7, 8; John xi. 42; Isa. liii. 11, 12.

25. *My praise* shall be *of thee.* That is, I will praise thee. I will call to remembrance thy goodness, and will unite with others in celebrating thy faithfulness and loving-kindness. ¶ *In the great congregation.* See Notes on ver. 22. ¶ *I will pay my vows before them that fear him.* In the presence of his worshippers. That is, he would keep the vows which in his afflictions he had made, that he would praise and serve God. These vows or promises were of the nature of a *debt* which he says he would remember to pay. Of the Redeemer, this need not be understood personally, but it means that as the result of his prayer having been heard, the worship of God would be celebrated by those who feared him. The solemn worship of the people of God—the praises which *they* offer to the Most High—may be regarded as worship paid by the Redeemer himself, for he does it *in* the persons and services of those whom he redeemed. All the praises which proceed from their hearts and lips are the fruit of his "vows," of his fidelity, and his prayers.

26. *The meek shall eat and be satisfied.* The word *meek*—עֲנָוִים, *anavim*—means here rather *afflicted,*

LORD that seek him: your heart shall live for ever.

27 All the ends of the world shall remember and turn unto the LORD; and all the kindreds of the nations shall worship before thee.

28 For the kingdom *is* the LORD'S, and he *is* the governor among the nations.

29 All *they that be* fat upon earth shall eat and worship: all they that go down to the dust shall bow before him: and none

---

distressed, miserable. This is its usual meaning. It is employed sometimes in the sense of *mild* or *meek* (comp. Num. xii. 3); but it here manifestly denotes the afflicted; the poor; the distressed. When it is said that they would "eat and be satisfied," the idea is that of prosperity or abundance; and the statement is, that, as the result of the Redeemer's work, blessings in abundance would be imparted to the poor and the distressed—those who had been destitute, forsaken, and friendless. ¶ *They shall praise the* LORD *that seek him.* Those that worship God, or the pious, shall see abundant cause to praise God. They will not merely call upon him by earnest prayer, but they will render him thanks for his mercies. ¶ *Your heart shall live for ever.* The hearts of those that worship God. Their hearts would not faint or be discouraged. They would exult and rejoice continually. In other words, their joy and their praise would never die away.

27. *All the ends of the world.* All parts of the earth; all nations. The earth is frequently represented in the Scriptures as having limits or boundaries; as spread out; as having corners, etc. Comp. Isa. xi. 12; Jer. ix. 26; xxv. 23; xlix. 32; Rev. vii. 1. This language is in accordance with the prevailing modes of thinking, in the same way as we say, "the sun rises;" "the sun sets," etc. ¶ *Shall remember.* The nations are often represented as *forgetting* God; that is, they act as if they had once known him, and had then forgotten him. See Job viii. 13; Ps. ix. 17; l. 22; Rom. i. 21. Here it is said that they would again call God to remembrance; that is, they would worship him as the true God. ¶ *And turn unto the* LORD. Turn away from their idols to worship the living God. ¶ *And all the kindreds of the nations.* All the *families.* The numerous families upon the earth that constitute the one great family of mankind. ¶ *Shall worship before thee.* Shall worship in thy presence; that is, shall worship thee. The language is derived from the act of worshipping God in the tabernacle or the temple, before the visible symbol of his presence there. As applicable to the Redeemer, this language is in accordance with what is uniformly said of him and his work, that the world would be converted to the living and true God. Comp. Notes on Ps. ii. 8.

28. *For the kingdom* is *the* LORD'S. The dominion belongs of right to Jehovah, the true God. See Matt. vi. 13; Ps. xlvii. 7, 8. ¶ *And he* is *the governor among the nations.* He is the rightful governor or ruler among the nations. This is an assertion of the absolute *right* of Jehovah to reign over the nations of the earth, and the expression of an assurance on the part of the Messiah that, as the consequence of his work, this empire of Jehovah over the nations would be actually established. Comp. Notes on Dan. vii. 13, 14, 27; and on 1 Cor. xv. 24–28.

29. *All* they that be *fat upon the earth.* The general meaning of this verse is, that *all classes of persons* will come and worship the true God;—not the poor and needy only, the afflicted, and the oppressed, but the rich and the prosperous. There are *three* classes mentioned as representing all:—(1) the rich and prosperous; (2) they who bow down to the dust, or

can keep alive his own soul.
30 A seed shall serve him; it shall be accounted to the LORD for a generation.

31 They shall come, and shall declare his righteousness [c] unto a people that shall be born, that he hath done *this*.

c Rom. iii. 21—26.

the crushed and the oppressed; (3) those who are approaching the grave, and have no power to keep themselves alive. The first class comprises those who are mentioned here as being *fat*. This image is often used to denote prosperity: Judg. iii. 29; Job xv. 27; Ps. xvii. 10; lxxiii. 4 (Heb.); Deut. xxxi. 20; xxxii. 15. The meaning is, that the rich, the great, the prosperous would be among the multitudes who would be converted to the living God. ¶ *Shall eat and worship.* This expression is derived from the custom of offering sacrifices, and of feasting upon portions of the animal that was slain. In accordance with this, the blessings of salvation are often represented as a *feast* to which all are invited. See Notes on Isa. xxv. 6. Comp. Luke xiv. 16. ¶ *All they that go down to the dust.* All those descending to the dust. Those who are bowed down to the dust; who are crushed, broken, and oppressed;—the poor, the sad, the sorrowful. Salvation is for them, as well as for the rich and the great. ¶ *Shall bow before him.* Shall worship before the true God. ¶ *And none can keep alive his own soul.* Or rather, and he who cannot keep his soul (that is, himself) alive. So the Hebrew properly means, and this accords better with the connexion. The class here represented is composed of those who are ready to perish, who are about to die,—the aged—the infirm—the sick—the dying. These, thus helpless, feeble, and sad, shall also become interested in the great plan of salvation, and shall turn unto the Lord. These classes would represent *all* the dwellers on the earth; and the affirmation is equivalent to a statement that men of all classes would be converted, and would partake of the blessings of salvation.

30. *A seed shall serve him.* A people; a race. The word used here, and rendered *seed*—זֶרַע, *zera*—means properly *a sowing;* then, a planting, a plantation; then, seed sown—of plants, trees, or grain; and then, a generation of men,—children, offspring, posterity: Gen. iii. 15; xiii. 16; xv. 5, 13; *et al.* Hence it means a race, stock, or family. It is used here as denoting those who belong to the family of God; his children. Comp. Isa. vi. 13; lxv. 9, 23. The meaning here is, that, as the result of the work performed by the sufferer, many would be brought to serve God. ¶ *It.* To wit, the seed mentioned; the people referred to. ¶ *Shall be accounted to the Lord for a generation.* The word here rendered *Lord* is not *Jehovah*, but *Adonai*,—a word which is often used as a name of God,—and should not be printed here in small capitals. Prof. Alexander renders this, it seems to me improperly, "It shall be related of the Lord to the next generation." So De Wette and Hengstenberg. But the common rendering appears to me to furnish a better signification, and to be more in accordance with the meaning of the original. According to this the idea is, that the seed—the people referred to—would be reckoned to the Lord as a generation of his own people, a race, a tribe, a family pertaining to *him*. They would be regarded as such by him; they would be so estimated by mankind. They would not be a generation of aliens and strangers, but a generation of his people and friends. Comp. Ps. lxxxvii. 6.

31. *They shall come.* That is, there were those who would thus come. *Who* these would be is not specified. The obvious sense is, that some *would* rise up to do this; that the succession of such men would be kept up from age to age, making known these great facts and truths to succeeding

generations. The *language* would be applicable to a class of men called, from age to age, to proclaim these truths, and set apart to this work. It is a *fair* application of the verse to refer it to those who have been actually designated for such an office,—the ministers of religion appointed to keep up the memory of the great work of redemption in the world. Thus understood, the passage is a proper carrying out of the great truths stated in the psalm—that, in virtue of the sufferings of the Redeemer, God would be made known to men; that his worship would be kept up in the earth; that distant generations would serve him. ¶ *And shall declare his righteousness.* No language could better describe the actual office of the ministers of the Gospel as appointed to set forth the "righteousness" of God, to vindicate his government and laws, and to state the way in which men may be made righteous, or may be justified. Comp. Rom. i. 17; iii. 26. ¶ *Unto a people that shall be born.* To future generations. ¶ *That he hath done* this. That God has done or accomplished what is stated in this psalm; that is, on the supposition that it refers to the Messiah, that he has caused an atonement to be made for mankind, or that redemption has been provided through the sufferings of the Messiah.

I have given what seems to me to be a fair exposition of this psalm, referring it wholly to the Messiah. No part of the interpretation, on this view of the psalm, seems to me to be forced or unnatural, and as thus interpreted it seems to me to have as fair and obvious an applicability to him as even the liii. chapter of Isaiah, or any other portion of the prophecies. The *scene* in the psalm is the *cross*, the Redeemer suffering for the sins of man. The main features of the psalm relate to the course of thoughts which then passed through the mind of the Redeemer; his sorrow at the idea of being abandoned by God; his confidence in God; the remembrance of his early hopes; his emotions at the taunts and revilings of his enemies; his consciousness of prostrated strength; his feelings as the soldiers pierced his hands and his feet, and as they proceeded to divide his raiment; his prayer that his enemies might not be suffered to accomplish their design, or to defeat the work of redemption; his purpose to make God known to men; his assurance that the effect of his sufferings would be to bring the dwellers on the earth to serve God, and to make his name and his righteousness known to far distant times. I regard the whole psalm, therefore, as applicable to the Messiah alone; and believing it to be inspired, I cannot but feel that we have here a most interesting and affecting account, given long before it occurred, *of what actually passed through the mind of the Redeemer when on the cross*,—an account more full than we have anywhere else in the Bible. Other statements pertain more particularly to the *external* events of the crucifixion; here we have a record in anticipation of what actually passed through *his own mind* in those hours of unspeakable anguish when he made an atonement for the sins of the world.

PSALM XXIII.

This psalm is asserted in the title to have been composed by David, and there is nothing in its contents contrary to this supposition, as there is nothing in it that would lead us necessarily to ascribe it to him. The contents of the psalm indeed correspond with the facts of his history, and with the recollections of his early life as a shepherd; but it is such as might have been composed by any one who *had* been, and in fact by any one though he had *not* been, a shepherd, as the images in it are such as are common in all poetry. Still, there is nothing to lead us to doubt that it was written by David.

It is wholly uncertain on what occasion the psalm was composed, as there are in the psalm no historical references, no indications of time, and no allusions to any circumstances in the life of the author. It is impossible even to determine whether it was composed in a time of prosperity or adversity; whether

PSALM XXIII.

A Psalm of David.

THE LORD *is* my [d] shepherd; I shall not [e] want.

[d] Isa. xl. 11; John x. 11, 14.
[e] Ps. lxxxiv. 11.

when the author was persecuted, or when he was prosperous and triumphant. The only *apparent* allusion to any circumstance of the poet's life is in ver. 6, where he says, as the crowning joy which he anticipated, that he would "dwell in the house of the Lord for ever,"—from which it has been inferred by some that he was then in exile. But this allusion is of too general a character to justify this inference with certainty. Such a hope might be expressed by any one in any circumstances, as the highest desire of a pious heart. Kimchi supposes that the psalm was composed by David in the wilderness of Hareth (1 Sam. xxii. 5); and that it pertained to the people of Israel, and to their return from exile. But this is mere conjecture. The Chaldee Paraphrase applies the psalm to the Hebrew people when delivered from captivity and exile, as a song of triumph on their return to their own land. Rüdinger, and J. D. Michaelis, suppose that it refers to the time when David had obtained a complete victory over all his enemies—when the rebellion of Absalom was quelled, and when he was seated quietly on his throne. Probably if we are to attempt to fix a time, it was at that period of his life—an advanced period—when the recollection of the merciful interposition of God in his behalf so often manifested, would suggest the brightest image of his earlier years, the watchful care which he as a shepherd had extended over his own flock—a care which God had now extended over him in the perils of his own life. Still, all this is no more than conjecture.

The psalm has always been regarded as one of exquisite beauty. The main subject is the watchful care which God had extended over the author, and the consequent assurance which he felt that God would still watch over him, and supply all his need. The *leading thought*—the essential idea—is, his full belief that God would provide for him, and that he would never be left to want. This is the thought with which the psalm commences: "The Lord is my shepherd; *I shall not want*:" and this thought is carried through the psalm. It is illustrated by two facts or images: (*a*) That God was his shepherd; that he had always manifested towards him the care which a shepherd takes of his flock, vers. 1-3; and (*b*) That he had prepared a table before him in the very presence of his enemies, or that he had abundantly provided for him in their very sight, and when they were endeavouring to destroy him,—thus giving him the assurance that he never would leave him, ver. 5.

The psalm, therefore, may be regarded as consisting of two main parts:

I. The general subject of the psalm—the confidence of the author in God—the assurance that he would always so provide for him that he would not want, ver. 1.

II. The grounds or reasons for this confidence, vers. 2-6. These are two-fold:

(1.) An argument derived from the care of God over him as a shepherd, vers. 2-4.

(*a*) The statement of the fact, vers. 2, 3,

(*b*) The argument, ver. 4. From his experience of the Divine care in the past, he says that he would not be afraid even to descend into the valley of death.

(2.) An argument derived from the fact that God had provided for him in the very presence of his enemies, vers. 5, 6.

(*a*) The statement of the fact; or a reference to his life, during which God had shown the same care and goodness *as if* He had spread a table for him even in the sight of his enemies, ver. 5.

(*b*) The confident assurance, derived from that fact, that God *would* follow him with goodness and mercy all the days of his life; that his future course would be *as if* he were always to dwell in the house of the Lord, ver. 6.

1. *The* LORD is *my shepherd.* Comp. Gen. xlix. 24, "From thence is the shepherd, the stone of Israel;" Ps. lxxx. 1, "Give ear, O Shepherd of Israel." See also Notes on John x. 1—14. The comparison of the care which God extends over his people to that of a shepherd for his flock is one that would naturally occur to

2 He maketh me to lie down in [1] green pastures: he leadeth me beside the still [2] waters.

3 He restoreth my soul: he leadeth me in the paths of righteousness for his name's sake.

1 *pastures of tender grass.*

2 *waters of quietness.*

those who were accustomed to pastoral life. It would be natural that it should suggest itself to Jacob (Gen. xlix. 24), and to David, for both of them had been shepherds. David, in advanced years, would naturally remember the occupations of his early life; and the remembrance of the care of God over him would naturally recall the care which he had, in earlier years, extended over his flocks. The *idea* which the language suggests is that of tender care; protection; particular attention to the young and the feeble (comp. Isa. xl. 11); and providing for their wants. All these things are found eminently in God in reference to his people. ¶ *I shall not want.* This is the main idea in the psalm, and this idea is derived from the fact that God is a shepherd. The meaning is, that, as a shepherd, he would make all needful provision for his flock, and evince all proper care for it. The words *shall not want,* as applied to the psalmist, would embrace everything that could be a proper object of desire, whether temporal or spiritual; whether pertaining to the body or the soul; whether having reference to time or to eternity. There is no reason for supposing that David limited this to his temporal necessities, or to the present life, but the idea manifestly is that God would provide *all* that was needful for him always. Comp. Ps. xxxiv. 9, "There is no want to them that fear him." This idea enters essentially into the conception of God as the shepherd of his people, that *all* their real wants shall be supplied.

2. *He maketh me to lie down in green pastures.* Marg., *pastures of tender grass.* The Hebrew word rendered *pastures* means usually *dwellings,* or *habitations.* It is applied here properly to *pastures,* as places where flocks and herds lie down for repose. The word rendered in the margin *tender grass*—דֶּשֶׁא, *deshe*—refers to the first shoots of vegetation from the earth—young herbage—tender grass—as clothing the meadows, and as delicate food for cattle, Job vi. 5. It differs from ripe grass ready for mowing, which is expressed by a different word—חָצִיר, *hhatzir.* The idea is that of calmness and repose, as suggested by the image of flocks *lying down on the grass.* But this is not the only idea. It is that of flocks that lie down on the grass *fully fed* or *satisfied,*—their wants being completely supplied. The exact point of contemplation in the mind of the poet, I apprehend, is that of a flock in young and luxuriant grass, surrounded by abundance, and, having satisfied their wants, lying down amidst this luxuriance with calm contentment. It is not merely a flock enjoying repose; it is a flock whose wants are supplied, lying down in the midst of abundance. Applied to the psalmist himself, or to the people of God generally, the idea is, that the wants of the soul are met and satisfied, and that, in the full enjoyment of this, there is the conviction of abundance,—the repose of the soul at present satisfied, and feeling that in such abundance want will be always unknown. ¶ *He leadeth me beside the still waters.* Marg., *waters of quietness.* Not stagnant waters, but waters not tempestuous and stormy; waters so calm, gentle, and still, as to suggest the idea of repose, and such as prompt to repose. As applied to the people of God, this denotes the calmness—the peace—the repose of the soul, when salvation flows as in a gently running stream; when there is no apprehension of want; when the heart is at peace with God.

3. *He restoreth my soul.* Literally, "He causes my life to return." De

4 **Yea, though I walk through the valley of the shadow of death, I will fear no evil: for thou** *f* ***art*** **with me; thy rod and thy staff they comfort me.**

f Isa. xliii. 2.

Wette, "He quickens me," or causes me to live. The word *soul* here means life, or spirit, and not the soul in the strict sense in which the term is now used. It refers to the spirit when exhausted, weary, or sad; and the meaning is, that God quickens or vivifies the spirit when thus exhausted. The reference is not to the soul as wandering or backsliding from God, but to the life or spirit as exhausted, wearied, troubled, anxious, worn down with care and toil. The heart, thus exhausted, he re-animates. He brings back its vigour. He encourages it; excites it to new effort; fills it with new joy. ¶ *He leadeth me in the paths of righteousness.* In right paths, or right ways. He conducts me in the straight path that leads to himself; he does not suffer me to wander in ways that would lead to ruin. In reference to his people it is true (*a*) that he leads them in the path by which they *become* righteous, or by which they are *justified* before him; and (*b*) that he leads them in the way of *uprightness* and *truth.* He guides them in the way to heaven; his constant care is evinced that they *may* walk in that path. ¶ *For his name's sake.* For his own sake; or, that his name may be honoured. It is not primarily on their account; it is not solely that they may be saved. It is that he may be honoured (*a*) in their being saved at all; (*b*) in the manner in which it is done; (*c*) in the influence of their whole life, under his guidance, as making known his own character and perfections. Comp. Isa. xliii. 25; xlviii. 9; lxvi. 5; Jer. xiv. 7. The feeling expressed in this verse is that of confidence in God; an assurance that he would always lead his people in the path in which they should go. Comp. Ps. xxv. 9. This he will always do if men will follow the directions of his word, the teachings of his Spirit, and the guidance of his providence. None that thus submit to him ever go astray.

4. *Yea, though I walk through the valley of the shadow of death.* The meaning of this in the connexion in which it occurs is this:—"God will lead and guide me in the path of righteousness, even though that path lies through the darkest and most gloomy vale—through deep and dismal shades—in regions where there is no light, as if death had cast his dark and baleful shadow there. It is still a right path; it is a path of safety; and it will conduct me to bright regions beyond. In that dark and gloomy valley, though I could not guide myself, I will not be alarmed; I will not be afraid of wandering or of being lost; I will not fear any enemies there,—for my Shepherd is there to guide me still." On the word here rendered *shadow of death*—צַלְמָוֶת, *tzalmaveth*—see Notes on Job iii. 5; Isa. ix. 2. The word occurs besides only in the following places, in all of which it is rendered *shadow of death:* Job x. 21, 22; xii. 22; xvi. 16; xxiv. 17 (twice); xxviii. 3; xxxiv. 22; xxxviii. 17; Ps. xliv. 19; cvii. 10, 14; Jer. ii. 6; xiii. 16; Amos v. 8. The idea is that of death casting his gloomy shadow over that valley—the valley of the dead. Hence the word is applicable to any path of gloom or sadness; any scene of trouble or sorrow; any dark and dangerous way. Thus understood, it is applicable not merely to death itself—though it embraces that—but to any or all the dark, the dangerous, and the gloomy paths which we tread in life: to ways of sadness, solitude, and sorrow. All along those paths God will be a safe and certain guide. ¶ *I will fear no evil.* Dark, cheerless, dismal as it seems, I will dread nothing. The true friend of God *has* nothing to fear in that dark valley. His great Shepherd will accompany him there, and can lead him safely through,

5 Thou preparest a table before me in the presence of mine enemies: thou [1] anointest my head with oil; my cup runneth over.

[1] *makest fat.*

however dark it may appear. The true believer has nothing to fear in the most gloomy scenes of life; he has nothing to fear in the valley of death; he has nothing to fear in the grave; he has nothing to fear in the world beyond. ¶ *For thou* art *with me.* Thou wilt be with me. Though invisible, thou wilt attend me. I shall not go alone; I shall not be alone. The psalmist felt assured that if God was with him he had nothing to dread there. God would be his companion, his comforter, his protector, his guide. How applicable is this to death! The dying man *seems* to go into the dark valley alone. His friends accompany him as far as they can, and then they must give him the parting hand. They cheer him with their voice until he becomes deaf to all sounds; they cheer him with their looks until his eye becomes dim, and he can see no more; they cheer him with the fond embrace until he becomes insensible to every expression of earthly affection, and then he seems to be alone. But the dying believer is *not* alone. His Saviour God is with him in that valley, and will never leave him. On his arm he can lean, and by his presence he will be comforted, until he emerges from the gloom into the bright world beyond. All that is needful to dissipate the terrors of the valley of death is to be able to say, "Thou art with me." ¶ *Thy rod and thy staff.* It may not be easy to mark the difference between these two words; but they would seem probably to refer, the latter to the *staff* which the shepherd used in walking, and the former to the *crook* which a shepherd used for guiding his flock. The image is that of a shepherd in attendance on his flock, with a staff on which he leans with one hand; in the other hand the *crook* or rod which was the symbol of his office. Either of these also might be used to guard the flock, or to drive off the enemies of the flock. The *crook* is said (see Rosenmüller, *in loc.*) to have been used to seize the legs of the sheep or goats when they were disposed to run away, and thus to keep them with the flock. "The shepherd invariably carries a rod or staff with him when he goes forth to feed his flock. It is often bent or hooked at one end, which gave rise to the shepherd's crook in the hand of the Christian bishop. With this staff he rules and guides the flock to their green pastures, and defends them from their enemies. With it also he corrects them when disobedient, and brings them back when wandering." (The Land and the Book, vol. i., p. 305.) ¶ *They comfort me.* The sight of them consoles me. They show that the Shepherd is there. As significant of his presence and his office, they impart confidence, showing that he will not leave me alone, and that he will defend me.

5. *Thou preparest a table.* The image is now changed, though expressing the general idea which is indicated in the first verse of the psalm, "I shall not want." The evidence or proof of this in the previous verses is, that God was a shepherd, and would provide for him as a shepherd does for his flock; the evidence here is that God had provided a table, or a feast, for him in the very presence of his enemies, and had filled his cup with joy. The word *table* here is synonymous with *feast;* and the meaning is, "thou providest for my wants." There *may* be an allusion here to some particular period of the life of the psalmist, when he was in want, and when he perhaps felt an apprehension that he would perish, and when God had unexpectedly provided for his wants; but it is impossible now to determine to what occasion he thus refers. There were numerous occasions in the life of

6 Surely goodness and mercy shall follow me all the days of my life; and I will dwell in the house of the LORD [1] for ever.

[1] *to length of days.*

David which would be well represented by this language, *as if* God had provided a meal for him in the very *presence* of his foes, and in *spite* of them. ¶ *Before me.* For me. It is spread in my presence, and *for* me. ¶ *In the presence of mine enemies.* That is, in spite of them, or so that they could not prevent it. They were compelled to look on and see how God provided for him. It was manifest that this was from God; it was a proof of the Divine favour; it furnished an assurance that he who had done this would never leave him to want. The friends of God are made to triumph in the very presence of their foes. Their enemies are compelled to see how he interposes in their behalf, how he provides for them, and how he defends them. Their final triumph in the day of judgment will be in the very presence of all their assembled enemies, for in their very presence he will pronounce the sentence which will make their eternal happiness sure, Matt. xxv. 31—36. ¶ *Thou anointest my head with oil.* Marg., as in Heb., *makest fat.* That is, thou dost pour oil on my head so abundantly that it seems to be made fat with it. The expression indicates abundance. The allusion is to the custom of anointing the head on festival occasions, as an indication of prosperity and rejoicing (see Notes on Matt. vi. 17; Luke vii. 46), and the whole is indicative of the Divine favour, of prosperity, and of joy. ¶ *My cup runneth over.* It is not merely *full*; it runs over. This, too, indicates abundance; and from the abundance of the favours thus bestowed, the psalmist infers that God would always provide for him, and that he would never leave him to want.

6. *Surely goodness and mercy shall follow me.* God will bestow them upon me. This is the *result* of what is stated in the previous verses. The effect of God's merciful dealings with him had been to lead his mind to the assurance that God would always be his shepherd and friend; that he would never leave him to want. ¶ *All the days of my life.* Through all its changes; in every variety of situation; until I reach its close. Life indeed would end, and he does not venture to conjecture when that would be; but as long as life should continue, he felt confidently assured that everything needful for him would be bestowed upon him. The language is the utterance of a heart overflowing with joy and gratitude in the recollection of the past, and full of glad anticipation (as derived from the experience of the past) in regard to the future. ¶ *And I will dwell in the house of the* LORD *for ever.* Marg., as in Hebrew, *to length of days.* The expression, I think, does not refer to eternity or to heaven, but it is parallel with the former expression "All the days of my life;" that is, he would dwell in the house of the Lord as long as he lived,—with the idea added here, which was not in the former member of the sentence, that his life *would be* long, or that he hoped and anticipated that he would live long on the earth. The phrase here used, "I will dwell in the house of the Lord," is one that is several times employed in the Psalms as indicative of the wish of the psalmist. Thus in Psalm xxvii. 4, "One thing have I desired of the Lord, that will I seek after; that I may dwell in the house of the Lord all the days of my life." Ps. xxvi. 8, "Lord, I have loved the habitation of thy house, and the place where thine honour dwelleth." Ps. lxv. 4, "Blessed is the man whom thou choosest, and causest to approach unto thee, that he may dwell in thy courts." Ps. lxxxiv. 4, "Blessed are they that dwell in thy house." (Comp. also vers. 1, 3, and 10 of Psalm lxxxiv).

The *language* here is obviously taken from the employment of those who had their habitation near the tabernacle, and afterwards the temple, whose business it was to attend constantly on the service of God, and to minister in his courts. We are not to suppose of David that he anticipated such a residence in or near the tabernacle or the house of God; but the meaning is, that he anticipated and desired a life *as if* he dwelt there, and *as if* he was constantly engaged in holy occupations. His life would be spent *as if* in the constant service of God; his joy and peace in religion would be *as if* he were always within the immediate dwelling-place of the Most High. This expresses the desire of a true child of God. He wishes to live *as if* he were always engaged in solemn acts of worship, and occupied in holy things; he desires peace and joy in religion *as if* he were constantly in the place where God makes his abode, and allowed to partake of his smiles and friendship. In a very important sense it *is* his privilege so to live even on earth; it *will* certainly be his privilege so to live in heaven: and, full of grateful exultation and joy, every child of God may adopt this language as his own, and say confidently, "Goodness and mercy will follow me all the days of my life here, and I shall dwell in the house of the Lord for ever,"—for heaven, where God dwells, will be his eternal home.

PSALM XXIV.

There is no reason to doubt that the title of this psalm, which ascribes it to David, is correct. A portion of the psalm (vers. 3–6) has a strong resemblance to Psalm xv., and doubtless was composed by the same author.

The occasion on which the psalm was composed is not designated; but from its contents it was evidently on some public occasion of great solemnity; probably on the removal of the ark of the covenant into its appointed place in Jerusalem, where it was to abide permanently; a solemn entrance of Jehovah, as it were, into the place of his permanent abode, vers. 7–10. This could not have been the temple; for (*a*) that was not erected in the time of David; and (*b*) the description (vers. 7–10) is rather that of entering into a *city* than into a temple or a place of public worship, for the psalmist calls on the "*gates*" to lift up their heads,—an expression more suitable to a city than to the doors of a tabernacle or a temple. According to this view, no occasion seems more appropriate than that of removing the ark from the house of Obed-edom to "the city of David," or to Jerusalem, as described in 2 Sam. vi. 12–17. David indeed placed the ark "in the midst of the tabernacle which he had pitched for it" on Mount Zion (2 Sam. vi. 17), but the particular reference of the psalm would rather seem to be to the entrance of the ark into the city than into the tabernacle. It was probably designed to be sung as the procession approached the city where the ark was destined to remain. The occasion of thus taking up the ark into the holy hill where it was to abide seems to have suggested the inquiry, who would be fitted to ascend the holy hill where God abides, and to stand in his presence, vers. 3–6.

The psalm properly consists of three parts:—

I. An ascription of praise to God as the Maker and Upholder of all things, vers. 1, 2. He is represented as the proprietor of the whole earth, and as having a right to all that there is in the world, since he has made the earth and all which it contains. This universal claim, this recognition of him as Lord of all, would be peculiarly appropriate in bringing up the symbol of his existence and his power, and establishing his worship in the capital of the nation.

II. An inquiry, who would ascend into the hill of the Lord, and stand in his holy place;—who could be regarded as worthy to engage in his worship, and to be considered as his friend? vers. 3–6. This part of the psalm accords in the main with Ps. xv.; and the inquiry and the answer would be peculiarly appropriate on an occasion such as that on which the psalm appears to have been composed. In asserting God's claim to universal dominion (vers. 1, 2), and in introducing the symbols of his power into the place where he was to be recognised and adored (vers. 7–10), nothing could be more suitable than the question who would be regarded as qualified to worship before him; that is, who would be regarded as his friends. The essential

PSALM XXIV.

A Psalm of David.

1 THE earth *is* the LORD'S, *g* and the fulness thereof; the world, and they that dwell therein:

g Ps. l. 12.

thing here asserted to be requisite, as in Ps. xv., is purity of heart and life,—things essential to the evidence of piety under every dispensation, patriarchal, Mosaic, Christian.

III. A responsive song on the entrance of the procession with the ark into the city, vers. 7-10. This consists of two strophes, to be sung, it would seem most probable, by responsive choirs:—

First strophe, vers. 7, 8.

(*a*) The call on the gates to lift up their heads, that the King of glory might come in.

(*b*) The response: Who is this King of glory?

(*c*) The answer: Jehovah, mighty in battle.

Second strophe, vers. 9, 10.

(*a*) The call on the gates to lift up their heads, that the King of glory might come in.

(*b*) The response: Who is this King of glory?

(*c*) The answer: Jehovah of hosts.

1. *The earth* is *the* LORD'S. The whole world belongs to God. He is the Creator of the earth, and therefore its proprietor; or, in other words, "the property vests in him." It belongs to him in a sense somewhat similar to our right of property in anything that is the production of our hands, or of our labour or skill. We claim that as our own. We feel that we have a right to use it, or to dispose of it, as we choose. No other man has a right to take it from us, or to dictate to us how we shall employ it. Thus God, in the highest possible sense, has a right to the earth, and to all which it produces, as being all of it the creation of his hands, and the fruit of his culture and skill. He has a right to dispose of it as he pleases;—by fire, or flood, or tempest;—and he has an equal right to direct man in what way *he* shall employ that portion of the productions of the earth which may be entrusted to him. All the right which any man has to any portion of the earth's surface, or to what is treasured up in the earth, or to what it is made to produce, is subordinate to the claims of God, and all should be yielded up at his bidding, whether he comes and claims it to be employed in his service, or whether he comes and sweeps it away by fire or flood; by the locust, or by the palmer-worm. ¶ *And the fulness thereof.* All which it contains; everything which goes to *fill up* the world:—animals, minerals, vegetables, men. All belong to God, and he has a right to claim them for his service, and to dispose of them as he pleases. This very language, so noble, so true, and so fit to be made conspicuous in the eyes of men, I saw inscribed in a place where it seemed to be most appropriate, and most adapted to arrest and direct the thoughts of men—on the front of the Royal Exchange in London. It was well to remind the great merchants of the largest commercial city in the world of the truth which it contains; it does much to describe the character of the British nation that it should be inscribed in a place so conspicuous, and, as it were, on the wealth of that great capital. ¶ *The world.* The word here used—תֵּבֵל, *tebel*—is a poetic word, referring to the earth considered as fertile and inhabited,—the *habitable* globe; the same as the Greek, οἰκουμένη. ¶ *And they that dwell therein.* All the inhabitants of the earth, embracing men and animals of all kinds. Comp. Ps. l. 10, 11. God has a claim on men—on their services, on their talents, on all that they can acquire by labour and skill; he has a right to all that fly in the air, or that walk the earth, or that swim in the sea. On the occasion on which it is supposed that this psalm was written, in bringing up the ark of God, and placing it in the tabernacle provided for it in the capital of the nation, no

2 For he hath founded it upon the seas, and established it upon the floods.
3 Who [h] shall ascend into the hill of the LORD? or who shall stand in his holy place?
4 [1] He that hath clean hands, and a pure heart; who hath not lifted up his soul unto vanity; nor sworn deceitfully.

h Ps. xv.

1 *the clean of hands.*

sentiment could be more appropriate than that which would recognise the universal supremacy of God.

2. *For he hath founded it upon the seas.* That is, the earth, or the habitable world. The ground of the claim to the earth and all that it contains, which is here asserted, is the fact that God had created it, or "founded" it. The language here used—"he hath *founded* it," that is, he has laid the foundation of it, "upon the seas" and "the floods"—is in accordance with the usual mode of speaking of the earth in the Scriptures as laid upon a foundation,—as a house is raised on a firm foundation. See Notes on Job xxxviii. 6. As the earth appeared to be surrounded by water, it was natural to speak of it as *founded* also upon the waters. There is probably an allusion here to the statement in Gen. i. 9, 10, where the waters are said to have been so gathered together that the dry land appeared. Above all the waters the earth was established, so as to become the abode of plants, animals, and men. ¶ *And established it upon the floods.* The streams; the torrents. The earth has been elevated above them, so as to be a residence for animals and for men. The essential thought is, that this earth has become what it is by the fact that God has founded it;—and, therefore, what it produces belongs of right to him.

3. *Who shall ascend into the hill of the* LORD? Mount Zion; called the hill of the Lord, because it was the place designated for his worship, or the place of his abode. See Notes on Ps. xv. 1. The idea here is, "Who shall ascend there with a view of abiding there? who is worthy to dwell there?" The question is equivalent to asking, What constitutes true religion? What is required for the acceptable worship of God? What will prepare a man for heaven? ¶ *Or who shall stand in his holy place?* In the tabernacle, or in the place where he is worshipped. Comp. Notes on Ps. i. 5. Who is worthy to stand before God? Who has the qualifications requisite to constitute the evidence of his friendship?

4. *He that hath clean hands.* In the parallel passage in Ps. xv. 2, the answer to the question is, "He that walketh uprightly, and worketh righteousness." The sentiment is substantially the same there as in the passage before us. The meaning is, that he who would be recognised as a friend and worshipper of Jehovah must be an upright man; a man not living in the practice of iniquity, but striving always to do that which is right. The *hands* are the instruments by which we accomplish anything; and hence to have clean hands is equivalent to being upright. See Job xvii. 9; Isaiah i. 15; lix. 3; Acts ii. 23; Ps. xxvi. 10. The margin here, as the Hebrew, is *the clean of hands.* ¶ *And a pure heart.* Not merely he whose external conduct is upright, but whose heart is pure. The great principle is here stated which enters always into true religion, that it does not consist in outward conformity to law, or to the mere performance of rites and ceremonies, or to external morality, but that it controls the heart, and produces purity of motive and of thought. ¶ *Who hath not lifted up his soul unto vanity.* Unto that which is *vain,* or which is *false.* This expression might refer to one who had not devoted himself to the worship of an idol,—regarded as vain, or as nothing (1 Cor. viii. 6; Isa. xli. 24; Ps. cxv. 4–8); or to one who had not

5 He [i] shall receive the blessing from the LORD, and righteousness from the God of his salvation.

6 This *is* the generation of them that seek him, that seek thy face, [1] O Jacob. Selah.

i Isa. xxxiii. 15—17.
[1] Or, O God of *Jacob*.

embraced that which is false and vain in opinion; or to one who had not sworn falsely, or taken the name of God in vain, Ex. xx. 7. The probable meaning is, that he has not set his heart on vain things, or that which is false. He has sought after substantial truth, alike in the object of worship, in that which he professes to believe, and in the statements and promises which he makes to others. He aims to secure that which is true and real. He is in no sense "carried away" with that which is unreal and false. ¶ *Nor sworn deceitfully.* This is one form of that which had been just specified—his love of truth. The idea here is, that he has not affirmed, under the solemnities of an oath, that which was false; and that he has not, under similar solemnities, promised what he has not performed. He is a sincere man; a man seeking after the true and the real, and not running after shadows and falsehood; a man true to God and to his fellow-creatures; a man whose statements are in accordance with facts, and whose promises may be always relied on. In the parallel passage, in Ps. xv. 2, the statement is, "he that speaketh the truth in his heart." See Notes on that passage.

5. *He shall receive the blessing from the* LORD. Literally, "He shall bear away a blessing from Jehovah." The blessing here referred to means His favour and friendship. He shall be recognised and treated as his. In other words, God bestows his favour on those who possess the character here referred to. ¶ *And righteousness from the God of his salvation.* He shall be regarded and treated as righteous. Or, he shall obtain the Divine approval as a righteous man. The idea of the psalmist would seem to be, not that he would obtain this as if it were a gift, but that he would obtain the Divine *approval* of his character as righteous; he would be recognised and dealt with as a righteous man. He would come to God with "clean hands and a pure heart" (ver. 4), and would be welcomed and treated as a friend of God. The wicked and the impure could not hope to obtain this; but he who *was* thus righteous would be treated according to his real character, and would meet with the assurances of the Divine favour. It is as true now as it was in the days of the psalmist, that it is only the man who is in fact upright and holy that can obtain the evidences of the Divine approval. God will not regard one who is living in wickedness as a righteous man, nor will he admit such a man to his favour here, or to his dwelling-place hereafter.

6. *This* is *the generation of them that seek him.* This describes the race of those who seek him; or, this is their character. The word *generation* here is used evidently in the sense of *race, people,* or *persons.* This is the character or description of the *persons* who seek his favour; or, this is the character of his true friends. The phrase *to seek God* is often used as descriptive of true piety: Ps. ix. 10; xiv. 2; lxiii. 1; Prov. viii. 17; Matt. vi. 33; vii. 7. It indicates an earnest desire to know him and to obtain his favour. It denotes also humility of mind, and a sense of dependence on God. ¶ *That seek thy face, O Jacob.* Marg., O *God of* Jacob. De Wette understands this as meaning that they would seek the face of God *among* his people; or that they who belonged to the race of Jacob, and who were sincere, thus sought the face of God. There is supposed to be, according to this interpretation, a distinction between the true and the false Israel; between those who professed to be the people of God and those who really

7 Lift up your heads, O ye gates; and be ye lift up, ye everlasting doors; and the King of glory shall come in.

8 Who *is* this King of glory? The LORD strong and mighty, the LORD mighty in battle.

were his people (comp. Rom. ix. 6–8). It seems to me that the word is not used here as it is in the margin to denote the "*God* of Jacob," which would be a harsh and an unusual construction, but that it is in apposition with the preceding words, as denoting what constituted the true Jacob, or the true people of God. "This is the generation of them that seek him; this is the true Jacob, that seek thy face, O Lord." That is, this is the characteristic of all who properly belong to the race of Jacob, or who properly belong to God as his true people. The sense, however, is not materially affected if we adopt the reading in the margin.

7. *Lift up your heads, O ye gates.* Either the gates of the city, or of the house erected for the worship of God; most probably, as has been remarked, the former. This may be supposed to have been uttered as the procession approached the city where the ark was to abide, as a summons to admit the King of glory to a permanent residence there. It would seem not improbable that the gates of the city were originally made in the form of a portcullis, as the gates of the old castles in the feudal ages were, not to *open*, but to be *lifted up* by weights and pullies. In some of the old ruins of castles in Palestine there are still to be seen deep grooves in the *posts* of the gateway, showing that the door did not open and shut, but that it was drawn up or let down. (Land and the Book, vol. i. p. 376. One such I saw at Carisbrooke Castle in the Isle of Wight; and they were common in the castles erected in the Middle Ages.) There were some advantages in this, as they could be suddenly *let down* on an enemy about to enter, when it would be difficult to close them if they were made to open as doors and gates are commonly made. Thus understood, the "heads" of the gates would be the top, perhaps ornamented in some such way as to suggest the idea of a "head," and the command was that these should be elevated to admit the ark of God to pass. ¶ *And be ye lift up, ye everlasting doors.* The doors of a city or sanctuary that was now to be the permanent place of the worship of God. The ark was to be fixed and settled there. It was no longer to be moved from place to place. It had found a final home. The idea in the word "everlasting" is that of permanence. The place where the ark was to abide was to be the enduring place of worship; or was to endure as long as the worship of God in that form should continue. There is no evidence that the author of the psalm supposed that those doors would be literally *eternal*, but the language is such as we use when we say of anything that it is permanent and abiding. ¶ *And the King of glory shall come in.* The glorious King. The allusion is to God as a King. On the cover of the ark, or the mercy seat, the symbol of the Divine presence—the Shekinah—rested; and hence it was natural to say that God would enter through those gates. In other words, the cover of the ark was regarded as his abode—his seat—his throne; and, as thus occupying the mercy-seat, he was about to enter the place of his permanent abode. Comp. Ex. xxv. 17, 20, 22.

8. *Who* is *this King of glory?* This is probably the response of a portion of the choir of singers. The answer is found in the other part of the verse. ¶ *The* LORD *strong and mighty.* Jehovah, strong and mighty,—describing him by his most exalted attributes as a God of power. This is in accordance with the idea in vers. 1, 2, where he is represented as the Creator and the Proprietor of all the earth. Perhaps, also, there is an allusion to the fact that he is mighty, as

9 Lift up your heads, O ye gates; even lift *them* up, ye everlasting doors; and the King of glory shall come in.

10 Who is this King of glory? The LORD of hosts, he *is* the King of glory. Selah.

distinguished from idols which have no power. ¶ *The* LORD *mighty in battle.* Who displays his power eminently in overthrowing hostile armies;—perhaps in allusion to the victories which had been won when his people were animated in war by the presence of the ark in the midst of their armies, and when the victory could be properly traced to the fact that the ark, the symbol of the Divine presence, was with them, and when, therefore, the victory would be properly ascribed to Jehovah himself.

9. *Lift up your heads,* etc. The repetition here is designed to give force and emphasis to what is uttered. The response in ver. 5 is slightly varied from the response in ver. 8; but the same general sentiment is expressed. The design is to announce in a solemn manner that the symbol of the Divine presence and majesty was about to be introduced into the place of its permanent abode, and that this was an event worthy to be celebrated;—that even the gates of the city should voluntarily open themselves to admit the great and glorious King who was to reign there for ever.

10. *Who is this King of glory?* See Notes on ver. 8. ¶ *The* LORD *of hosts, he* is *the King of glory.* On the meaning of the phrase, "the Lord of hosts," see Notes on Isa. i. 9. The essential idea is, that God rules over the universe of worlds considered as marshalled in order, or arrayed as hosts or armies are for battle. All are under his command. The stars in the sky, that seem to be marshalled and led forth in such perfect and beautiful order,—the inhabitants of heaven in their different orders and ranks,—all these acknowledge him, and submit to him as the supreme God. In the close of the psalm, therefore, there is an exact accordance with the thought in the beginning, that God is the Sovereign Ruler of the universe, and that he should everywhere be recognised and regarded as such. The entrance of the ark of the covenant into the place provided for it as a permanent residence was a fit occasion to proclaim this thought; and this *is* proclaimed in the psalm in a manner befitting so solemn an occasion and so sublime a truth.

PSALM XXV.

This purports to be a psalm of David, and there is no reason to doubt that he was its author. There are no indications, however, of the occasion on which it was composed, nor is it possible now to ascertain that occasion. It is probably one of those which were composed in his leisure moments, with no outward existing cause—designed to express the feelings of piety in the calm contemplation of God and his perfections.

The peculiarity of the psalm is, that it is the first of that class of psalms which are known as *alphabetical,* in which the first word of each verse begins with one of the letters of the Hebrew alphabet. One design of this mode of composition *may* have been to assist the memory; but it is probable that the prevailing reason was that it was regarded as a poetic beauty thus to arrange the letters of the alphabet. Such arts of poetry are common in all languages. Occasionally in these psalms the order of the letters is slightly changed; in other instances, some of the letters are omitted, while the general structure is observed. Specimens of this mode of composition occur in Ps. xxxiv., xxxvii., cxi., cxii., cxix., cxlv.; in Proverbs xxxi., from the tenth verse to the end of the chapter; and in the Lamentations of Jeremiah, the whole of which book is composed on this plan, except the last chapter. The same mode of composition is common in Syrian and Persian poetry. See Assemani Biblioth. Orient. III., Pt. 1, p 63, 328. Comp. Lowth's Lectures on Heb. Poetry, Lect. xxii.; and Grotii Prolegomm. ad Com. in Psalmos, p. 81.

In the psalm before us, the general

order of the Hebrew alphabet is observed, with the following exceptions:—the two first verses commence with the letter א, *Aleph*, the first letter of the Hebrew alphabet; while the second letter, ב, *Beth*, is omitted. The letters ו, *Vau*, and ק, *Koph*, are also omitted, while two verses begin with the letter ר, *Resch;* and at the close of the psalm, after the letter ת, *Tau*—the last letter of the Hebrew alphabet,—another verse is added, beginning with the letter פ, *Phe.* We cannot account for these variations. Capellus supposes that it arises from the haste and want of attention of transcribers, and suggests a plan by which the alphabetical arrangement in this psalm could be restored to proper order. See Rosenmüller, Scholia in Ps. xxv., p. 633. J. D. Michaelis supposes that the authors of the psalm allowed to themselves some liberty in the arrangement, and that the proper letter of the alphabet was sometimes in the middle of the verse rather than at the beginning. But it is impossible to assign the reasons which may have existed for the want of perfect regularity in the composition of the psalm, and the deviations from the exact alphabetical order which occur. Those deviations are very slight, and do not affect the general character of the composition. Of course this poetic beauty cannot be perceived in a translation, and must be lost to all except to Hebrew scholars.

The general *plan* of these psalms seems to be, not to follow out one particular thought, or to dwell on one subject, but to bring together such independent expressions of pious feeling as could be conveniently arranged in this manner. Accordingly in the psalm before us we have a considerable variety of subjects introduced,—all *suggestive*, or all indicating the kind of thoughts which will pass through a pious mind in moments of relaxation, and *unbending*, when the thoughts are allowed to flow freely or without restraint from the will. The current of thought in such moments is often a more sure indication of the true state of the heart, and of the real character, than what occurs in our more studied and laboured habits of thinking; and a man may often look to these trains of thought as most certainly indicating the actual condition of his heart.

Among the thoughts thus suggesting themselves to the mind of the psalmist in this season of relaxation, and as indicating the real state of his heart, the following may be noticed:—

(1) Confident trust in God, and a feeling that that trust would not be disappointed, vers. 1-3.

(2) A desire to be led in the way of truth, vers. 4, 5.

(3) A desire that God, in his treatment of him, would remember His own merciful character, and not the sins of the psalmist, vers. 6, 7.

(4) A belief that God will guide those who trust him, vers. 8, 9.

(5) Confidence in God in all his ways, ver. 10.

(6) Prayer for the pardon of sin, ver. 11.

(7) An expression of belief that God will teach and guide those who fear him, vers. 12, 13.

(8) The assurance that the secret of the Lord is with them that fear him, ver. 14.

(9) Prayer for deliverance from all trouble, vers. 15-21.

(10) Prayer for the redemption of the people of God; for their complete deliverance from evil; for the salvation of the church, ver. 22.

The psalm thus expresses the feelings of a pious mind when running over a great variety of subjects, apparently with little connexion, or united only by a very slender thread of association; such thoughts as occur to one when the mind is allowed a free range, and follows out easy suggestions with no great effort to restrain the mind by the stricter rules of thinking, or when the mind allows itself to be easily drawn along from one subject to another, and finds, in each one that occurs, something to be thankful for; or to pray for; or to rejoice over; or to anticipate with pleasure; or to hope for; or to be penitent for; or to contemplate with gratitude and love. The thoughts of wicked men, when their minds are thus unbent and unstrung, recur to images of pollution and sin; they gloat over past indulgences; they recall the images of sensual pleasures; they bring before the fancy new and untried scenes of pollution; they revel in the anticipated pleasures of gaiety and sensuality. Perhaps there is nothing that more clearly indicates the real state of a man's heart than the kind of recollections, imaginings, and anticipations into which the mind falls in such a relaxed, or what some might call an

PSALM XXV.

A Psalm of David.

UNTO thee, O LORD, do I lift up my soul.

2 O my God, I trust in thee: let me not be ashamed; [i] let not mine enemies triumph over me.

3 Yea, let none that wait on thee be ashamed: let them be ashamed which transgress without cause.

i Ps. xxii. 4, 5; Isa. xlix. 23.

---

idle, state of the mind;—just as we judge of a stream when it flows gently as left to its own course, not when it is dammed up, or forced into new channels, or swelled by rains, or made into artificial rills and water-falls, or employed to turn mills, or diverted, contrary to its natural flow, even into beautiful gardens.

1. *Unto thee,* O LORD, *do I lift up my soul.* In meditation; in gratitude; in praise. The idea is, that the thoughts are lifted up from earth and earthly subjects to God. This is the beginning of the meditation; this gives character, perhaps, to the psalm. The state of mind is that of one who turns cheerfully away from earthly themes, and opens his mind to more lofty and hallowed influences. The mind *begins* with God; and, beginning with this, the current of thought is allowed to flow on, gathering up such ideas as would come in under this general purpose. Opening the mind to this influence, thoughts would flow in upon the soul embracing a wide range, and perhaps not very closely connected among themselves, but all of which would be fitted to raise the heart to God in meditation, thankfulness, and praise.

2. *O my God, I trust in thee.* This is the first thought,—a feeling that he *had* true confidence in God, and that in all the duties of life, in all his trials, and in all his hopes for the future, his reliance was on God alone. ¶ *Let me not be ashamed.* That is, let me never be so forsaken by thee as to have occasion for shame that I *have* thus trusted in thee. The prayer is not that he might never be ashamed to avow and confess his trust in God, but that he might *find* God to be such a helper and friend that he might never be ashamed on account of the trust which he had put in him, as if it had been a false reliance; that he might not be disappointed, and made to feel that he had done a foolish thing in confiding in one who was not able to help him. See the word explained in the Notes on Job vi. 20. Comp. Isa. xxx. 5; Jer. viii. 9; xiv. 3, 4. ¶ *Let not mine enemies triumph over me.* This explains what the psalmist meant by his prayer that he might not be *ashamed,* or put to shame. He prayed that he might not be vanquished by his foes, and that it might not appear that he had trusted in a Being who was unable to defend him. Applied now to us, the prayer would imply a desire that we may not be so overcome by our spiritual foes as to bring dishonour on ourselves and on the cause which we profess to love; that we may not be held up to the world as those who are unable to maintain the warfare of faith, and exposed to scorn as those who are unfaithful to their trust; that we may not be so forsaken, so left to trial without consolation, so given over to sadness, melancholy, or despair, as to leave the world to say that reliance on God is vain, and that there is no advantage in being his friends.

3. *Yea, let none that wait on thee be ashamed.* To "wait on the Lord" is an expression denoting true piety, as indicating our dependence on him, and as implying that we look to him for the command that is to regulate our conduct and for the grace needful to protect and save us. Comp. Isa. xl. 31. See also Isa. viii. 17; xxx. 18; Ps. xl. 1; lxix. 3. This petition is indicative of the wish of the pious heart that none who profess to serve God may ever be put to shame; that they may never be overcome by sin; that they may never fall under the power of temptation; that they may

4 Show [k] me thy ways, O LORD; teach me thy paths.
5 Lead me in thy truth, and teach me: for thou *art* the God of my salvation; on thee do I wait all the day.

k Isa. ii. 3; Jer. l. 5.

not fail of eternal salvation. ¶ *Let them be ashamed which transgress without cause.* This does not imply that any sinners transgress otherwise than without cause, or that they have any good reason for sinning; but it brings into view a prominent thought in regard to sin, that it *is* without cause. If the wicked *had* any good reason for their course of life,—if they were compelled to do wrong,—if the temptations under which they act were so powerful that they could not resist them,—if they were not voluntary in their transgressions,—then true benevolence would demand of us the prayer that they might *not* be confounded or put to shame. But as none of these circumstances occur in the case of the sinner, there is no want of benevolence in praying that all the workers of evil may be put to confusion; that is, that they may not triumph in an evil course, but that their plans may be defeated, and that they may be arrested in their career. There is no benevolence in desiring the triumph of wickedness; there is no want of benevolence in praying that all the plans of wicked men may be confounded, and all the purposes of evil be frustrated. True benevolence requires us to pray that all their plans *may* be arrested, and that the sinner may *not* be successful in his career. A man may be certain that he is acting out the principles of benevolence when he endeavours to prevent the consummation of the plans and the desires of the wicked.

4. *Show me thy ways, O* LORD. The "ways" of God are his methods of administering the affairs of the world; his dispensations; the rules which he has prescribed for himself in the execution of his plans; the great laws by which he governs the universe. Deut. xxxii. 4, "All his ways are judgment; a God of truth and without iniquity, just and right is he." The prayer of the psalmist is, that he may be able to understand the methods of the Divine government; the principles on which God bestows happiness and salvation; the rules which he has been pleased to prescribe for human conduct; the arrangements by which he confers favours on mankind; the scheme by which he saves men. The idea evidently is that he might understand so much of this as to regulate his own conduct aright; that he might not lean to his own understanding, or trust to his own guidance, but that he might ever be under the guidance and direction of God. ¶ *Teach me thy paths.* The paths which thou dost take; to wit, as before, in administering the affairs of the world. The prayer is expressive of a desire to be wholly under the direction of God.

5. *Lead me in thy truth.* In the way which thou regardest as truth, or which thou seest to be true. Truth is eternal and unchanging. What God sees and regards as truth *is* true, for he sees things as they are; and when we have the Divine estimate of anything, we understand what the thing is. It is not that he *makes* it to be true, but that he *sees* it to be true. Such is the perfection of his nature that we have the utmost assurance that what God regards as truth *is* truth; what he proclaims to be right *is* right. It is then *His* truth, as he adopts it for the rule of his own conduct, and makes it known to his creatures to guide them. ¶ *And teach me.* As this would be understood by the psalmist, it would be a prayer that God would teach him by his law as then made known; by his Spirit in the heart; by the dispensations of his providence. As applicable to us, it is a prayer that he would instruct us by all the truths then made known, and all that have

6 Remember, O LORD, thy
[1] tender mercies and thy loving-
kindnesses; for they *have been*
ever of old.

7 Remember not the sins of
my [l] youth, nor my transgressions: according [m] to thy mercy
remember thou me, for thy goodness' sake, O LORD.

[1] *bowels*, Isa. lxiii. 15.

l Job xiii. 26.
m Ps. li. 1.

since been revealed; by his Spirit in its influences on our hearts; by the events which are occurring around us; by the *accumulated* truth of ages;—the knowledge which by all the methods he employs he has imparted to men for their guidance and direction. ¶ *For thou* art *the God of my salvation.* The word *salvation* is not to be understood here in the sense in which it is now commonly used, as denoting deliverance from sin and future ruin, but in the more general sense of *deliverance*—deliverance from danger and death. The phrase is synonymous with *preservation,* and the idea is that the psalmist regarded God as his preserver; or that he owed his protection and safety in the time of danger to Him alone. ¶ *On thee do I wait.* That is, I rely on thee; or, I am dependent on thee. He had no other source of reliance or dependence. ¶ *All the day.* Continually, always. He was *really* dependent on him at all times, and he *felt* that dependence. It is always true that we are dependent on God for everything; it is not true that we always *feel* this. It was a characteristic of the piety of the psalmist that he *did* feel this.

6. *Remember, O* LORD. That is, In thy future treatment of me, bring to remembrance what thou hast done, and treat me in the same manner still. The language is that of one who felt that God had always been kind and gracious, and who asked for the future a continuance of the favours of the past. If we would recall the goodness of God in the past, we should find enough to lay the foundation of prayer in reference to that which is to come. If we saw and understood fully all that has happened to us, we should need to offer no other prayer than that God might deal with us in the future as he has done in the past. ¶ *Thy tender mercies.* Marg., as in Heb., *thy bowels.* The Hebrew word means *the inner parts,* regarded by the Hebrews as the seat of the affections. See Notes on Isa. xvi. 11. ¶ *And thy loving-kindnesses.* Thy tokens of favour; thy acts of mercy and compassion. ¶ *For they* have been *ever of old.* "For from eternity are they." The language is that of a heart deeply impressed with a sense of the goodness of God. In looking over his own life, the author of the psalm saw that the mercies of God had been unceasing and constant towards him from his earliest years. In words expressive of warm love and gratitude, therefore, he says that those acts of mercy had never failed—had been from eternity. His thoughts rise from the acts of God toward himself to the character of God, and to His attributes of mercy and love; and his heart is full of the idea that God is *always* good; that it belongs to His very nature to do good.

7. *Remember not the sins of my youth.* In strong contrast with God, the psalmist brings forward his own conduct and life. He could ask of God (ver. 6) to remember His own acts—what *He himself* had done; but could not ask him to remember *his* conduct—*his* past life. He could only pray that this might be forgotten. He did not wish it to come into remembrance before God; he could not ask that God would deal with him according to that. He prays, therefore, that he might not be visited as he advanced in life with the fruits of his conduct in early years, but that all the offences of that period of his life might be forgiven and forgotten. Who is there that cannot with deep feeling join in this prayer? Who is there that has reached the

8 Good and upright *is* the LORD: therefore will he teach sinners in the way.

9 The meek will he guide in judgment, and the meek will he teach his way.

period of middle or advanced life, who would be willing to have the follies of his youth, the plans, and thoughts, and wishes of his early years brought again to remembrance? Who would be willing to have recalled to his own mind, or made known to his friends, to society around him, or to assembled worlds, the thoughts, the purposes, the wishes, the *imaginings* of his youthful days? Who would dare to pray that he might be treated in advancing years as he treated God in his own early life? Nay, who would venture to pray that God would treat him in the day of judgment as he had treated the friends of his childhood, even the father that begat him, or the mother that bare him? Our hope in regard to the favour of God is that he will *not* summon up the thoughts and the purposes of our early years; that he will *not* treat us as if he remembered them; but that he will treat us as if they were forgotten. ¶ *Nor my transgressions.* The sins of my early years. ¶ *According to thy mercy remember thou me.* Deal with me, not according to strict justice, but according to mercy. Deal with me indeed according to thy nature and character; but let the attribute of mercy be that which will be the guide rather than the attribute of justice. ¶ *For thy goodness' sake.* In order that thy goodness or benevolence may be displayed and honoured —not primarily and mainly that *I* may be saved, but that thy character may be seen to be good and merciful.

8. *Good and upright* is *the* LORD. His character is benevolent, and he is worthy of confidence. He is not merely *good,* but he is equal and just in his dealings with men. This latter attribute is no less a reason for confidence in his character than the former. We need a God who is not merely benevolent and kind, but who is just and faithful; whose administration is based on principles of truth and justice, and in whose dealings, therefore, his creatures can repose unlimited confidence. ¶ *Therefore will he teach sinners.* Because he is good and upright, we may approach him with the assurance that he will guide us aright. His *goodness* may be relied on as furnishing evidence that he will be *disposed* to do this; his *uprightness* as furnishing the assurance that the path in which he will lead us will be the best path. We could not rely on mere benevolence, for it might lack wisdom and firmness, or might lack power to execute its own purposes; we can rely on it when it is connected with a character that is infinitely upright, and an arm that is infinitely mighty. ¶ *In the way.* In the right way—the way in which they should go, the path of truth, of happiness, of salvation.

9. *The meek will he guide.* The humble, the teachable, the prayerful, the gentle of spirit—those who are willing to learn. A proud man who supposes that he already knows enough cannot be taught; a haughty man who has no respect for others, cannot learn of them; a man who is willing to believe nothing cannot be instructed. The first requisite, therefore, in the work of religion, as in respect to all kinds of knowledge, is a meek and docile spirit. See Matt. xviii. 3. ¶ *In judgment.* In a right judgment or estimate of things. It is not merely in the administration of justice, or in doing *right,* but it is in judging of truth; of duty; of the value of objects; of the right way to live; of all on which the mind can be called to exercise judgment, or to come to a decision. ¶ *And the meek will he teach his way.* The way in which he would have them to go. The *methods* by which God does this are (1) By his word or law, (*a*) laying down there the principles which are to guide human conduct, and (*b*) in numerous cases furnishing specific

10 All the paths of the LORD *are* mercy and truth unto such [n] as keep his covenant and his testimonies.

n Hos. xiv. 9.

11 For [o] thy name's sake, O LORD, pardon mine iniquity; for it *is* [p] great.

o Ps. lxxix. 9; Ezek. xxxvi. 22, 32; 1 John ii. 12. *p* Rom. v. 15—21.

rules for directing our conduct in the relations of life; (2) by his Spirit, (*a*) disposing the mind to candour, (*b*) enlightening it to see the truth, and (*c*) making it honest and sincere in its inquiries; (3) by his providence,—often indicating, in an unexpected manner, to those who are sincere in their inquiries after truth and duty, what he would have them to do; and (4) by the advice and counsel of those who have experience,—the aged and the wise,—those who have themselves been placed in similar circumstances, or who have passed through the same perplexities and embarrassments. By all these methods a man who goes to God in humble prayer, and with a proper sense of dependence, may trust that he will be guided aright; and it is not probable that a case could occur in which one who should honestly seek for guidance by these helps, might not feel assured that God would lead him aright. Having used these means, a man may feel assured that God will not leave him to error.

10. *All the paths of the* LORD. All the ways that the Lord takes; all that he commands; all that he does. The "paths of the Lord" denote the course in which he himself walks, or his dealings with his creatures. In the previous verse, the psalmist had said that the Lord would teach *His way* to the "meek;" he now says that all His ways are ways of mercy and of truth; or that all will be found to be in the direction of mercy and of truth. ¶ Are *mercy and truth.* In all his dealings with those who "keep his covenant" he shows himself to be at the same time merciful and true:—compassionate towards their errors; faithful to his own promises. ¶ *To such as keep his covenant.* To those who are his friends; to those who are faithful to him. This expression is often used to denote those who are the true people of God, Gen. xvii. 9, 10; Ex. xix. 5; Deut. xxix. 9; Ps. cxxxii. 12. The word *covenant* here is equivalent to *command* or *law;* and the idea is, that if they keep his laws they will find him to be merciful and true. On the meaning of the word *covenant,* see Notes on Acts vii. 8; Heb. viii. 8; ix. 16, 17. ¶ *And his testimonies.* The word *testimony* in the Scripture, in this connexion, refers to that to which God bears witness as *true;* or that which he has declared to be truth. In this sense the phrase means here those who maintain his truth; or who abide by what he has pronounced to be true. The word is very often used in the Scriptures to denote the truth of God and the commandments of God. In all such cases there is the underlying idea that the command or the statement referred to is that to which God bears witness as true or right.

11. *For thy name's sake, O* LORD. See Notes on Ps. xxiii. 3. The idea here is that God would do this on his own account, or for the honour of his own name. This is *a* reason, and one of the main reasons, why God ever pardons iniquity. It is that the honour of his name may be promoted; that his glorious character may be displayed; that he may *show* himself to the universe to be merciful and gracious. There are, doubtless, other reasons why he pardons sin—reasons drawn from the bearing which the act of mercy will have on the welfare of the universe; but still the main reason is, that his own honour will thus be promoted, and his true character thus made known. See Notes on Isa. xliii. 25; xlviii. 9. Comp. Ps. vi. 4; and verse 7 of this psalm. ¶ *Pardon mine iniquity.* This prayer seems to have been offered in view of the remembered

12 What man *is* he that feareth the LORD? him [q] shall he teach in the way *that* he shall choose.

q Ps. xxxii. 8; xxxvii. 23.

13 His soul shall [1] dwell at ease; and his seed shall inherit [r] the earth.

[1] *lodge in goodness.* *r* Ps. xxxvii. 11, 22.

transgressions of his early years, ver. 7. These recollected sins apparently pressed upon his mind all through the psalm, and were the main reason of the supplications which occur in it. Comp. vers. 16—18. ¶ *For it is great.* As this translation stands, the fact that his sin was great was a *reason* why God should pardon it. This is a reason, because (*a*) it would be felt that the sin was so great that it could not be removed by any one but God, and that unless *forgiven* it would sink the soul down to death; and (*b*) because the mere fact of its magnitude would tend to illustrate the mercy of the Lord. Undoubtedly these *are* reasons why we may pray for the forgiveness of sin; but it may be doubted whether this is the exact idea of the psalmist, and whether the word *although* would not better express the true sense,—"*although* it is great." It is true that the general sense of the particle here rendered "for"—כִּי, *ki*—is *because* or *since;* but it may also mean *although,* as in Ex. xiii. 17, "God led them not the way through the land of the Philistines, *although* — (כִּי) — that was near," *i.e.* that was nearest, or was the most direct way. So in Deut. xxix. 19, "I shall have peace, *though* — (כִּי) —I walk in the imagination of mine heart." Also Josh. xvii. 18, "Thou shalt drive out the Canaanites, *though* — (כִּי)—they have iron chariots, and *though* they be strong." Thus understood, the prayer of the psalmist here is, that God would pardon his offences *although* they were so great. His mind is fixed on the *greatness* of the offences; on the obstacles in the way of pardon; on his own unworthiness; on the fact that he had no claim to mercy; and he presents this strong and earnest plea that God would have mercy on him *although* his sins were so numerous and so aggravated. In this prayer all can join; this is a petition the force of which all true penitents deeply feel.

12. *What man* is *he.* Who is he. The statement in this verse is intended to include every man; or to be universal. Wherever one is found who has the character here referred to, or whoever he may be, of him what is here affirmed will be true, that God will lead him in the way that he shall choose. ¶ *That feareth the* LORD. That is, a true worshipper of Jehovah, or that is truly a pious man: Ps. v. 7. ¶ *Him shall he teach.* He will guide, or instruct him. See ver. 9. ¶ *In the way* that *he shall choose.* The way that the man ought to choose; or, in other words, in the right way. It is not the way that *God* shall choose, but the way that the pious man ought to choose: God will so instruct him that he shall find the true path.

13. *His soul shall dwell at ease.* Marg., *shall lodge in goodness.* So the Hebrew. The idea is that of one *at home;* one who finds a comfortable and safe resting-place; one who is not a wanderer or a vagrant. The word rendered in the text *at ease,* and in the margin *goodness,* means *good;* and the idea is that of a good or safe condition as compared with that of one who wanders abroad without a shelter, or of one who has lost his way, and has no one to guide him. As contrasted with such an one, he who fears God, and who seeks his guidance and direction, will be like a man in his own comfortable and quiet home. The one is a condition of safety and of ease; the other, a condition of anxiety, doubt, trouble. Nothing could better describe the calmness, peace, and conscious security of the man who has found the truth and who serves God,—as compared with the state of that man who

14 The secret *s* of the LORD *is* with them that fear him; and [1] he will show them his covenant.
15 Mine eyes *are* ever toward the LORD; for he shall [2] pluck my feet out of the *t* net.
16 Turn *u* thee unto me, and have mercy upon me; for I *am* desolate and afflicted.

s Prov. iii. 32; John vii. 17; Eph. i. 9, 18.
[1] Or, *his covenant to make them know* it.
[2] *bring forth.*

t Ps. cxxiv. 7, 8. *u* Mic. vii. 19.

has no religion, no fear of God, no hope of heaven. ¶ *And his seed.* His posterity; his family. ¶ *Shall inherit the earth.* Originally this promise referred to the land of Canaan, as a promise connected with obeying the law of God: Ex. xx. 12. It came then to be synonymous with outward worldly prosperity; with length of days, and happiness in the earth. See it explained in the Notes on Matt. v. 5.

14. *The secret of the* LORD. On the word here rendered *secret,* see Notes on Job xv. 8. It properly means a couch or cushion; and then, a *divan* or circle of friends sitting together; then, deliberation or consultation; then, familiar intercourse, intimacy; and then, a *secret,*—as if it were the result of a private consultation among friends, or something which pertained to them, and which they did not wish to have known. It is rendered *secret* in Gen. xlix. 6; Job xv. 8; xxix. 4; Ps. xxv. 14; Prov. iii. 32; xi. 13; xx. 19; xxv. 9; Amos iii. 7;—*counsel* in Ps. lv. 14; lxiv. 2; lxxxiii. 3; Jer. xxiii. 18, 22;—and *assembly* in Ps. lxxxix. 7; cxi. 1; Jer. vi. 11; xv. 17; Ezek. xiii. 9. The word *friendship* would perhaps express the meaning here. The sense is, that those who fear the Lord are admitted to the intimacy of friendship with him; are permitted to come into his presence, and to partake of his counsels; are allowed free access to him; or, as it is more commonly expressed, have *fellowship* with him. Comp. 1 John i. 3. The language is such as would be applied to the intimacy of friends, or to those who take counsel together. The language belongs to a large class of expressions denoting the close connexion between God and his people. ¶ *With them that fear him.* With those who truly and properly reverence him, or who are his true worshippers: Ps. v. 7; Job i. 1. ¶ *And he will show them his covenant.* Marg., *And his covenant to make them know* it. The meaning is, that God will impart to them the true knowledge of his covenant; or, in other words, he will enable them to understand what there is in that covenant, or in its gracious provisions, that is adapted to promote their happiness and salvation. The word *covenant* here is the same term which is commonly used to describe the arrangements which God has made for the salvation of men: see ver. 10. Whatever there is in that arrangement to promote the happiness and salvation of his people, he will cause them to understand.

15. *Mine eyes* are *ever toward the* LORD. This is an indication of the habitual state of mind of the psalmist. He had said that God would lead and guide those who were meek, gentle, teachable, humble; and he now says that this was his habitual state of mind. He constantly looked to God. He sought his direction. In perplexity, in doubt, in difficulty, in danger, in view of death and the future world, he looked to God as his guide. In other words, in reference to himself, he carried out the principles which he had stated as constituting true religion. It was a religion of dependence on God, for man's only hope is in him. ¶ *For he shall pluck my feet out of the net.* Marg., *bring forth.* Comp. Notes on Ps. ix. 15, 16; x. 9. The *net* here is that which had been laid for him by the wicked. He trusted in God alone to deliver him from it.

16. *Turn thee unto me.* The Hebrew rather means *look upon me.*

17 The troubles of my heart are [u] enlarged: *O* bring thou me out of my distresses.

u Hab. iii. 17—19.

18 Look upon mine affliction and my pain; and forgive all my sins.

19 Consider mine enemies; for

The idea, however, is that the face of God was, as it were, turned in another direction, or that he was not attentive to him; and he prays that he would turn and behold him; that he would *see* him in his trouble. ¶ *And have mercy upon me.* The psalmist seems to have felt that *if* God would look upon him he *would* pity him. He would see his case to be so sad that he would show him compassion,—as, when we see an object of distress, "the eye affects the heart." ¶ *For I am desolate.* The word here rendered *desolate*—יָחִיד, *yahhid*—means properly *one alone, only;* and then, one who *is alone,* or who is solitary, forsaken, wretched. There is no deeper sadness that ever comes over the mind than the idea that we are *alone* in the world; that we have not a friend; that no one cares for us; that no one is concerned about anything that may happen to us; that no one would care if we should die; that no one would shed a tear over our grave. ¶ *And afflicted.* In what way we do not know. David, however, was very often in circumstances when he could use this language. The other parts of the psalm show that the "affliction" to which he here refers was that which arose from the recollection of the sins of his early life, and from the designs and purposes of his enemies.

17. *The troubles of my heart.* The sorrows which spring upon the heart,—particularly from the recollections of sin. ¶ *Are enlarged.* Have become great. They increased the more he reflected on the sins of his life. ¶ O *bring thou me out of my distresses.* Alike from my sins, and from the dangers which surround me. These two things, external trouble and the inward consciousness of guilt, are not infrequently combined. Outward trouble has a tendency to bring up the remembrance of past transgressions, and to suggest the inquiry whether the affliction is not a Divine visitation for sin. Any one source of sorrow may draw along numerous others in its train. The laws of association are such that when the mind rests on one source of joy, and is made cheerful by that, numerous other blessings will be suggested to increase the joy; and when one great sorrow has taken possession of the soul, all the lesser sorrows of the past life cluster around it, so that we seem to ourselves to be wholly abandoned by God and by man.

18. *Look upon mine affliction and my pain.* See ver. 16. This is a repetition of earnest pleading—*as if* God still turned away from him, and did not deign to regard him. In trouble and distress piety thus pleads with God, and *repeats* the earnest supplication for his help. Though God *seems* not to regard the prayer, faith does not fail, but renews the supplication, confident that he will yet hear and save. ¶ *And forgive all my sins.* The mind, as above remarked, connects trouble and sin together. When we are afflicted, we naturally inquire *whether* the affliction is not on account of some particular transgressions of which we have been guilty; and even when we cannot trace any *direct* connexion with sin, affliction suggests the general fact that we *are* sinners, and that *all* our troubles are originated by that fact. One of the benefits of affliction, therefore, is to call to our remembrance our sins, and to keep before the mind the fact that we are violators of the law of God. This connexion between suffering and sin, in the sense that the one naturally suggests the other, was more than once illustrated in the miracles wrought by the Saviour. See Matt. ix. 2.

19. *Consider mine enemies.* See ver. 2. It is evident that *one* source

they are many; and they hate me with [1] cruel hatred.

20 O keep my soul, and deliver me; let me not be ashamed: for I put my trust in thee.

[1] *hatred of violence.*

21 Let integrity and uprightness preserve me; for I wait on thee.

22 Redeem [v] Israel, O God, out of all his troubles.

v Ps. cxxx. 8.

---

of the trouble referred to in the psalm was the fact that he had cruel foes, and that he was apprehensive of their designs. The train of thought seems to be, in accordance with the remarks above, that enemies actually surrounded him, and threatened him, and that this fact suggested the inquiry whether this was not permitted on account of his sins. *This* had led him to think of the sins of his past life, going back as far as his youth (ver. 7), as if these calamities, even in advanced life, were on account of those early offences. ¶ *For they are many.* Who and what they were, we have now no means of ascertaining. See Notes on ver. 16. ¶ *And they hate me with cruel hatred.* Marg., as in Heb., *hatred of violence.* It was such hatred as tended to violence; such that they could not restrain it. It sought his destruction, and was ready to break out at any moment.

20. *O keep my soul.* My *life;* or, keep *me.* The allusion is to *all* the perils which encompassed him, whether arising from his foes or his sins; and the prayer is, that the Divine protection might be commensurate with the danger; that is, that he might not be destroyed, either by his enemies or by the sins which he had committed. ¶ *And deliver me.* Save me; rescue me. ¶ *Let me not be ashamed.* See ver. 2. ¶ *For I put my trust in thee.* This is urged as a *reason* why he should be delivered and saved. The idea seems to be, that the honour of God would be concerned in protecting one who fled to him; who confided in him; who relied on him. Thus, when the helpless and the oppressed have so much confidence in our character and our ability as to fly to us in the time of trouble, it is a proper reason for them to ask our protection that they do confide in us. Our character becomes involved in the matter, and they may safely trust that we shall feel ourselves under obligations to act in conformity with the confidence reposed in us. It is thus that the poor and the oppressed confide in the good; thus that a sinner confides in God.

21. *Let integrity and uprightness preserve me.* The word here rendered *integrity* means properly *perfection.* See it explained in the Notes on Job i. 1. The language here may refer either (*a*) to God—as denoting *his* perfection and uprightness, and then the psalmist's prayer would be that he, a righteous God, would keep him; or (*b*) to his own integrity and uprightness of character, and then the prayer would be that *that* might be the means of keeping him, as the ground of his safety, under the government of a righteous God; or, (*c*) which I think the more probable meaning, it may be the utterance of a prayer that God would show himself upright and perfect in protecting one who put his trust in him; one who was wronged and injured by his fellow-men; one who fled to God for refuge in time of persecution and trouble. It was not exactly the Divine perfections, as such, on which he relied; nor was it the integrity and purity of his own life; but it was the government of God, considered as just and equal, as bearing on himself and those who had wronged him. ¶ *For I wait on thee.* That is, I depend on thee, or I rely on thee. This is a reason why he pleaded that God would preserve him. See Notes on ver. 20.

22. *Redeem Israel.* Redeem or save thy people,—the word *Israel* here being used, as elsewhere, to denote

the people of God. ¶ *Out of all his troubles.* Save thy people from persecution, and from trial of all kinds. The prayer of the psalmist had, before this, related mainly to himself. He had made mention of his own troubles and sorrows, and had earnestly sought relief. The psalm, however, closes appropriately with a reference to others; to all the people of God who might be in similar circumstances. Religion is not selfish. The mind under the influence of true piety, however intensely it may feel its own trouble, and however earnestly it may pray for deliverance, is not forgetful of the troubles of others; and prayers for their comfort and deliverance are freely mingled with those which the afflicted children of God offer for themselves. This verse may be, therefore, taken as an illustration of the nature of true piety:—piety that seeks the welfare of all; piety that does not terminate in itself alone; piety that desires the happiness of all men, especially the deliverance of the suffering and the sad. It should, however, be added that this verse is no part of the alphabetical series in the psalm,—that having been ended, in ver. 21, with the last letter of the Hebrew alphabet. This verse commences with the Hebrew letter פ, P. Some have supposed that it was added to the psalm when it was prepared for public use, in order to make what was at first applicable to an individual appropriate as a part of public worship,—or because the sentiments in the psalm, originally having reference to one individual, were as applicable to the people of God generally as to the author of the psalm. There is some plausibility in this conjecture.

PSALM XXVI.

The title affirms this to be a psalm of David, and there is no reason to doubt the correctness of the superscription; but there are no indications by which we can determine on what occasion it was written.

It is not difficult, however, to ascertain from its contents the state of mind in which it was composed; and as that state of mind is not uncommon among those who are the professed people of God, the psalm will be useful in all ages of the world. The state of mind is that in which there is deep solicitude in regard to personal piety, or on the question whether the evidences of our piety are genuine, and are such as we may rely on as warranting our hope of salvation. In this state of mind, and under this deep solicitude, the psalmist appeals to God to search him, or to judge in his case; he then recounts the evidences on which he relied as a ground for concluding that he was truly a friend of God; and then expresses the earnest desire of his heart *to be* found among the friends of God, and not to be united in character or in destiny with the wicked.

The psalm, therefore, properly consists of three parts:—

I. A solemn appeal to God, or an earnest prayer that *He* would examine and judge of the evidences of piety on which the psalmist was accustomed to rely, vers. 1, 2. He was conscious of integrity or uprightness of intention, but he still felt that there was a possibility that he might deceive himself, and he therefore prays that God would search his heart and try his reins,—that *He* would examine the evidences of his personal piety, and save him from delusion.

II. A statement of the evidences on which he relied, vers. 3-8.

These evidences were the following:

(1) That God's loving-kindness was before his eyes, and that he had walked in his truth, ver. 3.

(2) That he had not been the companion of the wicked, nor had he delighted to associate with them, vers. 4, 5.

(3) The desire of his heart to approach the altar of God with purity, and to celebrate the praises of God;—or his delight in public worship, vers. 6, 7.

(4) That he had loved the place where God dwelt, or the habitation of his house, ver. 8.

III. His earnest wish to be found among the friends of God, or to have his portion with them, vers. 9–12.

(1) His *prayer* that this might be his lot, vers. 9, 10.

(2) His *purpose* to walk with the just and the holy, or to be found among the friends of God, vers. 11, 12.

In reference to all this, he asks the guidance and direction of God; he prays for the searching of his eye; he pleads

PSALM XXVI.

A Psalm of David.

JUDGE me, O LORD; for I have walked in mine integrity: I have trusted also in the LORD; *therefore* I shall not slide.

2 Examine [w] me, O LORD, and prove me; try [x] my reins and my heart.

w Ps. cxxxix. 23. *x* Zech. xiii. 9.

---

that God would enable him sincerely to carry out these desires and purposes of his soul. The psalm is a beautiful illustration of the nature of true religion, and of the desire of a truly pious man that all the evidences of his piety—all which is his ground of reliance—may be submitted to the searching eye of God.

1. *Judge me, O* LORD. That is, determine in regard to my case whether I am truly thy friend, or whether the evidences of my piety are genuine. The psalmist asks an examination of his own case; he brings the matter before God for Him to decide; he submits the facts in regard to himself to God, that He may pronounce upon them whether they constitute evidence of real piety. ¶ *For I have walked in mine integrity.* On the word *walk*, see Notes on Ps. i. 1. The word *integrity* here is the same which is elsewhere rendered *perfection.* See Notes on Job i. 1. Comp. Ps. xxxvii. 37. See also Ps. vii. 8; xxv. 21; where the word is rendered, as here, *integrity.* It means here *uprightness, sincerity.* This is the first thing which he brings before God for him to examine—the consciousness that he had endeavoured to live an upright life; and yet it is referred to as if he was sensible that he *might* have deceived himself, and therefore he prays that God would determine whether his life had been really upright. ¶ *I have trusted also in the* LORD. Of this, likewise, he felt conscious; but this too he desired to submit to God. Trust in Jehovah, and an upright life, constituted the evidence of piety, or were the constituents of true religion according to the views of the Hebrews, as they are the constituents of true religion everywhere; and the purpose of the psalmist was to ascertain whether his piety was really of that character. ¶ Therefore *I shall not slide.* If these are really traits of my character, if I really possess these, I shall not be moved. My feet will be firm, and I shall be secure. Or this may be regarded as a further declaration in regard to himself, as indicating firm confidence in God, and as meaning that he was conscious that he would not be moved, or would not swerve in this purpose of life. And yet the next verse shows that, with all this confidence as to his own character, he felt that there was a *possibility* of his having deceived himself; and, therefore, he pleaded that God would search and try him.

2. *Examine me, O* LORD. The meaning of this verse is, that he asked of God a strict and rigid examination of his case. To express this, the psalmist uses three words—*examine; prove; try.* These words are designed to include the modes in which the reality of anything is tested, and they imply together that he wished the most *thorough* investigation to be made; he did not shrink from *any* test. He evidently felt that it was essential to his welfare that the most rigid examination should be made; that the exact truth should be known; that if he was deceived, it was best for himself that he should not be left under the delusion, but that, understanding his own case, he might be led to secure his salvation. The word rendered *examine* means, *to try, to prove,* and is applicable especially to metals: Jer. ix. 7; Zech. xiii. 9. It means here, "Apply to me such tests as are applied to metals in order to determine their genuineness and their value." ¶ *And prove me.* A word of similar import. In the original meaning of the word there is a reference to *smell;* to try by the smell; to ascertain the qualities of an object by the smell. Hence it comes

3 For thy loving-kindness *is* before mine eyes; and I have walked in thy truth.

4 I [y] have not sat with vain persons, neither will I go in with dissemblers.

y Ps. i. 1.

to be used in a more general sense to denote any way of ascertaining the quality of an object. ¶ *Try my reins.* The word here rendered *try* is one that is most commonly applied to metals; and the three words together express the earnest desire of the psalmist that God would examine into the evidences of his piety—those evidences to which he immediately refers—and apply the proper kind of tests to determine whether that piety was genuine. The word rendered *reins* means properly the *kidneys,* and hence it is used to denote the inward part, the mind, the soul—the seat of the desires and the affections. See Notes on Ps. vii. 9; xvi. 7. We speak now of the *heart* as the seat of the affections or of love. The Hebrews more commonly spoke of the heart as the seat of intelligence or knowledge, and the reins or the "bowels" as the seat of the affections. In itself there was no more impropriety in their speaking of the reins or kidneys as the seat of the affections than there is of our speaking of the heart in that manner. Neither of them is strictly correct; and both modes of speech are founded on popular usage.

3. *For thy loving-kindness* is *before mine eyes.* Thy favour or friendship is constantly before me, in the sense that it is the object of my desire. I wish to secure it; I long to know whether I have sufficient evidence that it is mine. This is a reason why he desires that God would search him. The favour or the friendship of God was an object of intense desire with him. He had evidence on which he relied, and which seemed to him to be satisfactory, that God was his friend. But the object was so great, the matter was so important, the danger of self-deception was so imminent, that he did not dare to trust his own judgment, and he prayed that God would search him. The thought here is, that it was a steady purpose of his life to secure the favour of God. His eye was never turned from this. It was always before him. ¶ *And I have walked in thy truth.* I have embraced the truth; I have regulated my life by the truth. This is the first thing to which he refers. He was certain that this had been his aim. Comp. Notes on 3 John 4. See also 2 Kings xx. 3. One of the first characteristics of piety is a desire to know what is true, and to live in accordance with the truth. The psalmist was conscious that he had *arrived* at this, and that he had endeavoured to make it a ruling principle in his conduct. Whether he *had* done this, or whether he had deceived himself in the matter, was what he now wished to submit to the all-searching eye of God.

4. *I have not sat with vain persons.* That is, I have not been found among them; I have not made them my companions. See Notes on Ps. i. 1. The word "*vain*" here is in contrast with those who are sincere and true. The expression would be applied to men who are false and hollow; to those who have no sincerity or solidity of character; to those who are hypocrites and pretenders. The psalmist urges it as one evidence of his attachment to God that he had not been found among that class of persons, either as making them his companions, or as taking part with them in their counsels. ¶ *Neither will I go in with dissemblers.* Neither will I walk with them; neither will I be found in their company. The word here rendered *dissemblers* means properly those who are *hidden* or *concealed;* then, those who hide their purposes or designs from others, or who conceal their real character and intentions. Thus used, the word denotes hypocrites, whose real character is *concealed* or *hidden* from the world. The psalmist says

5 I have hated the congregation of evil-doers; and will not sit with the wicked.

6 I will wash [z] mine hands in innocency: so will I compass thine altar, O LORD:

7 That I may publish with the

z Ex. xxx. 19, 20.

that he had not associated with such men, but that his companionship had been with the open, the frank, the sincere. On this he relied as one evidence of his piety; and this *is* always an evidence of true religion. See Notes on Ps. i. 1.

5. *I have hated.* We have here the same evidence of his piety repeated in another and a stronger form. In the previous verse he had merely stated that he had not been found among that class of persons, or that he had not made them his companions. He here says positively that he disapproved of their principles; that he hated the purpose for which they gathered themselves together; that he had no sympathy whatever with them. ¶ *The congregation of evil-doers.* All such assemblages as were gathered together for wicked purposes; for sin and revelry; to plot wickedness; to injure men; to oppose God. ¶ *And will not sit with the wicked.* That is, I will not be associated with them. This was the fixed purpose of his soul; and this was then, as it is now, an evidence of true piety. This, moreover, is an *indispensable* evidence of piety. He who *does* thus sit with the wicked; who makes them his companions and friends; who unites with them in their plans and purposes; who partakes with them in their peculiar amusements and pursuits, cannot possibly be a pious man. If he mingles with such men at all, it must be only as demanded by the necessities of social or civil life; or in the transactions of business; or for the purpose of doing them good. If it is for other purposes, if he makes them his chosen companions and friends, he gives the clearest evidence that his heart is with them, and that it is *not* with God.

6. *I will wash mine hands in innocency.* The psalmist here refers, as another evidence of his piety, to the fact that it was a ruling purpose of his life to be pure, to worship and serve his Maker in purity. He had stated that he had no sympathy with the wicked, and that he did not make them his companions; he now states what his preferences were, and where his heart was to be found. He had loved, and he still loved the worship of God; he delighted in the pure service of the Most High. Washing the hands is an emblem of purity. So Pilate (Matt. xxvii. 24) "took water, and washed his hands before the multitude, saying, I am innocent of the blood of this just person." Comp. Deut. xxi. 6, 7. The word rendered *innocency* means properly *cleanness, purity;* and perhaps the allusion here is to water that is perfectly pure. The sense of the passage is, that he would endeavour to make himself pure, and would thus worship God. He would not come, practising iniquity, or cherishing sin in his heart. He would banish all from his mind and heart and life that was wrong, and would come with true love to God, and with the spirit of a sincere worshipper. ¶ *So will I compass thine altar, O* LORD. In this manner, and with this spirit, I will worship thee. The word *compass* may either mean that he would *embrace* it by throwing his arms around it, or that he would *go round* it with others in a solemn procession in worship. The idea is, that he would come to the altar of God with his offering in sincerity and truth. It was to himself one evidence of sincere piety that he so purposed in his heart, or that he was conscious of a desire to worship God in purity and truth. This desire is always an indication of true piety.

7. *That I may publish with the voice of thanksgiving.* Literally, "that I may cause to be heard;" that is, that I may make known to others. The

voice of thanksgiving, and tell of all thy wondrous works.

8 LORD, I have loved [a] the habitation of thy house, and the place where [1] thine honour dwelleth.

9 [2] Gather not my soul with sinners, nor my life with [3] bloody men;

a Ps. xxvii. 4; lxxxiv. 1, 2.
1 *of the tabernacle of thine honour.*

2 Or, *take not away.* 3 *men of blood.*

idea is, that he would make known to others what he had learned of God; or that he would make known to them the delights of his service, and seek to win them to his worship. This he would do with a thankful remembrance of the favours which he had himself enjoyed, or as an expression of his gratitude for the mercies which had been conferred on him. As expressive of his gratitude to God, he would endeavour to win others also to his service. ¶ *And tell of all thy wondrous works.* The wonderful things which thou hast done,—thy works of creation, providence, and salvation. His own mind was deeply impressed with the greatness of God's works, and he would desire to make the Divine doings known as far as possible in the world. Comp. Ps. xxii. 22; lxvi. 16; cxlv. 5, 6. This is always one of the evidences of true piety. They who have been impressed properly with a sense of the greatness and goodness of God; they who have experienced his pardoning mercy and forgiving grace, desire always to make these things known to others, and to invite them also to partake of the mercies connected with the Divine favour. Comp. John i. 45.

8. LORD, *I have loved the habitation of thy house.* I have loved to dwell in thy house. See Notes on Ps. xxiii. 6. The psalmist often refers to his delight in the house of God,—the place of public worship; his love to be there united with the people of God in the solemn services of religion. Comp. Ps. lxxxiv. 1, 2, 4, 10; xxvii. 4. ¶ *And the place where thine honour dwelleth.* Marg., *the tabernacle of thine honour.* This *might* indeed refer to the tabernacle; and the idea might be that he loved the place where that rested in its wanderings. But the more correct meaning is, that he loved the place where the "glory" of God—the Shekinah—the symbol of his presence—rested; that is, the place where God was pleased to manifest himself, and where he dwelt. Wherever that was, he found pleasure in being there; and that he *did* thus love the place where God manifested himself, was to his own mind an evidence of true piety. It *is* always an evidence of piety, for there can be no true religion where the soul does *not* find pleasure in the worship of God. A man who does *not* delight in such a service here, is not prepared for heaven, where God eternally dwells.

9. *Gather not my soul with sinners.* Marg., *take not away.* The word rendered *gather,* means properly to *collect;* to *gather,*—as fruits, Exod. xxiii. 10; ears of grain, Ruth ii. 7; money, 2 Kings xxii. 4. There is the idea of assembling together, or collecting; and the meaning here is, that he desired not to be united with wicked men, or to be regarded as one of their number. It does not refer particularly, as I apprehend, to death, as if he prayed that he might not be cut down with wicked men; but it has a more general meaning,—that he did not wish either in this life, in death, or in the future world, to be united with the wicked. He desired that his lot might be with those who feared God, and not with those who were his foes. He was united with those who feared God now; he desired that he might be united with them for ever. This is expressive of true religion; and this prayer must go forth really from every pious heart. They who truly love God must desire that their lot should be with his friends, alike in this world and in the world to come, however poor, and humble, and despised they may be;—not with sinners, however prosperous, or honoured, or

10 In whose hands *is* mischief,
and their right hand is [1] full of
bribes.
11 But as for me, I will walk
in mine integrity: redeem me,
and be merciful unto me.
12 My foot [b] standeth in an
even place: in the congregations
will I bless the Lord.

[1] *filled with.* [b] Ps. xl. 2.

gay, or rich, they may be. The word *my soul* here is synonymous with *me;* and the meaning is, he desired that *he himself* should not thus be gathered with sinners. It is the same word which is commonly rendered *life.* ¶ *Nor my life.* This word properly means *life;* and the prayer is, that his life might not be taken away or destroyed with that class of men. He did not wish to be associated with them when he died or was dead. He had preferred the society of the righteous; and he prayed that he might die as he had lived, united in feeling and in destiny with those who feared and loved God. ¶ *With bloody men.* Marg., *men of blood.* Men who shed blood—robbers, murderers,—a term used to denote the wicked. See Notes on Ps. v. 6.

10. *In whose hands* is *mischief.* The word here rendered *mischief,* means properly *purpose, counsel, plan;* then, an evil purpose, *mischief, wickedness, crime.* The idea is, either that they intended to do mischief, and that they employed their hands to accomplish it, or that the fruit or result of their wicked plans was in their hands; that is, they had in their possession what they had secured by robbery, or plunder, or dishonesty. ¶ *And their right hand is full of bribes.* Marg., *filled with.* The word here rendered *bribes* means properly a *gift,* or *present;* and then, a gift offered to a judge to procure an unjust sentence, 2 Kings xvi. 8; Prov. vi. 35; Exod. xxiii. 8; Deut. x. 17. The general meaning is that he did not desire to be associated either with men who openly committed crime, or with those who could be corrupted in the administration of justice.

11. *But as for me.* The Hebrew is, "and I." But there is evidently a contrast between what he purposed to do, and the course of life pursued by those to whom he had just referred; and this is correctly expressed in our translation, "*But* as for me." It is a statement of his profession of piety, and of his purpose to lead a religious life. He *meant*—he solemnly *purposed*—to lead a holy life. ¶ *I will walk.* I will live a life of integrity. See Notes on Ps. i. 1. ¶ *In mine integrity.* Heb., in my *perfection.* See Notes on Ps. vii. 8; Job i. 1. The idea is that he intended to live a life of uprightness. ¶ *Redeem me.* From sin; from trouble; from death. The word *redeem* here implies that he did not claim to be *perfect* in the most absolute sense, even when he expressed his purpose to lead a life of integrity. He felt still that he was a sinner, and that he was dependent on redeeming mercy for salvation. On the word *redeem,* see Notes on Ps. xxv. 22; Isa. xxix. 22. Comp. Notes on Isa. xliii. 3. ¶ *And be merciful to me.* In connexion with redemption. The prayer for mercy is always an acknowledgment of guilt, and the plea here shows that with all his purposes of holy living, and notwithstanding all that he had referred to in the psalm as evidence of uprightness of intention and integrity of life, he still felt that he was a sinner, and that his only hope was in the mercy of God.

12. *My foot standeth in an even place.* The word rendered *even place* —מִישׁוֹר, *mishor*—means properly *righteousness,* or *justice;* then, *evenness,* a *level region,* a *plain:* Isa. xl. 4; xlii. 16. De Wette renders it, "in a right path." The idea is, either that he was standing now on smooth and level ground; or that he was walking in a straight path, in contradistinction from the crooked and perverse ways of the wicked;

that is, he had found now a level road where he might walk securely. The latter is probably the true meaning. He had been anxious about his condition. He had been examining the evidences of his piety. He had had doubts and fears. He had seen much to apprehend, and he had appealed to God to determine the question on which he was so anxious,—whether his hope was built on a solid foundation. His path in these inquiries, and while his mind was thus troubled, was like a journey over a rough and dangerous road—a road of hills and vallies—of rocks and ravines. Now he had found a smooth and safe path. The way was level. He felt secure; and he walked calmly and safely along, as a traveller does who has got over dangerous passes and who feels that he is on level ground. The idea is, that his doubts had been dissipated, and he now felt that his evidences of piety were well founded, and that he was truly a child of God. ¶ *In the congregations will I bless the* LORD. In the assemblies of his people will I praise him. Comp. Ps. xxii. 22. The meaning is, that in the great assembly he would offer special praise that God had resolved his doubts, and had given him so clear evidence that he was truly his friend. He would go to the house of God, and there render him public praise that he had been able to find the evidence which he desired. No act could be more appropriate than such an act of praise, for there is nothing for which we should render more hearty thanks than for any evidence that we are truly the friends of God, and have a well-founded hope of heaven. The whole psalm should lead us carefully to examine the evidences of our piety; to bring before God all that we rely on as proof that we are his friends; and to pray that he will enable us to examine it aright; and, when the result is, as it was in the case of the psalmist,—when we can feel that we have reached a level place and found a smooth path, then we should go, as he did, and offer hearty thanks to God that we *have* reason to believe we are his children and are heirs of salvation.

PSALM XXVII.

This purports to be "A Psalm of David," and there is no reason to think that the inscription is not correct. But the occasion on which it was composed is wholly unknown. There is no intimation of this in the title, and there are no historical marks in the psalm which would enable us to determine this. There were not a few occasions in the life of David when all that is expressed in the psalm *might* have been said by him,—as there are many occasions, in the lives of all, to which the sentiments of the psalm would be appropriate. The Septuagint version has the title, "A Psalm of David before his anointing," --- πρὸ τοῦ χρισθῆναι. Grotius supposes the occasion to have been the anointing in Hebron, when he was first inaugurated as king, 2 Sam. ii. 4. Rosenmüller refers it to the last anointing, 2 Sam. v. 3. Many of the Jewish expositors refer the psalm to the last days of David, when he was delivered from death by the intervention of Abishai, 2 Sam. xxi. 16, 17. But there is no internal evidence that the psalm was composed on either of these occasions, and it is now impossible to ascertain the time or the circumstances of its composition.

The general object of the psalm is to excite in others confidence in God from the experience which the psalmist had of His merciful interposition in times of trouble and danger, ver. 14. The author of the psalm had had some marked evidence of the Divine favour and protection in seasons of peril and sorrow (ver. 1); and he makes use of this as an argument running through the psalm to lead others to repose on God in similar circumstances. It may have been that at the time of composing the psalm he was still surrounded by enemies, and exposed to danger; but if so, he expresses the utmost confidence in God, and gratefully refers to His past interposition in similar circumstances as full proof that all his interests would be secure.

The contents of the psalm are,—

I. An expression of confidence in God as derived from his own experience of His merciful interposition in times of danger, vers. 1-3. He had been in peril at some time which is not specified, and had been rescued; and from this gracious

PSALM XXVII.

A Psalm of David.

THE LORD [c] is my light and my salvation; whom shall I fear? the LORD *is* the strength of my life; of whom shall I be afraid?

2 When the wicked, *even* mine enemies and my foes, [1] came upon me to eat up my flesh, they stumbled and fell.

c Mic. vii. 7, 8.

1 *approached against.*

interposition he argues that it would be safe always to trust in God.

II. The expression of a desire to dwell always where God is; to see his beauty there; to inquire further after him; to offer sacrifices; and to praise him, vers. 4–6. The psalmist had seen so much of God that he desired to see yet more; he had had such experience of his favour that he wished always to be with him; he had found so much happiness in God that he believed that all his happiness was to be found in His presence, and in His service.

III. An earnest prayer that God would hear him; that he would grant his requests; that he would save him from all his enemies; that he would lead him in a plain path, vers. 7–12. This is founded partly on his own past experience, that when God had commanded him to seek his face he had obeyed (ver. 8), and it is connected with the fullest assurance that God would protect him, even should he be forsaken by father and mother (ver. 10).

IV. The conclusion—the exhortation to wait on the Lord, vers. 13, 14. This exhortation is derived from his own experience. He says that he himself would have fainted if he had not confided in God and hoped in His mercy, when there was no other hope (ver. 13); and, in view of that experience, he encourages all others to put their trust in Him (ver. 14).

1. *The* LORD *is my light.* He is to me the source of light. That is, he guides and leads me. Darkness is the emblem of distress, trouble, perplexity, and sorrow; light is the emblem of the opposite of these. God furnished him such light that these troubles disappeared, and his way was bright and happy. ¶ *And my salvation.* That is, he saves or delivers me. ¶ *Whom shall I fear?* Comp. Rom. viii. 31. If God is on our side, or is for us, we can have no apprehension of danger. He is abundantly able to protect us, and we may confidently trust in him. No one needs any better security against the objects of fear or dread than the conviction that God is his friend. ¶ *The* LORD is *the strength of my life.* The support of my life. Or, in other words, he keeps me alive. In itself life is feeble, and is easily crushed out by trouble and sorrow; but as long as *God* is its strength, there is nothing to fear. ¶ *Of whom shall I be afraid?* No one has power to take life away while he defends me. God is to those who put their trust in him a stronghold or fortress, and they are safe.

2. *When the wicked,* even *mine enemies and my foes, came upon me.* This refers, doubtless, to some particular period of his past life when he was in very great danger, and when God interposed to save him. The margin here is, *approached against me.* The literal rendering would be, "in the drawing near against me of the wicked to eat up my flesh." The reference is to some period when they purposed an attack on him, and when he was in imminent danger from such a threatened attack. ¶ *To eat up my flesh.* As if they would eat me up. That is, they came upon me like ravening wolves, or hungry lions. We are not to suppose that they literally purposed to eat up his flesh, or that they were cannibals; but the comparison is one that is drawn from the fierceness of wild beasts rushing on their prey. Comp. Ps. xiv. 4. ¶ *They stumbled and fell.* They were overthrown. They failed in their purpose. Either they were thrown into a panic by a false fear, or they were overthrown in battle. The language would be rather applicable to the former, as if by some alarm they were thrown into consternation. Either they differed

3 Though an host should encamp against me, my heart shall not fear; though war should rise against me, in this *will* I *be* confident.

4 One *thing* have I desired of the LORD, that will I seek after; that I may dwell [d] in the house of the LORD all the days of my life, to behold [e] the [1] beauty of the LORD, and to enquire in his temple.

d Ps. lxv. 4. e Ps. lxiii. 2.

1 Or, *delight*.

among themselves and became confused, or God threw obstacles in their way and they were driven back. The general idea is, that *God* had interposed in some way to prevent the execution of their purposes.

3. *Though an host.* Though an *army;* that is, any army, or any number of men in battle array. The past interposition of God in similar times of trouble and danger was to him a sufficient security that he had nothing to fear. ¶ *Should encamp against me.* In battle array, or prepared for battle. ¶ *My heart shall not fear.* He would not tremble; he would not feel that there was anything of which to be afraid. God had shown himself superior to the power of hostile armies, and the psalmist felt assured that he might confide in him. ¶ *Though war should rise against me.* Though it should be proclaimed, and though all preparation should be made for it, I will not be afraid. ¶ *In this* will *I* be *confident.* In such a case, in such an extremity or emergency, I would calmly trust in God. He would apprehend no danger, for he had seen that the Lord could deliver him.

4. *One* thing *have I desired of the* LORD. One main object; one thing that I have specially desired; one thing which has been the object of my constant wish. This ruling desire of his heart the psalmist has more than once adverted to in the previous psalms (comp. Ps. xxiii. 6; xxvi. 8); and he frequently refers to it in the subsequent psalms. ¶ *That will I seek after.* As the leading object of my life; as the thing which I most earnestly desire. ¶ *That I may dwell in the house of the* LORD. See Notes on Ps. xxiii. 6. ¶ *All the days of my life.* Constantly; to the end. Though engaged in other things, and though there were other objects of interest in the world, yet he felt that it would be supreme felicity on earth to dwell always in the temple of God, and to be employed in its sacred services, preparatory to an eternal residence in the temple above. To him the service of God on earth was not burdensome, nor did he anticipate that he would ever become weary of praising his Maker. How can a man be prepared for an eternal heaven who finds the worship of God on earth irksome and tedious? ¶ *To behold the beauty of the* LORD. Marg., *the delight.* The word rendered *beauty* here—נֹעַם, *noam*—means properly *pleasantness;* then, *beauty, splendour;* then, *grace, favour.* The reference here is to the beauty or loveliness of the Divine character as it was particularly manifested in the public worship of God, or by those symbols which in the ancient worship were designed to make that character known. In the tabernacle and in the temple there was a manifestation of the character of God not seen elsewhere. The whole worship was adapted to set forth his greatness, his glory, and his grace. Great truths were brought before the mind, fitted to elevate, to comfort, and to sanctify the soul; and it was in the contemplation of those truths that the psalmist sought to elevate and purify his own mind, and to sustain himself in the troubles and perplexities of life. Comp. Ps. lxxiii. 15—17. ¶ *And to inquire in his temple.* Or tabernacle. The *word* here used would be applicable to either, considered as the *palace* or the residence of Jehovah. As the temple was not, however, built at

5 For [f] in the time of trouble
he shall hide me in his pavilion:
in the secret of his tabernacle
shall he hide me: he shall set
me up upon a rock.

6 And now shall mine head be
lifted up above mine enemies
round about me: therefore will I
offer in his tabernacle sacrifices
of [1] joy; I will sing, yea, I will
sing praises unto the LORD.

f Isa. iv. 5, 6. 1 *shouting.*

this time, the word must here be understood to refer to the tabernacle. See Notes on Ps. v. 7. The meaning of the passage is, that he would wish to seek instruction, or to obtain light on the great questions pertaining to God, and that he looked for this light in the place where God was worshipped, and by means of the views which that worship was adapted to convey to the mind. In a manner still more direct and full may we now hope to obtain just views of God by attendance on his worship. The Christian sanctuary — the place of public worship—is the place where, if anywhere on earth, we may hope to have our minds enlightened; our perplexities removed; our hearts comforted and sanctified, by right views of God.

5. *For in the time of trouble.* When I am surrounded by dangers, or when affliction comes upon me. ¶ *He shall hide me.* The word here used means to hide; to secrete; and then, to defend or protect. It would properly be applied to one who had fled from oppression, or from any impending evil, and who should be *secreted* in a house or cavern, and thus rendered safe from pursuers, or from the threatening evil. ¶ *In his pavilion.* The word *pavilion* means *tent* or *tabernacle.* The Hebrew word —סֻכָּה, *sukkah*—means properly a booth, hut, or cot formed of green branches interwoven: Jonah iv. 5; Job xxvii. 18; see Notes on Isa. iv. 6. Then it is applied to tents made of skins: Lev. xxiii. 43; 2 Sam. xi. 11. It thus is used to denote the tabernacle, considered as the dwelling-place of God on earth, and the meaning here is, that God would hide him as it were in his own dwelling; he would admit him near to himself; he would take care that he should be protected as if he were one of his own family;—as a man protects those whom he admits to his own abode. ¶ *In the secret of his tabernacle.* In the most retired and private part of his dwelling. He would not merely admit him to his premises; not only to the vestibule of his house; not only to the open court, or to the parts of his house frequented by the rest of his family; but he would admit him to the private apartments—the place to which he himself withdrew to be alone, and where no stranger, and not even one of the family, would venture to intrude. Nothing could more certainly denote friendship; nothing could more certainly make protection sure, than thus to be taken into the private apartment where the master of a family was accustomed himself to withdraw, that he might be alone; and nothing, therefore, can more beautifully describe the protection which God will give to his friends than the idea of thus admitting them to the secret apartments of his own dwelling-place. ¶ *He shall set me up upon a rock.* A place where I shall be secure; a place inaccessible to my enemies. Comp. Ps. xviii. 1, 2; xix. 14 (*margin*); lxi. 2; lxxi. 3. The meaning is, that he would be *safe* from all his enemies.

6. *And now shall mine head.* Now shall *I* be exalted. So we say that in affliction a man bows down his head; in prosperity he lifts it up. This verse expresses the confident expectation that he would be enabled to triumph over all his foes, and a firm purpose on his part, as the result of this, to offer sacrifices of praise to his great deliverer. ¶ *Above mine enemies round about me.* All my enemies, though they seem even to encompass

7 Hear, O LORD, *when* I cry with my voice: have mercy also upon me, and answer me.

8 [1] *When thou saidst*, Seek ye my face; my heart said unto thee, Thy face, LORD, will I seek.

9 Hide not thy face *far* from me; put not thy servant away in anger: thou hast been my help; leave me not, neither forsake me, O God of my salvation.

[1] Or, *My heart said unto thee, Let my face seek thy face.*

me on every side. ¶ *Therefore will I offer in his tabernacle.* In his tent, his dwelling-place: referring here, undoubtedly, to *the tabernacle* as a place where God was worshipped. ¶ *Sacrifices of joy.* Marg., as in the Hebrew, *of shouting.* That is, he would offer sacrifices accompanied with loud sounds of praise and thanksgiving. There is nothing wrong in shouting for joy when a man is delivered from imminent danger, nothing wrong in doing so when he feels that he is rescued from the peril of eternal ruin. ¶ *I will sing, yea, I will sing praises unto the* LORD. This language is that which comes from a full heart. He is not contented with saying merely that he would *sing.* He repeats the idea; he dwells upon it. With a heart overflowing with gratitude he would go and give utterance to his joy. He would repeat, and dwell upon, the language of thanksgiving.

7. *Hear, O* LORD, when *I cry with my voice.* This earnest prayer seems to have been prompted by a returning sense of danger. He had had assurance of the Divine favour. He had found God ready to help him. He did not doubt but that he would aid him; yet all this did not prevent his calling upon him for the aid which he needed, but rather stimulated him to do it. With all the deep-felt conviction of his heart that God was ready and willing to assist him, he still felt that he had no reason to hope for his aid unless he called upon him. The phrase "when I cry with my voice" refers to the fact that he prayed audibly or aloud. It was not mental prayer, but that which found expression in the language of earnest entreaty.

8. When thou saidst, *Seek ye my face*, etc. Marg., *My heart said unto thee, Let my face seek thy face.* The literal translation would be, "To Thee hath said my heart, Seek ye my face; thy face, O Lord, will I seek." De Wette thus expresses the idea, "Of thee my heart thinks (in regard to the command to seek thy face), thy face, Lord, I will seek." Our translators have given the correct meaning, though the original is quite obscure. The passage is designed to denote the state of the mind, or the disposition, in regard to the commands of God. The command or precept was to seek God. The prompt purpose of the mind or heart of the psalmist was, that he would do it. He *immediately* complied with that command, as it was a principle of his life—one of the steady promptings of his heart—that he would do this. The heart asked no excuse; pleaded for no delay; desired no reason for not complying with the command, but at once assented to the propriety of the law, and resolved to obey. This related undoubtedly at first to prayer, but the *principle* is applicable to all the commands of God. It is the prompting of a pious heart immediately and always to obey the voice of God, no matter what his command is, and no matter what sacrifice may be required in obeying it.

9. *Hide not thy face* far *from me.* Comp. Notes on Ps. iv. 6. To "hide the face" is to turn it away with displeasure, as if we would not look on one who has offended us. The favour of God is often expressed by "lifting the light of his countenance" upon any one,—looking complacently or *pleasedly* upon him. The reverse of this is expressed by hiding the face, or by turning it away. The word "*far*" introduced by the translators does not aid the sense of the passage.

10 When my father and my mother forsake me, then the LORD will [1] take me up.

11 Teach me thy way, O LORD, and lead me in a [2] plain path, because of [3] mine enemies.

12 Deliver me not over unto the will of mine enemies; for false witnesses are risen up against me, and such as breathe out cruelty.

[1] *gather me*, Isa. xl. 11.

[2] *way of plainness*, Ps. xxvi. 12.

[3] *those which observe me*, Ps. v. 8.

¶ *Put not thy servant away in anger.* Do not turn me off, or put me away in displeasure. We turn one away, or do not admit him into our presence, with whom we are displeased. The psalmist prayed that he might have free access to God as a friend. ¶ *Thou hast been my help.* In days that are past. This he urges as a reason why God should still befriend him. The fact that he *had* shown mercy to him, that he had treated him as a friend, is urged as a reason why he should now hear his prayers, and show him mercy. ¶ *Leave me not.* Do not abandon me. This is still a proper ground of pleading with God. We may refer to all his former mercies towards us; we may make mention of those mercies as a reason why he should now interpose and save us. We may, so to speak, *remind* him of his former favours and friendship, and may plead with him that he will complete what he has begun, and that, having once admitted us to his favour, he will never leave or forsake us.

10. *When my father and my mother forsake me.* If they should do it. The psalmist supposes it possible that this might occur. It does occur, though very rarely; but the psalmist means to say that the love of God is stronger and more certain than even that of a father or mother, since he will *never* forsake his people. Though every other tie that binds heart to heart should dissolve, this will remain; though a case might occur in which we could not be sure of the love that naturally springs out of the most tender earthly relationships, yet we can always confide in his love. See Notes on Isa. xlix. 15. ¶ *Then the* LORD *will take me up.* Marg., *will gather me.* The margin expresses the usual meaning of the word. It is sometimes used as referring to the hospitable reception of strangers or wanderers into one's house: Judges xix. 15, 18; Joshua xx. 4. The meaning here is, that if he should be forsaken by his nearest earthly friends, and be an outcast and a wanderer, so that no one on earth would take him in, the Lord would then receive him.

11. *Teach me thy way, O* LORD. See Notes on Ps. xxv. 4, 5. ¶ *And lead me in a plain path.* Marg., *a way of plainness.* That is, a straight or smooth path. In other words, he prayed that he might be enabled to act wisely and right; he desired that God would teach him what he should do. ¶ *Because of mine enemies.* Marg., *those which observe me.* The translation in the text expresses the true sense. The word which is used is derived from a verb that signifies *to twist; to twist together;* and then, to oppress; to treat as an enemy. Here it refers to those who would treat him harshly or cruelly; and he prays that God would show him how to act in view of the fact that he was surrounded by such foes. They were harsh and cruel; they sought to overcome him; they laid snares for him. He knew not how to act so as to escape from them, and he therefore pleads that God would instruct and guide him.

12. *Deliver me not over unto the will of mine enemies.* Let them not accomplish their desires in regard to me; let them not be able to carry out their purposes. The word here rendered *will* means properly *soul,* but it is here used evidently to denote *wish* or *desire.* Comp. Ps. xxxv. 25. ¶ *For false witnesses are risen up against me.* Men who would lay false

13 *I had fainted,* unless I had believed to [g] see the goodness of the LORD in the land of the living.

14 Wait on the LORD; be of good courage, and he shall strengthen thine heart: wait, I say, on the LORD.

g Ps. cxviii. 17, 18.

charges against him, or who would wrongfully accuse him. They charged him with crimes which he never committed, and they persecuted him as if he were guilty of what they alleged against him. ¶ *And such as breathe out cruelty.* That is, they meditate violence or cruel treatment. They are intent on this; they pant for it. Saul of Tarsus thus "*breathed out* threatenings and slaughter against the disciples of the Lord." See Notes on Acts ix. 1.

13. I had fainted, *unless I had believed.* The words "I had fainted" are supplied by the translators, but they undoubtedly express the true sense of the passage. The psalmist refers to the state of mind produced by the efforts of his enemies to destroy him, as mentioned in ver. 12. So numerous, mighty, and formidable were they, that he says his only support was his faith in God; his belief that he would yet be permitted to see the goodness of God upon the earth. In this time of perplexity and trial he *had* confidence in God, and believed that He would uphold him, and would permit him to see the evidences of His goodness and mercy while yet on the earth. What was the *ground* of this confidence he does not say, but he had the fullest belief that this would be so. He may have had some special assurance of it, or he may have had a deep internal conviction of it, sufficient to calm his mind; but whatever was the source of this confidence it was that which sustained him. A similar state of feeling is indicated in the remarkable passage in Job, ch. xix. 25–27. See Notes on that passage. ¶ *To see the goodness of the* LORD *in the land of the living.* That is, that I should *live,* and yet see and enjoy the tokens of the Divine favour here upon the earth.

14. *Wait on the* LORD. This is the sum of all the instruction in the psalm; the main lesson which the psalm is designed to convey. The object is to induce others, from the experience of the psalmist, to trust in the Lord; to rely upon him; to come to him in trouble and danger; to wait for his interposition when all other resources fail. Comp. Ps. xxv. 3. ¶ *Be of good courage.* The Hebrew word here means, *be strong.* That is, do not faint. Do not be dismayed. Still hope and trust in the Lord. ¶ *He shall strengthen thine heart.* He will strengthen *thee.* He will enable you to perform your duties, and to triumph over your enemies. See Notes on Isa. xl. 31. ¶ *Wait, I say, on the* LORD. Repeating an idea with which the heart was full; a lesson resulting from his own rich experience. He dwells upon it as a lesson which he would fix deeply in the mind, that in all times of danger and difficulty, instead of despondency, instead of sinking down in despair, instead of giving up all effort, we should go forward in the discharge of duty, putting our trust solely in the Lord.

PSALM XXVIII.

This psalm is entitled "A Psalm of David;" and there is no reason for doubting the correctness of the inscription. But, as in some of the previous psalms, neither the title nor the contents contain any intimation as to the time or the circumstances of its composition.

It has, in some respects, a strong resemblance to Ps. xxvi. The leading idea in this, as in that, is the strong affection of the author for those who feared and loved God; his strong desire to be associated with them in character and destiny; his earnest wish that he might not be drawn away from them, and that his lot might not be with the wicked. It would seem from the psalm itself, especially from ver. 3, that it was

PSALM XXVIII.

A Psalm of David.

UNTO thee will I cry, O LORD my rock; be not silent [1] to me: lest, *if* thou be silent to me, I become like them that go down into the pit.

2 Hear the voice of my supplications, when I cry unto thee, when [h] I lift up my hands toward [2] thy holy oracle.

[1] *from.* [h] Ps. cxxxviii. 2.
[2] Or, *the oracle of thy sanctuary.*

---

composed when its author was under some powerful temptation from the wicked, or when there were strong allurements offered by them which tended to lead him into the society of those who were strangers to God; and, under this temptation, he urges this earnest prayer, and seeks to bring before his own mind considerations why he should *not* yield to these influences.

The contents of the psalm, therefore, may be presented in the following analysis:—

I. The consciousness of danger so pressing upon him as to lead him to break out in an earnest cry to God, vers. 1, 2.

II. The source of his anxiety or his danger; and his earnest prayer that he might not be left to the powerful temptation, and be drawn into the society of the wicked, ver. 3.

III. Considerations which occurred to the mind of the psalmist himself why he should *not* yield to the temptation, or why he should *not* be associated with the wicked. These considerations are stated in vers. 3-5. They are drawn from the character and the certain destiny of the wicked.

IV. A sense of relief, or a feeling that God *had* answered his prayer, and that he was safe from the danger, vers. 6, 7.

The psalm is peculiarly appropriate to those who are in danger of being led away by the acts of the ungodly,—or who are under strong temptations to be associated with the gay, the sensual, and the worldly,—or to whom strong inducements are offered to mingle in their pleasures, their vices, and their follies. They who before their conversion were the companions of the ungodly; they who were devoted to guilty pleasures but have been rescued from them; they who have contracted habits of intemperance or sensuality in the society of the dissolute, and who feel the power of the habit returning upon them, and are invited by their former associates to join them again,—are in the condition contemplated in the psalm, and will find its sentiments appropriate to their experience.

1 *Unto thee will I cry.* That is, under the consciousness of the danger to which I am exposed—the danger of being drawn away into the society of the wicked. In such circumstances his reliance was not on his own strength; or on his own resolutions; on his own heart; or on his fellowmen. He felt that he was safe only in God, and he appeals to Him, therefore, in this earnest manner, to save him. ¶ *O* LORD *my rock.* See Notes on Ps. xviii. 2. ¶ *Be not silent to me.* Marg., *from me.* So the Hebrew. The idea is that of one who will not speak to us, or who will not attend to us. We pray, and we look for an *answer* to our prayers, or, as it were, we expect God to *speak* to us; to utter words of kindness; to assure us of his favour; to declare our sins forgiven. ¶ *Lest, if thou be silent to me.* If thou dost not answer my supplications. ¶ *I become like unto them that go down into the pit.* Like those who die; or, lest I be crushed by anxiety and distress, and die. The word *pit* here refers to the grave. So it is used in Ps. xxx. 3; lxxxviii. 4; Isa. xxxviii. 18; xiv. 15, 19. The meaning is, that if he did not obtain help from God he despaired of life. His troubles would overwhelm and crush him. He could not bear up under them.

2. *Hear the voice of my supplications.* It was not mental prayer which he offered; it was a petition uttered audibly. ¶ *When I lift up my hands.* To lift up the hands denotes supplication, as this was a common attitude in prayer. See Notes on 1 Tim. ii. 8. ¶ *Toward thy holy oracle.* Marg., as in Hebrew, *toward the oracle of thy holiness.* The word *oracle* as used here denotes the place where the answer to prayer is given.

3 Draw [i] me not away with the wicked, and with the workers of iniquity; which speak peace to their neighbours, but mischief *is* in their hearts.

i Ps. cxxv. 5.

The Hebrew word—דְּבִיר, *debir*—means properly the inner sanctuary of the tabernacle or the temple, the place where God was supposed to reside, and where he gave responses to the prayers of his people:—the same place which is elsewhere called the Holy of Holies. See Notes on Heb. ix. 3—14. The Hebrew word is found only here and in 1 Kings vi. 5, 16, 19, 20, 21, 22, 23, 31; vii. 49; viii. 6, 8; 2 Chron. iii. 16; iv. 20; v. 7, 9. The idea here is that he who prayed stretched out his hands toward that sacred place where God was supposed to dwell. So we stretch out our hands towards heaven—the sacred dwelling-place of God. Comp. Notes on Ps. v. 7. The Hebrew word is probably derived from the verb to *speak;* and, according to this derivation, the idea is that God spake to his people; that he *communed* with them; that he answered their prayers from that sacred recess,—his peculiar dwelling-place. See Ex. xxv. 22; Num. vii. 89.

3. *Draw me not away with the wicked.* See Notes on Ps. xxvi. 9. The prayer here, as well as the prayer in Ps. xxvi. 9, expresses a strong desire *not* to be united with wicked men in feeling or in destiny—in life or in death—on earth or in the future world. The reason of the prayer seems to have been that the psalmist, being at this time under a strong temptation to associate with wicked persons, and feeling the force of the temptation, was apprehensive that he should be left to *yield* to it, and to become associated with them. Deeply conscious of this danger, he earnestly prays that he may not be left to yield to the power of the temptation, and fall into sin. So the Saviour (Matt. vi. 13) has taught us to pray, "And lead us not into temptation." None who desire to serve God can be insensible to the propriety of this prayer. The temptations of the world are so strong; the amusements in which the world indulges are so brilliant and fascinating; they who invite us to partake of their pleasures are often so elevated in their social position, so refined in their manners, and so cultivated by education; the propensities of our hearts for such indulgences are so strong by nature; habits formed before our conversion are still so powerful; and the prospect of worldly advantages from compliance with the customs of those around us are often so great,—that we cannot but feel that it is proper for us to go to the throne of grace, and to plead earnestly with God that he will keep us and not suffer us to fall into the snare. Especially is this true of those who before they were converted had indulged in habits of intemperance, or in sensual pleasures of any kind, and who are invited by their old companions in sin again to unite with them in their pursuits. Here all the power of the former habit returns; here often there is a most fierce struggle between conscience and the old habit for victory; here especially those who are thus tempted need the grace of God to keep them; here there is special appropriateness in the prayer, "Draw me not away with the wicked." ¶ *And with the workers of iniquity.* In any form. With those who do evil. ¶ *Which speak peace to their neighbours.* Who speak words of friendliness. Who *seem* to be persuading you to do that which is for your good. Who put on plausible pretexts. They appear to be your friends; they profess to be so. They use flattering words while they tempt you to go astray. ¶ *But mischief* is *in their hearts.* They are secretly plotting your ruin. They wish to lead you into such courses of life in order that you may fall into sin; that you may dishonour religion; that you may disgrace your profession; or that they may in some way profit by your compliance with

4 Give them according to their deeds, and according to the wickedness of their endeavours: give them after the work of their hands; render to them their desert.
5 Because [k] they regard not the works of the LORD, nor the operation of his hands, he shall destroy them, and not build them up.
6 Blessed *be* the LORD, because he hath heard the voice of my supplications.
7 The LORD *is* my strength

k Job xxxiv. 26, 27.

their counsels. So the wicked, under plausible pretences, would allure the good; so the corrupt would seduce the innocent; so the enemies of God would entice his friends, that they may bring shame and reproach upon the cause of religion.

4. *Give them according to their deeds.* Deal righteously with them. Recompense them as they deserve. ¶ *And according to the wickedness of their endeavours.* Their designs; their works; their plans. ¶ *Give them after the work of their hands.* Reward them according to what they *do.* ¶ *Render to them their desert.* A just recompense. This whole verse is a prayer that God would deal *justly* with them. There is no evidence that there is anything of vindictiveness or malice in the prayer. In itself considered, there is no impropriety in praying that *justice* may be done to the violators of law. See General Introduction, § 6.

5. *Because they regard not the works of the* LORD. What the Lord *does* in creation; in his providence; through his commands and laws; and by his Spirit. They do not find pleasure in his works; they do not give heed to the intimations of his will in his providential dealings; they do not listen to his commands; they do not yield to the influences of his Spirit. ¶ *Nor the operation of his hands.* What he is now doing. The sense is essentially the same as in the former member of the sentence. ¶ *He shall destroy them.* He will pull them down, instead of building them up. They expose themselves to his displeasure, and he will bring deserved punishment upon them. ¶ *And not build them up.* He will not favour them; he will not give them prosperity. Health, happiness, salvation are to be found only in conformity with the laws which God has ordained. Neither can be found in violating those laws, or in any other method than that which he has ordained. Sooner or later the violation of law, in regard to these things, and in regard to everything, must lead to calamity and ruin.

6. *Blessed* be *the* LORD, *because he hath heard the voice of my supplications.* This is one of those passages which frequently occur in the Psalms, when there has been an earnest and anxious prayer offered to God, and when the answer to the prayer seems to be immediate. The mind of the anxious and troubled pleader becomes calm; the promises of God are brought directly to the soul; the peace which was sought is obtained; and he who began the psalm with deep anxiety and trouble of mind, rejoices at the close of it in the evidences of the Divine favour and love. What thus happened to the psalmist frequently occurs now. The answer to prayer, so far as giving calmness and assurance to the mind is concerned, is often immediate. The troubled spirit becomes calm; and whatever may be the result in other respects, the heart is made peaceful and confiding, and feels the assurance that all will be well. It is sufficient for us to feel that God *hears* us; for if this is so, we have the assurance that all is right. In this sense, certainly, it is right to look for an immediate answer to our prayers. See Notes on Isa. lxv. 24; Dan. ix. 21.

7. *The* LORD is *my strength.* See Notes on Ps. xviii. 1. ¶ *And my*

and my shield: my heart trusted in him, and I am helped; therefore my heart greatly rejoiceth, and with my song will I praise him.

8 The LORD *is* [1] their strength, and he *is* the [2] saving strength of his anointed.

9 Save thy people, and bless *l* thine inheritance: [3] feed them also, and lift them up for ever.

[1] Or, *his*. [2] *strength of salvations*.

l 1 Kings viii. 51, 53. [3] Or, *rule*, Mic. vii. 14.

shield. See Notes on Ps. iii. 3. Comp. Ps. xxxiii. 20; lix. 11; lxxxiv. 9; lxxxix. 18; Gen. xv. 1. ¶ *My heart trusted in him.* I trusted or confided in him. See Ps. xiii. 5. ¶ *And I am helped.* I have found the assistance which I desired. ¶ *Therefore my heart greatly rejoiceth.* I greatly rejoice. I am happy. He had found the assurance of the Divine favour which he desired, and his heart was glad. ¶ *And with my song will I praise him.* I will sing praises to him. Comp. Ps. xxii. 25.

8. *The* LORD is *their strength.* Marg., *his strength.* The Hebrew is, *their strength*, or *strength to them.* The allusion is to the people of God. The course of thought seems to be, that the psalmist, having derived in his own case assistance from God, or having found God a strength to him, his mind turns from this fact to the general idea that God was the strength of *all* who were in similar circumstances; or that all his people might confide in Him as he had done. ¶ *And he* is *the saving strength.* Marg., as in Heb., *strength of salvations.* That is, In him is found the strength which produces salvation. See Notes on Ps. xxvii. 1. ¶ *Of his anointed.* See Notes on Ps. ii. 2; xx. 6. The primary reference here is doubtless to the psalmist himself, as one who had been anointed or set apart to the kingly office; but the connexion shows that he intended to include *all* the people of God, as those whom he had consecrated or set apart to his service. See 1 Peter ii. 5, 9.

9. *Save thy people.* All thy people. The psalm appropriately closes with a prayer for all the people of God. The prayer is offered in view of the deliverance which the psalmist had himself experienced, and he prays that all the people of God might experience similar deliverance and mercy. ¶ *And bless thine inheritance.* Thy heritage; thy people. The Hebrew word properly means *taking possession of anything; occupation.* Then it comes to mean *possession; domain; estate*: Num. xviii. 21. Thus it is used as applied to the territory assigned to each tribe in the promised land: Josh. xiii. 23. Thus also it is applied to the people of Israel—the Jewish nation—as the *possession* or *property* of Jehovah; as a people whom he regarded as his own, and whom, as such, he protected: Deut. iv. 20; ix. 26, 29. In this place the people of God are thus spoken of as his peculiar possession or property on earth; as that which he regards as of most value to him; as that which belongs to him, or to which he has a claim; as that which cannot without injustice to him be alienated from him. ¶ *Feed them also.* Marg., *rule.* The Hebrew word refers to the care which a shepherd extends over his flock. See Psalm xxiii. 1, where the same word, under another form—*shepherd*—is used. The prayer is, that God would take the same care of his people that a shepherd takes of his flock. ¶ *And lift them up for ever.* The word here used may mean *sustain* them, or *support* them; but it more properly means *bear*, and would be best expressed by a reference to the fact that the shepherd carries the feeble, the young, and the sickly of his flock in his arms, or that he lifts them up when unable themselves to rise. See Notes on Isa. xl. 11; lxiii. 9. The word *for ever* here means simply *always*:—in all circumstances; at all times. In other words, the psalmist prays that God would *always* mani-

PSALM XXIX.

A Psalm of David.

1 GIVE [m] unto the LORD, O ye mighty, give unto the LORD
[n] glory and strength.

m Ps. xcvi. 7—9; 1 Chron. xvi. 28, 29.
1 *sons of the mighty*, Ps. lxxxix. 6.
n Rev. v. 11—14.

fest himself as the friend and helper of his people, as He had done to him. It may be added here, that what the psalmist thus prays for *will* be done. God *will* save his people; he *will* bless his heritage; he *will* be to them a kind and faithful shepherd; he *will* sustain, comfort, uphold, and cherish them always,—in affliction; in temptation; in death; for ever. They have only to trust in him, and they will find him more kind and faithful than the most tender shepherd ever was to his flock.

PSALM XXIX.

This also purports to be a psalm of David, and it has every mark of being his production. It is designed to set forth the majesty and glory of God, especially as manifested in a thunder-storm, and was evidently composed in view of such an exhibition of his power and glory. It is one of the sublimest descriptions of a storm of thunder and lightning anywhere to be found. It is not possible to ascertain the particular occasion on which it was composed, nor is it necessary to do this in order to enter into the spirit and to appreciate the beauty of the psalm. Occasions occur in every country which furnish an illustration of the psalm; and its meaning can be appreciated by all.

The psalm has a universal applicability. It may be regarded as having been designed to show what feelings men should have in a violent storm, when the thunder rolls over sea and land, and when the lightnings flash along the sky; the effects which should be produced amidst such scenes; the influence of religion in keeping the mind from alarm,—lifting up the soul in adoration of the great God,—and inspiring confidence in One who has power to control elements so fearful. Amidst all the terrors of the tempest the mind of the psalmist was calm. The effect of it was to lead him to confide in the power of God, and to fill his soul with adoring views of him. We need not dread the fury of the elements when we know that they are under the absolute control of a Being of infinite goodness, truth, mercy, and love. If these fearful elements raged without control; if they were independent of God; if they were restrained by no laws; if the thunder rolled and the lightning played by mere caprice, or under the dominion of chance, well might we tremble.

The psalm properly consists of three parts:—

I. The duty of ascribing praise and glory to God; of giving to him the glory due to his name; of worshipping him in the beauty of holiness, vers. 1, 2.

II. The description of the storm, vers. 3-9. The thunder is seven times spoken of as "the voice of the Lord" (comp. Rev. x. 3, "And when he had cried, *seven* thunders uttered their voices");—and some peculiar effect is referred to as resulting from the utterance of that voice. It is "upon the waters;" it is "powerful;" it is "full of majesty;" it "breaks the cedars;" it "divides the flames of fire;" it "shakes the wilderness;" it "makes the hinds to calve," and "discovereth the forests."

III. The impression that should be produced by the whole scene. The Lord presides over the floods; the Lord is king for ever; the Lord is able to give strength to his people; the Lord will bless his people with peace, vers. 10, 11. In *such* a God his people may put confidence; under the protection of One who can arm himself with such power, and who can control such elements, his people have nothing to fear; in contending with such a God—one who can sweep the earth with desolation,—who can direct the playing lightnings where he pleases,—who can cause his voice to echo over hills, and vales, and floods, over the sea and the land, producing dismay and consternation,—his enemies can have nothing to hope.

1. *Give unto the* LORD. Ascribe unto Jehovah; or, recognise him as entitled to what is here ascribed to him. The word cannot be understood, as it is commonly with us, to denote the imparting to another, or granting to another what he does not now possess—for God is always in posses-

2 Give unto the LORD the [1] glory due unto his name; worship the LORD in [2] the beauty [o] of holiness.

[1] honour of his name.
[2] Or, his glorious sanctuary.

3 The voice of the LORD *is* upon the waters: the God of glory thundereth; the LORD *is* upon [3] many waters.

o Ps. xc. 17; 2 Chron. xx. 21. [3] Or, *great.*

sion of what is here ascribed to him. ¶ *O ye mighty.* Marg., as in Heb., *ye sons of the mighty.* The Hebrew word here used—אֵלִים— is the plural form of one of the names of God—אֵל. The word means properly *strong, mighty, a mighty one, a hero;* then, *strength, might, power;* and then it is applied to God as *the Mighty One,* the Almighty. (*Gesenius.*) In the plural form, the word means *mighty ones, heroes, gods:* Exod. xv. 11; xviii. 11; Dan. xi. 36. The phrase *sons of the mighty* is used only here and in Ps. lxxxix. 6. The allusion is undoubtedly to the angels as being in an eminent sense the sons of God, or of the mighty ones; and they are referred to here under that appellation as being themselves endowed with power or strength. Comp. Ps. ciii. 20, "Bless the Lord, ye his angels, that excel in strength;" marg., *mighty in strength.* In view of the wonderful exhibitions of God's power in the storm—exhibitions far above the power of the most exalted of His creatures, the psalmist calls upon the angels, the most exalted of them, to acknowledge the existence of a power so much beyond their own. ¶ *Glory and strength.* Majesty and might. Acknowledge him as the God of glory; as endowed with power. That is, learn from the manifestations of the power evinced in the storm how great is the power and the glory of God.

2. *Give unto the* LORD *the glory due unto his name.* Marg., *the honour of his name.* The honour of his name is that which is due to it, or which properly belongs to it. The *name* is put here, as it often is, for God himself; and the meaning is, "Ascribe to God the honour that is properly his due." This is a claim addressed to the angels; it is a claim certainly not less binding on men. It is practically a call on all creatures in the universe to ascribe due honour to God. ¶ *Worship the* LORD. This exhortation is made particularly in view of the manifestations of his power in the storm. The idea is, that one who is capable of putting forth such power as is displayed in a tempest, has a claim to adoration and praise. ¶ *In the beauty of holiness.* Marg., *in* his *glorious sanctuary.* The Hebrew phrase would properly mean *holy beauty.* Some have supposed that it means *in holy adorning,* or in such consecrated vestments as were worn by priests in the sacred services of the sanctuary, or when they came into the presence of Jehovah. So De Wette understands it. But the more probable interpretation is that which refers it to the state of the heart—the *internal* ornament—with which we should approach God,—to a holy and pure state of mind—that beauty or appropriateness of the soul which consists in holiness or purity. Of this the external clothing of the priesthood was itself but an emblem, and this is that which God desires in those who approach him in an act of worship. It may be added that there is no *beauty* like this; that there is no external comeliness, no charm of person or complexion, no adorning of costly robes, that can be compared with this. It is this which God seeks, and with this he will be pleased, whether under a less or more attractive external form; whether under rich and costly raiment, or under the plain and decent clothing of poverty.

3. *The voice of the* LORD. The voice of Jehovah. There can be no doubt that the expression here, which is seven times repeated in the psalm, "the voice of Jehovah," refers to thunder; and no one can fail to see the appropriateness of the expression. In heavy thunder it seems as if God

4 The voice of the LORD *is* [1] powerful; the voice of the LORD *is* [2] full of majesty.

[1] *in power.* [2] *in majesty.*

5 The voice of the LORD breaketh the cedars; yea, the LORD breaketh the cedars of Lebanon.

spake. It comes from above. It fills us with awe. We know, indeed, that thunder as well as the other phenomena in the world, is produced by what are called "natural causes;" that there is no miracle in thunder; and that really God does not *speak* any more in the thunder than he does in the sighing of the breeze or in the gurgling of the rivulet;—but (*a*) he *seems* more impressively to speak to men in the thunder; and (*b*) he may not improperly be regarded *as* speaking alike in the thunder, in the sighing of the breeze, *and* in the gurgling stream. In each and all of these ways God *is* addressing men; in each and all there *are* lessons of great value conveyed, as if by his own voice, respecting his own existence and character. Those which are addressed to us particularly in thunder, pertain to his power, his majesty, his greatness; to our own weakness, feebleness, dependence; to the ease with which he could take us away, and to the importance of being prepared to stand before such a God. ¶ Is *upon the waters.* The word "*is*" is supplied here by our translators. The whole passage might be read as an exclamation: *The voice of Jehovah upon the waters!* It is the utterance of one who is overpowered by a sudden clap of thunder. The mind is awed. God seems to speak; his voice is heard rolling over the waters. The psalm was most likely composed in view of the sea or a lake—not improbably in view of the Mediterranean, when a storm was passing over it. A thunder-storm is sublime anywhere, in mountain scenery or on the plains, on the land or on the ocean; but there are circumstances which give it peculiar grandeur at sea, when the thunder seems to *roll* along with nothing to check or break it, and when the sublimity is increased by the solitude which reigns everywhere on the ocean. ¶ *The God of glory.* The glorious God. See Notes on Ps. xxiv. 7–10. ¶ *The* LORD is *upon many waters.* Jehovah himself seems to be on the ocean. His voice is heard there, and he himself appears to be there. The margin here is, *great waters.* This would seem to imply that the psalm was composed in view of waters more extended than a lake or a river, and sustains the idea above expressed, that it was in view of the great waters which must have been so familiar to the mind of the sacred writer—the waters of the Mediterranean.

4. *The voice of the* LORD is *powerful.* Marg., as in Hebrew, *in power.* That is, is mighty; or, has strength. Allusion may be made to what seems to be the effect of thunder in prostrating trees, or tearing off their limbs, or it may be merely to the loud sound of the thunder. ¶ Is *full of majesty.* Marg., as in Hebrew, *in majesty.* That is, it is grand, sublime, overpowering.

5. *Breaketh the cedars.* The thunder prostrates the lofty trees of the forest. The psalmist speaks as things appeared, attributing, as was natural, and as was commonly done, that to the thunder which was really produced by the lightning. It is now fully known that the effect here referred to is not produced by thunder, but by the rapid passage of the electric fluid as it passes from the cloud to the earth. *That* power is so great as to rive the oak or the cedar; to twist off their limbs; to prostrate their lofty trunks to the ground. The psalmist speaks of thunder as accomplishing this, in the same way that the sacred writers and all men, even scientific men, commonly speak, as when we say, the sun rises and sets,—the stars rise and set, etc. Men who should undertake in all cases to speak with scientific accuracy, or in the strict language of science, would

6 He maketh them also to skip like a calf; Lebanon and Sirion like a young unicorn.

7 The voice of the LORD [1] divideth the flames of fire.

8 The voice of the LORD shaketh the wilderness; the LORD shaketh the wilderness of Kadesh.

1 *cutteth out.*

---

be unintelligible to the mass of mankind; perhaps on most subjects they would soon cease to speak at all,—since they themselves would be in utter doubt as to what *is* scientific accuracy. Men who require that a revelation from God should always use language of strict scientific precision, really require that a revelation should anticipate by hundreds or thousands of years the discoveries of science, and use language which, when the revelation was given, would be unintelligible to the mass of mankind; nay, which would be always unintelligible to a large portion of the race,—since men ordinarily, however much the exact truths of science may be diffused, do not learn to use such exactness of speech. As long as men have occasion to speak on the subject at all they will probably continue to say that the sun rises and sets; that the grass grows; and that water runs. ¶ *Breaketh the cedars of Lebanon.* "Cedars are mentioned as the loftiest forest trees, and those of Lebanon as the loftiest of their species."—*Prof. Alexander.* The cedars of Lebanon are often referred to in the Scriptures as remarkable for their size and grandeur: 1 Kings iv. 33; v. 6; Ps. xcii. 12; Ezra iii. 7.

6. *He maketh them also to skip like a calf.* That is, the cedars of Lebanon. Comp. Ps. cxiv. 4, "The mountains skipped like rams, and the little hills like lambs." Ps. lxviii. 16, "Why leap ye, ye high hills?" The meaning is plain. The lightning tore off the large branches, and uprooted the loftiest trees, so that they seemed to play and dance like calves in their gambols. Nothing could be more strikingly descriptive of *power.* ¶ *Lebanon and Sirion.* Sirion was the name by which Mount Hermon was known among the Sidonians: Deut. iii. 9, "Which Hermon the Sidonians call Sirion." It is a part of the great range of Anti-libanus. ¶ *Like a young unicorn.* On the meaning of the word here used, see Notes on Ps. xxii. 21. The illustration would be the same if *any* young wild animal were referred to.

7. *Divideth the flames of fire.* Marg., *cutteth out.* The Hebrew word—חָצַב, *hhatzab*—means properly *to cut, to hew, to hew out;* as, for example, stones. The allusion here is undoubtedly to lightning; and the image is either that it seems to be cut out, or cut into tongues and streaks,—or, more probably, that the *clouds* seem to be cut or hewed so as to make openings or paths for the lightning. The eye is evidently fixed on the clouds, and on the sudden flash of lightning, as if the clouds had been *cleaved* or *opened* for the passage of it. The idea of the psalmist is that the "voice of the Lord," or the thunder, seems to cleave or open the clouds for the flames of fire to play amidst the tempest. Of course this language, as well as that which has been already noticed (ver. 5), must be taken as denoting what *appears* to the eye, and not as a scientific statement of the reality in the case. The rolling thunder not only shakes the cedars, and makes the lofty trees on Lebanon and Sirion skip like a calf or a young unicorn, but it rends asunder or cleaves the clouds, and *cuts out* paths for the flames of fire.

8. *Shaketh the wilderness.* Causes it to shake or to tremble. The word here used means properly to dance; to be whirled or twisted upon anything; to twist—as with pain—or, to writhe; and then, to tremble, to quake. The forests are made to tremble or quake in the fierceness of the storm,—referring still to what

9 The voice of the LORD maketh the hinds [1] to calve, and discovereth the forests: and [o] in his temple [2] doth every one speak of *his* glory.

10 The LORD sitteth upon the flood; [p] yea, the LORD sitteth [q] King for ever.

[1] Or, *be in pain.* [o] Ps. lxiii. 2.
[2] Or, *every whit of it uttereth.*
[p] Gen. viii. 1, 2. [q] Ps. ii. 6—9.

the thunder *seems* to do. ¶ *The wilderness of Kadesh.* As in referring (vers. 5, 6) to the effect of the storm on lofty trees, the psalmist had given poetic beauty to the description by *specifying* Lebanon and Sirion, so he here refers, for the same purpose, to a particular forest as illustrating the power of the tempest—to wit, the forest or wilderness of *Kadesh.* This wilderness or forest was on the south-eastern border of the Promised Land, towards Edom; and it is memorable as having been the place where the Israelites twice encamped with a view of entering Palestine from that point, but whence they were twice driven back again,—the first time in pursuance of the sentence that they should wander forty years in the wilderness,—and the second time, from the refusal of the king of Edom to allow them to pass through his territories. It was from Kadesh that the spies entered Palestine. See Num. xiii. 17, 26; xiv. 40–45; xxi. 1–3; Deut. i. 41–46; Judges i. 7. Kadesh was on the northern border of Edom, and not far from Mount Hor. See Robinson's Biblical Researches in Palestine, vol. ii. pp. 582, 610, 662; Kitto, Cyclo. Bib. Lit., art. *Kadesh;* and the Pictorial Bible on Num. xx. 1. There seems to have been nothing *special* in regard to this wilderness which led the author of the psalm to select it for his illustration, except that it was well known and commonly spoken of, and that it would thus suggest an image that would be familiar to the Israelites.

9. *The voice of the* LORD *maketh the hinds to calve.* The deer. The object of the psalmist here is to show the effects of the storm in producing consternation, especially on the weak and timid animals of the forest. The effect here adverted to is that of fear or consternation in bringing on the throes of parturition. Comp. Job xxxix. 1, 3. No one can doubt that the effect here described may occur in the violence of a tempest; and perhaps no image could more vividly describe the terrors of the storm than the consternation thus produced. The margin here is, *to be in pain.* The Hebrew means *to bring forth,* referring to the pains of parturition. ¶ *And discovereth the forests.* The word here used means *to strip off, to uncover;* and, as used here, it means to strip off the leaves of the forest; to make the trees bare—referring to an effect which is often produced by a violent storm. ¶ *And in his temple doth every one speak of* his *glory.* Marg., *every whit of it uttereth,* etc. The word here rendered *temple* does not refer in this place to the tabernacle, or to the temple at Jerusalem, but rather *to the world itself,* considered as the residence or dwelling-place of God. Perhaps the true translation would be, "And in his temple everything says, Glory!" That is, in the dwelling-place of God,—the world of nature,—the sky, the earth, the forests, the waters, everything in the storm, echoes *glory, glory!* All these things declare the glory of God; all these wonders—the voice of God upon the waters; the thunder; the crash of the trees upon the hills; the shaking of the wilderness; the universal consternation; the leaves stripped from the trees and flying in every direction,—all proclaim the majesty and glory of Jehovah.

10. *The* LORD *sitteth upon the flood.* God is enthroned upon the flood, or presides over it. The obvious meaning is, that God is enthroned upon the storm, or presides over that which produces such consternation. It is not undirected; it is not the result

11 The LORD will give strength [r] unto his people; the LORD will bless his people with [s] peace.

[r] Isa. xl. 29—31.

[s] Ps. lxxxv. 8, 10.

of chance or fate; it is not produced by mere physical laws; it is not without restraint—without a ruler—for Jehovah presides over all, and all this may be regarded as his throne. Comp. Notes on Ps. xviii. 7–11. See also Ps. xcvii. 2. The word here used is commonly applied to the deluge in the time of Noah, but there would be an obvious unfitness in supposing here that the mind of the psalmist referred to that, or that the course of thought would be directed to that, and it is most natural, therefore, to suppose that the reference is to the floods above—the vast reservoirs of waters in the clouds, pouring down, amidst the fury of the tempest, floods of rain upon the earth. ¶ *The* LORD *sitteth King for ever.* This is an appropriate close of the entire description; this is a thought which tends to make the mind calm and confiding when the winds howl and the thunder rolls; this accords with the leading purpose of the psalm—the call on the sons of the mighty (ver. 1) to ascribe strength and glory to God. From all the terrors of the storm;—from all that is fearful, on the waters, in the forests, on the hills, when it would seem as if everything would be swept away,—the mind turns calmly to the thought that *God* is enthroned upon the clouds; that he presides over all that produces this wide-spread alarm and commotion, and that he *will* reign for ever and ever.

11. *The* LORD *will give strength unto his people.* This is a practical application of the sentiments of the psalm, or a conclusion which is fairly to be derived from the main thought in the psalm. The idea is, that the God who presides over the tempest and the storm, the God who has such power, and can produce such effects, is abundantly able to uphold his people, and to defend them. In other words, the application of such amazing power will be to protect his people, and to save them from danger. When we look on the rolling clouds in the tempest, when we hear the roaring of the thunder, and see the flashing of the lightning, when we hear the oak crash on the hills, and see the waves piled mountains high, if we feel that God presides over all, and that he controls all this with infinite ease, assuredly we have no occasion to doubt that he can protect us; no reason to fear that his strength cannot support us. ¶ *The* LORD *will bless his people with peace.* They have nothing to fear in the tempest and storm; nothing to fear from anything. He will bless them with peace *in* the tempest; he will bless them with peace through that power by which he controls the tempest. Let them, therefore, not fear in the storm, however fiercely it may rage; let them not be afraid in any of the troubles and trials of life. *In* the storm, and *in* those troubles and trials, he can make the mind calm; *beyond* those storms and those troubles he can give them eternal peace in a world where no "angry tempest blows."

PSALM XXX.

This is said to be "A Psalm or Song at the dedication of the house of David." There is no reason to call in question the correctness of this inscription, though it cannot be certain that it was prefixed by the author himself. The words of the title are found in the Hebrew, and it is to be presumed that they were affixed to the psalm by some one of the inspired writers.

It is clearly implied in the title, though not expressly affirmed, that David was the author of the psalm, for it is to be presumed that he would himself compose the hymn or song that was to be used at the dedication of his own dwelling. In fact, the title, as Rosenmüller has remarked, might not improperly be read, "A Psalm, a song of dedication of a house, of David," so that the words "A Psalm of David" might not improperly be regarded as united.

It is not absolutely certain what occasion is referred to in the psalm. Some have supposed that the tabernacle is meant; but the tabernacle was dedicated long before the time of David. Others, and among them several Jewish interpreters, have supposed that it was prepared in order to be sung either at the dedication of the temple which Solomon built, or the dedication of that which was erected after the return from the Babylonish captivity. Others have supposed that it was intended to be used at the dedication of the house or palace which David built for himself on Mount Zion, 2 Sam. v. 11. It was usual for the Hebrews to "dedicate" a house when it was finished; that is, to devote it in a solemn manner to God, probably with appropriate religious exercises. Deut. xx. 5, "What man is there that hath built a new house, and hath not dedicated it? let him go and return to his house, lest he die in the battle, and another man dedicate it." Comp. also Neh. xii. 27. Others, as Rosenmüller and Prof. Alexander, suppose that the psalm was designed to be used at the dedication of the altar reared by David on the "threshing-floor" of Ornan, which David purchased at the time of the pestilence which came upon the people for his sin in numbering the people, 1 Chron. xxi. 15-26. But there is no certain evidence of this. Apart from the incongruity of calling an altar a "*house*," the circumstances are not such as to lead us to believe that the psalm was composed for that occasion. The allusion in the psalm is rather to a previous state of depression, trouble, and sorrow, such as occurred in the life of David *before* he conquered his enemies, and *before* he was peaceably established on his throne,—and to the joy which he felt when he *had* triumphed over his foes, and *was* peacefully established as king in Jerusalem. All the circumstances seem to me to accord best with the time when David erected a house for his own abode—a palace—on Mount Zion, and to the act of dedicating such a house to God. See 2 Sam. v. 9-12; vii. 1, 2. It may be added that that was properly called "the house of David"—a name which could be given neither to the altar erected on the threshing-floor of Ornan, nor to the tabernacle, nor to the temple.

But although the psalm was composed for the purpose of being used at the dedication of his "house," it was in view of some important circumstances of his past life, and particularly of his feelings in time of dangerous illness, and of his obligation on his recovery to devote himself to God. In the dedication of his house to God he recurs with deep interest to that period of his life, and dwells with grateful satisfaction on the goodness of God manifested in his restoration to health. On entering his new abode, he seems to have felt that there was a special propriety in his recognising the fact that he owed his life to God; his life, not only in general, but in this special act of goodness, by which he had been raised up from the borders of the grave. *His former condition of calamity and sorrow as contrasted with his present happy and prosperous condition*, therefore, suggested the train of thought in the psalm at the dedication of his house. In the course of the psalm, as illustrating his feelings, he adverts to the following points:—(1.) His former state of self-confidence or security when he was in health, and when he thought his "mountain" stood "strong," vers. 6, 7. (2.) His sickness as a means of humbling him, and teaching him his dependence, vers. 2, 3. (3.) His prayer for deliverance when he was sick, vers. 2, 8—10. (4.) His deliverance as an act of God vers. 2, 3, 11. (5.) His obligation to give thanks to God for his mercy, vers. 1, 4, 12. These would suggest most appropriate topics of meditation on entering a new abode, and looking forward to the vicissitudes which might and which would probably occur there.

That the allusion in the psalm is to *sickness*, seems to me to be evident from vers. 2, 3, and 9, though at what time of life this occurred, or what was the particular form of disease, we are not informed. From vers. 3 and 9, however, it is certain that it was a *dangerous* illness; that he anticipated death; and that he was saved from death only in answer to fervent prayer. The psalm, therefore, in this respect, has a resemblance to Ps. vi., xxxv., and xli.—psalms composed also in view of sickness. In a book claiming to be from God, and designed for all mankind in a world where sickness so abounds, it was to be expected that there would be allusions to disease as well as to other forms of affliction, and that in the examples of ancient saints suffering on beds of pain, we should be able to find illustrations of proper pious feeling; that we should be

PSALM XXX.

A Psalm *and* Song *at* the dedication of the house of David.

I WILL extol thee, O LORD; for thou hast lifted me up, and hast not made my foes to rejoice over me.

2 O LORD my God, I cried unto thee, and thou hast healed me.

---

directed by their example to the true sources of consolation, and should be made acquainted with the lessons which God designs to teach us in sickness.

The direct contents of the psalm are as follows:—

I. The author recounts the signal mercy of God to him in the time of his danger. God had lifted him up, and had not allowed his enemies to exult over his death, vers. 1-3.

II. He calls upon others to unite with him in praising God, and especially in view of the truth that affliction, as endured by the people of God, would not continue long, and that it would certainly be followed by peace and joy, as the light of the morning will certainly follow the darkest night, vers. 4, 5.

III. He adverts again, in illustration of this, to his former state, saying that there was a time when he thought he should never be moved; when he supposed that his "mountain" stood "strong," and that he was secure; but that God had hid his face, and troubled him, teaching him *not* to confide in his own strength, or in the mere fact that he was prosperous, vers. 6, 7.

IV. He adverts to his earnest prayer in the time of his affliction, and recounts the substance of that prayer, vers. 8-10. The *argument* which he then urged was that there could be no "profit" or advantage to God "in his blood," or in his being cut off; that the "dust," that is, the dead, could not praise him or declare his truth. He, therefore, prayed that God would keep him alive, that he might honour Him upon the earth.

V. In vers. 11, 12, he refers to the fact that the prayer was heard, and to the reason why it was heard. God had turned his mourning into dancing; he had put off his sackcloth, and girded him with gladness. The reason why God had done this was, that his "glory," that is, his tongue (marg.), might give praise to God, and not be silent; and, in view of all the goodness of God to him, he expresses his purpose to praise God for ever.

It will be seen, therefore, that the contents of the psalm are every way suitable to the occasion supposed to be referred to,—the dedication of his house to God. On entering such a habitation for the first time it was proper to recall the past scenes of his life,—his perils and troubles; it was proper to acknowledge the goodness of God in delivering him from those perils and troubles; it was proper to express his solemn purpose to serve God *in* that dwelling, and to consecrate himself and all that he had to him and to his service evermore. What was proper for the royal author of this psalm is proper for all; and there can be nothing more appropriate when we have erected a house to dwell in than to dedicate it to God, with a suitable recollection of his dealings with us in our past life, and to pray that *He* may also condescend to dwell with us there.

1. *I will extol thee.* Literally, *I will exalt thee;* that is, he would make God first and supreme in his thoughts and affections; he would do what he could to make Him known; he would elevate Him high in his praises. ¶ *For thou hast lifted me up.* To wit, from the state of danger in which I was (vers. 2, 3). The Hebrew word here used means properly to draw out, as from a well; and then, to deliver, to set free. As God had thus lifted *him* up, it was proper that he should show his gratitude by *lifting up* or extolling the name of God. ¶ *And hast not made my foes to rejoice over me.* Hast not suffered them to triumph over me; that is, thou hast delivered me from them. He refers to the fact that he had been saved from a dangerous illness, and that his enemies had not been allowed to exult over his death. Comp. Notes on Ps. xli. 5.

2. *O* LORD *my God,* I *cried unto thee.* In the time of trouble and danger. ¶ *And thou hast healed me.* Thou didst restore me to health. The language here evidently refers to the fact that he had been sick, and had then been restored to health.

3 O LORD, thou[s] hast brought up my soul from the grave: thou hast kept me alive, that I should not go down to the pit.
4 Sing unto the LORD, O ye saints of his, and give thanks[1] at the remembrance of his holiness.
5 For[2] his anger *endureth but* a moment; in his favour *is* life: weeping may endure[3] for a night, but[4] joy *cometh* in the morning.

s Isa. xxxviii. 17. [1] Or, *to the memorial.*

[2] there is but *a moment in his anger.* [3] *in the evening.* [4] *singing.*

3. *O* LORD, *thou hast brought up my soul from the grave.* My life; me. The meaning is, that he had been in imminent danger of death, and had been brought from the borders of the grave. The word here rendered *grave* is *Sheol*—a word which, properly used, commonly denotes the region of the dead; the under-world which is entered through the grave. Comp. Notes on Isa. xiv. 9; Ps. vi. 5. ¶ *Thou hast kept me alive, that I should not go down to the pit.* More literally, "thou hast caused me to live from them which go down to the pit; that is, thou hast distinguished me from them by keeping me alive. The word *pit* here means the same as the grave. See Notes on Ps. xxviii. 1.

4. *Sing unto the* LORD, *O ye saints of his.* This call upon others to give thanks to God is in view of the mercy which he had experienced. He invites them to unite with him in celebrating the praises of that God who had showed him so much mercy. It was not because *they* had been benefited by these tokens of the Divine favour; but (*a*) because when we *are* partakers of the Divine mercy, we desire that others may assist us in giving utterance to the praise due to God; and (*b*) because others may learn from the mercies bestowed on us that God *is* worthy of praise, or may see in his dealings with us an argument for his goodness; and may, therefore, appropriately unite in his praise. Thus religion diffuses its influence on all around us, and tends to *unite* the hearts of many in every manifestation of the character of God. Infidelity is solitary and dissocial; religion is social; and, no matter on whom the favour is bestowed, its effect is to unite the hearts of many to each other and to God. ¶ *And give thanks at the remembrance of his holiness.* Marg., *to the memorial.* The Hebrew is, *to the memory of his holiness.* The sense is, in calling to recollection the acts of his holiness, or his holy perfections. Comp. Notes on Ps. xxii. 3. The word *holiness* here is used in a large sense as denoting, not so much the hatred of sin, as benevolence, kindness, mercy,—the Divine compassion towards those who are in trouble or danger. It is true that it *is* a proper subject of rejoicing and praise that God is a holy God, a God of truth and justice, a God who cannot look upon sin but with abhorrence, a God in whose nature is combined every possible perfection; but that is not the exact idea here. The word refers to his compassion, goodness, kindness; and to the acts by which that had been manifested to the psalmist, as laying a proper foundation for gratitude and praise.

5. *For his anger* endureth but *a moment.* Marg., There is but *a moment in his anger.* So the Hebrew. That is, his anger endures but a short time, or brief period. The reference here is to the troubles and sorrows through which the psalmist had passed, as compared with his subsequent happiness. Though at the time they might have seemed to be long, yet, as compared with the many mercies of life, with the joy which had succeeded them, and with the hopes now cherished, they seemed to be but for a moment. God, according to the view of the psalmist, is not a Being who cherishes anger; not one who lays it up in his mind; not one who is unwilling to show mercy and kindness:—he is a Being who is disposed to be merciful, and though

6 And in my prosperity I said, I shall never be moved.

7 LORD, by thy favour thou [t] hast [1] made my mountain to

t Ps. xviii. 35, 36.

1 settled strength for my mountain.

he may be displeased with the conduct of men, yet his displeasure is not cherished and nourished, but passes away with the occasion, and is remembered no more. ¶ *In his favour* is *life.* It is his nature to impart life. He spares life; he will give eternal life. It is, in other words, not his nature to inflict death; death is to be traced to something else. Death is not pleasing or gratifying to him; it is pleasing and gratifying to him to confer life. His favour secures life; death is an evidence of his displeasure,—that is, death is caused by sin leading to his displeasure. If a man has the favour of God, he is sure of life; if not life in this world, yet life in the world to come. ¶ *Weeping may endure for a night.* Marg., *in the evening.* So the Hebrew. The word here rendered *endure* means properly *to lodge, to sojourn,* as one does for a little time. The idea is, that weeping is like a stranger—a wayfaring man —who lodges for a night only. In other words, sorrow will soon pass away to be succeeded by joy. ¶ *But joy* cometh *in the morning.* Marg., *singing.* The margin expresses the force of the original word. There will be singing, shouting, exultation. That is, if we have the friendship of God, sorrow will always be temporary, and will always be followed by joy. The morning will come; a morning without clouds; a morning when the sources of sorrow will disappear. This often occurs in the present life; it will always occur to the righteous in the life to come. The sorrows of this life are but for a moment, and they will be succeeded by the light and the joy of heaven. Then, if not before, all the sorrows of the present life, however long they may appear to be, will seem to have been but for a moment; weeping, though it *may* have made life here but one unbroken night, will be followed by one eternal day without a sigh or a tear.

6. *And in my prosperity I said, I shall never be moved.* I shall never be visited with calamity or trial. This refers to a past period of his life, when everything seemed to be prosperous, and when he had drawn around him so many comforts, and had apparently made them so secure, that it seemed as if they could never be taken from him, or as if he had nothing to fear. To what precise period of his life the psalmist refers, it is now impossible to ascertain. It is sufficient to say, that men are often substantially in that state of mind. They have such vigorous constitutions and such continued health; their plans are so uniformly crowned with success; everything which they touch so certainly turns to gold, and every enterprise so certainly succeeds; they have so many and such warmly-attached friends; they have accumulated so much property, and it is so safely invested,—that it seems as if they were never to know reverses, and they unconsciously suffer the illusion to pass over the mind that they are never to see changes, and that they have nothing to dread. They become self-confident. They forget their dependence on God. In their own minds they trace their success to their own efforts, tact, and skill, rather than to God. They become worldly-minded, and it is necessary for God to teach them how easily he can sweep all this away,—and thus to bring them back to a right view of the uncertainty of all earthly things. Health fails, or friends die, or property takes wings and flies away; and God accomplishes his purpose,—a purpose invaluable to them,—by showing them their dependence on himself, and by teaching them that permanent and certain happiness and security are to be found in Him alone.

7. LORD, *by thy favour thou hast made my mountain to stand strong.* Marg., *settled strength for my moun-*

stand strong: thou didst hide thy face, *and* I was troubled.

u Ps. xxxiv. 6.

8 I cried [u] to thee, O LORD; and unto the LORD I made supplication.

tain. This refers, I apprehend, to his former state of mind; to his confidence in that which constituted his prosperity as referred to in the previous verse; to his feeling, in that state, that everything pertaining to himself was safe; to his freedom from any apprehension that there would be any change. The word *mountain* seems to be used as denoting that on which he relied as his security or strength, as the mountain, or the inaccessible hills, constituted a refuge and security in times of danger. See Ps. xviii. 1, 2, 33; xxvii. 5. It does not refer to Mount Moriah, or Mount Zion, as some have supposed, for the passage relates to a former period of his life when these were not in his possession; but he speaks of himself as having, through the favour of God, put himself into a strong position,—a position where he feared no enemy and no change; where he thought himself entirely secure,—the state of *prosperity* to which he had referred in the previous verse. In that state, however, God showed him that there was no real security but in his favour: security not in what a man can draw around himself, but in the favour of God alone. ¶ *Thou didst hide thy face.* That is, at the time when I was so confident, and when I thought my mountain stood so strong, and that I was so secure. Then I was shown how insecure and uncertain was all that I relied on, and how absolutely, after all that I had done, I was dependent for safety on God. To *hide the face* is synonymous in the sacred writings with the withdrawing of favour, or with displeasure. See Notes on Ps. xiii. 1. Comp. Ps. civ. 29. ¶ And *I was troubled.* I was confounded, perplexed, agitated, terrified. I was thrown into sudden fear, for all that I had so confidently relied on, all that I thought was so firm, was suddenly swept away. We do not know what this was in the case of the psalmist. It may have been the strength of his own fortifications; it may have been the number and discipline of his army; it may have been his own conscious power and skill as a warrior; it may have been his wealth; it may have been his bodily health,—in reference to any of which he may have felt as if none of these things could fail. When that on which he so confidently relied was swept away, he was agitated, troubled, anxious. The same thing may occur now, and often does occur, when men rely on their own strength; their health; their wealth. Suddenly any of these may be swept away; suddenly they *are* often swept away, to teach such men—even good men—their dependence on God, and to show them how vain is every other refuge.

8. *I cried to thee, O* LORD. That is, when those reverses came, and when that on which I had so confidently relied was taken away, I called upon the Lord; I uttered an earnest cry for aid. The prayer which he uttered on the occasion is specified in the following verses. The idea here is, that he was not driven *from* God by these reverses, but *to* him. He felt that his reliance on those things in which he had put his trust was vain, and he now came to God, the true source of strength, and sought His protection and favour. This was doubtless the design of the reverses which God had brought upon him; and this will always be the effect of the reverses that come upon good men. When they have placed undue reliance on wealth, or health, or friends, and when these are taken away, the effect will be to lead them to God in earnest prayer. God designs to bring them back, and they *do* come back to him. Afflictions are always, sooner or later, effectual in bringing good men back to God. The sinner is often driven *from* God by trial; the good man is brought back to find his strength and comfort *in*

9 What profit *is there* in my blood, when I go down to the pit? Shall the dust praise thee? shall it declare thy truth?

10 Hear, O LORD, and have mercy upon me: LORD, be thou my helper.

11 Thou hast turned [v] for me my mourning into dancing: thou hast put off my sackcloth, and girded me with gladness;

v Ps. cxxvi. 1, 2; Isa. lxi. 3.

God. The one complains, and murmurs, and is wretched; the other prays, and submits, and is made more happy than he was in the days of his prosperity.

9. *What profit* is there *in my blood.* That is, What profit or advantage would there be to thee if I should die? What would be *gained* by it? The argument which the psalmist urges is that he could better serve God by his life than by his death; that his death, by removing him from the earth, would prevent his rendering the service which he might by his life. The same argument is presented also in Ps. vi. 5 (see Notes on that verse), and is found again in lxxxviii. 10—12, and in the hymn of Hezekiah, Isa. xxxviii. 18, 19. See Notes on that passage. The prayer here used is to be understood, not as a prayer at the time of the composition of the psalm, but as that which the psalmist employed at the time when he thought his mountain stood strong, and when God saw fit to humble him by some calamity—perhaps by a dangerous illness, vers. 6, 7. ¶ *When I go down to the pit?* To the grave; or, If I should go down to the grave. Notes on ver. 3. ¶ *Shall the dust praise thee?* That which turns to dust; the lifeless remains. See Notes on Ps. vi. 5. ¶ *Shall it declare thy truth?* Can a lifeless body stand up in defence of the truth, or make that truth known to the living? This shows on what his heart was really set, or what was the prevailing desire of his soul. It was to make known the truth of God; to celebrate his praise; to bring others to an acquaintance with him. It cannot be denied that the statement here made is founded on obscure views, or on a misconception of the condition of the soul after death—a misconception which we are enabled to correct by the clearer light of the Christian religion; but still there is a truth here of great importance. It is, that whatever *we* are to do for making known the character and perfections of God on earth,—for bringing others to the knowledge of the truth, and saving their souls,—is to be done *before* we go down to the grave. *Whatever* we may do to honour God in the future world—in the vast eternity on which we enter at death,—yet all that we are to do in this respect on earth is to be accomplished before the eyes are closed, and the lips are made dumb, in death. We shall not return to do what we have omitted to do on earth; we shall not come back to repair the evils of an inconsistent life; we shall not revisit the world to check the progress of error that we may have maintained; we shall not return to warn the sinners whom we neglected to warn. Our work on earth will be soon done,—and done finally and for ever. If we are to offer prayer for the salvation of our children, neighbours, or friends, it is to be done in this world; if we are to admonish and warn the wicked, it is to be done here; if we are to do anything by personal effort for the spread of the Gospel, it is to be done before we die. Whatever we may do in heaven, these things are not to be done there; for when we close our eyes in death, our personal efforts for the salvation of men will cease for ever.

10. *Hear, O* LORD, *and have mercy upon me*, etc. This, too, is the prayer which he uttered in the calamities adverted to in ver. 7. It is a cry for mercy founded on the idea referred to in ver. 9.

11. *Thou hast turned for me.* In my behalf. That is, God had heard his prayer; he had brought his troubles to an end; he had caused his

12 To the end that *my* [1] glory may sing praise to thee, and not be silent. O LORD my God, I will give thanks unto thee for ever.

[1] i.e. *tongue*, or, *soul*, Ps. xvi. 9.

sorrows to be succeeded by correspondent joy. ¶ *My mourning into dancing.* Joy, exultation, every expression of rejoicing, had been made to succeed his deep sorrows. Comp. ver. 5. It was this which he commemorated at the dedication of his house; this joy succeeding scenes of sorrow that he now called to remembrance as he entered the place which he had reared for a permanent abode. The contrast of his circumstances now—in a palace, with every comfort of plenty and peace around him—with his former circumstances which had been so sad, made it proper for him thus to celebrate the goodness of God. ¶ *Thou hast put off my sackcloth.* That which I wore, or had girded around me, as an emblem of sorrow, or in the time of my mourning. See Notes on Isa. iii. 24; Job xvi. 15; and Matt. xi. 21. ¶ *And girded me with gladness.* Instead of a girdle of sackcloth he had been clothed in a gay and festive dress, or with such a dress—girded with an elegant girdle—as was worn on joyous and festive occasions. See Notes on Matt. v. 38—41.

12. *To the end that* my *glory may sing praise to thee.* Marg., my *tongue*, or my *soul.* De Wette renders it, *my heart.* The Chaldee Paraphrase, "that the honourable of the world may praise thee." The LXX. and the Latin Vulgate, *my glory.* The reference is, undoubtedly, to what the psalmist regarded as most glorious, honourable, exalted, in himself. There is no evidence that he referred to his *tongue* or his *heart* particularly, but the expression seems to be equivalent to *my highest powers*—all the powers and faculties of my nature. The *tongue* would indeed be the instrument of uttering praise, but still the reference is rather to the exalted powers of the soul than to the instrument. Let all that is capable of praise within me, all my powers, be employed in celebrating the goodness of God. ¶ *And not be silent.* Be employed in praise. ¶ *O* LORD *my God, I will give thanks unto thee for ever.* Comp. Notes on Isa. xxxviii. 20. This verse states the purpose which the psalmist now saw that God intended to accomplish by his dealings with him in the varied scenes of his past life; and his own purpose now as he entered his new abode. *The purpose of God*, in all these various dealings—in the prosperity which had been bestowed on him (vers. 6, 7); in the reverses and trials by sickness or otherwise which had come upon him (vers. 3, 7); and in the deliverance which God had granted him in answer to his prayers (vers. 2, 3, 10, 11)—was, that he should learn to praise the Lord. *His own purpose* now, as he entered his new habitation and dedicated it to God, was, to praise God with his highest powers for ever:—to consecrate all that he had to his gracious preserver; to make his house, not a habitation of gaiety and sin, but an abode of serious piety—a home where the happiness sought would be that which is found in the influence of religion. It is scarcely necessary to add that every new dwelling should be entered by a family with feelings similar to these; that the first act of the head of a family on entering a new habitation—whether it be a palace or a cottage—should be solemnly to consecrate it to God, and to resolve that it shall be a house where His praises shall be celebrated, and where the influence of religion shall be invoked to guide and sanctify all the members of the household.

PSALM XXXI.

This psalm is addressed to "the chief Musician," and purports to be a psalm of David. On the meaning of the phrase "To the chief Musician," see Notes on the title to Ps. iv. There can be no doubt that the inscription which ascribes it to David is correct, and that he was the author. The occasion, however, on

PSALM XXXI.

To the chief Musician. A Psalm of David.

1 IN [w] thee, O LORD, do I put my trust; let me never be ashamed: deliver me in thy [x] righteousness.

w Ps. lxxi. 1—4. x Ps. cxliii. 1.

which it was composed is unknown, and cannot now be ascertained. Most of the Jewish and many Christian interpreters have supposed that it was written when David was in the wilderness of Maon, and when, having been betrayed (as to the place of his retreat) by the Ziphites, he was hotly pursued by Saul and his host, 1 Sam. xxiii. 19-26. There is, however, no particular reason for referring it to this period of his life, for there were many occasions to which it would be equally applicable.

Its general purpose is to inspire confidence in God in other hearts,—from the experience of the psalmist,—from that manifested favour by which he had been brought through his troubles. See vers. 23, 24. The psalm refers to the dangers which surrounded its author at the time referred to; his fears and apprehensions in those dangers; his calm confidence in God amid his dangers; the deliverance from trouble which was vouchsafed to him; his joy and gratitude for deliverance; and the lessons which others might learn in their trials from the Divine dealings towards him in his. That the psalmist was in trouble or danger when he penned this psalm there can be no reason to doubt; that he prayed earnestly at that time for deliverance is clear; but it is also plain that in the psalm he refers to former troubles, and to the deliverance which God had granted to him in *those* troubles, and that he seeks and derives consolation and assurance from the dealings of God with him then. In some parts of the psalm he refers to his present afflictions; in other parts to the trials of other days, and to his deliverances in those trials; in the entire psalm he inculcates the duty of confiding in God, from his own experience of his mercy, and from his own reliance on him.

The contents of the psalm are as follows:—

I. Prayer to God for deliverance from his sufferings and his enemies, on the ground of his confidence in Him, and his previous experience of His mercy, vers. 1-8.

II. Description of his troubles and of the calamities under which he was oppressed; or an enumeration of his present distresses, vers. 9-13. He says that he is in trouble, and that his eye is consumed with grief, ver. 9; that his life is spent with grief, and his years with sighing, that his strength failed, and that his bones were consumed, ver. 10; that he is a reproach among his neighbours and an object of dread to his acquaintances, or that they fled from him, he was so abject, forsaken, and afflicted, ver. 11; that he was forsaken and forgotten like a dead man who had passed away from the recollection of mankind, ver. 12; that he was slandered, and that men conspired together to take away his life, ver. 13.

III. Calm confidence in God in these times of trouble; or a calm committing of all into his hands, under an assurance which he felt that all would be well, vers. 14—20. He says that he trusted in God, ver. 14; and that his times were in the hand of God, ver. 15; he prays that God would deliver him, vers. 15--18; he finds comfort and peace in the assurance of the Divine goodness and mercy, ver. 19; and in the assurance that God would hide them that trusted in him from the pride of man, and would keep them safely in his pavilion, ver. 20.

IV. Thanks for deliverance, vers. 21, 22. He seems to have *found* the deliverance, even while he prayed, or to have had such an assurance of it that he could speak of it as if it were already his. He felt that he had been hasty in supposing that he would be cut off, and seems to have reproached himself for even a momentary doubt in regard to the goodness of God, ver. 22.

V. The lesson furnished to others by his experience, vers. 23, 24. It is a lesson of encouragement to all in similar circumstances, prompting them to be of good courage; to be cheered by his example and experience; never to despond; never to cease to trust God. Because *he* had found God to be a refuge and strength, he calls upon all others to believe that they would also find him such if they likewise trusted in him.

1. *In thee, O* LORD, *do I put my trust.* This is the ground of the petitions which follow; or the reason

2 Bow down thine ear to me; deliver me speedily: be thou [1] my strong rock, for an house of defence to save me.
3 For thou *art* my rock and my fortress: therefore for thy name's sake lead me and guide me.
4 Pull me out of the net that they have laid privily for me; for thou *art* my strength.
5 Into [y] thine hand I commit my spirit: thou hast redeemed me, O LORD God of truth.

1 *to me for a rock of strength.*
y Luke xxiii. 46; Acts vii. 59.

why the psalmist thus appeals to God. It was his firm confidence in him; in his character; in his promises; in his ability to deliver him in the time of danger. Comp. Notes on Ps. vii. 1. ¶ *Let me never be ashamed.* That is, let me never have occasion to be ashamed for having put this confidence in thee. Let thy dealings towards me be such as to show that my confidence was well founded. The word is not used here in the sense of being unwilling to confess his faith in God, or his love for Him, as it is often now (comp. Rom. i. 16; v. 5; 2 Tim. i. 12), but in the sense of being so *disappointed* as to make one ashamed that he *had* thus relied on that which was unworthy of confidence. See Notes on Job vi. 20; comp. also Isa. xxx. 5; Jer. ii. 26; xiv. 3, 4. The psalmist prays that God would interpose in his behalf in answer to his prayers, and that he would show that He was worthy of the confidence which he had reposed in him, or that He was a God who might be trusted in the time of trial; in other words, that he might not be subjected to the reproach of the wicked for having in his troubles relied on such a God. ¶ *Deliver me in thy righteousness.* In the manifestation of thy righteous character; in the exhibition of that character *as* righteous; as doing justice between man and man; as pronouncing a just sentence between me and my enemies.

2. *Bow down thine ear to me.* As he does who inclines his ear towards one whom he is willing to hear, or whom he is desirous of hearing. See Notes on Ps. xvii. 6. ¶ *Deliver me speedily.* Without delay. Or, *Hasten* to deliver me. It is right to pray to be delivered from all evil; equally right to pray to be delivered *at once.* ¶ *Be thou my strong rock.* Marg., *to me for a rock of strength.* See Notes on Ps. xviii. 1, 2, 46. ¶ *For an house of defence to save me.* A fortified house; a house made safe and strong. It is equivalent to praying that he might have a secure abode or dwelling-place.

3. *For thou* art *my rock and my fortress.* See Notes on Ps. xviii. 2. ¶ *Therefore for thy name's sake.* For the sake of thine own honour, or for the glory of thy name. See Notes on Ps. xxiii. 3. That is, since thou *art* my rock and my defence—since I put my trust in thee—show, by leading and guiding me, that my trust is well founded, or that this *is* thy character, and that thou wilt be true and faithful to those who commit their all to thee. See Notes on ver. 1.

4. *Pull me out of the net.* See Notes on Ps. ix. 15. ¶ *That they have laid privily for me.* That my enemies have laid for me. The phrase "laid privily" refers to the custom of *hiding* or *concealing* a net or gin, so that the wild beast that was to be taken could not see it, or would fall into it unawares. Thus his enemies designed to overcome him, by springing a net upon him at a moment when he was not aware of it, and at a place where he did not suspect it. ¶ *For thou* art *my strength.* My stronghold. My hope of defence is in thee, and thee alone.

5. *Into thine hand I commit my spirit.* The Saviour used this expression when on the cross, and when about to die: Luke xxiii. 46. But this does not prove that the psalm had originally a reference to him, or

6 I have hated them that regard [z] lying vanities: but I trust in the LORD.

z Jonah ii. 8.

that he meant to intimate that the words originally were a prophecy. The language was appropriate for him, as it is for all others in the hour of death; and His use of the words furnished the highest illustration of their *being* appropriate in that hour. The act of the psalmist was an act of strong confidence in God in the midst of dangers and troubles; the act of the Saviour was of the same nature, commending his spirit to God in the solemn hour of death. The same act of faith is proper for all the people of God, alike in trouble and in death. Comp. Acts vii. 59. The word *spirit* may mean either *life*, considered as the animating principle, equivalent to the word *myself;* or it may mean more specifically the *soul*, as distinguished from the body. The sense is not materially varied by either interpretation. ¶ *Thou hast redeemed me.* This was the ground or reason why the *psalmist* commended himself to God; this reason was not urged, and could not have been by the Saviour, in his dying moments. *He* committed his departing spirit to God as his Father, and in virtue of the work which he had been appointed to do, and which he was now about finishing, as a Redeemer;—*we* commit our souls to him in virtue of having been redeemed. This is proper for us, (*a*) because he *has* redeemed us; (*b*) because we have been redeemed *for* him, and we may ask him to take his own; (*c*) because this is a ground of safety, for *if* we have been redeemed, we may be certain that God will keep us; and (*d*) because this is the only ground of our security in reference to the future world. What *David* may have understood by this word it may not be easy to determine with certainty; but there is no reason to doubt that he *may* have used it as expressive of the idea that he had been recovered from the ruin of the fall, and from the dominion of sin, and had been made a child of God. Nor need we doubt that he had such views of the way of salvation that he would feel that he was redeemed only by an atonement, or by the shedding of blood for his sins. To all who are Christians it is enough to authorise them to use this language in the midst of troubles and dangers, and in the hour of death, that they have been redeemed by the blood of the Saviour; to none of us is there any other safe ground of trust and confidence in the hour of death than the fact that Christ has died for sin, and that we have evidence that we are interested in his blood. ¶ *O* LORD *God of truth.* True to thy promises and to thy covenant-engagements. As thou hast promised life and salvation to those who are redeemed, they may safely confide in thee. See Notes on 2 Cor. i. 20.

6. *I have hated them that regard lying vanities.* This is evidently stated as a *reason* for the prayer offered in the previous verses. It is a reference by the psalmist to his own past life; to his general aim and conduct. The meaning is, that he had been a friend of God; that he had separated himself from wicked men; and he now prays in return for His protection and interposition. The sentiment is similar to that which occurs in Ps. xxvi. 3, 4, 5. See Notes on that passage. The word rendered *regard* here means to observe, to keep, to attend upon; and the reference is to those who show honour to what is here called "lying vanities;" that is, those who attend upon them, or who show them favour. The "lying vanities" are probably *idols*, and the allusion is to those who attended on the worship of idols as distinguished from those who worshipped the true God. Idols are often represented as false,—as vain, or vanity,—as a lie,—in contradistinction from that which is true and real. See Notes on 1 Cor. viii. 4. There is peculiar emphasis in the language used here as denoting the *utter* worth-

7 I will be glad and rejoice in thy mercy: for thou hast considered my trouble; thou hast known [a] my soul in adversities;

8 And hast not shut me up into the hand of the enemy: thou [b] hast set my feet in a large room.

9 Have mercy upon me, O LORD, for I am in trouble; mine eye is consumed with grief, *yea*, my soul and my belly.

10 For [c] my life is spent with grief, and my years with sighing: my strength faileth because of mine iniquity, and my bones are consumed.

a Ps. cxlii. 3. *b* Ps. xviii. 19. *c* Ps. cii. 3, etc.

lessness and vanity of idols. The language means *vanities of emptiness;* denoting that they were *utterly* vain and worthless. ¶ *But I trust in the* LORD. In Jehovah, the true God, as distinguished from idols.

7. *I will be glad and rejoice in thy mercy.* I will triumph and joy in thy mercy; that is, in the mercy which he had already experienced, and in that which he still hoped to enjoy. He had had abundant proofs of that mercy; he hoped for still further proofs of it; and he says that he would find his joy in that, and not in what idols could give. ¶ *For thou hast considered my trouble.* In times past and now. He felt assured that his prayer would be regarded, and that God would relieve and deliver him. ¶ *Thou hast known my soul in adversities.* In the troubles that have come upon me. That is, God had seen and known all the feelings of his heart in the time of adversity;—his sorrow and anxiety; his hope and trust; his unmurmuring spirit; his feeling of entire dependence on God, and his belief that he would interpose to save him. God had not turned away from him, but had shown that he regarded with interest all his feelings, his desires, his hopes. It is much, in the time of trouble, to know that all our feelings are understood by God, that he sees all our sorrows, and that he will not be regardless of them. There are no states of mind more interesting than those which occur in adversities; there is no one who can fully understand the soul in adversities but God; there is no one but God who can wholly meet the wants of the soul in such seasons.

8. *And hast not shut me up into the hand of the enemy.* Hast not delivered me into his hand, or into his power. See margin 1 Sam. xvii. 46; xxiv. 18; xxvi. 8. ¶ *Thou hast set my feet in a large room.* In a large place. Thou hast made me free, or set me at liberty. See Notes on Ps. iv. 1; xviii. 19, 36.

9. *Have mercy upon me, O* LORD, *for I am in trouble.* The nature and sources of his trouble are specified in the verses following. He seems to have regarded all his trouble as the result of sin, either the sin of his heart, of which he alone was conscious, or of some open act of sin, that had been the means of bringing this affliction upon him, ver. 10. As a consequence of this, he says that he was subjected to the reproach of his enemies, and shunned by his neighbours and his acquaintances; that he was forgotten by them like a dead man out of mind; that he was exposed to the slander of others, and that they conspired against his life, vers. 11–13. In view of all this he calls earnestly upon God to save him in his troubles, and to be his helper and friend. ¶ *Mine eye is consumed with grief.* That is, with weeping. See Notes on Ps. vi. 7. ¶ *Yea, my soul.* That is, my spirit, my life, my mind. My powers are weakened and exhausted by excessive grief. ¶ *And my belly.* My bowels: regarded as the seat of the affections. See Notes on Isa. xvi. 11; comp. Ps. xxii. 14. The effect of his grief was to exhaust his strength, and to make his heart sink within him.

10. *For my life is spent with grief.* The word here rendered *spent* does not mean merely *passed,* as it is commonly now used, as when we say we *spent* our time at such a place, or in

11 I was a reproach among all mine enemies, but especially among my neighbours, [d] and a fear to mine acquaintance: they that did see me without fled from me.

12 I am forgotten as a dead

d Job xix. 13.

such a manner, but in the more proper meaning of the word, as denoting *consumed, wasted away*, or *destroyed.* See the word כָּלָה as used in Jer. xvi. 4; Lam. ii. 11; Ps. lxxxiv. 2 (Heb. 3); cxliii. 7; lxix. 3 (Heb. 4); Job xi. 20. ¶ *And my years with sighing.* That is, my years are wasted or consumed with sighing. Instead of being devoted to active toil and to useful effort, they are exhausted or wasted away with a grief which wholly occupies and preys upon me. ¶ *My strength faileth because of mine iniquity.* Because of the trouble that has come upon me for my sin. He regarded all this trouble—from whatever quarter it came, whether directly from the hand of God, or from man—as the fruit of *sin.* Whether he refers to any particular sin as the cause of this trouble, or to the sin of his nature as the source of all evil, it is impossible now to determine. As, however, no particular sin is specified, it seems most probable that the reference is to the sin of his heart—to his corrupt nature. It is common, and it is not improper, when we are afflicted, to regard *all* our trials as fruits of sin; as coming upon us as the result of the fall, and as an evidence that we *are* depraved. It is certain that there is no suffering in heaven, and that there never would be any in a perfectly holy world. It is equally certain that all the woes of earth are the consequence of man's apostacy; and it is proper, therefore, when we are afflicted, even though we cannot trace the affliction to any *particular* offence, to trace it all to the existence of evil, and to regard it as among the proofs of the Divine displeasure against sin. ¶ *And my bones are consumed.* That is, are decayed, worn out, or wasted away. Even the solid framework of my body gives way under excessive grief, and all my strength is gone. See Ps. xxxii. 3; cii. 3.

11. *I was a reproach among all mine enemies.* That is, he was subjected to their reproaches, or was calumniated and reviled by them. See Notes on Ps. xxii. 6. ¶ *But especially among my neighbours.* I was reproached by none more than by my neighbours. They showed special distrust of me, and manifested special unkindness, even more than my enemies did. They turned away from me. They abandoned me. They would not associate with me. They regarded me as a disgrace to them, and forsook me. Comp. Job xix. 13–15, and the Notes on that passage. ¶ *And a fear to mine acquaintance.* An object of dread or terror, so that they fled from me. ¶ *They that did see me without.* In the streets, or in public—out of my own house. Not only those in my own dwelling—the members of my family—regarded me in this manner, but passers in the streets—those whom I accidentally met—turned from me and fled in disgust and horror. It is not possible now to determine at what time in the life of the psalmist this occurred, or to ascertain the exact circumstances. There were, doubtless, times when with the saddest feelings he could say that all this was true of him. His troubles in the time of his persecutions by Saul, and still more probably his trials in the time when Absalom rebelled against him, and when he was driven away from his throne and his capital, would furnish an occasion when this would be true. If the latter was the occasion, then we can see how naturally he would connect all this with his "*iniquity,*" and regard it as the consequence of his sin in the matter of Uriah,—a sin which would probably be always in his recollection, and which he would ever onward regard as lying at the foundation of all his afflictions.

12. *I am forgotten as a dead man*

man out of mind: I am like a [1] broken vessel.

13 For I have heard the slander of many: fear *was* on every side: while they took counsel together against me, they devised to take away my life.

[1] *vessel that perisheth.*

out of mind. Like the man who is dead, and who has passed away from the recollection of mankind. Comp. Ps. lxxxviii. 4, 5. The Hebrew is, "as a dead man *from the heart;*" that is, from the memory or recollection of men, so as to be no more remembered; no more regarded. The expression is nearly the same in meaning as our common English proverb: *out of sight, out of mind.* The allusion is to the fact that a man who is dead is soon forgotten. He is missed at first by a few friends, while the rest of the world knows little about him, or cares little about him. He is no longer seen where he has been accustomed to be seen, at the place of business, in the social circle, in the scenes of amusement, in the streets, or in public assemblies. For a short period a vacancy is created which attracts attention and causes regret. But the world moves on. Another comes to fill his place, and soon his absence ceases to be a subject of remark, or a cause of regret; the world says little about him, and soon he altogether ceases to be remembered. At no distant time the rude board with his name written on it, or the marble sculptured with all the skill of art, falls down. The passing traveller casts an eye upon the *name* of him who slept his last sleep there, and neither knows nor cares who he was.

> "The gay will laugh
> When thou art gone, the solemn brood of care
> Plod on, and each one as before will chase
> His favourite phantom."—*Bryant.*

> "On my grassy grave
> The men of future times will careless tread,
> And read my name upon the sculptured stone;
> Nor will the sound, familiar to their ears,
> Recall my vanish'd memory."
> *Henry Kirke White.*

It is sad to reflect that this is to be *our* lot; but so it is. It would cast a most gloomy shade over life if this was to be the *end* of man, and if he passed from existence as soon as he passes from the recollection of the living. The idea of the psalmist here is, that, in the circumstances to which he referred, he had been forgotten by mankind, and he uses the most striking image which could be employed to convey that idea. ¶ *I am like a broken vessel.* Marg., as in Hebrew, *like a vessel that perisheth.* That is, like a vessel made of clay—a piece of pottery—that is easily broken and rendered worthless. This is a favourite comparison with Jeremiah. See ch. xxii. 28; xlviii. 38; Lam. iv. 2. Comp. also Ps. ii. 9; Isa. xxx. 14; Hosea viii. 8.

13. *For I have heard the slander of many.* The reproach; the false accusations; the unjust aspersions. We are here more definitely informed as to another of the sources of the trouble that came upon him. It was *slander.* He had already referred to *two* sources of trouble;—one (ver. 11) that he was *reproached* by his friends and neighbours, and that his society was shunned by them; a second, that he was *forgotten* by those who ought to have remembered him, and that they treated him as though he were dead, ver. 12. The third is referred to now; to wit, that he was the subject of *slander,* or of false reports. What was the *nature* of those false charges we are not informed. But it is not needful that we should know precisely what they were. It is enough, in order to see the depth and aggravation of his trouble, to know that he *was* exposed to this; and that, to all that he had to endure from other sources, there was this added,—that his name was reproached and cast out as evil,—that he was subjected to *slander,*

> "Whose edge is sharper than the sword; whose tongue
> Outvenoms all the worms of Nile; whose breath
> Rides on the posting winds; and doth belie
> All corners of the world."
> *Cymbeline,* Act iii., Sc. iv.

14 But I trusted in thee, O LORD: I said, Thou *art* my God.

15 My times *are* in thy hand: deliver me from the hand of my enemies and from them that persecute me.

16 Make [e] thy face to shine upon thy servant: save me for thy mercies' sake.

e Numb. vi. 25, 26.

¶ *Fear* was *on every side.* From the causes already specified. He knew not whom to trust. He seemed to have no friend. He was afraid, therefore, of every one that he met. ¶ *While they took counsel together against me.* See Notes on Ps. ii. 2. They entered into a conspiracy or combination. ¶ *They devised to take away my life.* They devised measures, or they laid a plot, thus to kill me. These are the grounds of the earnest prayer which he urges in ver. 9: "Have mercy upon me, O Lord, *for I am in trouble.*"

14. *But I trust in thee, O* LORD. In these times of trial—when (ver. 9) his eye was consumed with grief; when (ver. 10) his years were spent with sighing, his strength failed, and his bones were consumed; when (ver. 11) he was a reproach among his neighbours, and dreaded by his acquaintances; when (ver. 12) he was forgotten as a dead man; and when (ver. 13) he was surrounded with causes of alarm. Then he trusted in God. His confidence did not fail. He believed that God was his Father and Friend; that He was on the throne; that He could protect and defend him; and he left himself and his cause with Him. In such circumstances as these there is no other sure refuge but God; at such times the strength of faith is shown, and then is seen pre-eminently the power and value of religion. ¶ *I said, Thou* art *my God.* Thou art all that is implied in the name "God;" and thou art mine. He felt assured that God would not forsake him, though men did; that he might confide in Him, though his earthly friends all turned away. There is always *One* who will not leave or forsake us; and the friendship and favour of that One is of more value to us than that of all other beings in the universe combined.

15. *My times* are *in thy hand.* That is, I said this in my trouble; when my friends forsook me, and when my enemies came around me and threatened my life. The meaning is, that all that pertained to him was under the control and at the disposal of God. He would *live* as long as God should please. It was His to give life; His to preserve it; His to take it away. All in relation to life,—its origin—its continuance—its changes —its seasons—childhood, youth, middle age, old age,—all was in the hand of God. No one, therefore, could take his life before the time that had been appointed by God, and he might calmly commit the whole to him. This we may feel in all seasons of life and in all times of danger; of sickness; of feebleness. We shall live as long as God has appointed; we shall pass through such changes as he directs; we shall die when and where and how he chooses. In the faithful discharge of our duty, therefore, we may commit all these things to him, and leave all at his disposal. ¶ *Deliver me from the hand of mine enemies.* That is, since all these things are under thy control; since thou hast power over my life and over all that pertains to me, I pray that thy power may be exerted in my behalf, and that my life may be rescued from danger. This was his prayer in the midst of his troubles, and this prayer was heard.

16. *Make thy face to shine upon thy servant.* That is, show me thy favour, or be kind and merciful to me. See Notes on Ps. iv. 6. ¶ *Save me for thy mercies' sake.* On account of thy mercy; or that thy mercy may be manifested. This is always a just ground of appeal to God by a sinner or a sufferer, that God would make our sins and trials an *occasion* for displaying his own character. There are,

17 Let me not be ashamed, O LORD; for I have called upon thee: let the wicked be ashamed, *and* let them be [1] silent in the grave.

18 Let the lying lips be put to silence, which speak [2] grievous things proudly and contemptuously against the righteous.

19 *Oh* how great *f* *is* thy goodness, which thou hast laid up for them that fear thee; *which* thou hast wrought for them that trust in thee before the sons of men.

[1] Or, *cut off for.* [2] *a hard thing.* *f* Isa. lxiv. 4.

indeed, other grounds of appeal; but there is no one that is more pure or exalted than this.

17. *Let me not be ashamed, O* LORD, *for I have called upon thee.* That is, I have reposed entire confidence in thee, and in thy promises, in the time of trial; let now the result be such as to show that I had reason thus to trust in thee; that thy character is such that the persecuted and the afflicted *may* always find thee to be a safe and secure refuge. In other words, Let me not be disappointed, and thus be made *ashamed* before men, as if I had put my trust where no relief was to be found, or where there was nothing to authorize an act of unreserved confidence. See Notes on Ps. xxv. 2, 3. ¶ *Let the wicked be ashamed.* Let them be disappointed in that on which they had put their trust; let it be seen that they, in their wicked plans, had no safe ground of confidence. They rely on their strength; their skill; their courage; their resources; and not on God. Let it now be seen that these things constitute no safe ground of trust, and let not others be encouraged to follow their example by any success that shall attend them in their designs. ¶ And *let them be silent in the grave.* Marg., *let them be cut off for the grave.* Heb., *for Sheol.* The more correct translation is that which is in the text, *Let them be silent.* That is, let them go down to the grave—to *Sheol*—to the *underworld*—to the *land of silence.* On the meaning of the word here used–*Sheol*, the grave—see Notes on Isa. xiv. 9; comp. Notes on Job x. 21, 22; and on Ps. xvi. 10. This is represented as a land of *silence.* This idea is derived from *the grave*, where the dead repose in silence; and the meaning here is, let them be cut off and consigned to that land of silence. It is a prayer that the wicked may not triumph.

18. *Let the lying lips be put to silence.* See Notes on Ps. xii. 2, 3. The lips which speak lies. The reference here is especially to those who had spoken in this manner against the psalmist himself, though he makes the language general, or prays in general that God would silence all liars:—a prayer certainly in which all persons may properly join. ¶ *Which speak grievous things.* Marg., *a hard thing.* The Hebrew word—עָתָק, *âthâk*—means *bold, impudent, wicked.* Gesenius, *Lex.* The phrase here means, therefore, to speak wickedly, or to speak in a bold, reckless, impudent manner; that is, without regard to the truth of what is said. ¶ *Proudly and contemptuously.* Heb., in pride and contempt:—that is, in a manner which shows that they are proud of themselves and despise others. Slander always perhaps implies this. Men are secretly proud of themselves; or they *desire* to cherish an exalted opinion of themselves, and to have others entertain the same opinion of them; and hence, if they cannot exalt themselves by their own merit, as they wish, they endeavour to humble others below their real merit, and to a level lower than themselves, by detraction.

19. Oh *how great* is *thy goodness.* That is, in view of the Divine protection and favour in such cases, or when thus assailed. The psalmist seems to have felt that it was an inexpressible privilege thus to be permitted to appeal to God with the assurance of the

20 Thou shalt hide them in the secret of thy presence from the pride of man; thou [g] shalt keep them secretly in a pavilion from the strife of tongues.

g Job v. 21.

Divine protection. In few circumstances do men feel more grateful for the opportunity of appealing to God than when they are reviled and calumniated. As there is nothing which we feel more keenly than calumny and reproach, so there can be no circumstances when we more appreciate the privilege of having such a refuge and friend as God. ¶ *Which thou hast laid up.* Which thou hast *treasured* up, for so the Hebrew word means. That is, goodness and mercy had been, as it were, *treasured up* for such an emergency,—as a man treasures up food in autumn for the wants of winter, or wealth for the wants of old age. The goodness of God is thus a treasure garnered up for the wants of his people—a treasure always accessible; a treasure that can never be exhausted. ¶ *For them that fear thee.* Or *reverence* thee,—fear or reverence being often used to denote friendship with God, or religion. See Notes on Ps. v. 7. ¶ Which *thou hast wrought for them.* Which thou hast *made* for them (Heb.); or, which thou hast secured *as if* by labour; that is, by plan and arrangement. It was not by chance that that goodness had been provided; God had done it in a manner resembling the act of a man who lays up treasure for his future use by plan and by toil. The idea is, that all this was the *work* of a benevolent God; a God who had carefully anticipated the wants of his people. ¶ *For them that trust in thee.* Who rely on thee in trouble, in danger, and in want;—who feel that their *only* reliance is on thee, and who *do* actually trust in thee. ¶ *Before the sons of men.* That is, Thou hast wrought this in the presence of the sons of men, or in the presence of mankind. God had not only laid it up in secret, making provision for the wants of his people, but he had wrought out this deliverance before men, or had shown his goodness to them openly. The acts of benevolence or goodness in the case were—*first,* that he had *treasured up* the resources of his goodness by previous arrangement, or by anticipation, for them; and *second,* that he had *wrought out* deliverance, or had *manifested* his goodness by interposing to save, and by doing it openly that it might be seen by mankind.

20. *Thou shalt hide them in the secret of thy presence.* See Notes on Ps. xxvii. 5. The phrase "secret of thy presence" means thy "secret presence." The Hebrew is, *the secret of thy face;* and the idea is, that he would hide them, or withdraw them from public view, or from the view of their enemies, into the very place where he himself dwelt, so that they would be before him and near him; so that his eye would be upon them, and that they would be certain of his protection. The language here is the same as in Ps. xxvii. 5, except that the word *face* or *presence* is used here instead of the word *tabernacle.* The idea is the same. ¶ *From the pride of man.* The Hebrew word here rendered *pride*—רֹכֶס, *rōkēs*—means properly *league* or *conspiracy;* then, *snares* or *plots.* It occurs nowhere else in the Scriptures, though the corresponding verb—רָכַס, *rakas*—occurs twice, meaning to *bind on* or *to,* Ex. xxviii. 28; xxxix. 21. The word here means *league* or *conspiracy,* and the idea is, that when the wicked form a conspiracy, or enter into a league against the righteous, God will take them, as it were, into his own immediate presence, and will protect them. ¶ *Thou shalt keep them secretly.* Thou wilt *hide* them as with thyself. ¶ *In a pavilion.* In thy tent, or dwelling-place. See Notes on Ps. xxvii. 5. ¶ *From the strife of tongues.* Slander; reproach; calumny. This does not mean the strife of tongues among themselves, or their contentions with each other,

21 Blessed *be* the LORD; for he hath showed me his marvellous kindness in a [1] strong city.
22 For I said in my haste, I am cut off [h] from before thine eyes: nevertheless thou heardest the voice of my supplications, when I cried unto thee.
23 O love the LORD, all ye his saints: *for* the LORD preserveth the faithful, and plentifully rewardeth the proud doer.

[1] Or, *fenced.*

h Job xxxv. 14.

but the united clamours of the whole against himself. God would guard the righteous from their reproaches, or their efforts to ruin them by slander. Comp. Ps. xxxvii. 5, 6.

21. *Blessed* be *the* LORD. An expression of thanksgiving for the evidence that God had heard him in his troubles, and had answered him. ¶ *For he hath showed me his marvellous kindness.* Literally, *He has made his mercy wonderful;* that is, he has showed me such mercy as to be an object of admiration and astonishment. It was not ordinary kindness, such as is shown to men every day; it was so uncommon—so far beyond all expectation—so separate from second causes and the agency of man—so marked in its character—as to fill the mind with wonder. ¶ *In a strong city.* Marg., *fenced city.* This may mean either that he had thus placed him literally in a strongly fortified city where he was safe from the fear of his enemies; or, that he had interposed in his behalf, and had given him protection *as if* he had brought him into such a strongly fortified place. Jarchi supposes that the city of *Keilah* (1 Sam. xxiii. 7) is here intended. But this is improbable. All that the passage necessarily implies is, that God had given him protection *as if* he had been placed in a strongly-fortified town where he would be safe from danger.

22. *For I said in my haste.* In my fear; my apprehension. The word rendered *haste* means properly that terror or alarm which causes one to flee, or to endeavour to escape. It is not *haste* in the sense of an opinion formed too quickly, or formed rashly; it is *haste* in the sense of terror leading to sudden flight, or an effort to escape. See an illustration of this idea in the case of David himself, in 1 Sam. xxiii. 26. ¶ *I am cut off.* That is, I shall certainly be cut off or destroyed. ¶ *From before thine eyes.* Either, in thy very presence; or, so that I shall not be admitted into thy presence. I shall be cut down, and suffered no more to come before thee to worship thee. Comp. Notes on Ps. vi. 5. ¶ *Nevertheless thou heardest*, etc. Contrary to my apprehensions, I was heard and delivered. God's mercy went *beyond* the psalmist's faith,—as it often does to His people now, far beyond what they hope for; far beyond what they even pray for; far beyond what they believe to be possible;—so far beyond all this, as to make the result, as in the case of David (ver. 21), a matter of wonder and astonishment.

23. *O love the* LORD, *all ye his saints.* This is the *application* of all the truths suggested in the psalm. The experience of the psalmist had shown the wisdom of trusting in God in times of danger and trouble, and had laid the foundation for a proper exhortation to others to imitate his example; an argument why all the people of God should love him, and should be of good courage. The reason here assigned for their loving the Lord is, that he preserves those who are faithful to him, and "rewards the proud doer." This *is* a reason for loving God, or for putting our trust in him,—though the psalmist does not say that this is the *only* reason for doing it. The meaning here is, that the dealings of God toward the psalmist had established this truth in regard to the character of God, that he *does* preserve the faithful, and *does* punish the proud, and that this fact constitutes a reason why all his

24 Be of good courage, and he shall strengthen your heart, all ye that hope in the LORD.

people should confide in him. ¶ *For the* LORD *preserveth the faithful.* The faithful;—those who put their trust in him; those who do not give up in despondency and despair in time of danger and trouble; those who do not forsake him even though for a time he *seems* to forsake them. What God looks for mainly in his people is confidence; faithfulness; trust; fidelity. ¶ *And plentifully rewardeth. Abundantly* rewards. Literally, *in plenty.* That is, his punishment does not fall short of the desert of the wicked man. It is ample or full. He does *full* justice. ¶ *The proud doer.* "The man *working pride.*" The reference is to the man who is confident in himself; who seeks to aggrandise himself, and who in doing this is regardless of the rights of others.

24. *Be of good courage.* See a similar exhortation at the close of a psalm, in Ps. xxvii. 14. Comp. Notes on that verse. As the result of all his own experience of the goodness of God, and of His gracious interposition in the time of danger, the psalmist exhorts others to be encouraged, and to feel assured that God would not leave or forsake them. ¶ *And he shall strengthen your heart.* He will animate you; he will enable you to meet trial and opposition; he will keep you from becoming faint and disheartened. ¶ *All ye that hope in the* LORD. All that put their trust in him, or all whose expectation is from him. It is a characteristic of true piety that all *hope* centres in God, or that the soul feels that there *is* no other ground of hope. (*a*) The truly pious man despairs of success in anything else, or from any other quarter, for he feels that God alone can give success. (*b*) He *does* hope in God—in reference to all that is needful for himself as an individual; all that will be for the good of his family; all that will tend to bless the world; all that he desires in heaven. Hope in God cheers him, sustains him, comforts him; makes life happy and prosperous; and makes death calm, serene, triumphant.

PSALM XXXII.

This psalm is ascribed to David, and there is no reason to doubt the correctness of the superscription to that effect.

The *occasion* on which it was composed, however, is not intimated, nor is there any way now of ascertaining it. That David refers to his own experience is manifest from the psalm itself, vers. 3-5; but whether to his experience at the time of his conversion, or to his experience in the matter of Bathsheba and Uriah—his deep guilt—his anguish of spirit on that occasion—the remorse of conscience which he felt when the guilt of that sin was brought home to his conscience; or whether he refers to some other occasion of his life when he was troubled at the remembrance of sin, it is impossible now to determine.

The *design* of this psalm is manifest. It is to show the blessedness of the forgiveness of sin. This is done by showing, in the first place, the pain, distress, and anguish, resulting from the conviction of guilt. Then follows a statement of the effects consequent on a frank and full confession of guilt in giving peace to the mind, and relieving the distress caused by the remembrance of guilt. It is remarkable that this psalm refers so much to the *inward* feelings; and that it contains no reference to any external acts,—to Jewish sacrifices and offerings. It pertains to the soul and to God; to the inward work of penitence and pardon; to the sorrow of conviction and to the peace of forgiveness; and it shows that there *was* among the Hebrews a just idea of the nature of religion as a spiritual transaction between the soul and God. Even De Wette recognises this, and sees in the psalm an illustration of the nature of faith and its bearing on salvation, and an illustration of the nature of true reconciliation with God. "In this psalm," says he, "as well as in Ps. li. and others, Judaism *nears itself*—*nähert sich*—to Christianity; it elevates itself from the mere legal to the moral." The psalm thus furnishes an illustration of the nature of true conversion to God, and is of value—as such an illustration

PSALM XXXII.

A Psalm of David, [1] Maschil.

1 BLESSED [i] *is he whose* transgression *is* forgiven, *whose* sin *is* covered.

[1] Or, *giving instruction.*
i Rom. iv. 6—8.

—to all men; while it also shows that true religion, under all dispensations, is essentially the same.

The psalm is composed of the following parts:—

I. A statement of the blessings of forgiveness, as the leading thought of the psalm, vers. 1, 2.

II. A description of the state of mind, when under conviction for sin, vers. 3, 4.

III. The effect of confession of sin, resulting in a sense of forgiveness and peace, ver. 5.

IV. Encouragement to others in similar circumstances, derived from the example of the psalmist, or from the fact that *he* found peace and pardon when he called upon God, ver. 6.

V. An expression of confidence in God as a refuge and hiding-place in time of trouble, ver. 7.

VI. The proper spirit which they should have who are thus brought up from the depths of guilt; and the way in which they should receive the guidance and direction which will be afforded them, vers. 8, 9. The psalmist undertakes to instruct them; and says that they should cherish a spirit of humility and docility,—not the fierce spirit of the untamed horse, or the spirit of the obstinate mule.

VII. The blessedness of trusting in the Lord, as the result of the experience of the psalmist in this time of sorrow for sin, vers. 10, 11.

The word *Maschil* in the title-מַשְׂכִּיל, is derived from the verb—שָׂכַל, *sakhal*—meaning properly *to look at, to behold, to view;* and then, to be prudent, circumspect; to act prudently or circumspectly, as one does who looks attentively and carefully at objects; then it means to be intelligent, prudent, wise. The participle, which is the form used here (causat. of Hiph.), means *making wise or prudent,* or *conveying instruction;* and this title is given to this psalm, as well as to many others, as conveying the idea that the psalm was adapted *to make wise,* or to impart instruction; and the sense would be well expressed by our phrase, *didactic song.* The title is prefixed also to the following psalms: xlii., xliv., xlv., lii., liii., liv., lv., lxxiv., lxxxviii., lxxxix., cxlii. It would be difficult now, however, to discover from the contents of the psalms themselves why the title was affixed to these particularly rather than to many others. Probably this was determined, by those who collected and arranged the psalms, according to some rules that are not now known to us.

1. *Blessed* is he, etc. On the meaning of the word *blessed,* see Notes on Ps. i. 1. See the passage explained in the Notes on Rom. iv. 7, 8. The word *blessed* here is equivalent to *happy:*—"Happy *is* the man;" or "happy is the condition—the state of mind—happy are the prospects, of one whose sins are forgiven." His condition is happy or blessed (*a*) as compared with his former state, when he was pressed or bowed down under a sense of guilt; (*b*) in his real condition, as that of a pardoned man—a man who has nothing now to fear as the result of his guilt, or who feels that he is at peace with God; (*c*) in his hopes and prospects, as now a child of God and an heir of heaven. ¶ Whose *transgression* is *forgiven.* The word rendered *forgiven* means properly to lift up, to bear, to carry, to carry away; and sin which is forgiven is referred to here *as if* it were borne away,—perhaps as the scapegoat bore off sin into the wilderness. Comp. Ps. lxxxv. 2; Job vii. 21; Gen. l. 17; Num. xiv. 19; Isa. ii. 9. ¶ Whose *sin* is *covered.* As it were *covered over;* that is, concealed or hidden; or, in other words, so covered that it will not appear. This is the idea in the Hebrew word which is commonly used to denote the atonement,—כָּפַר, *kaphar,*—meaning *to cover over;* then, to overlook, to forgive; Gen. vi. 14; Ps. lxv. 3; lxxviii. 38; Dan. ix. 24. The original word here, however, is different — כָּסָה, *kasah*—though meaning the same,—*to cover.* The idea is, that the sin would be, as it were, covered over, hidden, concealed, so that it would no

2 Blessed *is* the man unto whom the LORD imputeth [k] not iniquity, and in whose spirit *there is* no guile.

3 When I kept silence, my bones waxed old through my roaring all the day long.

k 2 Cor. v. 19.

longer come into the view of either God or man; that is, the offender would be regarded and treated *as if* he had not sinned, or *as if* he had no sin.

2. *Blessed* is *the man unto whom the* LORD *imputeth not iniquity.* Whose sin is not *reckoned* to him, or *charged* on him. The reference here is *to his own sin.* The idea is not, that he is happy on whom God does not charge the guilt of other men, but that he is happy who is not charged *with his own guilt,* or who is treated *as if* he had no guilt; that is, as if he were innocent. This is the true idea of justification. It is, that a man, although he *is* a sinner, and *is conscious* of having violated the law of God, is treated *as if* he had not committed sin, or as if he were innocent; that is, he is pardoned, and his sins are remembered against him no more; and it is the purpose of God to treat him henceforward as if he were innocent. The act of pardon does not change the *facts* in the case, or *make him innocent,* but it makes it proper for God to treat him *as if* he were innocent. The sin will not be re-charged upon him, or reckoned to his account; but he is admitted to the same kind of treatment to which he would be entitled if he had always been perfectly holy. See Notes on Rom. i. 17; iii. 24; iv. 5; v. 1. ¶ *And in whose spirit* there is *no guile.* Who are sincere and true. That is, who are not hypocrites; who are conscious of no desire to cover up or to conceal their offences; who make a frank and full confession to God, imploring pardon. The *guile* here refers to the matter under consideration. The idea is not who are *innocent,* or *without guilt,* but who are sincere, frank, and honest in making *confession* of their sins; who keep nothing back when they go before God. We cannot go before him and plead our innocence, but we may go before him with the feeling of conscious sincerity and honesty in making confession of our guilt. Comp. Ps. lxvi. 18.

3. *When I kept silence.* The psalmist now proceeds to state his condition of mind *before* he himself found this peace, or before he had this evidence of pardon; the state in which he felt deeply that he was a sinner, yet was unwilling to confess his sin, and attempted to conceal it in his own heart. This he refers to by the expression, "When I kept silence;" that is, before I confessed my sin, or before I made mention of it to God. The condition of mind was evidently this:—he had committed sin, but he endeavoured to hide it in his own mind; he was unwilling to make confession of it, and to implore pardon. He hoped, probably, that the conviction of sin would die away; or that his trouble would cease of itself; or that time would relieve him; or that employment—occupying himself in the affairs of the world—would soothe the anguish of his spirit, and render it unnecessary for him to make a humiliating confession of his guilt. He thus describes a state of mind which is very common in the case of sinners. They know that they *are* sinners, but they are unwilling to make confession of their guilt. They attempt to conceal it. They put off, or try to remove far away, the whole subject. They endeavour to divert their minds, and to turn their thoughts from a subject so painful as the idea of guilt—by occupation, or by amusement, or even by plunging into scenes of dissipation. Sometimes, often in fact, they are successful in this; but, sometimes, as in the case of the psalmist, the trouble at the remembrance of sins becomes deeper and deeper, destroying their rest, and wasting their strength, until they make humble confession, and *then* the mind finds rest. ¶ *My bones waxed old.* My strength

4 For day and night thy hand was heavy upon me: my moisture is turned into the drought of summer. Selah.

5 I acknowledged my sin unto thee, and mine iniquity have I not hid. I said, I [l] will confess

l 1 John i. 9.

failed; my strength was exhausted; it seemed as if the decrepitude of age was coming upon me. The word here used, and rendered *waxed old,* would properly denote *decay,* or the wearing out of the strength by slow decay. All have witnessed the prostrating effect of excessive grief. ¶ *Through my roaring.* My cries of anguish and distress. See Notes on Ps. xxii. 1. The meaning here is, that his sorrow was so great as to lead to loud and passionate cries; and this well describes the condition of a mind under deep trouble at the remembrance of sin and the apprehension of the wrath of God. ¶ *All the day long.* Continually; without intermission.

4. *For day and night.* I found no relief even at night. The burden was constant, and was insupportable. ¶ *Thy hand was heavy upon me.* Thy hand seemed to press me down. It weighed upon me. See Job xiii. 21; Ps. xxxix. 10. It was the remembrance of guilt that troubled him, but that seemed to him to be the hand of God. It was God who brought that guilt to his recollection; and God *kept* the recollection of it before his mind, and on his heart and conscience, so that he could not throw it off. ¶ *My moisture.* The word here used —לְשַׁד, *leshad*—means properly *juice* or *sap,* as in a tree; and then, *vital-moisture,* or, as we should say, *life-blood.* Then it comes to denote vigour or strength. ¶ *Is turned into the drought of summer.* Is, as it were, all dried up. I am—that is, I was at the time referred to—like plants in the heat of summer, in a time of drought, when all moisture of rain or dew is withheld, and when they dry up and wither. Nothing could more strikingly represent the distress of mind under long-continued conviction of sin, when all strength and vigour seem to waste away.

5. *I acknowledged my sin unto thee.* That is, I *then* confessed my guilt. I had borne the dreadful pressure as long as I could. I had endeavoured to conceal and suppress my conviction, but I found *no* relief. The anguish became deeper and deeper; my strength was failing; I was crushed under the intolerable burden, and when I could no longer bear it I went and made humble confession, and found relief. The verb here used is in the future tense, "I *will* acknowledge my sin;" but in order to a correct understanding of it, it should be regarded as referring to the state of mind *at the time* referred to in the psalm, and the resolution which the psalmist *then* formed. The words "I *said*" should be understood here. This he expresses in a subsequent part of the verse, referring doubtless to the same time. "I said," or I formed a resolution to this effect. The idea is, that he could find no relief in any other way. He could not banish these serious and troublous thoughts from his mind; his days and nights were spent in anguish. He resolved to go to God and to confess his sin, and to see what relief could be found by such an acknowledgment of guilt. ¶ *And mine iniquity have I not hid.* That is, I did not attempt *then* to hide it. I made a frank, a full confession. I stated it all, without any attempt to conceal it; to apologise for it; to defend it. *Before,* he had endeavoured to conceal it, and it was crushing him to the earth. He now resolved to confess it all, and he found relief. ¶ *I said.* I formed the resolution. ¶ *I will confess my transgressions unto the* LORD. I will no longer attempt to hide them, or to suppress the convictions of guilt. I will seek the only proper relief by making confession of my sin, and by obtaining forgiveness. This resolu-

my transgressions unto the LORD; and thou forgavest the iniquity of my sin. Selah.

6 For [m] this shall every one that is godly pray unto thee in a time [1] when thou mayest be [n] found: surely in the floods of great waters [o] they shall not come nigh unto him.

m 1 Tim. i. 16. 1 *of finding.* n Isa. lv. 6. o Isa. xliii. 2.

tion was substantially the same as that of the prodigal son: "I will arise and go to my father, and will say unto him, Father, I have sinned," Luke xv. 18. ¶ *And thou forgavest the iniquity of my sin.* He found that God was willing to pardon; he no sooner made confession than he obtained the evidence of pardon. All the *guilt,* or the "*iniquity*" of his sin, was at once forgiven; and, as a consequence, he found peace. In what way he *had* evidence that his sin was forgiven he does not state. It *may* have been in his case by direct revelation, but it is more probable that he obtained this evidence in the same way that sinners do now, by the internal peace and joy which follows such an act of penitent confession. In regard to this, we may observe,—(*a*) the very act of making confession tends to give relief to the mind; and, in fact, relief never can be found when confession is not made. (*b*) We have the assurance that when confession *is* made in a proper manner, God *will* pardon. See Notes on 1 John i. 9. (*c*) When such confession is made, peace will flow into the soul; God will show himself merciful and gracious. The peace which follows from a *true* confession of guilt before God, proves that God *has* heard the prayer of the penitent, and *has* been merciful in forgiving his offences. Thus, without any miracle, or any direct revelation, we may obtain evidence that our sins are washed away, which will give comfort to the soul.

6. *For this.* With reference to this state of mind, or to this happy result; or, encouraged by my example and my success. The idea seems to be that others would find, and might find, encouragement from what had occurred to him. In other words, his case had furnished an illustration of the way in which sinners are pardoned, and a proof of the mercy of God, which would be instructive and encouraging to others in similar circumstances. The conversion of one sinner, or the fact that one sinner obtains pardon, becomes thus an encouragement to all others; for (*a*) pardon is always to be obtained in the same manner essentially,—by humble and penitent confession of sin, and by casting ourselves entirely on the offered mercy of God; and (*b*) the fact that *one* sinner has been pardoned, is full proof that others may obtain forgiveness also, for God is unchangeably the same. All those, therefore, who *have* been pardoned and saved in the world have become examples to the rest, and have furnished full proof that all others *may* be pardoned and saved if they will come in the same manner. See Notes on 1 Tim. i. 16. ¶ *Every one that is godly.* The original word here used would properly mean those who are pious, or who are already converted. It is the common word used in the Scriptures to denote *saints,* and is usually so translated. But, as used here, it would seem rather to denote those who are *inclined* to be pious, or who are seeking how they may become pious; in other words, those who are *religiously disposed.* The encouragement is to those who feel that they are sinners; who desire some way of relief from the burden of sin; who are convinced that there is no other source of relief but God, and who are disposed to make the same trial which the psalmist did,—to find peace by making confession of sin. All such persons, the psalmist says, might see in his case encouragement to come thus to God; all such would find him willing to pardon. ¶ *In a time when thou mayest be found.* Marg., as in

7 Thou [p] *art* my hiding-place;
thou shalt preserve me from
trouble; thou shalt compass me
about with songs [q] of deliverance.
Selah.

p Ps. cxliii. 9.

8 I will instruct thee, [r] and
teach thee in the way which thou
shalt go: I will [1] guide thee with
mine eye.

q Ex. xv. 1, etc.; Rev. xv. 2, 3.
1 *counsel* thee, *mine eye* shall be *upon thee.*

Heb., *in a time of finding.* That is, they would find *that* to be a propitious time, or a time of mercy. It does not mean that there were appointed or set times in which God would be gracious; or that there were seasons when he was disposed to *give audience* to men, and seasons when he *could not* be approached; but the meaning is, that whenever they came thus—with this penitent feeling, and this language of confession — they would find *that* the time of mercy. The idea is not that God is any more disposed to show mercy at one time than another, but that they would find him *always* ready to show mercy when they came in that manner:—*that* would be the time to obtain his favour; *that* "the time of finding." The real time of *mercy*, therefore, for a sinner, is the time when he is willing to come as a penitent, and to make confession of sin. ¶ *Surely in the floods of great waters.* In times of calamity —as when floods of water spread over a land; or in a time of judgment— when such floods sweep everything away. The reference here is, doubtless, to the floods that will come upon the ungodly—upon a wicked world. The illustration is drawn probably from the deluge in the time of Noah. So, when God shall sweep away the wicked in his wrath,—when he shall consign them to destruction in the day of judgment,—the pardoned sinner will be safe. ¶ *They shall not come nigh unto him.* He will be secure. He shall not be swept off with others. Safe, as a forgiven man, — safe as a child and a friend of God,— he shall be protected as Noah was in the great deluge that swept off a guilty world. A pardoned man has nothing to fear, though flood or fire should sweep over the world.

7. *Thou* art *my hiding-place.* See Notes on Ps. ix. 9; xxvii. 5. The idea is that he would be safe under the protection of God. The general allusion is to concealment from an enemy, but the immediate reference is to sin, and the consequences of sin. By fleeing to God he would be secure against all the evils which sin brings upon men. ¶ *Thou shalt preserve me from trouble.* Particularly the trouble which comes from guilt;— sadness and sorrow in the remembrance of sin; apprehension of the wrath of God in the world to come; the consequences of guilt in that unseen and eternal world. ¶ *Thou shalt compass me about with songs of deliverance.* With songs expressive of deliverance or salvation. It is not merely one song or a single expression of gratitude; — in his pathway to another world he will be attended with songs and rejoicings; he will seem to be surrounded with songs. He himself will sing. Others, redeemed like him, will sing, and will seem to chant praises because *he* is redeemed and forgiven. All nature will seem to rejoice over his redemption. Nature is full of songs. The birds of the air; the wind; the running stream; the ocean; the seasons —spring, summer, autumn, winter; hills, valleys, groves,—all, to one redeemed, *seem* to be full of songs. The feeling that we are pardoned fills the universe with melody, and makes the heaven and the earth seem to us to be glad. The Christian is a happy man; and he himself being happy, all around him sympathizes with him in his joy.

8. *I will instruct thee.* Many interpreters have understood this to refer to God,—as if he were now introduced as speaking, and as saying that he would be the guide of those who thus submitted to him, and who sought him by penitence and confes-

9 Be ye not as the horse, [r] *or* as the mule, *which* have no understanding; whose mouth must be held in with [s] bit and bridle, lest they come near unto thee.

r Prov. xxvi. 3.

s James iii. 3.

sion. But it is more natural to regard the psalmist as still speaking, and referring to his own experience as qualifying him to give counsel to others, showing them how *they* might find peace, and with what views and feelings they should come before God if they wished to secure his favour. He had himself learned by painful experience, and after much delay, how the favour of God was to be obtained, and how deliverance from the distressing consciousness of guilt was to be secured; and he regards himself as now qualified to teach others who are borne down with the same consciousness of guilt, and who are seeking deliverance, how they may find peace. It is an instance of one who, by personal experience, is fitted to give instruction to others; and the psalmist, in what follows, does merely what every converted man is qualified to do, and should do, by imparting valuable knowledge to those who are inquiring how they must be saved. Comp. Ps. li. 12, 13. ¶ *And teach thee in the way which thou shalt go.* The way which you are to take to find pardon and peace; or, the way to God. ¶ I *will guide thee with mine eye.* Marg., *I will counsel* thee, *mine eye* shall be *upon thee.* The margin expresses the sense of the Hebrew. The literal *meaning* is, "I will counsel thee; mine eye shall be upon thee." De Wette, "my eye shall be directed towards thee." The *idea* is that of one who is telling another what way he is to take in order that he may reach a certain place; and he says he will watch him, or will keep an eye upon him; he will not let him go wrong.

9. *Be ye not as the horse.* The horse as it is by nature—wild, ungoverned, unwilling to be caught and made obedient. The counsel referred to in the previous verse is here given; and it is, that one who wishes to obtain the favour of God should not be as the wild and unbroken horse, an animal that can be subdued only by a curb, but should evince a calm, submissive spirit—a spirit *disposed* to obey and submit. If he becomes a subject of God's government, he is not to be subdued and held as the horse is —by mere force; there must be the cheerful submission of the will. Men are not brought into the service of God by physical power; they are not kept there by an iron *curb.* They come and yield themselves willingly to his law; they *must* come with that spirit if they would find the favour of God. ¶ Or *as the mule.* The mule is distinguished for its obstinacy, and this is evidently the ground of comparison here. The meaning is, be tractable, gentle, yielding; submit to the guidance and direction of God and his truth. ¶ Which *have no understanding.* That cannot be controlled by reason and conscience. They are governed only by power and by fear. Men have reason and conscience, and they should allow themselves to be controlled by appeals *to* their reason and to their moral sense. They are not made to be governed as brutes are. As they *have* a higher nature, they should permit themselves to be governed by it. ¶ *Whose mouth must be held in with bit and bridle.* More literally, "in bit and bridle is their ornament to restrain them;" that is, the trappings or the ornaments of the horse and the mule consist of the bridle and the bit, the purpose of which is to restrain or control them. The allusion, however, is not to the bit and bridle *as* an "*ornament,*" but as the ordinary trappings of the mule and the horse. ¶ *Lest they come near unto thee.* Or rather, "because of its not approaching thee;" that is, because the horse and the mule will not come to thee of their own accord, but must be restrained and controlled.

10 Many [s] sorrows *shall be* to the wicked: but he [t] that trusteth in the LORD, mercy shall compass him about.

s Ps. xvi. 4; 1 Tim. vi. 10.

11 Be glad in the LORD, and rejoice, ye righteous: and shout for joy, all *ye that are* upright in heart.

t Jer. xvii. 7, 8.

10. *Many sorrows* shall be *to the wicked.* The meaning here is, probably, that those who will *not* submit themselves to God in the manner which the psalmist recommends; who *are* like the horse and the mule, needing to be restrained, and who are to be restrained only by force, will experience bitter sorrows. The psalmist may refer here, in part, to sorrows such as he says he himself experienced when he attempted to suppress the convictions of guilt (vers. 3, 4); and partly to the punishment that will come upon the impenitent sinner for his sins. The sorrows referred to are probably both internal and external; those arising from remorse, and those which will be brought upon the guilty as a direct punishment. ¶ *But he that trusteth in the* LORD. He that has faith in God; he that so confides in him that he goes to him with the language of sincere confession. ¶ *Mercy shall compass him about.* Shall surround him; shall attend him; shall be on every side of him. It shall not be only in one respect, but in all respects. He shall be *surrounded* with mercy—as one is surrounded by the air, or by the sunlight. He shall find mercy and favour everywhere,—at home, abroad; by day, by night; in society, in solitude; in sickness, in health; in life, in death; in time, in eternity. He shall walk amidst mercies; he shall die amidst mercies; he shall live in a better world in the midst of eternal mercies.

11. *Be glad in the* LORD. Rejoice in the Lord. Rejoice that there is a God; rejoice that he is such as he is; rejoice in his favour; find your joy—your supreme joy—in him. Comp. Notes on Phil. iii. 1; iv. 4. ¶ *Ye righteous.* You who are willing to go to him and confess your sins; you who are willing to serve and obey him. See Notes on ver. 6. The meaning is, that those who are disposed to confess their sins, and are willing to submit to him without being compelled by force, as the horse and the mule are, will find occasion for rejoicing. They will find a God who is worthy of their love, and they will find true happiness in him. ¶ *And shout for joy.* Give expression to your joy. Let it not remain merely in the heart; but give it utterance in the language of song. If any of the dwellers on earth have occasion for the loud utterances of praise, they are those who are redeemed; whose sins are forgiven; who have the hope of heaven. If there is any occasion when the heart should be full of joy, and when the lips should give forth loud utterances of praise, it is when one pressed down with the consciousness of guilt, and overwhelmed with the apprehensions of wrath, makes confession to God, and secures the hope of heaven. ¶ *All* ye that are *upright in heart.* That is, who are sincere in your confession of sin, and in your desires to secure the favour of God. Such have occasion for joy, for to such God will show himself merciful, as He did to the psalmist when *he* made confession of sin; to such God will give the tokens of his favour, and the hope of heaven, as he did to *him.* The experience of the psalmist, therefore, as recorded in this psalm, should be full of encouragement to all who are burdened with a sense of sin. Warned by his experience, they should not attempt to conceal their transgressions in their own bosom, but they should go at once, as he was constrained at last to go, and make full and free confession to God. So doing, they will find that God is not slow to pardon them, and to fill their hearts with peace, and their lips with praise.

PSALM XXXIII.

REJOICE [u] in the LORD, O ye righteous: *for* praise is comely for the upright.

2 Praise the LORD with harp: sing unto him with the [v] psaltery *and* an instrument of ten strings.

u Ps. xcvii. 12 Phil. iv. 4.
v Ps. cl. 3, 4.

PSALM XXXIII.

This psalm has no title prefixed to it, and it is not possible to determine with certainty who was the author, or on what occasion it was written. There is nothing in the psalm that has any special allusion to David, nor is there reference to any circumstances which would enable us to determine when it was composed. It has, indeed, no particular allusion to the Jewish religion, or to the prevailing mode of worship in that land, and is, in fact, so *general* in its sentiments and in its descriptions, that it might have been written at any period of the Jewish history, or even in any land. As it is found *among* the Psalms of David, and is between psalms which are both ascribed to David, we may presume that it was believed to have been composed by him; and there is nothing in it that is at variance with that belief. It is really but a carrying out of the sentiment with which the preceding psalm closes; and it has been conjectured that the intimate relation of the two psalms may have been the reason why the title to the latter of them was omitted.

The psalm properly consists of three parts:—I. an exhortation to praise God; II. reasons why he should be praised; and III. the expression of a purpose thus to praise him.

I. An exhortation to praise God, vers. 1-3. In this there is a call on the righteous to praise him with songs and with musical instruments,—the harp, the psaltery, the instrument of ten strings;—a call to make use of the best powers of music in all its varied forms in his service.

II. Reasons for thus praising him, vers. 4-19.

(1) His general character for goodness and truth, vers. 4, 5.

(2) The fact that he made the universe;—or, the wisdom and power displayed by him in creation, vers. 6-9.

(3) The stability of his counsel or purposes, vers. 10, 11.

(4) The blessings which he bestows upon those who acknowledge him to be their God—blessings of care, protection, and deliverance in danger, vers. 12-19.

III. The purpose of the writer, and of those who were associated with him, thus to praise God, vers. 20-22.

The psalm is thus one that is appropriate to the people of all lands and times, and will be better appreciated in proportion as men become more and more acquainted with God in the wisdom, the power, and the skill which he has shown in the works of creation, and in his providential government of the world.

1. *Rejoice in the* LORD, *O ye righteous.* This is the sentiment with which the preceding psalm closes. See Notes on Ps. xxxii. 11. ¶ *For praise is comely for the upright.* Is befitting, suitable, proper. That is, the upright—the righteous—have abundant cause for praise, and it is for them a suitable employment, or one which becomes them. A man who *is* upright, or who *is* a righteous man, has in this very fact much which lays a foundation for praise, for the fact that he has such a character is to be traced to the grace of God, and this in itself is a more valuable possession than gold or kingly crowns would be. That he is not an open violator of the law of God; that he is not intemperate; that he is not the victim of raging lusts and passions; that he is not a dishonest man; that he is not profane; that he is not an infidel or a scoffer;—that he *is* a pious man,—a redeemed man,—a man of good character,—an heir of heaven,—is *the* highest blessing that could be conferred on him; and he who has been saved from outbreaking transgression and crime in a world like this, and has been enabled to live an upright life, has eminently occasion to praise and bless God. Assuredly for such a man praise is an appropriate employment; for such a man it is "comely."

2. *Praise the* LORD *with harp.* For a description of the *harp*, see Notes on Isa. v. 12. ¶ *Sing unto him with*

3 Sing[w] unto him a new song;
play skilfully with a loud noise.
4 For the word of the LORD *is*
right; and all his works *are done*
in truth.
5 He loveth righteousness and
judgment: the earth is full[x] of
the [1] goodness of the LORD.

w Ps. cxliv. 9; Rev. v. 9.

x Ps. cxix. 64. [1] Or, *mercy*.

the psaltery. For the meaning of this word, also, see Notes on Isa. v. 12, where the word is rendered *viol.* ¶ And *an instrument of ten strings.* The word "*and*" is supplied here by the translators as if, in this place, a third instrument was referred to, distinct from the harp and the psaltery. The more correct rendering, however, would be, "a psaltery (or lyre) of ten strings." The same construction occurs in Ps. cxliv. 9. In Ps. xcii. 3, however, the two words are separately used as denoting different instruments. The *lyre* or psaltery was probably not always made with the same number of strings, and it would seem that the one that was made of *ten* strings had something peculiar about it as an instrument of uncommon sweetness or power. Hence it is particularly designated here; and the idea is that the instruments of especial power and sweetness should be on this occasion employed in the service of God.

3. *Sing unto him a new song.* A song specially composed for this occasion; expressive of the peculiar feelings suggested by this occasion, or appropriate to this new manifestation of the Divine goodness and mercy. Such occasions, exhibiting some new phase of the Divine goodness, demanded new language appropriate to them. So now, new hymns of praise, and new tunes in music, are demanded to meet the ever-varying manifestations of the mercy of God; and as the church is extended in the world, its modes of praise must be adapted to the new state of things which will arise. Nothing could be more absurd than to attempt to restrict the church in its praises to the exact words which were used in the time of David, or to the music which was employed then. Comp. Notes on Rev. v. 9. The expression "*new song*" occurs several times in the Psalms, showing that new hymns of praise were composed as adapted to some new manifestation of the goodness of God: Ps. xl. 3; xcvi. 1; xcviii. 1; cxliv. 9; cxlix. 1. Compare also Isa. xlii. 10. ¶ *Play skilfully with a loud noise.* Literally, *Do well to play;* or, *do well in playing.* That is, do the work well, or with all the skill of music. The word rendered *loud noise,* means properly *a shout of joy* or rejoicing: Job viii. 21; 1 Sam. iv. 5. It is especially applied to the sound or clangour of trumpets: Lev. xxv. 9; xxiii. 24; Num. xxix. 1. There is rather the idea of *rejoicing* than of *noise* in the word. The meaning is that the music should be such as would be expressive of the highest joy.

4. *For the word of the* LORD is *right.* The command; the law; the promise of God. Whatever he *says* is right; or, is true. It is worthy of universal belief; and should, therefore, be a reason for praise. The fact that God *says* a thing is the highest proof that it is true. ¶ *And all his works* are done *in truth.* Or rather, *in faithfulness.* That is, All that he does is executed faithfully. He does all that he promises, and all that he does is such as to claim universal confidence. Whatever he does is, from the very fact that *he* does it, worthy of the confidence of all his creatures. None, however they may be affected by what he does, have any reason to doubt that it is perfectly right. God is the only Being of whom we have any knowledge, concerning whom we can feel this certain assurance.

5. *He loveth righteousness.* See Ps. xi. 7. ¶ *And judgment.* Justice. ¶ *The earth is full of the goodness of the* LORD. Marg., *mercy.* So the Hebrew. That is, his mercy or goodness is manifest everywhere. Every

6 By [y] the word of the LORD
were the heavens made: and all
[z] the host of them by the breath
of his mouth.
7 He [a] gathereth the waters of
the sea together as an heap: he
layeth up the depth [b] in storehouses.
8 Let all the earth fear the
LORD; let all the inhabitants of
the world stand in awe of him.
9 For he spake, [d] and it was

y Heb. xi. 3. *z* Gen. ii. 1. *a* Job xxvi. 10. *b* Job xxxviii. 8—11. *c* Jer. x. 7. *d* Gen. i. 3, etc.

part of the earth bears witness that he is good.

6. *By the word of the* LORD. By the command of God: Gen. i. 3, 6, etc. See Notes on ver. 9. ¶ *Were the heavens made.* That is, the starry heavens; the worlds above us: Gen. i. 1. ¶ *And all the host of them.* All their *armies.* The stars are represented as armies or marshalled hosts, led forth at his command, and under his direction,—as armies are led forth in war. See Gen. ii. 1; comp. Notes on Isa. i. 9. ¶ *By the breath of his mouth.* By his word or command—as our words issue from our mouths with our breath. The idea here is, that God is the Creator of all things; and, as such, has a claim to praise; or, that *as* Creator he is entitled to adoration. To this he is entitled from the *fact* that he has made all things, and from the *manner* in which it has been done—the wisdom, power, goodness, skill, with which it has been accomplished.

7. *He gathereth the waters of the sea together as an heap.* The Hebrew word here rendered *gathereth* is a participle;—*gathering.* The design is to represent this as a continuous act; an act not merely of the original creation, but constantly occurring. The reference is to the power by which the waters are gathered and kept together; the continual power which prevents their overspreading the earth. The word rendered *heap*—נֵד, *Ned*—means properly a heap or *mound,* and is applied to the waves of the sea heaped up together like mounds. Comp. Josh. iii. 13, 16; Ex. xv. 8: Ps. lxxviii. 13. He collected those waters, and kept them in their places, as if they were solid matter. This denotes the absolute control which God has over the waters, and is thus a most striking illustration of his power. ¶ *He layeth up the depth in storehouses.* The abysses; the deep waters; the masses of water. He places them where he pleases; he disposes of them as the farmer his grain, or the rich man his treasures. The caverns of the ocean—the ocean-beds—are thus vast reservoirs or treasure-houses for the reception of the waters which God has chosen to deposit there. All this is proof of his amazing power, and all this lays a proper foundation for praise. Occasions for gratitude to him may be found in every world that he has made; in every object that has come from his hand; and nothing more *obviously* suggests this than his wondrous power over the waters of the ocean—collecting them, restraining them, controlling them, as he pleases.

8. *Let all the earth.* All the inhabitants of the earth. ¶ *Fear the* LORD. Worship and adore a Being of so great power. See Notes on Ps. v. 7. ¶ *Let all the inhabitants of the world.* The power displayed in the works of creation appeals to *all* alike. ¶ *Stand in awe of him.* Reverence or adore him. The expression is equivalent to *worship,*—fear or reverence entering essentially into the idea of worship.

9. *For he spake, and it was* done. The word "*done,*" introduced here by our translators, enfeebles the sentence. It would be made more expressive and sublime as it is in the original:—"He spake, and it was." That is, Its existence depended on his word; the universe sprang into being at his command; he had only to speak, and it arose in all its grandeur where before there was nothing. There is

done; he commanded, and it stood fast.

10 The Lord [1] bringeth the counsel of the heathen to nought; he [d] maketh the devices of the people of none effect.

11 The counsel [e] of the Lord standeth for ever, the thoughts of his heart to [2] all generations.

[1] *maketh frustrate.* [d] Isa. xliv. 25. [e] Isa. xlvi. 10.

[2] *generation and generation.*

here an undoubted allusion to the account in Genesis of the work of creation,—where the statement is that all depended on the command or the word of God: ch. i. 3, 6, 9, 11, 14, 20, 24, 26. Nothing more sublime can be conceived than the language thus employed in the Scriptures in describing that work. No more elevated conception can enter the human mind than that which is implied when it is said, God *spoke* and all this vast and wonderful universe rose into being. ¶ *He commanded.* He gave order; he required the universe to appear. ¶ *And it stood fast.* Or rather, *stood.* That is, it stood forth; it appeared; it rose into being. The idea of its "standing *fast*" is not in the original, and greatly enfeebles the expression.

10. *The* Lord *bringeth the counsel of the heathen to nought.* Marg., *maketh frustrate.* The Hebrew word means to *break,* or to *annul.* The word here rendered *heathen* means *nations;* and the idea is that God, by his own overruling purpose and providence, frustrates the designs of the nations of the earth; that he carries forward his own designs and purposes in spite of theirs; that their plans avail nothing when they come in competition with his. *Their* purposes must yield to *his.* Comp. Notes on Isa. viii. 9, 10; and xix. 3. All the plans and purposes of the nations of the earth that conflict with the purposes of God will be vain; all those plans, whatever they may be, will be made subservient under his Providence to the promotion of his great designs. ¶ *He maketh the devices of the people of none effect.* That is, he renders them vain, unsuccessful, ineffectual. The word *people* here is synonymous with *nations,* and the idea is, that whatever may be the thoughts and purposes of men, if they are opposed to the plans of God, or if they do not tend to promote his glory, they will be rendered futile or vain. God is a great and glorious Sovereign over all, and he will make everything subordinate to the promotion of his own great designs.

11. *The counsel of the* Lord. The purpose of the Lord. ¶ *Standeth for ever.* It will be carried out. It will never be changed. There can be no *superior* counsel or will to change it, as is the case with the plans of men; and no purposes of any beings *inferior* to himself—angels, men, or devils—can affect, defeat, or modify his eternal plans. No changes in human affairs can impede his plans; no opposition can defeat them; no progress can supersede them. ¶ *The thoughts of his heart.* The things which he has *designed,* or which he intends shall be accomplished. ¶ *To all generations.* Marg., as in Heb., *to generation and generation.* That is, from one generation of men to another; or, to all time. The plans of God are not changed by the passing off of one generation and the coming on of another; by new dynasties of kings, or by the revolutions that may occur in states and empires. Men can seldom cause *their* plans to be carried forward beyond the generation in which they live; and they can have no security that coming generations, with their own plans, will not abolish or change all that has been devised or purposed before. No man can make it certain that his own will, even in regard to *property,* will be carried out in the generation that succeeds him. No monarch can make it certain that his plans will be perfected by his successors. Schemes devised with the profoundest care and the highest wisdom may be set

12 Blessed [f] *is* the nation whose God *is* the LORD; *and* the people *whom* he hath chosen for his own inheritance.
13 The LORD looketh from heaven; he [g] beholdeth all the sons of men.
14 From the place of his habitation he looketh upon all the inhabitants of the earth.
15 He [h] fashioneth their hearts

f Ps. lxv. 4. *g* Prov. xv. 3. *h* Prov. xxii. 2.

aside by those who are next in power; and no individual can hope that coming ages will feel sufficient interest in him or his memory to carry on his plans. Who feels now any obligation to carry out the projects of Cæsar or Alexander? How long since have all their plans passed away! So it will be with all who are now playing their parts on the earth! But none of these things affect the purposes of Him who will continue to live and to carry out his own designs when all the generations of men shall have passed away.

12. *Blessed* is *the nation.* For the meaning of the word *blessed,* see Notes on Ps. i. 1. The idea here is, that the nation referred to is happy, or that its condition is desirable. What is true of a nation is also as true of an individual. ¶ *Whose God* is *the* LORD. Whose God is Jehovah,—for so this is in the original Hebrew. That is, the nation which worships Jehovah, and is under his protection. This is evidently said to distinguish such a nation from those which worshipped false gods or idols. Such a nation is blessed or happy, because (*a*) he is a *real* God, the true God, and not an imagination or fiction; (*b*) because his laws are just and good, and their observance will always tend to promote the public welfare and prosperity; (*c*) because his protection will be vouchsafed to such a nation; and (*d*) because his worship, and the influence of his religion, will tend to diffuse virtue, intelligence, purity, and truth, over a land, and thus will promote its welfare. ¶ And *the people* whom *he hath chosen for his own inheritance.* Chosen to be *his;* or, his portion. The primary reference here is undoubtedly to the Hebrew people, called his *inheritance:* Deut. iv. 20; ix. 26; xxxii. 9; Ps. lxxiv. 2; lxxviii. 62, 71; or *heritage,* Ps. xciv. 5; Jer. xii. 7, 9; but what is here affirmed of that people is true also of all other people who worship the true God.

13. *The* LORD *looketh from heaven.* Heaven is represented as his abode or dwelling; and from that place he is represented as looking down upon all the nations of the earth. The meaning here is, that he sees all that dwell upon the earth, and that therefore all that worship him are under his eye. He knows their wants, and he will watch over them to protect them. It is not merely to the abstract truth that God *sees* all who dwell upon the earth that the psalmist means to refer; but that those who are his friends, or who worship him, are all under his eye, so as to enjoy his watchful care and attention. ¶ *He beholdeth all the sons of men.* All the descendants of *Adam,*—for this is the original. There is no improbability in supposing that the word *Adam* here (usually meaning *man*) is employed as a proper name to denote the great ancestor of the human race, and that the psalmist means to refer to the race *as* one great family descended from a common ancestor, though scattered abroad over the face of the world.

14. *From the place of his habitation.* From his dwelling,—heaven. ¶ *He looketh down.* He continually sees. The sentiment is repeated here to show that no one can escape his eye; that the condition, the characters, the wants of all are intimately known to him, and that thus he *can* watch over his people—all that love and serve him—and *can* guard them from danger. See vers. 18, 19.

15. *He fashioneth their hearts*

alike; he considereth all their works.
16 There [i] is no king saved by the multitude of an host: a mighty man is not delivered by much strength.
17 An horse [k] *is* a vain thing for safety: neither shall he deliver *any* by his great strength.
18 Behold, the eye [l] of the LORD *is* upon them that fear

i Ps. xliv. 3—7.
k Prov. xxi. 31; Hos. xiv. 3.
l 1 Pet. iii. 12.

alike. That is, one as well as another; or, one as really as another. No one is exempt from his control, or from all that is implied in the word *fashioneth.* The meaning is not that their hearts are made to *resemble* each other, or to be *like* each other, whether in goodness or in wickedness,—but that all alike *are* made by him. The idea in the word "*fashioneth*" here is not that of *creating*, in the sense that He *makes* the heart by his own power what it is, whether good or bad;—but that, as he has *formed* the hearts of all men, he must see what is *in* the heart, or must behold all the purposes and thoughts of men. The Maker of the human heart must understand what is in it; and therefore He must have a clear understanding of the purposes and designs of men. This idea is carried out in the latter member of the sentence, "he *considereth* all their works," and is substantially the same as in the expression (Ps. xciv. 9), "He that planted the ear, shall he not hear? He that formed the eye, shall he not see?" ¶ *He considereth all their works.* He understands all that they do; he marks, or attends to, all that is done by them. The purpose here is to state the universal sovereignty of God. He made all things; he presides over all things; he sees all things; he is the source of safety and protection to all.

16. *There is no king saved by the multitude of an host.* By the number of his armies. His safety, however numerous and mighty may be his forces, is in God alone. He is the great Protector, whatever means men may use to defend themselves. The most numerous and the best organized armies cannot secure a victory. It is, after all, wholly in the hands of God. A wasting sickness in a camp may defeat all the plans of war; or success in battle may depend on contingencies which no commander could anticipate or provide against. A mutiny in a camp, or a panic on the battle-field, may disconcert the best-laid schemes; or forces may come against an army that were unexpected; or storm and tempest may disarrange and frustrate the entire plan of the campaign. See Eccl. ix. 11. ¶ *A mighty man.* A strong man; a giant,—as Goliath of Gath. *Strength* is not the only thing necessary to secure a victory. ¶ *Is not delivered by much strength.* By the mere fact that he is strong. Other things are needed to ensure success; and God has power so to arrange events that mere strength shall be of no avail.

17. *An horse.* The reference here is undoubtedly to the war-horse. See Notes on Ps. xx. 7. ¶ Is *a vain thing.* Literally, is a *lie.* That is, he cannot be confided in. ¶ *For safety.* For securing safety in battle. He is liable to be stricken down, or to become wild and furious so as to be beyond the control of his rider; and however strong or fleet he may be, or however well he may be "broken," yet none of these things make it certain that the rider will be safe. *God* is the only being in whom perfect confidence can be reposed. ¶ *Neither shall he deliver* any *by his great strength.* Safety cannot be found in his mere *strength*, however great that may be. These illustrations are all designed to lead the mind to the great idea that safety is to be found in God alone, vers. 18, 19.

18. *Behold, the eye of the* LORD is *upon them that fear him.* He watches over them, and *he* guards

him, upon them that hope in his mercy;
19 To deliver their soul from death, and to keep them alive in [m] famine.
20 Our [n] soul waiteth for the LORD; he *is* our help and our shield.
21 For [o] our heart shall rejoice in him, because [p] we have trusted in his holy name.
22 Let thy mercy, O LORD, be upon us according as we hope in thee.

m Ps. xxxvii. 19. n Ps. cxv. 9—11. o Zec. x. 7; John xvi. 22. p Isa xxv. 9.

them from danger. His eye is, in fact, upon all men; but it is directed with special attention to those who fear him and trust in him. Their security is in the fact that the eye of God is upon them; that he knows their wants; that he sees their dangers; that he has ample ability to deliver and save them. ¶ *Upon them that hope in his mercy.* Upon the pious; upon his friends. The expression is a very beautiful one. It describes the true state of a pious heart; it in fact characterises the whole of religion, for we imply all that there is in religion on earth when we say of a man, that—conscious of his weakness and sinfulness—*he hopes in the mercy of God.*

19. *To deliver their soul from death.* To preserve their *lives,*—for so the word *soul* is to be understood here. The meaning is, to keep them alive. That is, God is their protector; he guards and defends them when in danger. ¶ *And to keep them alive in famine.* In times of want. Comp. Job v. 20. He can provide for them when the harvests fail. Famine was one of the evils to which the inhabitants of Palestine, and of Oriental countries generally, were particularly exposed, and it is often referred to in the Scriptures.

20. *Our soul waiteth for the* LORD. This and the subsequent verses to the end of the psalm refer to the people of God, expressing their faith in him in view of the considerations suggested in the former part of the psalm. The language is expressive of the general character of piety. True piety leads men to wait on the Lord; to depend on him; to look to his interposition in danger, sickness, poverty, want; to rely on him for all that is hoped for in this life, and for salvation in the life to come. Comp. Ps. lxii. 1; xxv. 3. ¶ *He is our help.* Our aid; our helper. Comp. Ps. x. 14; xxii. 11; xxx. 10. ¶ *And our shield.* See Notes on Ps. v. 12. That is, he will defend us from our enemies, *as if* he threw his shield between us and them.

21. *For our heart shall rejoice in him.* See Notes on Ps. xiii. 5. ¶ *Because we have trusted in his holy name.* In *him,*—the *name* often being put for the person himself. See Notes on Ps. xx. 1. The idea is (*a*) that the fact of our having put our trust in God is in itself an occasion of joy or rejoicing; (*b*) that the result will be joy, for we shall never be disappointed. It will always, and in all circumstances, be a source of joy to any one that he *has* put his trust in the name of God.

22. *Let thy mercy, O* LORD, *be upon us.* Let us find or obtain thy mercy or thy favour. ¶ *According as we hope in thee.* It may be remarked in regard to this,—(*a*) it is but *reasonable* that we should look for the favour of God *only* as we trust in him, for we could not with propriety expect his favour beyond the measure of our confidence in him. (*b*) This may be regarded as the *most* that we are entitled to hope from God. We have no reason to suppose that he will go *beyond* our wishes and prayers, or that he will confer favours on us which we neither expect nor desire. (*c*) One of the reasons why the people of God are no *more* blessed, or why they receive no *more* favours from him, may be found in what is here suggested. As they expect little,

they obtain little; as they have no intense, burning, lofty desire for the favour of God, either for themselves personally, or for their families, or for the world, so they obtain but slight tokens of that favour. (*d*) The true principle, therefore, on which God is willing to bestow his favours, and which will be the rule that he will observe, is, that if men desire much, they will obtain much; that if they have large expectations, they will not be disappointed; and that God is willing to bestow his mercies on his people and on the world to the utmost of their desires and hopes. Comp. Ps. lxxxi. 10, "Open thy mouth wide, and I will fill it." Ps. xxxvii. 4, "Delight thyself in the Lord, and he shall give thee the desires of thy heart." How intense and fervent, then, should be the prayers and the petitions of the people of God! How earnest the supplications of sinners that God would have mercy on them!

PSALM XXXIV.

This psalm purports, by its title, to have been written by David, and there is no reason to call in question the correctness of the inscription. It is not probable that the title was given to the psalm by the author himself; but, like the other inscriptions which have occurred in many of the previous psalms, it is in the Hebrew, and was doubtless prefixed by him who made a collection of the Psalms, and expresses the current belief of the time in regard to its author. There is nothing in the psalm that is inconsistent with the supposition that David was the author, or that is incompatible with the circumstances of the occasion on which it is said to have been composed.

That occasion is said to have been when David "changed his behaviour before Abimelech." The circumstance here referred to is, undoubtedly, that which is described in 1 Sam. xxi. 10-15. David, for fear of Saul, fled to Gath, and put himself under the protection of Achish (or Abimelech), the king of Gath. It soon became known who the stranger was. The fame of David had reached Gath, and a public reference was made to him by the "servants of Achish," and to the manner in which his deeds had been celebrated among the Hebrews: "Did they not sing one to another of him in dances, saying, Saul hath slain his thousands, and David his ten thousands?" 1 Sam. xxi. 11. David was apprehensive that he might be betrayed, and be delivered up by Achish to Saul, and he resorted to the device of feigning himself mad, supposing that this would be a protection; that either from pity Achish would shelter him; or, that as he would thus be considered harmless, Saul would regard it needless to secure him. He, therefore, acted like a madman, or like an idiot. He "scrabbled on the doors of the gate, and let his spittle fall down upon his beard." The device, though it may have saved him from being delivered up to Saul, had no other effect. Achish was unwilling to harbour a madman; and David left him, and sought a refuge in the cave of Adullam: 1 Sam. xxi. 15; xxii. 1. It is not necessary, in order to a proper understanding of the psalm, to attempt to vindicate the conduct of David in this. Perfect honesty would doubtless, in this case, as in all others, have been better in regard to the result as it is certainly better in respect to a good conscience. The question of adopting *disguises*, however, when in danger, is not one which it is always easy to determine.

It is by no means necessary to suppose that the psalm was written *at that time*, or *when* he thus "changed his behaviour." All that the language of the inscription properly expresses is, that it was with reference to that occasion, or to the danger in which he then was, or in remembrance of his feelings at the time, as he recalled them afterwards; and that it was in view of his own experience in going through that trial, and of his deliverance from that danger. In the psalm itself there is no allusion to his "change of behaviour;" and the design of David was not to celebrate that, or to vindicate that, but to celebrate the goodness of God in his deliverance as it was effected at that time. In the psalm David expresses no opinion about the measure which he adopted to secure his safety; but his heart and his lips are full of praise in view of the fact that he *was* delivered. It is, moreover, fairly implied in the inscription itself, that the psalm was composed, not at that time, but subsequently:—"A Psalm of David, when he changed his behaviour before Abimelech, *who drove him away, and he departed.*" The obvious construction of this would be that the psalm was composed *after* Abimelech had driven him away.

The *name* of the king of Gath at the time is said, in the text of the inscription or title, to have been Abimelech; in the margin, it is Achish. In 1 Sam. xxi. it is *Achish* in the text, and *Abimelech* in the margin. It is not at all improbable that he was known by both these names. His personal name was doubtless *Achish*; the hereditary name—the name by which the line of kings of Gath was known—was probably Abimelech. Thus the general, the hereditary, the family name of the kings of Egypt in early times was Pharaoh; in later times Ptolemy. In like manner the kings of Pontus had the general name of Mithridates; the Roman emperors, after the time of Julius Cæsar, were *the Cæsars*; and so, not improbably, the general name of the kings of Jerusalem may have been Adonizedek, or Melchizedek; and the name of the kings of the Amalekites, Agag. We have evidence that the general name Abimelech was given to the kings of the Philistines (Gen. xx., xxvi.) as early as the time of Abraham; and it is certainly not impossible or improbable that it became a hereditary name, like the names Pharaoh, Ptolemy, Mithridates, and Cæsar. A slight confirmation of this supposition may be derived from the signification of the name itself. It properly means *father of the king*, or *father-king;* and it might thus become a common title of the kings in Philistia. Thus, also, the term *Padisha* (Pater, Rex) is given to the kings of Persia, and the title *Atalik* (father) to the khans of Bucharia. (Gesenius, *Lex.*)

This psalm is the second of the alphabetical psalms, or the psalms in which the successive verses begin with one of the letters of the Hebrew alphabet. See introd. to Ps. xxv. The arrangement is regular in this psalm, except that the letter ו, *Vau*, is omitted, and that, to make the number of the verses equal to the letters of the Hebrew alphabet, an additional verse is appended to the end, commencing, as in the last verse of Ps. xxv., with the letter פ, *p*.

The psalm consists essentially of four parts, which, though sufficiently connected to be appropriate to the one occasion on which it was composed, are so distinct as to suggest different trains of thought.

I. An expression of thanksgiving for deliverance (vers. 1-6); concluding with the language, "This poor man cried, and the Lord heard him, and saved him out of all his troubles." From this it has been supposed, as suggested above, that the psalm was composed *after* David had left the court of Abimelech, and not *at the time* when he was feigning madness.

II. A general statement about the privilege of confiding in God, as derived from his own experience; and an exhortation to others, founded on that experience, vers. 7-10.

III. A special exhortation to the *young* to trust in the Lord, and to pursue a life of uprightness, vers. 11-14. The psalmist professes himself able to instruct them, and he shows them that the way to attain to prosperity and to length of days is to lead a life of virtue and religion. What he had himself passed through—his deliverance in the time of trial—the recollections of his former life,—all suggested this as an invaluable lesson to the young. From this it would seem not to be improbable that the psalm was written at a considerable period after what occurred to him at the court of the king of Gath, and perhaps when he was himself growing old, —yet still in view of the events at that period of his life.

IV. A general statement that God will protect the righteous; that their interests are safe in his hands; that they may confidently rely on him; that though they may be afflicted, yet God will deliver them from their afflictions, and that he will ultimately redeem them from all their troubles, vers. 15-22.

The general purport and bearing of the psalm, therefore, is to furnish an argument for trusting in God in the time of trouble, and for leading such a life that we *may* confidently trust him as our Protector and Friend.

In the title, the words "a psalm" are not in the original. The original is simply of *David*, לְדָוִד, or *by David*,—without denoting the character of the production, whether it was to be regarded as a *psalm*, or some other species of composition. ¶ *When he changed his behaviour*. The word *behaviour* does not quite express the meaning of the original word, nor describe the fact as it is related 1 Sam. xxi. The Hebrew word — טַעַם, *taam* — means properly, *taste, flavour of food;* then intellectual taste, judgment, discernment, under-

PSALM XXXIV.

A Psalm of David, when he changed his behaviour before [1] Abimelech; who drove him away, and he departed.

I WILL bless the LORD at all *q* times: his praise *shall* continually *be* in my mouth.

2 My soul shall make her boast *r* in the LORD: the *s* humble shall hear *thereof*, and be glad.

[1] Or, *Achish*, 1 Sam. xxi. 13.
q Eph. v. 20. *r* 1 Cor. i. 31. *s* Ps. cxix. 74.

standing; and in this place it would literally mean, "*he changed his understanding*;" that is, he feigned himself mad. This corresponds precisely with the statement of his conduct in 1 Sam. xxi. 13. ¶ *Before Abimelech.* Marg., *Achish.* As remarked above, this latter is the proper or personal name of the king. ¶ *Who drove him away.* See 1 Sam. xxi. 15.

1. *I will bless the* LORD. I will praise him; I will be thankful for his mercies, and will always express my sense of his goodness. ¶ *At all times.* In every situation of life; in every event that occurs. The idea is, that he would do it publicly and privately; in prosperity and in adversity; in safety and in danger; in joy and in sorrow. It would be a great principle of his life, expressive of the deep feeling of his soul, that God was *always* to be regarded as an object of adoration and praise. ¶ *His praise* shall *continually* be *in my mouth.* I will be constantly uttering his praises; or, my thanks shall be unceasing. This expresses the *purpose* of the psalmist; and this is an indication of the nature of true piety. With a truly pious man the praise of God is constant; and it is an indication of true religion when a man is *disposed* always to bless God, whatever may occur. Irreligion, unbelief, scepticism, worldliness, false philosophy, murmur and complain under the trials and amidst the dark things of life; true religion, faith, love, spirituality of mind, Christian philosophy, see in God always an object of praise. Men who have no real piety, but who make pretensions to it, are disposed to praise and bless God in times of sunshine and prosperity; true piety always regards him as worthy of praise—in the storm as well as in the sunshine; in the dark night of calamity, as well as in the bright days of prosperity. Comp. Job xiii. 15.

2. *My soul shall make her boast in the* LORD. I myself will rejoice and exult in him. The word "*boast*" here refers to that on which a man would value himself; that which would be most prominent in his mind when he endeavoured to call to remembrance what he could reflect on with most pleasure. The psalmist here says that when *he* did this, it would not be wealth or strength to which he would refer; it would not be his rank or position in society; it would not be what he had done, nor what he had gained, as pertaining to this life. His joy would spring from the fact that there *was* a God; that he was *such* a God, and that he could regard him as *his* God. This would be his chief distinction—that on which he would value himself most. Of all the things that we can possess in this world, the crowning distinction is, that we have a God, and that he is such a being as he is. ¶ *The humble shall hear* thereof. The poor; the afflicted; those who are in the lower walks of life. They should hear that *he* put his trust in God, and *they* should find joy in being thus directed to God as their portion and their hope. The psalmist seems to have referred here to that class particularly, because (*a*) they would be more likely to appreciate this than those of more elevated rank, or than those who had never known affliction; and (*b*) because this would be specially fitted to impart to them support and consolation, as derived from his own experience. *He* had been in trouble. He had been encompassed with dangers. He had been mercifully protected and delivered. He was about to state how it had been done. He was sure that they who were in the circum-

3 O magnify [t] the LORD with me, and let us exalt his name together.

4 I sought [u] the LORD, and he heard me, and delivered me from all my fears.

5 They [1] looked unto him, and were lightened; and their faces were not ashamed.

t Luke i. 46, etc.
u Luke xi. 9.

1 Or, *flowed.*

stances in which he had been would welcome the truths which he was about to state, and would rejoice that there might be deliverance for them also, and that they too might find God a protector and a friend. Calamity, danger, poverty, trial, are often of eminent advantage in preparing the mind to appreciate the nature, and to prize the lessons of religion. ¶ *And be glad.* Rejoice in the story of my deliverance, since it will lead them to see that they also may find deliverance in the day of trial.

3. *O magnify the* LORD *with me.* This seems to be addressed primarily to the "humble,"—those referred to in the previous verse. As they could appreciate what he would say, as they could understand the nature of his feelings in view of his deliverance, he calls on them especially to exult with him in the goodness of God. As he and they had common calamities and trials, so might they have common joys; as they were united in danger and sorrow, so it was proper that they should be united in joy and in praise. The word *magnify* means literally *to make great,* and then, to make great in the view of the mind, or to regard and treat as great. The idea is, that he wished all, in circumstances similar to those in which he had been placed, to have a just sense of the greatness of God, and of his claims to love and praise. Comp. Ps. xxxv. 27; xl. 17; lxix. 30; lxx. 4; Luke i. 46. ¶ *And let us exalt his name together.* Let us unite in *lifting up* his name; that is, in raising it above all other things in our own estimation, and in the view of our fellow-men; in so making it known that it shall rise above every other object, that all may see and adore.

4. *I sought the* LORD, *and he heard me.* That is, on the occasion referred to in the psalm, when he was exposed to the persecutions of Saul, and when he sought refuge in the country of Abimelech or Achish: 1 Sam. xxi. The idea is, that at that time he did not confide in his own wisdom, or trust to any devices of his own, but that he sought the protection and guidance of God, alike when he fled *to* Gath, and when he fled *from* Gath. ¶ *And delivered me from all my fears.* From all that he apprehended from Saul, and again from all that he dreaded when he found that Abimelech would not harbour him, but drove him from him.

5. *They looked unto him.* That is, they who were with the psalmist. He was not alone when he fled to Abimelech; and the meaning here is, that each one of those who were with him looked to God, and found light and comfort in Him. The psalmist seems to have had his thoughts here suddenly turned from himself to those who were with him, and to have called to his remembrance how they *all* looked to God in their troubles, and how they all found relief. ¶ *And were lightened.* Or, *enlightened.* They found light. Their faces, as we should say, *brightened up,* or they became cheerful. Their minds were made calm, for they felt assured that God would protect them. Nothing could better express what often occurs in the time of trouble, when the heart is sad, and when the countenance is sorrowful,—a dark cloud apparently having come over all things,—if one thus looks to God. The burden is removed from the heart, and the countenance becomes radiant with hope and joy. The margin here, however, is, "*They flowed* unto him." The Hebrew word, נָהַר, *nahar,* means

6 This [v] poor man cried, and the LORD heard *him*, and saved [w] him out of all his troubles.

v Ps. iii. 4. w 2 Sam. xxii. 1.

7 The angel [x] of the LORD encampeth round about them that fear him, and delivereth them.

x Heb. i. 14.

sometimes *to flow, to flow together,* Isa. ii. 2; Jer. xxxi. 12; li. 44; but it also means *to shine, to be bright;* and thence, *to be cheered, to rejoice,* Isa. lx. 5. This is probably the idea here, for this interpretation is better suited to the connexion in which the word occurs. ¶ *And their faces were not ashamed.* That is, they were not ashamed of having put their trust in God, or they were not disappointed. They had not occasion to confess that it was a vain reliance, or that they had been foolish in thus trusting him. Comp. Notes on Job vi. 20; Ps. xxii. 5; Rom. ix. 33; 1 John ii. 28. The idea here is, that they found God to be all that they expected or hoped that he would be. They had no cause to repent of what they had done. What was true of them will be true of all who put their trust in God.

6. *This poor man cried.* The psalmist here returns to his own particular experience. The emphasis here is on the word *this*: "*This* poor, afflicted, persecuted man cried." There is something much more touching in this than if he had merely said "I," or "I myself" cried. The language brings before us at once his afflicted and miserable condition. The word *poor* here—עָנִי, *ani*—does not mean "poor" in the sense of a want of wealth, but "poor" in the sense of being afflicted, crushed, forsaken, desolate. The word *miserable* would better express the idea than the word *poor.* ¶ *And the* LORD *heard* him. That is, heard in the sense of *answered.* He regarded his cry, and saved him.

7. *The angel of the* LORD. The angel whom the Lord sends, or who comes, at his command, for the purpose of protecting the people of God. This does not refer to any *particular* angel as one who was specifically called "the angel *of the Lord,*" but it may refer to any one of the angels whom the Lord may commission for this purpose; and the phrase is equivalent to saying that *angels* encompass and protect the friends of God. The word *angel* properly means a *messenger,* and then is applied to those holy beings around the throne of God who are sent forth as his *messengers* to mankind; who are appointed to communicate his will, to execute his commands; or to protect his people. Comp. Notes on Matt. xxiv. 31; Job iv. 18; Heb. i. 6; John v. 4. As the word has a general signification, and would denote in itself merely a messenger, the qualification is added here that it is an "angel *of the Lord*" that is referred to, and that becomes a protector of the people of God. ¶ *Encampeth.* Literally, *pitches his tent.* Gen. xxvi. 17; Ex. xiii. 20; xvii. 1. Then the word comes to mean *to defend; to protect:* Zech. ix. 8. The idea here is, that the angel of the Lord protects the people of God as an army defends a country, or as such an army would be a protection. He "pitches his tent" near the people of God, and is there to guard them from danger. ¶ *About them that fear him.* His true friends, friendship for God being often denoted by the word *fear* or *reverence.* See Notes on Job i. 1. ¶ *And delivereth them.* Rescues them from danger. The psalmist evidently has his own case in view, and the general remark here is founded on his own experience. He attributes his safety from danger at the time to which he is referring, not to his own art or skill; not to the valour of his own arm, or to the prowess of his followers, but to the goodness of God in sending an angel, or a company of angels, to rescue him; and hence he infers that what was true of himself would be true of others, and that the general statement might be made

8 O taste [y] and see that the
LORD *is* good: blessed [z] *is* the
man *that* trusteth in him.

y 1 Pet. ii. 3.

9 O fear the LORD, ye his
saints: for *there is* no want to
them that fear him.

z Ps. ii. 12.

which is presented in this verse. The doctrine is one that is frequently affirmed in the Scriptures. Nothing is more clearly or constantly asserted than that the angels are employed in defending the people of God; in leading and guiding them; in comforting them under trial, and sustaining them in death;—as it is also affirmed, on the other hand, that wicked angels are constantly employed in leading men to ruin. Comp. Notes on Dan. vi. 22; Heb. i. 14. See also Genesis xxxii. 1, 2; 2 Kings vi. 17; Ps. xci. 11; Luke xvi. 22; xxii. 43; John xx. 12. It may be added that no one can prove that what is here stated by the psalmist may *not* be literally true at the present time; and to *believe* that we are under the protection of angels may be as philosophical as it is pious. The most lonely, the most humble, the most obscure, and the poorest child of God, *may* have near him and around him a retinue and a defence which kings never have when their armies pitch their tents around their palaces, and when a thousand swords would at once be drawn to defend them.

8. *O taste and see.* This is an address to others, founded on the experience of the psalmist. He had found protection from the Lord; he had had evidence of his goodness; and he asks now of others that they would make the same trial which he had made. It is the language of piety in view of personal experience; and it is such language as a young convert, whose heart is filled with joy as hope first dawns on his soul, would address to his companions and friends, and to all the world around; such language as one who has had any special comfort, or who has experienced any special deliverance from temptation or from trouble, would address to others. Lessons, derived from our own experience, we may properly recommend to others; the evidence which has been furnished *us* that God is good, we may properly employ in persuading others to come and taste his love. The word *taste* here —טָעַם, *taam*—means properly to try the flavour of anything, Job xii. 11; to eat a little so as to ascertain what a thing is, 1 Sam. xiv. 24, 29, 43; Jonah iii. 7; and then to perceive by the mind, to try, to experience, Prov. xxxi. 18. It is used here in the sense of making a trial of, or testing by experience. The idea is, that by putting trust in God—by testing the comforts of religion—one would so thoroughly see or perceive the blessings of it—would have so much happiness in it—that he would be led to seek his happiness there altogether. In other words, if we could but get men to make a *trial* of religion; to enter upon it so as really to understand and experience it, we may be certain that they would have the same appreciation of it which we have, and that they would engage truly in the service of God. If those who are in danger would look to him; if sinners would believe in him; if the afflicted would seek him; if the wretched would cast their cares on him; if they who have sought in vain for happiness in the world, would seek happiness in him,—they would, one and all, so surely find what they need that they would renounce all else, and put their trust alone in God. Of this the psalmist was certain; of this all are sure who have sought for happiness in religion and in God.

"Oh make but trial of His love;
Experience will decide
How bless'd are they—and only they—
Who in His truth confide."

¶ *Blessed* is *the man* that *trusteth in him.* Comp. Notes on Ps. ii. 12.

9. *O fear the* LORD. Reverence him; honour him; confide in him. Comp. Ps. xxxi. 23. ¶ *Ye his saints.* His holy

10 The young lions do lack, and suffer hunger: but they that seek the LORD shall not want any good *thing*.

ones. All who profess to be his friends. This exhortation is addressed especially to the saints, or to the pious, because the speaker professed to be a friend of God, and had had personal experience of the truth of what he is here saying. It is the testimony of one child of God addressed to others, to encourage them by the result of his own experience. ¶ *For there is no want to them that fear him.* All their wants will be abundantly supplied. Sooner or later all their real necessities will be met, and God will bestow upon them every needed blessing. The statement here cannot be regarded as absolutely and universally true,—that is, it cannot mean that they who fear the Lord will never, in any instance, be hungry or thirsty, or destitute of raiment or of a comfortable home; but it is evidently intended to be a *general* affirmation, and is in accordance with the other statements which occur in the Bible about the advantages of true religion in securing temporal as well as spiritual blessings from God. Thus, in 1 Tim. iv. 8, it is said, "Godliness is profitable unto all things, having promise of the life that now is, and of that which is to come." Thus, in Isa. xxxiii. 16, it is said of the righteous man, "Bread shall be given him; his waters shall be sure." And so, in Ps. xxxvii. 25, David records the result of his own observation at the end of a long life, "I have been young, and now am old; yet have I not seen the righteous forsaken, nor his seed begging bread." But while these statements should not be interpreted as affirming absolutely that *no* child of God will ever be in want of food, or drink, or raiment, or home, or friends, yet it is *generally* true that the wants of the righteous are supplied, often in an unexpected manner, and from an unexpected source. It *is* true that virtue and religion conduce to temporal prosperity; and it is almost universally true that the inmates of almshouses and prisons are neither the pious, nor the children of the pious. These houses are the refuge, to a great extent, of the intemperate, the godless, and the profligate,—or of the families of the intemperate, the godless, and the profligate; and if all such persons were to be discharged from those abodes, our almshouses and prisons would soon become tenantless. A community could most easily provide for *all* those who have been trained in the ways of religion, but who are reduced to poverty by fire, or by flood, or by ill health; and they would most cheerfully do it. Nothing can be more true than that if a man wished to do all that could be done in the general uncertainty of human affairs to *secure* prosperity, it would be an advantage to him to be a virtuous and religious man. God never blesses or prospers a sinner *as such*, though he often does it *notwithstanding* the fact that he is a sinner; but he does and will bless and prosper a righteous man *as such*, and *because* he is righteous. Compare Notes on 1 Tim. iv. 8.

10. *The young lions do lack and suffer hunger.* That is, they often do it, as compared with the friends of God. The allusion is especially to the *young* lions who are not able to go forth themselves in search of food. Perhaps the idea is, that they are dependent on the older lions—their parents—for the supply of their wants, as the pious are dependent on God; but that the result shows *their* reliance to be often vain, while that of the pious never is. The old lions may be unable to procure food for their young; God is never unable to provide for the wants of his children. If their wants are in any case unsupplied, it is for some other reason than because God is *unable* to meet their necessities. The word *lack* here—רוּשׁ, *rûsh*—means to be poor; to suffer want; to be needy: Prov. xiv. 20; xviii. 23. ¶ *But they that seek*

11 Come, ye children, hearken unto me: I will teach you the fear of the LORD.

12 What [a] man *is he that* desireth life, *and* loveth *many* days, that he may see good?

a 1 Pet. iii. 10, etc.

the LORD. That seek him as their friend; that seek his favour; that seek what they need from him. To *seek God* is a phrase which is often used to denote true piety. It means that we wish to know him; that we desire his friendship; and that we seek all our blessings from him. ¶ *Shall not want any good* thing. Any real good. God is able to supply every want; and if anything is withheld, it is always certain that it is not because God could not confer it, but because he sees some good reasons why it should not be conferred. The real good; what we most need; what will most benefit us,–will be bestowed on us; and universally it may be said of all the children of God that everything in this world and the next will be granted that is *really* for their good. They themselves are often not the best judges of what will be for their good; but God is an infallible judge in this matter, and he will certainly bestow what is best for them.

11. *Come, ye children.* From persons in general (ver. 8),—from the saints and the pious (ver. 9),—the psalmist now turns to children—to the young,—that he may state to *them* the result of his own experience, and teach them from that experience how they may find happiness and prosperity. The original word here rendered *children* properly means *sons;* but there can be no doubt that the psalmist meant to address the young in general. There is no evidence that he especially designed what is here said for his own sons. The counsel seems to have been designed for *all* the young. I see no reason for supposing, as Rosenmüller, De Wette, and Professor Alexander do, that the word is here used in the sense of *disciples, scholars, learners.* That the word *may* have such a meaning, there can be no doubt; but it is much more in accordance with the scope of the psalm to regard the word as employed in its usual sense as denoting the young. It is thus a most interesting address from an aged and experienced man of God to those who are in the morning of life—suggesting to them the way by which they may make life prosperous and happy. ¶ *Hearken unto me.* Attend to what I have to say, as the fruit of my experience and observation. ¶ *I will teach you the fear of the* LORD. I will show you what constitutes the true fear of the Lord, or what is the nature of true religion. I will teach you how you may so fear and serve God as to enjoy his favour and obtain length of days upon the earth.

12. *What man* is he that *desireth life?* That desires to live long. All men naturally love life; and all naturally desire to live long; and this desire, being founded in our nature, is not wrong. Life is, in itself, a good,—a blessing to be desired; death is in itself an evil, and a thing to be dreaded, and there is nothing wrong, in itself, in such a dread. Equally proper is it to wish *not* to be cut down in early life; for where one has before him an eternity for which to prepare, he feels it undesirable that he should be cut off in the beginning of his way. The psalmist, therefore, does not put this question because he supposes that there were any who did *not* desire life, or did *not* wish to see many days, but in order to fix the attention on the inquiry, and to prepare the mind for the answer which was to follow. By thus putting the question, also, he has implicitly expressed the opinion that it *is* lawful to desire life, and to wish to see many days. ¶ And *loveth* many *days.* Literally, *loving days.* That is, who so loves days, considered as a part of life, that he wishes they may be prolonged and multiplied. ¶ *That he*

13 Keep thy tongue from evil, and thy lips from speaking guile.
14 Depart [b] from evil, and do good; seek peace, [c] and pursue it.
15 The eyes of the LORD *are* upon the righteous, and his ears *are open* unto their cry.

b 2 Tim. ii. 19.
c Matt. v. 9.

may see good. That he may enjoy prosperity, or find happiness. In other words, who is he that would desire to understand the way by which life may be lengthened out to old age, and by which it may be made happy and prosperous? The psalmist proposes to answer this question,—as he does in the following verses, by stating the results of what he had experienced and observed.

13. *Keep thy tongue from evil.* From speaking wrong things. Always give utterance to truth, and truth alone. The meaning is, that this is one of the methods of lengthening out life. To love the truth; to speak the truth; to avoid all falsehood, slander, and deceit, will contribute to this, or will be a means which will tend to prolong life, and to make it happy. ¶ *And thy lips from speaking guile.* Deceit. Do not *deceive* others by your words. Do not make any statements which are not true, or any promises which you cannot and will not keep. Do not flatter others; and do not give utterance to slander. Be a man characterised by the love of truth; and let all your words convey truth, and truth only. It cannot be doubted that this, like all other virtues, would tend to lengthen life, and to make it prosperous and peaceful. There is no vice which does not tend to abridge human life, as there is no virtue which does not tend to lengthen it. But probably the specific idea here is, that the way to avoid the enmity of other men, and to secure their favour and friendship, is to deal with them truly, and thus to live in peace with them. It is true, also, that God will bless a life of virtue and uprightness, and though there is no absolute certainty that any one, however virtuous he may be, may not be cut off in early life, yet it is also true that, other things being equal, a man of truth and integrity will be more likely to live long—(as he will be more certain to make the most of life) — than one who is false and corrupt.

14. *Depart from evil.* From all evil; from vice and crime in every form. ¶ *And do good.* Do good to all men, and in all the relations of life. ¶ *Seek peace.* Strive to live in peace with all the world. Comp. Notes on Rom. xii. 18. ¶ *And pursue it.* Follow after it. Make it an object of desire, and put forth constant efforts to live in peace with all men. There can be no doubt that this is appropriate advice to one who wishes to lengthen out his days. We have only to remember how many are cut down by indulging in a quarrelsome, litigious, and contentious spirit, —by seeking revenge,—by quarrels, duels, wars, and strife,—to see the wisdom of this counsel.

15. *The eyes of the* LORD are *upon the righteous.* This is another of the ways in which the psalmist says that life will be lengthened out, or that those who desire life may find it. The Lord will be the protector of the righteous; he will watch over and defend them. See Notes on Job xxxvi. 7. ¶ *And his ears* are open *unto their cry.* That is, when in trouble and in danger. He will hear them, and will deliver them. All this seems to be stated as the result of the experience of the psalmist himself; *he* had found that the eyes of God had been upon him in his dangers, and that His ears had been open when he called upon Him (ver. 6); and now, from his own experience, he assures others that the way to secure life and to find prosperity is to pursue such a course as will ensure the favour and protection of God. The general thought is, that virtue

16 The face [d] of the LORD *is* against them that do evil, to cut off the remembrance of them from the earth.

17 *The righteous* cry, and the LORD heareth, [e] and delivereth them out of all their troubles.

d Ezek. xiv. 7, 8. *e* Isa. lxv. 24.

and religion,—the love of truth, and the love of peace,—the favour and friendship of God, will tend to lengthen out life, and to make it prosperous and happy. All the statements in the Bible concur in this, and all the experience of man goes to confirm it.

16. *The face of the* LORD. This phrase is synonymous with that in the previous verse: "The eyes of the Lord." The meaning is, that the righteous and the wicked are alike under the eye of God; the one for protection, the other for punishment. Neither of them can escape his notice; but at all times, and in all circumstances, they are equally seen by him. ¶ Is *against them that do evil.* The wicked; all that do wrong. In the former verse the statement is, that the eyes of the Lord are "*upon*" the righteous, that is, for their protection;—in this case, by a change of the preposition in the original, the statement is, that his face is "*against*" them that do evil, that is, he observes them to bring judgment upon them. ¶ *To cut off the remembrance of them from the earth.* To cut off themselves,—their families,—and all memorials of them, so that they shall utterly be forgotten among men. Comp. Ps. cix. 13—15. So, in Prov. x. 7, it is said, "The memory of the just is blessed; but the name of the wicked shall rot." Two things are implied here: (1) That it is *desirable* to be remembered after we are dead. There is in us a deep-rooted principle, of great value to the cause of virtue, which prompts us to *desire* that we may be held in grateful recollection by mankind after we have passed away; that is, which prompts us to do something in our lives, the remembrance of which the world will not "willingly let die." *Milton.*—(2) The other idea is, that there is a state of things on earth which has a tendency to cause the remembrance of the wicked to die out, or to make men forget them. There is nothing to make men desire to retain their recollection, or to rear monuments to them. Men *are* indeed remembered who are of bad eminence in crime; but the world will forget a wicked man just as soon as it can. This is stated here as a reason particularly addressed to the young (ver. 11) why *they* should seek God, and pursue the ways of righteousness. The motive is, that men will *gladly* retain the remembrance of those who are good; of those who have done anything worthy to be remembered, but that a life of sin will make men desire to forget as soon as possible all those who practise it. This is not a low and base motive to be addressed to the young. That is a high and honourable principle which makes us wish that our names should be cherished by those who are to live after us, and is one of the original principles by which God keeps up virtue in the world,—one of those arrangements, those safeguards of virtue, by which we are prompted to do right, and to abstain from that which is wrong. It is greatly perverted, indeed, to purposes of ambition, but, in itself, the desire not to be forgotten when we are dead contributes much to the industry, the enterprise, and the benevolence of the world, and is one of the most efficacious means for preserving us from sin.

17. The righteous *cry, and the* LORD *heareth.* That is, one of the advantages or benefits of being righteous is the privilege of crying unto God, or of calling on his name, with the assurance that he will hear and deliver us. No one has ever yet fully appreciated the *privilege* of being permitted to call upon God; the privilege of prayer. There is no bless-

18 The LORD *is* [1] nigh unto them that are of a broken heart; and saveth [2] such as be of a contrite spirit.

19 Many *are* the afflictions of the righteous: but the LORD delivereth him out of them all.

20 He keepeth all his bones: not one of them is broken.

[1] *to the broken of heart.*
[2] *the contrite of spirit.*

ing conferred on man in his present state superior to this; and no one can fully understand the force of the argument derived from this in favour of the service of God. What a world would this be—how sad, how helpless, how wretched—if there were no God to whom the guilty, the suffering, and the sorrowful might come; if God were a Being who never heard prayer at all; if he were a capricious Being who might or might not hear prayer; if he were a Being governed by fitful emotions, who would now hear the righteous, and then the wicked, and then neither, and who dispensed his favours in answer to prayer by no certain rule! ¶ *And delivereth them out of all their troubles.* (1.) He often delivers them from trouble in this life in answer to prayer. (2.) He will deliver them literally from "all" trouble in the life to come. The promise is not, indeed, that they shall be delivered from *all* trouble on earth, but the idea is that God is able to rescue them from trouble here; that he often does it in answer to prayer; and that there will be, in the case of every righteous person, a sure and complete deliverance from all trouble hereafter. Comp. Notes on ver. 6: see ver. 19.

18. *The* LORD is *nigh unto them that are of a broken heart.* Margin, as in Hebrew, *to the broken of heart.* The phrase, "*the Lord is nigh,*" means that he is ready to hear and to help. The language is, of course, figurative. As an Omnipresent Being, God is equally near to all persons at all times; but the language is adapted to our conceptions, as we feel that one who is near us can help us, or that one who is distant from us cannot give us aid. Comp. Notes on Ps. xxii. 11. The phrase, "them that are of a broken heart," occurs often in the Bible. It refers to a condition when a burden *seems* to be on the heart, and when the heart *seems* to be crushed by sin or sorrow; and it is designed to describe a consciousness of deep guilt, or the heaviest kind of affliction and trouble. Comp. Ps. li. 17; Isa. lvii. 15; lxi. 1; lxvi. 2. ¶ *And saveth such as be of a contrite spirit.* Margin, as in Hebrew, *contrite of spirit.* The phrase here means the spirit as *crushed* or *broken down;* that is, as in the other phrase, a spirit that is oppressed by sin or trouble. The world abounds with instances of those who can fully understand this language.

19. *Many* are *the afflictions of the righteous.* This is not intended to affirm that the afflictions of the righteous are more numerous or more severe than the afflictions of other men, but that they *are* subjected to much suffering, and to many trials. Religion does not exempt them *from* suffering, but it sustains them *in* it; it does not deliver them from all trials in this life, but it supports them in their trials, which it teaches them to consider as a preparation for the life to come. There are, indeed, sorrows which are peculiar to the righteous, or which come upon them in virtue of their religion, as the trials of persecution; but there are sorrows, also, that are peculiar to the wicked,—such as are the effects of intemperance, dishonesty, crime. The latter are more numerous by far than the former; so that it is still true that the wicked suffer more than the righteous in this life. ¶ *But the* LORD *delivereth him out of them all.* See Notes on ver. 17.

20. *He keepeth all his bones.* That is, he preserves or guards the righteous. ¶ *Not one of them is broken.*

21 Evil shall slay the wicked; and they that hate the righteous shall be [1] desolate.

22 The LORD redeemeth the soul of his servants; and none *f* of them that trust in him shall be desolate.

[1] Or, *guilty*. *f* Ps. lxxxiv. 11, 12.

Perhaps there is a direct and immediate allusion here to what the psalmist had himself experienced. In *his* dangers God had preserved him, so that he had escaped without a broken bone. But the statement is more general, and is designed to convey a truth in respect to the usual and proper effect of religion, or to denote the advantage, in reference to personal safety in the dangers of this life, derived from religion. The language is of a *general* character, such as often occurs in the Scriptures, and it should, in all fairness, be so construed. It cannot mean that the bones of a righteous man are *never* broken, or that the fact that a man has a broken bone proves that he is not righteous; but it means that, as a general principle, religion conduces to safety, or that the righteous are under the protection of God. Comp. Matt. x. 30, 31. Nothing more can be demanded in the fair interpretation of the language than this.

21. *Evil shall slay the wicked.* That is, his own wicked conduct will be the cause of his destruction. His ruin is not arbitrary, or the mere result of a Divine appointment; it is caused by sin, and is the regular and natural consequence of guilt. In the destruction of the sinner, there will not be any one thing which cannot be explained by the supposition that it is the regular effect of sin, or what sin is, in its own nature, fitted to produce. The one will measure the other; guilt will be the measure of all that there is *in* the punishment. ¶ *And they that hate the righteous.* Another term for the wicked, or a term designating the character of the wicked in one aspect or view. It is true of all the wicked that they must hate the righteous in their hearts, or that they are so opposed to the character of the righteous that it is proper to designate this feeling as *hatred.* ¶ *Shall be desolate.* Margin, *shall be guilty.* Professor Alexander and Hengstenberg render this, as in the margin, *shall be guilty.* De Wette, *shall repent.* Rosenmüller, *shall be condemned.* The original word—אָשַׁם, *asham*—means properly to fail in duty, to transgress, to be guilty. The primary idea, says Gesenius (*Lex.*), is that of *negligence,* especially in going, or in gait, as of a camel that is slow or faltering. Then the word means to be held or treated as faulty or guilty; and then, to bear the consequences of guilt, or to be punished. This seems to be the idea here. The word is sometimes synonymous with another Hebrew word— יָשַׁם, *yasham*—meaning to be desolate; to be destroyed; to be laid waste: Ezek. vi. 6; Joel i. 18; Ps. v. 10. But the usual meaning of the word is undoubtedly retained here, as signifying that, in the dealings of Providence, or in the administering of Divine government, such men will be held to be guilty, and will be treated accordingly; that is, that they will be punished.

22. *The* LORD *redeemeth the soul of his servants.* The literal meaning of this is, that the Lord rescues the lives of his servants, or that he saves them from death. The word *redeem* in its primary sense means to let go or loose; to *buy* loose, or to ransom; and hence, to redeem with a price, or to rescue in any way. Here the idea is not that of delivering or rescuing by a *price,* or by an offering, but of rescuing from danger and death by the interposition of the power and providence of God. The word *soul* here is used to denote the entire man, and the idea is, that God will *rescue* or *save* those who serve and obey him. They will be kept from destruction. They will not be held and

regarded as guilty, and will not be treated as if they were wicked. As the word *redeem* is used by David here it means God will save his people;—without specifying the *means* by which it will be done. As the word *redeem* is used by Christians now, employing the ideas of the New Testament on the subject, it means that God will redeem his people by that great sacrifice which was made for them on the cross. ¶ *And none of them that trust in him shall be desolate.* Shall be held and treated as *guilty*. See ver. 21, where the same word occurs in the original. They shall not be held to be guilty; they shall not be punished. This is designed to be in contrast with the statement respecting the wicked in ver. 21. The psalm, therefore, closes appropriately with the idea that they who trust the Lord will be ultimately safe; that God will make a distinction between them and the wicked; that they will be ultimately rescued from death, and be regarded and treated for ever as the friends of God.

PSALM XXXV.

This psalm is ascribed to David. The title in the original, לְדָוִד — "*by* David," or, "*of* David"—is without anything to designate the occasion on which it was composed, or anything to mark the character of the psalm, as distinguished from others. Occasionally in the titles of the psalms there is a special reference to the circumstances in which the psalm was composed, as in Ps. iii., vii., xviii., xxx., xxxiv.; and, much more frequently, there is something added in the title to distinguish the character of the psalm, either in its own nature, or in its adaptedness to music, as in Ps. iv., v., vi., ix., xvi., xxii. In this case, however, there is nothing in the title that furnishes any information on either of these points.

There is nothing in the psalm itself that will enable us to determine with any accuracy the occasion on which it was written. By some it has been referred to the time of the persecution of David by Saul; by others, to the opposition which he encountered from Ahithophel, or Shimei, or to the ingratitude of Mephibosheth (2 Sam. xvi. 3); by others it has been referred to the rebellion of Absalom; and others have referred it to the Messiah, as prophetically descriptive of what would occur to him. The psalm can be intelligently interpreted on either of the former suppositions, but there is no evidence that it had any direct reference to the Messiah. The only place in the New Testament in which it could be alleged that any part of it is applied to Christ, is John xv. 25, where it is said, "But this cometh to pass, that the word might be fulfilled which is written in their law, They hated me without a cause." By those who suppose that the psalm refers to the Messiah, it is said that this is a quotation from ver. 19 of this psalm. But it may be remarked in regard to this (*a*) that the language of the psalm in that verse is different from that used in John, the language of the former being, "Neither let them wink with the eye that hate me without a cause;" and (*b*) that the language in John is a much more literal quotation from Ps. lxix. 4, "They that hate me without a cause," etc.,—a psalm which undoubtedly has reference to the Messiah. De Wette supposes that the psalm is not properly ascribed to David, and says that it is not "worthy" of him. He supposes that it was composed after the death of David, by an inferior poet. He furnishes, however, no reason for this opinion, except that which is derived from his own feelings,—"*nach meinem Gefühle*.' The time and occasion on which the psalm was composed are not, however, of material consequence. As it would be appropriate to any of the occasions above referred to, so it is appropriate to numerous occasions which arise in the history of individuals; and it is, therefore, of so general a character that it may be useful in the church at all times.

What is apparent in the psalm—the central idea, and that which makes it so useful—is, that it was composed with reference to the treatment which the author received from those who had been his professed friends:—from those to whom he had shown kindness in their troubles; to whom he had been a friend and a brother, but who had now turned against him. In the times of prosperity they had been his professed friends, and had partaken freely and largely of his hospitality; when they were afflicted he had shown them sympathy and kindness; but when reverses

PSALM XXXV.

A Psalm of David.

PLEAD [g] *my cause,* O LORD, with them that strive with me: fight against them that fight against me.

g Lam. iii. 58.

came upon him, they forsook him, and joined with his calumniators, persecutors, and accusers. The psalm, therefore, has a special applicability to trials of that nature. It expresses the feelings and views of the author in regard to his own sorrows, as springing from such ingratitude, and his earnest prayer to God to interpose in his behalf,—the rolling of the sorrows of his pained and oppressed heart upon the arm of his unchanging Friend, the mighty and merciful God. As occasions similar to those referred to in the psalm not unfrequently occur in the world, it was important that in the volume of inspiration an *example* should be furnished of the manner in which piety is to meet such a form of trial.

The psalm consists of the following parts:—

I. The prayer, vers. 1-10. This is (*a*) an earnest appeal to God for his interposition, vers. 1-3; (*b*) a solemn imprecation of Divine vengeance on his enemies, or a prayer that they may receive from the hand of God just retribution for their crimes, vers. 4-8; (*c*) the expression of a determined purpose on his part to triumph in God, or to ascribe praise to God for his interposition, vers. 9, 10.

II. The description of the character and conduct of his enemies, vers. 11-16. They were (*a*) false witnesses against him, or calumniators, ver. 11; (*b*) they had rendered to him evil for good, or had been guilty of base ingratitude, ver. 12; (*c*) in their troubles he had been to them as a brother, vers. 13, 14; but (*d*) they had forgotten all this in his adversity, and had united with the vile and the abandoned—with revellers and drunkards, in pouring contempt on his name, and in reproaching his character, vers. 15, 16.

III. An earnest appeal to God, in view of these circumstances, to interpose and deliver him; to show that He was the patron and friend of those who were calumniated and injured, vers. 17-28. This appeal is founded on such arguments as the following:—(*a*) That God *seemed* now to be looking on, and taking no interest in a righteous cause, or in the cause of one who was oppressed and wronged, ver. 17; (*b*) that his interposition would lead the psalmist to render him praise, ver. 18; (*c*) that those who had so much injured and wronged him seemed to enjoy the Divine favour, and were at ease, vers. 19, 20; (*d*) that God had seen all this, and still saw it, and that it became him to interpose in his behalf, vers. 21-23; (*e*) that it was inconsistent for God to suffer the wicked to triumph over the righteous, or that they should be allowed to exult as if they had swallowed them up, vers. 24-26; and (*f*) that it was desirable that, under the government of God, they who were truly righteous should receive such tokens of the Divine favour and protection that they could rejoice in God, and render him appropriate praise, vers. 27, 28.

1. *Plead* my cause, *O* LORD. The word *plead* means, properly, to argue in support of a claim, or against the claim of another; to urge reasons for or against; to attempt to persuade one by argument or supplication;—as, to plead for the life of a criminal, that is, to urge reasons why he should be acquitted or pardoned; and then, to supplicate with earnestness in any way. The original word here used, —רִיב, *rib*—meads to contend, strive, quarrel; and then, to contend before a judge, to manage or plead a cause. The idea here is, that the psalmist desires that God would undertake his cause *against* those who had risen up against him, *as if* it were managed before a tribunal, or before a judge, and God should be the advocate. The same word is used, in another form, in the other member of the sentence—"with them that *strive*—יְרִיבַי—against me." The idea is, that *they* were *pleading* against him, or were urging arguments, as it were, before a tribunal or a judge, why he should be condemned. They were his bitter opponents, engaged in bringing all manner of false accusations against him, and seeking his condemnation. The psalmist felt that he could not

2 Take hold of shield and buckler, and stand up for mine help.
3 Draw out also the spear, and stop *the way* against them that persecute me: say unto my soul, I *am* thy salvation.

manage his own cause against them; and he, therefore, pleads with God that *he* would interpose, and stand up for him. ¶ *Fight against them that fight against me.* The same idea substantially occurs here as in the former member of the verse. It is a prayer that *God* would undertake his cause; that he would exert his power against those who were opposed to him.

2. *Take hold of shield and buckler.* That is, Arm thyself as if for the contest. It is a prayer, in a new form, that God would interpose, and that he would go forth as a warrior against the enemies of the psalmist. On the word *shield*, see Notes on Ps. v. 12. Comp. Notes on Eph. vi. 16. On the word *buckler*, see Notes on Ps. xviii. 2. These terms are derived from the armour of a warrior, and the prayer here is that God would appear in that character for his defence. ¶ *And stand up for my help.* As a warrior stands up, or stands firm, to arrest the attack of an enemy.

3. *Draw out also the spear.* The word here rendered *draw out* means properly to pour out; to empty; and it is applied to the act of emptying sacks, Gen. xlii. 35; to emptying bottles, Jer. xlviii. 12; to drawing a sword from a sheath, Ex. xv. 9; Lev. xxvi. 33; Ezek. v. 12. It is applied to a *spear* either as drawing it out of the place where it was kept, or as stretching it out for the purposes of attack. The former probably is the meaning, and the idea is, that David prayed God to *arm himself*—as a warrior does—in order to defend him. The spear was a common weapon in ancient warfare. It was sometimes so short that it could be brandished as a sword in the hand, or hurled at an enemy, 1 Sam. xviii. 11; xix. 10; xx. 33; but it was usually made as long as it could be to be handled conveniently. The spear was a weapon of *attack.* The parts of armour referred to in ver. 2 were designed for defence. The idea of the psalmist is that of a warrior prepared alike for attack or defence. ¶ *And stop the way against them that persecute me.* The words *the way* are not in the original. The word rendered *stop*—סְגֹר, *segor*—means properly to shut, to close, as a door or gate, Job iii. 10; 1 Sam. i. 5; Gen. xix. 6, 10. The idea here, according to the usage of the word, is, Shut or close up the way against those that persecute me. So Gesenius renders it. Grotius, Michaelis, De Wette, and others, however, regard the word as a noun, signifying the same as the Greek—σάγαρις—a two-edged sword, such as was used by the Scythians, Persians, and Amazons. Herod. vii. 64. See Rosenmüller *in loc.* It is not so rendered, however, in any of the ancient versions. The LXX. render it, "And shut up against those that persecute me;" the Vulgate, "Pre-occupy against those that persecute me;" the Chaldee, "Shut up against those that persecute me." The correct idea probably is that which is given in the common version. The psalmist prays that God would go forth to meet his enemies; that he would arrest and check them in their march; that he would hedge up their way, and that he would thus prevent them from attacking him. ¶ *Say unto my soul, I am thy salvation.* Say to *me*, I will save you. That is, Give me some assurance that thou wilt interpose, and that thou wilt guard me from my enemies. Man only wants this assurance to be calm in respect to any danger. When God says to us that he will be our salvation; that he will protect us; that he will deliver us from sin, from danger, from hell, the mind may and will be perfectly calm. To a believer he gives this assurance; to all he is willing to give it. The

4 Let [h] them be confounded and put to shame that seek after my soul: let them be turned back and brought to confusion that devise my hurt.

5 Let them be as chaff [i] before the wind: and let the angel of the Lord chase *them*.

6 Let their way be [1] dark and slippery; and let the angel of the LORD persecute them.

7 For without cause have they hid for me their net *in* a pit, *which* without cause they have digged for my soul.

h Ps. lxxi. 24. *i* Ps. i. 4.
[1] *darkness and slipperiness.*

whole plan of salvation is arranged with a view to furnish such an assurance, and to give a pledge to the soul that God *will* save. Death loses its terrors then; the redeemed man moves on calmly, — for in all the future—in all worlds—he has nothing now to fear.

4. *Let them be confounded.* That is, Let them, through thy gracious interposition in my behalf, be so entirely overcome and subdued that they shall be *ashamed* that they ever made the effort to destroy me; let them see so manifestly that God is on my side that they will be covered with confusion for having opposed one who was so entirely the object of the Divine protection and care. See Notes on Ps. vi. 10; xxv. 2, 3. Comp. Notes on Job vi. 20. ¶ *That seek after my soul.* My life. That seek to destroy me. ¶ *Let them be turned back.* In their attempts to pursue me. Do thou interpose and turn them back. ¶ *And brought to confusion.* Put to shame; or made ashamed,—as they are who are disappointed and thwarted in their schemes.

5. *Let them be as chaff before the wind.* As chaff is driven away in winnowing grain. See Notes on Ps. i. 4. ¶ *And let the angel of the* LORD *chase* them. Drive them away, or scatter them. Angels are often represented in the Scriptures as agents employed by God in bringing punishment on wicked men. See 2 Kings xix. 35; Isa. xxxvii. 36; 1 Chron. xxi. 12, 30; 2 Sam. xxiv. 16.

6. *Let their way be dark.* Marg., as in Heb., *darkness.* That is, let them not be able to see where they go; what danger they incur; what is before them. The idea is that of persons who wander in the night, not knowing what is before them, or what danger may be near. The succession of images and figures here is terrific. The representation is that of persons scattered as the chaff is before the wind; pursued by the angel seeking vengeance; and driven along a dark and slippery path, with no guide, and no knowledge as to the precipices which may be before them, or the enemies that may be pressing upon them. ¶ *And slippery.* Marg., as in Heb., *slipperiness.* This is a circumstance which adds increased terror to the image. It is not only a *dark* road, but a road made slippery by rains; a road where they are in danger every moment of sliding down a precipice where they will be destroyed. ¶ *And let the angel of the* LORD *persecute them.* Pursue or follow them. The word *persecute* we use now in the sense of subjecting one to pain, torture, or privation, on account of his religious opinions. This is not the meaning of the word used here. It is simply to *follow* or *pursue.* The image is that of the avenging angel following on, or pursuing them in this dark and slippery way; a flight in a dark and dangerous path, with a destroying angel close in the rear.

7. *For without cause have they hid for me their net* in *a pit.* See Notes on Ps. vii. 15; ix. 15. This figure is derived from hunting. The idea is that of digging a pit or hole for a wild beast to fall into, with a net so concealed that the animal could not see it, and that might be suddenly drawn over him so as to secure him. The reference here is to plans that are laid to entrap and ruin others: plots that

8 Let destruction [k] come upon
him [1] at unawares; and let his
net that he hath hid catch himself:
into that very destruction
let him fall.
9 And my soul shall be joyful
in the LORD: it shall rejoice in
his salvation.
10 All my bones shall say,
LORD, who *is* like unto thee, which
deliverest [l] the poor from him
that is too strong for him, yea,
the poor and the needy from him
that spoileth him?

[1] which *he knoweth not of.*
k 1 Thess. v. 3. *l* Prov. xxii. 22, 23.

are concocted so as to secure destruction before one is aware. The psalmist says that, in his case, they had done this without *cause*, or without any sufficient reason. He had done them no wrong; he had given them no show of excuse for their conduct. ¶ Which *without cause they have digged for my soul.* For my life. That is, they have digged a pit into which I might fall, and into which they designed that I should fall, though I have never done anything to give them occasion thus to seek my destruction.

8. *Let destruction come upon him at unawares.* Marg., which *he knoweth not of.* So the Hebrew. The meaning is, Let destruction come upon him when he is not looking for it, or expecting it. ¶ *And let his net that he hath hid catch himself.* See Notes on Ps. vii. 15, 16. The psalmist prays here that the same thing may occur to his enemy which his enemy had designed for him. It is simply a prayer that they might be treated as they purposed to treat him.

9. *And my soul shall be joyful in the* LORD. That is, *I* shall be joyful, or will rejoice. This is said in anticipation of the interposition of God in destroying his enemies, and in delivering him from danger. It is not joy in the destruction of others; it is joy that he himself would be delivered. Our own deliverance from the hand of our enemies *may* involve the necessity of their being cut off. What we rejoice in, in such a case, is not their ruin, but our own deliverance; and for this it can never be improper to give thanks. The psalmist says that he would rejoice *in the Lord.* It would not be in his own skill or valour, but in what God had done to save him. See Notes on Ps. xxxiv. 2. ¶ *It shall rejoice in his salvation.* For the salvation or deliverance that he brings to me.

10. *All my bones shall say.* A similar expression occurs in Ps. li. 8: "That the bones which thou hast broken may rejoice." The *bones* are here put for the frame; the whole man. See Notes on Ps. xxxii. 3. The idea is, that he had been crushed and overborne with trouble and danger, so that his very frame—that which sustained him—had given way. He says now that if God would interpose in the manner which he prays for, he would be relieved of the insupportable burden, and his whole nature would rejoice. ¶ *Who is like unto thee.* Who can bring deliverance like God. Comp. Notes on Isa. xl. 18. ¶ *Which deliverest the poor,* etc. Who rescues the poor from the hand of the mighty. That is, (*a*) who is there that *would* interpose as God does in behalf of the poor and the down-trodden? (*b*) who is there that *could* save them as he does? In his power, and in his willingness to aid, there is no one like God. The word rendered *poor* here rather means one who is afflicted, or crushed by trial. ¶ *Yea, the poor and the needy.* The word here rendered *poor* is the same as that which occurs in the former member of the sentence. The word rendered *needy* is that which is commonly used to denote the *poor* in the usual sense of the term—one who is in want. The reference is to David, who was afflicted by persecution, and at the same time was in want of the comforts of life. ¶ *From him that spoileth him.* From him that would plunder and rob him.

11 [1] False witnesses [m] did rise up: they [2] laid to my charge *things* that I knew not.

12 They rewarded me evil for good, *to* the [3] spoiling of my soul.

13 But as for me, when they were sick, my clothing *was* sackcloth: I [4] humbled my soul with fasting; and my prayer returned into mine own bosom.

1 *witnesses of wrong.*

m Ps. xxvii. 12; Matt. xxvi. 59—61.
2 *asked me.* 3 *depriving.* 4 Or, *afflicted.*

---

11. *False witnesses did rise up.* Marg., *witnesses of wrong.* The Hebrew is, "witnesses of *violence,*" חָמָס, *hamas.* That is, they were persons who, in what they said of me, were guilty of injustice and wrong. Their conduct was injurious to me as an act of *violence* would be. ¶ *They laid to my charge.* Marg., as in Heb., *they asked me.* The word *asked* here seems to be used in the sense of *demand;* that is, they demanded an *answer* to what was said. The usage appears to have been derived from courts, where the forms of trial may have been in the way of question and answer,—the mode of accusation having been in the form of *asking* how a thing was, or whether it was so; and the defence being regarded as an *answer* to such an inquiry. Hence it is synonymous with our expression of laying to the charge of any one; or of accusing any one. ¶ Things *that I knew not.* Of which I had no knowledge; which never came into my mind. What those charges were the psalmist does not specify; but it is not uncommon for a good man to be falsely accused, and we are certain that such things occurred in the life of David.

12. *They rewarded me evil for good.* They recompensed, or returned evil instead of good. The manner in which they did it he states in the following verses. ¶ To *the spoiling of my soul.* Marg., *depriving.* The Hebrew word means *the being forsaken,* or *abandoned.* The idea is, that owing to this conduct he was forsaken or abandoned by all in whom he might have put confidence.

13. *But as for me.* The psalmist now contrasts their conduct with his own. He refers to the recollections of his past life, and to the acts of kindness which he had shown to them in times of trouble, as more deeply marking the evils of their own conduct now. ¶ *When they were sick.* Comp. Notes on Job xxx. 25. It would seem from this that the persons referred to, who now treated him with so much ingratitude, were those with whom he had been formerly intimately associated, or whom he had regarded as his personal friends, since it cannot be supposed that this deep sympathy would have been shown for those who were altogether strangers to him. ¶ *My clothing* was *sackcloth.* Comp. Notes on Ps. xxx. 11. The meaning is, that he showed the deepest sympathy in their distress by putting on the emblems of humiliation or mourning. It was also with reference to prayer in their behalf, and to fasting, that he put on these marks of grief. The idea is, that he did all that was understood to be connected with the deepest humiliation before God, and that would fit the mind for earnest prayer in their behalf. He felt that their restoration to health—that the preservation of their lives—depended on God, and he most earnestly and fervently pleaded in their behalf. ¶ *I humbled my soul with fasting.* Marg., *afflicted;* so the Hebrew properly means. The word *soul* here is equivalent to *self;* I afflicted myself. He subjected himself to the pains of hunger, that he might be better prepared to offer fervent and acceptable prayer. Among the Hebrews fasting and prayer were much more closely connected than they are with Christians. See Dan. ix. 3; Matt. xvii. 21; Luke ii. 37. ¶ *And my prayer returned into mine own bosom.* De Wette explains this

14 I [1] behaved myself [2] as though *he had been* my friend *or* brother: I bowed down heavily, as one that mourneth *for his* mother.

[1] *walked.*
[2] *as a friend, as a brother to me.*

as meaning, "I prayed with my head sunk on my bosom;" that is, with the head bowed down, so that the prayer which went out of his lips seemed to return again to his own bosom—that earnest prayer which one offers when the head is bowed with sorrow. A posture somewhat similar to this is referred to in the case of Elijah, 1 Kings xviii. 42: "And he cast himself down upon the earth, and put his face between his knees." The posture of prayer with the head reclining towards the bosom is common among the Mohammedans, *Reland* de Religione Mohammetica, p. 87. Jarchi explains this as meaning that he sought the same for those who were now his enemies which he would for himself, or that he desired that that should come into his own bosom which he sought for them. Prof. Alexander supposes that this means, according to a traditional interpretation of the Jews, that he desired that the prayer which he offered might redound to his own advantage: "My prayer shall not be lost, it shall return in blessings to the heart which prompted it." There can be no reason to doubt that this is true *in fact;* and that prayer offered for others *does* bring back blessings to those who offer it. But to suppose that this was the *motive* in the case is to suppose that the psalmist was wholly selfish, and would take away the very point of his observation about his prayer—that it was dictated by the sincerest love for them and true sympathy for their sufferings. The most simple interpretation, therefore, is that which supposes that the prayer was offered under such a burden of grief on account of their sufferings, that his head sank on his bosom; or, in other words, that the prayer which was offered was such as is presented when the heart is most burdened and most sad.

14. *I behaved myself.* Marg., as in Heb., *I walked.* The word *walk,* in the Scriptures, is often used to denote a course of conduct; the way in which a man lives and acts: Phil. iii. 18; Gal. ii. 14; 1 Thes. iv. 12; 2 Thess. iii. 11. It is not improperly rendered here, *I behaved myself.* ¶ *As though* he had been *my friend* or *brother.* Marg., as in Heb., *as a friend, as a brother to me.* This shows that these persons were not his near *relations,* but that they were his intimate friends, or were supposed to be so. He felt and acted towards them as though they had been his nearest relations. ¶ *I bowed down heavily.* Prof. Alexander renders this, "Squalid I bowed down." The word rendered "I bowed down" refers to the condition of one who is oppressed with grief, or who sinks under it. All have felt this effect of grief, when the head is bowed; when the frame is bent; when one under the pressure throws himself on a couch or on the ground. The word rendered *heavily* — קֹדֵר, *kodair* — is derived from a word — קָדַר, *kadar* — which means to be turbid or foul, as a torrent: Job vi. 16; and then, to mourn, or to go about in filthy garments or sackcloth as mourners: Job v. 11; Jer. xiv. 2; Ps. xxxviii. 6; xlii. 9; and then, to be of a dirty, dusky colour, as the skin is that is scorched by the sun: Job xxx. 28. It is rendered *black* in Jer. iv. 28; viii. 21; 1 Kings xviii. 45; Jer. xiv. 2; *blackish,* Job vi. 16; *dark,* Joel ii. 10; Micah iii. 6; Ezek. xxxii. 7, 8; *darkened,* Joel iii. 15; *mourn* and *mourning,* Job v. 11; xxx. 28; Ps. xxxviii. 6; xlii. 9; xliii. 2; Ezek. xxxi. 15; and *heavily* only in this place. The *idea* here is that of one appearing in the usual aspect and habiliments of mourning. He had a sad countenance; he had put on the garments that were indicative of grief; and thus he

15 But in mine [1] adversity they rejoiced, and gathered themselves together; *yea*, the abjects [n] gathered themselves together against me, and I knew *it* not; they did tear *me*, and ceased not.

[1] *halting.*

[n] Job xxx. 1, 8, etc.

walked about. ¶ *As one that mourneth* for his *mother.* The psalmist here evidently designs to illustrate the depth of his own sorrow by a reference to the deepest kind of grief which we ever experience. The sorrow for a mother is peculiar, and there is no grief which a man feels more deeply or keenly than this. We have but one mother to lose, and thousands of most tender recollections come into the memory when she dies. While she lived we had always *one* friend to whom we could tell everything,—to whom we could communicate all our joys, and of whose sympathy we were certain in all our sorrows, however trivial in their own nature they might be. Whoever might be indifferent to us, whoever might turn away from us in our troubles, whoever might feel that our affairs were not worth regarding, we were sure that *she* would not be the one; we were always certain that she would feel an interest in whatever concerned us. Even those things which we felt could be scarcely worth a father's attention we could freely communicate to her, for we were sure there was nothing that pertained to us that was too insignificant for her to regard, and we went and freely told all to her. And then, how much has a mother done for us! All the ideas that we have of tenderness, affection, self-denial, patience, and gentleness, are closely connected with the recollection of a mother, for we have, in our early years, seen more of these things in her than in perhaps all other persons together. Though, therefore, we weep when a father dies, and though, in the formation of our character, we may have been more indebted to him than to her, yet our grief for him when he dies is different from that which we feel when a mother dies. We, indeed, reverence and honour and love him, but we are conscious of quite a different feeling from that which we have when a mother is removed by death.

15. *But in mine adversity they rejoiced.* Marg., as in Hebrew, *halting.* That is, when reverses and troubles came upon me; when, in my journey of life, I seemed to stumble. ¶ *And gathered themselves together.* Not to help me, but to oppose me, and to deride me. ¶ Yea, *the abjects gathered themselves together against me.* The word rendered *abjects*—נֵכִים, *naichim*—has been very variously rendered. The LXX. render it *μάστιγες, scourges;* so the Vulgate, *flagella.* Our translators evidently regarded it as meaning the low, the vile, the outcasts of society; but this idea is not necessarily implied in the Hebrew word. The word used here is derived from a verb—נָכָה, *nachah*—which means to smite, to strike, to beat; and it would be correctly rendered in this place, *those smiting,* or *beating:—the smiters.* But probably the allusion is to the *tongue*—to those who, as it were, smite or beat with the tongue; that is, who rail or revile: those who are slanderous. Compare Jer. xviii. 18; Gesenius (*Lex.*). Others have supposed that it means *lame;* that is, those who limp or halt—meaning that all classes of persons gathered themselves together. But probably the true idea is that which is expressed above, that he was surrounded by slanderers and revilers. ¶ *And I knew* it *not.* Hebrew, "I knew not;" that is, I knew nothing of what they accused me of; I was wholly ignorant of the charges brought against me. See Notes on ver. 11. ¶ *They did tear* me. See Notes on Job xvi. 9. The idea here is that they *tore* or *rent* with words; or, as we say in English, they "tore him in pieces;" that is, they railed at, or reviled him, tearing his character in pieces. ¶ *And ceased not.* It was not one act only;

16 With hypocritical mockers in feasts, they gnashed [o] upon me with their teeth.

o Lam. ii. 16; Acts vii. 54.
1 only one.

17 Lord, how long wilt thou look on? rescue my soul from their destructions, my [1] darling from the [p] lions.

p Ps. xxii. 20.

it was continuous and unceasing. They did it when alone; and they gathered themselves together to do it; they countenanced and encouraged one another.

16. *With hypocritical mockers in feasts.* The word rendered *hypocritical* here—חָנֵף, *hhanaiph*—properly means men *profane, impious, abandoned.* It refers to such persons as are commonly found in scenes of revelry. The words rendered "mockers at feasts," it is scarcely possible to render literally. The word translated, "*mockers*," —לַעֵג, *Laaig* — means properly one who stammers, or who speaks a foreign language; then, a jester, mocker, buffoon. The word rendered *feasts*—מָעוֹג, *Maog*—means *a cake of bread;* and the whole phrase would denote *cake-jesters; table-buffoons* — those, perhaps, who act the part of jesters at the tables of the rich for the sake of good eating. *Gesenius.*—The meaning is, that he was exposed to the ribaldry or jesting of that low class of men; that those with whom he had formerly been on friendly terms, and whom he had admitted to his own table, and for whom he had wept in their troubles, now drew around themselves that low and vulgar class of parasites and buffoons for the purpose of ridiculing or deriding him. ¶ *They gnashed upon me with their teeth.* The act of gnashing with the teeth is expressive of anger or wrath. See Notes on Job xvi. 9; comp. Matt. viii. 12; xiii. 42, 50; xxii. 13; xxiv. 51; xxv. 30; Luke xiii. 28. The meaning here is that they connected the expressions of anger or wrath with those of derision and scorn. The one is commonly not far from the other.

17. *Lord, how long wilt thou look on?* How long wilt thou witness this without interposing to deliver me, and to punish those who treat me thus? God saw it all. He was able to save him that was thus persecuted and opposed. And yet he did not interpose. He *seemed* to pay no attention to it. He *appeared* to be indifferent to it. The psalmist, therefore, asks *how long* this was to continue. He did not doubt that God *would*, at some time, interpose and save him; but what was so mysterious to him was the fact that he looked so calmly on,—that he saw it all, and that he did not interpose when he could so easily do it. The same question we may now ask, and may constantly ask, in regard to the wickedness in the world,—*and no one can answer it.* No one can tell why God, when he sees the state of things on earth, *is* so calm (comp. Notes on Isa. xviii. 4), and apparently so indifferent; why he does *not* hasten to deliver his people, and to punish the wicked. "Even so, Father, for so it seemeth good in thy sight," is all the answer that can be given to this inquiry. Yet it should have occurred to the psalmist, and it should be observed now, that the fact that God *seems* to be indifferent to the state of things, does not *prove* that he *is* indifferent. There is an eternity to come, in which there will be ample time to adjust human affairs, and to develop fully the Divine character and counsels. ¶ *Rescue my soul from their destructions.* My life from the destruction which they are aiming to accomplish. ¶ *My darling.* Marg., *my only one.* See Notes on Ps. xxii. 20. The reference here is to *his own soul* or life. It is the language of tenderness addressed to himself. He had but one soul or life, and that was dear to him, as an only child is dear to its parent. ¶ *From the lions.* Enemies, described as lions; having the fierceness and savage fury of lions. In Ps. xxii. 20 it is, "from

18 I will give thee thanks in the great congregation: I will praise thee among [1] much people.
19 Let not them that are mine enemies [2] wrongfully rejoice over me; *neither* let them wink with the eye that [q] hate me without a cause.
20 For they speak not peace; but they devise [r] deceitful matters against *them that are* quiet in the land.
21 Yea, they opened their

[1] *strong.* [2] *falsely.* *q* John xv. 25.

r Matt. xii. 24.

the power of the dog." The idea is the same in both places. Compare Notes on Ps. xxii. 20.

18. *I will give thee thanks*, etc. That is, When I am delivered I will publicly express my gratitude and joy. Comp. Ps. xxii. 25; xviii. 49. ¶ *I will praise thee among much people.* Marg., *strong.* So the Hebrew. The idea here is, *strong in respect to numbers;* that is, when a large body of people should be assembled together.

19. *Let not them that are mine enemies wrongfully rejoice over me.* Marg., *falsely.* Literally, "My enemies of falsehood;" that is, who are *falsely* my foes; who have no just cause for being opposed to me. Comp. Matt. v. 11. David was conscious that he had done them no wrong, or that he had given no occasion for their conduct towards him, and hence his prayer is simply a request that *justice* might be done. ¶ Neither *let them wink with the eye.* Comp. Notes on Job xv. 12. See also Prov. vi. 13; x. 10. The word rendered *wink* means properly to tear or cut asunder; and then, to cut with the teeth, to bite; and hence the phrase *to bite the lips*, as an expression of malice, or mischief-making: Prov. xvi. 30; and to bite or pinch the eyes, that is, to press the eyelids together in the manner of biting the lips,—also a gesture of malice or mischief. So Gesenius, *Lex.* But perhaps the more probable meaning is that of *winking* literally; or giving a significant wink of the eyes as an expression of triumph over any one. In this sense the term is often used now. ¶ *That hate me without a cause.* To whom I have given no occasion for opposition. In the case under consideration the psalmist regarded himself as entirely innocent in this respect.

20. *For they speak not peace.* They seek a quarrel. They are unwilling to be on good terms with others, or to live in peace with them. The idea is that they were *disposed* or *inclined* to quarrel. Thus we speak now of persons who are *quarrelsome.* ¶ *They devise deceitful matters.* Literally, "they think of words of deceit." That is, they set their hearts on misrepresentation, and they study such misrepresentations as occasions for strife with others. They falsely represent my character; they attribute conduct to me of which I am not guilty; they pervert my words; they state that to be true which never occurred, and thus they attempt to justify their own conduct. Almost all the quarrels in the world, whether pertaining to nations, to neighbourhoods, to families, or to individuals, are based on some *misrepresentation* of facts, designed or undesigned, and could have been avoided if men had been willing to look at facts as they are, or perfectly understood each other. ¶ *Against* them that are *quiet in the land.* That are disposed to be quiet, or that are inclined to live in peace with those around them. The word rendered *quiet* means literally those who are *timid;* then, those who shrink back, and gather together from fear; then, those in general who are disposed to be peaceful and quiet, or who are indisposed to contention and strife. David implicitly asserts himself to be one of that class;—a man who preferred peace to war, and who had no disposition to keep up a strife with his neighbours.

21. *Yea, they opened their mouth*

mouth wide against me, *and* said,
Aha, [s] aha! our eye hath seen *it*.
22 *This* thou hast seen, O LORD;
keep not [t] silence: O Lord, be
not far from me.
23 Stir [u] up thyself, and awake
to my judgment, *even* unto my
cause, my God and my Lord.
24 Judge [v] me, O LORD my
God, according to thy righteousness;
[w] and let them not rejoice
over me.
25 Let them not say in their
hearts, [1] Ah, so would we have it;
let them not say, We have swallowed
him up.

s Ps. xl. 15. t Ps. l. 21; Isa. lxv. 6. u Ps. lxxx. 2.
v 1 Pet. ii. 23. w 2 Thess. i. 6.
1 *ah, ah, our soul!*

wide against me. See Notes on Ps. xxii. 13. ¶ *And said, Aha, aha!* See Ps. xl. 15; lxx. 3. The language is that which we use when we *detect* another in doing wrong,—in doing what he meant to conceal. ¶ *Our eye hath seen it.* We are not dependent on the reports of others. We have seen it with our own eyes. We have found you out. We cannot be mistaken in regard to it. The reference is to some supposed *detection* of misconduct on the part of David, and the joy and triumph of such a supposed detection.

22. This *thou hast seen, O* LORD. Thou hast seen what they have done, as they profess to have seen what I have done (ver. 21). Thine eye has been upon all their movements, as they say that theirs has been upon mine. Comp. Notes on ver. 17. ¶ *Keep not silence.* That is, Speak; rebuke them; punish them. God *seemed* to look on with unconcern. As we express it, he *said nothing*. He appeared to pay no attention to what was done, but suffered them to do as they pleased without interposing to rebuke or check them. Comp. Notes on Psalm xxviii. 1. ¶ *O Lord, be not far from me.* Comp. Notes on Ps. x. 1.

23. *Stir up thyself.* Arouse thyself as if from sleep. See Ps. xliv. 23. ¶ *And awake to my judgment.* To execute judgment for me, or to render me justice. A similar petition (almost in the same words) occurs in Ps. vii. 6. See Notes on that passage. ¶ Even *unto my cause.* In my behalf; or, in the cause which so nearly pertains to me.

24. *Judge me, O* LORD *my God.* Pronounce judgment, or judge between me and my enemies. Comp. Notes on Ps. xxvi. 1. ¶ *According to thy righteousness.* That is, *rightly*. Let there be a righteous judgment. The character of God, or the righteousness of God, is the highest standard of equity and justice, and the psalmist asks that he would manifest his real character as judge in interposing in behalf of an injured and oppressed man, and doing justice to him. When we are *right* in our own cause we may ask a just God to interpose and determine between us and our enemies according to his own nature. As between ourselves and our fellow-men we may bring our cause with this plea before a righteous God; as between ourselves and God, we can make no appeal to his *justice*, but our only hope is in his *mercy*. ¶ *And let them not rejoice over me.* Let them not carry out their purposes; let them not be successful, so that they can appeal to the result *as if* they were right, and thus obtain a triumph over me. Comp. ver. 19.

25. *Let them not say in their hearts.* Let them not congratulate themselves on the result; let them not feel that they have triumphed; let them not, under thy government, come off victorious in doing wrong. ¶ *Ah, so would we have it.* Marg., as in Heb., *Ah, our soul.* That is, It is just as we thought it was; just as we desired it should be; that is exactly our mind in the case. God has permitted us to triumph, and he has showed that we are right in the matter. He has decided the thing in our favour, and

26 Let them be ashamed and brought to confusion together that rejoice at mine hurt: let them be clothed [x] with shame and dishonour that magnify *themselves* against me.

27 Let them shout for joy, and be glad, that favour my [1] righteous cause; yea, let them [y] say continually, Let the LORD be magnified, which hath pleasure in the prosperity of his servant.

28 And [z] my tongue shall speak of thy righteousness *and* of thy praise all the day long.

x Ps. cxxxii. 18. *y* Ps. lxx. 4. [1] *righteousness.* *z* Ps. xxxiv. 1.

it is just as it should be. ¶ *Let them not say, We have swallowed him up.* See Notes on Ps. xxi. 9. The meaning is, We have entirely destroyed him,—as Korah, Dathan, and Abiram were destroyed by being swallowed up in the earth, Num. xvi. 31–35. Comp. Lam. ii. 16.

26. *Let them be ashamed,* etc. See Notes on ver. 4. ¶ *That magnify* themselves *against me.* Who seek to exalt themselves over me; to make themselves great by humbling and destroying me. They hope to rise on my ruin.

27. *Let them shout for joy.* That is, Let me be delivered; let my friends see that God is on my side, and that they have occasion to rejoice in his merciful interposition in my behalf. ¶ *That favour my righteous cause.* Marg., as in Heb., *my righteousness.* The reference is to those who considered his cause a just one, and who were his friends. ¶ *Yea, let them say continually.* Let this be a constant subject of grateful reflection,—a perpetual source of joy to them,—that God *has* interposed in my behalf, and has shown that my cause was a just one. ¶ *Let the* LORD *be magnified.* Be regarded as great, exalted, glorious. Let the effect be to elevate their conceptions of the character of God by the fact that he has thus interposed in a righteous cause, and has shown that he is the friend of the wronged and the oppressed. ¶ *Which hath pleasure in the prosperity of his servant.* Who delights to make his friends prosperous and happy. Let them see that this *is* the character of God, and let them thus be led to rejoice in him evermore.

28. *And my tongue shall speak of thy righteousness.* That is, I will praise thee as a righteous God. ¶ And *of thy praise.* Of that which is a ground or reason for praise. I will speak continually of that in God and in his doings which make it proper that he should be praised. ¶ *All the day long.* Continually; constantly. Every new proof of the kindness of God to him would lead to new acts of praise; and his life, as ours should be, would be a continual expression of thanksgiving.

PSALM XXXVI.

The *title* to this psalm is, "To the chief Musician, *A Psalm* of David the servant of the LORD." On the meaning of the phrase "To the chief Musician." see Notes on the title to Ps. iv. The words "A Psalm" are supplied by the translators. The original is simply "of," or "by David," as in Ps. xi., xiv., xxv., xxvi., and others, without indicating whether it is a *psalm* or a *prayer*. In many instances the *character* of the psalm is indicated by the title, as in Ps. iii., iv., v., vi., and others, "*A Psalm* of David;" in Ps. vii., "*Shiggaion* of David;" Ps. xvi., "*Michtam* of David;" Ps. xvii., "*A Prayer* of David," etc. etc. The meaning of the title here is simply that this was *composed* by David, without indicating anything in regard to the *contents* or *character* of the psalm. The addition in the title, "The servant of the Lord," occurs also in the title to Ps. xviii. See Notes on that title. This seems to have been added here, as in Ps. xviii., for some reason which rendered it proper to remark that the psalm was composed by one who was a "servant" or a friend of Jehovah, and who was setting forth something that was peculiarly connected with that service, or was suggested by it,—as expressing either the *feelings* of one who served God; or as showing the *result* of serving

PSALM XXXVI.

To the chief Musician. *A Psalm* of David the servant of the Lord.

THE transgression of the wicked saith within my heart, *that there is* no fear of God before his eyes.

God. In Ps. xviii. the latter seems to have been the prominent idea; in the psalm before us the former seems to be the main thought; *and the psalm is properly an expression of the feelings of one who is truly engaged in the service of God.* As such, its instructions are valuable at all times, and in all ages.

The *occasion* on which the psalm was composed is not known. There is nothing in the title to indicate this, or in the psalm itself, and conjecture is vain. Amyraldus supposed that it had reference to the time of Saul, and especially to the time when he seemed to be friendly to David, but when he secretly harboured malice in his heart, and sought to destroy him, and to the fact that David saw his real designs through all the professions of his friendship and confidence. See Rosenmüller's Introd. to the Psalms. It is certainly *possible* that this may have been the occasion on which the psalm was composed; but there are no circumstances in the psalm which make this absolutely certain, and there were many occasions in the life of David when the description in one part of the psalm (vers. 1-4) would have been applicable to the character and designs of his enemies, as the description in the remainder of the psalm would have been applicable to his own.

The psalm consists of three parts:—

I. A description of the character of the wicked, referring doubtless to some persons who were, or who had been, plotting the ruin of the author of the psalm;—a general description of human depravity, drawn from the character of those whom the psalmist had particularly in his eye, vers. 1-4.

II. A description of the mercy of God, and an expression of strong confidence in that mercy;—particularly, a description of the character of a merciful God as a refuge in times when depravity prevails, and in times of darkness; an expression of strong confidence that light will ultimately come forth from him, and that they will find security who put their trust under the shadow of his wings, vers. 5-9.

III. A prayer of the psalmist that he might experience the mercy of God in this case, and an expression of firm conviction that God would interpose in his behalf, vers. 10-12. He is so confident of this—so certain that it would occur—that he speaks of it as if it were already done.

1. *The transgression of the wicked.* There is considerable difficulty in respect to the grammatical construction of the Hebrew in this verse, though the general sense is plain. The main idea undoubtedly is, that the fair explanation of the conduct of the wicked, or the fair inference to be derived from that conduct was, that they had no fear of God before them; that they did in no proper way regard or fear God. The psalmist introduces himself as looking at the *conduct* or the *acts* of the wicked, and he says that their conduct can be explained, in his judgment, or "in his heart," in no other way than on this supposition. The word "transgression" here refers to some open and public act. What the particular act was the psalmist does not state, though probably it had reference to something which had been done to himself. What is here said, however, with particular reference to his enemies, may be regarded as a general truth in regard to the wicked, to wit, that their conduct is such that the fair interpretation of what they do is, that there is no "fear of God before their eyes," or that they have no regard for his will. ¶ *Saith.* This word—נְאֻם, *neum*—is a participle from a verb, נָאַם *naam*, meaning to mutter; to murmur; to speak in a low voice; and is employed especially with reference to the Divine voice in which the oracles of God were revealed to the prophets. Comp. 1 Kings xix. 12. It is found most commonly in connexion with the word *Lord* or *Jehovah*, expressed by the phrase "Saith the Lord," as if the oracle were the voice of Jehovah. Gen. xxii. 16; Num. xiv. 28; Isa. i.

2 For he flattereth himself in his own eyes, [1] until his iniquity be found to be hateful.

[1] *to find his iniquity to hate.*

24; iii. 15, *et sæpe.* It is correctly rendered here *saith*; or, the *saying* of the transgression of the wicked is, etc. That is, this is what their conduct *says*; or, this is the fair interpretation of their conduct. ¶ *Within my heart.* Heb., *in the midst of my heart.* Evidently this means in my judgment; in my apprehension; or, as we should say, "So it seems or appears to me." My heart, or my judgment, puts this construction on their conduct, and can put no other on it. ¶ That there is *no fear of God.* No reverence for God; no regard for his will. The sinner acts without any restraint derived from the law or the will of God. ¶ *Before his eyes.* He does not see or apprehend God; he acts as if there were no God. This is the *fair* interpretation to be put upon the conduct of the wicked *everywhere* — that they have no regard for God or his law.

2. *For he flattereth himself in his own eyes.* He puts such an exalted estimate on himself; he so overrates himself and his own ability in judging of what is right and proper, that he is allowed to pursue a course which ultimately makes his conduct odious to all men: the result is *so* apparent, and *so* abominable, that no one can doubt what he himself is. The foundation or the basis of all this is an overweening confidence *in himself*—in his own importance; in his own judgment; in his own ability to direct his course regardless of God. The *result* is such a development of character, that it cannot but be regarded as hateful or odious. There is, indeed, considerable obscurity in the original. A literal translation would be, "For he has made smooth to him in his eyes to find his iniquity to hate." The ancient interpretations throw no light on the passage. The word rendered *flattereth*—חָלַק, *hhalak*—means to be smooth; then, to be smooth in the sense of being bland or flattering: Hosea x 2; Ps. v. 9; Prov. xxviii. 23; ii. 16; vii. 5. Here the meaning is, that he commends himself to himself; he overestimates himself; he ascribes to himself qualities which he does not possess,—either (*a*) by supposing that what he does must be right and proper, or (*b*) by overestimating his strength of virtue, and his power to resist temptation. He does this until God suffers him so to act out his own nature, and to show what he is, that his course of life is *seen* by himself and by others to be odious. ¶ *In his own eyes.* As if his eyes were looking upon himself, or his own conduct. *We* act so as to be seen by others; thus *he* is represented as acting as if he *himself* were looking on, and sought to commend himself to himself. ¶ *Until his iniquity be found to be hateful.* Margin, as in Hebrew, *to find his iniquity to hate.* Professor Alexander renders this, "As to (God's) finding his iniquity (and) hating (it);" that is (as he supposes the meaning to be), that he flatters himself that God will not find out his iniquity and hate it, or punish it. De Wette renders it, "that he does not find and hate his guilt;" that is, he so flatters himself in what he does, that he does not *see* the guilt of what he is doing, and hate it. He is blind to the real nature of what he is doing. But it seems to me that the true construction is that which is given by our translators. The real difficulty rests on the interpretation of the preposition in the word לִמְצֹא, *limtzo* — "until he find." If the interpretation proposed by De Wette were the true one, the preposition should have been מ instead of ל,—(מִמְּצֹא instead of לִמְצֹא). The preposition here used (ל) often has the sense of *even unto, until.* Comp. Ezek. xxxix. 19; Isa. vii. 15; and this idea seems best to comport with the connexion. The idea, according to this, is that he overestimates himself; he prides him-

3 The words of his mouth *are* iniquity and deceit: he hath left off to be wise, *and* to [a] do good.

4 He deviseth [1] mischief upon his [b] bed; he setteth himself in a way *that is* not good: he abhorreth [c] not evil,

5 Thy mercy, O LORD, *is* in the heavens, *and* thy faithfulness *reacheth* unto the clouds.

a Jer. iv. 22. *b* Prov. iv. 16. [1] Or, *vanity*. *c* Ps. xcvii. 10.

self on his own strength and goodness, he confides in his own wisdom and power, he pursues his course of conduct trusting in himself, until he is suffered to act out what is really in his heart,—and his conduct becomes hateful and abominable,—until he can no longer conceal what he really is. God suffers him to act out what he had endeavoured to cover over by his own flattery. Men who pride themselves on their own cunning and strength,—men who attempt to conceal their plans from the world,—are often thus suffered to develop their character so that the mask is taken off, and the world is allowed to see how vile they are at heart.

3. *The words of his mouth* are *iniquity and deceit.* Are false and wicked. See Notes on Ps. xii. 2. His words do not fairly represent or express what is in his heart. ¶ *He hath left off to be wise.* To act wisely; to do right. ¶ And *to do good.* To act benevolently and kindly. This would seem to imply that there had been a change in his conduct, or that he was not what he once professed to be, and appeared to be. This *language* would be applicable to the change in the conduct of Saul towards David after he became envious and jealous of him (1 Sam. xviii.); and it is *possible,* as Amyraldus supposed, that this may have had particular reference to him. But such instances of a change of feeling and conduct are not very uncommon in the world, and it may doubtless have happened that David experienced this more than once in his life.

4. *He deviseth mischief upon his bed.* Margin, as in Hebrew, *vanity.* That is, when he lies down; when he is wakeful at night; he plots some scheme of iniquity—some vain, wicked enterprise. So in Prov. iv. 16, "For they sleep not, except they have done mischief; and their sleep is taken away, unless they cause some to fall." ¶ *He setteth himself.* That is, he takes his stand or his position; he assumes this attitude. See Ps. ii. 2, "The kings of the earth *set themselves,*" where the same word occurs. The meaning is that what is done by him is the result of a calm and deliberate purpose. It is not the effect of passion or temporary excitement, but it is a deliberate act in which the mind is *made up* to do the thing. The conduct here referred to is thus distinguished from rash and hasty acts, showing that this is the settled character of the man. ¶ *In a way* that is *not good.* In a bad or wicked way; in a way in which no good can be found; in conduct which allows of no redeeming or mitigating circumstances, and for which there can be no apology. ¶ *He abhorreth not evil.* He has no aversion to evil. He is not in any manner deterred from doing anything *because* it is wrong. The fact that it is sinful is not allowed to be a consideration affecting his mind in determining what he shall do. In other words, the moral quality of an action does not influence him at all in making up his mind as to how he shall act. If it is right, it is by accident, and not because he prefers the right; if it is wrong, that fact does not in any way hinder him from carrying his purpose into execution. This is, of course, the very essence of depravity.

5. *Thy mercy,* O LORD, is *in the heavens.* This commences the second part of the psalm,—the description of the character of God in contrast with the character of the wicked man. The meaning here is, evidently, that the mercy of God is very exalted; to the very heavens, as high as the

6 Thy righteousness *is* like the
[1] great mountains; thy judgments *are* a great [d] deep: O
LORD, thou preservest man and beast.

[1] *mountains of God.* [d] Rom. xi. 33.

highest object of which man can conceive. Thus we speak of virtue as *exalted*, or virtue of the *highest kind*. The idea is not that the mercy of God is *manifested* in heaven, for, mercy being favour shown to the guilty, there is no occasion for it in heaven; nor is the idea that mercy, as shown to man, has its *origin* in heaven, which is indeed true in itself; but it is, as above explained, that it is of the most exalted nature; that it is as high as man can conceive. ¶ And *thy faithfulness.* Thy *truthfulness;* thy fidelity to thy promises and to thy friends. ¶ Reacheth *unto the clouds.* The clouds are among the highest objects. They rise above the loftiest trees, and ascend above the mountains, and seem to lie or roll along the sky. The idea here, therefore, as in the first part of the verse, is, that it is elevated or exalted.

6. *Thy righteousness.* Thy justice; that is, the justice of God considered as residing in his own nature; his justice in his laws; his justice in his providential dealings; his justice in his plan of delivering man from sin; his justice to the universe in administering the rewards and penalties of the law. ¶ Is *like the great mountains.* Marg., as in Heb., *the mountains of God.* The name *God* is thus, in the Scriptures, often given to that which is great or exalted, as God is the greatest Being that the mind can form any conception of. So in Ps. lxxx. 10: "The boughs thereof were like the goodly cedars,"—in the Heb., *cedars of God.* Connecting his name with *mountains* or *cedars,* we have the idea of *strength* or *greatness,* as being peculiarly the work of the Almighty. The idea here is, that as the mountains are the most stable of all the objects with which we are acquainted, so it is with the justice of God. It is as fixed as the everlasting hills. ¶ *Thy judgments.* The acts and records which are expressive of thy judgment in regard to what is right and best; that judgment as it is expressed in thy law, and in thy dealings with mankind. The *judgment* of God in any matter may be expressed either by a declaration or by his acts. The latter is the idea now most commonly attached to the word, and it has come to be used almost exclusively to denote *afflictive* dispensations of his Providence, or expressions of his displeasure against sin. The word is not used in that exclusive sense in the Scriptures. It refers to *any* Divine adjudication as to what is right, whether expressed by declaration or by act, and would include his adjudications in favour of that which is right as well as those against that which is wrong. ¶ Are *a great deep.* The word rendered *deep* here means properly wave, billow, surge; then, a mass of waters, a flood, a deep; and the phrase *great deep* would properly refer to the ocean, its *depth* being one of the most remarkable things in regard to it. The *idea* here is, that as we cannot fathom the ocean or penetrate to its bottom, so it is with the judgments of God. They are beyond our comprehension, and after all our efforts to understand them, we are constrained, as in measuring the depths of the ocean, to confess that we cannot reach to the bottom of them. This is true in regard to his law, in regard to the principles of his government as he has declared them, and in regard to his actual dealings with mankind. It could not be otherwise than that in the administration of an infinite God there must be much that man, in his present state, could not comprehend. Comp. Job xi. 7–9; Isa. lv. 8, 9. ¶ O LORD, *thou preservest man and beast.* Literally, thou wilt *save;* that is, thou savest them from destruction. The idea is, that he keeps them alive; or that life, where it is continued, is always continued by his agency. The psalmist evidently sees in the fact here stated an illus-

7 How [1] excellent *is* thy loving-kindness, O God! therefore the children of men put their trust under the shadow of thy wings.

[1] *precious*, 1 Pet. ii. 7.
e Ps. lxv. 4.

8 They [e] shall be [2] abundantly satisfied with the fatness of thy house; and thou shalt make them drink of the river [f] of thy pleasures.

[2] *watered.* *f* Rev. xxii. 17.

tration of what he had just said about the *greatness* of God in his providential agency and his general government. He was struck with his greatness, and with the incomprehensible nature of his power and agency, in the fact that he kept alive continually so many myriads of creatures upon the earth—so many hundred millions of human beings—so many thousand millions of wild beasts, reptiles, fishes, birds, and insects—all dependent on him; that he provided for their wants, and that he protected them in the dangers to which they were exposed. And who *can* comprehend the extent of his law, and the wonderfulness of his Providence, in thus watching over and providing for the multitudes of animated beings that swarm in the waters, in the air, and on the earth?

7. *How excellent.* Margin, as in Hebrew, *precious.* The word here used is one that would be applicable to precious stones (1 Kings x. 2, 10, 11); or to the more costly kind of stones employed in building, as marble (2 Chron. iii. 6); and then, anything that is *costly* or *valuable.* The meaning is, that the loving-kindness of God is to be estimated only by the value set on the most rare and costly objects. ¶ Is *thy loving-kindness.* Thy mercy. The same word is used here which occurs in ver. 5, and which is there rendered *mercy.* It is not a *new* attribute of God which is here celebrated or brought into view, but the same characteristic which is referred to in ver. 5. The repetition of the word indicates the state of mind of the writer of the psalm, and shows that he *delights* to dwell on this; he naturally turns to this; his meditations begin and end with this. While he is deeply impressed by the "faithfulness," the "righteousness," and the "judgment" of God, still it is his "mercy" or his "loving-kindness" that is the beginning and the ending of his thoughts; to this the soul turns with ever new delight and wonder when reflecting on the character and the doings of God. Here *our* hope begins; and to this attribute of the Almighty, when we have learned all else that we *can* learn about God, the soul turns with ever new delight. ¶ *Therefore.* In view of that mercy; or *because* God is a merciful God. It is not in his *justice* that we can take refuge, for we are sinners, but the foundation of all our hope is his mercy. A *holy* creature could fly to a holy Creator for refuge and defence; he who has given himself to Him, and who has been pardoned, can appeal to his "faithfulness;" but the refuge of a sinner, as such, is only his *mercy;* and it is only to that mercy that he can flee. ¶ *The children of men.* Literally, "the sons of man;" that is, the human race, considered as descended from their great ancestor, or as one family. The meaning is not that all the children of men actually *do* thus put their trust in the mercy of God—for that is not true; but (*a*) all *may* do it *as* the children of men, or as men; and (*b*) all who *do* "put their trust under the shadow of his wings" confide in his *mercy* alone, as the ground of their hope. ¶ *Under the shadow of thy wings.* As little, helpless birds seek protection under the wings of the mother-bird. See Notes on Matt. xxiii. 37; comp. Deut. xxxii. 11, 12.

8. *They shall be abundantly satisfied.* Margin, *watered.* That is, all who thus put their trust in the *mercy* of God. The Hebrew word—רָוָה, *ravah*—means to drink to the full; to be satisfied, or sated with drink; or to be satisfied or filled with

9 For [g] with thee *is* the fountain of life: in [h] thy light shall we see light.

g Jer. ii. 13; John iv. 10, 14. h 2 Cor. iv. 6.

water, as the earth or fields after an abundant rain: Isa. xxxiv. 7; Ps. lxv. 10. The state referred to by the word is that of one who was thirsty, but who has drunk to the full; who feels that his desire is satisfied: (*a*) he has found that which is *adapted* to his wants, or which *meets* his wants, as water does the wants of one who is athirst; (*b*) he has found this *in abundance.* There is no lack, and he partakes of it in as large measure as he chooses. So the weary and thirsty traveller, when he finds in the desert a "new and untasted spring," finds that which he needs, and drinks freely; and so the sinner—the dying man—the man who feels that there is nothing in the world that can satisfy him, (1) finds in the provisions of the gospel that which exactly meets the wants of his nature, and (2) he finds it in abundance. ¶ *With the fatness.* The word here used means properly *fatness* or *fat:* Judges ix. 9. Then it means *fat food,* or *sumptuous food,* Job xxxvi. 16; Isa. lv. 2; Jer. xxxi. 14. It is connected here with the word *drink,* or *drink in,* because this kind of food was *sucked* in at the mouth, and the mode of partaking of it resembled the act of drinking. *Gesenius.*—The allusion is the same as that which so often occurs in the Scriptures, where the provisions of salvation are represented as a *feast,* or where the illustration is drawn from the act of eating or drinking. ¶ *Of thy house.* Furnished by thy house, or in the place of public worship. God is represented as the Head or Father of a family, and as providing for the wants of his children. Comp. Ps. xxiii. 6; xxvii. 4. ¶ *And thou shalt make them drink.* In allusion to the provisions of salvation considered as adapted to satisfy the wants of the thirsty soul. ¶ *Of the river.* The abundance. Not a running fountain; not a gentle bubbling rivulet; not a stream that would soon dry up; but a "*river,*"—large; full; overflowing; inexhaustible. ¶ *Of thy pleasures.* Furnishing happiness or pleasure such as *thine* is. The pious man has happiness of the same *kind* or *nature* as that of God. It is happiness in holiness or purity; happiness in doing good; happiness *in* the happiness of others. It is in this sense that the friend of God partakes of *his* pleasure or happiness. Comp. 2 Peter i. 4. The following things, therefore, are taught by this verse:—(1) that God is happy; (2) that religion makes man happy; (3) that his happiness is of the same *kind* or *nature* as that of God; (4) that this happiness is *satisfying* in its nature, or that it meets the real wants of the soul; (5) that it is abundant, and leaves no want of the soul unsupplied; and (6) that this happiness is to be found in an eminent degree in the "house of God," or is closely connected with the public worship of God. It is there that God has made provision for the wants of his people; and advancement in religion, and in the comforts of religion, will always be closely connected with the fidelity with which we attend on public worship.

9. *For with thee* is *the fountain of life.* The fountain or source from which all life flows. All living beings derive their origin from thee, as streams flow from fountains; all that is properly *called* life proceeds from thee; everything which makes life *real* life,—which makes it desirable or happy,—has its origin in thee. The psalmist evidently meant here to include more than mere *life* considered as animated existence. He recalls what he had referred to in the previous verses—the various blessings which proceeded from the mercy and loving-kindness of God, and which were attendant on his worship; and he here says that *all* this—*all* that makes man happy—all that can properly be regarded as *life*—proceeds from God. Life literally, in man and in all animated beings; life spi-

10 O [1] continue thy loving-kindness unto them that know thee; and thy righteousness to the upright in heart.

11 Let not the foot of pride come against me, and let not the hand of the wicked remove me.

12 There are the workers of iniquity fallen: they are cast down, and shall not be able to rise.

[1] *draw out at length.*

ritually; life here, and life hereafter,—all is to be traced to God. ¶ *In thy light shall we see light.* As thou art the Source of light, and all light proceeds from thee, so we shall be enabled to see light, or to see what is true, only as we see it in thee. By looking to thee; by meditating on thy character; by a right understanding of thyself; by being encompassed with the light which encompasses thee, we shall see light on all those great questions which perplex us, and which it is so desirable that we should understand. It is not by looking at ourselves; it is not by any human teaching; it is not by searching for information *away from thee,* that we can hope to have the questions which perplex us solved; it is only by coming to thyself, and looking directly to thee. There is no other source of real light and truth but God; and in the contemplation of himself, and of the light which encompasses him, and in that alone, can we hope to comprehend the great subjects on which we pant so much to be informed. All away from God is dark; all near him is light. If, therefore, we desire light on the subjects which pertain to our salvation, it must be sought by a direct and near approach to him; and the more we can lose ourselves in the splendours of his throne, the more we shall understand of truth. Compare 1 John i. 5; Rev. xxi. 23; xxii. 5; 1 Pet. ii. 9.

10. *O continue.* Marg., as in Heb., *draw out at length.* The Hebrew word means *to draw;* hence, *to draw out,* in the sense of *continuing* or *prolonging.* Comp. Ps. lxxxv. 5; cix. 12; Jer. xxxi. 3. The desire of the psalmist here is, that God would make the manifestation of his loving-kindness *continuous* or *perpetual* to his people; that it might not be fitful and interrupted, but always enduring, or constant. It is the utterance of a prayer that his favour might *always* be manifested to his friends. ¶ *Thy loving-kindness.* Thy mercy, vers. 5, 7. ¶ *Unto them that know thee.* That are thy friends. The word *know* is often used to denote true religion: John xvii. 3; Phil. iii. 10; Eph. iii. 19; 2 Tim. i. 12. ¶ *And thy righteousness.* Thy favour; thy protection. That is, show to them the righteousness, or the glory of thy character. Deal with them according to those just principles which belong to thy character. Comp. Notes on 1 John i. 9. ¶ *To the upright in heart.* Those who are pure and holy in their intentions or their purposes. Comp. Ps. vii. 10. All true uprightness has its seat in the heart, and the psalmist prays that God would show his continued favour to those whom he sees to be true in heart to himself.

11. *Let not the foot of pride come against me.* The foot of the proud man. The word rendered "come *against* me" more properly means, "come not *upon* me;" and the meaning is, Let me not be *trampled down* as they who are vanquished in battle are *trodden down* by their conquerors. Comp. Notes on Ps. xviii. 40. ¶ *And let not the hand of the wicked remove me.* Let no efforts of the wicked do this. The *hand* is the instrument by which we accomplish anything, and the reference here is to the efforts which the wicked might make to destroy him. The prayer is, that he might be *firm* and *unmoved* amid all the attempts which might be made to take his life.

12. *There are the workers of iniquity fallen.* The meaning of this seems to be, that the psalmist saw his prayer answered already. He speaks as if that which he desired and had prayed

for was already done, and as if he himself saw it. He was so certain that it would be done, he had such an assurance that his prayer would be answered, that he seemed, by faith, to see the events already occurring before his own eyes, and felt that he might speak of what he prayed for as if it were already granted. Such is the nature of faith; and such strong confidence in God, and in his faithfulness to his promises, may all have who pray in faith. It is remarkable, as has been observed already in reference to the Psalms, how often a psalm *begins* in depression and *ends* in triumph; how often the author is desponding and sad as he surveys, at the beginning of the psalm, the troubles which surround him, and how in the progress of the psalm the clouds disperse; the mind becomes calm; and the soul becomes triumphant. ¶ *They are cast down, and shall not be able to rise.* They are utterly overthrown. Their discomfiture is complete. They shall never be able to rally again. So faith looks on all enemies of truth and righteousness as hereafter to be utterly overthrown, and it regards this as so certain that it may speak already in the exulting language of victory. So certainly will all the spiritual foes of those who trust in God be vanquished, —so certainly will the righteous triumph,—that, on the wings of faith, they may look beyond all conflicts and struggles, and see the victory won, and break forth into songs of exulting praise. Faith often converts the promises into reality, and in the bright anticipations and the certain hopes of heaven sings and rejoices as if it were already in our possession,—anticipating only by a few short days, weeks, or years, what will certainly be ours.

PSALM XXXVII.

This psalm is entitled simply "of David," or "by David"—לְדָוִד. In the original title there is no intimation, as in Ps. iii., iv., vii., xvi., xvii., whether it is a *psalm* or some other species of composition, but the idea is merely that it is *a composition* of David, or that David was its *author*.

This is one of the *alphabetical* psalms: see introd. to Ps. xxv. In this psalm the peculiarity of the composition is, that the successive letters of the alphabet occur at the beginning of every other verse, the first, the third, the fifth, etc. The exceptions are at vers. 7, 20, 29, 34. In ver. 29 the letter צ—*tzaddi* —occurs instead of ע, *ain*;—and in vers. 7, 20, and 34, the letter introduces only a single verse. It is not possible now to account for these irregularities in the structure of the psalm. J. J. Bellermann (in dem Versuch über die Metrik der Hebräer, p. 117, seq.) endeavoured from conjecture to restore the regular series of verses by changing a portion of them; but there is no authority for this from the manuscripts, and the probability is, that the author of the psalm did not observe *entire* accuracy in this respect, but that he made use of the successive Hebrew letters only as a *general* guide in controlling the mode of the composition. In this psalm the succession of *letters* does not in any way denote a succession or a variety of *subjects*.

The occasion on which the psalm was composed is not mentioned in the title, nor is there anything in the psalm itself to fix it to any particular period of the life of David. Like Ps. lxxiii., it seems to have been suggested by a contemplation of the character and designs of the wicked, and especially of the fact that they are permitted to live, and that they enjoy, under the Divine administration, so much prosperity. The psalm is designed to meet and remove the perplexity arising from that fact, not (it would seem) as a *personal* matter in the case of the psalmist, or because the author of the psalm was himself suffering any wrong from the wicked, but as a perplexity often arising from the general fact. This fact has perplexed and embarrassed reflecting men in all ages, and it has been an object of earnest solicitude to find a solution of it, or a method of reconciling it with the administration of a pure and righteous God. The purpose of this psalm seems to have been to furnish in some degree a solution of the difficulty, or to calm down the mind in its contemplation. The psalm begins, therefore, with the general counsel, "Fret not thyself because of evil doers, neither be thou envious against the

PSALM XXXVII.

A Psalm of David.

FRET [i] not thyself because of evil-doers, neither be thou envious [k] against the workers of iniquity.

i 1 Sam. i. 6; Prov. xxiv. 19.
k Ps. lxxiii. 3.

workers of iniquity," ver. 1. This may be regarded either as counsel addressed to some one,—either a real or an imaginary person,—whose mind was thus agitated, or who was disposed to fret and murmur on account of this,—and, on that supposition, the drift of the psalm is to calm down such a mind; or it may be regarded as the address or counsel of *God* directed to the psalmist himself in *his* state of perplexity and embarrassment on the subject. From some things in the psalm (vers. 25, 35, 36) it seems most probable that the former is the true supposition.

The points in the psalm are the following:—

I. The main subject of the psalm,—the exhortation not to "fret" or be troubled on account of evil-doers and the workers of iniquity; not to allow the mind to be anxious in regard to the fact that there are such persons, or in regard to their plans, or to their prosperity in the world,—for they are soon to be cut down and pass away, vers. 1, 2.

II. The state of mind which should be cherished in such cases,—*calm confidence in God in the faithful performance of duty*, vers. 3-8. We are to trust in the Lord, and do good, ver. 3; to find our happiness in God, ver. 4; to commit our way to him in all our perplexities and troubles, vers. 5, 6; to rest secure in him, waiting patiently for his interposition, ver. 7; and to cease from all wrathful or revengeful feelings in reference to the wicked, ver. 8.

III. The reasons for this state of mind, vers. 9-40.

These reasons, without being kept entirely distinct, are two in number,—

(1.) The future doom of the wicked, vers. 9-15. The general idea here is, that they will be cut off, and soon pass away; that they will not secure ultimate success and prosperity, but that their wicked conduct will recoil on themselves, and overwhelm them in destruction.

(2.) The ultimate prosperity of the righteous, vers. 16-40. This is illustrated from various points of view, and with special reference to the experience of the psalmist. After some general statements in regard to the happy lot of the righteous (vers. 16-24), he refers to his own observation, during a long life, respecting the comparative effects of a wicked and a righteous course. This is shown in two respects:—

(*a*) The protection and care of Providence over the righteous, vers. 25, 26. He says that he had been young, and that he was then an aged man, but that in his long life he had never seen the righteous forsaken, nor his children begging bread.

(*b*) The providence of God as against the wicked, vers. 35, 36. He says that he had seen the wicked man in great power, and flourishing like a tree, but he soon passed away, and could no more be found upon the earth.

The general argument in the psalm, therefore, is that righteousness, the fear of God, *religion*, has a tendency to promote ultimate happiness, and to secure length of days and real honour upon the earth; that the prosperity of the wicked is temporary, and that however prosperous and happy they may seem to be, they will be ultimately cut off and made miserable.

It remains only to add that this psalm was composed when David was an old man (ver. 25); and apart, therefore, from the fact that it is the work of an inspired writer, it has special value as expressing the result of the observations of a long life on a point which perplexes the good in every age.

1. *Fret not thyself.* The Hebrew word here means properly to burn, to be kindled, to be inflamed, and is often applied to anger, as if under its influence we become *heated:* Gen. xxxi. 36; xxxiv. 7; 1 Sam. xv. 11; 2 Sam. xix. 43. Hence it means to fret oneself, to be angry, or indignant. Comp. Prov. xxiv. 19. We should perhaps express the same idea by the word *worrying* or *chafing*. The state of mind is that where we are worried, or envious, because others are prosperous and successful, and we are not. The idea is, therefore, closely allied with that in the other part of the verse, "neither be thou *envious*."

2 For they shall soon be cut down like the grass, and wither as the green herb.

3 Trust in the LORD, and do good: *so* shalt thou dwell in the land, and [1] verily thou shalt be fed.

[1] *in truth* or *stableness.*

¶ *Because of evil-doers.* Wicked men:—(*a*) at the fact that there *are* wicked men, or that God suffers them to live; (*b*) at their numbers; (*c*) at their success and prosperity. ¶ *Neither be thou envious.* Envy is pain, mortification, discontent, at the superior excellence or prosperity of others, accompanied often with some degree of malignant feeling, and with a disposition to detract from their merit. It is the result of a comparison of ourselves with others who are more highly gifted or favoured, or who are more successful than we are ourselves. The feeling referred to here is that which springs up in the mind when we see persons of corrupt or wicked character prospered, while we, endeavouring to do right, are left to poverty, to disappointment, and to tears.

2. *For they shall soon be cut down like the grass.* As the grass in the field is cut down by the mower; that is, however prosperous they may seem to be now, they are like the grass in the meadow which is so green and luxuriant, but which is soon to fall under the scythe of the mower. Their prosperity is only temporary, for they will soon pass away. The idea in the word rendered *soon*—מְהֵרָה, *mehairah*—is that of *haste* or *speed:* Ps. cxlvii. 15; Num. xvi. 46; Deut. xi. 17. The thought is not that it will be done immediately, but that *when* it occurs it will be a quick and rapid operation,—as the grass falls rapidly before the mower. ¶ *And wither as the green herb.* When it is cut down. That is, not as the dry and stinted shrub that grows in the desert of sand, but like the herb that grows in a garden, or in a marsh, or by the river, that is full of juices, and that needs abundant water to sustain it—like the flag or rush (comp. Job viii. 11)—and that withers almost instantly when it is cut down. The rapidity with which things *wilt* is in proportion to the rapidity of their growth, so the prosperity of a sinner is suddenly blasted, and he passes away. Comp. Ps. xc. 5, 6.

3. *Trust in the* LORD. Confide in him; rest on him. Instead of allowing the mind to be disturbed and sad, because there are wicked men upon the earth; because they are prosperous and apparently happy; because they may injure you in your person or reputation (ver. 6), calmly confide in God. Leave all this in his hands. Feel that he rules, and that what he permits is wisely permitted; and that whatever may occur, it will all be overruled for his own glory and the good of the universe. ¶ *And do good.* Be engaged always in some work of benevolence. (*a*) If there are wicked men in the world, if wickedness abounds around us, there is the more reason for our endeavouring to do good. If others are doing evil, we should do good; if they are wicked, we cannot do a better work than to do good to them, for the best way of meeting the wickedness of the world is to do it good. (*b*) The best way to keep the mind from murmuring, chafing, and fretting, is to be always engaged in doing good; to have the mind always occupied in something valuable and useful. Each one should have so much of his own to do that he will have no time to murmur and complain, to allow the mind to prey on itself, or to *corrode* for want of employment. ¶ So *shalt thou dwell in the land.* This would be more correctly translated as a command: "Dwell in the land." That is, abide safely or securely in the land,—referring, perhaps, to "the land" as the land of promise—the country given to the people of God. The idea is, that they should abide there calmly and securely; that they should not worry themselves because there were

4 Delight [l] thyself also in the
LORD; and he shall give thee
the desires of thine heart.
5 [1] Commit thy way unto the
LORD; trust also in him, and he
shall bring *it* to pass:
6 And [m] he shall bring forth

[l] Isa. lviii. 14.

[1] *roll thy way upon*, Ps. xxii. 8.
[m] Mic. vii. 8, 9.

---

wicked men upon the earth, and because they were successful, but that they should be thankful for their inheritance, and partake gratefully of the bounties which they receive from the hand of God. Comp. Notes on Matt. v. 5. ¶ *And verily thou shalt be fed.* Marg., *in truth* or *stableness.* The *literal* meaning would be, "Feed on truth." The word rendered *fed* is here in the imperative mood. It properly means to feed, as a flock; and then, to feed upon anything in the sense of delighting in, or taking pleasure in anything, as if we found our support or sustenance in it; and here it means, doubtless, *Feed on truth;* that is, seek after truth; find delight in it; let it be the food of your souls. The word here rendered *verily* means, as in the margin, *truth:* and the meaning is, that they should seek after truth, and find their support and comfort in that. There are, then, in this verse, four things prescribed as duty, in order to keep the mind calm in view of the fact that wickedness abounds in the world: (1) to confide in God; (2) to be actively employed in doing good; (3) to abide calmly and gratefully in the land which God has given *us;* (4) to seek after *truth,* or a true view of the character and government of God as the great Ruler. If men would do these things, there would be little murmuring and fretting in the world.

4. *Delight thyself also in the* LORD. The word rendered *delight* means properly to live delicately and effeminately; then, to be tender or delicate; then, to live a life of ease or pleasure; then, to find delight or pleasure in anything. The meaning here is, that we should seek our happiness in God—in his being, his perfections, his friendship, his love. ¶ *And he shall give thee the desires of thine heart.* Literally, the *askings,* or the *requests* of thy heart. What you really *desire* will be granted to you. That is, (*a*) the fact that you seek your happiness in him will *regulate* your desires, so that you will be *disposed* to ask only those things which it will be proper for him to grant; and (*b*) the fact that you *do* find your happiness in him will be a reason why he will grant your desires. The fact that a child loves his father, and finds his happiness in doing his will, will do much to regulate his own *wishes* or *desires,* and will at the same time be a *reason* why the father will be disposed to comply with his requests.

5. *Commit thy way unto the* LORD. Marg., as in Heb., *Roll thy way upon the Lord.* Comp. Notes on Ps. xxii. 8, where the marg., as the Heb., is, *He rolled himself on the Lord.* See also 1 Pet. v. 7. The idea is that of rolling a heavy burden from ourselves on another, or laying it upon him, so that he may bear it. The burden which we have not got strength to bear we may lay on God. The term *way* means properly the act of treading or going; then, a way or path; then, a course of life, or the manner in which one lives; and the reference here is to the whole course of life, or all that can affect life; all our plans or conduct; all the issues or results of those plans. It is equivalent here to *lot* or *destiny.* Everything, in regard to the manner in which we live, and all its results, are to be committed to the Lord. ¶ *Trust also in him.* See ver. 3. ¶ *And he shall bring* it *to pass.* Heb., *He shall do it.* That is, He will bring it to a proper issue; He will secure a happy result. He will take care of your interests, and will not permit you to suffer, or to be ultimately wronged. The thing particularly referred to here, as appears from the next verse, is reputation or character.

thy righteousness as the light, and thy judgment as the noon-day.

7 [1] Rest in the LORD, and wait [n] patiently for him: fret not thyself because of him who prospereth in his way, because of the man who bringeth wicked devices to pass.

[1] *be silent to.*
n Prov. xx. 22; Lam. iii. 25, 26.

6. *And he shall bring forth thy righteousness as the light.* That is, if you are slandered; if your character is assailed, and seems for the time to be under a cloud; if reproach comes upon you from the devices of wicked men in such a way that you cannot meet it,—then, if you will commit the case to God, he will protect your character, and will cause the clouds to disperse, and all to be as clear in reference to your character and the motives of your conduct as the sun without a cloud. There are numerous cases in which a man cannot meet the assaults made on his reputation, in which he cannot trace to its source a slanderous accusation, in which he cannot immediately explain the circumstances which may have served to give the slanderous report an appearance of probability, but in which he may be perfectly conscious of innocence; and, in such cases, the only resource is to commit the whole matter to God. And there is nothing that may be more safely left with him; nothing that God will more certainly protect than the injured reputation of a good man. Under his administration things will ultimately work themselves right, and a man will have all the reputation which he deserves to have. But he who spends his life in the mere work of defending himself, will soon have a reputation that is not much worth defending. The true way for a man is to do his duty—to do right always—and then commit the whole to God. ¶ *And thy judgment.* Thy just sentence. That is, God will cause justice to be done to your character. ¶ *As the noon-day.* The original word here is in the *dual* form, and means properly *double-light;* that is, the strongest, brightest light. It means *noon,* because the light is then most clear and bright. The idea is, that he will make your character perfectly clear and bright. No cloud will remain on it.

7. *Rest in the* LORD. Marg., *Be silent to the Lord.* The Hebrew word means to be dumb, silent, still: Job xxix. 21; Lev. x. 3; Lam. iii. 28. Hence to be silent *to* any one; that is, to listen to him in silence; and the idea in the phrase here, "*be silent to Jehovah,*" is that of waiting in silent patience or confidence for his interposition; or, in other words, of leaving the whole matter with him without being anxious as to the result. ¶ *And wait patiently for him.* For his bringing the matter to a proper issue. He may seem to delay long; it may appear strange that he does not interpose; you may wonder that he should suffer an innocent man to be thus accused and calumniated; but you are not to be anxious and troubled. God does not always interpose in behalf of the innocent at once; and there *may be* valuable ends to accomplish in reference to yourself,—in the discipline of your own spirit; in bringing out in your case the graces of gentleness, patience, and forgiveness; and in leading you to examine yourself and to understand your own character, —which may make it proper that he should *not* interpose immediately. It may be added that, however important *time* seems to us, it is of no consequence to God; *nullum tempus occurrit* (as the lawyers say), to him; and more important results *may* be secured by delay than would be gained by an immediate interposition in correcting the evil and redressing the wrong. All that the promise implies is that justice *will be done,* but whether sooner or later must be left to him; and that our character will be *finally* safe in his hands. ¶ *Fret not thyself.* See Notes on ver. 1. ¶ *Because of*

8 Cease from anger, and forsake wrath; fret not thyself in any wise to do evil.
9 For evil-doers shall be cut off: but those that wait upon the LORD, they shall inherit the earth.
10 For yet a little while, and

him who prospereth in his way. Because a wicked man has a prosperous life, or is not at once dealt with as he deserves. ¶ *Because of the man who bringeth wicked devices to pass.* Because the man is allowed to accomplish his purposes of wickedness, or is not arrested at once in his schemes of guilt.

8. *Cease from anger.* That is, in reference to the fact that there *are* wicked men, and that they are permitted to carry out their plans. Do not allow your mind to be excited with envious, fretful, wrathful, or murmuring feelings against God because he bears patiently with them, and because they are allowed a temporary prosperity and triumph. Be calm, whatever may be the wickedness of the world. The supreme direction belongs to God, and he will dispose of it in the best way. ¶ *And forsake wrath.* That is, as above, in regard to the existence of evil, and to the conduct of wicked men. ¶ *Fret not thyself in any wise.* See ver. 1. Let the mind be entirely calm and composed. ¶ *To do evil.* So as to lead you to do evil. Do not allow your mind to become so excited that you will indulge in harsh or malignant remarks; or so as to lead you to do wrong to any man, however wicked he may be. See always that *you* are right, whatever others may be, and do not allow their conduct to be the means of leading you into sin in any form. Look to your own character and conduct first.

9. *For evil-doers shall be cut off.* See ver. 2. This will be the termination of their course. They shall not ultimately prosper. God will order all things in equity, and though such men now seem to be prosperous, and to be the objects of the Divine favour, yet all this is temporary. The day of retribution will certainly come, and they will be dealt with as they deserve. The reference here probably is to judgment in this life, or to the fact that God will, as a general law, show his disapprobation of the course of the wicked by judgments inflicted on them in this world. See Ps. lv. 23, "Bloody and deceitful men shall not live out half their days." Prov. x. 27, "The years of the wicked shall be shortened." Comp. Job xv. 32. The idea here is that wicked men will be cut down before they reach the ordinary term of human life, or before they would be cut off if they were *not* wicked. Comp. vers. 35, 36. This is not indeed universally true, but there are instances enough of this kind to establish it as a *general* rule. Intemperance, voluptuousness, the indulgence of violent passions, and the crimes proceeding therefrom, shorten the lives of multitudes who, but for these, might have lived long on the earth. As it is a *general* rule that virtue, piety, the fear of God, temperance, honesty, and the calmness of spirit which results from these, tend to lengthen out life, so it is certain that the opposites of these tend to abridge it. Neither virtue nor piety indeed make it absolutely certain that a man will live to be old; but vice and crime make it morally certain that he will not. At all events, it is true that the wicked *are* to live but a little while upon the earth; that they soon *will*, like other men, be cut down and removed; and therefore we should not fret and murmur in regard to those who are so soon to pass away. Comp. Ps. lxxiii. ¶ *But those that wait upon the* LORD. The pious; they who fear God and serve him. ¶ *They shall inherit the earth.* Comp. Notes on ver. 3. See also vers. 11, 22, 25.

10. *For yet a little while, and the wicked* shall *not* be. The time will soon come when they shall pass away. The language "shall not be" cannot mean that they will cease to *exist* alto-

the wicked *shall* not *be;* yea, thou shalt diligently consider his place, and it *shall* not *be.*

11 But [o] the meek shall inherit the earth, and shall delight themselves in the abundance of peace.

12 The wicked [1] plotteth against the just, and gnasheth upon him with his teeth.

13 The LORD shall laugh at him; for he seeth that his day is coming.

o Matt. v. 5.

[1] Or, *practiseth.*

gether, for the connexion does not demand this interpretation. All that is intended is that they would be no longer on the earth; they would no longer live to give occasion for anxious thoughts and troubled feelings in the hearts of good men. ¶ *Yea, thou shalt diligently consider his place.* The place where he lived; the house in which he dwelt; the office which he filled; the grounds which he cultivated. ¶ *And it* shall *not* be. Or rather, perhaps, as in the former member of the verse, *he is not.* That is, you will not see *him* there. His seat at the table is vacant; he is seen no more riding over his grounds; he is no more in the social circle where he found his pleasure, or in the place of business or of revelry:—you are impressed with the feeling that *he is gone.* You look where he was, but he is not there; you visit every place where you have been accustomed to see him, *but he is gone.* Alas! *where* has he gone? Comp. Job xiv. 10.

11. *But the meek shall inherit the earth.* See Notes on ver. 3. On the meaning of the word here rendered *meek,* see Notes on Ps. ix. 12, where it is rendered *humble.* The word properly denotes those who are afflicted, distressed, needy; then, those who are of humble rank in life; then, the mild, the gentle, the meek. The term here is a general one to denote those who are the friends of God, considered as meek, mild, gentle, humble, in contradistinction from the wicked who are proud and haughty; perhaps also, in this connexion, in contrast with the wicked as prosperous in life. It was probably this passage that the Saviour quoted in Matt. v. 5. ¶ *And shall delight themselves.* (*a*) Shall *prefer* what is here referred to as the source of their happiness, or as in accordance with the desires of their hearts; (*b*) shall *find* actual delight or happiness in this. Though not rich and prospered in this world as the wicked often are, yet they will have their own sources of enjoyment, and will find happiness in that which they prefer. ¶ *In the abundance of peace.* In abundant peace. In the tranquillity and quietness in which they spend their lives, in contrast with the jealousies, the contentions, and the strifes which exist among the wicked even when prosperous. They will have peace with God (Ps. xxix. 11; lxxxv. 8; cxix. 165; Rom. v. 1); they will have peace in their own consciences; they will have peace in the calmness of a quiet and contented spirit; they will have peace with those around them, as they have no passions to gratify, and no object to secure, which will excite the envy, or stir up the wrath, of others.

12. *The wicked plotteth against the just.* Marg., *practiseth.* The Hebrew word means to plot; to lie in wait; to plan; to purpose; to devise. See Ps. xxxi. 13. The meaning is, that wicked men lay their plans against the righteous, but that they will not be able to carry them out, or accomplish them, for they will be cut off, and the Lord will protect his friends. ¶ *And gnasheth upon him with his teeth.* An expression of rage or anger. See Notes on Ps. xxxv. 16.

13. *The* LORD *shall laugh at him.* See Notes on Ps. ii. 4. That is, he will regard all his attempts as vain—as not worthy of serious thought or care. The language is that which we use when there is no fear or apprehension felt. It is not that God is unfeeling, or that he is disposed to

14 The wicked have drawn out the sword, and have bent their bow, to cast down the poor and needy, *and* to slay [1] such as be of upright conversation.

15 Their sword shall enter into their own heart, and their bows shall be broken,

16 A [p] little that a righteous man hath *is* better than the riches of many wicked.

[1] *the upright of way.* p Prov. xv. 16.

deride man, but that he regards all such efforts as vain, and as not demanding notice on the ground of anything to be apprehended from them. ¶ *For he seeth that his day is coming.* The day of his destruction or overthrow. He sees that the wicked man cannot be ultimately successful, but that destruction is coming upon him. There is nothing ultimately to be apprehended from his designs, for his overthrow is certain.

14. *The wicked have drawn out the sword.* That is, they have prepared themselves with a full purpose to destroy the righteous. ¶ *And have bent their bow.* Literally, "have *trodden* the bow," in allusion to the method by which the bow was bent: to wit, by placing the foot on it, and drawing the string back. ¶ *To cast down the poor and needy.* To cause them to fall. ¶ And *to slay such as be of upright conversation.* Marg., as in Heb., *the upright of way.* That is, those who are upright in their manner of life, or in their conduct.

15. *Their sword shall enter into their own heart.* Their purposes will recoil on themselves; or they will themselves suffer what they had devised for others. See the same sentiment expressed in Ps. vii. 15, 16; ix. 15; comp. Esther vii. 10. ¶ *And their bows shall be broken.* They will be defeated in their plans. God will cut them off, and not suffer them to execute their designs.

16. *A little that a righteous man hath.* Literally, *Good is a little to the righteous, more than,* etc. Our translation, however, has expressed the sense with sufficient accuracy. There are two things implied here: (*a*) that it happens not unfrequently that the righteous *have* little of the wealth of this world; and (*b*) that this little is to them of more real value, accompanied, as it is, with higher blessings, than the more abundant wealth which the wicked often possess. It is better to have but little of this world's goods *with* righteousness, than it is to have the riches of many wicked men—or the wealth which is often found in the possession of wicked men—with their ungodliness. It is not always true, indeed, that the righteous are poor; but *if* they are poor, their lot is more to be desired than that of the wicked man, though he is rich. Comp. Luke xvi. 19—31. ¶ Is *better than the riches of many wicked.* Of many wicked men. The small property of *one* truly good man, with his character and hopes, is of more value than would be the aggregate wealth of *many* rich wicked men with their character and prospects. The word rendered riches here—הָמוֹן, *hamon*—means properly noise, sound, as of rain or of a multitude of men; then, a multitude, a crowd of people; and then, a *multitude* of possessions; that is, riches or wealth. The allusion here is not, as Professor Alexander supposes, to the tumult or bustle which often attends the acquisition of property, or to the disorder and disquiet which attends its possession, but simply to the *amount* considered as large, or as accumulated or brought together. It is true that its acquisition is often attended with bustle and noise; it is true that its possessor has not often the peace and calmness of mind which the man has who has a mere competence; but the simple thought here is that, in reference to the amount, or the actual possession, it is better, on the whole, to have what the poor, pious man has, than to have what many wicked men have, if it were all

17 For the arms [q] of the
wicked shall be broken: but the
LORD upholdeth the righteous.
18 The LORD knoweth the days
of the upright; and their inheritance [r] shall be for ever.
19 They shall not be ashamed
in the evil time; and in the days
of famine they shall be satisfied.
20 But the wicked shall perish,
and the enemies of the LORD

q Ezek. xxx. 21, etc. r 1 Pet. i. 3, 4.

gathered together. It does more to make a man happy on earth; it furnishes a better prospect for the life to come.

17. *For the arms of the wicked shall be broken.* See Notes on Ps. x. 15. The *arm* is the instrument by which we accomplish a purpose; and the meaning here is, that that will be broken on which the wicked rely, or, in other words, that their plans will fail, and that they will be disappointed,—as a man is rendered helpless whose arms are broken. Compare Notes on Job xxxviii. 15. ¶ *But the* LORD *upholdeth the righteous.* The Lord will sustain and strengthen him. While the plans of the wicked will be defeated, while they themselves will be overthrown, and fail to accomplish their purposes of wickedness, the Lord will uphold the righteous, and enable them fully to carry out *their* plans. Their great scheme or purpose of life, the promotion of the glory of God, and the salvation of their own souls, will be fully accomplished,—for in that purpose God will be their helper and friend.

18. *The* LORD *knoweth the days of the upright.* See Notes on Ps. i. 6. He knows how long they will live, and all that will happen to them. He sees their whole course of life; he sees the end. It is implied here that his eyes are on *all* the allotted days of their life; on all that has been ordained for them in the whole course of their life; and that nothing can *shorten* the days appointed to them. The wicked expect to live, hope to live, make their arrangements to live; but their eyes cannot rest on the future, and they cannot see the end,—cannot tell precisely when they will be cut off. Some unexpected calamity—something which they cannot foresee—may come upon them, and cut short their days long before the expected time; but this cannot happen in respect to Him whose eyes are on the righteous. Nothing can prevent their reaching the time which *he* has fixed as the termination of their lives. ¶ *And their inheritance shall be for ever.* Shall be permanent, enduring. Perhaps all that was implied in this language, as it was used by the psalmist, was that they would *continue,* or would not be cut off as the wicked are; that is, that righteousness would contribute to length of days upon the earth (comp. ver. 9); yet the *language* suggests a higher idea, and is applicable to the righteous in respect to the promise that they will be put in *everlasting* possession of that which they "inherit" from God; that is, that they will be literally blessed for ever. They will have a sure inheritance on earth, and it will endure to all eternity in another world.

19. *They shall not be ashamed in the evil time.* In times of calamity and trouble. The word *ashamed* here refers to disappointment; as when one goes to a fountain or stream for water and finds it dried up. See Notes on Job vi. 20, and Ps. xxv. 2, 3. The idea here is, that when times of trouble and calamity come, in seasons of famine or want, they will find their expectations, arising from confidence in God, fully met. Their wants will be supplied, and they will find him to be their friend. ¶ *And in the days of famine they shall be satisfied.* Their wants shall be supplied. God will provide for them. See ver. 25. This is in accordance with the general promises which are made in the Scriptures, that God will provide for the wants of those that trust in him. See Notes on ver. 3.

20. *But the wicked shall perish.* The general sentiment here is the same as in Ps. i., that the righteous

shall be as the [1] fat of lambs: they shall consume; into smoke shall they consume away.

[1] *preciousness.*

21 The wicked borroweth, and payeth not again: but the righteous showeth mercy, and giveth.

shall be prospered and saved, and that the wicked shall perish. See Notes on Ps. i. 4, 5. The word *perish* here would be applicable to any form of destruction,—death here, or death hereafter,—for it is equivalent to the idea that they shall be *destroyed.* Whether the psalmist means here to refer to the fact that they will be cut off from the earth, or will be punished hereafter in the world of woe, cannot be determined from the word itself. It is most probable, as appears from other parts of the psalm, that he refers particularly to the fact that they will be cut down in their sins; that their lives will be shortened by their crimes; that they will by their conduct expose themselves to the displeasure of God, and thus be cut off. The *word* used, however, would also express the idea of destruction in the future world in any form, and may have a significance beyond anything that can befall men in this life. Comp. 2 Thess. i. 8; Matt. xxv. 46. ¶ *And the enemies of the* LORD. All the enemies of God; all who can properly be regarded as his foes. ¶ Shall be *as the fat of lambs.* Marg., *the preciousness of lambs.* Gesenius renders this, *like the beauty of the pastures.* Professor Alexander, *like the precious* (part) *of lambs;* that is, the sacrificial parts, or the parts that were consumed in sacrifice. De Wette, *as the splendour of the pasture.* The Vulgate and the LXX. render it, "the enemies of the Lord, as soon as they are honoured and exalted, shall fail as if they were smoke." Rosenmüller renders it as it is in our common version. It is not easy to determine the meaning. The word rendered *fat*—יְקָר, *yakar*—means properly that which is precious, costly, weighty, as precious gems; then, anything dear, beloved, or valuable; then, that which is honoured, splendid, beautiful, rare. It is in no other instance rendered *fat;* and it cannot be so rendered here, except as *fat* was considered valuable or precious. But this is a forced idea. The word כַּר, *kar*, properly and commonly means a *lamb;* but it also may mean the *pasture* or *meadow* where lambs feed. Psa. lxv. 13: "The *pastures*—כָּרִים, *karim*—are clothed with flocks." Isa. xxx. 23, "In that day shall thy cattle feed in large *pastures*"—where the same word occurs. It seems to me, therefore, that the interpretation of Gesenius, De Wette, and others, is the correct interpretation, and that the idea is, that the wicked in their pride, beauty, and wealth, shall be like the meadow covered with grass and flowers, soon to be cut down by the scythe of the mower, or by the frosts of winter. This image often occurs: Matt. vi. 30; Ps. xc. 5, 6; Isa. xl. 6–8; James i. 10; 1 Pet. i. 24. ¶ *They shall consume.* The word here used means to be completed or finished; to be consumed or spent, as by fire, or in any other manner; to pine away by weeping, Lam. ii. 11; to vanish as a cloud or smoke, Job vii. 9. ¶ *Into smoke.* The meaning here is not that they will vanish as the fat of lambs does in sacrifice, but simply that they will pass away as smoke entirely disappears. All that there was of them—their wealth, their splendour, their power—shall utterly vanish away. This is spoken in contrast with what would be the condition of the righteous.

21. *The wicked borroweth, and payeth not again.* This is probably intended here, not so much to describe the *character* as the *condition* of the wicked. The idea is, that he will be in such a condition of want that he will be under a necessity of borrowing, but will not have the means of repaying what he has bor-

22 For *such as be* blessed of him shall inherit the earth; and *they that be* cursed of him shall be cut off.

23 The steps [s] of a *good* man are [1] ordered by the LORD; and he delighteth in his way.

s Prov. xvi. 9. [1] Or, *established*.

rowed, while the righteous will not only have enough for himself, but will have the means of showing mercy to others, and of *giving* to them what they need. The ability to lend to others is referred to as a part of the promise of God to his people, and as marking their condition as a prosperous one, in Deut. xv. 6: "And thou shalt lend unto many nations, and shalt not borrow." Comp. ch. xxviii. 12, 44. It is true, however, as a characteristic of a wicked man, that he will often be *disposed* to borrow and not pay again; that he will be *reckless* about borrowing and careless about paying; and that it is a characteristic of a good or upright man that he will not borrow when he can avoid it, and that he will be punctual and conscientious in paying what he has borrowed. ¶ *But the righteous showeth mercy, and giveth.* That is, in this connexion, he is not under the necessity of borrowing of others for the supply of his wants. He has not only enough for himself, but he has the means of aiding others, and has the disposition to do it. It is his *character* to show favours, and he has the means of gratifying this desire. ¶ *And giveth.* Imparts to others. He has enough for himself, and has also that which he can give to others. Of course all this is designed to be *general.* It does not mean that this will *universally* be the case, but that the tendency of a life of piety is to make a man prosperous in his worldly affairs; to give him what he needs for himself, and to furnish him with the means, as he has the disposition, to do good to others. Other things being equal, the honest, temperate, pure, pious man will be the most prosperous in the world: for honesty, temperance, purity, and piety produce the industry, economy, and prudence on which prosperity depends.

22. *For* such as be *blessed of him.* They who are his true friends. ¶ *Shall inherit the earth.* See ver. 9. ¶ *And* they that be *cursed of him.* His enemies. ¶ *Shall be cut off*: ver. 9. This verse suggests a thought of great importance, in advance of that which had been suggested before. It is that, after all, the difference in the ultimate condition of the two depends on the question whether they have, or have not, *the favour of the Lord.* It is not on the mere fact of their own skill, but it is on the fact that the one has secured the Divine favour, and that the other has not. It is not by mere human virtue, irrespective of God, that the result is determined; but it is that one is the friend of God, and the other not. This consideration will be found in the end to enter *essentially* into all the distinctions in the final condition of mankind.

23. *The steps of a* good *man are ordered by the* LORD. Marg., *established.* The word rendered *ordered* means to stand erect; to set up; to found; to adjust, fit, direct. The idea here is, that all which pertains to the journey of a good man through life is directed, ordered, fitted, or arranged by the Lord. That is, his course of life is under the Divine guidance and control. The word *good* has been supplied here by our translators, and there is nothing corresponding to it in the original. It is simply there, "the steps of man are ordered," etc. Yet there can be no doubt that a good or pious man is particularly referred to, for the connexion demands this interpretation. The word *steps* here means his course of life; the way in which he goes. ¶ *And he delighteth in his way.* In his course of life; and, therefore, he blesses him. The general idea is that he is the object of the Divine favour, and is under the care of God.

24 Though [t] he fall, he shall not be utterly cast down: for the LORD upholdeth *him with* his hand.

t Mic. vii. 8.

25 I have been young, and *now* am old; yet [u] have I not seen the righteous forsaken, nor his seed begging bread.

u Isa. xxxiii. 16; Heb. xiii. 5, 6.

24. *Though he fall.* That is, though he is sometimes disappointed; though he is not always successful; though he may be unfortunate,—yet this will not be final ruin. The word here does not refer to his falling into *sin*, but into misfortune, disappointment, reverses, calamities. The image is that of a man who is walking along on a journey, but who stumbles, or falls to the earth—a representation of one who is not always successful, but who finds disappointment spring up in his path. ¶ *He shall not be utterly cast down.* The word here used—טוּל, *tul*—means *to throw down at full length, to prostrate;* then, *to cast out, to throw away.* Comp. Isa. xxii. 17; Jer. xvi. 13; xxii. 26; Jonah i. 5, 15. Here it means that he would not be *utterly* and *finally* prostrated; he would not fall so that he could not rise again. The calamity would be temporary, and there would be ultimate prosperity. ¶ *For the Lord upholdeth* him with *his hand.* It is by no power of his own that he is recovered, but it is because, even when he falls, he is held up by an invisible hand. God will not suffer him to sink to utter ruin.

25. *I have been young.* The idea in this whole passage is, "I myself have passed through a long life. I have had an opportunity of observation, wide and extended. When I was a young man I looked upon the world around me with the views and feelings which belong to that period of existence; when in middle life, I contemplated the state of things with the more calm and sober reflections pertaining to that period, and to the opportunities of wider observation; and now, in old age, I contemplate the condition of the world with all the advantages which a still wider observation and a longer experience give me, and with the impartial judgment which one has who is about to leave the world. And the result of all is a conviction that religion is an advantage to man; that God protects his people; that he provides for them; that they are more uniformly and constantly blessed, even in their worldly affairs, than other men, and that they do not often come to poverty and want." There is a sad kind of feeling which a man has when he is constrained to say, "I *have been* young;" for it suggests the memory of joys, and hopes, and friends, that are now gone for ever. But a man may have some claim to respect for his opinions when he is constrained to say it; for he can bring to the coming generation such results of his own experience and observation as may be of great value to those who *are* "young." ¶ *And* now *am old.* This demonstrates that this psalm was one of the later productions of its author; and the psalm has an additional value from this circumstance, as stating the results of a long observation of the course of affairs on the earth. Yet there is much that is solemn when a man is constrained to say, "I *am* old." Life is nearly ended. The joys, the hopes, the vigour of youth, are all gone. The mature strength of manhood is now no more. The confines of life are nearly reached. The next remove is to another world, and that now *must* be near; and it is a solemn thing to stand on the shores of eternity; to look out on that boundless ocean, to feel that earth, and all that is dear on earth, is soon to be left *for ever.* ¶ *Yet have I not seen the righteous forsaken.* Forsaken by God; so forsaken that he has not a friend; so forsaken that he has nothing with which to supply his wants. ¶ *Nor his seed begging bread.* Nor his children beggars. This was a remarkable testimony; and though it cannot be

26 *He is*[1] ever merciful, and lendeth: and his seed *is* blessed.

[1] *all the day.*

27 Depart from evil, and do good; and dwell for evermore.

affirmed that the psalmist meant to say literally that he had *never*, in any instance, met with such a case—for the language may have been intended as a general statement,—yet it *may* have been true to the letter. In the course of a long life it may have occurred that he had *never* met with such a case,—and if so, it was a remarkable proof of the correctness of the general remarks which he was making about the advantage of piety. It is not now universally true that the "righteous" are not "forsaken," in the sense that they do not want, or in the sense that their children are not constrained to beg their bread, but the following things, are true: (*a*) that religion tends to make men industrious, economical, and prudent, and hence tends to promote prosperity, and to secure temporal comforts; (*b*) that religion *of itself* impoverishes no one, or makes no one the poorer; (*c*) that religion saves from many of the expenses in life which are produced by vicious indulgence; and (*d*) that, as a general rule, it saves men and their children from the necessity of public begging, and from the almshouse. Who are the inmates of the poor-houses in the land? Who are the beggars in our great cities? Here and there, it may be, is one who is the child of pious parents, reduced by sickness or misfortune, or a want of practical good sense,—for religion does not alter the constitution of the mind, and does not impart the *skill* or *talent* on which so much of the success in life depends; but the great mass of persons in our almshouses, and of beggars in the streets, are themselves intemperate, or are the wives and children of the intemperate. They consist of those whom religion, as it would have made them virtuous and industrious, would have saved from rags and beggary. It may not now be literally true that any one who has been young, and who is become old, could say that he had not once seen the righteous forsaken nor his seed begging bread; but the writer of these lines, who has this day—the day on which he pens them (Dec. 1, 1859)—reached the sixty-first year of his life, and who is constrained to say "I *have been* young," though he may feel a reluctance to add, "but now *am* old," can say, as the result of his own observation in the world, that, as a great law, the children of the pious are *not* vagrants and beggars. As a great law, they are sober, industrious, and prosperous. The vagrants and the beggars of the world are from other classes; and whatever may be the bearing of religion on the destinies of men in the future world, in this world the effect is to make them virtuous, industrious, prudent, and successful in their worldly affairs, so that their children are not left to beggary and want, but to respectability and to competence.

26. He is *ever merciful*. Marg., as in Heb., *all the day*. That is, it is his character; he is constantly in the habit of showing kindness. He does not do it at intervals, or only occasionally, but it is this that marks the character of the man. He is known by this. The word *merciful* here means kind, compassionate, benignant,—and particularly in this respect, that he is willing to *lend* to others when he has the means. ¶ *And lendeth.* The wicked man *borrows*, but does not pay again (ver. 21); the righteous man *lends* to his neighbour. ¶ *And his seed* is *blessed.* His children; his posterity, as the result of this conduct on his part. The effect of what he does passes over from him to them, conveying rich blessings to them.

27. *Depart from evil, and do good.* This is the sum of all that is said in the psalm; the great lesson inculcated and enforced by all these references to the effects of good and evil conduct. All these results—all that men

28 For [v] the LORD loveth judgment, and forsaketh not his saints; they are preserved [w] for ever: but [x] the seed of the wicked shall be cut off.

29 The righteous shall inherit the land, and dwell therein for ever.

30 The [y] mouth of the righteous speaketh wisdom, and his tongue talketh of judgment.

31 The law of his God *is* in his [z] heart: none of his [1] steps shall slide.

32 The wicked watcheth the

v Isa. xxx. 18. w 1 Pet. i. 5. x Isa. xiv. 20. y Matt. xii. 35. z Deut. vi. 6; Isa. li. 7. 1 Or, *goings*.

experience themselves, and all the effects of their conduct on their posterity, enforce the great practical lesson that we should do good and avoid evil. These *results* of conduct are among the means which God employs to induce men to do right, and to abstain from what is wrong. ¶ *And dwell for evermore.* That is, dwell in the land: meaning (in accordance with the general drift of the psalm) that righteousness will be connected with length of days and with prosperity; that its effects will be permanent on a family, descending from one generation to another. See Notes on ver. 3.

28. *For the* LORD *loveth judgment.* That is, God loves that which is right; he loves to do right. The idea is, that such a recompense as is here adverted to,—that on the one hand, in rewarding with prosperity a pure and upright life—and that, on the other, in cutting off the wicked—is right and proper in itself; and that as God *loves* to do right, these consequences respectively may be expected to follow in regard to the righteous and the wicked. Comp. Ps. xi. 7. ¶ *And forsaketh not his saints.* He manifests his sense of that which is right, by not forsaking his saints. ¶ *They are preserved for ever.* They are ever under his paternal eye, and he will keep them. It *will* be literally true that they will be preserved *for ever*, that they will *never* be suffered to perish. ¶ *But the seed of the wicked shall be cut off.* See Notes on Ps. xxi. 10. Comp. ver. 22.

29. *The righteous shall inherit the land.* See ver. 3. The word *inherit* suggests the idea that they are *heirs*, and that God will treat them as his children. ¶ *And dwell therein for ever.* Vers. 3, 18, 27.

30. *The mouth of the righteous speaketh wisdom.* That is, It is a characteristic of the righteous to speak *wise things;* not to utter folly. His conversation is serious, earnest, true, pure; and his words are faithful, kind, and just. This, as a part of human conduct, is one of the reasons why God will bless him with prosperity and length of days. ¶ *And his tongue talketh of judgment.* That is, of just or righteous things. See Matt. xii. 35.

31. *The law of his God* is *in his heart.* That is, he loves it; he thinks of it; he makes it the inward rule of his conduct: Deut. vi. 6; Ps. xl. 8. The word *law* here is a general term for the truth of God,—for all that he has revealed to guide men. As long as that truth is in the heart; as long as it is the object of love; as long as it is suffered to guide and control us, so long will our words and conduct be right. ¶ *None of his steps shall slide.* Marg., *goings.* The idea is, that his course will be firm and steady. He will not fall into sin, and his life will be prosperous and happy. This is in accordance with the general sentiment in the psalm, that religion tends to promote prosperity, happiness, and length of days on the earth.

32. *The wicked watcheth the righteous,* etc. Observes closely; looks out for him; has his eye on him, seeking an opportunity to slay him. See Notes on Ps. x. 8, 9. The sense is, that the wicked are the enemies of the righteous, and seek to do them wrong. It is a characteristic of the

righteous, and seeketh to slay him.

33 The LORD [a] will not leave him in his hand, nor condemn [b] him when he is judged.

34 Wait [c] on the LORD, and keep his way, and he shall exalt thee to inherit the land: when the wicked are cut off, thou shalt see *it*.

a 2 Pet. ii. 9. b Rom. viii. 1, 34. c ver. 7.

wicked that they seek to destroy the righteous. This was manifested in the case of the prophets; in the case of the apostles; in the case of the Saviour; and it has been so manifest in the deaths of the martyrs, and all the persecutions which the Church has suffered, as to justify the general declaration that it is one of the characteristics of a wicked world that it desires to do this.

33. *The* LORD *will not leave him in his hand.* Comp. 2 Peter ii. 9. That is, He will rescue him out of the hand of the wicked; he will not leave him, so that the wicked shall accomplish his purpose. The psalmist here undoubtedly means to refer mainly to what will occur in the present life—to the fact that God will interpose to deliver the righteous from the evil designs of the wicked, as he interposes to save his people from famine and want. The meaning is not that this will *universally* occur, for that would not be true; but that this is the *general* course of things; this is the tendency and bearing of the Divine interpositions and the Divine arrangements. Those interpositions and arrangements are, on the whole, favourable to virtue, and favourable to those who love and serve God; so much so that it is an *advantage* even in the present life to serve God. But this will be absolutely and universally true in the future world. The righteous will be *wholly* and *for ever* placed beyond the reach of the wicked. ¶ *Nor condemn him when he is judged.* Literally, He will not regard or hold him to be *guilty* when he is judged. He will regard and treat him as a righteous man. This may refer either (*a*) to a case where a judgment is pronounced on a good man *by his fellow-men*, by which he is condemned or adjudged to be guilty—meaning that God will not so regard and treat him; or (*b*) to the final judgment, when the cause comes *before God*—meaning that then he will regard and treat him as righteous. Both of these are true; but it seems probable that the former is particularly referred to here. De Wette understands it in the latter sense; Rosenmüller in the former. Rosenmüller remarks that the idea is, that the wicked, when he is not permitted to assail the righteous by violence, makes his appeal to the courts, and seeks to secure his condemnation there, but that God will not permit this. As he has saved him from violence, so he will interpose and save him from an unrighteous condemnation in the courts. This seems to me to be the true idea. Of course, this is to be understood only in a *general* sense, or as marking the *general* course of things under the Divine administration. On this subject, comp. Dr. Taylor's Lectures on Moral Government; vol. i., pp. 252—262. See also Butler's Analogy, *passim*.

34. *Wait on the* LORD. See Notes on ver. 9. Let your hope be from the Lord; depend wholly upon him; have such confidence in him as to expect his gracious interposition in your behalf. ¶ *And keep his way.* Or, walk in the path which he commands. Do not turn from that at any time. Do not allow any temptation, or any opposition, to cause you to swerve from that path. ¶ *And he shall exalt thee to inherit the land.* See vers. 3, 9, 18. ¶ *When the wicked are cut off, thou shalt see* it. This implies that they would certainly be cut off, and that the righteous would be permitted to see the result of a course

35 I [d] have seen the wicked in great power, and spreading himself like a [1] green bay tree.

d Job v. 3; Isa. xiv. 14—19.

36 Yet he passed away, and, lo, he *was* not: yea, I sought him, but he could not be found.

[1] Or, *tree that groweth in his own soil.*

of righteousness and one of wickedness. It is not necessarily implied that they would have any satisfaction in seeing the punishment of the wicked; but the meaning is, that they would be permitted to live so as to *see* that one course of life tended to secure the favour of God, and another to incur his displeasure; that there was an advantage in virtue and religion in this life; and the certainty that they would see this is adverted to as a *motive* for leading a life of piety. The result is so sure that a man may, if he live long, see it himself; and the fact that this is so should be an inducement for his leading a holy life. The psalmist proceeds, in vers. 35, 36, to illustrate this idea from his own observation.

35. *I have seen.* I have had an opportunity, in my long life (ver. 25), of witnessing the accuracy of the statement just made, that a righteous man may live to see a confirmation of the truth that wickedness, however prosperous the wicked man may be, will lead to ultimate ruin,—as I have had an opportunity of seeing (vers. 25, 26) the effect of a course of righteousness on the ultimate prosperity and happiness of its possessor. The same experience, with the same result, is referred to in Job v. 3. ¶ *In great power.* The word here used—עָרִיץ, *aritz*—means properly *terrible; inspiring terror.* It is applied to God in Jer. xx. 11; and to powerful nations, Isa. xxv. 3. It is also used in a bad sense, as denoting violent, fierce, lawless, or a tyrant, Isa. xiii. 11; xxv. 4, 5; Job xv. 20; xxvii. 13. Here it may be used in the sense of one who was prosperous and mighty, and as referring to a man who wielded vast power; but there is connected with that also, undoubtedly, the idea that that power was wielded, not for purposes of benevolence, but for injustice, oppression, and wrong. It was a *wicked* man that was thus powerful. ¶ *And spreading himself.* The word here used means properly to be naked; to make naked; to empty; then, to pour oneself out; and then, to spread oneself abroad. It is applied here to a tree that seems to pour itself out, or to spread itself out in every direction,—sending its limbs aloft, and its branches far on every side. ¶ *Like a green bay tree.* Marg., *a green tree that groweth in its own soil.* The *bay tree* is a species of laurel, but there is no evidence that the original word here refers particularly to this, or specifically to any other tree. The original word—אֶזְרָח, *ezrahh*—is derived from זָרַח, *zarahh*, to rise; and then, to spring up as a plant does, and it properly means here, as expressed in the margin, *a native tree;* that is, a tree that grows in its own soil, or that has not been transplanted. Then, also, it comes to denote a native; one born in the country, not a foreigner: Lev. xvi. 29; xviii. 26, *et al.* The *idea* here is that a tree which thus remains in its own soil is more vigorous, and will attain to a larger growth, than one which is transplanted; and thus the figure becomes an emblem of a prosperous and mighty man. *Perhaps,* also, there is included here, respecting the *man,* the idea that he has grown up where he is; that he has not been driven from place to place; that he has had uniform prosperity; that on the very soil which gave him birth he has risen to rank, to wealth, to power. His *life* has been spent in tranquil scenes, where everything seemed to be stable and secure; what his *end* will be, the psalmist states in the next verse.

36. *Yet he passed away.* Comp. Notes on Job xx. 5. The allusion here, of course, is to the *man,* and not to the *tree,* though the grammatical

37 Mark the perfect *man*, and behold the upright: for the end [c] of *that* man *is* peace.

c Prov. xiv. 32.

construction might refer to either. The idea is that he passed out of view —*he was gone;* he had no permanent abode on earth, but with all his pomp and splendour he had disappeared. Neither his prosperity, his greatness, nor his wealth, could secure him a permanent abode on earth. It might be said, also, in reply to this, that the good man passes away and is not. That is true. But the meaning here is, that this occurs *so much more frequently* in the case of a wicked man, or that wickedness is followed so often in this life by the judgment of God in cutting him off, as to show that there is a moral government, and that that government is administered in favour of the righteous, or that it is an advantage in this life to be righteous. It cannot be meant that this is *universally* so here, but that this is the *general* rule, and that it is *so* constant as to show that God *is* on the side of virtue and religion. ¶ *And lo, he* was *not.* He was no more; there was no longer any such person. The word "*lo*" implies that there was some degree of surprise, or that what had occurred was not looked for or expected. The observer had seen him in great power, flourishing, rich, honoured; and, to his astonishment, he soon passed entirely away. ¶ *Yea, I sought him, but he could not be found.* This is intended to *confirm* what had been just said, or to show how completely he had disappeared. It might be supposed, perhaps, that his removal was only temporary—that he was still somewhere upon the earth; but the psalmist says that after the most diligent search, he could not find him. He had disappeared entirely from among men.

37. *Mark the perfect* man. In contrast with what happens to the wicked. The word *perfect* here is used to designate a righteous man, or a man who serves and obeys God. See Notes on Job i. 1. The word *mark* here means *observe, take notice of.* The argument is, "Look upon that man in the end, in contrast with the prosperous wicked man. See how the close of life, in his case, differs from that of a wicked man, though the one may have been poor and humble, and the other rich and honoured." The *point* of the psalmist's remark turns on the *end*, or the *termination* of their course; and the idea is, that the end of the two is such as to show that there is an advantage in religion, and that God is the friend of the righteous. Of course this is to be understood in accordance with the main thought in the psalm, as affirming what is of *general* occurrence. ¶ *And behold the upright.* Another term for a pious man. Religion makes a man upright; and if a man is *not* upright in his dealings with his fellow-man, or if what he professes does not make him do *right*, it is the fullest proof that he has no true piety, 1 John iii. 7, 8. ¶ *For the end of* that *man* is *peace.* De Wette renders this, Denn Nachkommen hat der Mann Friedens;—"For a future has the man of peace." So it is rendered by the Latin Vulgate: Sunt reliquiæ homini pacifico. So the LXX. So also Hengstenberg, Rosenmüller, and Prof. Alexander. Tholuck renders it, as in our version, "It shall go well at last to such a man." It seems to me that the connexion demands this construction, and the authority of Tholuck is sufficient to prove that the Hebrew will admit of it. The word rendered *end* — אַחֲרִית, *ahharith* — means properly the last or extreme part; then, the end or issue of anything,—that which comes *after* it; then, the after time, the future, the hereafter: Isa. ii. 2; Micah iv. 1; Gen. xlix. 1; Dan. x. 14. It may, therefore, refer to *anything* future; and would be well expressed by the word *hereafter;*—the *hereafter* of such a man. So it is rendered *my last end* in Num. xxiii. 10; *latter end,* Num. xxiv. 20; *their end,* in Ps. lxxiii.

38 But [f] the transgressors shall be destroyed together: the end of the wicked shall be cut off.

39 But the salvation of the righteous *is* of the LORD; *he is* their strength in the time of trouble.

40 And the LORD shall help them, and deliver them; he [g] shall deliver them from the wicked, and save them, because they trust in him.

f Matt. xiii. 30.
g Dan. iii. 17—28.

17. It *might*, therefore, refer to all the future. The connexion—the contrast with what happens to the wicked, vers. 36, 38—would seem to imply that it is used here *particularly* and *especially* with reference to the close of life. The contrast is between the course of the one and that of the other, and between the *termination* of the one course and of the other. In the one case, it is ultimate disaster and ruin; in the other, it is ultimate peace and prosperity. The one *issues in*, or is *followed by* death and ruin; the other is succeeded by peace and salvation. Hence the word may be extended without impropriety to *all* the future,—the whole hereafter. The word *peace* is often employed in the Scriptures to denote the effect of true religion, (*a*) as implying reconciliation with God, and (*b*) as denoting the calmness, the tranquillity, and the happiness which results from such reconciliation, from his friendship, and from the hope of heaven. See John xiv. 27; xvi. 33; Rom. v. 1; viii. 6; Gal. v. 22; Phil. iv. 7. The meaning here, according to the interpretation suggested above, is, that the *future* of the righteous man—the whole future—would be peace; (*a*) as a general rule, peace or calmness in death as the result of religion; and (*b*) in the coming world, where there will be perfect and eternal peace. As a *usual* fact religious men die calmly and peacefully, sustained by hope and by the presence of God; as a *universal* fact, they are made happy for ever beyond the grave.

38. *But the transgressors.* Sinners; violators of the law of God. ¶ *Shall be destroyed together.* The word *together* here—יַחְדָּו, *yahhdav*—means properly a *union of them;* then, together—either (*a*) in one place, Gen. xiii. 6,—or (*b*) at one time, Ps. iv. 8; or (*c*) all as one, Ps. xiv. 3,—or (*d*) mutually with one another, as when men strive together, Deut. xxv. 11. The idea here is, that one would be destroyed as well as another; that there would be no exception; that they would go to the same ruin. They might be destroyed at different times, or in different modes, but it would be the same destruction in the end. ¶ *The end of the wicked.* The *future* of the wicked. The same word is used here which occurs in ver. 37, as applied to the righteous. The meaning is, that while the *future* of the one would be peace, the *future* of the other would be a *cutting off*, or destruction. ¶ *Shall be cut off.* That is, *they* shall be cut off; or, there will be a cutting off. This means here, evidently, (*a*) that as an ordinary fact they would be cut down before they had reached the full limit of their course, vers. 35, 36; (*b*) in the future world they would be cut off from hope and happiness for ever.

39. *But the salvation of the righteous* is *of the* LORD. Or, salvation comes to the righteous from the Lord. While the wicked are cut off, the righteous shall be safe. There are evidently two ideas here: (1) that there *will be* salvation to the righteous, while the wicked are cut off; (2) that this comes from the Lord, and not from themselves. It is not owing to any power of their own that they are safe, but is solely because they are kept by the Lord. ¶ He is *their strength in the time of trouble.* See Notes on Ps. ix. 9; xviii. 2.

40. *And the* LORD *shall help them.* He will interpose to defend them when they are in danger and in trouble.

¶ *And deliver them.* Rescue them from their dangers, and from the power of the wicked. ¶ *He shall deliver them from the wicked.* From all the attempts of the wicked to destroy them. ¶ *And save them.* Or, preserve them. He will keep them to everlasting life. ¶ *Because they trust in him.* They rely on him, and not on themselves. This verse is a summing up of the sentiments of the psalm, and is designed to confirm the main thought which runs through it, to wit, that we should not fret, or murmur, or repine at the prosperity of wicked men, ver. 1. The reason ultimately assigned for this is, that whatever may be the danger of the righteous from the designs of wicked men, they will in the end be safe. It will go well with them, for the Lord will keep them. The general course of thought in the psalm is, that, whatever prosperity the wicked now have, it is temporary, for they will soon be cut off; and that whatever troubles now come upon the righteous, they too are temporary, and that their *hereafter* — their *futurity* — will be blessedness and peace. There *is* a moral government: God is the friend of the righteous; along the path of the present life there are proofs that he is so, and beyond the present life he will show himself to be so in their eternal peace. He is the enemy of the wicked; there are evidences in the present life that he is so, and this will be fully and finally manifested in their destruction in the future world. The argument in the psalm, indeed, is mainly drawn from the *present life,*—from what there is to encourage virtue and goodness in the blessings which religion scatters on earth, and by the peaceful termination of the course—as well as from what there is to discourage wickedness and vice, in the fact that the wicked will be cut down and pass away. The argument is, that if this life were all, there are encouragements here to virtue and goodness. In Ps. lxxiii., which in some respects resembles this psalm, the argument which satisfied the mind of the troubled psalmist — troubled at the prosperity of the wicked — is drawn mainly from the future world. Here it is drawn chiefly from the present life; and the main thought here—the practical lesson from the psalm—is, that even with reference to the life that now is—to its security, to its peace, to its blessedness, and to its happy close—it is an advantage to be righteous. It is better to have God for our friend in life, and our support in death, than to have all the external prosperity of wicked men.

PSALM XXXVIII.

I. *Author of the psalm.*—The psalm purports to have been written by David, and there is no reason to doubt that it was composed by him. There is no tradition to the contrary, and there is nothing in the psalm inconsistent with such a supposition.

II. *The title.*—The psalm is said in the title to be designed "to bring to remembrance." The same title occurs in Ps. lxx., though there is no resemblance between the two, except that they both have reference to the attempts and purposes of the enemies of David, and to trials in different forms which had come from them. The Latin Vulgate renders this, "A Psalm of David, for remembrance concerning the Sabbath." The Septuagint renders it in the same manner. The Arabic: "In which there is a mention of the sabbath." Whence these allusions to the sabbath were derived is unknown, as there is nothing in the Hebrew corresponding with them. The Chaldee Paraphrase has prefixed, "For a good memorial concerning Israel." The Hebrew term used—לְהַזְכִּיר, *lehazkir*—means simply *for bringing to remembrance,* or for reminding. The meaning is, that it is a record for the purpose of *reminding;* that is, of keeping up the *remembrance* of something which had occurred in his own experience, and which might be useful to himself or to others; the record of some valuable lessons which had been learned from what he had experienced in the trials referred to. Comp. Gen. xl. 14; 1 Kings xvii. 18; Ezek. xxi. 24. Gesenius (*Lex.*) renders it, "To bring to remembrance, sc., oneself with God." Grotius says of it, "This psalm is designed to inculcate the perpetual remembrance of David and his sin, and of the pardon that was granted." There can be no doubt that the psalm had this design of making a permanent record of an important event in the life of the author, or of his *experience* in a time of great calamity; but why this title was affixed only to this psalm and to Ps. lxx. is wholly unknown. There are many other psalms to which, it would seem, the title might have been prefixed with equal propriety, as containing important reminiscences of trials, and of religious experience under those trials.

III. *Occasion of the psalm.*—The particular time or occasion on which the psalm was composed is unknown. There are no recorded events in the life of David to which this psalm would be *particularly* applicable, though, in a life of trial and suffering such as his was, there can be no doubt that there may have been many such occasions. It is impossible now, however, to fix the exact time or occasion with any degree of accuracy or probability. What is known is, that it was with reference to sickness (vers. 3-8, 10, 11), and to the neglect which was evinced, and the cruel treatment which he received, in sickness (vers. 11, 12, 19, 20).

IV. *The contents of the psalm.*

(1.) The psalm describes the condition of one who was suffering from *sickness*, vers. 2, 3, 5, 7, 8, 10, 11. Some have supposed that this is merely *figurative* language, and that it is designed to represent calamity, trouble, sorrow, heavily pressing upon him *as if* he were sick; others have supposed that it is intended to refer, not to David, but to the people of Israel as afflicted and persecuted, represented under the image of one suffering from disease; but the most natural and obvious interpretation is to regard it as a literal description of one who was suffering under some form of disease. There were doubtless occasions in the long life of David when this actually occurred; and there are occasions in the lives of the people of God of a similar kind, sufficiently numerous to make it proper that an inspired record of the experience of a good man thus suffering should be preserved, as an example of the proper spirit to be manifested in sickness. What was the *character* or *nature* of that sickness may appear in the examination of the particular expressions in the record.

(2.) The condition of the sufferer as aggravated by two things:

(*a*) By the neglect of his friends,—by their turning away from him in his trials, ver. 11;

(*b*) By the efforts of his enemies,—taking advantage of his sickness, and bringing against him accusations which he was not then able to meet, ver. 12.

(3.) He himself traces all these trials, arising either from his disease or from the attacks of his enemies, to his own sins, and regards them all as the expression of the Divine displeasure against his transgressions, vers. 3, 4, 5, 18. The effect of his suffering from sickness was to bring his sins to remembrance—an effect not uncommon, and, under the Providence of God, not undesigned—though he may have erred, as the afflicted often do, in supposing that his sickness was a *specific punishment* for sin, or was intended to correct him for some *particular* transgression.

(4.) His own calmness and meekness in respect to the charges which, amid his other trials, his enemies brought against him, vers. 13, 14. He says that he was like a deaf man that did not hear, and like a dumb man that did not open his mouth. He *seemed* not to hear anything that was said to his disadvantage, and he was as silent as though he had been dumb.

(5.) His earnest prayer for the interposition of God in these circumstances of sickness and trial, vers. 15-22. He says that his only help is in God, ver. 15; he prays that God will not allow his enemies to triumph over him, ver. 16; he says that he is ready to halt, or that his strength is nearly exhausted, and he fears that his patience will utterly give way, ver. 17; he says that he will confess all his sin, ver. 18; he refers to the fact that his enemies are "lively," and are on the alert for his fall, vers. 19, 20; and in view of all this, he earnestly calls on God to save him, vers. 21, 22.

There is a striking resemblance between this psalm and Ps. vi., in the general structure, and in some of the particular expressions. Both appear to have been composed in a time of sickness, though not probably in the *same* sickness; and both express substantially the same feelings. The forty-first psalm, also, appears to have been composed on a similar occasion. In a revelation adapted to mankind, and designed to be applicable in its instructions and promises to the various conditions in which men are placed on the earth, it was to be presumed that there would be a not un-

PSALM XXXVIII.

A Psalm of David to bring to *h* remembrance.

O LORD, rebuke me not in thy wrath; neither chasten me in thy hot displeasure.

2 For thine arrows *i* stick fast in me, and thy hand presseth me sore.

3 *There is* no soundness in my flesh, because of thine anger; neither *is there any* [1] rest in my bones, *k* because of my sin.

h Ps. lxx., *title.* *i* Job vi. 4.

[1] *peace,* or, *health.* *k* Ps. li. 8.

frequent reference to the sick bed—to the trials on a couch of languishing. And in an inspired book of *devotion*, like the book of Psalms, designed to illustrate the nature of piety in the various and diversified situations of life, the object of a revelation could not be fully accomplished without an illustration of the feelings of piety in the time of sickness, and in the prospect of death,—for such scenes must occur in the world, and it is eminently in such scenes that we desire to know what is the proper feeling to be cherished; what true religion *is* at such a time; what it will do to sustain and comfort the soul. The book of Psalms, therefore, would not have been complete without such an illustration of the nature of piety; and hence it was every way probable that psalms like this would be composed, and every way improbable that no such psalms would be found in a book of inspired devotion. It seems to me, therefore, unnatural, and not demanded by any proper views of interpretation, to regard this psalm, and the other similar psalms, as De Wette, Hengstenberg, Rosenmüller and others do, and as the Chaldee Paraphrase and Jarchi do, as descriptive of *general calamity, Unglück;*—or of calamity coming upon *a people*—rather than a *particular* affliction in the form of sickness coming upon *an individual.* The great value of the book of Psalms consists in the fact that it furnishes illustrations of the nature and power of true religion in all the varied circumstances of the lives of individual friends of God.

1. *O* LORD, *rebuke me not in thy wrath.* See Notes on Ps. vi. 1, where the same language occurs, except in the change of a single Hebrew *word,* i. e., *wrath,* though expressing the same *idea.* ¶ *Neither chasten me in thy hot displeasure.* See Notes on Ps. vi. 1. The Hebrew in both is the same, except that in this place the negative particle is omitted, but without affecting the sense. It is not improbable that the one was copied from the other, or that this was composed with the language of the former in the memory. Thus we often use language with which we are familiar, as being well adapted to express our ideas.

2. *For thine arrows stick fast in me.* See Notes on Job vi. 4. The word rendered *stick fast*—נָחַת, *nahhath*—means properly to go or come down; to descend; and the literal idea here would be, "thine arrows come down upon me." It is not so much the idea of their *sticking fast* when in the wound or flesh; it is that they come down upon one, and pierce him. The meaning is, that he was afflicted *as if* God had wounded him with arrows,—arrows which pierced deep in his flesh. Comp. Notes on Ps. xlv. 5. The allusion is to the disease with which he was afflicted. ¶ *And thy hand presseth me sore.* The same word is here used which in the former part of the verse is rendered *stick fast.* The idea is, that the hand of God had *descended* or *come down* upon him, prostrating his strength, and laying him on a bed of pain.

3. There is *no soundness in my flesh.* There is no sound place in my flesh; there is no part of my body that is free from disease. The word here used—מְתֹם, *methom*—occurs only in Judges xx. 48, where it is rendered *men;* in Isa. i. 6, and in this place, where it is rendered *soundness.* See Notes on Isa. i. 6. It means that the body was wholly diseased; but what was the nature of the disease we are not informed. It would seem, however, that it was some cutaneous disease, or some disease that produced outward and loathsome erup-

4 For mine iniquities are gone over mine [l] head; as an heavy burden they are too heavy for me.

l Ezra ix. 6.

tions that made his friends withdraw from him, vers. 7, 11; comp. Ps. xli. 8. ¶ *Because of thine anger.* That is, he regarded this as a punishment for sin; a specific manifestation of the Divine displeasure on account of some particular offence or act of transgression. He does not refer, however, to the particular sin which he regarded as the cause of his sickness, and it is probable that this is just an instance of that state of mind, often morbid, in which we consider a particular calamity that comes upon us as a special proof of the Divine displeasure. There are, undoubtedly, cases when sickness may be properly thus regarded;—but it should be observed that, as this is not the universal rule in regard to sickness and other trials,—as they come upon us under general laws, and because in sweeping over a community they often fall upon the righteous as well as the wicked,—we should not infer at once, when *we* are sick or otherwise afflicted, that it is for any *particular* sin, or that it is proof of any special displeasure of God against us. It is undoubtedly right to regard *all* affliction as having a close connexion with sin, and to allow any calamity to *suggest* to us the idea of our depravity, for sin is the original cause of all the wretchedness and woe on earth; but under this general law we cannot always determine the *particular* reason why calamity comes on *us.* It may have other purposes and ends than that of being a specific *punishment* for our offences. ¶ *Neither* is there any *rest in my bones.* Marg., *peace* or *health.* The Hebrew word means *peace.* The idea is, that there was no comfort; no rest. His bones were filled with constant pain. The flesh *and the bones* constitute the entire man; and the idea here is, that he was universally diseased. The disease pervaded every part of the body. ¶ *Because of my sin.* Regarding his sin as the immediate cause of his suffering. In a general sense, as has been remarked above, it is not wrong to regard sin as the cause of all our misery, and we may allow our suffering to be, in some degree, a measure or gauge of the evil of sin. The error consists in our regarding a particular form of trial as the punishment of a particular sin. The effect in the case of the psalmist was undoubtedly to bring to remembrance his sins; to impress his mind deeply with a sense of the evil of sin; to humble him at the recollection of guilt. This effect is not improper or undesirable, provided it does not lead us to the conclusion, often erroneous, that our affliction has come upon us on account of a particular transgression. That *may* be so indeed; but the idea that that is the universal rule in regard to affliction is one which we are not required to entertain. See Notes on Luke xiii. 1–5.

4. *For mine iniquities are gone over mine head.* This is merely an enlargement of the idea suggested in the last verse—that his present sickness was to be traced to his sin, and that he was suffering the punishment for sin. The idea is here that his sins were very numerous and very aggravated. They had risen up around him, or had so accumulated that the mass rose, like waves of the sea, above his head. A somewhat similar idea—though the thought there refers rather to the *number* of sins than the *degree* of guilt—occurs in Ps. xl. 12: "Mine iniquities . . . . are more than the hairs of my head." ¶ *As an heavy burden,* etc. That is, they are so heavy that I cannot bear them, and my frame has sunk under them. This might mean either that the *sense* of sin was so great that he could not bear up under it, but had been crushed by it (comp. Ps. xxxii. 3, 4); or that on account of sin, *as if* it were a heavy weight, he had been crushed by disease.

5 My wounds [m] stink, *and* are corrupt because of my foolishness.

6 I am [1] troubled; I am bowed down greatly; I go mourning all the day long.

7 For my loins are filled with a loathsome *disease;* and *there is* no soundness in my flesh.

m Isa. i. 5, 6. [1] *wearied.*

The general idea is, that the real *cause* of his sickness was the fact that he was a great sinner, and that God was punishing him for it.

5. *My wounds stink.* The word rendered *wounds* here means properly the swelling or wales produced by stripes. See Notes on Isa. i. 6; liii. 5. The meaning here is, that he was under *chastisement* for his sin; that the stripes or blows on account of it had not only left a mark and produced a swelling, but that the skin itself had been broken, and that the flesh had become corrupt, and the sore offensive. Many expositors regard this as a mere figurative representation of the sorrow produced by the consciousness of sin; and of the loathsome nature of sin, but it seems to me that the whole connexion rather requires us to understand it of bodily suffering, or of disease. ¶ And *are corrupt.* The word here used—מָקַק, *makak*—means properly to melt; to pine away; and then, to flow, to run, as sores and ulcers do. The meaning here is, My sores run; to wit, with corrupt matter. ¶ *Because of my foolishness.* Because of my sin, regarded as folly. Comp. Notes on Ps. xiv. 1. The Scripture idea is that sin is the highest folly. Hence the psalmist, at the same time that he confesses his sin, acknowledges also its foolishness. The idea of sin and that of folly become so blended together,—or they are so entirely synonymous,—that the one term may be used for the other.

6. *I am troubled.* Marg., *wearied.* The Hebrew word means to bend, to curve; then, to be distorted, to writhe with pain, convulsions, and spasms. In Isa. xxi. 3, the same word is rendered, "*I was bowed down* at the hearing of it;" that is, Sorrow so took hold of him, that at the intelligence he writhed with pain as a woman in travail. So here it means that he was bent, or bowed down, or that he writhed in pain as the result of his iniquities. ¶ *I am bowed down greatly.* Comp. Ps. xxxv. 14. The word means properly to bow down; then, to be brought low; to be depressed with pain, grief, sorrow: Ps. x. 10; Isa. ii. 11. ¶ *I go mourning all the day long.* Constantly; without any intermission. On the word rendered *go mourning*—קָדַר, *kadar*—see Notes on Ps. xxxv. 14. The idea here is, that, on account of sin, he was crushed and bowed down as a mourner is with his sorrows, and that he appeared constantly as he walked about with these badges of grief and heavy sorrow. The disease which he had, and which was so offensive to himself (ver. 5), and to others (ver. 11), was like the filthy and foul garments which mourners put on as expressive of their sorrow. See Notes on Job i. 20; ii. 8.

7. *For my bones are filled with a loathsome* disease. This would seem to indicate the *seat* of the disease, though not its nature. The word here used, according to Gesenius (*Lex.*), properly denotes the internal muscles of the loins near the kidneys, to which the fat adheres. The word rendered *loathsome*—the word *disease* being supplied by our translators—is derived from קָלָה, *kalah,* a word which means to roast, to parch, as fruit, grain, etc.; and then, in the form used here, it means scorched, burned; hence, a burning or inflammation; and the whole phrase would be synonymous with *an inflammation of the kidneys.* The *word* here used does not imply that there was any eruption, or ulcer, though it would seem from ver. 5 that this was the fact, and that the inflammation had produced this effect. ¶ *And* there is

8 I am feeble and sore broken: I have [n] roared by reason of the disquietness of my heart.
9 Lord, all my desire *is* before [o] thee: and my groaning is not hid from thee.
10 My heart panteth, my strength faileth me: as for the light [p] of mine eyes, it also is [1] gone from me.
11 My lovers and my friends stand aloof [q] from my [2] sore; and my [3] kinsmen stand [r] afar off.

n Ps. xxxii. 3. *o* Ps. cxlv. 19. *p* Lam. v. 17. [1] *not with.* *q* Matt. xxvi. 56; Luke x. 31, 32. [2] *stroke.* [3] Or, *my neighbours.* *r* Luke xxiii. 49.

no soundness in my flesh. See ver. 3. His disease was so deep-seated and so pervading, that there did not seem to be *any* soundness in his flesh. His whole body seemed to be diseased.

8. *I am feeble.* The word here used means properly to be cold, or without warmth; and then, to be torpid or languid. Comp. Gen. xlv. 26. Would not this be well represented by the idea of a *"chill"*? ¶ *And sore broken.* This word means to break in pieces; to beat small; to crush; and then it may be used to denote being broken in spirit, or crushed by pain and sorrow: Isa. lvii. 15; liii. 5; xix. 10. ¶ *I have roared.* I have cried out on account of my suffering. See Notes on Ps. xxii. 1. ¶ *By reason of the disquietness of my heart.* The word here rendered *disquietness* means properly a *roaring*, as of the sea: Isa. v. 30; and then, a groaning, or roaring, as of the afflicted. Here the *heart* is represented as *roaring* or *crying out.* The lips only gave utterance to the deeper groanings of the heart.

9. *Lord, all my desire* is *before thee.* That is, Thou knowest all that I would ask or that I need. This is the expression of one who felt that his only hope was in God, and that He fully understood the case. There was no need of repeating the request. He was willing to leave the whole case with God. ¶ *And my groaning is not hid from thee.* My sighing; the expression of my sorrow and anguish. As God certainly heard these sighs, and as He wholly understood the case, David hoped that He would mercifully interpose in his behalf.

10. *My heart panteth.* The word rendered *panteth*, in its original form, means properly to go about; to travel around; and then, to travel around as a merchant or pedlar, or for purposes of traffic: Gen. xxiii. 16; xxxvii. 28; xlii. 34. Applied to the heart, as it is here, it means to move about rapidly; to palpitate; to beat quick. It is an expression of pain and distress, indicated by a rapid beating of the heart. ¶ *My strength faileth me.* It is rapidly failing. He regarded himself as rapidly approaching death. ¶ *As for the light of mine eyes.* My vision; my sight. ¶ *It also is gone from me.* Marg., as in Heb., *is not with me.* This is usually an indication of approaching death; and it would seem from all these symptoms that he appeared to be drawing near to the end of life. Comp. Ps. xiii. 3; vi. 7; xxxi. 9.

11. *My lovers.* See Notes on Ps. xxxi. 11. The reference here is to those who professed to be his friends. ¶ *And my friends.* The word here used means properly an acquaintance, a companion, a friend, Job ii. 11; xix. 21; then, a lover, a friend, a neighbour. The phrase here would be synonymous with our word *kinsmen.* ¶ *Stand aloof.* They are unwilling to come near me; they leave me to suffer alone. ¶ *From my sore.* Marg., *stroke.* The Hebrew word means properly a stroke, a blow, Deut. xvii. 8; xxi. 5; then a stroke in the sense of calamities or judgments, such as God brings upon men: Gen xii. 17; Ex. xi. 1. The meaning here is, that they stand aloof from him, or refuse to come near him, as if he were afflicted with some contagious disease. ¶ *And my kinsmen.* Marg., *neighbours.* The Hebrew word here used —קָרוֹב, *karob*—means properly near,

12 They also that seek after my life lay snares *for me:* and they that seek my hurt speak mischievous things, and imagine deceits all the day long.
13 But [s] I, as a deaf *man*, heard not; and *I was* as a dumb man *that* openeth not his mouth.
14 Thus I was as a man that heareth not, and in whose mouth *are* no reproofs.

s 2 Sam. xvi. 10, etc.; Isa. xlii. 19, 20.

nigh; spoken of a place, Gen. xix. 20; then of time, Isa. xiii. 6; then of kindred or affinity, Num. xxvii. 11; and then of friendship, meaning our intimate acquaintance—as we should say, those who are *near* to us, Job xix. 14. The word would be applicable to neighbours or to warm personal friends.

12. *They also that seek after my life.* This was a new aggravation of his affliction, that those who were his enemies now sought to accomplish their purposes against him with better hopes of success, by taking advantage of his sickness. ¶ *Lay snares* for me. On the meaning of this phrase, see Notes on Ps. ix. 15. The idea here is that they sought this opportunity of ensnaring or entrapping him so as to ruin him. They took advantage of the fact that he was weak and helpless, and of the fact that he was forsaken or abandoned by his friends, to accomplish his ruin. *How* this was done is not stated. It might have been by their coming on him when he was thus helpless; or it might have been by endeavouring in his weak condition to extort confessions or promises from him that might be turned to his ruin. An enemy may hope to succeed much better when the one opposed is sick than when he is well, and may take advantage of his weak state of body and mind, and of the fact that he seems to be forsaken by all, to accomplish what could not be done if he were in the enjoyment of health, or sustained by powerful friends, or by a public opinion in his favour. ¶ *And they that seek my hurt.* They who seek to injure me. ¶ *Speak mischievous things.* Slanderous words. They charge on me things that are false, and that tend to injure me. The very fact that he was thus afflicted, they might urge (in accordance with a prevailing belief, and with the conviction of the psalmist also, vers. 3–5) as a proof of guilt. This was done by the three friends of Job; and the enemies of the psalmist may thus have taken advantage of his sickness to circulate false reports about him which he could not then well meet. ¶ *And imagine deceits.* Imagine or feign deceitful things; things which they know to be false or unfounded. ¶ *All the day long.* Constantly. They seem to have no other employment. See Ps. xxxv. 20.

13. *But I, as a deaf* man, *heard not.* I was *as if* I had been deaf, and did not hear them or know what they were about. I took no notice of what they did any more than if I had not heard them. That is, he did not reply to them; he did not become angry; he was as calm and patient as if they had said nothing. ¶ *And* I was *as a dumb man* that *openeth not his mouth.* As if I were a man that could not speak. I was perfectly silent under all this persecution. Comp. 2 Sam. xvi. 10. How eminently true was this of the Saviour! Isa. liii. 7; 1 Peter ii. 23; Matt. xxvi. 63; xxvii. 12, 14.

14. *Thus I was as a man that heareth not.* The sentiment in the former verse is repeated here to show the greatness of his patience and forbearance, or to fix the attention on the fact that one who was so calumniated and wronged could bear it patiently. ¶ *And in whose mouth* are *no reproofs.* As a man who *never* reproved another; who, whatever might be the wrong which he endured, never replied to it; as he would be who was *incapable* of reproof, or who had no *faculty* for reproving. The whole of this is de-

15 For [1] in thee, O LORD, do I hope: thou wilt [2] hear, O LORD my God.

16 For I said, *Hear me,* lest *otherwise* they should rejoice over me: when my foot slippeth, they magnify *themselves* against me.

17 For I *am* ready [3] to halt,

[1] *thee do I wait for.* [2] Or, *answer.* [3] *for halting.*

signed to show his entire patience under the wrongs which he suffered.

15. *For in thee, O* LORD, *do I hope.* This shows the reason or ground of his patience. He committed his whole cause to God. He believed that God would take care of his reputation, and that he would vindicate him. See Ps. xxxvii. 5, 6. He had no doubt that He would protect his character, and that, notwithstanding the reproaches of his enemies, his true character would at last be made to shine forth, so that all men would see that he had been unjustly aspersed. The exact idea here is expressed, and the sentiment was beautifully and perfectly illustrated, in what is said of the Lord Jesus:—"Who, when he was reviled, reviled not again; when he suffered, he threatened not; but committed himself to him that judgeth righteously," 1 Peter ii. 23. ¶ *Thou wilt hear, O* LORD *my God.* Marg., as in Heb., *answer.* The idea is, that God would answer his prayers, and that his character would, in answer to those prayers, be set right before the world.

16. *For I said.* This is the prayer to which he referred in the previous verse. He prayed that he might not be permitted to fall away under the influence of his sins and sufferings; that his faith might remain firm; that he might not be allowed to act so as to justify the accusations of his enemies, or to give them occasion to rejoice over his fall. The entire prayer (vers. 16–18) is one that is based on the consciousness of his own weakness, and his liability to sin, if left to himself; on the certainty that if God *did* not interpose, his sins would get the mastery over him, and he would become in his conduct all that his enemies desired, and be in fact all that they had falsely charged on him. ¶ Hear me, *lest* otherwise *they should rejoice over me.* Literally, "For I said, lest they should rejoice over me." It is the language of earnest desire that they might *not* thus be allowed to rejoice over his fall. The same sentiment occurs substantially in Ps. xiii. 3, 4. The motive is a right one; alike (*a*) in reference to ourselves personally—that our foes may not triumph over us by the ruin of our character; and (*b*) in reference to its bearing on the cause of virtue and religion—that that cause may not suffer by our misconduct; comp. Ps. lxix. 6. ¶ *When my foot slippeth.* (*a*) When my foot really *has* slipped, or when *I have* committed sin (as the psalmist did not deny that he had done, vers. 3, 4, 5, 18); or (*b*) when it *might* occur *again* (as he felt was possible); or (*c*) *if* I deviate in the slightest degree from perfect virtue; *if* I inadvertently do anything wrong. The slipping of the foot is an indication of the want of firmness, and hence it comes to represent the falling into sin. ¶ *They magnify* themselves *against me.* See Ps. xxxv. 26. They exult over me; they triumph; they boast. They *make themselves great* on my fall, or by my being put down. This he says (*a*) they were *disposed* to do, for they had shown a disposition to do it whenever he had fallen into sin; (*b*) he apprehended that they *would* do it again, and they had already begun to magnify themselves against him, *as if* they were certain that it would occur. He did not deny that there was ground to fear this, for he felt that his strength was almost gone (ver. 17), and that God only could uphold him, and save him from justifying all the expectations of his enemies.

17. *For I* am *ready to halt.* Marg., as in Heb., *for halting.* The word from which the word used here is derived means properly to lean on one side, and then to halt or limp. The

and my sorrow *is* continually before me.

18 For I will declare mine iniquity; I will be sorry [t] for my sin.

19 But mine enemies [1] *are* lively, *and* they are strong; and they that hate me wrongfully are multiplied.

20 They also that render evil for good are mine adversaries; because I follow *the thing that* good *is*.

t 2 Cor. vii. 9, 10.
[1] being *living, are strong.*

meaning here is, that he was like one who was limping along, and who was ready to fall; that is, in the case here referred to, he felt that his strength was almost gone, and that he was in continual danger of falling into sin, or sinking under his accumulated burdens, and of thus giving occasion for all that his enemies said of him, or occasion for their triumphing over him. Men often have this feeling,—that their sorrows are so great that they cannot hope to hold out much longer, and that if God does not interpose they *must* fall. ¶ *And my sorrow* is *continually before me.* That is, my grief or suffering is unintermitted. Probably the reference here is particularly to that which *caused* his grief, or which was the source of his trouble—his sin. The fact that he was a sinner was never absent from his mind; *that* was the source of all his trouble; *that* was what so pressed upon him that it was likely to crush him to the dust.

18. *For I will declare mine iniquity.* That is, he was not disposed to hide his sin. He would make no concealment of the fact that he regarded himself as a sinner. He admitted this to be true, and he admitted that his sin was the cause of all his troubles. It was the fact that he was a sinner that so painfully affected his mind; and he was not disposed to attempt to conceal it from any one. ¶ *I will be sorry for my sin.* I will not deny it; I will not apologise for it. I admit the truth of what my conscience charges on me; I admit the correctness and the propriety of the Divine judgment by which I have been afflicted on account of my sin; I desire to repent of all my transgressions, and to turn from them. Comp. Lev. xxvi. 41. The calamity brought upon the psalmist for his sin had produced the desired effect in this respect, that it had brought him to true repentance; and now, with the full confession of his sin, he was anxious only lest he should fall utterly, and should give his enemies, and the enemies of the truth, the occasion to triumph over him which they desired.

19. *But mine enemies* are *lively*, etc. De Wette renders this, "My enemies live and are strong." The word translated *lively*—חַיִּים, *hhayyim*—means properly *living, being alive.* The literal translation would be, "My enemies, being alive, are strong." The idea is, that while he was weak and apparently near to death, they were in the full vigour of life and health. They were able to engage in active efforts to accomplish their purposes. They could take advantage of his weakness; and he could not contend with them, for he was no *match* for them. In every respect they had the advantage of him; and he prays, therefore, for the Divine interposition in his behalf. ¶ *And they that hate me wrongfully.* Heb., *falsely.* See Ps. xxxv. 19. ¶ *Are multiplied.* They are numerous. They are constantly increasing.

20. *They also that render evil for good.* They whose characteristic it is to return evil for good, are opposed to me. This implies that those who were now seeking his ruin had been formerly benefited by him. They were persons who cherished no grateful recollection of favours bestowed on them, but who found a pleasure in persecuting and wronging their benefactor. Comp. Ps. xxxv. 12–16. ¶ *Are my adversaries.* Are now opposed to me; have become my enemies. ¶ *Because I follow* the thing

21 Forsake me not, O LORD: O my God, be not far from me.

22 Make haste [1] to help me, O Lord my salvation.

[1] *for my help.*

that *good* is. This properly means, Because I follow the good. The Hebrew word rendered *because*—תַּחַת, *tahhath*—means properly the lower part; what is underneath; then, below; beneath. The idea here is, that the *underlying reason* of what they did was that he followed good, or that he was a righteous man; or, as we say, This was *at the bottom* of all their dealings with him. Sinner as he felt he was (and as he acknowledged he was) before God, and true as it was that his *sickness* was brought upon him by God for his sinfulness, yet the reason why *men* treated him as they did, was that he was a friend of God—a religious man; and their conduct, therefore, was sheer persecution. We may, with entire consistency, be very humble before God, and acknowledge that we deserve all that *He* brings upon us; and yet, at the same time, we may be sensible that we have not wronged men, and that *their* conduct toward us is wholly undeserved, is most ungrateful, is sheer malignity against us.

21. *Forsake me not, O* LORD. That is, Do not leave me in my troubles, my sickness, my sorrow. Leave me not to die; leave me not to murmur and dishonour thee; leave me not to the reproaches of my enemies. ¶ *O my God, be not far from me.* See Ps. xxxv. 22. Comp. Ps. x. 1; xiii. 1.

22. *Make haste to help me.* Marg., as in Heb., *for my help.* This is an earnest prayer that God would come immediately to his rescue. ¶ *O Lord my salvation.* See Notes on Psalm xxvii. 1. The effect, therefore, of the trials that came upon the psalmist was to lead him to cry most earnestly to God. Those sorrows led him to God. This is one of the designed effects of affliction. Trouble never accomplishes its proper effect unless it leads us to God; and anything that *will* lead us to him is a gain in the end. The deeper our trouble, therefore, the greater may be the ultimate good to us; and at the end of life, when we come to look over all that has happened in our journey through this world, that on which we may look back with most satisfaction and gratitude may be the sorrows and afflictions that have befallen us,—for these will be then seen to have been among the chief instrumentalities by which we were weaned from sin; by which we were led to the Saviour; by which we were induced to seek a preparation for heaven. No Christian, when he comes to die, ever feels that he has been too much afflicted, or that any trial has come upon him for which there was not occasion, and which was not designed and adapted to do him good.

PSALM XXXIX.

This psalm purports to be a Psalm of David, but the special occasion in his life when it was composed is not specified, and it cannot now be ascertained. It was evidently, like the previous psalm, in a time of affliction, but to what particular affliction it refers is unknown. It is, however, of so general a character, and expresses feelings which so often spring up in the mind of the afflicted, that it is adapted for general use in the world, and nothing would be gained, perhaps, if we *could* ascertain the particular trial in the life of the author of the psalm to which it had referred. On the meaning of the phrase in the title, "To the chief Musician," see Notes on the title to Ps. iv. The addition to that in this place, "to Jeduthun," implies, according to the rendering in our common version, that *Jeduthun*, at the time when the psalm was composed, occupied that position; and this is probable. The word Jeduthun means properly *praising, celebrating;* but here it is used evidently as a proper name, and designates some one who was placed over the music, or who had charge of it. The reference is to one of the choristers appointed by David. Jeduthun is expressly mentioned, among others, as having been appointed for this service, 1 Chron. xvi.

41: "And with them Heman and Jeduthun . . . to give thanks to the Lord." So, also, ver. 42: "And with them Heman and Jeduthun, with trumpets and cymbals for those that should make a sound, and with musical instruments of God." See, also, 1 Chron. xxv. 6; 2 Chron. xxxv. 15. It would seem, also, from Neh. xi. 17, that his descendants held the same office in his time.

The psalm was composed by one who was in trouble, and who had such thoughts in his affliction that he did not dare to express them for fear that they would do injury to the cause of religion. He was sad and dispirited. He could not understand the reason of the Divine dealings. He did not know why he was thus afflicted. He did not see the justice, the propriety, or the benevolence of the Divine arrangements by which the life of man was made so short and so vain, and by which he was called to suffer so much. There was, in his case, a conscious spirit of complaining against the Divine arrangements; or there was so much that, in his view, was mysterious and apparently inconsistent with benevolence in the Divine dealings, that he did not dare to express what was going on in his own mind, or to give vent to the secret thoughts of his soul; and he therefore resolved that he would keep silence, and would say nothing on the subject, especially when the wicked were before him. He bore this as long as he could, and then he gave vent to his suppressed emotions, and sought comfort in prayer.

The psalm, therefore, consists of two parts:—

I. His purpose to keep silence; to say nothing; to suppress the emotions which were struggling in his bosom, or not to give utterance to what was passing in his mind, lest, by such an expression, he should strengthen and confirm the wicked in what they were thinking about, or in their views of God. So far did he carry this, that he says he resolved to hold his "peace *even from good*;" that is, he resolved that he would say *nothing*, lest he should be tempted to say something which would injure the cause of religion, and which he would have occasion to regret, vers. 1, 2.

II. The fact that he was constrained to speak; that he could not confine his thoughts to his own bosom; that he was in such anguish that he *must* find relief by giving utterance to what was passing in his soul. This occupies the remainder of the psalm, vers. 3-13. This part of the psalm embraces the following points:—

(1.) The depth and anguish of his feeling; the fact that his feelings became so intense, like a pent-up fire in his bosom, that he could not but speak and make known his thoughts, ver. 3.

(2.) The utterance in words of the thoughts which he had been cherishing, which gave him so much trouble, and which he had been unwilling to express before the wicked, lest he should confirm them in their views about God and his dealings, vers. 4-6. These thoughts pertained to his contemplation of human life,—its brevity, its vanity, and its sorrows; to his doubts and perplexities about the purpose for which such a being as man was made; and to the darkness of his own mind concerning the reasons why God had made man thus, and why he dealt thus with him. Why was life so short? Why was it so vain? Why was it so full of sorrow?

(3.) His earnest appeal to God in this state of mind, vers. 7-13.

(*a*) He says that his only hope was in God, ver. 7.

(*b*) He asks for deliverance from his transgressions—that is, here, from the calamities which had come upon him for his sins, ver. 8.

(*c*) He says that he had been dumb before God, and had endeavoured not to murmur at his dealings, ver. 9.

(*d*) He refers to the fact that when God undertakes to rebuke man for his iniquity, man cannot stand before him —that his beauty is made to consume away like a moth, vers. 10, 11.

(*e*) He earnestly cries, therefore, to God, and prays that he would deliver him, vers. 12, 13. He asks for strength in these struggles and trials, before he should go forth and be no more.

The psalm will be found to express feelings which often pass through the minds of even good men in regard to the mysteries of our condition here, and will be found to be adapted to calm down those feelings which often arise in the soul, and which could not be expressed without doing injury by paining the hearts of the good, and by confirming the wicked in their notions; to silence the murmurings of the heart; and to bring the soul into a state of humble acquiescence before God under a recognition that all the events of life are controlled by his hand.

PSALM XXXIX.

To the chief Musician, *even* to *u* Jeduthun.
A Psalm of David.

I SAID, I will take heed to my ways, that I sin not with my tongue: *v* I will keep [1] my mouth with a bridle, while *w* the wicked is before me.

u 1 Chron. xvi. 41.

v Prov. xxi. 23; James iii. 2, etc.
[1] *a bridle*, or, *muzzle for my mouth.*
w Col. iv. 5.

1. *I said.* This refers to a resolution which he had formed. He does not say, however, at what time of his life the resolution was adopted, or how long a period had elapsed from the time when he formed the resolution to the time when he thus made a record of it. He had formed the resolution on some occasion when he was greatly troubled with anxious thoughts; when, as the subsequent verses show, his mind was deeply perplexed about the Divine administration, or the dealings of God with mankind. It would seem that this train of thought was suggested by his own particular trials (vers. 9, 10), from which he was led to reflect on the mysteries of the Divine administration in general, and on the fact that man had been subjected by his Creator to so much trouble and sorrow,—and that, under the Divine decree, human life was so short and so vain. ¶ *I will take heed to my ways.* To wit, in respect to this matter. I will be cautious, circumspect, prudent. I will not offend or pain the heart of others. The particular thing here referred to was, the resolution not to give utterance to the thoughts which were passing in his mind in regard to the Divine administration. He felt that he was in danger, if he stated what he thought on the subject, of saying things which would do injury, or which he would have occasion to regret, and he therefore resolved to keep silent. ¶ *That I sin not with my tongue.* That I do not utter sentiments which will be wrong, and which I shall have occasion to repent; sentiments which would do injury to those who are already *disposed* to find ground of complaint against God, and who would thus be furnished with arguments to confirm them in their views. Good men often have such thoughts passing through their minds;—thoughts reflecting on the government of God as unequal and severe; thoughts which, if they were suggested, would tend to confirm the wicked and the sceptical in their views; thoughts which they hope, in respect to themselves, to be able to calm down by meditation and prayer, but which would do only unmitigated harm if they were communicated to other men, especially to wicked men. ¶ *I will keep my mouth with a bridle.* The word here used means rather a *muzzle*, or something placed *over* the mouth. The bridle is to restrain or check or guide the horse; the muzzle was something to bind or fasten the mouth so as to prevent biting or eating. Deut. xxv. 4: "Thou shalt not muzzle the ox when he treadeth out the corn." See Notes on 1 Cor. ix. 9. The meaning here is, that he would restrain himself from uttering what was passing in his mind. ¶ *While the wicked is before me.* In their presence. He resolved to do this, as suggested above, lest if he should utter what was passing in his own mind,—if he should state the difficulties in regard to the Divine administration which he saw and felt,—if he should give expression to the sceptical or hard thoughts which occurred to him at such times, it would serve only to confirm them in their wickedness, and strengthen them in their alienation from God. A similar state of feeling, and on this very subject, is referred to by the psalmist (Ps. lxxiii. 15), where he says that if he should utter what was really passing in his mind, it would greatly pain and offend those who were the true children of God; would fill their minds with doubts and difficulties which might never occur to themselves: "If I say, I will speak thus;

2 I was dumb with silence: I held my peace, *even* from good; and my sorrow was [1] stirred.

[1] *troubled.*

behold, I shall offend against the generation of thy children." As illustrations of this state of feeling in the minds of good men, and as evidence of the fact that, as in the case of the psalmist, their existence in the mind, even in the severest and the most torturing form, is not proof that the man in whose bosom they arise is not a truly pious man, I make the following extracts as expressing the feelings of two of the most sincere and devoted Christian men that ever lived,—both eminently useful, both in an eminent degree ornaments to the Church,—Cecil and Payson:—"I have read all the most acute, and learned, and serious infidel writers, and have been really surprised at their poverty. The process of my mind has been such on the subject of revelation, that I have often thought Satan has done more for me than the best of them; for I have had, and could have produced, arguments that appeared to me far more weighty than any I ever found in them against revelation." *Cecil.*—Dr. Payson says in a letter to a friend:—"There is one trial which you cannot know experimentally: it is that of being obliged to preach to others when one doubts of everything, and can scarcely believe that there is a God. All the atheistical, deistical, and heretical objections which I meet with in books are childish babblings compared with those which Satan suggests, and which he urges upon the mind with a force which seems irresistible. Yet I am often obliged to write sermons, and to preach when these objections beat upon me like a whirlwind, and almost distract me."

2. *I was dumb with silence.* Comp. Ps. xxxviii. 13. The addition of the words "with silence," means that he was *entirely* or *absolutely* dumb; he said nothing at all. The idea is, that he did not allow himself to give utterance to the thoughts which were passing in his mind in regard to the Divine dealings. He kept his thoughts to himself, and endeavoured to suppress them in his own bosom. ¶ *I held my peace,* even *from good.* I said nothing. I did not even say what I *might* have said in vindication of the ways of God. I did not even endeavour to defend the Divine character, or to explain the reasons of the Divine dealings, or to suggest any considerations which would tend to calm down the feelings of complaint and dissatisfaction which might be rising in the minds of other men as well as my own. ¶ *And my sorrow was stirred.* The anguish of my mind; my trouble. The word "*stirred*" here, rendered in the margin *troubled,* means that the very fact of attempting to suppress his feelings,—the purpose to say nothing in the case,—was the means of increased anguish. His trouble on the subject found no vent for itself in words, and at length it became so insupportable that he sought relief by giving utterance to his thoughts, and by coming to God to obtain relief. The state of mind referred to here is that which often occurs when a man broods over his own troubled thoughts, and dwells upon things which are in themselves improper and rebellious. We are under no necessity of endeavouring to vindicate the psalmist in what he here did; nor should we take his conduct in this respect as our example. He evidently himself, on reflection, regarded this as wrong; and recorded it not as a pattern for others, but as a faithful transcript of what was passing at the time through his own mind. Yet, wrong as it was, it was what often occurs even in the minds of good men. Even they, as in the cases referred to above, often have thoughts about God and his dealings which they do not dare to express, and which it would do harm to express. They, therefore, hide them in their own bosom, and often experience just what the psalmist did,—increased trouble and perplexity from the very purpose to

3 My heart was hot within me: while I was musing the fire burned: *then* spake I with my tongue,

4 LORD, make me to know mine end, and the measure of my days, what it *is*; *that* I may know [1] how frail I *am*.

[1] Or, *what time I have* here.

suppress them. They should go at once to God. They may say to *him* what it would not be proper to say to men. They may pour out all their feelings before him in prayer, with the hope that *in* such acts of praying, and in the answers which they will receive to their prayers, they may find relief.

3. *My heart was hot within me.* My mind became more and more excited; my feelings more and more intense. The attempt to suppress my emotions only more and more enkindled them. ¶ *While I was musing the fire burned.* Literally, "*in my meditation the fire burned.*" That is, while I was dwelling on the subject; while I was agitating it in my mind; while I thought about it,—the flame was enkindled, and my thoughts found utterance. He was unable longer to suppress his feelings, and he gave vent to them in words. Comp. Jer. xx. 9; Job xxxii. 18, 19. ¶ Then *spake I with my tongue.* That is, in the words which are recorded in this psalm. He gave vent to his pent-up feelings in the language which follows. Even though there *was* a feeling of murmuring and complaining, he sought relief in stating his real difficulties before God, and in seeking from him direction and support.

4. LORD, *make me to know mine end.* This expresses evidently the substance of those anxious and troubled thoughts (vers. 1, 2) to which he had been unwilling to give utterance. His thoughts turned on the shortness of life; on the mystery of the Divine arrangement by which it had been made so short; and on the fact that so many troubles and sorrows had been crowded into a life so frail and so soon to terminate. With some impatience, and with a consciousness that he had been indulging feelings on this subject which were not proper, and which would do injury if they were expressed *before men,* he now pours out these feelings before God, and asks what *is* to be the end of this; how long this is to continue; when his own sorrows will cease. It was an impatient desire to know when the end would be, with a spirit of insubmission to the arrangements of Providence by which his life had been made so brief, and by which so much suffering had been appointed. ¶ *And the measure of my days, what it* is. How long I am to live; how long I am to bear these accumulated sorrows. ¶ That *I may know how frail I* am. Marg., *What time I have* here. Prof. Alexander renders this, *when I shall cease.* So De Wette. The Hebrew word here used—חָדֵל, *hhadail*—means *ceasing to be;* hence, *frail;* then, destitute, left, forsaken. An exact translation would be, "that I may know at what (time) or (point) I am ceasing, or about to cease." It is equivalent to a prayer that he might know when these sufferings—when a life so full of sorrow—would come to an end. The language is an expression of impatience; the utterance of a feeling which the psalmist knew was not right in itself, and which would do injury if expressed before men, but which the intensity of his feelings would not permit him to restrain, and to which he, therefore, gives utterance before God. Similar expressions of impatience in view of the sufferings of a life so short as this, and with so little to alleviate its sorrows, may be seen much amplified in Job iii. 1–26; vi. 4–12; vii. 7; xiv. 1–13. Before we *blame* the sacred writers for the indulgence of these feelings, let us carefully examine our own hearts, and recall what has passed through our own minds in view of the mysteries of the Divine administration; and

5 Behold, thou hast made my days *as* an handbreadth; and [x] mine age *is* as nothing before thee: verily every man [1] at his best state *is* altogether vanity. Selah.

x Ps. xc. 4, etc.

6 Surely every man walketh in [2] a vain show; surely they are disquieted in vain: he [y] heapeth up *riches*, and knoweth not who shall gather them.

[1] *settled.* [2] *an image.*
y Eccles. ii. 18, etc; Luke xii. 20, 21.

let us remember that one great object of the Bible is to *record* the actual feelings of men — not to *vindicate* them, but to show what human nature *is* even in the best circumstances, and what the human heart is when as yet but partially sanctified.

5. *Behold, thou hast made my days as an handbreadth.* Literally, "Lo, handbreadths hast thou given my days." The word rendered *handbreadth* means properly the spread hand; the palm; the hand when the four fingers are expanded. The word is then used to denote anything very short or brief. It is one of the smallest natural measures, as distinguished from the "foot"—*i. e.* the length of the foot; and from the cubit,—*i. e.* the length of the arm to the elbow. It is the *shortness* of life, therefore, that is the subject of painful and complaining reflection here. Who has not been in a state of mind to sympathise with the feelings of the psalmist? Who is there that does not often wonder, when he thinks of what he could and would accomplish on earth if his life extended to a thousand years, and when he thinks of the great interests at stake in reference to another world which God has made dependent on so short a life? Who can at all times so calm down his feelings as to give utterance to no expressions of impatience that life is so soon to terminate? Who is there that reflects on the great interests at stake that has not asked the question *why* God has not given man more time to prepare for eternity? ¶ *And mine age.* Or, my life. The word here used—חֶלֶד, *hheled*—means properly *duration of life*, lifetime; and then, life itself; Job xi. 17. ¶ Is *as nothing.* That is, it is so short that it seems to be nothing at all. ¶ *Before thee.* As over against thee; that is, in comparison with thee. Comp. Isa. xl. 17, "All nations *before him* are as nothing;" that is, over against him, or in comparison with him. When the two are placed together, the one seems to be as nothing in the presence of the other. So the life of man, when placed by the side of the life of God, seems to be absolutely nothing. ¶ *Verily every man at his best state is altogether vanity.* Marg., *settled.* The idea is, that every man is *constituted* vanity. Literally, "All vanity every man is constituted." There seems to be nothing but vanity; and this is the result of a Divine constitution or arrangement. The idea expressed in our common version, "at his best state," however true in itself, is not in the original. The thoughts in the original are (*a*) that all men are vanity; that is, life is so short, and man accomplishes so little, that it seems to be perfect vanity; and (*b*) that this is the result of the Divine constitution under which man was made. It was the fact that man has been *so made* which gave so much trouble to the mind of the psalmist.

6. *Surely every man walketh in a vain show.* Marg., *an image.* The word rendered *vain show* — צֶלֶם, *tzelem*—means properly a shade, a shadow; and then, an image or likeness, as shadowing forth any real object. Then it comes to denote an idol, 2 Kings xi. 18; Amos v. 26. Here the idea seems to be that of an *image*, as contradistinguished from a *reality;* the shadow of a thing, as distinguished from the substance. Man seems to be like an image, a shadow, a phantom,—and not a real object, walking about. He is a form, an appearance, that soon vanishes away like

7 And now, LORD, what wait I for? my hope *is* in thee.

8 Deliver me from all my transgressions; make me not the

a shadow. ¶ *Surely they are disquieted in vain.* That is, they are actively engaged; they bustle about; they are full of anxiety; they form plans which they execute with much toil, care, and trouble; yet for no purpose worthy of so much diligence and anxious thought. They are busy, bustling *shadows*—existing for no real or substantial purposes, and accomplishing nothing. "What shadows we are, and what shadows do we pursue," said the great orator and statesman, Edmund Burke; and what a striking and beautiful comment on the passage before us was that saying, coming from such a man, and from one occupying such a position. ¶ *He heapeth up* riches. The word here used means to heap up, to store up, as grain, Gen. xli. 35; or treasures, Job xxvii. 16; or a mound, Hab. i. 10. Here it undoubtedly refers to the efforts of men in accumulating wealth, or storing up property. This was the thing which struck the psalmist as the leading employment of these moving shadows,—a fact that would strike any one as he looks upon this busy world. ¶ *And knoweth not who shall gather them.* Who shall gather them to himself; to whom they will go when he dies. Comp. Job xxvii. 16–19; Eccles. ii. 18, 21; v. 13, 14; Luke xii. 20. The idea is, that it is not only vanity in itself, considered as the great business of life, to attempt to accumulate property,—seeing that this is not what the great object of life should be, and that a life thus spent really amounts to nothing,—but vanity in this respect also, that a man can have no absolute control over his property when he is dead, and he knows not, and cannot know, into whose hands his accumulated gains may fall. The facts on this subject; the actual distribution of property after a man is dead; the use often made of it, against which no man can guard,—should, together with other and higher motives, be a powerful consideration with every one, *not* to make the amassing of wealth the great business of life.

7. *And now,* LORD, *what wait I for?* From the consideration of a vain world,—of the fruitless efforts of man,—of what so perplexed, embarrassed, and troubled him,—the psalmist now turns to God, and looks to *him* as the source of consolation. Turning to him, he gains more cheerful views of life. The expression "What wait I for?" means, what do I now *expect* or *hope for;* on what is my hope based; where do I find any cheerful, comforting views in regard to life? He had found none in the contemplation of the world itself, in man and his pursuits; in the course of things so shadowy and so mysterious; and he says now, that he turns to God to find comfort in his perplexities. ¶ *My hope* is *in thee.* In thee alone. My reliance is on thee; my expectation is from thee. It is not from what I see in the world; it is not in my power of solving the mysteries which surround me; it is not that I can see the reason why these shadows are pursuing shadows so eagerly around me; it is in the God that made all, the ruler over all, that can control all, and that can accomplish his own great purposes in connexion even with these moving shadows, and that can confer on man thus vain in himself and in his pursuits that which will be valuable and permanent. The idea is, that the contemplation of a world so vain, so shadowy, so mysterious, should lead us away from all expectation of finding in that world what we need, or finding a solution of the questions which so much perplex us, up to the great God who is infinitely wise, and who can meet all the necessities of our immortal nature; and who, in his own time, can solve all these mysteries.

8. *Deliver me from all my transgressions.* Recognising, as in Ps. xxxviii. 3–5, his sins as the source of

reproach of the foolish.
9 I was dumb, I opened not my
mouth; because thou didst it.
10 Remove thy stroke away

all his troubles and sorrows. If his transgressions were forgiven, he felt assured that his trouble would be removed. His first petition, therefore, is, that his sins might be pardoned, with the implied conscious assurance that then it would be consistent and proper for God to remove his calamity, and deliver him from the evils which had come upon him. ¶ *Make me not the reproach of the foolish.* Of the wicked; of those who are foolish, *because* they are wicked. See Notes on Ps. xiv. 1. The prayer here is, that God would not suffer him to become an object of reproach to wicked and foolish men; that is, as the passage implies, that God would not so continue to treat him *as if* he were a sinner as to justify to themselves their reproaches of him as a wicked man. In other words, he prays that God would forgive his sin, and would withdraw his hand of affliction, so that even the wicked might see that he was not angry with him, but that he was an object of the Divine favour.

9. *I was dumb.* See Notes on ver. 2. Comp. Isa. liii. 7. The meaning here is, that he did not open his mouth to complain; he did not speak of God as if he had dealt unkindly or unjustly with him. ¶ *I opened not my mouth.* I kept entire silence. This would be better rendered, "I am dumb; I will not open my mouth." The meaning is, not that he had been *formerly* silent and uncomplaining, but that he was *now* silenced, or that his mind was now calm, and that he acquiesced in the dealings of Divine Providence. The state of mind here, it should be further observed, is not that which is described in ver. 2. There he represents himself as dumb, or as restraining himself from uttering what was in his mind, because he felt that it would do harm, by encouraging the wicked in their views of God and of his government; here he says that he was now silenced—he acquiesced—he had no disposition to say anything against the government of God. He was dumb, not by putting a *restraint* on himself, but because he *had* nothing to say. ¶ *Because thou didst it. Thou* hast done that which was so mysterious to me; that about which I was so much disposed to complain; that which has overwhelmed me with affliction and sorrow. It is now, to my mind, a sufficient reason for silencing all my murmurs, and producing entire acquiescence, that it has been done by *thee.* That fact is to me sufficient proof that it is right, and wise, and good; that fact makes my mind calm. *The best proof that anything is right and best is that it is done by God.* The most perfect calmness and peace in trouble is produced, not when we rely on our own reasonings, or when we attempt to comprehend and explain a mystery, but when we direct our thoughts simply to the fact that *God has done it.* This is the highest reason that can be presented to the human mind, that what is done is right; this raises the mind above the mysteriousness of *what* is done, and makes it plain that it *should* be done; this leaves the reasons *why* it is done, where they should be left, with God. This consideration will calm down the feelings when nothing else would do it, and dispose the mind, even under the deepest trials, to acquiescence and peace. I saw this verse engraved, with great appropriateness, on a beautiful marble monument that had been erected over a grave where lay three children that had been suddenly cut down by the scarlet fever. What could be more suitable in such a trial than such a text? What could more strikingly express the true feelings of Christian piety—the calm submission of redeemed souls—than the disposition of parents, thus bereaved, to record such a sentiment over the grave of their children?

10. *Remove thy stroke away from*

from me: I am consumed by the
[1] blow of thine hand.
11 When thou with rebukes
dost correct man for iniquity,
thou makest [2] his beauty to consume away like a moth: surely
every man *is* vanity. Selah.
12 Hear my prayer, O LORD,
and give ear unto my cry; hold
not thy peace at my tears: for I
am a stranger with thee, *and* a

[1] *conflict.*

[2] *that which is to be desired in him to melt away.*

me. And yet this calm submission, as expressed in ver. 9, does not take away the *desire* that the hand of God may be removed, and that the suffering that is brought upon us may cease. Perfect submission is not inconsistent with the prayer that, if it be the will of God, the calamity may be removed: Luke xxii. 42. On the word here rendered *stroke* — נֶגַע, *naiga* — see Notes on Ps. xxxviii. 11. It is equivalent here to chastisement, or judgment. It refers to the trial which he was then enduring, whatever it was, which had given occasion to the feelings that he says (ver. 1, 2) he had felt bound to suppress when in the presence of the wicked, but in reference to which he had learned entirely to acquiesce (ver. 9). From that trial itself he now prays that he may be delivered. ¶ *I am consumed.* I am wasting away. I cannot long bear up under it. I must sink down to the grave if it is not removed. See ver. 13. ¶ *By the blow of thine hand.* Marg., as in Heb., *conflict.* That is, the blow which God brings on any one when he has, as it were, a *strife* or a *conflict* with him. It is designed here to express his affliction, as if God had *struck* him.

11. *When thou with rebukes.* The word here rendered *rebukes* means properly (*a*) proof or demonstration; (*b*) confutation or contradiction; (*c*) reproof or admonition by words; (*d*) reproof by correction or punishment. This is the meaning here. The idea of the psalmist is, that God, by punishment or calamity, expresses his sense of the evil of human conduct; and that, under such an expression of it, man, being unable to sustain it, melts away or is destroyed. ¶ *Dost correct man for iniquity.* Dost punish man for his sin; or dost express thy sense of the evil of sin by the calamities which are brought upon him. ¶ *Thou makest his beauty.* Marg., *That which is to be desired in him.* The Hebrew means *desired, delighted in;* then, something desirable, pleasant; a delight. Its meaning is not confined to *beauty.* It refers to *anything* that is to man an object of desire or delight,—strength, beauty, possessions, life itself. All are made to fade away before the expressions of the Divine displeasure. ¶ *To consume away like a moth.* Not as a moth is consumed, but as a moth consumes or destroys valuable objects, such as clothing. See Notes on Job iv. 19. The beauty, the vigour, the strength of man is marred and destroyed, as the texture of cloth is by the moth. ¶ *Surely every man is vanity.* That is, he is seen to be vanity—to have no strength, no permanency—by the ease with which God takes away all on which he had prided himself. See Notes on ver. 5.

12. *Hear my prayer, O* LORD, *and give ear unto my cry.* That is, in view of my affliction and my sins; in view, also, of the perplexing questions which have agitated my bosom; the troublous thoughts which passed through my soul, which I did not dare to express before man (vers. 1, 2), but which I have now expressed before thee. ¶ *Hold not thy peace.* Be not silent. Do not refuse to answer me; to speak peace to me. ¶ *At my tears.* Or rather, at my weeping; as if God heard the voice of his weeping. Weeping, if unmurmuring, is of the nature of prayer, for God regards the sorrows of the soul as he sees them. The weeping penitent, the weeping sufferer, is one on whom we may suppose God looks with

sojourner, as all my fathers *were*.
13 O spare me, that I may recover strength, before I go hence, and be no more.

---

compassion, even though the sorrows of the soul do not find *words* to give utterance to them. Comp. Notes on Job xvi. 20. See also Rom. viii. 26. ¶ *For I* am *a stranger*. The word used — גֵּר, *gair* — means properly a sojourner; a foreigner; a man living out of his own country: Gen. xv. 13; Ex. ii. 22. It refers to a man who has no permanent home in the place or country where he now is; and it is used here as implying that, in the estimation of the psalmist himself, he had no permanent abode on earth. He was in a strange or foreign land. He was passing *to* a permanent home; and he prays that God would be merciful to him as to a man who *has* no home—no permanent abiding place — on earth. Comp. Notes on Heb. xi. 13; 1 Peter ii. 11. ¶ And *a sojourner*. This word has substantially the same signification. It denotes one living in another country, without the rights of a citizen. ¶ *As all my fathers* were. All my ancestors. The allusion is doubtless derived from the fact that the patriarchs Abraham, Isaac, and Jacob thus lived as men who had no permanent home here,—who had no possession of soil in the countries where they sojourned,—and whose whole life, therefore, was an illustration of the fact that they were *on a journey*—a journey to another world. 1 Chron. xxix. 15,—"For we are strangers before thee, and sojourners, as were all our fathers; our days on the earth are as a shadow, and there is none abiding." Comp. Notes on Heb. xi. 13–15.

13. *O spare me.* The word here used—from שָׁעָה, *shaah* — means *to look;* and then, in connexion with the preposition, *to look away from;* and it here means, *Look away from me;* that is, Do not come to inflict death on me. Preserve me. The idea is this: God seemed to have fixed his eyes on him, and to be pursuing him with the expressions of his displeasure (comp. Job xvi. 9); and the psalmist now prays that he would *turn away his eyes*, and leave him. ¶ *That I may recover strength.* The word here used — בָּלַג, *balag* — means, in Arabic, to be bright; to shine forth; and then, to make cheerful, to enliven one's countenance, or to be joyful, glad. In Job ix. 27, it is rendered *comfort;* in Job x. 20, that I *may take comfort;* in Amos v. 9, *strengtheneth.* It is not used elsewhere. The idea is that of being *cheered up;* of being strengthened and invigorated before he should pass away. He wished to be permitted to recover the strength which he had lost, and especially to receive consolation, before he should leave the earth. He desired that his closing days might not be under a cloud, but that he might obtain brighter and more cheerful views, and have more of the consolations of religion before he should be removed finally from this world. It is a wish not to leave the world in gloom, or with gloomy and desponding views, but with a cheerful view of the past; with joyful confidence in the government of God; and with bright anticipations of the coming world. ¶ *Before I go hence.* Before I die. ¶ *And be no more.* Be no more upon the earth. Comp. Notes on Ps. vi. 5; xxx. 9. See also Notes on Job xiv. 1–12. Whatever may have been his views of the future world, he desired to be cheered and comforted in the prospect of passing away finally from earth. He was unwilling to go down to the grave in gloom, or under the influence of the dark and distressing views which he had experienced, and to which he refers in this psalm. A religious man, about to leave the world, should *desire* to have bright hopes and anticipations. For his own comfort and peace, for the honour of religion, for the glory of God, he should not leave those around under the impression that religion does no-

thing to comfort a dying man, or to inspire with hope the mind of one about to leave the earth, or to give to the departing friend of God cheerful anticipations of the life to come. A joyful confidence in God and his government, when a man is about to leave the world, does much, very much, to impress the minds of others with a conviction of the truth and reality of religion, as dark and gloomy views can hardly fail to lead the world to ask what that religion is worth which will not inspire a dying man with hope, and make him calm in the closing scene.

PSALM XL.

This psalm, which purports to have been composed by David, is another of the psalms addressed or dedicated "to the chief Musician;" that is, which he is desired to adjust to the appropriate music; and it is, therefore, probably one that was particularly intended to be employed in the public worship of the Hebrews. On the meaning of this expression, see Notes to the inscription of Ps. iv.

There is no method of ascertaining with certainty on what occasion the psalm was composed. Doubtless it was in view of some of the trials which occurred in the life of David, since there were many of these to which the sentiments of the psalm may with propriety be applied. As it is impossible now, however, from anything in the psalm itself, to ascertain *which* of those afflictions were here referred to, or which suggested the psalm, conjecture would be useless; nor, if we could ascertain to what particular time of his life he made reference, would it furnish any material aid in interpreting the psalm. It is to be presumed, however, that there was a reference to *some* trouble or calamity in his own life; and even if it be supposed that the psalm was designed to refer wholly to the Messiah, and to be descriptive of *his* sufferings, still it is probable that the language employed was *suggested* by something in the life of the author of the psalm, and that he was led to contemplate the future sufferings of the Messiah in connexion with his own trials.

The contents of the psalm are as follows:—

(1.) A reference to some time of calamity or deep sorrow, represented by being in a horrible pit, from which he had been delivered in answer to prayer,—a deliverance so remarkable that the effect would be to lead many, on account of it, to praise God, vers. 1-3.

(2.) A statement of the blessedness of the man that made the Lord his trust, and put confidence in *him* rather than in the proud of the earth, or in those who were faithless or deceitful, ver. 4.

(3.) A grateful remembrance of the many works of the Lord;—evidently as laying the foundation of obligation to serve him in every way possible, and as a *reason* of the purpose of obedience immediately referred to, ver. 5.

(4.) A statement of what *he* had done, or what he proposed to do, as expressive of his sense of obligation, or of the service which God required of him, vers. 6-10. The speaker in the psalm says that God did not require of him sacrifice and offering—that is, the bloody sacrifices prescribed in the Hebrew ritual, ver. 6; that God had disposed him to obey, or had prepared him to render such obedience as was required—("Mine ears hast thou opened"), ver. 6; that he came to obey, in accordance with some prediction or previous record in regard to him, ver. 7; that he found his supreme pleasure in doing the will of God, ver. 8; and that, in pursuance of this arrangement and of this purpose, he had made known the will of God—had preached righteousness in the great congregation, and had faithfully declared the salvation of God, vers. 9, 10.

(5.) Prayers and supplications founded on these facts—on his trials; on his dangers; on the attempts of his enemies to destroy him; on his desire for the welfare and safety of the people of God, vers. 11-17. Particularly (*a*) prayer for his own deliverance from the troubles which encompassed him still, vers. 11-13; (*b*) prayer that those who were opposed to him might be abased and humbled, vers. 14, 15; (*c*) prayer that those who sought the Lord might rejoice and be glad, ver. 16; and (*d*) a prayer for himself, as poor and needy, on the grounds that God was his help and his deliverer, ver. 17.

A very important and difficult question occurs here. It is the question to whom the psalm originally referred.

On this question there have been the following opinions: (1) That it refers originally and exclusively to David; (2) that it had an original and exclusive reference to the Messiah; (3) that it is susceptible of a *double* application, part of the psalm having reference to David, and the other portion to the Messiah, as having been *suggested* by his own circumstances; and (4) that the portion of the psalm applied to the Messiah in Heb. x. 5-9 is applied by way of *accommodation*, or as expressing the meaning of the author of the epistle to the Hebrews, but without affirming on the part of the writer of that epistle that the psalm had originally any Messianic reference.

It would be too long to examine these opinions in detail; and all that is needful in this brief introduction to the psalm may be to state some reasons for what seems to me to be the true opinion, that the psalm had an original and exclusive reference to the Messiah, or that it is one of the compositions in the Old Testament, like Ps. ii., xxii., and Is. liii., which were designed by the Spirit of inspiration to describe the Messiah, as to some of his characteristics, and as to what he would suffer.

(1) There *are* such psalms, such portions of the Old Testament. This is admitted by all who believe in the inspiration of the Scriptures. The Messiah was the hope of the Jewish people. He was the subject of their most sublime prophecies. The nation was accustomed to look forward to him as their great Deliverer. In all times of national calamity they looked forward to the period when *he* would appear for their rescue. He was, so to speak, the "*hero*" of their national literature; the bright object in the future to which all the sacred writers looked forward; the glorious Saviour and Deliverer whose coming, and the anticipated benefit of whose coming, animated their lays, and cheered them in the darkest days of trouble and sorrow. Comp. Introd. to Isaiah, § 7.

(2) The author of the epistle to the Hebrews expressly applies a part of this psalm to the Messiah, Heb. x. 5-9. There can be no reasonable doubt that he quoted this with the belief that the psalm had original reference to him, and that he did not use the language by way of accommodation, for he was endeavouring to demonstrate a *point*, or to *prove* that what he was stating was true. This he does by referring to the passage in the psalm *as proof on the point then under consideration*. But there would have been no proof—no argument—in the case, if he had merely quoted language by way of accommodation, which had originally a different design. The very point of his quotation is based on the fact that he was adducing a passage which had original reference to the Messiah, and which might be *properly* quoted as characterizing his work. The proof (as derived from this fact) that the psalm had reference to the Messiah, consists of two things:—(*a*) That it is so applied by an inspired apostle, which, with all who admit his inspiration would seem to be decisive of the question; (*b*) that he so applied it, shews, in the circumstances, that this was an ancient and admitted interpretation. He was writing to those who had been Jews; to those whom he was desirous of convincing as to the truth of what he was alleging in regard to the notion of Hebrew sacrifices. For this purpose it was necessary to appeal to the Old Testament; but it cannot be supposed that he would adduce, as proof, a passage whose relevancy to the point would not be at once admitted. It may be presumed, therefore, that the passage was commonly applied by the Hebrews themselves to the purpose for which the apostle used it, or that the application, when made, was so plain and obvious that they would not call it in question.

(3) The entire psalm may be applied to the Messiah without anything forced or unnatural in the interpretation. This will be shewn, in detail, in the exposition of the psalm; but in the meantime it may not be improper to refer to the principal difficulties in such an application, and to the principal objections derived from this source against the idea that the psalm refers to the Messiah. The principal of these relate to the following points:—(*a*) In ver. 2 the speaker in the psalm says: "He brought me up also out of an horrible pit, and out of the miry clay, and set my feet upon a rock, and established my goings;" and on the ground of this, he gives thanks to God. But there is no real difficulty in supposing that this refers to the Messiah, and that it was actually fulfilled in the case of the Lord Jesus. His enemies often plotted against his life; they laid snares for him; they endeavoured to destroy him; his dangers may well be represented as "an horrible pit," and as "miry clay;" and his deliverance from those perils may well be compared with the case of one who is raised up from such a pit, and from the deep mire. Even supposing that this was designed to refer to the

personal experience of the psalmist himself, still the language would be figurative, and must be designed to refer to some danger, peril, or trouble that would be well represented by being thrown into such a pit, or sinking in miry clay. It cannot be supposed that the psalmist meant to say this had really and literally occurred in his own life. Without any impropriety, therefore, the language may be applied to the trials and dangers of the Messiah, and to the merciful interposition of God in delivering him. (*b*) The second objection or difficulty in referring it to the Messiah is derived from what is said in ver. 12: "Mine iniquities have taken hold on me, so that I am not able to look up; they are more than the hairs of my head; therefore my heart faileth me." But, in reference to the propriety of applying this to the Messiah, two remarks may be made: *First.* It may be true that the Messiah was so identified with men—became so truly a substitute for sinners—experienced in his own soul, in the deep sorrows of the atonement, so intensely the effects of their *sin*,—and so bore the sufferings that were expressive of the Divine sense of the evil of sin, that the language might be applied to him *as if* these sins were his own. He was treated *as if* they were his—as if he had been a sinner. He so made them his own, that it was proper he should be treated *as if* they were his, and that he might feel he was suffering *as if* they were his. It is true that they could not be literally transferred to him; it is true that in no proper sense of the term was he a sinner; it is true that in the just signification of the word he was *not* "guilty," and that God always saw he was personally innocent; but still it is true that, in the work of the atonement, he was treated *as if* he had been a sinner, and that, in this sense, he might speak of the sins for which he suffered as his own. He had voluntarily assumed them, and he was suffering for them *as if* they had been his. Thus we have in Isa. liii. 4-6 similar language applied to him: "He hath borne our griefs, and carried our sorrows;" "he was wounded for our transgressions, he was bruised for our iniquities; the chastisement of our peace was upon him;" "the Lord hath laid on him the iniquity of us all." If such language might properly be applied to him and his sufferings, then there could be no impropriety or incongruity in his regarding himself as so identified with sinful men, and as so truly bearing what was due to their sins, that he might speak of those sins *as if* they were his own, as one might speak of a debt incurred by a friend, and which he had brought himself under voluntary obligation to pay, *as if* it were his own, and might say, "it is no longer *his*, but *mine.*" The language of Scripture in regard to the relation of the Redeemer to sin is often so marked and striking as to suggest and to justify this language. See 2 Cor. v. 21; Gal. iii. 13. *Second.* It is possible, after all, that the word rendered *iniquities* in the psalm, means here merely *calamity*, *trouble*, *sorrow*. (See Notes on Heb. x. 5; and comp. Prof. Stuart on the Epistle to the Hebrews, Excursus xx., p. 594.) So the same word which is here used means, in 2 Sam. xvi. 12, "It may be that the Lord will look on mine *affliction*." The words *iniquity* and *calamity*—*sin* and *punishment*—are closely connected in the Scriptures; so closely that the one is often put for the other, and when a sacred writer speaks of his *sin*, he often means the suffering or calamity that has come upon him in consequence of his sin. So the Messiah may be understood here to mean that the calamities or woes which had come upon him in consequence of his taking upon him the sins of the world made it proper to say that his "iniquities"—the iniquities which he had assumed, or which, in the language of Isaiah, he "bore"—had "taken hold on him, so that he was not able to look up;" or, considering their great number, he might say, "they are more than the hairs of my head, therefore my heart faileth me." (*c*) A third objection to the application of the psalm to the Messiah is, that it cannot be supposed he would utter such imprecations on his enemies as are found in vers. 14, 15: "Let them be ashamed and confounded; let them be driven backward; let them be desolate." To this it may be replied, that such imprecations are as proper in the mouth of the Messiah as in the mouth of David; and that they are *improper* in neither. Both David and the Messiah *did* utter denunciations against the enemies of piety and of God. There is no evidence that there was any *malignant* feeling in either case; nor is it inconsistent with the highest benevolence to utter denunciation of guilt. God constantly does it in his word; and he as often does it in the dealings of his Providence. The wicked cannot walk

PSALM XL.

To the chief Musician. A Psalm of David.

I [1] WAITED patiently for the LORD: and he inclined unto me, and heard my cry.

[1] *In waiting I waited.*

through this world without meeting denunciations of their guilt on every hand, and there was no impiety in the fact that he who will pronounce a sentence in the great day of judgment on all guilty men, should apprize them beforehand of what would be sure to come upon them. The objections, then, are not of such a nature that it is improper to regard the psalm as wholly applicable to the Messiah.

(4) The psalm cannot be applied with propriety to David, nor do we know of any one to whom it can be applied but the Messiah. It was not true of David that he "had come to do the will" of God, in view of the fact that God did not require sacrifice and offerings, vers. 6, 7; it was not true that it was written of him "in the volume of the book," that he delighted to do the will of God, and that he had come into the world in view of the fact that it *had been* so written (vers. 7, 8); it was not true that it had been his characteristic work to "preach righteousness in the great congregation" (ver. 9); but all this *was* true of the Messiah. These expressions are such as can be applied only to him; and, taking all these circumstances together, the conclusion seems to be a proper one that the whole psalm had original reference to the Redeemer, and is to be interpreted as appplying to him alone.

There is a remarkable resemblance between the close of this psalm (vers. 13–17) and Ps. lxx. Indeed, that entire psalm is the same as the closing part of this one. Why that portion of the psalm before us is thus repeated, and why it is separated from this and made a psalm by itself, is wholly unknown. It cannot be supposed to be an error in transcribing, for the error would be too material, and would most certainly be detected. Perhaps it can best be accounted for by supposing the author of Ps. lxx. to have been in the state of mind, and in the circumstances there described, and by supposing that instead of writing a *new* psalm which would express his feelings, he found that this part of Ps. xl., already composed, would describe so exactly what he wished to express, and that he regarded it as so adapted to be a prayer by itself, that he therefore copied it. The fact that it was thus copied, and that the sentiments were repeated, does not in any manner detract from the supposition that it is inspired.

1. *I waited patiently for the* LORD. Marg., as in Heb., *In waiting I waited.* That is, *I continued to wait.* It was not a single, momentary act of expectation or hope; it was continuous; or, was persevered in. The idea is, that his prayer was not answered at once, but that it was answered after he had made repeated prayers, or when it seemed as if his prayers would not be answered. It is earnest, persevering prayer that is referred to; it is continued supplication and hope when there seemed to be no answer to prayer, and no prospect that it would be answered. ¶ *And he inclined unto me.* That is, ultimately he heard and answered me; or he turned himself favourably towards me, as the result of *persevering* prayer. The word "inclined" here means properly *bowed;* that is, he *bent forward* to hearken, or to place his ear near my mouth and to hear me. At first he seemed as one that would not hear; as one that throws his head backward or turns his head away. Ultimately, however, he bent forward to receive my prayer. ¶ *And heard my cry.* The cry or supplication which I made for help; the cry which I directed to him in the depth of my sorrows and my danger, ver. 2. As applied to the Redeemer, this would refer to the fact that in his sorrows, in the deep sorrows connected with the work of redemption, he persevered in calling on God, and that God heard him, and raised him up to glory and joy. See Matt. xxvi. 36–46. Comp. Notes on Heb. v. 7. The time supposed to be referred to, is *after* his sufferings were closed; *after* his work was done; *after* he rose from the dead. It is the language of grateful remembrance which we may suppose he uttered in the review of the amazing sorrows

2 He brought me up also out of [1] an horrible pit, out of the miry clay, and set my feet upon a rock, *and* established my goings.

3 And he hath put a new song in my mouth, *even* praise unto our God: many shall see *it*, and fear, and shall trust in the LORD.

[1] *a pit of noise.*

through which he had passed in making the atonement, and in the recollection that God had kept him in those sorrows, and had brought him up from such a depth of woe to such a height of glory.

2. *He brought me up also out of an horrible pit.* Marg., *A pit of noise.* The word here used means a pit; a cistern; a prison; a dungeon; a grave. This last signification of the word is found in Ps. xxviii. 1; xxx. 4; lxxxviii. 4; Isa. xxxviii. 18; xiv. 19. It may refer to any calamity—or to trouble, like being *in* a pit,—or it may refer to the grave. The word rendered *horrible*—שָׁאוֹן, *shâon*—means properly *noise, uproar, tumult,* as of waters; of a crowd of men; of war. Then it seems to be used in the sense of *desolation* or *destruction,* as applicable to the grave. De Wette understands it here of a pit, a cavern, or an abyss that roars or is tumultuous; that is, that is impassable. Perhaps this is the idea,—a cavern, deep and dark, where the waters roar, and which seems to be filled with horrors. So Rosenmüller understands it. The LXX. render it ἐκ λάκκου ταλαιπωρίας, *a lake of misery.* It is a deep and horrid cavern, where there is no hope of being rescued, or where it would seem that there would be certain destruction. ¶ *Out of the miry clay.* At the bottom of the pit. Where there was no solid ground—no rock on which to stand. See Jer. xxxviii. 6; Ps. lxix. 2, 14. ¶ *And set my feet upon a rock.* Where there was firm standing. ¶ And *established my goings.* Or, fixed my steps. That is, he enabled me to walk as on solid ground; he conducted me along safely, where there was no danger of descending to the pit again or of sinking in the mire. If we understand this of the Redeemer, it refers to that time when, his sorrows ended, and his work of atonement done, it became certain that he would never be exposed again to such dangers, or sink into such a depth of woes, but that his course ever onward would be one of safety and of glory.

3. *And he hath put a new song in my mouth.* See Notes on Ps. xxxiii. 3. The idea is, that he had given a new or fresh *occasion* for praise. The deliverance was so marked, and was such an addition to former mercies, that a new expression of thanks was proper. It was an act of such surprising intervention on the part of God that the language used on former occasions, and which was adapted to express the mercies then received, would not be sufficient to convey the sense of gratitude felt for the present deliverance. As applied to the Messiah, and referring (as it was supposed in the Notes on ver. 2) to his being raised up to glory after the depth of his sorrows, it would mean that *no* language hitherto employed to express gratitude to God would be adequate to the occasion, but that the language of a *new* song of praise would be demanded to celebrate so great an event. ¶ Even *praise unto our God.* "To *our* God;"—identifying himself, as the Messiah does, with his people, and expressing the idea that the new song of praise was appropriate to them as well as to *himself,*—since they would be benefited by his work, and since God was their God as well as his. Comp. John xx. 17. ¶ *Many shall see* it. Great numbers of the human race shall be made acquainted with the occasion which there was for such a song. ¶ *And fear.* Learn to reverence, to worship, to honour God, as the result of what had been done. ¶ *And shall trust in the* LORD. Shall confide in God; shall put their trust in him; shall become his true worshippers and

4 Blessed *is* that man that maketh the LORD his trust, and respecteth [z] not the proud, nor such as [a] turn aside to lies.

5 Many, O LORD my God, *are* thy [b] wonderful works *which* thou hast done, and [c] thy thoughts *which are* to us-ward: they cannot be reckoned up in order unto thee: *if* I would declare and speak *of them*, they are more than can be numbered.

z Ps. xv. 4. a Ps. cxxv. 5. b Job ix. 10.

c Jer. xxix. 11.

1 Or, *none can order them unto thee.*

friends;—(*a*) as the effect of this merciful interposition in behalf of him who had been thus in trouble or distress, and who was enabled to triumph; (*b*) as the result of the work accomplished by him. The effect of the Redeemer's sorrows, and of God's merciful help, would be that great numbers would learn to put their trust in God, or would become his true friends. No man, in fact, can compute the *numbers* of those who, in consequence of the work of the Messiah, will turn to God and become his true worshippers and friends.

4. *Blessed* is *that man that maketh the* LORD *his trust.* See Notes on Ps. xxxiv. 8. Comp. Ps. xxvii. 1. Literally here, "The blessings of the man who places Jehovah for his confidence;" that is, who makes Him his *security*, or who feels that his security for happiness and salvation is in Him. ¶ *And respecteth not the proud.* The haughty, or those who are confident in themselves. Literally, "who *looks* not to the proud;" that is, who does not depend on them for help and for salvation. ¶ *Nor such as turn aside to lies.* Who depart from the straight path, and incline to that which is false and deceitful. The reference is to those who are easily made to swerve from that which is true and honest to that which is delusive and false. Their integrity cannot be confided in. There is no security that they will be disposed to do right. The *idea* is, that the man who trusts in God is blessed or happy, as compared with one who trusts in *man*;—man confident in himself; man liable to fall into error; man who is easily led astray; man who is deceitful, and who cannot, therefore, be relied on. God is mighty, but not haughty; God never is drawn aside from the truth; he never deceives.

5. *Many, O* LORD *my God,* are *thy wonderful works* which *thou hast done.* Literally, "Many [things], O Lord my God, hast thou done; thy wonderful things and thy thoughts towards us, it is not [possible] to state unto thee." The recollection of the particular kindness shown to the speaker, as referred to in the previous verses, suggests the recollection of the *great number* of wonders that God had done for his people,—the acts of his kindness which it would be hopeless to attempt to recount before him. And who *could* enumerate and record all the acts of God's benevolence towards men in the works of creation, providence, and redemption; all that he has done in the history of the Church, and for the individual members of the Church in past times; all that he has done to save his people in the days of persecution; all that has been accomplished in our own individual lives? Obviously these things are beyond all power of enumeration by man. They can be admired now only in the gross; eternity alone will be sufficient for us to look at them and to recount them in detail. The phrase "wonderful works" means here remarkable interventions; things fitted to excite astonishment; things that surpass what man could have anticipated; things that could have been done only by God. ¶ *And thy thoughts* which are *to us-ward.* Toward us; or which pertain to us. The word "thoughts" here refers to the plans, purposes, arrangements of God designed for our welfare; the things that are the result of his *thinking* of our wants—of what we need—of what would do us good. See ver.

6 Sacrifice [d] and offering thou didst not desire; mine ears hast thou [1] opened: burnt-offering and sin-offering hast thou not required.

d Ps. li. 16; Heb. x. 4—10.
[1] *digged*, Ex. xxi. 6.

17. ¶ *They cannot be reckoned up in order unto thee.* Marg., *None can order them unto thee.* Literally, "There is no putting them in order before thee;" that is, there is no such arranging of them, or disposing of them in order, that they can all be brought into their proper place, so as to be perceived or numbered. The Hebrew word—עָרַךְ, *arach*—means properly, to place in a row; to put in order; to arrange; as, to put an army in battle array, or to draw it up for battle, Judges xx. 20, 22; to put words in order for an argument, or to arrange thoughts so as to present an argument, Job xxxii. 14; to set a cause in order before a judge, or to lay it before him, Job xiii. 18. The word also means to place together with anything, or by the side of anything,—that is, to make a comparison. Gesenius (*Lex.*) supposes that this is the idea here, and that the proper interpretation is, *Nothing can be compared unto thee.* But the other interpretation seems best to accord with the connexion, as referring to the wonderful works of God, and to his thoughts of mercy and goodness as being beyond the power of computation, or as too numerous to be brought into order and arrangement before the mind. ¶ If *I would declare and speak* of them. If I should attempt to speak of them; or to recount them. ¶ *They are more than can be numbered.* More than man can enumerate. They go beyond the power of language to express them. This is literally true. No language of man can describe what God has *done* and has *purposed* in fitting up this world as an abode for men, and in his mercy towards them

6. *Sacrifice and offering.* The first of the words here used—זֶבַח, *zebahh*—means properly a bloody-offering; the other—מִנְחָה, *minhhah*—an offering without blood, as a thank-offering. See Notes on Isa. i. 11. The four words employed in this verse—sacrifice, offering, burnt-offering, sin-offering—embrace all the species of sacrifice and offerings known among the Hebrews; and the idea here is, that no such offering as they were accustomed to offer was required of him who is here referred to. A higher service was needed. ¶ *Thou didst not desire.* The word here rendered *desire* means to incline to, to be favourably disposed, as in reference to doing anything; that is, to will, to desire, to please. The meaning here is, that he did not will this or wish it; he would not be pleased with it in comparison with obedience, or as a substitute for obedience. He preferred obedience to any external rites and forms; to all the rites and forms of religion prescribed by the law. They were of no value without obedience; they could not be substituted in the place of obedience. This sentiment often occurs in the Old Testament, showing that the design of all the rites then prescribed was to bring men *to* obedience, and that they were of no value without obedience. See Notes on Isa. i. 10—20; comp. 1 Sam. xv. 22; Ps. li. 16, 17; Hos. vi. 6; see also Notes on Heb. x. 5. ¶ *Mine ears hast thou opened.* Marg., *digged.* The Hebrew word—כָּרָה, *karah*—means *to dig;* as, to dig a well, Gen. xxvi. 25; to dig a sepulchre, Gen. l. 5. As used here this would properly mean, *mine ears hast thou digged out;* that is, thou hast so opened them that there is a communication with the seat of hearing; or, in other words, thou hast caused me to hear this truth, or hast revealed it to me. Comp. Isa. l. 5, "The Lord God hath opened mine ear, and I was not rebellious." The meaning here would be, that the ear had been opened, so that it was quick to hear. An indisposition to obey the will of God is

7 Then said I, Lo, I come: in [e] the volume of the book *it is* written of me,

e Luke xxiv. 44; John v. 39.

often expressed by the fact that the ears are *stopped:* Zech. vii. 11; Ps. lviii. 4, 5; Prov. xxi. 13. There is manifestly no allusion here, though that has been supposed by many to be the reference, to the custom of boring through the ear of a servant with an awl, as a sign that he was willing to remain with his master: Exod. xxi. 6; Deut. xv. 17. In that case the outer circle, or rim of the ear was *bored through* with an awl; here the idea is that of *hollowing out,* digging, excavating, that is, of making a passage *through,* so that one could hear; not the mere piercing of the outer ear. The essential idea is, that this truth had been communicated to him—that God preferred obedience to sacrifice; and that he had been made attentive to that truth, *as if* he had been before deaf, and his ears had been opened. The principal difficulty in the passage relates to its application in the Epistle to the Hebrews, ch. x. 5. That difficulty arises from the fact that the Septuagint translates the phrase here by the words "a body hast thou prepared me;" and that the author of the Epistle to the Hebrews founds an argument *on* that translation, with reference to the work of the Messiah. On this point, see the Notes on Heb. x. 5. It is perhaps not now possible to explain this difficulty in a way that will be entirely satisfactory. ¶ *Burnt-offering.* See Notes on Isa. i. 11. The peculiarity of this offering was that it was consumed by fire. ¶ *And sin-offering.* Sin-offering was an offering or sacrifice made specifically for *sin,* with a view to expiate either sin in general, or some specific act of sin. In the Mosaic law there are two kinds of these offerings prescribed;—*trespass-offerings,* or offerings for guilt or fault, denoted by the word אָשָׁם, *asham;* and sin-offering, denoted by the word used here. They are offerings which were consumed by fire, Lev. v. 1—19; vi. 1—7; xiv. 10. But the essential *idea* was that they were for *sin,* or for some act of guilt. In a general sense, this was true of all bloody offerings or sacrifices; but in these cases the attention of the worshipper was turned particularly to the fact of *sin* or transgression. ¶ *Thou hast not required.* That is, thou hast not required them as compared with obedience; in other words, thou hast preferred the latter. These offerings would not meet the case. More was necessary to be done than was implied in these sacrifices. They would not expiate sin; they would not remove guilt; they would not give the conscience peace. A higher work, a work implied in an act of *obedience* of the most exalted kind, was demanded in order to accomplish the work to be done. Comp. Ps. li. 16.

7. *Then said I.* In Heb. x. 7, the apostle applies this to the Messiah. See Notes on that verse. This is the most simple and satisfactory interpretation of the passage. The word "then" in this verse means, "since this is the case;" or, "things being thus." It does not refer to *time,* but to the condition of things. "Since it was certain that the work needful to be done could not be accomplished by bloody offerings—the sacrifice of animals,—under these circumstances I said;" that is, I resolved or purposed to come. ¶ *Lo, I come.* It is difficult to see how this could be applied to David; it is easy to see how it could be applied to the Messiah. When all bloody offerings under the law—all the sacrifices which men could make—did not avail to put away sin, it was true of the Messiah that he came into the world to perform a higher work that *would* meet the case—a lofty work of obedience, extending even unto death, Phil. ii. 8. This is precisely the use which the apostle makes of the passage in Heb. x. 7, and this is clearly the most obvious meaning. It is in no sense applicable to David; it is fully applicable to the Messiah. ¶ *In the*

8 I [f] delight to do thy will, O my God: yea, thy law *is* [1] within my heart.

f John iv. 34.
[1] *in the midst of my bowels.*

volume of the book. Literally, "in the *roll* of the book." See Notes on Luke iv. 17. The phrase would most naturally denote the *roll of the law;* but it might include *any* volume or roll where a record or prophecy was made. In a large sense it would embrace *all* that had been written at the command of God at the time when this was supposed to be spoken. That is, as spoken by the Messiah, it would include all the books of the Old Testament. See Notes on Heb. x. 7. ¶ It is *written of me.* It is recorded; or, there is a record made of *me;* to wit, in this respect, that his great delight would be to do the will of God. The proper interpretation of this expression must be, that there must be some record to be found in the "book" or "volume" referred to, which was *designed* to describe *him* in this respect, or which had an original reference to him. The meaning is not that there was a *general* record on the point of obedience which *might* be applied to him as well as to others, but that the record was *intended* to be applied to him, and to describe his character. This is one of the passages in the Psalms which cannot with any propriety be applied to David himself. There was no such antecedent record in regard to him; no statement in any "book" or "volume" that this would be his character. There is no promise — no intimation—in any of the books of Scripture written before the time of David that *he* would come to do the will of God with a view to effect that which could not be done by the sacrifices and offerings under the law. The reference of the language, therefore, must be to the Messiah—to some place where it is represented or affirmed that he would come to accomplish by his obedience what could not be done by the sacrifices and oblations made under the law. Thus understood, and regarded as the language of the Messiah himself, the reference might be to all the books of the Old Testament (for all were completed before he came), and not merely to those which had been written in the time of David. But still, it is true that no such declaration, in so many words, can now be found in any of those books; and the meaning must be that this was the language which was everywhere *implied* respecting the Messiah; that this was the substance of the description given of him; that this characterised his work as predicted there; — to wit, that when all sacrifices and offerings under the law failed; when they had all shown that they were not efficacious to put away sin, One would come to perform some higher work that *would* be effectual in putting away transgression, and that this work might, in the highest sense, be described as "obedience," or as "doing the will of God." This was true. The language and the institutions of the Old Testament contemplated him as the One who only could put away sin. The entire spirit of the Mosaic economy supposed that a Saviour would come to do the will of God by making an atonement for the sin of the world. The meaning then is, "I come to do thy will in making an atonement, for no other offering would expiate sin; that I would do this, is the language of the Scriptures in predicting my coming, and of the whole spirit and design of the ancient dispensation."

8. *I delight to do thy will, O my God.* To wit, in obeying the law; in submitting to all the trials appointed to me; in making an atonement for the sins of men. See Notes on Heb. x. 7. Comp. Phil. ii. 8; Matt. xxvi. 39. ¶ *Yea, thy law* is *within my heart.* Marg., *In the midst of my bowels.* So the Hebrew. The idea is, that the law of God was *within* him. His obedience was not exter-

9 I have preached *g* righteousness in the great congregation: lo, I have not refrained my lips, O LORD, thou knowest.

10 I have not hid *h* thy righteousness within my heart; I have declared thy faithfulness and thy salvation: I have not concealed thy loving-kindness and thy truth from the great congregation.

11 Withhold not thou thy tender mercies from me, O LORD: let thy loving-kindness and thy truth *i* continually preserve me.

g Luke iv. 16—22.
h Acts xx. 20, 27.
i Ps. lxxxv. 10.

nal, but proceeded from the heart. How true this was of the Redeemer it is not necessary here to say.

9. *I have preached righteousness in the great congregation.* I have maintained and defended the principles of righteousness and truth among assembled multitudes. It would be difficult to see how *this* could be applied to David himself, or on what occasion of his life this could be said of him; but no one can doubt that this is applicable to the Messiah. (*a*) He *was* a preacher. (*b*) He addressed vast multitudes. (*c*) Before them all, and at all times, he maintained and illustrated the great principles of "righteousness" as demanded by the law of God, and unfolded the way in which all those multitudes might become "righteous" before God. ¶ *Lo, I have not refrained my lips.* I have not closed my lips. I have not kept back the truth. ¶ *O* LORD, *thou knowest.* He could make this solemn appeal to God as the searcher of hearts, in proof that he had faithfully uttered all that had been required of him in making known the will of God. Comp. John xvii. 4, 6, 8, 14, 26.

10. *I have not hid thy righteousness within my heart.* The word *righteousness* here may denote the Divine *views* on the subject of righteousness, or *the Divine method of making man righteous;* that is, the method of justification, as the word is used in the New Testament. See Notes on Rom. i. 17. The word, as it might have been employed by David, would have been used in the former sense, as meaning that, knowing what God *requires* of men, he had not concealed that in his heart, or had not kept it to himself; as used by the Messiah, as I suppose it to be here, it would be employed in the latter sense, or perhaps embrace both. The idea would be, that he had not concealed in his own mind, or had not kept to himself, the knowledge which he had of the requirements of the law of God, or of the way in which man can be justified or regarded and treated as righteous in his sight. He had fully communicated this knowledge to others. It is not necessary to say that this was literally fulfilled in the work of the Redeemer. He spent his life in making known the great truths about the righteousness of God; he died that he might disclose to man a way by which God could consistently regard and treat men as righteous. See Notes on Rom. iii. 24–26. ¶ *I have declared thy faithfulness.* Thy truthfulness; I have showed that God is worthy of confidence. ¶ *And thy salvation.* Thy method of salvation, or of saving men. ¶ *I have not concealed thy loving-kindness.* Thy mercy or thy merciful disposition towards men. He had shown to the human race that God was a merciful Being; a Being who would pardon sin. ¶ *And thy truth.* The truth which thou hast revealed; the truth on all subjects which it was important for men to understand. ¶ *From the great congregation.* That is, as in ver. 9, the assembled multitudes—the throngs that gathered to hear the words of the Great Teacher. Comp. Matt. v. 1; xiii. 2; Luke viii. 4.

11. *Withhold not thou thy tender mercies from me, O* LORD. Do not restrain or hold back thy compassions. Let thy mercies—the expressions of thy love — flow out freely

12 For innumerable [k] evils have compassed me about: mine iniquities [l] have taken hold upon me, so that I am not able to look up: they are more than the hairs of mine head; therefore my heart [1] faileth me.

k Heb. iv. 15. *l* Ps. xxxviii. 4, etc.

[1] *forsaketh.*

towards me in connexion with what I have done. As applicable to the Redeemer, this is a prayer that God would bestow upon him in connexion with his work, and as a reward of his work, appropriate proofs of his goodness. And especially is this to be understood here as a prayer for support and deliverance in the sorrows that came upon him in the accomplishment of his work. The prayer is *intermediate* between the expression of his purpose to do the will of God when all other means of salvation had failed (vers. 6–8), and the sorrows or sufferings that *would* come upon him in the accomplishment of his work (vers. 12, 13). He saw himself at this point of his life, as represented in the psalm, as about to sink into the depth of woes. He had kept the law of God, and had by his obedience thus far done his will. He had made known the truth of God, and had declared his great message to the assembled multitude that had crowded his path, and thronged to hear him. He saw himself now about to enter the vale of sorrow; to plunge into that depth of the unutterable woes connected with the making of an atonement. He prayed, therefore, that, in these approaching sorrows, God would *not* withhold the expression of his tender mercy. The point of time, therefore, in the Redeemer's life which the verse before us occupies, is that awful and sorrowful hour when, his public work of teaching and of miracles finished, he was about to endure the agonies of Gethsemane and of the cross. ¶ *Let thy loving-kindness.* Thy mercy. ¶ *And thy truth.* Thy promises; thy plighted support and strength; thy fidelity. That is, he prayed that God would show himself true and faithful in bearing him through the great work of the atonement. ¶ *Continually.* Through the whole of these sorrows. Do not for a moment leave or forsake me. ¶ *Preserve me.* Keep me from sinking under these woes; from speaking any improper word; from shrinking back; from being overcome by the tempter; from failing in the great work now to be accomplished. As the Redeemer had a human as well as a Divine nature;—as he was man, with all human susceptibilities to suffering, it was not inappropriate that he should utter this prayer, and lift up his heart with the utmost earnestness to God, that he might not be forsaken in the consummation of the great work of his life, and that this work might not fail.

12. *For innumerable evils have compassed me about.* Have surrounded me, or have beset me on every side. The "evils" here referred to, understood as being those which came upon the Messiah, were sorrows that came upon him in consequence of his undertaking to do what could not be done by sacrifices and offerings (ver. 6); that is, his undertaking to save men by his own "obedience unto death." The *time* referred to here, I apprehend, is that when the full effects of his having assumed the sins of the world to make expiation for them came upon him; when he was about to endure the agonies of Gethsemane and Calvary. ¶ *Mine iniquities have taken hold upon me.* On this passage, as constituting one of the main objections, and the strongest objection, to the application of the psalm to the Messiah, and on the way in which such objection may be met, see introd. to this psalm (3 *b*). ¶ *So that I am not able to look up.* This is not the exact idea of the Hebrew word. That is simply, I am not able *to see;* and it refers to the dimness or failure of sight caused by distress, weakness, or old age.

13 Be pleased, O LORD, to deliver me: O LORD, make haste to help me.

14 Let them be ashamed and confounded together that seek after my soul to destroy it; let them be driven backward, and put to shame, that wish me evil.

15 Let them be desolate for a reward of their shame, that say unto me, Aha, aha!

---

1 Sam. iii. 2; iv. 15; 1 Kings xiv. 4; comp. Ps. vi. 7. The idea here is, not that he was unable to *look up*, but that the calamities which came upon him were so heavy and severe as to make his sight dim, or to deprive him of vision. Either by weeping, or by the mere pressure of suffering, he was so affected as almost to be deprived of the power of seeing. ¶ *They are more than the hairs of mine head.* That is, the sorrows that come upon me in connexion with sin. The idea is that they were innumerable,—the hairs of the head, or the sands on the seashore, being employed in the Scriptures to denote what cannot be numbered. See Ps. lxix. 4. Comp. Gen. xxii. 17; xxxii. 12; Josh. xi. 4; 2 Sam. xvii. 11. ¶ *Therefore my heart faileth me.* Marg., as in Heb., *forsaketh.* The idea is, that he sank under these sufferings; he could not sustain them.

13. *Be pleased,* O LORD, *to deliver me.* That is, in these troubles and sorrows. See Matt. xxvi. 39. The prayer is that, if possible, the cup of sorrow might be taken away. ¶ O LORD, *make haste to help me.* This is the same form of prayer, and referring, I suppose, to the same occasion as that which occurs in Ps. xxii. 19. See Notes on that verse.

14. *Let them be ashamed and confounded together.* See Notes on Ps. xxxv. 4, 26. This may be understood here rather as a confident expectation than a wish or desire. It implies the certainty that they *would* thus be ashamed and confounded; that is, that they would not be successful, or would be foiled in their purposes. But understood as a wish or prayer, it could not be improper. There is no sin in the wish that the wicked may not be successful in their plans, and may not be suffered to injure us. As the language of the Messiah it was in every way an appropriate prayer that the purposes of those who would defeat his design in coming into the world might be foiled,—for on the execution of that design depended the salvation of a lost race. ¶ *That seek after my soul to destroy it.* That seek after my life; that would destroy me. That is, they seek to kill me; they would take my life before the full time is come. As understood of the Messiah, this would refer to the times when his life was in danger, as it often was, before the full period had arrived for him to die: John vii. 6; Matt. xxvi. 18. The *purpose* of his enemies was to take his life; to prevent the spread of his doctrines; to check him in his work. The taking of his life at any time before the full period had arrived, or in any other way than that in which he had purposed to lay it down, would have been a defeat of his work, since in the plan of salvation it was contemplated that he *should* die at a certain time, and in a certain manner,—that he should die at the time which had been predicted by the prophets, and in such a mode as to make an atonement for sin. All this would have been defeated if, before that time came, he had been put to death by stoning, or in any of the numerous ways in which his life was threatened. ¶ *Let them be driven backward, and put to shame, that wish me evil.* Turned backward, as they are who are unsuccessful, or are defeated. Comp. John xviii. 6.

15. *Let them be desolate.* The word here employed means *to be astonished* or *amazed;* then, to be laid waste, or *made desolate.* As used here, it refers to their purposes, and the wish or prayer is that they might be wholly unsuccessful, or that in respect to success they might be like a waste

16 Let all those that seek thee rejoice and be glad in thee: let such as love thy salvation say continually, The LORD be magnified.

17 But I *am* poor and needy; *yet* the LORD thinketh [n] upon me: thou *art* my help and my deliverer; make no tarrying, O my God.

n ver. 5; 1 Pet. v. 7.

---

and desolate field where nothing grows. ¶ *For a reward.* The word here used—עֵקֶב, *aikeb*—means the *end*, the last of anything; then, the recompence, reward, wages, as being the *end*, the *result*, or *issue* of a certain course of conduct. That is, in this case, the "desolation" prayed for would be a proper recompence for their purpose, or for what they said. ¶ *Of their shame.* Of their shameful act or purpose; their act as deserving of ignominy. ¶ *That say unto me, Aha, aha.* That use language of reproach and contempt. This is a term of exultation over another; a word of rejoicing at the calamities that come on another; an act of joy over a fallen enemy: Ezek. xxv. 3.; see Notes on Ps. xxxv. 21, 25. As understood of the Messiah, this would refer to the taunts and reproaches of his enemies; the exultation which they manifested when they had him in their power,—when they felt secure that their vexations in regard to him were at an end, or that they would be troubled with him no more. By putting him to death they supposed that they might feel safe from further molestation on his account. For this act, this note of exultation and joy, on the part of the Jewish rulers, and of the people as stimulated by those rulers, the "desolation" which came upon them (the utter ruin of their temple, their city, and their nation) was an appropriate "reward." That desolation did not go *beyond* their desert, for their treatment of the Messiah,—as the ruin of the sinner in the future world will not go *beyond* his desert for having rejected the same Messiah as his Saviour.

16. *Let all those that seek thee.* All those who desire to know thee; to understand thy ways; to be thy friends. The phrase is used to denote the truly pious, because it is a characteristic of all such that they truly desire to be acquainted with God, and to find the way which leads to his favour. ¶ *Rejoice and be glad in thee.* (1) By finding thee, or securing the object which they sought; (2) *in* thee, as the source of all true comfort and joy. The prayer is that all such may be successful in *their* efforts, while those who have no such aim may be disappointed, ver. 14. ¶ *Let such as love thy salvation.* (*a*) Thy *method* of salvation, or the appointed way by which men may be saved; and (*b*) the *salvation* itself,—deliverance from the guilt and dominion of sin, and complete and eternal restoration to the favour of God. ¶ *Say continually, The* LORD *be magnified.* See Notes on Ps. xxxv. 27, where the same expression occurs.

17. *But I* am *poor and needy.* More literally, "I am afflicted and poor." The language would describe the condition of one who was afflicted and was at the same time poor; of one who had no resource but in God, and who was passing through scenes of poverty and sorrow. There were undoubtedly times in the life of David to which this language would be applicable; but it would be far more applicable to the circumstances in which the Redeemer was placed; and, in accordance with the interpretation which has been given of the other parts of the psalm, I suppose that this is designed to represent his afflicted and humble condition as a man of poverty and sorrow. ¶ *Yet the* LORD *thinketh upon me.* The Lord cares for me; he has not forgotten me. Man forsakes me, but he will not. Man leaves me to poverty and sorrow, but he will not. How true this was of the Redeemer, that the "Lord," the Father of mercies,

"thought" on him, it is not needful now to say; nor can it be doubted that in the heavy sorrows of his life this was a source of habitual consolation. To others also — to all his friends—this is a source of unspeakable comfort. To be an object of the *thoughts* of God; to be had in his mind; to be constantly in his remembrance; to be certain that he will not forsake us in our trouble; to be assured in our own minds that one so great as God is—the infinite and eternal One—will never cease to "think" on us, may well sustain us in all the trials of life. It matters little who *does* forsake us, if he does not; it would be of little advantage to us who *should* think on us, if he did not. ¶ *Thou* art *my help and my deliverer*. Implying the highest confidence. See Notes on Ps. xviii. 2. ¶ *Make no tarrying, O my God.* Do not linger or delay in coming to my assistance. The psalm closes with this prayer. Applied to the Redeemer, it indicates strong confidence in God in the midst of his afflictions and sorrows, with earnest pleading, coming from the depth of those sorrows, that God would interpose for him. The vision of the psalmist extended here no farther. His eye rested on a suffering Messiah,—afflicted, crushed, broken, forsaken—with all the woes connected with the work of human redemption, and all the sorrows expressive of the evil of sin clustering upon him, yet confident in God, and finding his last consolation in the feeling that God "*thought*" on him, and in the assurance that He would not ultimately forsake him. There is something delightful, though pensive, in the close of the psalm. The last prayer of the sufferer—the confident, earnest pleading—lingers on the ear, and we almost seem to behold the Sufferer in the depth of his sorrows, and in the earnestness of his supplication, calmly looking up to God as One that "thought" on him when all others had forgotten him; as a last, safe refuge when every other refuge had failed. So, in our sorrows, we may lie before the throne, calmly looking up to God with a feeling that we are *not* forgotten; that there is *One* who "thinks" on us; and that it is our privilege to pray to him that he would hasten to deliver us. All sorrow can be borne when we feel that *God* has not forgotten us; we may be calm when all the world forsakes us, if we can feel assured that the great and blessed God "thinks" on us, and will never cease to remember us.

PSALM XLI.

This psalm, ascribed to David, has, in its general design and spirit, a strong resemblance to Ps. xxxviii. The occasion on which it was composed is not certainly known; but, like that, it seems to have been when the author was suffering under bodily sickness, not improbably brought on him by mental sorrows caused by the ingratitude of his friends, or by those nearly related to him in life. It is certain that his bodily sufferings were either caused or aggravated by the neglect of his friends; by their cold treatment of him; by their ingratitude towards him; by the reports which they circulated in regard to him. See Ps. xxxviii. 11, 12; comp. Ps. xli. 5-9. It was this unkindness certainly which greatly increased his suffering, and which probably gave occasion to the psalm. Who the persons were that thus treated him with neglect and coldness cannot now be ascertained; nor is it necessary to know *who* they were in order to appreciate the meaning and the beauty of the psalm. Their conduct is so accurately and so feelingly described, that it would be no particular advantage to be made acquainted with their names.

The case, therefore, in the psalm is that of one who is sick; who is forsaken by his friends; who is subjected to unkind remarks alike when they are with him and when absent from him; of one, therefore, whose only refuge is God, and who looks to *him* for sympathy.

According to this view, the psalm may be conveniently divided into four parts:—

I. The psalmist dwells on the blessed character of one who *does* show compassion or kindness to the poor and the suffering; the blessedness of the man who *is* merciful, vers. 1-3. This is evidently a reflection *forced* upon him by

PSALM XLI.

To the chief Musician. A Psalm of David.

BLESSED *o is* he that considereth the 1 poor: the LORD will deliver him in 2 time of trouble.

o Prov. xiv. 21; Heb. vi. 10.
1 *weak*, or, *sick*. 2 *the day of evil*.

the opposite conduct of those whom he supposed he might have regarded as his friends, and to whom he had a right to look for sympathy and kindness. In his own mind, therefore, he *contrasts* their actual conduct with the character of the truly kind and merciful man, and is led, in few words, to describe the happiness which *would* follow if proper kindness were shown to the poor and the afflicted. He says that the effect of such conduct would be (*a*) that the Lord would deliver such an one in the time of trouble, ver. 1; (*b*) that the Lord would preserve him alive, ver. 2; (*c*) that he would be blessed upon the earth, ver. 2; (*d*) that the Lord would not deliver him to the will of his enemies, ver. 2; (*e*) that he would strengthen him on the bed of languishing, and would make his bed in his sickness, ver. 3.

II. An appeal to God for mercy, and for restoration to health, with an humble confession that it was for his own sin that he was suffering; and with a purpose not to attempt to justify himself, or to say that he had not deserved this at the hand of God, ver. 4. He makes no complaint of God, much as he had occasion to complain of his friends.

III. A statement in regard to the manner in which he had been treated in his sickness, vers. 5-9. (*a*) His enemies took occasion to speak evil of him, and to utter the wish, in a manner which would be most painful to a sufferer, that he might die, and that his name might perish, ver. 5. (*b*) If they came to see him in his sickness, instead of speaking words of kindness and comfort, they spoke only "vain" and unmeaning words; they sought occasion to gratify their own malignity by finding something in his manner, or in his language, which they could repeat to his disadvantage, ver. 6. (*c*) All that hated him took occasion now to *conspire* against him, to lay together all that they individually knew or could say that would be injurious to him, and to urge their individual causes of complaint against him in a general statement in regard to his character, ver. 7. (*d*) They especially sought to injure him by reporting that a disease clave to him which was the result of sin, perhaps of an irregular life, and that there was no prospect that he would be again restored to health; that the hand of God was upon him, and that he must sink to the grave, ver. 8. (*e*) All this was aggravated by the fact that his own familiar friend, some one who had enjoyed his confidence, and had partaken of the hospitality of his table, had abused his friendship, and was found among his detractors and calumniators, ver. 9.

IV. An earnest invocation of the mercy of God, and an expression of the confident assurance of his favour, closes the psalm, vers. 10-13.

This psalm, like Ps. xxxviii., which it so much resembles, is one that will be always eminently useful to those who are visited with sickness, and who, at the same time, are deprived of the sympathy in their sufferings which the afflicted so much need and desire, and who, instead of sympathy, are subjected to detraction and calumny, --their enemies taking advantage of their condition to circulate unfavourable reports in regard to them, and their heretofore professed friends withdrawing from them, and uniting with their calumniators and detractors. Such cases may not be *very* common in the world, but they occur with sufficient frequency to make it proper that, in a book claiming to be inspired, and designed to be adapted to all times and all classes of men, they should be referred to, and that we should be told what is the true source of consolation in such troubles. Indeed, a book professing to come from God would be defective in the highest degree if such a case were *not* provided for, and if suitable instructions for such an occasion had not been furnished by precept, or example, or both. On the phrase in the title, "To the chief Musician," see Notes on the title to Ps. iv.

1. *Blessed* is *he*. See Notes on Ps. i. 1. Literally, "Oh the blessings of him that considers the poor." The object is to describe the advantages of doing what is here said; or the excellence of the spirit which would be manifested in such a case, and the effect which this would have on his own happiness. These happy effects

2 The LORD will preserve him, and keep him alive; *and* he shall be blessed upon the earth: and [1] thou wilt not *p* deliver him unto the will of his enemies.

3 The LORD will strengthen him upon the bed of languishing:

[1] Or, *do not thou.* *p* Ps. xxxvii. 32, 33.

are described in the remainder of this verse, and in the two following verses. ¶ *That considereth.* The word here used—from שָׂכַל, *sachal*—means properly to look at, to behold; then, to be prudent or circumspect; then, to attend to; and then in general to act prudently, wisely, intelligently, in any case. Here it means to attend to; to show an interest in; to care for. The idea is that of *not* neglecting; *not* passing by; *not* being indifferent to; *not* being hard-hearted and uncharitable towards. ¶ *The poor.* Marg., *the weak*, or *the sick.* The word used in the Hebrew—דַּל, *dal*—means properly something hanging or swinging, as of pendulous boughs or branches; and then, that which is weak, feeble, powerless. Thus it comes to denote those who are feeble and helpless either by poverty or by disease, and is used with a general reference to those who are in a low or humble condition, and who need the aid of others. The statement here is of a *general* nature,—that he is blessed who shows proper sympathy for all of that class: for those who need the sympathy of others from any cause—poverty, sickness, a low condition, or trouble. The *particular* thing here referred to was a case of sickness; where one was borne down by disease, perhaps brought on by mental sorrow, and when he particularly needed the sympathy of his friends. See vers. 5–8. ¶ *The* LORD *will deliver him in time of trouble.* Marg., as in Heb., *in the day of evil.* This is the *first* happy effect or result of showing proper sympathy with others in their troubles. It is a statement of the general principle that the Lord will deal with us as we do with others. See this principle stated and illustrated in Ps. xviii. 24–26.

2. *The* LORD *will preserve him, and keep him alive.* This is a farther statement of the same principle, and it refers to a *general*, not a *universal* rule in the Divine administration, that acts of piety will be partially rewarded on the earth; or that the Divine favour will be shown to those who deal kindly with others. This principle is often referred to in the Scriptures. See Notes on Ps. i. 3; xxxvii. 3, 4, 11, 23–26, 37; comp. Matt. v. 5; 1 Tim. iv. 8. The *particular* application here is, that if any one showed kindness to him that was sick or enfeebled by disease, he might expect that God would interpose in his case under similar circumstances, and would "preserve" him, or "keep him alive." Of course this is to be regarded as a statement made under the general principle. It is not to be interpreted as teaching that this would be *universally* true, or that he who did this would never die, but the meaning is, that he might look for special Divine aid and favour, when he in turn should be sick. ¶ And *he shall be blessed upon the earth.* This is in accordance with the doctrine noticed above, and so often referred to in the Psalms and elsewhere, that the effect of religion will be to promote happiness and prosperity in this life. ¶ *And thou wilt not deliver him unto the will of his enemies.* Marg., *Do not thou deliver.* The margin, perhaps, expresses most correctly the sense of the original, but still it is an expression of the confident belief of the psalmist that this *will* not occur; a belief expressed here rather in the form of a prayer than of a direct assertion. The idea is, that he would find God to be a defender and a helper when he was attacked by his foes.

3. *The* LORD *will strengthen him upon the bed of languishing.* The word rendered *strengthen* here means

thou wilt [1] make all his bed in his sickness.
4 I said, [q] LORD, be merciful unto me; heal [r] my soul; for I have sinned against thee.
5 Mine enemies speak evil of me,

[1] *turn.* [q] Ps. xxxii. 5. [r] Ps. cxlvii. 3; Hos. vi. 1.

to support; to uphold; to sustain. The idea here is, that God would *enable* him to bear his sickness, or would impart strength — inward strength—when his body failed, or when but for this aid he must sink under his disease and die. The word rendered *languishing* means properly languor or sickness; and more generally something *sickening*; that is, something unclean, unwholesome, nauseating, Job vi. 6. The idea here, in accordance with what is stated above, is, that acts of religion will tend to promote our welfare and happiness in this life; and more particularly that the man who shows favour (ver. 1) to those who are weak, sick, helpless, will find in turn that God will support him when he is sick. Thus, Ps. xviii. 25, "With the merciful thou wilt show thyself merciful." ¶ *Thou wilt make all his bed in his sickness.* Marg., as in Heb., *turn.* So the LXX., ἔστρεψας. Luther renders it, "Thou dost help him." The idea is, that God will *turn* his bed or his couch; that is, that he will render favour like turning his couch, or making his bed when he is sick; or, in other words, he will relieve his suffering, and make him comfortable on his bed. It does not mean that he will turn his sickness to health, but that he will relieve and comfort him, as one is relieved and soothed on a sick bed by having his bed "made up." This, too, is in accordance with the general sentiment that God will show himself merciful to those who are merciful; kind to those who are kind. On the bed of languishing it will be much to be able to remember that we, in our health, have contributed to the comfort of the sick and the dying. (*a*) The recollection itself will do much to impart inward satisfaction then, for we shall then appreciate better than we did when we performed the act the value of this trait of character, and have a deeper sense of gratitude that we have been able to relieve the sufferings of others; (*b*) we may believe and trust that God will remember what we have done, and that he will manifest himself to us then as our gracious supporter and our comforter. It will not be because by our own acts we have *merited* his favour, but because this is his gracious purpose, and because it is in accordance with his nature thus to bestow kindness on those who have been kind to others.

4. *I said,* LORD. I said in my sickness, or in the trial referred to in the psalm. I called on God to be merciful to me when others had no mercy; to be near to me when others turned away; to save me when pressed down with disease on account of my sins. All that follows relates, like this passage, to what occurred when he was sick; to the thoughts that passed through his mind, and to the treatment which he then experienced from others. ¶ *Be merciful unto me.* In forgiving my sins, and restoring me to health. ¶ *Heal my soul.* In restoring my *soul* to spiritual health by forgiving the sin which is the cause of my sickness; or it may mean, Restore my *life,*—regarding his *life* as (as it were) diseased and in danger of extinction. The probability, however, is that he had particular reference to the *soul* as the word is commonly understood, or as designating *himself;* heal, or restore *me.* ¶ *For I have sinned against thee.* Regarding his sin as the cause of his sickness. See Notes on Ps. xxxviii. 3, 4, 5.

5. *Mine enemies speak evil of me.* They take occasion to speak evil of me in my weak and feeble state, thus adding to my sorrows. The word "*evil*" here refers to their calumnies or reproaches. They spoke of him as a bad man; as if it were desirable

When shall he die, and his name perish?

6 And if he come to see *me*, he [s] speaketh vanity: his heart gathereth iniquity to itself; *when* he goeth abroad, he telleth *it*.

s Prov. xxvi. 24, 25.

that he should die; that his influence in the world should come to an end, and that his name should be forgotten. ¶ *When shall he die.* "He is sick; sick on account of his sins; it seems certain that he will die; and it is desirable that such a man *should* die. But he seems to linger on, as if there were no hope of his dying." Nothing can be imagined more unkind, cutting, severe than this,—the desire that a man who is sick shall die, and be out of the way. Nothing could add more to the sorrows of sickness itself than such a wish; than to have it talked about among men—whispered from one to another—that such a man was a nuisance; that he was a bad man; that he was suffering on account of his sins; that it was desirable that his death should occur as soon as possible, and that all remembrance of him on earth should cease. ¶ *And his name perish.* That he should be forgotten altogether; that his name should be no more mentioned; that all the influence of his life should cease for ever. Of a truly bad man—a corrupter of the faith and the virtue of others—this *is* desirable, for the sooner such men are forgotten the better. Forgotten they will be (Prov. x. 7), but there is no more malignant feeling in regard to a good man, and especially when such a man is suffering under a severe disease, than the wish that he should die, and that his name should wholly fade away from recollection.

6. *And if he come to see* me. If he condescends to visit me in my sickness. The word "me" is not in the original; and perhaps the idea is not that he came to see the sufferer, but that he came to see *for himself*, though under pretence of paying a visit of kindness. His real motive was to make observation, that he might find something in the expressions or manner of the sufferer that would enable him to make a report unfavourable to him, and to confirm him in his impression that it was desirable such a man should die. He would come under the mask of sympathy and friendship, but really to find something that would confirm him in the opinion that he was a bad man, and that would enable him to state to others that it was desirable he should die. ¶ *He speaketh vanity.* He utters no expressions of sincerity and truth; he suggests nothing that would console and comfort me; his words are all foreign to the purpose for which a man should visit another in such circumstances, and are, therefore, vain words. What he says is mere pretence and hypocrisy, and is designed to deceive me, as if he had sympathy with me, while his real purpose is to do me mischief. ¶ *His heart gathereth iniquity to itself.* Or, in his heart he is gathering mischief. That is, in his heart, or in his secret purpose, under the pretence of sympathy and friendship, he is really aiming to gather the materials for doing me wrong. He is endeavouring to find something in my words or manner; in my expressions of impatience and complaining; in the utterances of my unguarded moments, when I am scarcely conscious—something that may be uttered in the honesty of feeling when a man thinks that he is about to die—some reflections of my own on my past life—some confession of sin, which he may turn to my disadvantage, or which may justify his slanderous report that I am a bad man, and that it is desirable that *such* a man should live no longer. Can anything be imagined more malicious than this? ¶ When *he goeth abroad, he telleth* it. Literally, he tells it to the street, or to those who are without. Perhaps his friends, as malicious as himself, are anxiously waiting without for his re-

7 All that hate me whisper together against me: against me do they devise [1] my hurt.

8 [2] An evil disease, *say they*, cleaveth fast unto him: and *now* that he lieth, he shall rise up no more.

[1] *evil to me.* [2] *A thing of Belial.*

port, and, like him, are desirous of finding something that may confirm them in their opinion of him. Or perhaps he designs to tell this to the friends of the sufferer, to show them now that they were deceived in the man; that although in the days of his health, and in his prosperity, he *seemed* to be a good man, yet that now, when the trial has come, and a real test has been applied, all his religion has been found false and hollow; his impatience, his complaining, his murmuring, and his unwillingness to die, all showing that he was a hypocrite, and was at heart a bad man. Comp. Notes on Job i. 9–11.

7. *All that hate me whisper together against me.* They talk the matter over where they suppose that no one can hear; they endeavour to collect and arrange all that can be said against me; they place all that they can say or think as individuals, all that they have separately known or suspected, into *common stock*, and make use of it against me. There is a *conspiracy* against me—a purpose to do me all the evil that they can. This shows that, in the apprehension of the sufferer, the one who came to see for himself (ver. 6) came as one of a company—as one deputed or delegated to find some new occasion for a charge against him, and that he had not to suffer under the single malignity of one, but under the combined malignity of many. ¶ *Against me do they devise my hurt.* Marg., as in Heb., *evil to me.* That is, they devise some report, the truth of which they endeavour to confirm by something that they may observe in my sickness which will be injurious to me, and which will prove to the world that I am a bad man—a man by whose death the world would be benefited. The slanderous report on which they seemed to agree is mentioned in the following verse,—that he was suffering under a disease which was directly and manifestly the result of a sinful life, and that it must be fatal.

8. *An evil disease.* Marg., *a thing of Belial.* The Hebrew is literally *a word of Belial.* This has been very variously understood and interpreted. The LXX. render it, λόγον παράνομον—a wicked word; "a wicked determination" (Thompson); that is, they formed a wicked purpose against him, to wit, by saying that he was now confined to his bed, and could not rise again. The Latin Vulgate renders it in a similar manner: Verbum iniquitum constituerunt adversum me. Luther, "They have formed a wicked device (*Bubenstück*) against me;" they behave in a knavish or wicked manner. De Wette, "Destruction (*Verderben*) or punishment (*Strafe*) is poured upon him." The term rendered *disease* means properly *word* or *thing;* and Professor Alexander renders it, "A word of Belial is poured upon him." The word rendered *evil*, *Belial*, means literally *without use*—בְּלִיַּעַל—from בְּלִי, *beli, not* or *without*, and יַעַל, *yaal, use* or *profit.* Then it means worthlessness, wickedness, destruction; and hence, in connexion with *man*, denotes one who is wicked, worthless, abandoned. It is difficult to determine its meaning here. The *connexion* (ver. 3) would seem to suggest the idea adopted by our translators; the *words* themselves would seem rather to convey the idea of some reproach, or harsh saying—some vain, wicked, malicious words that were uttered against him. That there was disease in the case, and that the psalm was composed in view of it, and of the treatment which the author experienced from those who had been his professed friends when suffering under it, seems to me to be manifest from vers. 1, 3, 4, 8; but it is probable that the reference in this

9 Yea, [1] mine own familiar friend, in whom I trusted, which [t] did eat of my bread, hath [2] lifted up *his* heel against me.

[1] *the man of my peace.*

[t] Job xix. 19; John xiii. 18. [2] *magnified.*

expression is not to the disease, but to the words or the conduct of his calumniators. It is evident from the pronoun *him*—the third person—that this refers, as our translators have indicated by the words "*say they*" to something that they *said* in regard to him; something which they affirmed as the result of their observations on his condition, vers. 6, 7. The true idea, therefore, I think is this:—"They say—that is, those who came to see me said—A 'word of evil'—*a sentence of evil or destruction*—is poured upon him. He is suffering under such a 'word of destruction;' or, such a word (that is, sentence) as will involve his destruction, by way of punishment for his sins; therefore all is over with him, and he must die. He can hope to rise no more." This would express the idea that they regarded his death as certain, for he seemed to be under a sentence which made that sure. ¶ *Cleaveth fast unto him.* Or rather, *is poured upon him.* The word here used—צוּק, *tzuk*—means (1) to be narrow, straitened, compressed; and then (2) to pour out—as metal is poured out (Job xxviii. 2), or as words are poured out in prayer (Isa. xxvi. 16). Here it would seem to mean that such a sentence was poured upon him, or that he had become *submerged* or swallowed up under it. It was like the pouring out of a torrent on him, overwhelming him with floods of water, so that he could not hope to escape, or to rise again. ¶ *And* now *that he lieth, he shall rise up no more.* There is no hope for him; no prospect that he will ever get up again. They felt that they might indulge their remarks, therefore, freely, as he would not be able to take revenge on them, and their expectations and hopes were about to be accomplished by his death. Comp. ver. 5. As a part of his sufferings, all this was aggravated by the fact that they regarded those sufferings as full proof of his guilt; that he could not reply to their accusations; and that he was about to die under that imputation.

9. *Yea, mine own familiar friend.* Marg., as in Heb., *the man of my peace.* The man with whom I was at peace; who had no cause of alienation from me; with whom I was associated in the most peaceful and friendly relations. ¶ *In whom I trusted.* He whom I made my confidential friend, and on whom I supposed I could rely in the time of trouble. ¶ *Which did eat of my bread.* This may either denote one who was supported by him as one of his family, or else one who partook of his hospitality. In the former case, if that is the meaning, he had a right to expect that, as a matter of gratitude, such an one would stand by him, and not be found among his enemies. In the latter case, if that is the meaning, he had a right to expect that one who had shared his hospitality would not be found among his foes. ¶ *Hath lifted up* his *heel* against me. Marg., as in Heb., *magnified.* So the LXX. and the Latin Vulgate. Luther renders this, "hath trodden me under his feet." The figure here is taken from a horse that turns and kicks him that had fed him. This passage is applied (John xiii. 18) to Judas, with the statement, in regard to him, that what he had done was done "that the Scripture might be fulfilled:" see Notes on that passage. It is not necessary to suppose that the Saviour meant to say that the passage in the psalm had *original* and *exclusive* reference to Judas; the phrase employed by the Saviour, "that the Scripture might be fulfilled," may have been used by him in that large sense in which these words are often used as denoting, either (*a*) that the

10 But thou, O LORD, be merciful unto me, and raise me up, that I may requite them.

11 By this I know that thou favourest me, because mine enemy doth not triumph over me.

language found in the Scriptures, and applicable originally to another case, *would properly express the idea*, or describe the fact; or (*b*) that the case referred to was *one of a class;* or that, as it was accomplished in the case of David, so in a similar sense it was accomplished in the case of the Saviour. In other words, Judas was regarded as belonging to the same class as the individual to whom the psalm refers. He was one to whom the language of the psalm was applicable; and the Saviour endured the same kind of suffering which the person did who is referred to in the psalm. Thus the *language* of the Scriptures, applicable to all such cases, received a complete fulfilment in Him. It is remarkable that, in the reference to Judas, the Saviour quotes only a part of the verse: "He that eateth bread with me." He omits, apparently from design, the former part of the verse in the psalm, "mine own familiar friend, in whom I trusted," as if he would not even *seem* to convey the idea that he ever regarded Judas as his intimate friend, or as if he had ever really "trusted" him. He conveys the idea that Judas had partaken largely of his favours, but not that He himself was ever really a stranger to the baseness of his heart, John vi. 64, 70.

10. *But thou, O* LORD, *be merciful unto me.* That is, give me strength; restore me from my sickness and weakness. ¶ *And raise me up.* From my bed of languishing. ¶ *That I may requite them.* That I may repay them; or may recompense them. The word here used—שָׁלַם, *shalam*—means properly, to be whole, sound, safe; then, in Piel, to make secure, or preserve in safety; and then, to complete, to make whole, to make good, to restore; and then, to make whole or to complete in the sense of *recompensing* or *requiting:*—to make the matter *equal.* It would be well expressed here by the familiar language, *giving them what they deserve.* But it is not *necessary* to understand this as indicating an unforgiving spirit. The writer *may* have meant to say that the persons who demeaned themselves in this manner *ought* to be punished; that the public good required it; and being a magistrate, he spoke as one appointed to administer the laws, and prayed for a restoration to strength, that he *might* administer justice in this and in all similar cases. It is *possible* also that he meant to say he would repay them by "heaping coals of fire on their heads"—by acts of kindness in place of the wrongs that they had done him (see Prov. xxv. 21, 22; comp Rom. xii. 20, 21); though I admit that this is not the obvious interpretation. But in order to show that this was uttered with a bad spirit, and under the promptings of revenge, it would be necessary to show that neither of these *supposable* interpretations *could be* the true one. It may be added here that we may not be required to vindicate all the expressions of personal feeling found in the Psalms in order to any just view of inspiration. See General Introduction, § 6 (6).

11. *By this I know.* Comp. Notes on Ps. xx. 6. This indicates a confident assurance that his prayer would be answered, and that he would be restored to health. How he had this assurance we are not informed, but it seems most probable that it was by an intimation conveyed to his mind by God himself. Comp., for a similar case, Phil. i. 25. See Notes on that passage. ¶ *That thou favourest me.* That thou dost delight in me; that thou art my friend. ¶ *Because mine enemy doth not triumph over me.* The word here rendered *triumph* properly means to shout, or to make a noise. As a sign of exultation, more especially in war: 1 Sam. xvii. 20. Here it means that his enemy would not

12 And as for me, thou upholdest me in mine integrity, and settest me before thy face for ever.

13 Blessed *be* [t] the LORD God of Israel from everlasting, and to everlasting. Amen, and Amen.

t Ps. lxxii. 18, 19.

secure a victory over him; or would not shout *as if* such a victory were obtained. That is, he felt assured now that all the machinations of his foes would be defeated; that all the hopes which they cherished that he was soon to die would be disappointed; that he himself would be recovered from his sickness, contrary to their malicious anticipations and desires. This he regarded as an evidence that God was his friend.

12. *And as for me.* Literally, "and I;" as if there were some verb understood. The reference is turned on himself; on all that was suggested by this train of remark as bearing on himself. The result of the whole was a firm assurance that God would sustain him, and that he would be established before God for ever. The train of thought is this: "And I—thou upholdest me." Perhaps the course of expression, if it had not been suddenly changed, would have been, "And I am sustained or held up." The thought, however, turns rather on *God* than on *himself*, and instead of carrying out the reference to himself so prominently, he turns to *God* as the source whence all this was derived. ¶ *Thou upholdest me.* Not merely in strengthening me in my sickness, but, what is more important, in vindicating my character against the aspersions which are cast upon it. Thou dost show that I *am* upright. ¶ *In mine integrity.* Literally, "in my *perfection.*" See Notes on Job i. 1. The word here means *uprightness, sincerity, probity.* He had been calumniated by his foes. His sickness had been regarded by them as a proof that he was a hypocrite or a stranger to God. If he had died, they would have urged that fact as evidence that he was the object of the Divine displeasure. His restored health was clear proof that their suggestions were false, and that he was not suffering for the cause which they alleged. God thus showed that he regarded him as upright and sincere. The claim is not that of *absolute perfection,* but only of a character of piety or integrity in opposition to the slanderous charges of his enemies. Comp. Ps. vii. 8; xxv. 21; xxvi. 1, 11. ¶ *And settest me before thy face for ever.* That is, Thou *wilt* do it. God would always have him in his presence, permit him always to dwell with him—the highest proof of his friendship.

13. *Blessed* be *the* LORD *God of Israel.* That is, Let the Lord God of Israel be *praised, honoured, adored.* The language is an expression of desire that all honour, all happiness, might be His. It is a recognition of God as the source of the mercies referred to, and an expression of the feeling that he is entitled to universal praise. The word *Israel* here refers to the people of God as descended from Jacob or Israel. ¶ *From everlasting, and to everlasting.* Through eternity, or eternal ages,—from all past duration to all future duration. The expression "*from* everlasting *to* everlasting," would embrace eternity; and the idea is that God is deserving of *eternal* praise. ¶ *Amen, and amen.* The word *amen* means properly *surely, certainly, truly,* and is a word expressive of solemn affirmation, or of the desire of the mind that this should be so. Its repetition is emphatic, expressing *strong* assent to what is said as certainly true, or as *eminently* the wish of the mind. This benediction marks the close of one of the five books into which the Psalms are commonly divided. See the General Introduction, § 3.

APPENDIX.

PSALM I.

3. *And whatsoever he doeth shall prosper.* Blessed is the man who hath such a promise as this. But we must not always estimate the fulfilment of a promise by our own eyesight. How often, if we judge by feeble sense, may we come to the mournful conclusion of Jacob, "All these things are against me!" For though we know our interest in the promise, yet we are so tried and troubled that sight sees the very reverse of what promise foretells. But to the eye of faith this word is sure, and by it we perceive that our works are prospered, even when everything seems to go against us. It is not outward prosperity which the Christian most desires and values; it is soul prosperity which he longs for. We often, like Jehoshaphat, make ships to go to Tarshish for gold, but they are broken at Ezion-geber; but even here there is a true prospering, for it is often for the soul's health that we should be poor, bereaved, and persecuted. Our worst things are often our best things. As there is a curse wrapped up in the wicked man's mercies, so there is a blessing concealed in the righteous man's crosses, losses, and sorrows. The trials of the saint are a divine husbandry, by which he grows and brings forth abundant fruit.—*Spurgeon.*

6. *But the way of the ungodly shall perish.* Not only shall they perish themselves, but their way shall perish too. The righteous carves his name upon the rock, but the wicked writes his remembrance in the sand. The righteous man ploughs the furrows of earth, and sows a harvest here which shall never be fully reaped till he enters the enjoyments of eternity; but as for the wicked, he ploughs the sea, and though there may seem to be a shining trail behind his keel, yet the waves shall pass over it, and the place that knew him shall know him no more for ever. The very way of the ungodly shall perish. If it exist in remembrance, it shall be in the remembrance of the bad; for the Lord will cause the name of the wicked to rot, to become a stench in the nostrils of the good, and to be only known to the wicked themselves by its putridity.—*Spurgeon.*

PSALM II.

7. *Thou art my Son; this day have I begotten thee.* For a full discussion of the doctrine of Christ's eternal sonship, with special reference to Mr. Barnes' peculiar views on it, the reader is referred to the supplementary notes under Rom. i. 4; Heb. i. 3. We insert here the admirable note of Dr. J. A. Alexander, which leaves nothing to be desired in so far as this text and its bearing on the question are concerned:—"Whether this be regarded as part of the decree or law itself, or as a mere preamble to it, the relation here described is evidently one which carried with it universal dominion as a necessary consequence, as well as one which justifies the use of the expression *My King* in ver. 6. It must be something more then than a figure for intense love or peculiar favour, something more than the filial relation which theocratic kings, and Israel as a nation, bore to God. Nor will any explanation of the terms fully meet the requisitions of the context except one which supposes the relation here described as manifest in time to rest on one essential and eternal. This alone accounts for the identification of the persons as possessing a common interest, and reigning with and in each other. This profound sense of the passage is no more excluded by the phrase *this day*, implying something recent, than the universality of Christ's dominion is excluded by the local reference to Zion. The point of time, like the point of space, is the finite centre of an

infinite circle. Besides, the mere form of the declaration is a part of the dramatic scenery or costume with which the truth is here invested. The ideas of a king, a coronation, a hereditary succession, are all drawn from human and temporal associations. *This day have I begotten thee*, may be considered, therefore, as referring only to the coronation of Messiah, which is an ideal one. The essential meaning of the phrase *I have begotten thee*, is simply this, *I am thy Father*. The antithesis is perfectly identical with that in 2 Sa. vii. 14, 'I will be his father and he shall be my son.' Had the same form of expression been used here, *this day am I thy Father*, no reader would have understood *this day* as limiting the mutual relation of the parties, however it might limit to a certain point of time the formal recognition of it. It must also be observed that even if *this day* be referred to the inception of the filial relation, it is thrown indefinitely back by the form of reminiscence or narration in the first clause of the verse. *Jehovah said to me*, but when? If understood to mean from everlasting or eternity, the form of expression would be perfectly in keeping with the other figurative forms by which the Scriptures represent things really ineffable in human language. The opinion that this passage is applied by Paul, in Ac. xiii. 33, to Christ's resurrection, rests upon a misapprehension of the verb *raised up*, which has this specific meaning only when determined by the context or the addition of the words *from the dead*, as in the next verse of the same chapter, which is so far from requiring the more general expressions of the preceding verse to be taken in the same sense, that it rather forbids such a construction, and shows that the two verses speak of different stages in the same great process: first, the raising up of Jesus in the same sense in which God is said to have raised him up in Ac. ii. 30; iii. 22, 26; vii. 37; *i.e.* bringing him into being as a man; and then the raising up from the dead, which the apostle himself introduces as another topic in Ac. xiii. 34. There is nothing, therefore, inconsistent with the statement that the psalmist here speaks of eternal sonship, either in the passage just referred to, or in Heb. v. 5, where the words are only cited to prove the solemn recognition of Christ's sonship, and his consequent authority, by God himself. This recognition was repeated, and, as it were, realized at our Saviour's baptism and transfiguration, when a voice from heaven said, 'This is my beloved Son, in whom I am well pleased, hear ye him!'"

Speaking of the psalm as a whole, the reader will be delighted with our author's admirable defence of the exclusively Messianic reference. Even Calvin, who still holds the foremost place among commentators on the Psalms, and who first applied the principle of types to the interpretation of the Messianic psalms, seems to have erred here. "As often happens," says Dr. Binnie, "the great reformer having got hold of a valuable principle, went to the extreme in the application of it. In no psalm except Ps. cx. did he find Christ set forth without some intervening type. In the second psalm he thinks there is an immediate reference to David, and in Ps. xlv. to the nuptials of Solomon; and in this he has been followed by many commentators of the highest standing. But the interpretation in both instances is, I venture to think, destitute of solid foundation. It is difficult, no doubt, to draw a line between the psalms which relate exclusively to Christ and those in which he is seen through the veil of some type. . . . There are passages in Isaiah (ch. ix. and xi. for example) in which Christ and his reign are celebrated in imagery wholly taken from David's reign, yet no one regards them as anything but direct predictions. There is no reason to deny the same character to Ps. ii. and xlv. To expound them as having a primary reference to David or Solomon is simply to introduce confusion and embarrassment."—*The Psalms: their History, Teachings, and Use*, p. 187.

We subjoin also the following remarks of Dr. Delitzsch:—"The two names of the future One in use in the time of Jesus, ὁ χριστός and ὁ υἱὸς τοῦ θεοῦ, Jn. i. 50; Mat. xxvi. 63 (in the mouth of Nathanael and of the high-priest), refer back to this psalm and Dan. ix. 25, just as ὁ υἱὸς τοῦ ἀνθρώπου incontrovertibly refers to Ps. viii. 5 and Dan. vii. 13. The view maintained by De Wette and Hupfeld, that the psalm is not applicable to the Christian conceptions of the Messiah, seems almost as though these were to be gauged according to the authoritative utterances of the professorial chair, and not according to the language of the apostles. Even in the Apocalypse, ch. xix. 15; xii. 5, Jesus appears exactly as this psalm represents him, as ποιμαίνων τὰ ἔθνη ἐν ῥάβδῳ σιδηρᾷ. The office of the Messiah is not only that of Saviour, but also of Judge. Redemption is the beginning, and the judgment the end of his work. It is to this end that the psalm refers."

PSALM III.

2. *Selah.* This is a musical pause, the precise meaning of which is not known. Some think it simply a rest, a pause in the music; others say it means "Lift up the strain—sing more loudly—pitch the tune upon a higher key—there is nobler matter to come, therefore retune your harps." Harp-strings soon get out of order and need to be screwed up again to their proper tightness, and certainly our heart-strings are evermore getting out of tune. Let *Selah* teach us to pray,

"O may my heart in tune be found
Like David's harp of solemn sound."

At least, we may learn that wherever we see *Selah*, we should look upon it as a note of observation. Let us read the passage which precedes and succeeds it with greater earnestness, for surely there is always something excellent where we are required to rest and pause and meditate, or when we are required to lift up our hearts in grateful song. "SELAH."—*Spurgeon.*

PSALM IV.

3. *The Lord hath set apart him that is godly for himself.* How happy all God's servants are! They are set apart as vessels of honour, (1) by a free, eternal, holy, unchangeable choice in Christ Jesus; (2) by a powerful, internal, spiritual regeneration; (3) by a perfect, irrepealable justification; (4) by a kind, wise, watchful Providence ordering everything in their lot, and distinguishing them in this, that all things work together for their good, making their sorrows more blessed than the joys of the wicked, and giving them the victory even in death; (5) such shall be openly and gloriously owned and set apart in the last day. They are set apart to God's service and honour and enjoyment here and hereafter.—*Wm. S. Plumer, D.D., LL.D.*

8. *I will both lay me down in peace, and sleep.* Sweet evening hymn! I shall not sit up to watch through fear, but I will lie down; and then I will not lie awake listening to every rustling sound, but I will lie down in peace and sleep, for I have nought to fear. He that hath the wings of God above him needs no other curtain. Better than bolts or bars is the protection of the Lord. Armed men kept the bed of Solomon, but we do not believe that he slept more soundly than his father, whose bed was the hard ground, and who was hunted by bloodthirsty foes. Note the word "only," which means that God alone was his keeper, and that though alone, without man's help, he was even then in good keeping, for he was "alone with God." A quiet conscience is a good bed-fellow. How many of our sleepless hours might be traced to our untrusting and disordered minds. They slumber sweetly whom faith rocks to sleep. No pillow so soft as a promise; no coverlet so warm as an assured interest in Christ.

O Lord, give us this calm repose on thee, that, like David, we may lie down in peace and sleep each night while we live; and joyfully may lie down in the appointed season, to sleep in death, to rest in God.—*Spurgeon.*

PSALM VI.

8. *For the Lord hath heard the voice of my weeping.* What a fine Hebraism, and what grand poetry it is in English! "He hath heard the voice of my weeping." Is there a voice in weeping! Does weeping speak! In what language doth it utter its meaning? Why, in that universal tongue which is known and understood in all the earth, and even in heaven above. When a man weeps, whether he be a Jew or Gentile, barbarian, Scythian, bond or free, it has the same meaning in it. Weeping is the eloquence of sorrow. It is an unstammering orator, needing no interpreter, but understood of all. Is it not sweet to believe that our tears are understood even when words fail! Let us learn to think of tears as liquid prayers, and of weeping as a constant dropping of importunate intercession, which will wear its way right surely into the very heart of mercy, despite the stony difficulties which obstruct the way. My God, I will weep when I cannot plead, for thou hearest the voice of my weeping.—*Spurgeon.*

9. *The Lord hath heard my supplication.* Never was a more mournful complaint uttered than that in the previous

verses, yet the psalmist finds relief in God. "How different is all this from the miserable shifts to which ungodly men are driven! In their extremity dreadful sullenness and remorse, alternate bluster and fainting, boasting and cowering, mark their state. Shortly before his death Byron said, 'Shall I sue for mercy?' Pausing a considerable time, he made this desperate answer to his own question: 'Come, come, no weakness; let's be a man to the last.' That miserable pupil of Voltaire, the pedantic King Frederick II. of Prussia, had lived to feed his ambition, and after remarkable successes was compelled to say: 'It is unhappy that all who suffer must flatly contradict Zeno, as there is none but will confess pain to be a great evil. It is noble to raise oneself above the disagreeable accidents to which we are exposed, and a moderate stoicism is the only means of consolation for the unfortunate. But whenever the stone, the gout, or the bull of Phalaris mix in the scene, the frightful shrieks which escape from the sufferers leave no doubt that pain is a real evil. . . . The heart is conscious of a wound, the stoic freely confesses; I should feel no pain, but I do feel it against my will, it consumes, it lacerates me; an internal feeling overcomes my strength, and extorts from me complaints and fruitless groans.'"—*Plumer*.

Conclusion of the Psalm. Many of the mournful psalms end in this manner, to instruct the believer that he is continually to look forward and solace himself with beholding that day when his warfare shall be accomplished; when sin and sorrow shall be no more; when sudden and everlasting confusion shall cover the enemies of righteousness; when the sackcloth of the penitent shall be exchanged for the robe of glory, and every tear become a sparkling gem in his crown; when to sighs and groans shall succeed the songs of heaven, set to angelic harps, and faith shall be resolved into the vision of the Almighty. —*Horne*.

PSALM VIII.

The author in this place maintains the same views on which we had occasion to remark in the supplementary note under Heb. ii. 6. The reader will find in it a somewhat full view of the principle on which Ps. viii. and others of the same class are in the New Testament applied to Christ. We find it difficult to persuade ourselves that "the psalm does not appear originally to have any designed reference to the Messiah," but contains only "the principle on which the apostle reasons in Heb. ii.;" as if he had said, We find here an illustration of a principle set forth in the Psalms. This method of interpretation seems to destroy the idea of prophecy entirely, or to reduce it to the level of mere accommodation of what was long ago said by certain old authors, to present or passing events. We subjoin the excellent note of Dr. Binnie:—Ps. viii. has a certain title to the foremost place amongst those which hold forth Christ under the veil of some type. For, in this instance, the type under which he is presented is the oldest of all the types, being no other than the common progenitor of the race. Adam, we know, was "the figure of him that was to come." He prefigured Christ in this very notable respect, that as he was the head and surety of the entire race, insomuch that in his fall they fell; so Christ is the head and surety of the entire church, insomuch that by his obedience they are constituted righteous, 1 Cor. xv. 21, 22. The primary scope of the psalm is to celebrate the condescending bounty of God displayed in endowing our nature in the person of Adam with such a rich heritage of privilege; crowning it with glory and honour, making it to have dominion over the works of his hands, and subjecting all things to its rule. "Excellent endowments (some one may say); but is it not mockery of our fallen condition to ask us to celebrate them now, after they have been forfeited by our apostasy from God?" The answer is, that they were forfeited, but are now restored. And the restoration is made in a way exactly corresponding to the manner of the original endowment. It is made to God's people in the person of their common Head and Surety by whose blood the lost heritage has been redeemed. The grant first made to the race in Adam, is made a second time to the church in Christ, the second Adam. Hence the remarkable way in which the epistle to the Hebrews cites the psalm, as if it had been a prediction regarding Christ. It celebrates the second Adam and his dominion, under the type of the first Adam and his.—P. 186.

Delitzsch gives the same view:—The dominion of the world lost to fallen man, and only retained by him in a ruined condition, is allotted to mankind, when redeemed by him, in fuller and more perfect reality. This dominion is not yet in the actual possession of mankind, but in the person of Jesus it now sits enthroned at the right hand of God. In him the idea of humanity is transcendently realized, *i.e.* according to a very much higher standard than that laid down when the world was founded. He has entered into the state—only a little (βραχύ τι) beneath the angels—of created humanity for a little while (βραχύ τι), in order to raise redeemed humanity above the angels. Everything (כֹּל) is really put under him with just as little limitation as is expressed in this psalm: not merely the animal kingdom, not merely the world itself, but the universe with all the ruling powers in it, whether they be in subjection or in hostility to God, yea, even the power of death, 1 Co. xv. 27; cf. Eph. i. 22.

2. *Out of the mouth of babes and sucklings.* There seems no end to be gained by denying the original reference to little children, seeing the principle involved undoubtedly is that God would accomplish great effects by those who were feeble and weak. "David," says Perowne very beautifully, "speaks literally of children. And so our Lord himself applies the words, Mat. xxi. 16. Even the faith of a little child is bulwark enough against the mischief of men of corrupt heart and perverted intellect. The stars above, and the lips of infants below, show forth his praise." So also Calvin, De Wette, and Alexander.

PSALM IX.

11. *Sing praises to the Lord, which dwelleth in Zion: declare among the people his doings.* Being full of gratitude himself our inspired author is eager to excite others to join the strain, and praise God in the same manner as he had himself vowed to do in the first and second verses. The heavenly spirit of praise is gloriously contagious, and he that hath it is never content unless he can excite all who surround him to unite in his sweet employ. Singing and preaching, as means of glorifying God, are here joined together; and it is remarkable that, connected with all revivals of gospel ministry, there has been a sudden outburst of the spirit of song. Luther's psalms and hymns were in all men's mouths; and in the modern revival under Wesley and Whitfield, the strains of Charles Wesley, Cennick, Berridge, Toplady, Hart, Newton, and many others, were the outgrowth of restored piety. The singing of the birds of praise fitly accompanies the return of the gracious spring of divine visitation through the proclamation of the truth. Sing on, brethren, and preach on, and these shall both be a token that the Lord still dwelleth in Zion. It will be well for us when coming up to Zion to remember that the Lord dwells among his saints, and is to be had in peculiar reverence of all those that are about him.—*Spurgeon.*

PSALM X.

8-10. *In the lurking places of the villages,* &c. That is, in concealed places, in the thicket, in the neighbourhood of towns, they lie in wait for the peaceable inhabitants, with the view of suddenly falling upon them, and killing or plundering them. Our own abode in the East gives us a lively idea of the condition of society which this describes. During the three years of our abode in Baghdad, it was invariably considered most dangerous for any one to venture alone beyond the walls of the city, which was felt as a great hardship, as entirely precluding us from those solitary suburban walks to which we had been accustomed at home. We were constantly hearing of persons who on venturing out had been plundered and sent home naked by the Arabs infesting the neighbourhood. They were roughly handled and sometimes slain if they offered the slightest resistance. At this place the evil was exhibited to us in the most distinct forms, and became familiar from being always present to the mind; but we remember few places we visited in South-western Asia in which it was not considered dangerous for a person who looked as if he had anything to lose, to venture out of the towns and villages.—*Pictorial Bible.*

The Arab robber lurks like a wolf among these sand-heaps, and often springs out suddenly upon the solitary traveller, robs him in a trice, and then plunges again into the wilderness of sand-hills and reedy downs, where pursuit is fruitless. Our friends are careful not to allow us to straggle about or lag behind; and yet it seems absurd to fear a surprise here—Khaifa before,

Acre in the rear, and travellers in sight on both sides. Robberies, however, do often occur, just where we now are. Strange country! and it has always been so. There are a hundred allusions to just such things in the history, the Psalms, and the prophets of Israel. A whole class of imagery is based upon them (Ps. x. 8–10). A thousand rascals, the living originals of this picture, are this day crouching and lying in wait all over the country to catch poor helpless travellers. You observe that all these people you meet or pass are armed; nor would they venture to go from Acre to Khaifa without their musket, although the cannon of the castles seem to command every foot of the way. Strange, most strange land! but it tallies wonderfully with its ancient story.—*The Land and the Book*, p. 314.

PSALM XII.

6. *The words of the Lord are pure words.* Not only all true, but all pure, "like silver tried in a furnace of earth" or crucible. It notes, 1st. The sincerity of God's word. Everything is really as it is there represented, and not otherwise; it doth not jest with us, nor impose upon us, nor has it any other design upon us but our own good. 2d. The preciousness of God's word. It is of great intrinsic value, like silver refined to the highest degree; it has nothing in it to depreciate it. 3d. The many proofs that have been given of its power and truth. It has been often tried; all the saints in all ages have trusted it, and so tried it, and it never deceived them or frustrated their expectation; but they have all set to their seal that God's word is true, with an *experto crede*,—"trust one that has made trial;" they have found it so. Probably this refers especially to those promises of succouring and relieving the poor and distressed. Their friends put them in hopes they will do something for them, and yet prove a broken reed. But the words of God are what we may rely upon; and the less confidence is to be put in men's words, let us with the more assurance trust in God's word.—*Henry.*

PSALM XIV.

1–3. *They are corrupt, . . . there is none that doeth good.* It is the first three verses that are cited by the apostle in support of the doctrine that "both Jews and Gentiles are all under sin," and that "the whole world is become guilty before God." And certainly the terms applied by the psalmist are quite as universal in their sweep as those of the apostle. Indeed this very fact, that the terms are so sweeping, has been urged as a reason why some construction less severe should be put upon the psalm. "The psalmist (it is argued) cannot mean that all men, without exception, are such as he describes. For we know that, in fact, they are not so. There is a congregation of the righteous. In the worst times, God has his seven thousand who abide faithful to him. And even beyond that circle there is much virtue to be found, much civil righteousness, much beautiful natural affection." The objection is plausible; nevertheless the apostle's interpretation is the only one that will stand. No doubt there is a congregation of the godly on earth; but they are what they are, not by nature, but by the grace of God; so that their godliness does not avail to mitigate our judgment regarding fallen human nature. And as for the natural virtues that still adorn the world and claim the admiration of men, they are vitiated before God by this, that there is no regard in them to his will. The gravamen of the psalmist's indictment against natural men is, that "they do not seek after God."

This one passage is sufficient to demonstrate original sin. For if all men, everywhere and always, turn away from God till his grace recover them, there must be some reason for doing so. A constant event indicates a law of nature. There must be in mankind a deep malignity of nature, an inborn ungodliness of heart.—*Dr. Binnie*, p. 243.

We refer the reader also to our supplementary note under Ro. iii. 10, where a somewhat full view is given of the bearing of the psalmist's words on the question of universal depravity. The remarks of Pres. Edwards on the point in his treatise on Original Sin are of special force and value.

PSALM XVI.

It is difficult to decide between the two views of direct Messianic reference and of typical reference. The direct reference to Christ seems supported by the language of Peter in Ac. ii. On the other hand, there is difficulty in carrying this principle throughout the psalm, where so much has a primary and manifest fulfilment in the person of David.

But whatever reference the psalmist may have had to his own circumstances, there can be no doubt that he was carried beyond himself. And he seems to have been perfectly conscious that it was so. The critical acumen and sound judgment displayed by Mr. Barnes, in his notes under ver. 10, have not been surpassed in any commentary that has come under our eye. We add the following from Dr. J. P. Smith and Dr. Hengstenberg:—

The structure of this remarkable psalm is derived from the consolation enjoyed by David, in his difficulties and sufferings, from his reliance upon the great promise which God had made to him. That promise involved a guarantee, that he himself should not be overcome or utterly circumvented by his personal enemies; and the cheering meditation upon the transcendent mercies of God to him was employed by the prophetic spirit as a vehicle for elevating his mind to the inspired contemplation of his great though unknown descendant. "He, therefore, being a prophet, and knowing that with an oath God had sworn to him, of the descendants of his body according to the flesh, to raise up the Christ, to seat him upon his throne; seeing this before, spake concerning the resurrection of the Christ." Hence the King of Israel glanced but slightly upon his own troubles and consolations, and passed on to the contemplation of the theme which absorbed all his thoughts and enraptured him into the visions of a glory that should at last fill the whole earth.—Smith's *Scripture Testimony to the Messiah*, p. 201.

It still remains for us, now that we have finished our exposition of the psalm, to investigate its Messianic import. That such an import does belong to it is certain, even apart from the testimonies of the New Testament. The situation evidently appears to be that of one who found himself in great danger, and whose life was threatened. But the psalmist does not rest with the hope of obtaining deliverance from that particular danger; his soul rises higher; he triumphs, not only over the danger then present, but over death itself, exclaims, "Death! where is thy sting? Hell! Where is thy victory?" The *ground* of hope is connected with that, which, for the moment, was necessary, and the hope itself is expressed more comprehensively. The assurance is declared quite generally, that death and the grave can exercise no power over him who is inwardly united to the living God: of this he is confident, nor for the present moment merely, but for ever, ver. 11; and on that account, certainly for the present also, in respect to which he primarily gives utterance to the general hope.

Apart from Christ this hope must be regarded as a chimera, which the issue would put to shame. David served God in his generation, and then he died, was buried, and corrupted. But in Christ, who has brought life and immortality to light, it becomes perfectly true. David, in Christ, could speak as he does here, with full right. Christ has conquered death, not merely for himself, but also for his members. His resurrection is the ground of our resurrection; for can the head fail to draw its members along with it? In so far as what is here hoped for to the members can only be experienced by them in consequence of its having been first experienced by the head, so far the psalm must be considered as a prophecy of Christ.

But how far David himself clearly understood the Messianic subject of this hope we cannot ascertain. That the prophecy in respect to Christ was for him not an altogether unknown one, the declaration of Peter in Ac. ii. 30, 31 implies; while Paul stands simply on the ground that the psalm was fully verified in Christ. That the heroes of the Old Testament, in their more elevated moments, were favoured with a deep insight into the mystery of the future redemption, is affirmed by our Lord himself, Jn. viii. 56. A more or less conscious connection between the hope of eternal life and the expectation of Christ, is attended with the less difficulty, as this connection constantly appears, where we find in later times the hope of eternal life expressed in Isaiah, Ezekiel, Daniel.—*Hengstenberg.*

The exclusively Messianic reference is defended by Principal Fairbairn in his *Typology*, vol. i. p. 132; and the principles laid down by him are worthy of careful attention on the part of students of prophecy.

PSALM XVII.

11, 12. *They have now compassed us in our steps*, &c. The whole passage gives a graphic picture of a person surprised, compassed, and dodged by enemies, eagerly watching to take him for a single moment at advantage. The images are derived from circumstances which are of no uncommon occurrence at the present day in Palestine. It forcibly reminds us of an adventure which occurred to Dr. Olin, when he unadvisedly strayed at some distance from the caravan near Jericho. "The traveller in these unfortunate countries hears so many tales of robbery and violence, that they cease to produce any feelings of alarm, or even to insure the necessary forethought and caution. It was hardly an hour after listening to such recitals that I left the camp unattended, and quite forgetful of danger, to examine some ancient aqueducts." Having examined them, he was about to proceed to the fountain of Elisha, when—"I was approached by two Bedouins, armed with matchlocks and short swords, in the usual manner. They were bareheaded, an unusual circumstance, the hair being shaven close, with the exception of a small lock left long according to the fashion of these barbarians. Two more villanous assassin-like knaves I do not remember to have met with. They pretended, when I first saw them, to be engaged in taking care of some horses which were grazing loose near by, but soon left them and advanced directly up to me. I felt the unpleasantness of my situation, and saw my gross imprudence in wandering a mile or more from the camp alone, and in a region which, I had such good reason to know, was full of robbers. It was too late, however, to retreat; and I had only to make the best of my situation, and learn more prudence for the future. I saluted my unwelcome visitors with a courteous salaam, at the same time stepping back a little, as they had approached nearly within arm's length. I had no weapons, not so much as a walking-stick. Franks, however, are believed by these people to go always well armed: an impression which I tried to confirm by putting my hand in my bosom, as if to see that my pistols were ready for service. At the same time I armed myself with a couple of heavy stones, with which I hoped, if necessary, to prevent mischief from the crazy matchlocks, which must be ignited by the aid of a flint and steel before becoming very formidable. The fellows halted, in seeming suspense as to what they should do. They looked at the encampment, a mile distant, but still conspicuously in view, and near enough for the report of a musket to be heard. They were very small men, even for Bedouins; and I thought they eyed my stature of six feet with an appearance of respect, which, under the circumstances, was certainly gratifying to me. After a season of suspense, which seemed to me to be tedious, they retreated a few paces, and after consulting together for a moment, commenced urging me to go with them to the wady that opens into the mountain near the Jerusalem road, pointing eagerly in that direction, and exclaiming, 'El deir, el ain,' as if acquainted with the objects of my visit. They even seemed disposed to take hold of my hands and lead me towards these interesting objects. I declined their civilities with a resolute tone, designing to let them know that I took them for robbers, and at the same time keeping near them, as the best position for the use of my weapons, should that become necessary. After some minutes they retired towards the Western Mountain, and I, when they were gone a good distance, commenced my return to the camp, at first very carelessly, as being in no hurry, but as soon as I thought prudent, at a quicker step. It was now after sunset. I crossed the ravine by walking along the channel of the lower aqueduct. Here I met several English gentlemen of our party, and heard from them of some additional robberies that had been committed during the afternoon upon some of the pilgrims who had proceeded without a guard a little beyond the camp."—*Pictorial Bible.*

15. *As for me, I will behold thy face in righteousness: I shall be satisfied, when I awake, with thy likeness.* David, in Ps. xvii., when his faith is subjected to a trial of the same sort as Asaph's, finds comfort in the same thought which was so helpful to his friend. Turning away from the "men of the world, whose portion is in this life," he makes this lofty profession of his hope. The strength of these testimonies (Ps. lxxiii. 24, 26; xvii. 15) to the faith of the psalmists does not lie within the scope of a merely grammatical interpretation. The expressions made use of do not by themselves absolutely compel us to reject the lower and temporal meaning, which accordingly is advocated by some commentators of great eminence. But, standing where they

stand, they naturally raise the mind to the higher meaning, and have done so in the vast majority of sober unbiassed readers ever since they were penned. Those words of David, for instance, in which he describes his enemies as "men of the world, whose portion is in this life," do they not by plain implication hold forth the godly as men who are *not* of this world, and whose portion is in another life? The words are exactly parallel to those of the apostle, in which, contrasting himself with many "whose end is destruction, whose god is their belly, who mind earthly things," he declares that "our conversation (that is, *our citizenship*, *our country*, πολιτευμα) is in heaven." This being the psalmist's meaning, is it for a moment to be supposed that when he goes on, as he does in the words that follow, to profess his faith in God with respect to the future, the jubilant hope he utters is bounded by the grave? Is it to be supposed that this soul, conscious of the divine image, of present communion with God, and of an interest in his love as its proper portion—is it to be supposed, I say, that such a man has no better hope to utter than that ere he finally quits the world—ere he bids farewell to the sun and the fair face of nature, and the sweet companionships of the earth—ere he passes to a land of darkness and silence, and deep forgetfulness, where the light of God's face will never shine—he shall be satisfied with some transient gleams of the divine favour? Can this be all that David means in comforting himself with the hope of a bright awakening, when he shall behold the face, and be satisfied with the likeness of God?—*Binnie.*

PSALM XVIII.

Ps. xviii. is undoubtedly Messianic. Apostolical authority concurs with internal evidence in showing that the person who speaks in it is Christ. Yet nothing can be more certain than that it is not predictive of Christ in the same high and exclusive sense as Ps. cx. It was written by David in thankful commemoration of the kindness of the Lord in delivering him "from the hand of all his enemies, and from the hand of Saul." Not only is there a superscription to that effect, but the whole poem is inserted in the history of David's reign, as a document relative to the period. Such having been the origin and primary intention of the poem, the question will be asked, On what principle do you refer to Christ a song in which, as you admit, David speaks of himself, his dangers, his marvellous escapes, the eventual establishment of his throne, and wide extension of his sway? This is a perfectly fair question. Since it is a question, moreover, which crosses the path of every careful student of the Bible, and is apt to cause serious perplexity, the discussion of it cannot be declined, even although it brings up some points which are amongst the most difficult in the whole domain of biblical theology.

When we classify the Messianic psalms, according to the "diverse manners" in which they severally speak of Christ, they arrange themselves into three principal groups. First, there is a large group, consisting of those in which Christ is present in the person of David or some other type; then there is a smaller one, consisting of psalms which relate to him directly and exclusively; lastly, there is a group of undefined extent, consisting of psalms in which the person who speaks is "Christ mystical," the whole Church, the head and the members together.

. . . David knew that Christ was to be born of his seed, and that he was to be a king after the manner of David as well as a priest after the manner of Melchizedek. Accordingly, we find that in the psalms which unfold his own experience, he is sometimes lifted above himself, and speaks in terms which, although they may perhaps admit of being applied to himself, are much more easily and naturally applied to our Lord. Thus Ps. xviii., the great song of thanksgiving for the mercies of his life, rises at the close into this strain:—"Therefore will I give thanks unto thee, O Lord, among the heathen, and sing praises unto thy name. Great deliverance giveth he to his King, and showeth mercy to his anointed, to David, and to his seed for ever." When these verses (49, 50) are quoted in the epistle to the Romans (ch. xv. 9) as a declaration on the part of Christ of his purpose to publish God's name amongst the Gentiles, the apostle is not to be understood as applying the words to Christ by way of arbitrary accommodation. No doubt the words are David's, and express his purpose to indite songs in which all nations might one day sing praise to the God of Abraham. But in the character in which he speaks throughout the psalm, he so exactly prefigured Christ, that the whole is applicable to Christ as truly as to himself; and in these concluding verses he is moved by the Holy Spirit to utter words which, although true of himself, were much more perfectly fulfilled in Christ. And this is what we mean when we entitle his song of thanksgiving a *typically Messianic* psalm.—*Binnie*, p. 178-183.

2. *The Lord is my rock*, &c. The two first names, and also the last, are taken from the natural state of Palestine, where the precipitous rocks surrounded by deep ravines afford protection to the flying,—comp. "He sets me upon a rock," in Ps. xxvii. 5, for, He delivers me, Ju. vi. 2; 1 Sa. xxiv. 22; 2 Sa. v. 8. The predilection for this figurative description of the divine protection, which may be recognized not merely in the threefold repetition, but also in its forming both the beginning and the end, inclosing all the others, appears to have had its origin in the persecution of Saul. Then David often had to betake to rocks for refuge. He grounded the hope of his security, however, not upon their natural inaccessibility, but his mind rose from the corporeal rock to the spiritual, which he beheld under the form of the corporeal. The mode of contemplation to which he then became familiarized would readily suggest such figurative designations of God, his Deliverer, as his Rock, his Fastness, his Stronghold. Placed upon this Rock, he could say: *non curo te Cæsar*, with infinitely better right than he who, according to Augustine on Psalm lxx., called from a high natural rock to the emperor as he passed beneath.—*Hengstenberg*.

3. *I will call on the Lord, who is worthy to be praised*. He would teach us by this that there is nothing so bad, so great, so mighty, so long-continued which may not be overcome by the power of God if we only put our trust therein. Likewise that we then preeminently had cause to hope in the power of God, that it would then be mighty in us, when many great, strong, and constant evils forcibly press upon us, because it is a property of divine strength to help the little, the feeble, the dejected, not merely amid the evils of punishment, but also of guilt. For what sort of power were God's, if it could prevail over punishment alone, and not also over sin in us? So full is this passage of consolation; because the state of things it contemplates seems to be wholly against nature, and that one must abandon all hope, when not evil merely, but also great, weighty, and long-continued evil breaks in. . . . This doctrine is in tribulation the most ennobling and truly golden. One cannot believe what a powerful assistance such praise of God is in pressing danger. For the moment thou wilt begin to praise God, the evil also will begin to abate, the consoled heart will grow, and then will follow the calling upon God with confidence. There are people who cry to the Lord and are not heard, ver. 41. Why this? Because they do not praise the Lord when they cry to him, but go to him with reluctance; they have not represented to themselves how sweet the Lord is, but have looked only upon the bitterness. But no one gets deliverance from evil by simply looking upon his evil, and becoming alarmed at it; he can only do so by overcoming it, hanging upon the Lord, and having respect to his goodness. O doubtless a hard counsel! And a rare thing truly, in the midst of misfortune to conceive of God as sweet, and worthy of being praised, and when he has removed himself from us, and is incomprehensible, even then to regard him more strongly than our present misfortune which keeps us from regarding him. Only let every one try it, and endeavour at the praise of God, even though in little heart for it; he will presently experience an enlightment. For all other consolation profits not, or it profits in a deceitful manner; in other words, is highly injurious.—*Luther*.

6. *In my distress I called upon the Lord, and cried unto my God*. Prayer is that postern-gate which is left open even when the city is straitly besieged by the enemy; it is that way upward from the pit of despair to which the spiritual miner flees at once when the floods from beneath break forth upon him. Observe that he *calls*, and then *cries;* prayer grows in vehemence as it proceeds. Note also that he first invokes his God under the name of Jehovah, and then advances to a more familiar name, "My God;" thus faith increases by exercise, and he whom we at first viewed as Lord is soon seen to be our God in covenant. It is never an ill time to pray; no distress should prevent us from using the divine re-

medy of supplication. Above the noise of the raging billows of death, or the barking dogs of hell, the feeblest cry of a true believer will be heard in heaven. "*He heard my voice out of his temple, and my cry came before him, even into his ears.*" Far up within the bejewelled walls, and through the gates of pearl, the cry of the suffering suppliant was heard. Music of angels and harmony of seraphs availed not to drown or even impair the voice of that humble call. The King heard it in his palace of light unsufferable, and lent a willing ear to the cry of his own beloved child. O honoured prayer, to be able thus, through Jesus' blood, to penetrate the very ears and heart of Deity! The voice and the cry are themselves heard directly by the Lord, and not made to pass through the medium of saints and intercessors; "My cry came before *Him;*" the operation of prayer with God is immediate and personal. We may cry with confident and familiar importunity, while our Father himself listens.—*Spurgeon.*

7. *Then the earth shook and trembled.* In this and the following verses David describes by the sublimest expressions and grandest terms the majesty of God and the awful manner in which he came to his assistance. The representation of the storm in these verses must be allowed by all skilful and impartial judges to be truly sublime and noble, and in the genuine spirit of true poetry. The majesty of God, and the manner in which he is represented as coming to the aid of his favourite king, surrounded with all the powers of nature as his attendants and ministers, and arming (as it were) heaven and earth to fight his battles, and execute his vengeance, is described in the loftiest and most striking terms. The *shaking of the earth;* the trembling of the mountains and pillars of heaven; the *smoke* that drove out of his nostrils; the *flames* of devouring fire that flashed from his mouth; the *heavens bending* down to convey him to the battle; his riding upon a *cherub,* and rapidly flying on the *wings of a whirlwind;* his concealing his majesty in the *thick clouds* of heaven; the bursting of the *lightnings* from the *horrid darkness;* the *uttering of his voice* in *peals of thunder;* the *storm* of *fiery hail;* the *melting of the heavens,* and their dissolving into floods of *tempestuous rain;* the *cleaving of the earth,* and disclosing of the bottom of the hills, and the subterraneous channels or torrents of water, by the very breath of the nostrils of the Almighty,—are all of them circumstances which create admiration, excite a kind of horror, and exceed everything of this nature that is to be found in any of the remains of heathen antiquity. See Longinus on the *Sublime,* and Hesiod's description of Jupiter fighting against the Titans, which is one of the grandest things in all pagan antiquity, though upon comparison it will be found infinitely short of this description of the psalmist's, throughout the whole of which God is represented as a mighty warrior going forth to fight the battles of David, and highly incensed at the opposition his enemies made to his power and authority.

When he descended to the engagement, the very heavens bowed down to render his descent more awful; his *military tent* was *substantial darkness;* the *voice* of his *thunder* was the *warlike alarm* which sounded to the *battle;* the *chariot* in which he rode was the *thick clouds* of heaven, conducted by *cherubs,* and carried on by the irresistible force and rapid wings of an *impetuous tempest;* and the darts and weapons he employed were *thunderbolts, lightnings, fiery hail, deluging rains, and stormy winds!*

No wonder that when God thus arose all his enemies should be scattered, and those who hated him should flee before him. See Chandler, Delaney, and Lowth's ninth Prelection.—*Adam Clarke.*

10. *And he rode upon a cherub and did fly.* On the origin and meaning of the cherubim we quote the following from our article in Appendix to Stackhouse's *History of the Bible,* p. 1181, 1182:—"Mr. Layard thinks that the coincidence between the winged lions and bulls of Nineveh, and Ezekiel's figures does 'certainly lead to the inference that the symbols chosen by the prophet were borrowed from the Assyrian sculptures;' and in both cases he thinks the figures are emblems of the divinity or of his perfections.

"We feel disposed to regard the Assyrian compound animals as remains of the patriarchal religion. In the tabernacle and temple were set up over the mercy-seat, overshadowing it, figures called *cherubim.* These same figures were painted on the walls of the temple, and embroidered on its curtains, as they were on those of the tabernacle. Minute directions are given regarding every pin of the sacred structure—none regarding these. There is a simple command to introduce them. Our presumption is that they were well known. Indeed we read of 'cherubim' in connection with Eden, and the placing of cherubim before the garden intimates, according to the original, that he *set them in a tabernacle*, which formed the local and visible symbol of the divine presence. Now the prophet Ezekiel, in describing his compound figures (ch. x. 20), says, 'I knew they were the cherubim.' From all of which we conclude that the knowledge was handed down from patriarchal times, and that the form of the cherubim was so well known as to need no description, and that the Assyrians themselves were copyists from the original institute of the fathers of mankind. Originally the cherubim must have represented ministers or agents of providence; for symbols of the divine Being would not have been allowed, far less commanded, among the Jews."

33. *He maketh my feet like hinds' feet.* David points to the quick and unrestrained course of his conquests, just as already, in ver. 29, his springing over walls does not refer simply to David's personal deeds, but to what he did also by his army. In the second member, the heights are the hostile positions which David, in the strength of the Lord, surmounts. He names these heights *his* in faith; because he has the Lord for his helper, he considers them all beforehand as his possession, none as insurmountable. That we are not, with De Wette and others, to understand by the heights *places of refuge* is clear, not only from the context and parallelism, but also from the original passages in De. xxxii. 13, "He made him ride upon the high places of the earth;" and De. xxxiii. 29, "Thine enemies shall be found liars unto thee, and thou shalt tread upon their high places," in which the discourse is not of secure flight, but of resistless victory, as it is also in the passage, Hab. iii. 19, which has respect to our verse, "The Lord is my strength, and he makes my feet like the hinds', and he makes me to walk upon my high places."—*Hengstenberg.*

44. *As soon as they hear of me, they shall obey me.* Thus readily did the once struggling captain become a far-renowned victor, and thus easy shall be our triumphs. We prefer, however, to speak of Jesus. In many cases the gospel is speedily received by hearts apparently unprepared for it. Those who have never heard the gospel before have been charmed by its first message, and yielded obedience to it; while others, alas! who are accustomed to its joyful sound, are rather hardened than softened by its teachings. The grace of God sometimes runs like fire among the stubble, and a nation is born in a day. "Love at first sight" is no uncommon thing when Jesus is the wooer. He can write Cæsar's message without boasting, *Veni, vidi, vici;* his gospel is in some cases no sooner heard than believed. What inducements to spread abroad the doctrine of the cross!—*Spurgeon.*

PSALM XIX.

1. *The heavens declare,* &c. In the East the consideration of the heavens is peculiarly adapted to give a deep impression of the greatness of God as Creator. When C. Niebuhr, many years after his return from the East, lay in bed under the blindness and exhaustion of old age, "the glittering splendour of the nocturnal Asiatic sky, on which he had so often gazed, imaged itself to his mind in the hours of stillness, or its lofty vault and azure by day, and in this he found his sweetest enjoyment." The heavens and the firmament are personified, and the announcement of the glory of the Creator is attributed to them, which is apprehended in them by the pious mind. This personification is chosen with reference to the actual manifestation of God in the words contained in ver. 7–10. Instead of "the glory of God," Paul, in the passage, Ro. i. 20, which alludes to this here, has "eternal power and Godhead." That the firmament is identical with the heavens appears from Ge. i. 8. It is the vault of heaven, in which are sun, moon, and stars, the shining witnesses of God's glory, in reference to which he bears the name of Sabaoth, God of hosts.—*Hengstenberg.*

The engraving MIDNIGHT SKY represents the southern part of the starry vault seen as it appears if we turn our back to the circumpolar stars. This immense zone very nearly embraces half the horizon from east to west, passing by the south, and extending in altitude to the zenith. It comprises the most beautiful constellations and the most brilliant stars in the heavens. It is divided obliquely by the Milky Way. The annexed diagram will aid in understanding the following description.

Orion occupies nearly the middle view. This magnificent constellation forms a quadrilateral higher than it is broad, in the centre of which three stars of the second magnitude are arranged in a straight line. These are commonly called the Belt of Orion, and in Scotland the King's Elwand. Two of the stars of the quadrilateral, named

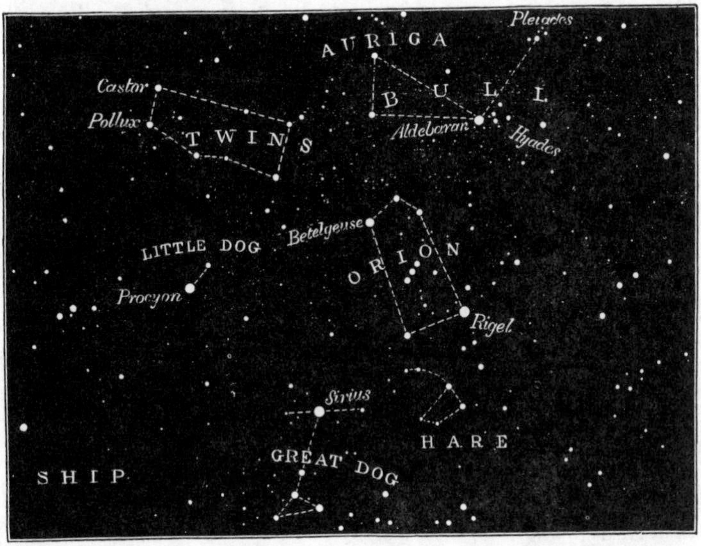

Betelgeuse and Rigel, are of the first magnitude. Betelgeuse is remarkable for the reddish tint of its light. Among the 115 stars visible to the naked eye, besides the two most brilliant, are included four of the second magnitude, and five between the second and the fourth.

In prolonging towards the north-west the line formed by the three stars in the Belt of Orion, the eye perceives a red star of the first magnitude: this is Aldebaran, the most beautiful star of the constellation Bull. Aldebaran is in the midst of a group of small stars named the Hyades. A little farther, in the same direction, will be found the Pleiades, so easy to recognize in the heavens by reason of the six stars visible to the naked eye, which compose this interesting group. The Bull contains 121 stars visible to the naked eye below the second magnitude.

If now we prolong towards the south-east of Orion, the line which has found for us Aldebaran on the north-west, we perceive near the edge of the Milky Way the constellation of the Great Dog, which includes Sirius, the most brilliant star in the two hemispheres, remarkable on account of its scintillation and by its dazzling whiteness.

Towards the east, and nearly at the same height as Betelgeuse, shines Procyon, on the other side of the Milky Way. This is a star of the first magnitude, and the most brilliant one in the constellation of the Little Dog. Betelgeuse, Sirius, and Procyon form a triangle, the three sides of which are nearly of the same apparent length. This circumstance enables us easily to recognize these stars. (*See above.*)

Above Procyon, and towards the zenith, Castor and Pollux point out the Twins, which include, besides these two stars of the first and second magnitudes, fifty-one stars visible to the naked eye. Towards the west, and by the side of the Pleiades, lies the constellation of the Ram, and a little below, those of the Whale and Eridanus, neither of which, in those parts visible to us in London, contain any stars of the first magnitude.

But while we are enumerating and contemplating this brilliant portion of the heavens, the stars defile across it, set, and disappear in the west, whilst others rise in the east, revealing new constellations. . . . Thus "night unto night sheweth knowledge."

3. *There is no speech nor language where their voice is not heard.* The author points to the powerfulness of the testimony which the heavens deliver of God's glory. How strongly must the traces of God's glory be impressed upon them when they need no speech to make him known as their Creator, when they need only to be dumb-heralds of the divine greatness, and still they declare and show forth. It is commonly supposed by those who follow this exposition, that the sense is first completed by the addition of the following verse: they are indeed speechless, yet still their preaching is understood throughout the whole earth, so loudly do they proclaim, by their mere existence, the glory of God. But this supposition is not a necessary one; just as well, and even better indeed, we can say that here the powerfulness of the testimony is represented, and there the wide compass of its territory. The more definite דברים (literally, *words*) is added to אמר (*speech*), which admits of a more general construction, in order to signify that the matter is here of a discourse in the more restricted sense. Luther, Calvin, and others, expound:—There is no speech and discourse where their language is not heard. Calvin—"He extends through a silent contrast the efficacy of this testimony which the heavens give to their Creator, as if he said—Although the nations are very different in language, yet the heavens have a common speech for instructing all in like manner, and nothing but carelessness prevents all from being taught at the mouth of this common teacher." But it is to be objected to this exposition that it takes אמר and דברים in the sense of *dialect*, *language*, in which the first certainly never occurs, nor is Ge. xi. 1 sufficient to establish it as properly belonging to the latter; that the speech and language would not be very fitly connected with the hearing; that it requires אמר to be taken in another sense than it was in ver. 2, and forcibly separates between מספרים and מגיד in ver. 1; and finally, that it destroys the parallelism which is manifestly formed between the expressions: there is not speech, and there are not words, and: their voice is not heard.—*Hengstenberg*.

4. *Their line is gone out through all the earth*, &c. This passage is quoted in Ro. x. 18, "But I say, Have they not heard? Yes, verily, their sound went into all the earth and their words unto the ends of the world." Hodge on this place in Romans remarks, "This verse, therefore, is to be considered as a strong declaration that what Paul had proved ought to be done, had in fact been accomplished. The middle wall of partition had been broken down, the gospel of salvation, the religion of God, was free from its trammels, the offers of mercy were as wide and general as the proclamation of the heavens. This idea the apostle beautifully and appositely expresses in the sublime language of Ps. xix. His object in using the words of the psalmist was, no doubt, to convey more clearly and affectingly to the minds of his hearers the idea that the proclamation of the gospel was now as free from all national or ecclesiastical restrictions, as the instructions shed down upon all people by the heavens under which they dwell. Paul, of course, is not to be understood as quoting the psalmist as though the ancient prophet was speaking of the preaching of the gospel. He simply uses scriptural language to express his own ideas, as is done involuntarily almost by every preacher in every sermon." But this is certainly yielding too much to the accommodation theory. Dean Alford's comment is worthy of regard here:—"It is remarkable that so few of the commentators have noticed (I have found it only in Bengel, and there but faintly hinted: Olsh., who defends the applicability of the text, does not even allude to it) that Ps. xix. is *a comparison of the sun, and glory of the heavens*, with the *Word of God*. As far as ver. 6 the glories of nature are described: then the great subject is taken up and the parallelism carried out to the end. So that the apostle has not, as alleged in nearly all the commentators, merely accommodated the text allegorically, but *taken it in its context*, and followed up the comparison of the psalm. As to the assertion of the preaching of the gospel having gone out into all

the world, when as yet a small part of it only had been evangelized, we must remember that it is not the *extent* so much as the *universality in character* of this preaching, which the apostle is here asserting; that Word of God, hitherto confined within the limits of Judea, had now broken those bounds and was preached in all parts of the earth. See Col. i. 6, 23." So also Thrupp:—"In his contemplation of the firmament he had discovered yet another proof that God had not yet poured forth the full measure of his gifts. The heavens told their story to all the nations of the earth: God's revealed law was restoring the souls and rejoicing the hearts of only a single people. Nor could the uncertainty be removed till the time when the knowledge of God's truth should be universally diffused. The approach of that time it was left to a later prophet openly to announce; when the God of Jacob should teach many people of his ways, when the law should go forth out of Zion, and the Word of the Lord from Jerusalem. But the same had in this psalm been indirectly heralded by David, in the stress laid by him on the universality of the testimony of God's creatures. And hence his words are by St. Paul actually quoted as a prophecy which was being fulfilled in the apostolic promulgation of the gospel."

5. *Which is as a bridegroom coming out of his chamber*, &c. I had occasion, a few weeks since, to take the early train from Providence to Boston, and for this purpose rose at two o'clock in the morning. Everything around was wrapt in darkness and hushed in silence, broken only by what seemed at that hour the unearthly clank and rush of the train. It was a mild, serene, midsummer's night—the sky was without a cloud—the winds were whist. The moon, then in the last quarter, had just risen, and the stars shone with a spectral lustre but little affected by her presence. . . . Such was the glorious spectacle as we entered the train. As we proceeded, the timid approach of twilight became more perceptible; the intense blue of the sky began to soften; the smaller stars, like little children, went first to rest; the sister beams of the Pleiades soon melted together; but the bright constellations of the west and north remained unchanged. Steadily the wondrous transfiguration went on. Hands of angels, hidden from mortal eyes, shifted the scenery of the heavens; the glories of night dissolved into the glories of the dawn. The blue sky now turned more softly gray; the great watch-stars shut up their holy eyes; the east began to kindle. Faint streaks of purple soon blushed along the sky; the whole celestial concave was filled with the inflowing tides of the morning light which came pouring down from above in one great ocean of radiance; till at length, as we reached the blue hills a flash of purple fire blazed out from above the horizon, and turned the dewy teardrops of flower and leaf into rubies and diamonds. In a few seconds the everlasting gates of the morning were thrown wide open, and the lord of day, arrayed in glories too severe for the gaze of man, began his state. . . . I am filled with amazement when I am told that in this enlightened age, and in the heart of the Christian world, there are persons who can witness this daily manifestation of the power and wisdom of the Creator, and yet say in their hearts, "There is no God."—*Everett.*

The bridegroom's ornaments and the giant's power are but faint images of the sun's mild splendour, and his swift penetrating light. All nature rejoices at his approach; the sweet melody of wood and grove hails his rising; before his face, the shadows of night flee away; wild beasts of the forest hasten to their retreats; and light, and cheerfulness, and happy industry revisit the habitations of men. Indeed one bright sun should for ever silence all cavillings respecting the fundamental truths of natural religion. "Where is your God? show him to me," said a proud heathen monarch to a devout Jew. "I cannot show you my God, but come with me and I will show you one of his messengers." Taking him to the open air he pointed him to the unclouded sun, and said, "Look at that." "I cannot, it pains my eyes," said the monarch. "Then," said the Jew, "how could'st thou look on the face of him, at whose rebuke the pillars of heaven tremble?"—*Plumer.*

7. *Converting the soul.* Making the man to be returned or restored to the place from which sin had cast him. The practical effect of the Word of God is to turn the man to himself, to his God, and to holiness; and the turn or conversion is not outward alone, "*the soul*" is moved and renewed. The great means of the conversion of sinners is

the Word of God, and the more closely we keep to it in our ministry the more likely are we to be successful. It is God's Word rather than man's comment on God's Word which is made mighty with souls. When the law drives and the gospel draws, the action is different but the end is one, for by God's Spirit the soul is made to yield, and cries, "Turn me, and I shall be turned." Try men's depraved nature with philosophy and reasoning, and it laughs your efforts to scorn, but the Word of God soon works a transformation.—*Spurgeon.*

12. *Secret faults.* Beware of committing acts which it will be necessary to conceal. There is a singular poem by Hood called *The Dream of Eugene Aram*—a most remarkable piece it is indeed, illustrating the point on which we are now dwelling. Aram had murdered a man, and cast his body into the river—"a sluggish water, black as ink, the depth was so extreme." The next morning he visited the scene of his guilt—

"And sought the black accursed pool,
With a wild misgiving eye;
And he saw the dead in the river bed,
For the faithless stream was dry."

Next he covered the corpse with heaps of leaves, but a mighty wind swept through the wood and left the secret bare before the sun—

"Then down I cast me on my face,
And first began to weep,
For I knew my secret then was one
That earth refused to keep;
On land or sea though it should be
Ten thousand fathoms deep."

In plaintive notes he prophesies his own discovery. He buried his victim in a cave, and trod him down with stones, but when years had run their weary round, the foul deed was discovered and the murderer put to death.

Guilt is a "grim chamberlain," even when his fingers are not bloody red. Secret sins bring fevered eyes and sleepless nights, until men burn out their consciences, and become in very deed ripe for the pit. Hypocrisy is a hard game to play at, for it is one deceiver against many observers; and for certain it is a miserable trade, which will earn at last, as its certain climax, a tremendous bankruptcy. Ah! ye who have sinned without discovery, "be sure your sin will find you out;" and bethink you, it may find you out ere long. Sin, like murder, will come out; men will even tell tales about themselves in their dreams. God has made men to be so wretched in their consciences that they have been obliged to stand forth and confess the truth. Secret sinner! if thou wantest the foretaste of damnation upon earth, continue in thy secret sins; for no man is more miserable than he who sinneth secretly, and yet trieth to preserve a character. Yon stag, followed by the hungry hounds with open mouths, is far more happy than the man who is pursued by his sins. Yon bird, taken in the fowler's net, and labouring to escape, is far more happy than he who hath weaved around himself a web of deception, and labours to escape from it, day by day making the toils more thick and the web more strong. Oh the misery of secret sins! One may well pray, "Cleanse thou me from secret faults."—*Spurgeon.*

PSALM XX.

The inscription shows that the psalm was composed by David; but though he was its author, there is no absurdity in his speaking of himself in the person of others. The office of a prophet having been committed to him, he with great propriety prepared this as a form of prayer for the use of the faithful. In doing this, his object was not so much to commend his own person, by authoritatively issuing a royal ordinance, enjoining upon the people the use of this prayer, as to show, in the exercise of his office as a teacher, that it belonged to the whole church to concern itself, and to use its endeavours that the kingdom which God had erected might continue safe and prosperous. Many interpreters view this prayer as offered up only on one particular occasion; but in this I cannot agree. The occasion of its composition at first may have arisen from some particular battle which was about to be fought, either against the Ammonites or against some other enemies of Israel. But the design of the Holy Spirit, in my judgment, was to deliver to the church a common form of prayer which, as we may gather from the words, was to be used whenever she was threatened with any danger. God commands his people in general to pray for kings; but there was a special reason, and one which did not apply to any other kingdom, why prayer was to be made in behalf of this kingdom; for it was only by the hand of David and his seed that God had determined to govern and maintain his people. It is particularly to be noticed that under the figure of this temporal kingdom there was described a government far more excellent on which the whole joy and felicity of the church depended. The object therefore which David had expressly in view was to exhort all the children of God to cherish such a holy solicitude about the kingdom of Christ as would stir them up to continual prayer in its behalf.—*Calvin.*

Nowhere does David's high sense of the dignity of his office shine more conspicuously forth than in the psalm to which we now proceed. It was obviously designed as a prayer to be used by the people in behalf of their king, whom they here address, proceeding forth to battle. Most modern critics join the Syrian translator in supposing that the occasion of the psalm was the commencement of the second campaign, conducted by David in person, of the war against the allied Ammonites and Syrians (2 Sa. x. 15–19). The proofs of this are first, its relation to the following psalm, which was probably composed on the final subjugation of the Ammonites; and secondly, the allusion to the enemy's reliance on their war-chariots and their cavalry, which formed the main strength of the Syrian host, and over which, in the campaign above mentioned, David signally triumphed. It has indeed been also urged that the words, "Now know I," &c. (ver. 5), imply a reference to some former victory, such as that which had been gained in the previous campaign over the united Syrians and Ammonites by Joab. But to this we can hardly assent. The words more probably express the feeling of confidence produced by the prayers and sacrifices that had just been offered; the faith of the suppliant rising into a sure anticipation of the issue. And it should also be noted that, although originally springing from the circumstances of a particular occasion, the psalm is sufficiently general in its character to have been sung again and again, even in its most literal acceptation, at the commencement of each new war. . . . This psalm, like Ps. xviii., is of a pre-eminently typical character. Its full sense was doubtless intended by David to culminate in the Messiah: it was a psalm of the future, its significance stretching far beyond the more immediate fulfilment, and from the first the more spiritually-minded among the Israelites could hardly have otherwise regarded it. But from the time that Zion's true King came to her, just, and having salvation, all doubt as to the true import of the psalm was removed. Messiah, having offered his one accepted sacrifice for sins, is now expecting till his enemies be made his footstool; and though himself seated at God's right hand in heaven, is in the person of his church gone forth upon earth conquering and to conquer. Confident in the Captain of her salvation, and sure that all his petitions to his Father will be accomplished, the church anticipates for herself a joyful career of victory, beseeching the King of heaven and earth so to hear her that the kingdoms of this world may become the kingdoms of his Christ, and thus be brought back to their rightful allegiance to himself.—*Thrupp.*

PSALM XXI.

The exclusively Messianic exposition, which has been defended by many of the older commentators, and latterly by Rosenmüller, in his 2d edition, is deprived by our view of the foundation which it was conceived to have in ver. 4, 7. It is opposed even by the undeniable reference which the psalm has to 2 Sa. vii. This admits of the application to Christ only in so far as the promise found its last and highest fulfilment in Him in whom the royal stem of David culminated, but at the same time imperiously demands the reference to Christ in this sense. Apart from Christ the words, "Thou givest him length of days for ever and ever," and "Thou settest him for blessing for ever," are nothing but an empty dream. —*Hengstenberg.*

The psalm could from the first have only applied to David in so far as the promises made to him would be ultimately realized in the person of Christ. It is of the same typical character with Ps. xviii. and xx. There are some who would regard it as applying to the Messiah alone, and would exclude, as in Ps. ii., all other reference. And they are able to appeal to the fact, that while in ver. 1–7 the king comes before us in the third person, and in ver. 8–12 in the second, he never throughout this psalm speaks in the first, and may therefore, as in Ps. ii., be viewed as entirely distinct from the psalmist. Yet it will generally be felt that the second and third persons are here but poetical or conventional substitutes for the first. There is to the king of this psalm no superhuman dignity ascribed. The perpetuity of life assigned him does not exclude the reference to David, provided only that he and his house be contemplated in their ideal unity. And the same remark applies also to the declaration that God had "set him to be blessings" (ver. 6, Eng. marg. rendering), which was so far true of David that it was of his lineage that the future Saviour of men was to spring.

To us there can indeed be little inducement to behold in the king of this psalm any but Christ. We must recollect, however, that it is in his church that his royalty is on earth chiefly displayed. Nay, in one point of view the person of Christ may here be regarded as almost merging in that of his church, contemplated as the perpetuation of the church of Israel; and the fullest commentary on the psalm will then be found in the sixtieth chapter of the prophecy of Isaiah. The pardon bestowed upon David after his sin will be a type of God's mercy to the church of Israel notwithstanding her apostasy: "In my wrath I smote thee, but in my favour have I had mercy on thee." The pledge of God's faithfulness in the birth of Solomon will be a type of God's glorification of Israel by raising up, of the seed of Abraham, him through whom the church was to become "an eternal excellency, a joy of many generations." Of the Ammonitish crown, which he had gained, even David could hardly have made mention had he not viewed it as a type of the riches of the Gentiles that were to form the diadem of the church, while his severities to the foes whom he had subdued were a testimony to the church. "The nation and kingdom that will not serve thee shall perish; yea, those nations shall be utterly wasted." If David's glory was great in God's salvation, this again was a pledge of the future glory with which the church should shine: "Arise, shine; for thy light is come, and the glory of the Lord is risen upon thee. For, behold, the darkness shall cover the earth, and gross darkness the people; but the Lord shall arise upon thee, and his glory shall be seen upon thee. And the Gentiles shall come to thy light, and kings to the brightness of thy rising." The honour laid upon the church of Christ was thus to consist in her being a light to the world; and this too had been implied in the psalm, in the words of ver. 6, already quoted, which had virtually repeated, though with a limitation to David and his house, the words of the promise to Abraham, "Thou shalt be a blessing . . . and in thee shall all families of the earth be blessed." For the fulfilment of the promises made through Nathan to David was manifestly designed to convey a general blessing to Israel, and to the world at large.—*Thrupp.*

3. *For thou preventest him with the blessings of goodness.* The word *prevent* formerly signified to precede or go before, and assuredly Jehovah preceded his Son with blessings. Before he died saints were saved by the anticipated merit of his death, before he came believers saw his day and were glad, and he himself had his delights with the sons of men. The father is so willing to give blessings through his Son, that instead of his being constrained to bestow his grace, he outstrips the mediatorial march of mercy. "I say not that I will pray the Father for you, for the Father himself loveth you." Before Jesus calls, the Father answers, and while he is yet speaking he hears. Mercies may be bought with blood, but they are also freely given. The love of Jehovah is not caused by the Redeemer's sacrifice, but that love, with its blessings of goodness, preceded the great atonement, and provided it for our salvation. Reader, it will be a happy thing for thee if, like thy Lord, thou canst see both providence and grace preceding thee, forestalling thy needs, and preparing thy path. Mercy, in the case of many of us, ran before our desires and prayers, and it ever outruns our endeavours and expectancies, and even our hopes are left to lag behind. Prevenient grace deserves a song; we may make one out of this sentence; let us try. All our mercies are to be viewed as *blessings;* gifts of a blessed God, meant to make us blessed; they are *blessings of goodness,* not of merit, but of free favour; and they come to us in a *preventing way,* a way of prudent foresight, such as only preventing love could have arranged. In this light the verse is itself a sonnet!—*Spurgeon.*

PSALM XXII.

There is yet another psalm for which

I would claim a place amongst those that are directly prophetical of Christ. I mean Ps. xxii. The majority of the best commentators, no doubt, regard it as referring throughout to David, and so rank it in the typical class. But the objections to that view are many, and, I think, unanswerable. For one thing, David's biography contains nothing corresponding to the account the Sufferer here gives of his tribulations (ver. 14-18). His enemies never "parted his garments among them or cast lots upon his vesture." Indeed, so inapplicable is the description to any Bible saint, that some who reject the direct reference to Christ are fain to attribute the psalm—in the teeth of all existing evidence—to "some afflicted person, otherwise unknown to us, during the captivity." Besides, even if it had been possible to find in the life of David or of some other saint a time of such sufferings as the psalm describes, those who see a primary reference to him would still have had to explain the remarkable hopes expressed in the latter part of it. The Sufferer, rising above the sense of his present sorrow, rejoices in the confident persuasion that, as the fruit of what he is now enduring, all the families of the earth shall one day be moved to return to the Lord, and to bow themselves down before him. This is a feature which so evidently points to the Man of Sorrows, that the great Jewish critics have betaken themselves to the same explanation by which they seek to get quit of the testimony of Isa. liii. to the cross of Christ. In both cases they labour to make out that the Sufferer described is the nation of Israel during the Babylonish captivity, and that the blessing so confidently anticipated to spring out of the sorrows of the chosen people was no other than that diffusion of the true religion which resulted from the dispersion of the exiles among the nations. The theory is ingenious, and it has been eagerly appropriated by the Rationalists. But there are things both in the prophecy and in the psalm that conclusively refute it. Thus, in the former, the Lord's righteous Servant whose sufferings are portrayed, instead of being identified with the people of Israel, is expressly contrasted with them (Isa. liii. 4-6.) In the psalm there is not only the same contrast (ver. 22, 23), but, from beginning to end, the terms in which the Sufferer's condition is described are too strongly individual to admit the hypothesis of personification. The only adequate and natural interpretation of the psalm is that which sees in it a lyrical prediction of the sufferings of Messiah and the glory that was to follow. No sufferer but one could, without presumption, have expected his griefs to result in the conversion of nations to God.

Moreover, it is not a vague description of a good man's sufferings that this great psalm sets forth. It goes into many details, and these so exactly corresponding to the sufferings of Christ, that the whole reads like a poetical version of the gospel history. (1.) The scene portrayed is a crucifixion, and just such a crucifixion as was witnessed at Calvary. The Sufferer cannot obtain the solace of retirement. He is encompassed by scornful men, who load him with reproaches. They deride the profession of his hope in God, and do so in terms which startle us by their identity with those actually employed by the crowds who encompassed the Lord's cross. All the dreadful accompaniments of crucifixion are seen;—the strength dried up like a potsherd—the bones out of joint—the burning thirst, making the tongue cleave to the jaws —the piercing of the hands and the feet[1]—the bones projecting so that one might count them—the parting of the garments by lot amongst the executioners. Surely the cross of Christ is here, and without the intervention of any type. (2.) Not only is the psalm cited by the evangelists as having been fulfilled in the crucifixion, but the Lord employed it himself (Mat. xxvii. 46) in expressing the anguish of his soul. "About the ninth hour he cried with a loud voice, saying, Eli, Eli, lama sabachthani? that is to say, My God, my God, why hast thou forsaken me?" Taking all the circumstances into account, it is a fair construction of this exclamation, to understand it with Augustine,[2] as equivalent to saying, The psalm was written concerning me. (3.) There is

1 This remarkable expression in ver. 16 is rendered by many of the modern critics, according to the Masoretic punctuation and the Jewish interpreters, "like a lion my hands and my feet;" but the usual translation is supported by all the ancient versions, and yields the better sense. Indeed, the other yields no tolerable sense at all. Compare Mr. Perowne's note.

2 *Enarratio* ii. in Ps. xxi. (xxii.) sec. 3.

in the psalm a singular alternation of deep dejection under present sorrow, and of solemn joy in the prospect of the blessings that are to accrue to all the nations. And this very alternation of conflicting sorrow and joy was seen in Christ, both on the cross and during the preceding week, John xii. 20–33. (4.) In one respect, the psalm stands alone in the Scriptures, and indeed in all religious literature. It is a cry out of the depths—the sorrowful prayer of One who is not only persecuted by man, but seems to himself, for the time, to be utterly forsaken of his God. Yet there is no confession of sin, no penitent sorrow, no trace of compunction or remorse. This distinguishes the psalm, quite unequivocally, not only from ordinary psalms of complaint, but from those in which Christ speaks in the person of David his type. The complaints found in them are never unaccompanied with confessions of sin. If David, or any other ancient saint, had written the twenty-second Psalm, as the expression of his own griefs and hopes, there would certainly have been audible in it some note of penitence.—*Binnie.*

1. *My God, my God, why hast thou forsaken me?* This was the startling cry of Golgotha: Eloi, Eloi, lama sabacthani. The Jews mocked, but the angels adored when Jesus cried this exceeding bitter cry. Nailed to the tree we behold our great Redeemer in extremities, and what see we? Having ears to hear let us hear, and having eyes to see let us see! Let us gaze with holy wonder, and mark the flashes of light amid the awful darkness of that mid-day midnight. First, our Lord's faith beams forth and deserves our reverent imitation; he keeps his hold upon his God with both hands and cries twice, *My God, my God!* The spirit of adoption was strong within the suffering Son of Man, and he felt no doubt about his interest in his God. Oh that we could imitate this cleaving to an afflicting God! Nor does the sufferer distrust the power of God to sustain him, for the title used—*El*—signifies *strength*, and is the name of the mighty God. He knows the Lord to be the all-sufficient support and succour of his spirit, and therefore appeals to him in the agony of grief, but not in the misery of doubt. He would fain know why he is left, he raises that question and repeats it, but neither the power nor the faithfulness of God does he mistrust. What an inquiry is this before us! *Why hast thou forsaken me?* We must lay the emphasis on every word of this saddest of all utterances. *Why?* what is the great cause of such a strange fact as for God to leave his own Son at such a time and in such a plight? There was no cause in him, why then was he deserted? *Hast;* it is done, and the Saviour is feeling its dread effect as he asks the question; it is surely true, but how mysterious! It was no threatening of forsaking which made the great Surety cry aloud, he endured that forsaking in very deed. *Thou:* I can understand why traitorous Judas and timid Peter should be gone, but *thou* my God, my faithful friend, how canst thou leave me? This is worst of all, yea worse than all put together. Hell itself has for its fiercest flame the separation of the soul from God. *Forsaken:* if thou hadst chastened I might bear it, for thy face would shine; but to forsake me utterly, ah! why is this? *Me:* thine innocent, obedient, suffering Son, why leavest thou *me* to perish? A sight of self seen by penitence, and of Jesus on the cross seen by faith, will best expound this question. Jesus is forsaken because our sins had separated between us and our God.—*Spurgeon.*

9. *Thou didst make me hope when I was upon my mother's breasts.* Augustine, in the first book of his *Confessions*, finds great enjoyment and consolation in similar reflections, where he praises God with devout admiration for his creation and birth, and extols the divine goodness in taking him up, and committing him to the care and attention of his mother. Although thoughts such as these may appear childish, effeminate, and unseasonable, for those who are in such pain and conflicts, yet experience here teaches us to remember these tender, cheerful, lovely works of God, to seek a place of refuge when suffering the hard bites of the wrath and of the rod of God, and to enjoy the sweet and pleasant milk of our mother's heart, and all these other acts of mercy which were shown during the years of infancy. Thus shall we, when brought into trouble, be led to think (as we are commanded to do) on the days of happiness gone by; when distress and suffering are upon us, we shall remember the great grace and goodness of God manifested to us in early youth; and

when we suffer as men, we shall reflect on what we enjoyed when children. . . . Try, and you will then understand what it is to see the divine majesty employed and taken up with childish, that is, with small, insignificant, yea contemptible works.—*Luther.*

16. *They pierced my hands and my feet.* The following admirable remarks, in reply to Dr. J. A. Alexander (who inclines to the translation—"like a lion," and observes that the sense would then be, "they surround my hands and my feet as they would a lion," or "as a lion would," *i.e.* with the strength and fierceness of a lion), are abridged from the *Bibliotheca Sacra* for 1851:—"That there is in the sacred writers an absence of explicit declaration on the subject of the piercing of the feet in crucifixion, may perhaps be admitted; but by no means can it be admitted that there is a '*singular* absence' of such allusions; for this would imply that there existed a demand for such 'explicit declaration' in the New Testament, which is by no means the fact. Whatever the custom in crucifying might have been, it was universally known in the time of Christ, and for centuries afterwards. Nor is it easy to imagine what occasion could exist, under such circumstances, that should require of the sacred writers the 'explicit declaration' referred to. The fact, however, that he was thus pierced is sufficiently referred to and implied. For example, in Mat. xxvii. 35, 36, we have precisely the occurrences which are mentioned in Ps. xxii. 17-19, 'They *crucified* him' (that is, agreeably to the usages of crucifixion as then universally known, they pierced his hands and feet by nailing them to the cross), 'and parted his garments,' &c. Then in Lu. xxiv. 39, 40, the same idea is most forcibly implied in Christ's words to his disciples, 'Behold my hands and my feet, that it is I myself:' ἴδετε τὰς χεῖράς μου καὶ τοὺς πόδας μου, ὅτι αὐτὸς ἐγώ εἰμι. It was by the marks which were visible in his hands and feet, therefore, that the disciples were to learn that he who then stood before them was he who had been crucified. . . .

"Dr. Alexander also considers it *very remarkable* that no citation or application of the clause occurs in any of the Gospels. But admitting it to be even so, what is there peculiarly remarkable herein? Is it not equally remarkable that Ge. xlix. 10, and Da. ix. 27, and other passages, are not quoted and applied? There can be no doubt that all such passages were adduced by the apostles in their disputes with the Jews, and that they were among those with which Apollos 'mightily convinced' them, and by which they were 'confounded' by Paul; but why they should have been formally quoted and applied in the New Testament does not appear. . .

"Gesenius candidly observes that 'all the ancient interpreters have taken כארי as a verb; and this is certainly possible if we regard כָּאֲרִי as the participle in Kal formed in the Chaldee manner, and in the plural number for כָּאֲרִים.' And he refers to two MSS. to prove that '*it was commonly held to be a verb.*' And in confirmation of this Vatablus declares that the ancient reading was twofold כָּאֲרִי and כָּרוּ; while according to the testimony of Genebrard, the Jews continued to write כָּאֲרִי in the margin and כָּארוּ in the text until the six hundredth year of the Christian era, and then began to insert the marginal reading into the text itself; and finally to omit כָּאֲרוּ altogether.

"It is scarcely possible to overestimate the weight and importance of the evidence furnished by the versions in favour of our position that the word in question is a verb. The limits allotted to this review are not sufficient to permit us to go thoroughly into this branch of the argument; and we can therefore do but little more than glance at it. We begin with the Septuagint, the most ancient of all versions, it having been made probably in the third century before the Christian era, and by Jews who unquestionably understood their own language. Now these interpreters rendered the clause in question by ὤρυξαν χεῖράς μου καὶ πόδας, *they pierced my hands and feet.* If therefore the word in dispute was then regarded as a noun, how is this rendering to be accounted for? Can any one suppose that such a rendering would have been given in defiance of MSS., common sense, common honesty, and directly in the face of the knowledge of every one who could read Hebrew? and also without any assignable inducement whatever? If it was not done in defiance of these things, we apprehend that there is but one other alternative—*it was done in accordance with the MSS., common sense, and honesty.* Add to this the fact that the Greek fathers all translate the word in a similar manner. Justin, in his dialogue with the shrewd and learned Jew Trypho, so translates it; so does the author of the *Questions to Antiochus*, Quest. 136, and Athanasius in his *Dialogue on the Trinity* and in his work on the *Incarnation*. Apollinaris, in his *Paraphrase*, thus renders it:

'Ημετέρους ὤρυξαν ὁμοῦ χεῖράς τε, πόδας τε.

"The Latin interpreters likewise uniformly render it as a verb. So Tertullian in innumerable places. Cyprian also, in his second book of *Testimonies against the Jews*, renders it by *effoderunt*. In the old Latin version of the Psalms made by Jerome from the Hebrew with the utmost care, the word is translated also as a verb: '*Fixerunt* manus meas, et pedes meas.' Now to this version there is a preface addressed to Sophronius by Jerome, in which he most confidently declares that he has not departed from the strict sense of the Hebrew in a single word; and he calls upon the Jews to show, if they were able, one instance of such departure.[1] Now let the reader ask himself whether Jerome (or any other man of sense or integrity) could have thus challenged such a scrutiny, and in a case where so glaring an error would, to his shame and mortification, have been at once detected by his bitter opposers the Jews, if in such a well-known instance as the one before us he had been conscious of having corrupted the text? The supposition is out of all question. Jerome knew that the Jews had *fastened* Jesus to the cross, and the Jews knew also that they had thus fastened him by piercing his hands and feet; and they likewise knew that all Christians applied this passage to that transaction. And yet under such circumstances Jerome thus challenges their scrutiny, and defies them to come forward and show that he had mistranslated a single word! The conclusion seems irresistible, that כָּאֲרוּ was either the reading of the then approved text, or כָּאֲרִי in Ps. xxii. was universally regarded as a verb.

"To all this may be added the strong fact that Aquila the Jew (a man of great industry, and thoroughly acquainted with Hebrew), who in the second century of the Christian era translated the Old Testament into Greek, renders the word not as a noun but verb; not indeed by ὤρυξαν, but by ᾔσχυναν, a word whose import in this connection (though Hengstenberg has strangely questioned it) involves the signification of *pierced*. At all events, he translates it as a verb, for this is the point before us. Here, then, was a most learned and eminent Jew thus translating from the approved text, or Kethibh of the Jews. What, then, must the reading of the Kethibh have been? Will any one say that it was כָּאֲרִי, and that this word is a noun? . . .

"There is one more consideration which certainly is of weight, and ought not to be overlooked in this connection. We refer to the following: In this same psalm everything else which our adorable Redeemer suffered while enduring the death of the cross is mentioned, and why then should not the piercing of his hands and feet be referred to? When in the deepest agony on the cross he repeated at least the first verse of the psalm.[2] In ver. 8, 9 he is represented as saying, 'All who see me laugh me to scorn; they shoot out the lip, they shake the head, saying, He trusted in the Lord that he would deliver him,' &c. In ver. 14, 'They gaped upon me with their mouths as a raging lion.' In ver. 16 he complains of thirst, and in ver. 19 says, 'They part my garments among them, and cast lots for my vesture.' Is it credible, then, that no reference should have been made to the excruciating agony which he endured from the piercing of his hands and feet? If Dr. Alexander's exposition of the word in question be the true one, *then there is no direct reference to this matter in the whole psalm.* Can this be believed?

"Not less forcible than touchingly beautiful are the following words of Luther: 'To us who believe in Christ, and who hold by the authority of the gospel that this whole psalm was spoken concerning him, it is easy to perceive that the proper reading of the passage is, '*they have pierced* my hands and my feet,' instead of '*as a lion* my hands and my feet.' For we would not en-

[1] "His words are, 'Certè confidenter dicam, et multos hujus operis testes citabo, me nihil duntaxat sententiæ Hebraica veritate mutâsse;' and, a little further on, he adds, 'Interroga quemlibet Hebraeorum.'"

[2] "Osiander (Dr. Lucas) and others of ancient times believed that Christ repeated *the whole psalm* while hanging on the cross; 'creditur Christus hunc psalmum totum in cruce recitasse,' says he, an idea which Coleridge and others in modern times have adopted."

deavour by means of the mysteries of the Scriptures to explain the things which are known to have occurred; but on the contrary would clear up the mystery by a reference to such things; that is, we would illustrate the Old Testament by the New (and not the New by the Old), and would determine what is the sense of the former by the obvious import of the latter: thus making them both to look towards Christ, as the two cherubim looked towards the mercy-seat. For God said by the prophet (Je. xxiii. 30), '*In the last days* ye shall understand my counsel;' but to Moses he said, 'Ye shall discern only my hinder parts.' Since, therefore, we are assured that Christ's hands and feet were pierced, and are equally certain also that this whole psalm applies to him; and since the sense of the passage not only strikingly accords herewith, but absolutely demands that the word be read, '*they pierced*' (especially since no rule of grammar forbids it), we may, without violence, and with perfect propriety, adopt this as its proper signification.' *Comment. in Ps.* xxii."

27. *Shall remember.* Andrew Fuller, in an excellent sermon on this verse, thus remarks regarding the nature of true conversion:—"It is to remember. . . . Perhaps the first religious exercise of mind of which we are conscious is reflection. A state of unregeneracy is a state of forgetfulness. God is forgotten. Sinners have lost all just sense of his glory, authority, mercy, and judgment, living as if there were no God, or as if they thought there was none. And when God is forgotten, there is no proper remembrance of themselves. Their own evil ways attract little or no attention. They go on adding sin to sin, and think scarcely anything about them. Even if some threatening judgment should have affrighted them into vows and resolutions to amend their lives, no sooner is the cloud dissipated than all is forgotten. But if ever we are brought to be the subjects of true conversion, we shall be brought to remember these things. This divine change is fitly expressed by the case of the prodigal, who is said to have *come to himself*, or to his right mind. If we thus come to ourselves, we shall think of the holiness, goodness, and forbearance of God, and be troubled. And if we think of God, we shall not forget our own evil ways. We shall remember, and be confounded, and never open our lips any more. The Holy Spirit makes use of divers means in conversion; but they all operate to bring the sinner to reflection. Sometimes he works by adverse providences. Thus it was with Joseph's brethren. They sold their brother for a slave, and framed a lie to deceive their father; and more than twenty years had elapsed when they went down into Egypt to buy corn. There they were treated roughly, and put in ward as though they were spies. In this situation they remembered and reflected upon their evil ways: 'And they said one to another, We are verily guilty concerning our brother.' Thus also Manasseh king of Judah, after a long life of the most awful wickedness, was reclaimed by an adverse providence. In the thorns of affliction he remembered the Lord God of his fathers, called upon his name, and obtained mercy. Frequently the Lord works by his word. In reading or hearing it, something lays hold of the heart; and the effect is the same. Peter's hearers (Ac. ii.) were brought to remember their evil doings, and to sue for mercy. We may read the Scriptures over and over, and hear hundreds of sermons, without any real profit, unless they operate in this way. If ever you hear to purpose, you will think but little of the preacher; your attention will be principally turned to yourselves. Sometimes, I believe, a sinner is converted without any apparent second cause. While sitting in his house, or walking by the way, his mind is insensibly drawn to think of its own evil courses: 'I thought on my ways,' says David, 'and turned my feet unto thy testimonies.' Whatever be the way in which we are brought, if it be by the word of God, we shall certainly be induced to remember those things which heretofore have been neglected and forgotten."

31. *He hath done this.* "The last word of our Saviour on the cross, τετέλεσται, evidently refers to this עשה, as His first exclamation is taken from the beginning of the psalm:—of all proofs of the profound significance of this whole thus bounded, this is the surest, giving, at the same time, the key to the variously misinterpreted word of our Saviour. According to this view, we are to regard *the work of God* as that which *was finished.* The last moment of suffering is the first of deliverance; and the expiring Saviour

here indicates that this is now at hand; that he has now received an answer, not in words but in deed, to the question, Why hast thou forsaken me? and that the morning dawn now succeeds the dark night. *The resurrection* certifies the exclamation: *It is finished.*"

The Hebrew is very elliptical. It seems as if עָשָׂה were here intentionally used in an absolute and indefinite way in order to fix our thoughts on the thing being done. A finger points to the scene, and a voice says, עָשָׂה, *q.d.* "*He has performed!*" Here is *deed*, not word only. Here is *fulfilment*, not promise only. The meek may eat and be filled! For lo! there is the thing done! performance of all that this psalm describes, of all that Jesus meant when he cried, "*It is finished.*" In that hour he saw his sufferings ended and his glory begun, and could proclaim victory through suffering. What a song of Zion is this! Messiah at every step! beginning with "Eli, Eli," and ending with τετέλεσται, "*It is finished.*"—*Andrew A. Bonar.*

PSALM XXIII.

The delightful picture of domestic piety that imparts such a charm to the book of Ruth is a memorial of the manners prevalent among David's immediate ancestors, and of the benign and heavenly influences that blessed his infancy and boyhood. I do not suppose that the twenty-third psalm was written in the psalmist's childhood, but it is at least a reminiscence of it, and brings vividly before us the scenes and the feelings which his memory recalled when it reverted to the golden morning of his life. We have good reason to believe that the regenerating hallowing grace of God's free Spirit accompanied—if indeed it did not anticipate—the teaching and godly nurture he received from his parents.—*Binnie.*

David has left no sweeter psalm than the short twenty-third. It is but a moment's opening of his soul; but, as when one, walking the winter street, sees the door opened for some one to enter, and the red light streams a moment forth, and the forms of gay children are running to greet the comer, and genial music sounds, though the door shuts and leaves the night black, yet it cannot shut back again all that the eyes, the ear, the heart, and the imagination have seen—so in this psalm, though it is but a moment's opening of the soul, are emitted truths of peace and consolation that will never be absent from the world. The twenty-third Psalm is the nightingale of the Psalms. It is small, of a homely feather, singing shyly out of obscurity; but, oh! it has filled the air of the whole world with melodious joy, greater than the heart can conceive. Blessed be the day on which that psalm was born! What would you say of a pilgrim commissioned of God to travel up and down the earth singing a strange melody, which, when one heard, caused him to forget whatever sorrow he had? And so the singing angel goes on his way through all lands, singing in the language of every nation, driving away trouble by the pulses of the air which his tongue moves with divine power. Behold just such an one! This pilgrim God has sent to speak in every language on the globe. It has charmed more griefs to rest than all the philosophy of the world. It has remanded to their dungeon more felon thoughts, more black doubts, more thieving sorrows, than there are sands on the sea-shore. It has comforted the noble host of the poor. It has sung courage to the army of the disappointed. It has poured balm and consolation into the heart of the sick, of captives in dungeons, of widows in their pinching griefs, of orphans in their loneliness. Dying soldiers have died easier as it was read to them; ghastly hospitals have been illuminated; it has visited the prisoner, and broken his chains, and, like Peter's angel, led him forth in imagination and sung him back to his home again. It has made the dying Christian slave freer than his master, and consoled those whom, dying, he left behind mourning, not so much that he was gone, as because they were left behind, and could not go too. Nor is its work done. It will go singing to your children and my children, and to their children, through all the generations of time; nor will it fold its wings till the last pilgrim is safe, and time ended; and then it shall fly back to the bosom of God, whence it issued, and sound on, mingled with all those sounds of celestial joy which make heaven musical for ever.—Beecher's *Life Thoughts.*

It has been said that what the nightingale is among birds, that is this divine ode among the Psalms, for it has sung sweetly in the ear of many a mourner in his night of weeping, and has bidden him hope for a morning of joy. I will venture to compare it also to the lark, which sings as it mounts, and mounts as it sings, until it is out of sight, and even then is not out of hearing. Note the last words of the psalm—"I will dwell in the house of the Lord for ever;" these are celestial notes, more fitted for the eternal mansions than for these dwelling-places below the clouds. Oh that we may enter into the spirit of the psalm as we read it, and then we shall experience the days of heaven upon the earth!—*Spurgeon.*

It is unnecessary to refer this psalm to any particular period of David's history. As the outpouring of a heart which has found perfect rest in God, it was most probably written in advanced years, after a long experience of God's goodness. Its language is coloured by the reminiscences of his past life. His own shepherd experience no doubt suggested the image of the former part; and in the latter we may perhaps trace a recollection, more or less distinct, of the circumstances mentioned in 2 Sam. xvii. 27-29, when, on David's coming to Mahanaim, during Absaloms' rebellion, he and his party were succoured and refreshed in their faintness and weariness through the kindness of Barzillai and other friends, who supplied their wants.—*Perowne.*

Of all the figures that are applied to God in the Old Testament, that of a shepherd is the most beautiful. "The other names sound somewhat too gloriously and majestically, and bring, as it were, an awe and fear with them when we hear them uttered. This is the case when the Scriptures call God our Lord, King, Creator. This, however, is not the case with the sweet word *shepherd.* It brings to the godly, when they read it or hear it, as it were, a confidence, a consolation or security, like the word *father.* We cannot better understand this consoling and lovely word than by going to nature, and learning carefully from her what are the dispositions and the properties of the sheep, and what the duty, the labour, the care of a good shepherd. A sheep can only live through the help, protection, and care of its shepherd. As soon as it loses him it is exposed to dangers of every kind, and must perish, for it cannot help itself. The reason is, it is a poor, weak, silly creature. But, weak creature though it be, it has the habit of keeping diligently near its shepherd, of depending upon his help and protection; it follows wherever he leads, and, if it can only be near him, it cares for nothing, is afraid of no one, but feels secure and happy, for it wants for nothing."—*Luther.*

1. *The Lord is my shepherd.* I never ride over these hills, clothed with flocks, without meditating upon this delightful theme. Our Saviour says that the good shepherd, when he putteth forth his own sheep, goeth before them, and they follow. This is true to the letter. They are so tame and so trained that they *follow* their keeper with the utmost docility. He leads them forth from the fold, or from their houses in the villages, just where he pleases. As there are many flocks in such a place as this, each one takes a different path, and it is his business to find pasture for them. It is necessary, therefore, that they should be taught to follow, and not to stray away into the unfenced fields of corn which lie so temptingly on either side. Any one that thus wanders is sure to get into trouble. The shepherd calls sharply from time to time, to remind them of his presence. They know his voice and follow on; but if a stranger call, they stop short, lift up their heads in alarm, and if it is repeated, they turn and flee, because they know not the voice of a stranger. This is not the fancy costume of a parable: it is simple fact. I have made the experiment repeatedly. The shepherd goes before, not merely to point out the way, but to see that it is practicable and safe. He is armed, in order to defend his charge; and in this he is very courageous. Many adventures with wild beasts occur not unlike that recounted by David (1 Sam. xvii. 34-36), and in these very mountains; for, though there are now no lions here, there are wolves in abundance; and leopards and panthers, exceeding fierce, prowl about these wild wadies. They not unfrequently attack the flock in the very presence of the shepherd, and he must be ready to do battle at a moment's warning. I have listened with intense interest to their graphic descriptions of downright and desperate fights with these savage beasts. And when the thief and the robber come (and come they do), the faithful shepherd has often to put his life in his hand to defend his flock. I

have known more than one case in which he had literally to lay it down in the contest. A poor faithful fellow last spring, between Tiberias and Tabor, instead of fleeing, actually fought three Bedawîn robbers, until he was hacked to pieces with their khanjars, and died among the sheep he was defending.—*The Land and the Book.*

2. *He maketh me to lie down in green pastures*, &c. This is but one of many beautiful passages of Scripture alluding to the practice of the eastern shepherds in leading their flocks from one region to another in search of green pasture. In winter and early spring the rains compel the roots and seeds of the desert to shoot, which in summer were kept down by excessive drought. But the moisture clothes the wilderness with verdure, and with the succulent and nutritive herbage on which the flocks luxuriate and prosper. And when the periodical drought returns to the wilderness, the shepherd leads off his flocks to the mountains, the streams, and the habitable districts, where herbage yet remains. Thus it is an important part of the eastern shepherd's character that he should possess such a knowledge of the country and its pasture-grounds as may enable him to move his flock from one point to another with the moral certainty of finding good pasturage in the place whither he is going. The bad, that is the ignorant shepherd, exposes his flock to the danger of perishing from hunger or fatigue: from hunger, if no pasture is found in the expected places; from fatigue, in hurrying the flock from one place to another, in the vague expectation of finding that which he knows not where to find.—*Pictorial Bible.*

4. *Thy rod and thy staff they comfort me.* The shepherd invariably carries a staff or rod with him when he goes forth to feed his flock. It is often bent or hooked at one end, which gave rise to the shepherd's crook in the hands of the Christian bishop. With this staff he rules and guides the flock to their green pastures, and defends them from their enemies. With it, also, he corrects them when disobedient, and brings them back when wandering. This staff is associated as inseparably with the shepherd as the goad is with the ploughman. David has an extended reference to the shepherd and his kind offices, and among them is an allusion to this rod: "Thy rod and thy staff they comfort me"—in every way in which these are employed by the good shepherd in the discharge of his office.—*The Land and the Book.*

5. *Thou anointest my head with oil.* This does not appear to refer to the regal anointing, but to the custom of anointing the head with oil and fragrant unguents on occasions of festivity and rejoicing. To anoint the head also was an honour paid to a distinguished guest; and, in Luke vii. 46, our Saviour seems to refer to the omission of it as rather inhospitable in his host, the Pharisee. The same customs as to anointing the head were in operation among the Greeks and Romans. At present, in Western Asia, people generally shave their heads, which has there put an end to these ancient usages. But they still subsist, more to the east, in India. "At their marriages and other festive times (says Roberts), the young and old may be seen with their long black tresses tied neatly on the crown of the head, shining and smooth, like polished ebony." The custom here alluded to is remarkably illustrated by a ceremony of which Captain Wilson describes himself as having been the object in India:—"I once had this ceremony performed on myself, in the house of a rich Indian, and in the presence of a large company. The gentleman of the house poured upon my hands and arms a delightful odoriferous perfume, put a golden cup into my hand, and poured wine into it till it ran over, assuring me at the same time that it was a great pleasure for him to receive me, and that I should find a rich supply in his house. I think the divine poet expressed his sense of the goodness of God by an allusion to this ceremony, or to one that very closely resembled it."—*Pictorial Bible.*

PSALM XXIV.

How far David himself recognized the prophetical import of his strains of praise, it is in the present instance difficult to determine. Yet in the whole Psalter there is hardly a psalm that can be regarded as more deeply prophetical than this. It is doubly prophetical. Alike portraying the characteristics of the true Israel, and celebrating the glory of Israel's God, it finds its perfect fulfilment in him who was himself at once both the one and the other, and whose ascension into heaven bore the double witness to his human obedience and his divine glory. As our Saviour was by his spotless innocence the only perfect representation of Israel, so on the other hand was it only in his power that the full glory of God was manifested to the world. His victory over death and hell proclaimed him the Lord strong and mighty, the Lord mighty in battle. His strength, infused by his Holy Spirit into the souls of his redeemed, proclaims him the Lord of hosts, the God of the armies of the true Israel; a title the justice of which will be more completely vindicated when the redeemed shall themselves have accomplished their victory, and when, freed from all stain of sin, they shall ascend whither their King of glory is ascended before them. As God's covenant people of olden time were a type of all who should truly serve him, so the victories of Israel's God and of his chosen armies over the Philistine invaders, were types of the spiritual victory of God manifest in the flesh, and in him of his Christian redeemed.

But in connection with this must not be overlooked the prophecy implicitly involved in the first verse of the psalm of the catholicity of God's true Israel. It is perhaps too much to suppose that David ever foresaw that God would one day recognize the equal holiness of every nation upon earth; for although in examining Ps. xix. we have seen that he discovered a stumbling-block in the restriction to a single people of the knowledge of God's truth, yet his utmost and latest anticipations in this respect seem from Ps. lxvii. to have gone no further than this, that God's special mercies to Israel would become a blessing and a joy to the Gentile world. The use, however, which St. Paul has made of the first verse in 1 Cor. x. 26 leaves no doubt that had *he* had occasion to furnish a general exposition of this psalm, he would have recognized in it the prophetical import assigned to it above; nor does the silence of the psalmist, who from the sphere of ideas in which he had been educated was disabled from pushing his words to their full consequences, afford any just ground for questioning the legitimacy of the interpretation thus placed upon them.—*Thrupp.*

The coming of the Lord of glory, the high demands upon his people originating therein, the absolute necessity to prepare worthily for his arrival, form the subject-matter of the psalm. It admits of applications far beyond the special occasion which called it forth. The Lord may be conceived of as constantly coming, in relation both to his church collectively and to his people individually. And his people therefore ought to be continually preparing to give him a suitable reception. Hence it follows that the Messianic interpretation, which in former times was so very prevalent, has an important element of truth in it. The coming of God to his kingdom took place in a manner infinitely more real at the appearance of Christ than it did at the entrance of the ark of the covenant. That lower occurrence was only the *shadow*, but the *body* was in Christ. At this truly real coming, which has different gradations—the coming in humility, the coming in spirit, and the coming in glory—the *demands* rise in proportion to the greater reality. The question, "Who shall ascend to the hill of the Lord, and who shall stand in his holy place?" becomes more solemn, and the command, "Lift up your heads, ye gates," is given in a louder tone.—*Hengstenberg.*

7-10. *Lift up your heads, O ye gates,* &c. We must now form to ourselves an idea of the Lord of glory, after his resurrection from the dead, making his entry into the eternal temple in heaven, as of old, by the symbol of his presence, he took possession of that figurative and temporary structure which once stood upon the hill of Sion. We are to conceive him gradually rising from Mount Olivet into the air, taking the clouds for his chariot and ascending up on high; while some of the angels, like the Levites in procession, attendant on the triumphant Messiah in the day of his power, demand that those everlasting gates and doors, hitherto shut and barred against the race of Adam, should be thrown open for his admission into the realms of bliss. "Lift up your heads, O ye gates; and be ye lift up, ye everlasting doors; and the King of glory shall come in." On hearing this voice of jubilee and exultation from the earth, the abode of misery and sorrow, the rest of the angels, astonished at the thought of a man claiming a right of entrance into their happy regions, ask from within, like the Levites in the temple, "Who is this King of glory?" To which question the attendant angels answer, in a strain of joy and triumph

—and let the church of the redeemed answer with them—"The Lord strong and mighty, the Lord mighty in battle;" the Lord Jesus, victorious over sin, death, and hell. Therefore we say, and with holy transport we repeat it, "Lift up your heads, O ye gates; and be ye lift up, ye everlasting doors; and the King of glory shall come in." And if any ask, "Who is the King of glory?" to heaven and earth we proclaim aloud—"The Lord of hosts;" all-conquering Messiah, Head over every creature, the Leader of the armies of Jehovah, "He is the King of glory." Even so, glory be to thee, O Lord most high! Amen. Hallelujah. —*Horne.*

Why is the song repeated? Why are the everlasting gates invited to lift up their heads a second time? We may not pretend here, or in any place, to know all the meaning of the divine Psalms. But what if the repetition of the verse was meant to put us in mind that our Saviour's ascension will be repeated also? He will not indeed die any more; death can no more have any dominion over him; "there remaineth no more sacrifice for sin." Neither of course can he rise again any more. But as he will come again at the end of the world, to judge the quick and the dead, so after that descent he will have to ascend again. And I say, this second ascension may be signified by the psalmist calling on the everlasting doors to lift up their heads a second time, and make way for the King of glory. Now observe the answer made this second time, "*Who is the King of glory? The Lord strong and mighty, the Lord mighty in battle. Lift up your heads, O ye gates; even lift them up, ye everlasting doors; and the King of glory shall come in. Who is this King of glory? The Lord of hosts, he is the King of glory.*" Before it was "*the Lord strong and mighty, the Lord mighty in battle;*" now it is "*The Lord of hosts.*" Christ ascending the first time, to intercede for us at his Father's right hand, is called "*The Lord mighty in battle.*" But Christ, ascending the second time, after the world hath been judged, and the good and bad separated for ever, is called "*the Lord of hosts.*" Why this difference in his divine titles? We may reverently take it, that it signifies to us the difference between his first and second coming down to earth, his first and second ascension into heaven. As in other respects his first coming was in great humility, so in this, that he came, in all appearance, alone. The angels were indeed waiting round him, but not visibly, not in glory. "He trode the wine-press alone, and of the people there was none with him." He wrestled with death, hell, and Satan alone. Alone he rose from the dead: alone, as far as man could see, he went up to heaven. Thus he showed himself "the Lord mighty in battle," mighty in that single combat which he, as our champion, our David, victoriously maintained against our great enemy. But when he shall come down and go up the second time, he will show himself "the Lord of hosts." Instead of coming down alone in mysterious silence, as in his wonderful incarnation, he will be followed by all the armies of heaven. "The Lord my God will come, and all his saints with him." "The Lord cometh with ten thousand of his saints." "The Son of Man will come in the glory of his Father, and all the holy angels with him." "Thousand thousands will stand around him, and ten thousand times ten thousand will minister unto him." Instead of the silence of that quiet chamber at Nazareth, and of the holy Virgin's womb, there will be the voice of the archangel and the trump of God accompanying him. Thus he will come down as the Lord of hosts, and as the Lord of hosts he will ascend again to his Father. After the judgment, he will pass again through the everlasting doors, with a greater company than before; for he will lead along with him, into the heavenly habitation, all those who shall have been raised from their graves and found worthy. Hear how the awful sight is described by one who will doubtless have a high place in that day near the Judge. The great apostle and prophet, St. Paul, says, "The Lord himself shall descend from heaven with a shout; and the dead in Christ shall rise first: then we which are alive and remain shall be caught up together with them in the clouds, to meet the Lord in the air, and so shall we ever be with the Lord."—*Keble.*

PSALM XXV.

The first of the alphabetical or acrostic psalms; on which class of psalms Dr. Binnie remarks:—The alphabetical psalms—the *psalmi abcedarii*, as the Latin fathers called them

—are nine in number; namely, Psalms ix. and x., xxv. and xxxiv., xxxvii., cxi. and cxii., cxix., cxlv. Perhaps the two that stand first should be marked as doubtful, for the acrostic is very imperfect; but an alphabetical arrangement is distinctly traceable, beginning with the first verse of the ninth psalm, and running on to the end of the tenth, two verses generally going to each letter of the alphabet. The circumstance that the two psalms are linked together so as to form one acrostic poem will explain the fact, so unusual in the First Book, that Psalm x. is unfurnished with a superscription. Doubtless, both psalms are from David's pen.

The twenty-fifth and thirty-fourth, both "psalms of David," form a pair of another sort. They are identical in structure, each consisting of twenty-two verses, being one for every letter of the Hebrew alphabet; with this curious peculiarity (found in both psalms), that one letter—*Vau*—is awanting, and the number is made up by the addition of a supplementary verse, having for its initial letter *Pe*, which is thus used a second time.

The hundred and eleventh and hundred and twelfth constitute a third pair, corresponding the one to the other, both in structure and theme.

The thirty-seventh, a "psalm of David," consists of forty verses. The acrostic is complete, two verses generally going to each letter. In the hundred and forty-fifth, also ascribed to David, there are twenty-one verses—one for every letter except *Nun*, which, for some unknown reason, is lacking. The hundred and nineteenth, as is well known, contains two-and-twenty stanzas of eight verses each. As the acrostic dominates in every verse, each letter occurs eight times over.

This acrostic way of writing is not confined to the Psalms; it is found both in the Proverbs and Lamentations. The Eulogy of the Virtuous Woman (Prov. xxxi. 10-31) is a regular acrostic of twenty-two verses. So also are the first and second chapters of the Lamentations. In the third chapter, which is likewise a long acrostic, there are three verses to each letter, making sixty-six in all. If it should seem strange that the heart-broken prophet restrained the flow of lamentations uttered because of the desolation of Zion within the limits of such an artificial kind of verse, it may be worth while to refer to our poet-laureate's *In Memoriam*. The measure chosen seems at first intolerably monotonous for a long poem; nevertheless the poet finds it well suited to express the sadness and desolation of his heart.

I cannot help thinking it is a pity that, except in the single instance of the hundred and nineteenth, no hint of their existence should have been suffered to appear in our Authorized Version. I will not take it upon me to affirm, with Ewald, that no version is faithful in which the acrostic is suppressed; but I do think that the existence of such a remarkable style of composition ought to be indicated in one way or another, and that some useful purposes are served by its being actually reproduced in the translation. No doubt there are difficulties in the way. The Hebrew alphabet differs widely from any of those now employed in Europe. Besides differences of a more fundamental kind, the Hebrew has only twenty-two letters for our twenty-six; and of the twenty-two a considerable number have no fellows in ours. An exact reproduction of a Hebrew acrostic in an English version is therefore impossible. The divergence between the alphabets is so great that it seems vain even to follow in English the *order* of the Hebrew letters. Dr. Delitzsch has industriously made an attempt of the sort in his German version, but with little success. The only feasible method is to omit from our alphabet the four letters that are of least frequent use, and make the two-and-twenty that remain stand for the two-and-twenty letters of the Hebrew. This may not suffice to meet the demands of a pedantic accuracy, but it will exhibit to the English reader the structure of the original, which is all that I propose.—*Binnie.*

The only lesson which the use of the *alphabetic* form may teach is this: that the Holy Spirit was willing to throw his words into all the moulds of human thought and speech; and whatever ingenuity man may exhibit in intellectual efforts, he should consecrate these to his Lord, making him the "*Alpha and Omega*" of his pursuits.—*Andrew A. Bonar.*

1. *Unto thee, O Lord, do I lift up my soul.* It is not easy to do this. We are naturally sluggish and grovelling. Who has not reason to acknowledge

with shame and sorrow, "my soul cleaveth unto the dust?" It is easy enough, in duty, to lift up our hands, and our eyes, and our voices; but it is another thing to come even to his seat, to enter into the secret of his tabernacle, and to hold intercourse with the God of heaven. And yet, without this, what is devotion? And how unanswerable will all our services be to the requisition of him who is a spirit, and seeketh such to worship him as worship him in spirit and in truth! And without this a real Christian is no more satisfied than God . . . And this marks the spiritual worshipper. He is not distinguished by always enjoying liberty and fervour in his holy exercises; but he mourns the want of them. . . . It is the spirituality of religion that befriends enjoyment. Nothing yields us pleasure but in proportion as the heart is engaged in the pursuit. How dull and how tiresome are those tasks, in which

"In vain to heaven we raise our cries,
And leave our souls behind."

But it is good to draw *near* to God. Then there is a sacred charm that keeps our thoughts from wandering. Then we attend on the Lord without distraction. Then we feel no weariness of Spirit. We call the Sabbath a delight. We find his words, and eat them. And our meditation of him is sweet.

And when such a worshipper comes forth, he will be ready to say to all he meets, "That which we have seen and heard declare we unto you, that ye also may have fellowship with us: and truly our fellowship is with the Father, and with his Son Jesus Christ." And *his* recommendations are likely to have some effect. For his profiting will appear unto all men. His face shines. His heart speaks. His life speaks. His character speaks. He must be impressive and influential. He will be felt—in the family—in the church—and in the world. He cannot but do good, even without pretension, without effort—

"When such a man, familiar with the skies,
Has filled his urn where those pure waters rise;
And once more mingles with us meaner things;
'Tis e'en as if an angel shook his wings—
Immortal fragrance fills the circuit wide,
Which tells us whence his treasures are supplied." —*Jay.*

16-18. *Turn thee unto me,* &c. Surely this book is addressed to the heart; and requires sensibility rather than talent to understand and explain it. How tender here is the language of David. And how instructive too. He was a sufferer, though a king and a man eminently godly. And his sorrows were not superficial, but deep and depressing—"the sorrows of the heart." And while hoping for their diminution, they were "enlarged." But he is a petitioner, as well as a sufferer; and those sorrows will never injure us that bring us to God. Three things he prays for. *First,* Deliverance. This we are allowed to desire, consistently with resignation to the divine will. But we must seek it not from creatures, but from God. "Call upon me in the day of trouble." *Secondly,* Notice. A kind look from God is desirable at any time, in any circumstances; but in affliction and pain, it is like life from the dead. Nothing cuts like the neglect of a friend in distress; nothing soothes like his calls and inquiries, and sympathies and tears. But to say—Thou, God, seest me:—to be assured that he is attentive to my condition and is smiling through the cloud; fills the heart, even in tribulation, with a peace that passeth all understanding. *Thirdly,* Pardon. Trials are apt to revive a sense of guilt. However the Christian may feel his sorrows, he will feel his sins much more. These, these are the burden, and the grief.

This was David's meaning; and I hope I can make it my own. If it be thy pleasure release me from my complaint. If not, and the distress is continued to try me, be near to afford me a sensible manifestation of thy favour; let me see thy countenance; let me hear thy voice saying, "I remember thee still." Or if this be denied, and I have no claim upon thee for such an indulgence, let me, for the Redeemer's sake, be absolved and justified. Remove my guilt, whatever becomes of my grief—grief *then* cannot be penal—cannot be injurious—

"If sin be pardoned, I'm secure,
Death hath no sting beside:
The law gives sin its damning power;
But Christ my ransom died."—*Jay.*

PSALM XXVI.

From the strength of the protestations of integrity and innocence here found, some have thought that this psalm must have its fulfilment in

Christ alone, and could not be at all applied to David. Fry's first remark is that "a psalm, commencing with a demand for justice at the tribunal of the Almighty, must necessarily belong to our righteous Advocate." Amyrald uses language nearly as strong. But Horne clears the matter sufficiently when he says that "we have here an appeal to God in behalf of injured innocence. . . . A trial of this sort might be desired by David, and may be desired by men, like him, conscious of their integrity as to the particular crimes charged upon them by the malice of their enemies. Christ alone could ask such a trial at large, as being equally free from every kind and degree of sin, and certain of receiving additional lustre from the increasing heat of the furnace." No doubt David, in his struggles for his crown and in the opposition of wicked men, was a type of Christ, and an example of all believers who should come after him. But under the charges brought against him, he would not do otherwise, if he spoke at all, than maintain his innocence.—*Plumer.*

1. *Judge me, O Jehovah.* A solemn appeal to the just tribunal of the heart-searching God, warranted by the circumstances of the writer, so far as regarded the particular offences with which he was wrongly charged. Worried and worn out by the injustice of men, the innocent spirit flies from its false accusers to the throne of Eternal Right. He had need have a clear case who dares to carry his suit into the King's Bench of heaven. Such an appeal as this is not to be rashly made on any occasion; and as to the whole of our walk and conversation, it should never be made at all, except as we are justified in Christ Jesus: a far more fitting prayer for a sinful mortal is the petition, "Enter not into judgment with thy servant."—*For I have walked in mine integrity.* He held integrity as his principle, and walked in it as his practice. David had not used any traitorous or unrighteous means to gain the crown, or to keep it; he was conscious of having been guided by the noblest principles of honour in all his actions with regard to Saul and his family. What a comfort it is to have the approbation of one's own conscience! If there be peace within the soul, the blustering storms of slander which howl around us are of little consideration. When the little bird in my bosom sings a merry song, it is no matter to me if a thousand owls hoot at me from without.—*Spurgeon.*

3. *Thy loving-kindness is before mine eyes.* And it may be well to follow David; and to keep the loving-kindness of God before our eyes also. This should be done in four ways:—First, As a subject of contemplation. The mind will be active; and it is our wisdom to regulate and sanctify our thoughts. People complain of the difficulty they feel in fixing their minds: but the duty would become easier by use—and surely they never can be at a loss for a theme. Let them take his loving-kindness and set it before their eyes. Let them observe it as it appears in the promises of his Word; in the history of his church; in their own experience. Let them pass from the instances of his loving-kindness to the qualities of it. Let them dwell upon its earliness, and fulness, and extensiveness, and seasonableness, and constancy.—Secondly, As a source of encouragement. We shall feel our want of it under a sense of our guilt, and unworthiness, and continued imperfections. It will give us everlasting consolation and good hope through grace; and boldness and access with confidence. We shall want it in our afflictions: nothing is so desirable in our sufferings as to see, not only the *hand*, but the *kindness* of God in them.—Thirdly, As an excitement to praise. It is afflicting to think how little the loving-kindness of God is acknowledged by those who are constantly partaking of it. How lamentable, says Leighton, is it, that a world so full of God's mercy should be so empty of his glory!—Lastly, We should keep his loving-kindness before our eyes as an example for our imitation. The Scripture calls upon us to be followers of God as dear children. And in what are we to resemble him? His moral, and not his natural perfections;—to be faithful as he is faithful—to be holy as he is holy—to be patient, and forgiving, and kind, like himself. You would do well to keep in view some of your fellow-creatures who feel that it is more blessed to give than to receive. Think of a Howard, a Thornton, a Reynolds. But God is love. We cannot equal him, but it is our happiness to resemble. He that dwelleth in love, dwelleth in God, and God in him.—*Jay.*

6. *I will wash mine hands in innocency.* The threefold Jehovah of the section is so divided, that it opens it, and concludes it, and stands here in the first verse of the second strophe,—the strophe of the *ascent* from morality to piety. *The hands* are considered, in the first clause, as the instruments of action: *innocence* is the spiritual water; compare Ps. lxxii. 13, where *the washing of the hands in innocency* corresponds to *cleansing the heart;* Job ix. 30, where instead of *innocency* there stands "potash;" and De. xxi. 6, and Mat. xxvii. 34, where the hands were washed in protestation of innocence. The psalmist describes himself as one *integer vitæ scelerisque purus.—Hengstenberg.*

9. *Gather not my soul with sinners.* He that would not be found amongst sinners in the other world, must take heed that he do not frequent their company in this. Those whom the constable finds wandering with vagrants, may be sent with them to the house of correction. "Lord," said a good woman on her death-bed, when in some doubt of her salvation, "send me not to hell amongst wicked men, for thou knowest I never loved their company all my life long." David deprecates their future doom upon the like ground, and argueth it as a sign of his sincerity: "*I have not sat with vain persons, neither will I go in with dissemblers. I have hated the congregation of evil-doers; and will not sit with the wicked. . . O gather not my soul with sinners.*" Lord, I have not loved the wicked so well as to sit with them for a little time, and shall I live with them for ever? I have not lain amongst them rotting on the earth; and wilt thou gather my soul with those sticks for the unquenchable fire of hell? Lord, I have been so far from liking, that thou knowest I have loathed the congregation of evil-doers. Do not I hate them that hate thee? Yea, I hate them with perfect hatred; and shall thy friends fare as thy foes? I appeal to thy Majesty, that my great comfort is in thy chosen. I rejoice only to be amongst thy children here, and shall I be excluded their company hereafter? "*O do not gather my soul with sinners,*" for the wine-press of thine eternal anger! Marcion, the heretic, seeing Polycarp, wondered that he would not own him. Do you not know me, Polycarp? Yea, saith Polycarp, "*Scio te esse primogenitum diaboli;*" "I know thee to be the first-born of the devil," and so despised him. —*George Swinnock.*

PSALM XXVII.

1. *Whom shall I fear?* The interrogation shows how highly David esteemed the divine protection, as he thus boldy exults against all his enemies and dangers; nor assuredly do we ascribe due homage to God, unless, trusting to his promised aid, we dare to boast of the certainty of our safety. Weighing, as it were, in scales the whole power of earth and hell, David accounts it all lighter than a feather, and considers God alone as far outweighing the whole.

Let us learn, therefore, to put such a value on God's power to protect us as to put to flight all our fears. Not that the minds of the faithful can, by reason of the infirmity of the flesh, be at all times devoid of fear; but immediately recovering courage, let us, from the high tower of our confidence, look down upon all our dangers with contempt. Those who have never tasted the grace of God tremble, because they refuse to rely upon him, and imagine that he is often incensed against them, or at least far removed from them. But with the promises of God before our eyes, and the grace which they offer, our unbelief does him grievous wrong, if we do not with unshrinking courage boldly set him against all our enemies. When God, therefore, kindly allures us to himself, and assures us that he will take care of our safety, since we have embraced his promises, or because we believe him to be faithful, it is meet that we highly extol his power, that it may ravish our hearts with admiration of himself. We must mark well this comparison, What are all creatures to God? Moreover, we must extend this confidence still farther, in order to banish all fears from our consciences, like Paul, who, when speaking of his eternal salvation, boldly exclaims, "If God be for us, who can be against us?"—*Calvin.*

4, 5. *One thing have I desired of the Lord,* &c. This (David's remarkable love for the tabernacle) was one of the strongly-marked features of his character. It impressed all who knew him, and, when he was gathered to his fathers, the generation that came after continued to speak with affection of "David and all his afflictions," all his anxious labours for the house of God—

how he lamented for the ark all the years it lay neglected at Kirjath-jearim —how he coveted its presence in his own city, as the fairest jewel in his diadem—how he pitched for it a tabernacle, and desired to build for it a temple. If David ever had a ruling passion, it was his zeal, his consuming zeal, for the house of God. He could say with rare truth, "The zeal of thine house hath eaten me up." How strongly is this expressed in the twenty-seventh psalm:—

One thing have I desired of Jehovah,
That will I seek after;
That I may dwell in the house of Jehovah,
All the days of my life;
To behold the beauty of Jehovah,
And to inquire in his temple.
For he shall conceal me in his tabernacle
In the day of evil:
He shall hide me in the hiding-place of his tent;
He shall set me upon a rock.

In David's position, and with his love for the tabernacle service, an uninspired poet would, to a certainty, have so framed his hymns that, however suitable to the typical dispensation, they would have become obsolete when the temple was given to the flames, and the cumbrous ritual, in which the fathers of the Old Testament worshipped God, was finally supplanted by a system of simple and spiritual ordinances. But David "spake as he was moved by the Holy Ghost;" and, accordingly, in his character of psalmist, we may say of him, with Augustine, that "although he lived under the Old Testament, he was not a man of the Old Testament." He seized on the spiritual elements and aspects of the tabernacle service, and wove these alone into the fabric of his songs; so that when "the things that might be shaken" were removed, the Psalms were found to belong to "the things which could not be shaken," and remained fixed in the worship of the catholic church.

14. *Wait on the Lord.* Thirty years ago, before "the Lord caused me to wander from my father's house," and from my native place, I put my mark upon this passage in Isaiah, "I am the Lord: they shall not be ashamed that wait for me." Of the many books I now possess, the Bible that bears this mark is the only one of them all that belonged to me at that time. It now lies before me; and I find that, although the hair which was then dark as night, has meanwhile become "a sable silvered," the ink which marked this text has grown into intensity of blackness as the time advanced, corresponding with, and in fact recording, the growing intensity of the conviction, that "they shall not be ashamed that wait for Thee." I believed it then; but I know it now; and I can write *probatum est* with my whole heart over against the symbol which that mark is to me of my ancient faith.

Looking back through the long period which has passed since I set my mark to these words—a period which forms the best and brightest, as well as the most trying and conflicting of all men's lives; it is a joy to me to be able to say, "I have waited for Thee, and have not been ashamed. Under many perilous circumstances, in many most trying scenes, amid faintings within and fears without, and under sorrows that rend the heart, and troubles that crush it down, I have waited for Thee; and, lo, I stand this day as one not ashamed."

Old scholars and divines were wont to write or paint up in their studies some favourite sentence from the sages of old, or some chosen text of Scripture. Those inclined to follow this custom could do no better than write up this one word, "WAIT." It is but a monosyllable; but it is fuller of meaning than any other word in the language, and it is applicable to all ages, and to all circumstances. At the first slight view, merely to "wait," seems so simple a thing, as scarcely entitled to be called a grace; and yet larger promises are made to it than to any other grace, except to faith; and hardly, indeed, with that exception, for the grace of "waiting" is part of the grace of faith,—is a form of faith,—is, as some would describe it, an effect of faith; or, more strictly, one of its most fruitful manifestations.—Kitto's *Daily Bible Illustrations.*

PSALM XXVIII.

The contents of the psalm throughout apply very well to David during the time of Absalom's rebellion, when, to all appearance, the design of God was that the lots of the righteous and the wicked should be exchanged; the people were brought into danger on account of the king; and the enemies especially were those who "spoke peace to their neighbours, while mischief was in their hearts." But, in the absence of all special historical circumstances, it is in the highest degree probable that the design of David in composing the psalm, was to draw out a form of prayer, grounded on his own experience at this time, for the use of his successors who should walk in the footsteps of his righteousness: compare Ps. xviii. 50. If this be the case, it is manifest, at the same time, that the psalm in reality possesses a didactic and hortatory character:—the righteous king, in a time of severe trouble, desires to set before his eyes the righteous judgment of God, which will not permit the righteous to be involved in the lot of the wicked, nor the wicked to go unpunished; to be calm and composed in dependence on this; and to wait with confident expectation for the help of God. This didactic tendency is particularly obvious in the fifth verse, where the form of address to God is abandoned.

The assertion of Ewald and Hitzig, that the portion from the 6th to the 9th verse was first written after the danger had gone past, is based on the false idea that the psalm has an individual character; proceeds from mistaking the nature of the transitions in the psalm; and overlooks the truth, that faith is the substance—the *ὑπόστασις*—of things hoped for, Heb. xi. 1.—*Hengstenberg.*

1. *Unto thee will I cry, O Lord my rock; be not silent to me*, &c. When we pray aright we will be concerned to get an answer in peace. Whoever leaves his prayer as the ostrich leaves her egg in the sand, and cares no more for it, does not pray at all. When Elijah prayed for rain, he sent his servant to "look toward the sea," to see if it was coming. Scott: "While others are troubling their fellow-creatures with unavailing complaints, believers should, under distresses, cry the more earnestly 'to the Rock of their salvation:' and they should not rest till they have received some satisfactory token that their prayers are heard; for if the Lord could refuse to answer them, their case would resemble that of those who have perished in their sins, to whose agonizing cries no gracious answer will be made for ever." Men can be in no worse state than to be where prayer is not heard.—*Plumer.*

PSALM XXIX.

Expositors have spoken confidently, yet diversely, as to the occasion of this psalm. Clarke: "It was probably written to commemorate the abundant rain which fell in the days of David, after the heavens had been shut up for three years, 2 Sa. xxi. 1-10;" Patrick: "This psalm seems to have been composed by David after some extraordinary great thunder, lightning, and rain: whereby (it is probable) God had so discomfited his enemies, and put their forces into such disorder, that he easily got the victory over them." With him agrees Dodd, who cites attention to the history given in 2 Sa. viii. in illustration. Pool favours the same view; and Morison mentions it with respect. Mudge is decidedly of the same opinion.

After his return from Palestine, M'Cheyne gave to Dr. James Hamilton of London an interpretation of this psalm, drawn from the natural scenery and the course of storms in the mountains of that land. . . . He says that in this psalm "the strength of Jehovah is celebrated, and the exemplification of it is evidently taken from a thunderstorm in Lebanon." Whatever may be thought of the correctness of this view, none can read either of these writers (M'Cheyne or Hamilton) without being struck with the exceedingly great beauty of the illustrations offered, and of the exquisite taste displayed in the method of presenting it.

But Hengstenberg says, "There is no ground for the idea that the psalm was occasioned by the sight of a thunderstorm. 'The freshness of the painting, the vigorous conceptions, and the rapid transition of the whole,' will give rise to this view only when low ideas are entertained of the power of poetry;" Alexander: "The superficial notion that this psalm is merely a description of a thunderstorm, or of Jehovah as the God of thunder, may be corrected by observing that the last verse gives the key-note to the whole composition."—*Plumer.*

It seems to be the general opinion of modern annotators, that this psalm is meant to express the glory of God as heard in the pealing thunder, and seen in an equinoctial tornado. Just as the eighth psalm is to be read by moonlight, when the stars are bright; as the nineteenth needs the rays of the rising sun to bring out its beauty, so this can be best rehearsed beneath the black wing of tempest, by the glare of the lightning, or amid that dubious dusk which heralds the war of elements. The verses march to the tune of thunderbolts. God is everywhere conspicuous, and all the earth is hushed by the majesty of his presence. The word of God in the law and gospel is here also depicted in its majesty of power. True ministers are sons of thunder, and the voice of God in Christ Jesus is full of majesty. Thus we have God's works and God's words joined together; let no man put them asunder by a false idea that theology and science can by any possibility oppose each other. We may, perhaps, by a prophetic glance, behold in this psalm the dread tempests of the latter days and the security of the elect people.

The first two verses are a call to adoration. From ver. 3—10 the path of the tempest is traced, the attributes of God's word are rehearsed, and God magnified in all the terrible grandeur of his power; and the last verse sweetly closes the scene with the assurance that the omnipotent Jehovah will give both strength and peace to his people. Let heaven and earth pass away, the Lord will surely bless his people.—*Spurgeon*.

The 29th Psalm surpasses all descriptions of a thunderstorm, including those of Lucretius, Virgil, and Byron, admirable as all those are. That of Lucretius is a hubbub of matter; the lightning is a mere elemental discharge, not a barbed arrow of vengeance; his system will not permit a powerful personification. Virgil's picture in his Georgics is superb, but has been somewhat vulgarized to our feelings by many imitations, and the old commonplaces about "Father Jove and his thunderbolts." Byron does not give us that overwhelming sense of unity which is the poetry of a thunderstorm —cloud answers to cloud, and mountain to mountain; it is a brisk and animated controversy in the heavens, but you have not the feeling of all nature bowing below the presence of one avenging power, with difficulty restrained from breaking forth to consume—of one voice creating the sounds—of one form hardly concealed by the darkness—of one hand grasping the livid reins of the passing chariot—and of one sigh of relief testifying to the feelings of gratitude on the part of nature and of man —when, in the dispersion of the storm, the one mysterious power and presence has passed away. It is this godhood of thunder which the Hebrew poet has expressed, and no other poet has. Like repeated peals, the name of the Lord sounds down all the 29th Psalm, solemnizing and harmonizing it all. . . . Thus are all the phenomena of the storm—from the agitated waters of the sea to the crashing cedars of Lebanon—from the depths of Bashan's forest, bared to its every fallen leaf, and every serpent's hole, in the glare of the lightning, to the premature calving of the hind—from the awe of the quaking wilderness, to the solemn peace and whispered worship of God's people in his temple—bound together by the name and presence of God as by a chain of living fire,—

> "When science, from creation's face,
> Enchantment's veil withdraws,
> What lovely visions yield their place
> To cold material laws."

True, but not merely *lovely*, but dreadful visions recede before the dawn of science; while the rainbow becomes less beautiful, the thunder becomes less sublime. But this poet seems not to feel, that, when science reaches its noonday, those visions shall return, for, indeed, they are something better than mere visions. The thunder, after all, *is* the voice of God. Every particle of that tempest is an instant emanation from a present Deity. Analyze electricity as strictly as you can, the question recurs, "What is it, whence comes it?" and the answer must be, From an inconceivable, illimitable power behind and within those elements—in one word, from God.—Gilfillan's *Bards of the Bible*.

3. *The voice of the Lord is upon the waters; the God of glory thundereth: the Lord is upon many waters.* The "Jehovah" of the first clause is supplemented in the second, and the "water" in the third. Thunder is "the voice of the Lord" only for believers. An ungodly Hebrew would assuredly not consider it as such. Every gentle breath of air is also the voice of the Lord: all nature proclaims his glory: God speaks in everything to men. But because our ears are dull of hearing, that especially is called his voice by which he speaks in loudest tones, and proclaims to us, in spite of all unwillingness on our part to hear, his omnipotence and his majesty. The "waters" are the clouds, "the waters which are above the firmament," Gen. i. 7; "the dark waters," Ps. xviii. 11; "the multitude of waters,"

Jer. x. 13: compare Ps. lxxvii. 17; Job xxxvi. 28. Several interpreters apply the term to the waters of the sea and rivers. But the word "many," in the last clause, is decisive against this: it shows that the waters form a part of the storm itself; for only in this case is their multiplicity of importance to the object in view, inasmuch as it serves to bring forward the greatness of God in the storm. The designation of God as "the God of glory," points back to ver. 1, 2, and shows that the description which begins in our verse, serves as a basis to the exhortation which is there addressed to the angels to praise the glory of God.—*Hengstenberg*.

David selects only those works of God which prove not only that the world was at first created by him, and is governed by his power, but which also awaken the torpid, and drag them, as it were, in spite of themselves, humbly to adore him; as even Horace was compelled, though he was not only a heathen poet, but an Epicurean and a vile contemner of Deity, to say of himself in one of his odes,—

"A fugitive from heaven and prayer,
I mocked at all religious fear,
Deep scienced in the mazy lore
Of mad philosophy; but now
Hoist sail, and back my voyage plough
To that blest harbour which I left before.

"For, lo! that awful heavenly Sire
Who frequent cleaves the clouds with fire,
Parent of day, immortal Jove;
Late through the floating fields of air,
The face of heaven serene and fair,
His thund'ring steeds and winged chariot drove," &c.
—*Hor. lib.* 1, *ode* 34, *Dr. Francis' Trans.*

Experience, too, tells us that those who are most daring in their contempt of God are most afraid of thunderings, storms, and such like violent commotions. With great propriety, therefore, does the prophet invite our attention to these instances which strike the rude and insensible with some sense of the existence of a God, and rouse them to action, however sluggish and regardless they are. He says not that the sun rises from day to day and sheds abroad his life-giving beams, nor that the rain gently descends to fertilize the earth with its moisture; but he brings forward thunders, violent tempests, and such things as smite the hearts of men with dread by their violence. God, it is true, speaks in all his creatures, but here the prophet mentions those sounds which rouse us from our drowsiness, or rather our lethargy, by the loudness of their noise. We have said that this language is chiefly directed to those who, with stubborn recklessness, cast from them, as far as they can, all thoughts of God. The very figures which he uses sufficiently declare, that David's design was to subdue by fear the obstinacy which yields not willingly otherwise. Thrice he repeats that God's voice is heard in great and violent tempests, and in the subsequent verse he adds, that it is full of power and majesty.—*Calvin.*

10, 11.

Jehovah sate throned above the flood:
Yea Jehovah sitteth throned a King for ever.
Jehovah giveth strength to his people.
Jehovah blesseth his people with peace.

FLOOD, *i.e.* the Deluge. The word here employed (מַבּוּל) occurs nowhere else, except in the story of the flood (Gen. vi.—xi.), and therefore refers, I cannot help thinking, to that great act of judgment, and not merely to a recent inundation caused by the storm, the mountain-torrents having been swollen by the rain, and having flooded the country. This might have happened. But the selection of so peculiar a word, as well as the fact that the verb is in the past tense, "*sate* throned," makes the other more probable.

Very beautiful is the conclusion of the psalm. If, in his heavenly temple above, all that are therein ascribe "glory" to God, upon earth too he manifested that glory. He sat as a King when he sent the flood of water to destroy the earth. He sits now, and for ever will sit, as King. As then he saved the righteous man from death, so now he watches over his people: for Jehovah is the God of Israel. It was he who, when the storm waxed strong, gave it its strength; it was he who, when it was hushed, spread over earth, and sea, and sky, the sweet Sabbath stillness of peace. And he whose almighty power was seen in the march of the tempest, whose voice was heard in its wildest uproar, and whose word stilled its fiercest war, shall he not give both strength and peace? Yea, Jehovah who is strong and mighty, will give his own strength to his people. And he who is the Prince of Peace will bless his people with peace. Thus the psalm begins, as Delitzsch says, with a *Gloria in excelsis*, and ends with a *Pax in terris*.—*Perowne.*

PSALM XXX.

Title. A psalm. A song of dedication (*for*) *the house. By David.* The construction, *house of David*, although not ungrammatical, is forced, as that idea would, according to usage, have been otherwise expressed in Hebrew. This construction has moreover given rise to the false notion, that the psalm has reference to the king's own dwelling, whereas *the house*, as an absolute phrase, can only mean the house of God. The historical occasion of the psalm is furnished by the narrative in 2 Sa. xxiv. and 1 Ch. xxi. David's presumption in numbering the people had been punished by a pestilence, which raged until the destroying angel had, in answer to the king's prayer, been required to sheathe his sword. The spot where this indication of God's mercy had been given, was immediately purchased by David, and consecrated by the erection of an altar, upon which he offered sacrifices and received the divine approbation in the gift of fire from heaven (1 Ch. xxi. 26). This place the king expressly calls the house of God (1 Ch. xxii. 1), either in the wide sense of the patriarchal *Bethel*, or as the designated site of the temple for which he immediately commenced his preparations (1 Ch. xxii. 2), and in reference to which this psalm might well be called a *song of dedication*, although naturally more full of the pestilence, and the sin which caused it, than of the sanctuary yet to be erected.—*J. A. Alexander.*

4. *Give thanks at the remembrance of his holiness.* Memory in this connection does not mean the power, or the act of remembering, but that which is remembered when we think of God, to wit, his glorious perfections, which are summed up in his *holiness.*—*J. A. Alexander.*

Since the fall, this attribute, which renders God so amiable in himself, and which draws forth the highest praises of heaven, makes him unlovely to an apostate creature. There is nothing the sinner thinks of with so much dislike as a perfection that justifies all his fears, and opposes all his inclinations and pursuits. What an enemy the world naturally is to the holiness of God may be seen in the practice of the heathens. Among all the heroes they deified, they advanced none for those qualities which approach the most nearly to it; but frequently for passions the most remote from it; and at best only for some physical power, valued, or useful in the concerns of this life. Esculapius was deified for his skill in curing diseases. Bacchus for the use of the grape. Vulcan for his operations in fire. Hercules for his destroying monsters. But not one of them all was advanced to this honour for the virtue of holiness, as if this property was beneath their notice in the formation of a deity; or they loved a god better that had nothing to do with it. It was upon this principle that they who are now saints "would" once themselves have "none of him;" and really said unto God, "Depart from us; we desire not the knowledge of thy ways." What a blessed evidence is it in their favour that they can now "glory in his holy name;" and "sing and give thanks at the remembrance of his holiness!" But such is the change they have experienced that they do contemplate him with pleasure as holy in all his ways, and righteous in all his works. It is a relief, a satisfaction to their minds in every perplexity in nature or providence, that the Judge of all the earth must do right. They delight in the law of God, which is holy, just, and good, after the inward man. The gospel appears to their minds glorious, "because therein is the righteousness of God revealed from faith to faith; that he might be just, and the justifier of him which believeth in Jesus." This attribute now smiles upon them. They have a vast interest and hope in it. As he is holy they can depend upon his truth; and are assured of the fulfilment of his word. They know that he who has said, "I will abundantly pardon," "I will never leave thee nor forsake thee," is a God that cannot lie. Yes, says the Christian, since he who loves me is purity itself, and his influence is almighty, he will sprinkle clean water upon me, and *I* shall be clean. He will destroy in me the sin which he infinitely hates. He will make me a *partaker* of his holiness, and render me meet for the inheritance of the saints in light.

6. *In my prosperity I said, I shall never be moved.* The deepest insight into the dangers of prosperity, and the necessity which thence arises for affliction, had previously been exhibited in the *law:* compare, for example, Deut.

xxxii. 15, "But Jeshurun waxed fat and kicked: thou art waxen fat, thou art grown thick, thou art covered with fatness; then he forsook God which made him, and lightly esteemed the Rock of his salvation:" but especially Deut. viii. 11-18, where almost every word agrees exactly with the case before us: "Beware that thou forget not the Lord thy God, lest when thou hast eaten and art full, and thine heart be lifted up, and thou say in thine heart, My power and the might of mine hand hath gotten me this wealth; but thou shalt remember the Lord thy God, for he it is that giveth thee power to get wealth." Besides Israel (compare Hos. xiii. 16, "According to their pasture so were they filled; they were filled, and their heart was exalted; therefore have they forgotten Me") and David, we have in the Old Testament a remarkable example of the dangers of prosperity in the case of Hezekiah, who stood so nobly when in adversity. These dangers are not only incident to worldly prosperity, but are also to be dreaded in a season of spiritual enjoyment. J. Arnd says: "Behold! we have here a very affecting warning in the example of beloved David, which should teach us to fear God during our days of prosperity, and never to be confident, or to put our dependence on earthly things. How did the prophets preach against the mighty kings and nations in their prophecies against Babylon and others! All those mighty nations, cities, and kings who depended on their own might and riches, have been broken and laid waste, and levelled with the ground; while, on the other hand, all who acted humbly, feared God, and cherished a sense of dependence on his grace, have been maintained, and shall continue to exist for ever. The sentence also is to be understood in a spiritual sense: many a one is so strong in faith, so spiritually minded, so joyful, so full of confidence, that he bids defiance to the devil and the world, and says, with David, "I will not fear though hundreds of thousands were encamped against me." But when our beloved God tries us a little, when he withdraws from us his grace, O then all is over with us, and we are ready to sink into hell, and to give up all for lost. This God does, that we may become acquainted with our own weakness, and may know that we are entirely dependent on divine grace." The Berleb. Bib.: "A change is necessary, in order that the soul may be brought to know that its firmness is entirely dependent on the strength which *God* has imparted. If its beautiful day had no evening, if its sun were never darkened, the soul would infallibly ascribe all to its own power and care. But as soon as God withdraws his sensible co-operation, evening and darkness destroy its beautiful day: and it then knows that everything comes from this source and sun, and that everything proceeds from the will of God, and through the working of his grace, without any merit on our own part at all."—*Hengstenberg.*

9. *Shall the dust praise thee? shall it declare thy truth?* It sounds harsh to speak of a misconception of the state of the soul after death, in connection with the name of David, as our author does in his comment on this verse. The true sense seems to be given by himself in the following sentence:—When he says that whatever we are to do for making known God *on earth*, must be done ere we descend to the grave (Ps. vi. 5; lxxxviii. 10, 12; Is. xxxviii. 18, 19). On the whole subject of the state of knowledge in early times on the future world, the reader is referred to the editor's preface in the first volume on Job.

Calvin *in loco* says, By inquiring in the end of the verse, *Shall the dust praise thee?* he does not mean that the dead are altogether deprived of power to praise God. If the faithful, while encumbered with a burden of flesh, exercise themselves in this pious duty, how should they desist from it when they are disencumbered and set free from the restraints of the body? It ought to be observed, therefore, that David does not professedly treat of what the dead do, or how they are occupied, but considers only the purpose for which we live in this world, which is this, that we may mutually show forth to one another the glory of God. Having been employed in this exercise to the end of our life, death at length comes upon us, and shuts our mouth.

PSALM XXXI.

The psalmist in dire affliction appeals to his God for help with much confidence and holy importunity, and ere long finds his mind so strengthened that he magnifies the Lord for his great goodness. Some have thought that the occasion in his troubled life which led to this psalm, was the treachery of the men of Keilah, and we have felt much inclined to this conjecture; but after reflection it seems to us that its very mournful tone and its allusion to his iniquity demand a later date, and it may be more satisfactory to illustrate it by the period when Absalom had rebelled, and his courtiers were fled from him, while lying lips spread a thousand malicious rumours against him. It is perhaps quite as well that we have no settled season mentioned, or we might have been so busy applying it to David's case as to forget its suitability to our own.—*Spurgeon.*

2. *Bow down thine ear to me.* Condescend to my low estate; listen to me attentively as one who would hear every word. Heaven with its transcendent glories of harmony might well engross the divine ear, but yet the Lord has an hourly regard to the weakest moanings of his poorest people.—*Spurgeon.*

5. *Into thine hand I commit my spirit.* Our Lord uttered these words on the cross, and this circumstance led many of the old expositors to apply the whole psalm directly to the Messiah. Huss repeated frequently on the way to the stake the words:—"Into thine hands I commend my spirit; thou hast redeemed me, my Lord Jesus, God of truth."

Upon the expression of confidence in the power and faithfulness of God, follows the expression of the singer's resolve. *My spirit* (*ruach*), more than my *soul* or *life* (*nephesh*). It is not only from sickness and death, but from sin and all ghostly enemies, that the man of God would be kept, and therefore he commends to God, not his body or his bodily life alone, but the life of his spirit, which is more precious (compare Is. xxxviii. 16, "life of my spirit"). *I commend* (παρατίθεμαι), *i.e.* place as a *deposit*, intrust. With these words our Lord breathed out his life, Lu. xxiii. 46, as he had before used words from another psalm in his agony on the cross. The first words were from a psalm (Ps. xxii.) which, typically at least, foreshadowed his sufferings; whereas this is not in the same way prophetical. But the Holy One of God, in that last hour of mortal agony, chose these words of one of his servants to express the solemn surrender of his life. And in so doing he gave them a new interpretation. The Jewish singer only meant by them that he put himself and all his hopes into the hands of God. Jesus meant by them, that *by his own act, of his own free will*, he gave up his spirit, and therewith his life, to the Father. Observe how the evangelists carefully choose their expressions: ἀφῆκεν τὸ πνεῦμα, Matt.; παρέδωκεν τὸ πν., John. And they who have died with their Lord have died with the same words on their lips. These were the last words of Polycarp, of Bernard, of Huss, of Jerome of Prague, of Luther, Melancthon, and many others. "Blessed are they," says Luther, "who die not only *for* the Lord, as martyrs, not only *in* the Lord, as all believers, but likewise *with* the Lord, as breathing forth their lives in these words, 'Into thy hand I commend my spirit.'"—*Perowne.*

David again declares his faith to God, and affirms that he had such high thoughts of his providence as to cast all his cares upon it. Whoever commits himself into God's hand and to his guardianship, not only constitutes him the arbiter of life and death to him, but also calmly depends on him for protection amidst all his dangers. The verb is in the future tense, "I will commit," and it unquestionably denotes a continued act, and is therefore fitly translated into the present tense. It is also to be observed that no man can possibly commit his life to God with sincerity but he who considers himself exposed to a thousand deaths, and that his life hangs by a thread, or differs almost nothing from a breath which passes suddenly away. David being thus at the point of despair, leaves nothing to himself to do but this—to go on his way, trusting in God as the keeper and governor of his life. It is marvellous that, although many things distress us all, scarcely one in a hundred is so wise as to commit his life into God's hand. Multitudes live from day to day as merry and careless as if they were in a quiet nest, free from all disturbance; but as soon as they encounter anything to terrify them, they are ready to die for anguish. It thus happens that they never betake themselves to God, either because they deceive themselves with vain delusions, flattering themselves that all will yet be well, or because they are so stricken with dread and stupified with amazement, that they have no desire for his fatherly care. Farther, as various tempests of grief disturb us, and even sometimes throw us down headlong, or drag us from the direct path of duty, or at least remove us from our post, the only remedy which exists for setting these things at rest, is to consider that God, who is the author of our life, is also its preserver. This then is the only means of lightening all our burdens, and preserving us from being swallowed up of overmuch sorrow. Seeing therefore that God condescends to undertake the care of our lives, and to support them, although they are often exposed to various sorts of death, let us learn always to flee to this asylum; nay, the more that any one is exposed to dangers, let him exercise himself the more carefully in meditating on it. In short, let this be our shield against all dangerous attacks,—our haven amidst all tossings and tempests,—that although our safety may be beyond all human hope, God is the faithful guardian of it; and let this again arouse us to prayer, that he would defend us and make our deliverance sure. This confidence will likewise make every man forward to discharge his duty with alacrity, and constantly and fearlessly to struggle onward to the end of his course. How does it happen that so many are slothful and indifferent, and that others perfidiously forsake their duty, but because, overwhelmed with anxiety, they are terrified at dangers and inconveniences, and leave no room for the operation of the providence of God?—*Calvin.*

7. *Thou hast known my soul in adversities.* God owns his saints when others are ashamed to acknowledge them; he never refuses to know his friends. He thinks not the worse of them for their rags and tatters. He does not misjudge them and cast them off when their faces are lean with sickness, or their hearts heavy with despondency. Moreover, the Lord Jesus knows us in our pangs in a peculiar sense, by having a deep sympathy towards us in them all; when no others can enter into our griefs from want of understanding them experimentally, Jesus dives into the lowest depths with us, comprehending the direst of our woes, because he has felt the same. Jesus is a physician who knows every case; nothing is new to him. When we are so bewildered as not to know our own state, he knows us altogether. He has known us, and will know us: O for grace to know more of him!—*Spurgeon.*

PSALM XXXII.

Most commentators suppose that David composed this psalm when he obtained forgiveness from God after his adultery with Bathsheba, and the death of Uriah, to which that sin led. The correctness of this view can scarcely be called in question. That the case represented in ver. 3 is no *fiction*, but *a reality*, is clear as day. The psalmist speaks in language far too definite of himself and of a particular case, to allow us to regard the matter as a fiction. Now, if the matter be a reality, no other circumstances can be referred to, except those above mentioned. All the characteristic features agree exactly. Here, as there, it is none of the common *sins of infirmity* that are spoken of, but a *dreadful transgression*, yea, an assemblage of dreadful transgressions: compare the expression in the 5th verse, "I will confess *my crimes* to the Lord," in which respect the transgression of David with Bathsheba, and the accompanying circumstances, are said to hold a peculiar place in the history of David, 1 Ki. xv. 5. Here, as there, we have a long continuance of impenitence: according to ver. 3, "the bones of the psalmist waxed old *continually;*" according to ver. 4, "the hand of the Lord was heavy upon him *day* and *night;*" and, according to the history, there elapsed nearly a whole year between the sin of David and the repentance. Here, as there, we have a sudden *transition:* confession of sin at once breaking out, and forgiveness immediately following. Compare ver. 5, "I acknowledged my sin unto thee, and I did not hide my iniquity; I said, I will confess my transgressions unto the Lord, and thou didst take away the guilt of my sin," with 2 Sa. xii. 13, "And David said to Nathan, I have sinned against the Lord. And Nathan said to David, The Lord forgiveth thy sin, thou shalt not die."—The reasons which have been adduced to show that the historical account given in Samuel is not wholly in accordance with the psalm, are easily set aside. David, it is said, according to that account, did not confess his sin, but had it brought before him by Nathan. But, even according to Samuel, David *did confess* his sin; and the circumstance that his confession was called forth by Nathan's address, did not detract from its character as a voluntary act. David must have arrived, within his own mind, even at the very threshold of repentance; otherwise the address of Nathan would not have produced the effect which it did. Nathan did not *originate* the confession, he only *set it loose.* In what other way can we explain the fact, that Nathan postponed the discharge of his duty towards the king for such a length of time after the sin was committed, except by assuming that he waited, according to the direction of God, for the crisis in David's mind? Inasmuch, therefore, as the address of Nathan occupied only a subordinate place, and was not the *ground*, but merely the *occasion* of David's confession, David might very well pass it over in silence in this psalm, in the same way in which he does in the 51st Psalm, which refers to the same circumstance. *Again*, stress is laid upon the circumstance, that the writer of this psalm is joyful at having obtained deliverance from the *punishment* of his sin, with which he had already been visited (ver. 6 and 7); whereas in 2 Sa. xii. David obtained forgiveness previous to the infliction of the punishment. But the punishment in deliverance from which the psalmist rejoices, is not one with which he had been already visited, but one which he dreaded, with which he was threatened,—one present, indeed, in the view of conscience, which already saw the angel with the flaming sword approaching, but in reality yet future. In ver. 6 it is said that "the floods shall not *reach* to the godly who prays at the right time to God for forgiveness of sin," but not that "they shall *turn* away from him;" and in ver. 7, the preceding clause, "Thou preservest me from *trouble*," leads us to consider the "songs of deliverance," as songs called forth by deliverance from *threatened* danger. Now, David had been visited with anxiety in regard to future punishment after his adultery with Bathsheba. Nathan's words, 2 Sa. xii. 10, "Now therefore the sword shall never depart from thine house, because thou hast despised me and taken the wife of Uriah," would not have produced such a dreadful impression on his mind, had not his conscience, before this, distinctly and repeatedly made the same announcement.

It has been frequently maintained that this psalm stands in opposition to the general point of view of the Old Testament. "It teaches inward reconciliation with God through faith; whereas, according to the theocratic view and practice, reconciliation is outward, and obtained by sacrifice." But there cannot be produced, out of the whole Old Testament, one single passage in which the doctrine that sacrifices of themselves, and apart from the state of mind of the offerers, are well-pleasing to God, is advanced, except for the purpose of vigorously opposing it. The law of Moses disowns this doctrine with complete decision. When, for example, in Le. xxvi. 31, it is said in reference to the ungodly, "I will not smell the savour of your sweet odours;" and when, in Ge. iv. 4, 5, we find that, along with an outward similarity, the offerings of Cain and Abel met with such different receptions from God, and that this difference is traced back to a difference in the persons; it is all but expressly asserted that sacrifices are regarded only as expressive of the mind within. Moreover, how could any such importance be attached to sacrifices, considered as such, when the value of all that man does is so repeatedly and so decidedly represented as dependent on his love to God? Compare Beitr. P. iii. p. 611. Now, just as *sacrifices* do not exclude *faith*, but faith is rather the *soul* of sacrifices, so faith does not exclude sacrifices. It is not a matter of any consequence, that David should have made no reference to them in this psalm, inasmuch as, although generally available in the case before us (compare on this Ps. li.), they occupy in every instance a very subordinate place.—*Hengstenberg.*

This is the second of the seven Penitential Psalms, as they are called, "which," says Selnecker, "St. Augustine used often to read with weeping heart and eyes, and which before his death he had written on the wall over against his sick-bed, that he might exercise himself therein, and find comfort therein in his sickness." St. Augustine's own words, "intelligentia prima est, ut te noris peccatorem," might stand as its motto.—*Perowne.*

Title, MASCHIL. There is yet another word, of frequent occurrence in the superscriptions, which claims a moment's notice. I refer to the term *Maschil*, which is prefixed to thirteen psalms. Our translators have not ventured to do more, in the *text*, than simply print the word in English characters; in the *margin*, however, they render it, as the Geneva version had done before them, "to give instruction." It would be going too far to affirm that this interpretation is subject to no doubt. Some good Hebraists take exception to it; so that perhaps our venerable translators did well to leave it untranslated. Still the interpretation they have set down in the margin, as it is the most ancient, so it is sustained by the great preponderance of authority.[1] It agrees remarkably with the contents of the 32d Psalm, which affords the earliest instance of its use; for that psalm is pre-eminently didactic. Its scope is to instruct the convicted soul how to obtain peace with God and be compassed about with songs of deliverance. The title, although prefixed only to a few, is less or more applicable to all the psalms. It holds forth as one of the purposes they were designed to serve, the edification of souls in the truth and ways of the Lord. It is true, as we may afterwards have occasion to show, that there is very little *revelation*, strictly so called, in this part of the divine word—little disclosure of new truth to the church. The psalter is rather the response of the church to God's revelations elsewhere made, than itself the vehicle of new revelations. But it is a very instructive response. Many, many a time has it happened that the psalms learned by a child at his mother's knee have deposited in his heart the seeds of divine knowledge, and kept them alive till they have sprung up long after in a harvest of salvation. The psalms, then, besides being songs and hymns, are designed "to give instruction."—*Binnie.*

2. *Imputeth not iniquity*, &c. "The true idea of justification is that a man, although he is a sinner, is treated as though he had not committed sin or as if he were innocent." But God treats no man as righteous without a sufficient ground for so doing; and the ground is the imputation of the righteousness of Christ. We are accepted "only for the righteousness of Christ imputed to us and received by faith alone." The author's views on imputation are somewhat peculiar, and have already been fully discussed by us in the supplementary notes on Rom. i. 17; iii. 24; iv. 3, 5; Gal. ii. 16, to which the reader is referred. We need scarcely add that it is an unhappy way of speaking to say that the "act of pardon does not change the *facts* in the case, or *make him innocent*, but it makes it proper for God to treat him *as if* he were innocent." It is not the act of pardon that makes the divine conduct in this matter "proper," but the righteousness of Christ, on which both the pardon and the subsequent treatment must for ever rest.—Ed.

The apostle's way of interpreting the text is remarkable. Finding David celebrating the *non-imputation of iniquity*, he construes this to mean the *imputation of righteousness*. Some have made bold to challenge the legitimacy of the construction, and have contended that the apostle quotes David's words by way of accommodation. But the interpretation is strictly correct. For what are the sins whose non-imputation is so gratefully celebrated? Are they the man's positive transgressions only? his sins of commission? That cannot be. For in that case the non-imputation would still leave the man under the ban of God's holy law. A sin of omission may sink a soul in perdition as surely as a sin of commission. "Inasmuch as ye did it *not*," will be the word of condemnation to many in the great day (Mat. xxv. 45). It must therefore be the non-imputation of all sins, of either kind, that David celebrates. Now, if God impute to a man neither his transgressions of the law, nor his omissions of duty, he treats him as a man who has fulfilled all righteousness; which is just to say, that he imputes to him righteousness without works (compare Chalmers' *Lectures on Romans*, at chap. iv. 6).

And this brings out very clearly the nature of the benefit which the Scriptures celebrate under the title of justification. It is forgiveness, and it is something more. When a pardon comes down from the crown to some condemned felon, it cancels the sentence and opens the prison door; but there its effect ceases. It does not restore the wretch to his former standing in society. He is a marked man for life. Very

[1] The LXX. and Vulgate are ambiguous, but Jerome in his version from the Hebrew renders it *eruditio;* and in this he is followed by the modern translators generally. Of recent critics, Gesenius and Hengstenberg render it *a didactic song*, Hupfeld *a doctrine* or *instruction*, and Delitzsch *a pious meditation.* Ewald and Mr. Perowne take the meaning to be, *a skilfully composed song*, *ein feines Lied*, and refer to Ps. xlvii. 7, where the same term is rendered "*with understanding.*"

different is the effect of the pardon God bestows on those who, trusting in his mercy, confess their sins. They are *justified* by their faith. For Christ's sake they are treated as righteous persons,—as persons who had perfectly obeyed the law. God imputes to them righteousness, even the righteousness of Christ in whom they trust. Well, it is to be observed, that although the ground of justification is not plainly declared in the Psalms,—could not be plainly declared till Christ died,—the truth of justification is distinctly revealed. And, as I said before, this truth, which comes up in the shape of a clear articulate statement in the thirty-second Psalm, underlies all the rest. The voice which makes itself heard in the songs of God's Israel, is not the voice of a prodigal who has been forgiven merely, and suffered to take a place among the servants of his father's house.—*Binnie.*

Imputeth. The word rendered *impute* first denotes the *reckoning, counting*, or imputing to men that which is supposed to be properly their own. Thus in Gen. xxxviii. 15; 1 Sa. i. 13; 2 Sa. xix. 19; "When he saw her he *thought* her to be an harlot;" "Eli *thought* that she had been drunken;" "Let not my Lord *impute* iniquity unto me." The word is used in the same sense in Lev. xvii. 4; Neh. xiii. 13, and elsewhere. It has this proper signification here. Then it signifies that there is reckoned, counted, imputed to one something which did not belong to him previous to such reckoning or imputation. So it is used in Num. xviii. 27: "And this your heave-offering shall be reckoned unto you, as though it were the corn of the threshing-floor, and as the fulness of the wine-press." See also Lam. iv. 2, and many other places. In the first case we regard and treat persons according to what they *personally* are; in the second, according to what they *relatively* are. To impute sin in the first sense "is to charge guilt upon the guilty in a judicial way, with a view to his being punished for it." To impute sin in the second sense, is to hold one liable in law for the acts of his representative. The doctrine of the Old and New Testaments on this point is the same. Thus Paul prayed that the sin of those who had deserted him might not be laid to their charge, 2 Tim. iv. 16. Here we have the word in its first sense. And in Phile. 18, we have it in its second sense: "If he hath wronged thee, or oweth thee aught, put that on my account." In all these cases the Hebrew and Greek words are those we render *impute.* God may and does charge upon the guilty their own sins; he may and does impute to Adam's posterity the sin of their federal head; he did impute to Christ the sins of his people; and he may and does impute to believers the righteousness of Christ. In all these cases the Scripture is clear, and the testimony and teaching of orthodox Christians is almost unvarying. The clause under consideration speaks of the *non-imputation* of sin. To *impute iniquity*, is to charge iniquity in condemnation, and to act accordingly. *Not to impute* sin is just the opposite. It is to remit the offence, pardon, forgive, absolve the sinner, cast his sins behind the back so as not to see them, bury them in the sea, remove them out of sight, blot them out so that they rise not in judgment to condemn him.—*Plumer.*

4. *The drought of summer.* We are not to suppose that the psalmist alludes to any season of extraordinary drought, but to the *ordinary* heat and dryness of the summer—to which the most extraordinary drought of our own summers cannot be compared. Near rivers and other sources of natural or artificial irrigation, verdure and beauty are preserved; but as no rain falls, the verdure of the unwatered plains soon disappears under the intense warmth of the season;—every flower fades, and every green thing withers; and a brown and arid desert alone remains, the parched herbage of which crackles beneath the feet of those who walk. A little rain, when it comes in its season, produces an equally rapid and marked change of an opposite character.—*Pictorial Bible.*

PSALM XXXIII.

A song of praise intended to excite and to express the confidence of Israel in Jehovah, and closely connected with the didactic psalm before it, the closing sentiment of which is here carried out. This intimate relation of the two psalms may account for the absence of a title in the one before us, as in the case of the ninth and tenth.—*Alexander.*

The psalm, along with the one before it, forms one pair. The chief reason for adopting this view is, that the psalm *begins* in the same strain as that with which the preceding one *concludes*, namely, an exhortation to rejoice in the

Lord: there, *Be glad in the Lord, and rejoice, ye righteous; and shout for joy, all ye that are upright in heart:* here, *Rejoice in the Lord, ye righteous; for praise is comely for the upright.* It is impossible to explain this circumstance by the supposition, that the collector of the Psalms placed the two together on account of the accidental resemblance between the concluding verse of the one, and the opening verse of the other. For the transition from the particular to the general in Ps. xxxii. takes place in such a striking and sudden manner, as to suggest the idea, that it was intended to prepare the way for passing on to a psalm of a general character. Another reason is, the want of a title in our psalm, though standing in the middle of an assemblage of psalms which are all designated psalms of David. This appearance met us in Ps. x., where we found strong reasons for regarding it and Ps. ix. as forming one pair. . . .

From these remarks, our view of the relation of the two psalms to each other will be as follows. David, inwardly and deeply moved by the proof of the glory of God, which he had obtained in the forgiveness of his dreadful offence, begins with praising it, in its present special manifestation. But his heart is so full, that he cannot be confined to this, but must take a wider range. He must unfold to Israel all that he has *generally* in God, especially God's protection and help against a hostile world. —*Hengstenberg.*

7. *He gathereth the waters of the sea together*, &c. He separated the *water* from the *earth;* and while the latter was collected into continents, islands, mountains, hills, and valleys, the former was collected into *one place*, and called *seas;* and by his all-controlling power and providence the waters have been retained in their place, so that they have not returned to drown the earth: and he has so adapted the *solar* and *lunar influence* exerted on the waters, that the tides are only raised to certain heights so that they cannot overflow the shores, nor become dissipated in the atmospheric regions. In this one economy there is a whole circle of science. The quantity of matter in the sun, moon, and in the earth are all adjusted to each other in this astonishing provision: the *course* of the *moon*, and the *diurnal* and *annual revolutions of the earth*, are all concerned here; and so concerned that it requires some of the nicest of the Newtonian calculations to ascertain the laws by which the whole is effected. —*Dr. Adam Clarke.*

PSALM XXXIV.

Title. A psalm of David, when he changed his behaviour before Abimelech; who drove him away, and he departed. Of this transaction, which reflects no credit upon David's memory, we have a brief account in 1 Sa. xxi. Although the gratitude of the psalmist prompted him thankfully to record the goodness of the Lord in vouchsafing an undeserved deliverance, yet he weaves none of the incidents of the escape into the narrative, but dwells only on the grand fact of his being heard in the hour of peril. We may learn from his example not to parade our sins before others, as certain vainglorious professors are wont to do, who seem as proud of their sins as old Greenwich pensioners of their battles and their wounds. David played the fool with singular dexterity, but he was not so real a fool as to sing of his own exploits of folly. In the original, the title does not teach us that the psalmist composed this poem at the time of his escape from Achish, the king, or Abimelech of Gath, but that it is intended to commemorate that event, and was suggested by it. It is well to mark our mercies with well-carved memorials: God deserves our best handiwork. David, in view of the special peril from which he was rescued, was at great pains with this psalm, and wrote it with considerable regularity, in almost exact accordance with the letters of the Hebrew alphabet. This is the second alphabetical psalm, the twenty-fifth being the first.

Division.—The psalm is split into two great divisions at the close of verse 10, when the psalmist, having expressed his praise to God, turns in direct address to men. The first ten verses are *a hymn*, and the last twelve *a sermon*. For further assistance to the reader we may subdivide thus: In verses 1 to 3 David vows to bless the Lord, and invites the praise of others; from 4 to 7 he relates his experience; and in 8, 9, 10 exhorts the godly to constancy of faith. In verses 11–14 he gives direct exhortation, and follows it up by didactic teaching from verses 15 to the close.—*Spurgeon.*

1. *I will bless the Lord at all times*, &c. It has frequently been observed

as a most beautiful and appropriate circumstance in the life and experience of David, the man of God, that the first notes of his harp should give forth praises at the very time "when he changed his behaviour (*i.e. concealed his intellect*, or disguised his reason) before Abimelech, who sent him away and he departed." Cast out again, homeless, friendless, helpless, David trudges along the highway of Philistia, with the world all before him, where to choose his place of rest; and though he knows not where to lay his head, he journeys on, singing, "I will bless the Lord! I will bless him at all times: his praise shall continually be in my mouth."—*A. A. Bonar*.

2. *My soul shall make her boast in the Lord.* Here we see that we may glory in him, though we are forbidden to glory in creatures, or in ourselves. . . And there are moments and frames when, surveying him in his works and perfections and promises, the believer can exult with joy unspeakable and full of glory. "What a friend have I! . . . What a shepherd! . . . What a God! . . . What a portion!"—*Jay*.

13. *Keep thy tongue from evil. Keep, hold back, restrain, vigilantly guard, preserve.* The same word is applied to *keeping* the commandments, *keeping* covenant, *keeping* the law, *keeping* the heart. This ought to be easy work; but sin has made it very difficult, and without divine grace, impossible, Ja. iii. 2–10. Yet we may not on that account be excused from our duty, Ja. i. 26. The ways in which men sin with the tongue are many. Laurentius says there are as many sins of the tongue as there are letters in the alphabet. Richard Baxter has catalogued thirty. Perhaps no form of sin more terribly destroys personal, domestic, social, and public peace and prosperity. "The tongue is a fire." It burns all who abuse it. It burns them up. Dreadful plagues befall it here and hereafter, Ps. lii. 5; cxx. 4. The two forms of sinful speaking noticed in the verse are *evil* and *guile*. The latter word is elsewhere in our version rendered *deceit, subtlety, treachery, craft*, and several times *guile*. *Evil*, elsewhere *mischief, wickedness, wrong* Hengstenberg: "In giving the details of the fear of God, the duties toward our neighbour are, according to David's usual way, dwelt upon with particular care, because there hypocrisy, which is so ready to appropriate to itself premises with which it has nothing to do, finds least scope for its exercise."—*Plumer*.

PSALM XXXV.

The psalmist, sorely distressed by malicious and ungodly enemies, prays the Lord for deliverance, promising cordial thanks if his prayer should be granted. The psalm falls into three strophes, in each of which the three elements of complaint, prayer, and promise of thanksgiving, are contained, and which are especially remarkable on this account, that each of these runs out into the vow of thanksgiving, ver. 1–10; ver. 11–18; ver. 19–28. The middle strophe, surrounded on each side by two decades, in which prayer predominates, is chiefly remarkable for an extended representation of the psalmist's distress, and of the black ingratitude of his enemies, which calls aloud for the divine retribution.

The relations of David's time manifestly form the ground of this psalm, which was composed, according to the superscription, by him. A more special ground may be obtained in 1 Sa. xxiv. 15, where a declaration of David to Saul is recorded, "The Lord therefore be judge, and judge between me and thee, and see and plead my cause, and deliver me out of thine hand,"—which coincides with the first verse of our psalm in very characteristic expressions. Still we are not to suppose, on this account, that the psalm possesses an individual character: what at first sight appears to carry this aspect, is soon perceived, by an experienced judgment, to be a mere individualizing. David speaks in the person of the righteous, from which view it is more easily explained how the truly Righteous One could appropriate this psalm to himself (Jn. xv. 25, comp. with ver. 19 here), an application, which led many of the older expositors to give to the psalm a direct and exclusive Messianic interpretation (comp. on the other hand, Introd. to Ps. xxii.) A casual synchronism between this psalm and the immediately preceding one is indicated by the agreement which ver. 6 and 7 present, the more remarkable as these two psalms are the only ones in which the Angel of the Lord, in a general way, occurs. But in both he appears entirely in the same character and connection.—*Hengstenberg*.

Like Psalm xxii., which it very

strongly resembles, Psalm xxxv. divides itself into three portions or strophes. . . . Nor is it only in its formal arrangement that this psalm thus resembles Psalm xxii. The ideal picture of the suppliant's distress in the second portion of the psalm is hardly less minutely and literally prophetical of the sufferings of our blessed Saviour than the picture in the corresponding portion of the great psalm of the crucifixion; though obscurities or ambiguities of translation, coupled with the fact of its being but once quoted in the New Testament (Jn. xv. 25), have rendered its details less familiar to Christian ears. The principal difference between the two psalms, prophetically regarded, is this, that whereas the prophecies of the one were literally verified in the scene of the crucifixion, those of the other found their literal fulfilment in the story of the condemnation. And this diversity of prophetical import is in perfect harmony with the difference between the fundamental burdens of complaint in the respective psalms. In Psalm xxii. the suppliant bewails his utter wretchedness; in Psalm xxxv. (probably composed at an earlier period) he only protests against the injustice to which he is submitting: in the one his God has forsaken him; in the other the Lord is still looking on, though forbearing as yet to redress his wrongs: "Be not thou far from me" is the prayer of the one; that of the other, "Plead thou my cause." Nor are the insults of the adversaries described in the latter psalm of so extreme a kind as those of the destroyers depicted in the former.

We may briefly run through the principal features in the picture which the psalmist has drawn. First of all, in ver. 11, we have the false witnesses rising up, laying to the suppliant's charge things that he knew not. And here, in order that we may once more beware of laying overmuch stress on the mere literal verification of the prophecy, let us observe that the false witness borne against Christ in the high-priest's palace, was but a type of that which the world is ever bearing against the doctrine and church of Christ, consisting, as it does, not in pure invention, but in a slight though all-important perversion of the truth. The next point in the description is the bitterness with which the suppliant's adversaries render him evil for good, yea even to depriving him of his life. We at once call to mind the persistency with which the multitude demanded of Pilate that Jesus should be crucified; and we may remember that among this very multitude there were probably some of those who had been present at the raising of Lazarus. And as regards the suppliant's former outpourings of love (ver. 13, 14) toward them that now persecuted him:—although the general spirit of loving-kindness here portrayed, not the details in which it manifested itself, be the point of real importance—still may we not reverently regard the mortal flesh which our Lord, the blessed Son of God, assumed (a mortal flesh of no form nor comeliness, of no beauty that men should desire him) as a sackcloth with which he was indeed clothed for the sicknesses and corruptions of the whole human race? May we not think of his long fasting for us in the wilderness? or of the many prayers which he must have urged for those who would not be saved, but which, failing of their immediate purpose, returned into his own bosom? May we not profitably call to mind how he had behaved himself to even his false apostle as to a very brother? How he had saluted him as friend, even at the very moment that he was betraying him? Or how he had wept, even as one that mourneth for his mother, over the approaching desolation of Jerusalem, whose children, had she only been willing, he would so often have gathered together as a hen gathereth her chickens under her wings? But from the records of his love we must return to the contemplation of his sufferings. In ver. 15 we read, "They have gathered themselves together upon me, smiters, and I know not;" *i.e.* "They have gathered themselves together upon me, to smite me, and to rejoice in the ignorance I display of the authors of each indignity that I suffer." St. Matthew's account of what passed in the high-priest's palace will supply us with the literal verification of these words: "Then did they spit in his face, and buffeted him; and others smote him with the palms of their hands, saying, Prophesy unto us, thou Christ, Who is he that smote thee?" Lastly, ver. 16 may be thus rendered: "While I am profaned with fictitious mockeries, they gnash upon me with their teeth;" and we have thus another yet more forcible prophecy of the deep hatred and the blasphemous affectation of scorn with which Christ should be treated when once in the power of his adversaries. . . . The prophecy was afterwards followed up by Isaiah, l. 6: "I gave my back to the smiters, and my cheeks to them that plucked off the hair: I hid not my face from shame and spitting." Here the mockery of justice which has been perpetrated comes to a head; and the picture is abruptly terminated, as at Ps. xxii. 19, by an earnest entreaty to God to advance to his servant's rescue. That rescue was vouchsafed when at the resurrection Christ was "*justified* in the Spirit."—*Thrupp.*

3. *Say unto my soul*, &c. Some expound these words thus: Declare to me by secret inspiration; and others, Make me to feel indeed that my salvation is in thy hand. In my opinion, David desires to have it thoroughly fixed in his mind, and to be fully persuaded that God is the author of his salvation. This he was unable, from the present aspect of things, to ascertain and determine; for such is the insensibility and dulness of our natures, that God often delivers us whilst we sleep and are ignorant of it. Accordingly he makes use of a very forcible manner of expression, in praying that God would grant him a lively sense of his favour, so that being armed with this buckler, he might sustain every conflict, and surmount every opposing obstacle; as if he had said, Lord, whatever may arise to discourage me, confirm me in this persuasion, that my salvation is assuredly in thee; and although temptations drive me hither and thither, recall my thoughts to thee in such a manner as that my hope of salvation may rise superior to all the dangers to which I shall be exposed; nay more, that I may become as infallibly certain as if thou hadst said it, that through thy favour I shall be saved.—*Calvin.*

5. *Let them be as chaff*, &c. Under the influence of inspiration, the psalmist sees the natural and righteous consequences of their wickedness, and viewing the case merely in itself, apart from personal feeling, speaks of this effect as desirable. The wish expressed is, to all intents and purposes, equivalent to a prediction or the affirmation of a general truth. The psalmist desires the destruction of these sinners precisely as God wills it; nor is it any harder to reconcile the certain fact that God allows some men to perish in his infinite benevolence.—*Alexander.*

14. *As one that mourneth for his mother.* This indication is particularly impressive, as illustrated by the existing state of feeling of sons towards their mothers in the East. The relations between the father and the son in early life are not calculated to call forth the tender feelings of the latter in any very eminent degree. The father is looked up to distantly; is respected, venerated, but seldom loved. The restraint and deference which characterize his limited intercourse with his father, direct all his tender affections with double force towards his mother; whose indulgence and attachment towards him are so continually evinced, as enable her to establish an influence over him which seldom terminates but with her life. He constantly turns to her with perfect confidence on all occasions in which his feelings are interested; he usually commits to her the choice of his wife or wives; and when he settles in life she commonly takes the charge of his domestic establishment, becomes the real head of his household, and remains his nearest counsellor and friend, as she had been in his childhood. This station is the highest object of woman's ambition in the East. It is as a mother, not as a wife, that she attains the most independent and honoured station to which the condition of society allows her to aspire; and this it is, principally, which makes a woman in the East so anxious to have male children, and so comparatively indifferent about daughters; and this also induces the mother to exert herself in every possible way to fix and cultivate her son's affection, and in which she seldom fails so to succeed that "to bow down heavily as one that mourneth for his mother," would at once be understood by an Oriental as expressing the utmost profundity of grief.—*Kitto.*

PSALM XXXVI.

Ps. xxxvi. stands in nearly the same relation to Ps. xxxv. as Ps. xxiii. to Ps. xxii. Its connection with the preceding psalm appears in this, that while in the one the worshipper had prayed God to plead his cause, he makes in the other particular reference to God's faithfulness and righteousness; and while in the former it was as the Lord's *servant* that he had specially implored protection, he expressly bestows upon himself that title in the superscription of the latter. His concluding prayers, moreover, in reference to his adversaries, coincide with those to which he had previously given utterance. Furthermore, as the language used by David to Saul at Engedi contained the substance of the petition in Ps. xxxv., so in the specious words with which Saul replied to David's remonstrances we find the basis of the sentiments ascribed to the wicked man in the opening of Ps. xxxvi.; as was noticed even by Theodoret. A similar view seems to have been taken by Bossuet, who prefixes to the psalm this heading: "Impiorum, qualis erat Saül, profunda malitia . . ." And to the occasion of the meeting at Engedi the psalm has been also referred by the Arabic translator. Indeed one might feel that in penning ver. 3 David mourned only too truly over the alteration which the indulgence of evil passions had produced in his father-in-law's once noble character. Leaving off to be wise and to do good, Saul was now condescending to iniquity and deceit; and had probably been devising mischief on that very bed on which he had been found asleep, and had been spared by the man whom he himself desired to slay.

A further proof of the occasion on which the psalm was composed, may be traced in the striking coincidence of its imagery with the natural features of the scenery round the fountain of Engedi, situate in a solitary oasis amidst a barrier of naked limestone precipices on the western bank of the Dead Sea. . . .

THE INTERPRETATION OF THE PSALM.—It begins by setting forth that SIN, speaking as an oracle to the wicked in his innermost heart, exerts a more powerful influence upon him than the terrors of God, which can only address him from without; and that like a false and deceitful prophet, making things smooth to him in his eyes, it prevents him from detecting his own iniquity and hating it. In contrast to this blindness which the wicked has brought upon himself is the ever-increasing light which is enjoyed by the righteous. We are thus led to the main theme. It is only the servant of the Lord, who drinks of the true fountain of life, and sees light in God's light, that can really appreciate or experience the Lord's mercy. He alone can discern God's lovingkindness speaking to him in all the varied scenes of nature around: he alone can call that lovingkindness his own, and can entreat, with the prayer of faith, that it may be still continued to him. With such an entreaty, and with a prophecy of the discomfiture of the wicked, the psalm concludes.—*Thrupp.*

1. *The transgression of the wicked.* His daring and wanton sin; his breaking the bounds of law and justice. *Saith within my heart, that there is no fear of God before his eyes.* Men's sins have a voice to godly ears. They are the outer index of an inner evil. It is clear that men who dare to sin constantly and presumptuously cannot respect the great Judge of all. Despite the professions of unrighteous men, when we see their unhallowed actions our heart is driven to the conclusion that they have no religion whatever. Unholiness is clear evidence of ungodliness. Wickedness is the fruit of an atheistic root. This may be made clear to the candid head by cogent reasoning, but it is clear already and intuitively to the pious heart. If God be everywhere, and I fear him, how can I dare to break his laws in his very presence? He must be a desperate traitor who will rebel in the monarch's own halls. Whatever theoretical opinions bad men may avow, they can only be classed with atheists, since they are such practically. Those eyes which have no fear of God before them now, shall have the terrors of hell before them for ever.—*Spurgeon.*

2. *For.* Here is the argument to prove the proposition laid down in the former verse. David here runs over the process of reasoning by which he had become convinced that wicked men have no proper idea of God or respect for him. God-fearing men see their sins and bewail them; where the reverse is the case we may be sure there is no fear of God. *He flattereth himself in his own eyes.* He counts himself a fine fellow, worthy of great respect. He quiets his conscience, and so deceives his own judgment as to reckon himself a pattern of excellence; if not for morality, yet for having sense enough not to be enslaved by rules which are bonds to others. He is the free-thinker, the man of strong mind, the hater of cant, the philosopher; and the servants of God are, in his esteem, mean-spirited and narrow-minded. Of all flatteries this is the most absurd and dangerous. Even the silliest bird will not set traps for itself; the most pettifogging attorney will not cheat himself. To smooth over one's own conduct to one's conscience (which is the meaning of the Hebrew) is to smooth one's own path to hell.

The descent to eternal ruin is easy enough, without making a glissade of it, as self-flatterers do. *Until his iniquity be found to be hateful.* At length he is found out and detested, despite his self-conceit. Rottenness smells sooner or later too strong to be concealed. There is a time when the leprosy cannot be hidden. At last the old house can no longer be propped up, and falls about the tenant's ears: so there is a limit to a man's self-gratulation; he is found out amid general scorn, and can no longer keep up the farce which he played so well. If this happen not in this life, the hand of death will let light in upon the covered character, and expose the sinner to shame and contempt.—*Spurgeon.*

7. *How excellent is thy lovingkindness, O God.* Here we enter into the Holy of Holies. Benevolence, and mercy, and justice are everywhere, but the excellence of that mercy only those have known whose faith has lifted the veil and passed into the brighter presence of the Lord; these behold the excellency of the Lord's mercy. The word translated *excellent* may be rendered "precious;" no gem or pearl can ever equal in value a sense of the Lord's love. This is such a brilliant as angels wear. Kings' regalia are a beggarly collection of worthless pebbles when compared with the tender mercy of Jehovah. David could not estimate it, and therefore, after putting a note of admiration, he left our hearts and imagination, and better still, our experience, to fill up the rest. He writes *How excellent!* because he cannot tell us the half of it. *Therefore the children of men put their trust under the shadow of thy wings.* The best of reasons for the best of courses. The figure is very beautiful. The Lord overshadows his people as a hen protects her brood, or as an eagle covers its young; and we as the little ones run under the blessed shelter and feel at rest. To cower down under the wings of God is so sweet. Although the enemy be far too strong for us, we have no fear, for we nestle under the Lord's wing. O that more of Adam's race knew the excellency of the heavenly shelter! It made Jesus weep to see how they refused it: our tears may well lament the same evil.—*Spurgeon.*

8. *Thy house.* The house of God is here neither, as some absurdly expound, the world, which is never so named, nor is it, as others suppose, a mere image of a divine storehouse; but it is here, as everywhere else, the national sanctuary, the tabernacle of meeting, in which the servants of the Lord spiritually dwell with him, and where they are tenderly cared for by him as the good householder. Comp. on Ps. xv. 1; xxiii. 6; xxiv. 3; xxvii. 4, 5; lxv. 4. Michaelis, correctly as to the sense: ecclesiae tuae. For the house of God was the image of the church. To it belong the treasures of salvation, of which God makes his people to partake.—In the second member there seems to be a reference to Gen. ii. 10, "And a river went out from Eden (delight) to water the garden," which is also alluded to in Jn. iv. 18; Eze. xlvii.; Zec. xiv. 8—passages in which the thought, the whole earth shall partake of the blessings of the kingdom of God, is represented under the image of a stream, which, issuing from Jerusalem, refreshes the dry and barren region around. Comp. Christol. P. II. p. 367. In the stream which of old watered the garden of Eden for the good of man, the psalmist saw the type of that stream of bliss with which God's love never ceases to refresh his people.—*Hengstenberg.*

12. *There are the workers of iniquity fallen.*—Here he derives confidence from his prayer, not doubting that he has already obtained his request. And thus we see how the certainty of faith directs the saints to prayer. Besides, still further to confirm his confidence and hope in God, he shows as it were, by pointing to it with the finger, the certain destruction of the wicked, even though it lay as yet concealed in the future. In this respect the adverb *there* is not superfluous; for while the ungodly boast of their good fortune and the world applaud them, David beholds by the eye of faith, as if from a watch-tower, their destruction, and speaks of it with as much confidence as if he had already seen it realized.—*Calvin.*

PSALM XXXVII.

This is another of the acrostic or alphabetical psalms. Dr. Binnie regrets that the existence of this remarkable style of composition is not indicated in our English translations; and he presents the English reader with a translation of the opening part of the thirty-seventh Psalm, constructed on the principle of exhibiting the Hebrew peculiarity to an English eye:—

1. At evil-doers fret not thyself,
At workers of iniquity be thou not envious.
2. For like the grass they shall soon be cut down,
And like the green herb they shall wither.

3. But trust thou in Jehovah and do good;
Inhabit the land and feed on faithfulness.
4. Delight thyself also in Jehovah;
And he shall give thee the petitions of thine heart.

5. Commit to Jehovah thy way;
Trust also in him, and he will effect it.
6. Yea, he shall bring out, as the light, thy righteousness,
And thy judgment as the noonday.

7. Dumb be thou before Jehovah, and wait patiently for him;
Fret not thyself at him who prospereth in his way,
At the man who practiseth plots.

8. Evermore desist from anger and forsake wrath;
Fret not thyself, only to do evil.
9. For evil-doers shall be cut off;
But those that wait upon Jehovah, they shall inherit the land.

10. For yet a little while, and the wicked is not:
Yea, thou shalt consider his place, and he is not there.
11. But the meek shall inherit the land,
And shall delight themselves in abundance of peace.

12. 'Gainst the righteous the wicked plotteth,
And gnasheth upon him with his teeth.
13. The Lord shall laugh at him,
For he seeth that his day will come.

1. *Fret not thyself*, &c. "How immediately does the prophet seize and hit upon the thoughts of the heart in this temptation, and take away all causes thereof, saying, at the first: O man, thou art angry, and hast cause for it, as thou thinkest, for there are wicked men who do unjustly, and commit much evil, while still they continue to prosper, so that nature thinks it has just cause to be angry. But not so, dear child; permit grace, and not nature here to rule; break thine anger, and be at rest for a little; let them go on doing evil and prospering; believe me it shall do thee no harm. Then if men ask: When shall things cease to be thus? Who can endure so long? He answers: For as the grass, &c. This is a beautiful similitude, terrible to hypocrites, and consoling to the afflicted. How entirely does it raise us out of our own sight, and place us in the sight of God! In our sight the multitude of hypocrites flourishes and grows, and covers the world so completely that they alone seem almost to exist; as the green grass covers and adorns the earth. But in God's sight what are they? Hay, that must presently be made; and the higher the grass grows, the nearer is it to the scythe and the haycock; even so the higher and farther the wicked spread and rise aloft, the nearer are they to destruction. Wherefore then shouldst thou be angry, when their wickedness and prosperity are of so short-lived a nature?"—*Luther*.

6. *He shall bring forth thy righteousness as the light*, &c. See holy David, Saul with all his kingly might could not destroy him. God brought David forth at last as a shining light, as the sun at noon-day; and what a bright light was David over the whole land! How thick a darkness fell upon our Lord Christ, the Sun of righteousness, in his holy sufferings and death; but in his glorious resurrection and ascension to heaven, and proclamation of the blessed gospel, the true light burst forth, and illuminated the whole earth, so that even the heathen walk in this light, and in the brightness which has proceeded from him.—*John Arndt*.

18. *The Lord knoweth the days of the upright; and their inheritance shall be for ever*. Everything here requires attention. The *persons*—"the upright." The upright mean those who are sincere; sincere in their dealings with their fellow-creatures, with their own souls, with their God. The character is equally rare and excellent. It admits of imperfection, but not of partiality; and is never found separate from the renewing of the Holy Ghost. The *period*—"their days." These are "known of

God." This knowledge being spoken of as a privilege, something more than mere intelligence must be intended. The meaning is, he knows them kindly and graciously; that he feels and will acknowledge his concern in them; and make them all work together for their good. He knows their number: he has appointed it: friends cannot enlarge, enemies cannot reduce it. He knows the nature of them—and he determines it. Have they days of affliction? He knows them: knows their source, their pressure, how long they have continued, the support they require, and the proper time to remove them. Have they days of danger? He knows them, and will be a refuge and defence in them. Have they days of duty? He knows them, and will furnish the strength and help they require. Have they days of inaction, when they are laid aside from their work by accident or disease? He knows them, and says to his servants, under every prevention, "It is well that it was in thy heart." Have they days of privation, when they are denied the ordinances of religion? He knows them, and will be a little sanctuary to his people in their losses. Have they days of declension and of age, in which their strength is fled and their senses fail, and so many of their connections have gone down to the dust—evil days, wherein they have no pleasure? He knows them, and says, "Even to old age I am he, and to hoar hairs will I bear and carry you." The *portion*—"their inheritance shall be for ever." So was not the inheritance of many of the angels in heaven; for they kept not their first estate. So was not the inheritance of Adam in Paradise; for the Lord drove out the man. So was not the inheritance of the Jews in Canaan; for the glory of all lands was made a desolation. So is not the inheritance of the man of the world; his portion is in this life. And what is this but a vapour, a shadow? Yet at the end of it he is stripped of all, and departs as naked as he came. But the Christian has not only being, health, riches, honour, peace, joy, friendship; but all these for ever.—*Jay.*

25. *I have been young, and now am old; yet have I not seen the righteous forsaken, nor his seed begging bread.* This was David's observation. It is not *my* observation just as it stands, for I have relieved the children of undoubtedly good men, who have appealed to me as common mendicants. But this does not cast a doubt upon the observation of David. He lived under a dispensation more outward and more of this world than the present rule of personal faith. Never are the righteous forsaken; that is a rule without exception. Seldom indeed do their seed beg bread; and although it does occasionally occur, through dissipation, idleness, or some such causes on the part of their sons, yet doubtless it is so rare a thing that there are many alive who never saw it. Go into the union house and see how few are the children of godly parents; enter the jail and see how much rarer still is the case. Poor ministers' sons often become rich. I am not old, but I have seen the families of the poor godly become rich, and have seen the Lord reward the faithfulness of the father in the success of the son, so that I have often thought that the best way to endow one's seed with wealth is to become poor for Christ's sake. In the Indian mission of the "Baptist Missionary Society" this is abundantly illustrated.—*Spurgeon.*

35. *I have seen the wicked in great power*, &c. A second time David turns to his diary, and this time in poetic imagery tells us of what he had observed. It were well if we too took notes of divine providences. *I have seen the wicked in great power.* The man was terrible to others, ruling with much authority, and carrying things with a high hand, a Cæsar in might, a Crœsus in wealth. *And spreading himself like a green bay-tree.* Adding house to house and field to field, rising higher and higher in the state. He seemed to be ever verdant like a laurel, he grew as a tree in its own native soil, from which it had never been transplanted. No particular tree is here meant, a spreading beech or a wide expanding oak may serve us to realize the picture; it is a thing of earth, whose roots are in the clay; its honours are fading leaves; and though its shadow dwarfs the plants which are condemned to pine beneath it, yet it is itself a dying thing, as the feller's axe shall prove. In the noble tree, which claims to be king of the forest, behold the grandeur of the ungodly to-day; wait awhile and wonder at the change, as the timber is carried away, and the very root torn from the ground.—*Spurgeon.*

A green bay tree. The word (אֶזְרָח ezrakh) occurs only in this text, and has been variously explained. Most of the rabbins, followed by Mudge, Waterland, Gesenius, Hengstenberg, and many others, prefer that which is given in our marginal reading, denoting an indigenous tree—implying the flourishing condition of that which grows in its native and congenial soil. This we certainly prefer. But the Septuagint, Vulgate, and some other ancient versions, followed by some good authorities, have "cedar." For the reading of "bay tree" we are not aware of any authority, except the very feeble one which is offered by some of the older of the modern versions, in this country and on the Continent. Images comparing the transitory nature of human hope and prosperity to the sudden blight and overthrow which so often befall the glory of the forest or the pride of the garden, are at once so beautiful and natural that they have been employed by poets of every country and age as often as by those of Israel. A passage in one of our own poets (Shakspeare) furnishes a beautiful paraphrase on the present text.

"This is the state of man: to-day he puts forth
The tender leaves of hopes; to-morrow blossoms,
And bears his blushing honours thick upon him;
The third day comes a frost, a killing frost,
And when he thinks, good easy man, full surely
His greatness is a-ripening, nips his root,
And then he falls." —*Kitto.*

PSALM XXXVIII.

This psalm tells the story of a bitter suffering. The suffering is both in body and in mind. The body is wasted by a cruel and loathsome disease, and the mind is full of anguish, arising partly from a deep sense of sin, and partly from the fear of relentless and now rejoicing enemies. Body and mind, in such circumstances, act and react upon one another. Mental anguish impairs the strength of the body; and bodily suffering and weakness make us less able to face with steady and resolute courage the horrors which crowd upon the mind.

To add to his distress, the sufferer is deserted even of his friends. They to whose kind offices he might naturally have looked at such a time, they who had been his friends in his health and prosperity, and who might now have watched by his sick-bed, and spoken words of comfort to him in his sorrow, turned coldly away and left him alone with his grief. A burning fever consumed him (ver. 7), his heart beat hotly, his eyes failed him, the bitter remembrance of his sin was with him; there was the consciousness and the fear of God's displeasure; and as if this were not enough, there was besides all this the utter loneliness, never so hard to bear as in such a season of bodily and mental prostration; the weary couch, never so weary as when no hand is there to smooth it; the pain of the disease, far more acutely felt because none offered sympathy; the terrors of conscience and of imagination, aggravated because they had to be endured in solitude. Suffering seems here to have reached its height. But out of the very midst of the furnace the sufferer can say, "Lord, before thee is all my desire; in thee, O Jehovah, have I hoped;" can cry with all the earnestness of a faith purified by affliction, "Leave me not, be not far from me, O Lord, my salvation."—*Perowne.*

The title correctly ascribes this psalm to David. The contents well agree with this. We know nothing of the particular circumstances under which it was written, except that its author was in deep distress. Hengstenberg: "Of any particular occasion there is found no trace in the psalm." Some have thought otherwise; but they have not well sustained their opinions. The title has claimed considerable attention. The Hebrew is well rendered in our version, though there is no objection to the renderings of others: *For remembrance; To commemorate; To call to mind; To remind.* But who is to be reminded? Hengstenberg: "Not, as is generally supposed, the psalmist himself, or the whole church, but God, who seemed to have forgotten the psalmist." With him agrees Alexander. Calvin: "The title indicates that David composed this psalm as a memorial for himself as well as others, lest he should too soon forget the chastisement by which God had afflicted him." Morison is of the opinion that "this psalm was composed by David as a memorial of the deep sorrow of mind when his spirit was burdened with the remembrance of some grievous offence against God." May it not have been as a remembrancer to God and also a memorial to himself? It is not likely that any part of the title has reference to the *music* with which the psalm was to be sung. —*Plumer*.

PSALM XXXIX.

"The most beautiful," says Ewald, "of all elegies in the Psalter." It is the sorrowful complaint of a heart not yet subdued to a perfect resignation, but jealous with a godly jealousy, lest it should bring dishonour upon its God, and longing for light from heaven to scatter its doubts. The holy singer had long pent up his feelings; and though busy thoughts were stirring within him, he would not give them utterance. He could not bare his bosom to the rude gaze of an unsympathizing world. And he feared lest, while telling his perplexities, some word might drop from his lips which would give the wicked an occasion to speak evil against his God. (This feeling is one the expression of which we have already had in the preceding psalm.) And when at last, unable to express his strong emotion, he speaks, it is to God and not to man. It is as one who feels how hopeless the problem of life is, except as seen in the light of God. It is with the deep conviction of personal frailty (ver. 6) and sinfulness (ver. 9), as well as of the frailty and sinfulness of all men. It is with the touching sadness of one who cannot be comforted. And yet the weeping eye is raised to heaven, and amidst all his grief and perplexity, notwithstanding all that is so dark and cheerless in the world, pilgrim and stranger as he is, the holy singer can still say, "My hope is in thee."—*Perowne*.

4. *Lord, make me to know mine end.* In what relation does the prayer stand to the perplexity which gave birth to it? Why does he ask, MAKE ME KNOW MINE END? It is not (as Hengst. supposes) an expression of impatience, "I am weary of this suffering: tell me when my life shall end, and so my suffering end;" nor is it an expostulation with God (as Kimchi and Calvin), as if he would say, "See how short my life is: is such a life long enough for all thou layest upon me?" Such interpretations are at variance with the tone of sad resignation which breathes through the psalm. It is rather this: Make me rightly to know and estimate the shortness and uncertainty of human life, that so, instead of suffering myself to be perplexed with all that I see around me, I may cast myself the more entirely upon thee," as indeed follows, "And now, Lord, what wait I for?"—*Perowne*.

6. *Surely every man walketh in a vain show.* Life is but a passing pageant. This alone is sure, that nothing is sure. All around us shadows mock us; we walk among them, and too many live for them as if the mocking images were substantial; acting their borrowed parts with zeal fit only to be spent on realities, and lost upon the phantoms of this passing scene. Worldly men walk like travellers in a mirage, deluded, duped, deceived, soon to be filled with disappointment and despair. *Surely they are disquieted in vain.* Men fret, and fume, and worry, and all for mere nothing. They are shadows pursuing shadows, while death pursues them. He who toils and contrives, and wearies himself for gold, for fame, for rank, even if he wins his desire, finds at the end his labour lost; for like the treasure of the miser's dream, it all vanishes when the man awakes in the world of reality. Read well this text, and then listen to the clamour of the market, the hum of the exchange, the din of the city streets, and remember that all this *noise* (for so the word means), this breach of quiet, is made about unsubstantial, fleeting vanities. Broken rest, anxious fear, over-worked brain, failing mind, lunacy, these are steps in the process of disquieting with many, and all to be rich, or, in other words, to load one's-self with the thick clay; clay, too, which a man must leave so soon. *He heapeth up riches, and knoweth not who shall gather them.* He misses often the result of his ventures, for there are many slips between the cup and the lips. His wheat is sheaved, but an interloping robber bears it away—as often happens with the poor Eastern husbandman; or, the wheat is even stored, but the invader feasts thereon. Many work for others all unknown to them. Especially does this verse refer to those all-gathering muckrakes, who in due time are succeeded by all-scattering forks, which scatter riches as profusely as their sires gathered them parsimoniously. We know not our heirs, for our children die, and strangers fill the old ancestral halls; estates change hands, and entail, though rivetted with a thousand bonds, yields to the corroding power of time. Men rise up early and sit up late to build a house, and then the stranger tramps along its

passages, laughs in its chambers, and forgetful of its first builder, calls it all his own. Here is one of the evils under the sun for which no remedy can be prescribed.—*Spurgeon.*

PSALM XL.

The reader will observe that Mr. Barnes ably advocates the exclusive Messianic reference; and his treatment of the whole psalm on this principle, as well as his reply to special objections, will carry many readers along with him. We give the following extracts, exhibiting the *principle* of interpretation respectively adopted by Alexander, Delitzsch, and Binnie. Dr. Binnie's principle, which seems to us, on the whole, best to meet all the difficulties of the case, is presented with singular clearness, force, and beauty.

"Since the ceremonies of the law are worthless, when divorced from habitual obedience, instead of offering mere sacrifice, I offer myself, to do whatever is prescribed to me in the written revelation of thy will." This is the spirit of every true believer, and is therefore perfectly appropriate to the whole class to whom this psalm relates, and for whom it was intended. It is peculiarly significant, however, when applied to Christ: first, because he alone possessed this spirit in perfection; secondly, because he sustained a peculiar relation to the rites, and more especially the sacrifices, of the law. David, or any other individual believer under the old economy, was bound to bring himself as an oblation, in completion, or in lieu of his external gifts; but such self-devotion was peculiarly important upon Christ's part, as the real sacrifice, of which those rites were only figures. The failure of any individual to render this essential offering insured his own destruction. But if Christ had failed to do the same, all his followers must have perished. It is not, therefore, an accommodation of the passage to a subject altogether different, but an exposition of it in its highest application, that is given in Heb. x. 5-10. The limitation of the words to Christ, as an exclusive Messianic prophecy, has the twofold inconvenience of forbidding its use by the large class of godly sufferers for whom it seems so admirably suited, and of requiring us to understand even the confession of sins as uttered in his person.—*Alexander.*

The Epistle to the Hebrews, ch. x. 5-9, interprets ver. 7-9 of this psalm (after the LXX.) as words of Messiah coming into the world. That this interpretation of the psalm is made on the typical principle, is evident from the second part of the psalm itself. Words spoken by David after his anointing, but while he is only as yet on the way to the throne, are so shaped by the Holy Spirit, the Spirit of prophecy, that they sound like words of the second David as he goes through sufferings to his glory—that David whose sacrifice of himself puts an end to the animal sacrifices, and whose person and work are the kernel and the star of the roll of the law.—*Delitzsch.*

There are psalms demonstrably Messianic which cannot well be assigned to either of the two classes we have surveyed. They are neither directly predictive of Christ, nor yet do they speak of him through some type. The two most prominent examples of this class are the sixteenth and the fortieth. Its characteristic features will be best illustrated by examining one of these. For various reasons I select the fortieth. This (ver. 5-9) is applied to Christ in the most unqualified way in the epistle to the Hebrews (ch. x. 4-10). There is no mistaking the view here taken of David's words. So plainly is the Messianic interpretation laid down, and so strongly is the argument of the epistle built upon it, that many eminent divines conclude that Christ must be the direct and exclusive subject of the psalm. The fatal objection to that view is, that the psalm contains one of those sorrowful confessions of sin, the absence of which has just been commented upon in the case of the twenty-second, ver. 12.

In explanation of this, we are reminded, no doubt, that Christ, though he knew no sin, was made sin for us: so that he was, in a very true sense, a sinner before God. This explanation is an old one. It is thus put by Augustine:—"He made our offences his offences, that he might make his righteousness our righteousness. Why should not he who took upon him the likeness of the sinner's flesh, take upon him also the likeness of the sinner's voice?" There is force in these suggestions, and they go far to explain the fact (to which we shall revert immediately), that in one and the same psalm we hear the voice both of the sinless Saviour and his sinning people. But it is pressing them too far to urge them as a reason why we should attribute to Christ words which, in their natural and obvious sense, are a sorrowful and shame-stricken confession of sin before God. The psalm is certainly not of the directly Messianic order.

Shall we set it down therefore among the typically Messianic class? This is a very common interpretation. According to it David is the person who speaks, but he speaks as a type of Christ, and therefore his words are attributed to Christ by the epistle to the Hebrews. But neither is this view satisfactory. David was not a type of Christ in his priesthood and sacrifice; and it is of these only, and not at all of the kingdom, that this psalm speaks. The person who here comes forward and declares his purpose to do the will of God, puts such a value on his obedience as neither David nor any mere man could, without presumption, have claimed for theirs. The true key to the psalm is to be found, not in the doctrine of the types, but rather in that of the mystical union between Christ and the church. It is a MYSTICALLY MESSIANIC psalm. This is the view taken by the ancient fathers, and especially Augustine. That great divine was penetrated with a sense of the unity which, through the grace of God, subsists between Christ and all his people, even the humblest and feeblest in the company of the saints. He is never weary of telling how, when the obscure disciples of Christ in Damascus were persecuted, the Lord resented it as a wrong done to himself, and thundered in the ear of the oppressor, "I am Jesus whom thou persecutest;" and how, when any poor saint is visited or fed, Christ takes the kindness as done to himself (Ac. xi. 5; Mat. xxv. 40). And he makes perpetual use of the principle in endeavouring to open up the Messianic element in the Psalter. The pages of his *Enarrationes* are thus made fragrant with the savour of the Bridegroom's name. Few will deny, indeed, that he presses the principle too far. He applies it to many places that can only be successfully explained on the typical principle. Nevertheless, the principle is a sound one, and is of great value in the interpretation of Scripture.

The difficulty to be explained in the class of psalms under consideration, is the seeming incongruity involved in the attributing of different parts of one and the same song to different persons,—one part to Christ, another part to his people,—while there is nothing in the context to indicate a change of subject. The mystical hypothesis explains it by pointing out, that there is such a union between Christ and his people as warrants their being thus conjoined in the same song. That he and they are conjoined in a real fellowship of life is most certain. "For as the body is one, and hath many members, and all the members of that one body, being many, are one body: so also is CHRIST. For by one Spirit are we all baptized into one body, whether we be Jews or Gentiles, whether we be bond or free" (1 Cor. xii. 12, 13; comp. Gal. iii. 16). The CHRIST here named is not the individual person of our Lord, but he and the church together,—Christ mystical, *totus Christus caput et corpus*. This mystical union has left its effects on many parts of Scripture. Thus, throughout the prophecies of Isaiah, one and the same title, "The Servant of the Lord," is used to denote sometimes the Lord Jesus himself (ch. xlii. 1; liii. 11); sometimes his people (ch. xlii. 19); sometimes the whole mystical body, including him and them together (ch. xlix. 1 -6). This no doubt wears an appearance of incongruity. But something of the kind is always found when diverse elements are conjoined in an intimate union. I sometimes speak of myself as an immortal creature, sometimes as a dying man. Why? Because my nature is not simple but composite. By my soul I am immortal; it is a "deathless principle:" by my body I am subject to corruption. Just so is it with the church. The Lord has taken his people into a union with himself, more intimate than that even of body and soul. He and they constitute one Christ. *And of that one Christ the psalter is the voice.* If in some psalms it is the members who speak and in others the Head, there are others again in which we can distinguish the speech of both. This furnishes the only satisfactory explanation of the remarkable conjoining of Christ and the church in the sixteenth and fortieth psalms. In the case of the latter the explanation is frankly accepted by Calvin, although he was as little tolerant of subtleties in the interpretation of Scripture as can well be imagined. "David (he observes) is not speaking here in his own name only, but is pointing out generally what is common to all God's children: but when he thus bringeth in the community of the church, we must ascend to him who is the head."

It is related in the gospel that the Lord Jesus joined with the disciples in singing the paschal Hallel; and there is no reason to suppose that his voice was ever mute when the psalms were sung in the synagogues of Nazareth or Capernaum on the Sabbath-days. He lifted up his soul to God along with "the praises of Israel" (Ps. xxii. 3); and he did not deem it necessary to refrain his voice when the melody descended to notes of contrite confession. There was no impropriety nor untruthfulness in his thus making use of words which, in their letter, were inapplicable to his case. There is hardly a psalm but contains things which are applicable only to some in the congregation; yet all who are present take part in the song. We do not enjoin the little children to be silent when the seventy-first Psalm is sung, although it is the song of old age; nor the aged men to be silent when the twenty-seventh is sung, although it is the prayer of a youth. The psalms are church songs, and all who belong to the church are to sing them. "Both young men and maidens, old men and children, let them praise the name of the Lord" (Ps. cxlviii. 12, 13). The ripe believer, who can triumph in the steadfast hope of God's glory, is to lend his voice to swell the song of the church when she cries to God out of the depths; and the penitent, who is still sitting in darkness, is not to refrain his voice when the church pours out in song her sense of God's love. The whole church has fellowship in the psalms. And from this fellowship the divine Head does not turn away. There are sentiments here and there in which he cannot perfectly participate. Nevertheless, the psalms are the voice of the body of which he is the Head, and therefore he joins in them. This simple fact, that the Lord Jesus sang the psalms,—how vividly does it represent the mystical union! When we sing the psalms, especially those in which the voice of Christ makes itself so distinctly audible as it is in the sixteenth and fortieth, it ought to affect our hearts to think that we are, in effect, sitting beside Christ, as the disciples did in the guest-chamber, and are singing along with him out of the same book.—*Binnie.*

1. *I waited patiently for the Lord,* &c. Patient waiting upon God was a special characteristic of our Lord Jesus. Impatience never lingered in his heart, much less escaped his lips. All through his agony in the garden, his trial of cruel mockings before Herod and Pilate, and his passion on the tree, he waited in omnipotence of patience. No glance of wrath, no word of murmuring, no deed of vengeance came from God's patient Lamb; he waited and waited on; was patient, and patient to perfection, far excelling all others who have according to their measure glorified God in the fires. Job on the dunghill does not equal Jesus on the cross. The Christ of God wears the imperial crown among the patient. Did the Only Begotten wait, and shall we be petulant and rebellious? *And he inclined unto me, and heard my cry.* Neither Jesus the head, nor any one of the members of his body, shall ever wait upon the Lord in vain. Mark the figure of inclining, as though the suppliant cried out of the lowest depression, and condescending love stooped to hear his feeble moans. What a marvel is it that our Lord Jesus should have to cry as we do, and wait as we do, and should receive the Father's help after the same process of faith and pleading as must be gone through by ourselves! The Saviour's prayers among the midnight mountains and in Gethsemane expound this verse. The Son of David was brought very low, but he rose to victory; and here he teaches us how to conduct our conflicts so as to succeed after the same glorious pattern of triumph. Let us arm ourselves with the same mind; and panoplied in patience, armed with prayer, and girt with faith, let us maintain the holy war.—*Spurgeon.*

5. *Many, O Lord,* &c. Read this verse and meditate on what he who is the Word suggests: "*God's thoughts towards us!*" The unnumbered multitude of his thoughts of love to us! The forests with their countless leaves, the grass on every plain and mountain of earth with its numberless blades, the sands on every shore of every river and ocean, the waves of every sea, and the drops of every wave of every sea, the stars of heaven; none of these, nor all combined, could afford an adequate idea of "*his thoughts towards us:*"—"*there is no comparison to thee*"—nothing wherewith to help out a statement. And the *depth of love* in every one of these thoughts!—*A. A. Bonar.*

9, 10. *I have preached righteousness,* &c. These remarkable words of the great prophet received a partial accomplishment in such sermons as the one which filled with astonishment the townspeople of Nazareth, amongst whom he had grown up; but their proper and full accomplishment is that which they are receiving year by year. In the gospel of Christ "the righteousness of God is revealed to faith," Ro. i. 17. Wherever that righteousness is faithfully declared, it matters not who the preacher may be, the message is Christ's, and it is to be received as his. In this connection, also, I may cite the classical text from the twenty-second Psalm (ver. 22):—

> I will declare thy name unto my brethren,
> In the midst of the congregation will I praise thee.

Our Lord had these words in his heart when he said in the guest-chamber, "I have declared unto them thy name, and will declare it," Jn. xvii. 26. They are a compendious summary of all he taught the disciples, and of all that he will continue by them to teach all generations. The drift of Christ's teaching is evermore *to declare to men God's name;* in other words, to set forth what they are to believe concerning God. But the peculiar glory of the psalmist's intimation of Christ's prophetical office lies in the golden words, *My brethren.* Christ teaches, in the midst of the church, not with the dazzling majesty of the Godhead, but in the milder radiance of the first-born of the many brethren. The words of the psalmist suggest, by contrast, the manner in which God's name was declared from Horeb, in the audience of the mighty congregation that filled the plain below. It was with thunder-peals, out of the thick darkness. The people found the weight of the glory insupportable, and entreated that Moses, their brother, might be constituted an internuntius to bear to them the word of the Lord. It was in allusion to that entreaty that, when Moses afterwards delivered the prediction respecting Christ, in which, for the first time, mention is made of his prophetical office, it ran in these terms: "The Lord thy God will raise up unto thee a prophet, from the midst of thee, of thy brethren, like unto me," De. xviii. 15; *of thy brethren,* so that his voice will not affright thee, any more than mine has done. In the psalm, the prophet thus announced takes up the promise, and repeats it in his own person: "I will declare thy name unto my brethren."—*Binnie.*

PSALM XLI.

1. *The Lord will deliver him in time of trouble.* The compassionate lover of the poor thought of others, and therefore God will think of him. God measures to us with our own bushel. Days of trouble come even to the most generous, and they have made the wisest provision for rainy days who have lent shelter to others when times were better with them. The promise is not that the generous saint shall have no trouble, but that he shall be preserved in it, and in due time brought out of it. How true was this of our Lord! never trouble deeper nor triumph brighter than his, and glory be to his name, he secures the ultimate victory of all his blood-bought ones. Would that they all were more like him in putting on bowels of compassion to the poor. Much blessedness they miss who stint their alms. The joy of doing good, the sweet reaction of another's happiness, the approving smile of Heaven upon the heart, if not upon the estate; all these the niggardly soul knows nothing of. Selfishness bears in itself a curse, it is a cancer in the heart; while liberality is happiness, and maketh fat the bones. In dark days we cannot rest upon the supposed merit of almsgiving, but still the music of memory brings with it no mean solace when it tells of widows and orphans whom we have succoured, and prisoners and sick folk to whom we have ministered.—*Spurgeon.*

3. *The Lord will strengthen him upon the bed of languishing.* The everlasting arms shall stay up his soul as friendly hands and downy pillows stay up the body of the sick. How tender and sympathizing is this image; how near it brings our God to our infirmities and sicknesses! Whoever heard this of the old heathen Jove, or of the gods of India or China? This is language peculiar to the God of Israel; he it is who deigns to become nurse and attendant upon good men. If he smites with one hand he sustains with the other. Oh, it is blessed fainting when one falls upon the Lord's own bosom, and is upborne thereby! Grace is the best of restoratives; divine love is the noblest stimulant for a languishing patient; it makes the soul strong as a giant, even when

the aching bones are breaking through the skin. No physician like the Lord, no tonic like his promise, no wine like his love. *Thou wilt make all his bed in his sickness.* What, doth the Lord turn bedmaker to his sick children? Herein is love indeed. Who would not consider the poor if such be the promised reward? A bed soon grows hard when the body is weary with tossing to and fro upon it, but grace gives patience, and God's smile gives peace, and the bed is made soft because the man's heart is content; the pillows are downy because the head is peaceful. Note that the Lord will make *all* his bed, from head to foot. What considerate and indefatigable kindness! Our dear and ever-blessed Lord Jesus, though in all respects an inheritor of this promise, for our sakes condescended to forego the blessing, and died on a cross and not upon a bed; yet, even there, he was after awhile upheld and cheered by the Lord his God, so that he died in triumph.

We must not imagine that the benediction pronounced in these three verses belongs to all who casually give money to the poor, or leave it in their wills, or contribute to societies. Such do well, or act from mere custom, as the case may be, but they are not here alluded to. The blessing is for those whose habit it is to love their neighbour as themselves, and who for Christ's sake feed the hungry and clothe the naked. To imagine a man to be a saint who does not consider the poor as he has ability, is to conceive the fruitless fig-tree to be acceptable; there will be sharp dealing with many professors on this point in the day when the King cometh in his glory.—*Spurgeon.*

END OF VOL. I.